VEGETAL ENTWINEMENTS IN PHILOSOPHY AND ART

VEGETAL ENTWINEMENTS IN PHILOSOPHY AND ART

A READER

EDITED BY GIOVANNI ALOI AND
MICHAEL MARDER

THE MIT PRESS
CAMBRIDGE, MASSACHUSETTS
LONDON, ENGLAND

The MIT Press would like to thank the anonymous peer reviewers who provided comments on drafts of this book. The generous work of academic experts is essential for establishing the authority and quality of our publications. We acknowledge with gratitude the contributions of these otherwise uncredited readers.

This book was set in Arnhem Pro and Frank New by Westchester Publishing Services. Printed and bound in the United States of America.

Library of Congress Cataloging-in-Publication Data

Names: Aloi, Giovanni, editor. | Marder, Michael, 1980– editor.
Title: Vegetal entwinements in philosophy and art : a reader / edited by Giovanni Aloi and Michael Marder.
Description: Cambridge, Massachusetts : The MIT Press, [2023] | Includes bibliographical references.
Identifiers: LCCN 2022036850 | ISBN 9780262047791
Subjects: LCSH: Plants (Philosophy) | Nature (Aesthetics)
Classification: LCC B105.P535 V44 2023 | DDC 113/.8—dc23/eng/20230202
LC record available at https://lccn.loc.gov/2022036850

10 9 8 7 6 5 4 3 2 1

publication supported by a grant from
The Community Foundation for Greater New Haven
as part of the **Urban Haven Project**

CONTENTS

ALTERNATIVE READING PATHWAYS

I ORIENTATIONS

II CROSS-POLLINATION

INTRODUCTION

Let's begin with an image, as much conceptual as it is aesthetic, entwining the domains of knowing and sensing. The image is that of a gigantic, perhaps cosmic, tree, often with an inverted morphology, according to which the roots stretch high above while branches and leaves extend below. In *The Bhagavad Gita*, the eternal *ashvattha* tree is a tree at once of life and of knowledge. Modeled on a fig or a banyan, it is a tree that is imperishable (*avyayam*), "having its roots above and branches below, / whose leaves are the (Vedic) hymns" (XV.1). Immediately, though, *ashvattha*'s hierarchical arrangement is put in question: "Below and above [*adhascordhvam*] its branches spread, / nourished by the qualities, with objects of the senses as sprouts; / and below its roots stretch forth / engendering action in the world of men" (XV.2). The realms above and below merge into a single domain above-below, *adhascordhvam*, just as living and knowing, sensing-thinking, and acting, are different parts of the same vegetal being.

In Hellenic antiquity, Plato and Plotinus probably received the conceptual image of the tree as a microcosm and a macrocosm of existence from Eastern thought, notably from Indian (the earlier Vedic as well as the later Mahabharata-based) and Zoroastrian traditions. In *Timaeus*, Plato pictures the human "not as an earthly but a heavenly plant," rooted by the thinking head in the realm of ideas above (90a–b). Plotinus figures "the Soul of All" in the shape of a tree, or, more precisely, "a great growing plant," with the lower parts embodied and the higher caring for the lower within the same sublime vegetal assemblage (*Enneads* IV.3.4, 25–30). Although the world tree migrates to ancient Greece and Hellenized Egypt, and although thinking and sensing are both mapped onto its organs, it is endowed with a rigid hierarchical structure, prioritizing abstract thought over sensory and nutritive capacities.

The Biblical heritage, too, adds another brushstroke to the portrait of the world as a tree. In Genesis 2:9, we read that in the Garden of Eden,

> God made grow out of the earth every tree that is pleasing to sight and good for food, and the tree of life [*'etz ha-chayim*] was within the Garden and the tree of knowledge of good and evil [*ve'etz ha-da'at tov va'ra'*].

In contrast to *The Bhagavad Gita*, the tree of life is distinct from the tree of knowledge, so much so that the original sin of eating a fruit from the tree of knowledge cuts human connections to the tree of life, connections said to be repaired in Christianity. The prototype of the eternal *ashvattha*, or fig tree, is associated in Judaism and Christianity with the first attempt to mitigate the consequences of sin by covering genitals with broad fig leaves.

The Edenic condition of the first humans is far from perfect when set against the backdrop of foundational narratives from other cultural traditions and the goals of subsequent mysticisms alike. A hypothetical recovery of the paradisiac state is still burdened by the original division between life and knowledge, including not only the "ethical" knowledge of good and evil but also that of life itself. The two central trees in Biblical Eden are separate and even mutually exclusive: to eat the forbidden fruit from one of them is to be expelled from the vicinity of the other. This division, in turn, cuts through and between the vegetal and the human, human vegetality and our humanity, sensing and knowing, art and philosophy. If we invoke "vegetal entwinements," it is in order to contribute in our modest way to the integration of these vital dimensions of existence.

A stumbling block in the way of such an integration is the attitude that is called, somewhat misleadingly, anthropocentrism. Without giving a second thought to the competing meanings and to the essential indeterminacy of *anthropos* (Greek for "human"), this largely unconscious attitude, privileging an exceptionally restricted notion of rationality, has considerably stifled thinking, feeling, and being in the world; it has undercut the potentialities of other-than-human, as well as of human, forms of life.

Anthropocentrism is ingrained in us. It has been passed on for millennia, from generation to generation, by teachers, parents, politicians, and the clergy. We are taught that nature is a resource to exploit; we are made to believe that only children should have an interest in all things natural; we are resigned before the fact that such things are not newsworthy unless disasters strike; we think it's normal for nature never to be a priority in urban planning; and we are constantly told that animals and plants were created for us to enjoy and dispose of as we see fit (recall in this context the Biblical "pleasing to sight and good for food"). The cultural framework provided by anthropocentrism is difficult to dismantle, an endeavor that requires a good dose of trust in speculative approaches to both art and philosophy.

For their part, traditional philosophical approaches to plants have supplied the ideological foundations for their unrestricted instrumental treatment. The theoretical gesture of situating vegetal life at the bottom of the metaphysical hierarchy implies that this life is less differentiated or individuated than animal or human vitalities, while obfuscating how it materially (and even psychically) sustains the rest of ontology. That said, we should not simply dismiss the views on plants held by key figures in Western philosophy, some of whom (like Plato and Plotinus) have been influenced by philosophies from other parts of the world. On the one hand, they reveal—if only negatively—what the root of the problem is and, therefore, may play an important part in the current reassessment of the place of plants and that of the human. On the other hand, the "unconscious" layer of philosophical writings on vegetal life includes resources for subverting their own explicit message insofar as they betray the irrepressible tendency of vegetality traversing other sorts of existence, whether animal or human.

Since the beginning of the new millennium, the sudden rise in popularity of human–animal studies and the excitement generated by posthuman perspectives have progressively destabilized Western anthropocentric certitude.[1] Grasping the importance of nonhuman agency has not proved an easy task, and what's more important, the hard work such a grasp entails has just begun. Now, plants might not be the last frontier of the exciting ontological turn that has swept the humanities over the past 20 years, but vegetal life is one of the most challenging. While mammals often provide anthropomorphic opportunities for representationally bridging the abyss that separates us from them, the utter alterity of plants seems much less generous, at least at first glance. Vegetal life often appears alien when viewed from our habitual perspective: the more or less clear separations between the inner and the outer, the individual and the collective, the organism and its environment, and indeed life and death simply do not apply.

So, why *look* at plants now? Philosophy and art seem to have simultaneously, if not synergically, come to the conclusion that anthropocentrism has impoverished our universe of meaning and also led to destruction of habitats and ecosystems. Furthermore, in an ongoing dialogue with philosophy, contemporary art is especially well situated to shape new conceptions of plants. It leads us to ask: How can we outline a thinking-sensing framework, in which to conceive plants and to be with plants while avoiding objectifying and pacifying tropes? How can art respond to the philosophies and sciences of plants, new and old, and, in a reciprocal relation, inspire our theoretical imagination relevant to vegetal capacities? What philosophical insights about vegetation could emerge from a sustained engagement with art?

Needless to say, both Western art and philosophy have to a certain degree failed plants by relegating them to the background of human concerns. Perhaps for this very reason the inverted morphology of upside-down trees also abounds in the work of many artists today. For instance, Darwin asked us to think of the plant as a kind of upside-down animal with its main sensitive organs below ground and sexual organs above.[2] The upside-down iconography is an invitation to look again and afresh beyond our inherited cultural structures. Shinji Turner-Yamamoto's site-specific installations of uprooted trees, inspired by Sumerian goddess Inanna-Ishtar, aim to make visible commonalities between plant and human life. Through different aesthetic approaches, Shirazeh Houshiary, Giuseppe Penone, Holt/Smithson, Henrik Hakansson, and many others have inverted arboreal forms to challenge our plant-blindness.[3] This inversion fruitfully complicates the encounter; it subverts and interferes with the objectifying powers of cultural constructs, while allowing for the emergence of knowledge that bypasses the field of botany and its taxonomical structures. Or, like in the case of Rodney Graham's photographs of upside-down oak trees, the whole of our perceptual/cognitive scope is uprooted, together with the representational systems we rely upon for the production of knowledge. In art, upside-down trees are stripped-bare vegetal bodies—potent and silent enigmas, philosophical questions, or simply monuments to the communicative inadequateness with regard to other forms of life that characterizes our species. But most of all, they stand as opportunities to surpass the representational and rational constrictions that have characterized our anthropocentric methods and knowledge.

Of great importance, in this context, is the implicit acknowledgment that the inscrutability of plants, their relatively simple anatomy and sessile existence should no longer be seen as markers of inferiority, but as fecund opportunities through which to rethink our relationship with the vegetal world, the land, and ecosystems. In light of these opportunities, artists have, since the beginning of the millennium, started to pry open a space from which new vegetal conceptions can emerge.[4]

The many de-objectifying aesthetic strategies contemporary artists have thus far devised are the first and all-important stage in combating plant-blindness in art. More recently, a growing number of artists have shifted their focus toward new notions of interconnectedness in order to foreground plants as crucial actors in bionetworks. They more readily seem to engage with what the American art theorist Hal Foster has identified as a change from qualitative—aesthetically and historically determined—internal affairs of art, to "interested art" that challenges the borders of contemporary cultural thought in what amounts to a meaningful shift from "medium-specific elaborations to debate-specific projects."[5] From bio art and installations to video work, artists have begun to focus on the human/vegetal/material/cultural entanglements that define our lives and, along with that, our planet.

Often straddling past and present histories, plants in art easily come to embody collective and individual memories, traumas, and identities. They help us visualize the elusive blueprints of colonial pasts that haunt the world today and trace back histories of exploitation and social injustice in order to confront what metanarratives have concealed. With this context in mind, plants in contemporary art are always political in the sense that they relentlessly trouble anthropocentric certainties, parameters, and limitations. In so doing, they often implicitly invite radical perceptual shifts and deep reconsiderations of subject–object relations. Here lies the subversive power of plants. Artists, curators, and art historians who today take plants seriously are aware of their material recalcitrance; of how they trouble hegemonic conceptions of time, intelligence, movement, and identity; and of how considering plants from new and creative perspectives might also bear the potential to foster more sustainable futures.

The current vegetal turn will be remembered as an extraordinarily unique time in the histories of both philosophy and art. And it is no coincidence that such a momentous shift should become manifest at a time of planetary crisis. Catastrophic climate change and the sixth mass extinction are only two of the most urgent anthropogenic issues our planet currently faces. No doubts are left: anthropocentrism is the *prima causa* of what today we call the Anthropocene.

According to current statistics, every day roughly 81,000 hectares, an area nearly 14 times the size of Manhattan, are destroyed to make space for agriculture and to produce timber. The rate of deforestation is such that about 36 football fields' worth of trees are lost every minute.[6] Of course, the destructive effects of deforestation are not limited to erosion and deterioration of soil or the loss of biodiversity. Even conservative estimates indicate that deforestation causes the loss of roughly 137 species of plants, insects, and other animals every day.[7] Approximately 20 percent of global greenhouse emissions are generated by deforestation. The loss of trees has a deep impact on the hydrological system of this planet too. Cleared forest leads to drier local climates because water is no longer channeled through tree roots and foliage into the atmosphere. This results in desertification and, at the same time, increased risks of flooding.

Rethinking our relationship with plants, reconsidering their vital place in the biosystems of this planet, and envisioning new modes of coexistence lie at the core of the possibility for more sustainable futures. The time has come to reconsider vegetal ontology and philosophy as such in the face of an ethical urgency. Nevertheless, as one of us has asked recently, "Are we writing and thinking about plants, in this collection and in numerous others, with such intensity and dedication because the forests are receding? Because we are losing vegetal variety, the biodiversity of the flora, in actuality? Are we trying to commemorate in thought what is disappearing in deed?"[8] The current nexus of art and philosophy articulated around plants needs to be envisioned in the context not only of ethical urgency but also of our undisguisable belatedness.

The field of critical plant studies has thus far created a slew of possibilities for scientific research, local traditions, Indigenous knowledges, history, geography, anthropology, philosophy, and aesthetics to intersect, inform each other, and lead transdisciplinary and transcultural dialogues. Art has simultaneously facilitated and problematized these junctions, often deliberately pushing against disciplinary and institutional boundaries and devising ever more sensitive epistemological frameworks capable of detecting what had, up until recently, been overlooked.

To outline this field, texts comprising *Vegetal Entwinements* are divided into six sections:

1. **Conceptions** includes writings that shape seemingly abstract notions of reality starting from (and returning to) plants. How does vegetal existence inform our ideas about being? In what ways can this kind of existence be an organizing (or a disorganizing) trope for thinking about existence as such? How do plant processes, images, and phenomena participate in philosophical and artistic constructions of the world? These are some of the questions raised in the first section.

2. **Methodologies** presents a variety of paths toward and through plant life and its reverberations in other beings, be they humans or animals, and ecosystems. The paths themselves, however, are not separate from the subject matter of the book: to move along them is already to adopt a vegetal point of view. In this section, we thus situate works that open new perspectives on plant life and give readers the tools to relate the nascent critical plant studies methodologies to their own practical and theoretical concerns and interests.

3. **Engagements** encompasses the mutual interactions of plants and humans in such areas as medicine, art, politics, and conservationism. The section includes case studies, as well as important historical and regional materials, on the largely overlooked, if indispensable, effects of plants on our most varied endeavors that, in their turn, affect the flora.

4. **Subjectivities** refers to the understanding of plants as subjects with their own experiences of and approaches to their environments. The chapters in this section range from those that attribute to plants a certain kind of personhood, soul, and autonomy, to those that conceive plant subjects as radically depersonalized, dispersed, multiple, and receptive.

5. **Intelligences** gathers key texts with the scientific and philosophical depictions of plants as intelligent organisms capable of (among other things) learning, remembering, anticipating the future, and making decisions. The most venturesome of these selections illuminate the thinking of plants that characterizes their modes of being beyond the limits of purely instrumental intelligence concerned with survival.

6. **Autobiographies** compiles accounts that mix autobiographies with reflections on and involvements with plants. Together, these writings open the possibility of an alternative, vegetal narrativization of our life stories and give plants a lead role in the constitution of human subjectivity. And, in a reciprocal fashion, moving plants from the background to the forefront of activities, through which we make sense of ourselves and our world, these accounts shed intimate light on "vegetal being."

As we were planning this *Reader*, in the course of ongoing discussions, it became evident that the structure of the book must be both well-defined and flexible, akin to that of many plants, promoting both stability and growth. However, we felt it would be wrong to resort to a single example of vegetal architecture in the hopes that it would provide a blueprint for the arrangement of key themes and ideas in plant studies. A branching tree structure is neither more nor less valuable or representative than, say, a knotted rhizome or a horizontal spread of grass at the levels of its blades and roots. While a different organization of the volume may at times resemble these and other plant figures, what we would like to highlight are vegetal tendencies and qualities rather than shapes. Briefly put, these tendencies and qualities are:

1. **The primacy of possibility.** Plants eschew the rigid architectonic molds of a shape, which would be fixed for their lifetime, starting at the embryonic stage. Instead, they continually develop, reconfiguring themselves, shedding some organs and adding new ones. A book on plants, following these tendencies of vegetal life, nurtures the possibilities of approaching its themes from different points of departure and cutting unexpected paths through the topics at hand. While remaining physically the same, it thus looks different on each reading.
2. **Nonhierarchical multiplicity.** Plants don't tend to establish a hierarchy among organs, but proliferate through a multiplication of existing structures by means of a growth called "modular." Similarly, a plant *Reader* refrains from prioritizing some of the thematic clusters, or modules, over others; a multiplication of interconnections between texts stimulates the *intensive* growth of its subject.
3. **Articulations.** Without a unified command center, plants are especially adept at articulating parts of themselves with each other and with parts of other plants and animals. While parts of this book are articulated among themselves in a coherent manner, they also appeal, beyond a given coherent narrative that slots them into their rightful places, to a logic of articulation that is as open-ended as it is determinate and specific.

To reflect these important considerations, the structure of our *Reader* focuses on historical, ontological, and relational approaches to plant life and its representations. We have conceived these groupings as essential components, through which our relations with plants have developed over time. However, we would also like to point out "alternative reading pathways" that might allow for branching out and rooting through, so to follow less prescriptive, more diverse and simultaneously coherent epistemic routes. We believe that such pathways would enable readers to identify specific content in order to draw novel connections between texts. And, perhaps more crucially, alternative reading pathways might live up to the playful plurality within vegetal being that offers a plethora of points of access without being exhausted in any one of them.

In order to indicate fresh approaches and facilitate different reading experiences, we have identified three additional reading itineraries readers might follow. In a shorthand, we call them "Orientations," "Cross-Pollination," and "Ecologies." Each names a vital theme or a methodological vein running through the book. "Orientations" refers to the possibility of recalibrating our being in the world in tandem with the life of plants or human–plant relations. It consists of such signposts as place, time, experience, ethics, and politics. "Cross-Pollination" signals the fecund encounters of distinct fields of study, modes of existence, or ways of relating to the environment, including such subthemes as composting, grafting, transcending, or healing. "Ecologies" unites plant-related topics bearing on climate change, social justice, decolonization, and diasporas. Following one of these threads—whether at the level of the collection as a whole or at the level of one of the subthemes—readers can explore how various conceptual and aesthetic lines grow and decay, how they metamorphose into each other and into still other lines hinted at but not explicitly present in the book.

For example, if your main interest is in the time of plants, which is a subtheme of the "Orientations" reading pathway, then you can read the chapters by Stefano Mancuso and Alessandra Viola, David Wood, Mark Payne, Elaine Gan, Lois Weinberger, and Wangari Maathai. These texts are to be found in every single main section of the book, and yet, by following their meandering tracks, you can imagine another structure of the *Reader*, one that suits your own theoretical and practical concerns and preoccupations. To facilitate your individual journey through the collection, we have provided an alternative table of contents at the beginning of the book that you can use to navigate pathways and subthemes; and we have included the main themes and subthemes at the end of each text. Our goal, then, is to devise a *Reader* that is vegetal not only in its content (as evinced by the table of contents) but also in its living form, which is actually a multiplicity of possible forms. This book in perpetual metamorphosis is an open invitation to you: Read like a plant!

Dr. Giovanni Aloi
School of the Art Institute of Chicago

Dr. Michael Marder
Ikerbasque and University of the Basque Country (UPV-EHU), Vitoria-Gasteiz

NOTES

1. Some key references on Human-Animal Studies: Giorgio Agamben, *The Open: Man and Animal* (Stanford: Stanford University Press, 2004); Giovanni Aloi, *Art & Animals* (London: I. B. Tauris, 2011); Giovanni Aloi, *Speculative Taxidermy* (New York: Columbia University Press, 2018); Steve Baker, *The Postmodern Animal* (London: Reaktion, 2000); Ron Broglio, *Surface Encounters: Thinking with Animals and Art* (Minneapolis: University of Minnesota Press, 2011); Jonathan Burt, *Animals in Film* (London: Reaktion, 2002); Matthew Calarco, *Zoographies: The Question of the Animal from Heidegger to Derrida* (New York: Columbia University Press, 2008); Jacques Derrida, *The Animal That Therefore I Am*, edited by M. L. Mallet (New York: Fordham University Press, 2006); Donna J. Haraway, *When Species Meet* (Minneapolis: University of Minnesota Press, 2008); Akira Mizuta Lippit, *Electric Animal: Toward a Rhetoric of Wildlife* (Minneapolis: University of Minnesota Press, 2000); and Susan McHugh, *Animal Stories: Narrating across Species Lines* (Minneapolis: University of Minnesota Press, 2011).
2. Charles Darwin, *The Power of Movement in Plants* (London: John Murray, 1880).
3. James H. Wandersee and Elisabeth E. Schussler, "Preventing Plant Blindness," *The American Biology Teacher* 61 no. 2, (1999): 82–86.
4. Giovanni Aloi (ed. and main author), *Why Look at Plants: The Botanical Emergence in Contemporary Art* (Laden: Brill, 2019).
5. Hal Foster, *Return of the Real* (Cambridge: MIT Press, 1996), xi.
6. Alina Bradford, "Deforestation: Facts, Causes and Impacts of Deforestation," *LiveScience*, March 4, 2015, https://www.123helpme.com/essay/Deforestation-Facts-Causes-And-Impacts-Of-Deforestation-524378.
7. Rhett A. Butler, "Rainforest Facts for 2021," September 12, 2021, https://rainforests.mongabay.com/facts/rainforest-facts.html.
8. Michael Marder, "Auto-Heteronomy: Thoreau's Circuitous Return to the Vegetal World," in *Dispersion: Thoreau and Vegetal Thought*, edited by Branka Arsic (London: Bloomsbury, 2021), 67.

I
CONCEPTIONS

1

THE PLANT: A STRANGER

Stefano Mancuso and Alessandra Viola

Human beings have lived with plants since our appearance on the earth about 200,000 years ago. Two hundred thousand years would seem to be enough time to get to know someone. But it hasn't been enough time for us to get to know plants. We know very little about the plant world, and we probably see plants in much the same way as the first *Homo sapiens* did.

This assertion, though patently indemonstrable, may be clarified with a simple example. Let's consider an animal—say, a cat—and try to describe its characteristics. What can we say about the cat? It's smart, clever, affectionate, sociable, opportunistic, agile, quick, and who knows how many other things. Now let's consider a plant—say, an oak tree—and describe its characteristics, too. What is there to say about an oak tree? It's tall, shady, knotty, fragrant . . . what else? At most, we could add some aesthetic qualities and appreciations of its usefulness. We certainly wouldn't include attributes referring to its "social dimension," whereas in the case of the cat we've said that it is sociable (though "individualistic" would also describe a cat's way of relating to its environment). We wouldn't attribute any sort of intelligence to a plant—whereas in the cat we recognize it easily—nor would it occur to us to call an oak affectionate!

And yet something's off about this. How is it possible that living beings that are unintelligent, without social aptitudes, and incapable of relating to their

From Stephano Mancuso and Alessandro Viola, *Brilliant Green* (Firenze-Milano: Giunti Editore S.p.A., 2013). Reproduced by permission of Island Press, Washington, DC.

environment, have survived and evolved on the planet? If plants really functioned so poorly, natural selection would have swept them away long ago!

But we don't need to look to the past as evidence; in the last several decades, science has been showing that plants are endowed with feeling, weave complex social relations, and can communicate with themselves and with animals, all of which we will explore in the following chapters. So why do human beings still see the plant world only as raw material, or a food source, or decor? What prevents us from going beyond this initial, superficial valuation of the life forms that populate it?

EUGLENA VERSUS PARAMECIUM: AN EVEN MATCH?

Besides cultural factors, two others influence our perception of the plant world: an evolutionary factor and a temporal one.

Let's start with the evolutionary factor and attempt an analysis, first by asking what we mean by the word *evolution*. Evolution refers to the slow, continuous process of adaptation to the environment, in the course of which a living organism develops the characteristics most suited to its survival. During this process, each species acquires or loses characteristics and capacities in relation to the kind of habitat in which it lives. Of course, all of this happens over very long periods of time, but it can lead to macroscopic changes between the original and the eventual organism. Evolution has played a fundamental role in differentiating animals from plants, and today it's part of the problem that keeps us from deeply knowing the plant kingdom.

To see this more clearly, let's take a step back.

We know that the first single-celled organisms that appeared on the planet were algae—that is, the plant kind of living things. Through photosynthesis, they created the oxygen that enabled life to spread over the earth. This included the emergence of eukaryotes, or animal cells.

In those days, as today, plant and animal cells were not as different as one might think. To be sure, plant cells are more complex, because compared to animal cells they have an additional organelle—the chloroplast—in which photosynthesis takes place; and a cell wall that surrounds the entire cell, making it far more robust than an animal cell. But these two differences aside, plant and animal cells are really very similar.

So how to explain the fact that when a single-celled plant organism is compared to a single-celled "animal" (so to speak), the latter is always considered more complex, more evolved—in a word, superior?

Let's compare two unicellular beings, one animal and one plant: the paramecium and the euglena. We're taking some license in calling the paramecium an animal since, along with other protozoa, it's now in a separate classification, the protists. But until a few years ago, for all intents and purposes, it was considered an animal: as the name *protozoa* implies (from the Greek *protos*, "first," and *zoon*, "animal"), it's a proto-animal.

The paramecium is a minuscule unicellular organism whose body is covered with cilia that act like oars, allowing it to swim and move around in the water. If you look at it under a microscope, you can't help being fascinated by its elegant evolution, and by movements that seem to imply elegant behavior. It's a true champion among living beings: a single cell, but capable of astonishing activity. Writing about another little amoeba-like unicellular animal, Herbert Spencer Jennings (1868–1947) in his book *Behavior of the Lower Organisms*, published in 1906, wondered whether we would be more apt to grant intelligence to the predatory amoeba if it were the size of a whale, and a potential threat to humans.

And in the other corner, we have another marvel of creation, a minuscule single-celled green alga: the euglena. It, too, can be classified with the protists, but without a doubt it has a plant nature.

Looking at such simple living organisms and discovering their extraordinary abilities can help us see what underlies our prejudiced view of the plant world. What do these unicellular organisms have in common, and how are they different from each other? Do the animals really have a minimal form of intelligence, but not the plants?

To get a general idea, let's start with the paramecium. For such a small organism, it has surprising abilities: for example, it can locate food and move to reach it.

Naturally, in order to live, the euglena needs energy, too. Normally, it supplies its energy needs through photosynthesis, like all plants, but if light is scarce, it doesn't give up: it transforms itself into a predator and behaves like an animal. It can locate food and move to reach it—yes, it's a plant, but it moves! This microscopic alga, in fact, swims with the aid of very thin flagella.

Obviously, both the paramecium and the euglena can reproduce. If you watch them moving in the water, there don't seem to be many differences between them.

But wait: there are electrical signals traversing the body of the paramecium, transmitting information across a single cell. For this reason, it's been called a "swimming neuron," which seems like a pretty good definition of a paramecium. But there are the same kind of electrical impulses going across the single-celled body of the euglena. So, they're even again.

Can the paramecium and the euglena do the same things? Does the match between plants and animals end in a draw? No way—but the outcome isn't what we would expect. The one with the ace up its sleeve isn't the paramecium but the euglena, which has another capacity that beats the competition hands-down: it can carry out photosynthesis. To improve this capacity, it has developed a rudimentary sense of sight, which allows it to intercept light frequencies and then to find the best position for receiving light.

But if the euglena can do everything a paramecium can do, and in addition, can see and produce energy by transforming light from the sun, why has no one ever called it a "swimming neuron" or some other epithet that expresses its exceptional abilities? Hard to say. There's no rational way to explain the general disregard for solid scientific evidence that plant cells have greater capacities than those of animal cells.

FIVE HUNDRED MILLION YEARS AGO

Returning to the evolutionary obstacle we mentioned at the beginning of the chapter, let's go back about 500 million years, when the differentiation between plants and animals began. The first organisms chose two divergent paths, which can be summed up thus: plants opted for a stationary lifestyle, animals for a nomadic one. It's interesting to note in passing that the same choice in favor of a stationary life gave birth to the first great civilizations.

Plants faced the necessity of obtaining from the earth, the air, and the sun everything they needed in order to live; animals, on the other hand, needed to feed on other animals or on plants, and for that purpose developed manifold movement capacities (running, flying, swimming, and so on). On this account plants are defined as "autotrophic" (from the Greek *autos*, "by itself," and *trophe*, "food"), that is, self-sufficient, not dependent on other living things for their survival; and animals as "heterotrophic" (from the Greek *eteros*, "other," and *trophe*, "food"), because they're not self-sufficient.

From generation to generation, this initial choice led to other fundamental differences between the animal and plant worlds, to the point that now they can be considered the yin and yang, the black and white, of ecosystems. Plants are stationary and animals are mobile; animals are aggressive, plants passive; animals are swift, plants slow. We could come up with dozens of such antithetical pairings, but they would amount to the same thing: life has evolved very differently in the plant world and the animal world over the past 500 million years.

The primitive choice to evolve as beings that are stationary or in motion led, over time, to an extraordinary differentiation in bodies and ways of life: animals have chosen to defend and feed themselves, and to reproduce, through motion (or flight), while plants have chosen to remain fixed in one place, which has imposed on them the necessity of finding solutions that are completely original, at least from our point of view (which, let's not forget, is an animal one).

PLANT IS A COLONY

To start with, being stationary and therefore subject to being preyed on by animals, plants developed a kind of "passive resistance" to external attack. Their bodies are constructed on a modular design, in which each part is important but none is truly indispensable. This structure represents a fundamental advantage vis-à-vis the animal kingdom, especially considering the number of herbivores on the planet and the impossibility of escaping their voracious appetites.

The first advantage of having a modular organization, to give just one example, is that, for a plant, being eaten isn't that big a deal! Could any animal say that?

The physiology of plants, as we will see, is based on different principles from that of animals. While animals have evolved to concentrate almost all their most important vital functions in a few organs such as the brain, lungs, stomach, and so on, plants have taken into account the reality of being easy prey, and avoided concentrating their faculties in a few neurological areas. It's a bit like not keeping all your money in one place, but instead dividing it up and hiding it in several places to minimize the loss in case of theft, or diversifying your investments to distribute risk. In short, a very wise move!

A plant's functions are not related to organs—which means plants breathe without having lungs, nourish themselves without having a mouth or stomach, stand erect without having a skeleton, and as we will soon see, make decisions without having a brain.

It's because of this very special physiology that large portions of a plant can be removed without putting its survival at risk: some plants can have up to 90 or 95 percent of themselves eaten, but then grow back normally from the small surviving nub. A meadow grazed on by an entire herd can grow back in a few days. You don't have to be an herbivore to experience this phenomenon; if you've ever tried to cut back an ivy or a wind weed, or even to clip your lawn, you know what we're talking about. So as an evolutionary strategy, plants, being stationary (or more properly speaking, sessile) organisms, have chosen to be composed of divisible parts in order to better withstand predators. Animals, on the other hand, which based their defensive strategies on movement from the outset, never developed regenerative capacities, or did so only in a few cases. Yes, a lizard can grow back its tail, but a foot, an arm, or its head, once cut off, doesn't grow back. But if part of a plant is removed, it generally not only survives, but sometimes even benefits: consider the rejuvenating effects of pruning. This characteristic is a direct result of its structure, which is very different from ours. A plant is made up of repeating modules: the branches, stem, leaves, and roots are all combinations of very simple modules, which essentially add on to each other independently, a little like Lego blocks.

True, a geranium on a terrace doesn't give that impression: it looks like a unique being. But if you take off a piece and then replant it—if you take a cutting, in gardener's parlance—the piece of geranium will put out new roots and grow into a new plant, whereas neither our arm nor an elephant's foot can regenerate a whole new organism or stay alive apart from the rest of the body.

It's no accident that we continually refer to ourselves as *individuals*: the term comes from the Latin *in* (which here means "not") and *dividuus* ("divisible"). Our body really is indivisible: if we're cut in half, the two halves can't live separately; they die. But if we cut a plant in half, the two parts can still live independently, for the simple reason that a plant isn't an individual. In fact, the right way to think about a tree, a cactus, or a shrub is not to compare it to a human being or any other animal, but to picture it as a colony. A tree is much more like a colony of bees or ants than an individual animal.

Though plants are very ancient, from this standpoint they also turn out to be exceptionally modern. One of the cardinal concepts underlying many of the technologies made possible by the advent of the Internet and based on the interconnection of groups (such as social networks) is that of so-called emergent properties, typical of superorganisms or swarm intelligences. These are properties that single entities develop only by virtue of the unitary functioning of the group; none of the individual components possesses their own—just as bees or ants, by forming colonies, develop a collective intelligence much greater than that of their individual members.

A PROBLEM OF TEMPOS

Let's return to the reasons that prevent us from recognizing plants for what they are—social organisms, sophisticated and highly evolved like us. There's another aspect to our inability to perceive the complex reality, one that has to do with time.

We all know that the average lifespan of living creatures varies considerably from species to species: a human being lives about 80 years; a bee less than two months; a giant tortoise more than 100 years. Beyond the variation in average life span, animals also have different vital rhythms: some hibernate; some move and reproduce much faster than we do, others much more slowly. It wouldn't seem to be that hard to recognize the existence of time scales very different from our own. But that isn't the case. A flow of events that gives rise to a time scale so slow as to be imperceptible to our eyes doesn't compute. While these adjectives are obviously meaningless in absolute terms, another way of putting it is that we are "fast" and plants are "slow." Very slow.

The difference in speed between us and them is so great that our perception can't grasp it. It's a bit like a *trompe l'oeil* or an optical illusion, but on a temporal scale. For example, we know very well that a plant moves to capture light, to distance itself from danger, and to seek support (in the case of the climbing plants). For decades, modern techniques of photography and film have enabled us to reconstruct plant movement, which Darwin had already discussed and validated. Today a quick Internet search will bring you to a video showing a flower opening or a shoot growing. Yet in our perception, plants remain "still."

The sight of these movies astounds us, it speaks to the existence of movements in plants, but it doesn't budge our unshakable conviction, partly instinctive, that these creatures are closer to the mineral world than to animal life. Our senses don't perceive plants moving, so we act as if they are inanimate objects. It makes no difference that we know they grow and therefore move; to us they're motionless because their movements escape our sight, and thus our deep understanding.

But what's the significance of our denial? In the hypertechnological society we live in, there are many things of which we have no direct (sensory) knowledge, but whose properties we don't doubt. Few people know how a television works, or a phone or a computer, but we wouldn't think of belittling their technical characteristics merely because we have no direct sensory experience of the ways they work. Our knowledge of the structure of the universe and the composition of matter is mediated by extremely complicated instruments. But who would think of denying the complexity of atomic structure, even though it's much more removed from our sense perception than the structure of plants? Of course, education plays an important role in this regard.

So why doesn't something similar happen with respect to plants? It doesn't seem improbable that there may be a kind of "psychological block" preventing any kind of cultural mediation that over time might mitigate this instinctive behavior on our part. We'll explain what we mean.

Our relationship with plants is one of absolute, primordial dependence, and in that sense it somewhat recalls the relationship of a child to its parents. While we're growing up, and especially in adolescence, we go through a period of totally denying our dependence on our parental figures that frees us to attain psychological autonomy, in preparation for actual autonomy, which will come many years later. It's not out of the question that a similar psychological mechanism enters into our relationships with plants. No one likes depending on another. Dependence coincides with a position of weakness and vulnerability that we don't enjoy contemplating. We may resent those we depend on, because they don't make us feel completely free. In short, we're so dependent on plants that we do everything we can not to think about them. Perhaps we don't wish to remember that our very survival is linked to the plant world, because that makes us feel weak—hardly masters of the universe! Of course, this argument is partly intended to be provocative, but it may be useful in clarifying the balance of power between us and the plant world.

LIFE WITHOUT PLANTS: IMPOSSIBLE

If plants disappeared from the earth tomorrow, human life would continue for no more than a few weeks, or at most months. Very soon, all higher forms of life would disappear from the planet. On the other hand, if we were the ones that disappeared, in a few years plants would repossess all the land previously taken over from the natural realm, and in a little less than a century every sign of our enduring civilization would be covered in green. Maybe this can help us take the measure of the relative importance, in biological terms, of plants and human beings. To use another metaphor: we could say that in biology we're still in a period which we could define as Aristotelian-Ptolemaic. Before the Copernican Revolution, people believed that Earth was at the center of the universe and all the celestial bodies revolved around it—a totally anthropocentric vision, which Galileo endeavored to subvert, and which took centuries to disappear from popular opinion. Well, we could say that biology finds itself in a more or less pre-Copernican situation. The reigning idea is that humans are the most important living beings and everything revolves around us: because we have imposed ourselves on the others, we're the absolute lords of nature. An intriguing and consoling vision . . . if only it were true!

In fact, our situation really isn't so stellar. The plant world alone represents more than 99.5 percent of the biomass of the planet. It's like saying that if 100 is the total weight of everything alive, according to various estimates, between 99.5 and 99.9 percent is composed of plants. Or to put it the other way around, of all living things, animals—humans included—represent only a trace (a scant 0.1 to 0.5 percent).

Despite determined human efforts at maximizing deforestation, plants are the incontestable queens of living things. And thank heaven! It is this relationship that makes life on Earth still possible.

As we know, plants are at the base of the food chain: everything we eat (meat and fish included) either is a plant or became what it is by feeding on plants. It might seem that humans have recourse to the full variety of plants for our nutrition, but this isn't the case. There are principally six plants from which we get most of our calories: sugar cane, corn, rice, wheat, potato, and soy. These and a few others form the nutritional base for almost all humans throughout the world. They are the so-called food plants, very special living beings.

Cultivating a plant is a little like raising an animal. Have you ever wondered why humans' carnivorous diet is based almost entirely on beef, chicken, and pork? Why hasn't any culture based its food on lion, gnu, wolf, bear, or snake? These animals are perfectly edible, on a par with cows and chickens. The answer, obviously, is that domesticated animals are easier to raise. A bear is excellent to eat but not easy to raise. Likewise, it's plain that not all plants lend themselves to intensive cultivation.

Comestible (edible) plants are numerous but most cannot be cultivated on an industrial scale because of the way they've evolved. They're wild, like tigers and bears. Dogs, on the other hand, evolved from wolves as a new species, through discovering that living symbiotically with humans was easier and more convenient than fighting for survival. Over the course of evolution an excellent, mutually satisfying collaboration came about: humans feed and take care of dogs and receive protection and companionship in return. Certain plants have adopted a similar evolutionary strategy: by feeding humans they have been protected from insects, provided with nourishment, and, especially, propagated until they've spread to the far reaches of the planet.

Alimentation is only the first and most intuitive link in our dependence on plants. Then, obviously, there's oxygen. We all know that the oxygen we breathe comes from plants and that our survival depends on the existence of oxygen in the air. But not everyone knows that a large part of the energy we use is also of plant origin, and that we have plants to thank for the energy which has been at our disposal for thousands of years.

Think about it: large quantities of the available energy sources on Earth were once concentrated inside plants, through the transformation of solar energy into chemical energy. This miraculous process, which we call photosynthesis, converts light rays and carbon dioxide present in the atmosphere into sugars, that is, molecules with a high energy content (as anyone on a low-calorie diet who's had to give them up knows). This is the first, fundamental phase in which, through successive transformations, the energy we consume is created, in one of the numerous forms it takes (from wood to charcoal, from petroleum to other combustible fuels).

At the turn of the last century, the Russian botanist Kliment Timiryazev (1843–1920) wrote, "The plant is the connecting link between the earth and the sun," and in fact, almost everything humans use for energy has always come from plants.

Practically speaking, fossil fuels (charcoal, hydrocarbons, oil, gas, and so on) are nothing but underground accumulations of energy from the sun which, during various geologic periods, plant organisms have put into the biosphere by means of photosynthesis. Far from being "minerals," as some persist in calling them, they're true organic deposits.

So after air and food, plants enrich us with another fundamental element: energy. This should be enough to make us worship everything green. And that's even without considering medicine. Practically our entire pharmacopoeia is obtained from molecules that are either produced by plants or synthesized by human beings copying plant chemistry.

Throughout the world, in Eastern and Western cultures, in advanced and developing countries, plants are a fundamental and indispensable component of medicine. Their benefit to human beings comes not only from the pharmacological use of many of the molecules they produce but also directly, in many different environmental contexts, through the positive effects of the presence of plants on our psychophysical well-being.

The benefits plants bring by producing oxygen, absorbing carbon dioxide and pollutants, and moderating climate have been known for a long time. But other ways plants can affect our well-being have been studied only recently, and the findings are remarkable: the presence of plants has been reported to reduce stress, increase attention, and speed recovery from illness. Simply seeing a plant induces calm and relaxation, as can be shown by measuring physiological parameters. Hospital patients with windows looking out on plants have less need for painkillers and are discharged sooner than patients with views of buildings or empty lots. This is why (for essentially economic reasons) many new hospitals built in northern Europe have spaces (sometimes an entire floor) devoted to plants, where patients can spend their time. In the United States, Boston Children's Hospital and the University of Maryland Rehabilitation and Orthopaedic Institute are two examples among many with gardens open to patients and other visitors.

The effects of the presence of plants on babies and children have been studied recently from a number of different perspectives. And the results of the first studies are striking, to say the least. One study at the University of Illinois at Urbana-Champaign, for example, looked at student performance on tests which they were asked to do in their rooms. The tests, which required some concentration, had clearly better outcomes for students whose windows looked out on green areas than for students with views of buildings.

Even more than university students, elementary school children show improved attention capacity in the presence of plants, as studies at a school in Florence, Italy, have demonstrated. What's more, there are fewer accidents on tree-lined streets, and there are fewer suicides and fewer violent crimes in neighborhoods with plenty of green spaces. In short, plants positively influence our mood, concentration, learning, and general well-being. The presence of plants seems indispensable even on long space missions, not just as food but for their relaxing effect.

The reasons why plants have these psychological benefits for us are still mostly unknown and may go back far in time, bound up in our unconscious awareness that without them life for our species wouldn't be possible. The calm that pervades us in their presence may be the echo of an ancestral awareness that everything we need and every chance for our survival dwells in the green world. Now as long ago.

Main Pathway: Orientations

Subthemes

Proceed to Experience, p. 145
Proceed to Time, p. 335

2

MAIMONIDES' PALM TREE

Michael Marder

Rabbi Moses Ben Maimon (abbreviated as Rambam and known in the Western world under the name Maimonides) performed for Judaism the same invaluable service as Aristotle rendered to ancient Greek philosophy. The classical philosopher presented a unified worldview, one both building on and disputing the theories of his predecessors; the rabbi from Cordoba systematized disparate religious laws into a colossal fourteen-tome *Code* titled *Mishneh Torah*, or *Repetition of the Torah*. For this reason, the disciples of Maimonides nicknamed him *ha-nesher ha-gadol'*, "the great eagle," as a tribute to the panoramic vision of the Law he bequeathed to future generations.

Maimonides also did not hesitate to descend from the heights of the Law to the minutiae of the everyday, proffering answers to the most obscure problems. He stipulated what was and was not permitted to the observers of Sabbath (the day of rest), came up with principles for resolving property disputes between neighbors and applied them to singular cases, and discussed the merits of boiling food in fruit juices. In light of his impressive macro- and microvision of the world, we may ask: What do plants look like from the perspective of the eagle, that is to say, from the eagle's-eye view of that teaching which purports to repeat the teaching of the Torah? And when zeroing in on any given plant species or a family of plants—say,

Originally published as Chapter 6, "Maimonides' Palm Tree," in Michael Marder, *The Philosopher's Plant: An Intellectual Herbarium* (New York: Columbia University Press, 2014), 97–114. Reprinted with permission.

Arecaceae, palm trees—what does Maimonides see from his preferred theological and philosophical vantage points?

The Book of Acquisition (Qinyan), contained within the fourteen-volume Code, details the rules governing sales and gifts as well as the rightful enjoyment and utilization of property. There Maimonides wants to ensure what we now call "sustainability," the chance for tree groves purchased specifically for felling to regenerate. So he requires that the buyer of olive trees leave untouched at least a stump and two shoots growing close to the ground. But "in the case of palm trees," he writes, the buyer "may dig and root them out because their stumps do not grow anew."[1] Palm trees are subject to absolute appropriation, which would leave no trace of their existence, except a hollow in the ground, once the felling operation is over. In stripping them of all legal protections, Maimonides thus exposes these trees to unlimited violence.

The Italian philosopher Giorgio Agamben coined the term *homo sacer* to refer to a human being reduced to the state of "bare life," exposed to unlimited violence, and handed over to the possibility of being killed with impunity (though not sacrificed).[2] Similarly, a palm tree in *The Book of Acquisitions* takes on the features of what we might call *arbor sacra*, a creature that is either barely alive or not deemed alive at all and that at any moment may be chopped down without care for the future. Palm trees grow in a permanent state of exception and, as we will soon realize, stand for all other trees and plants, excluded by Maimonides from the sphere of the living. They occupy the "zone of indistinction between nature and right,"[3] between life and death, between legal limits (within which they are nonetheless caught up) and unlimited violence.

The sentence by Maimonides I've quoted above is not the only mention of palm trees in laws regulating sales and other acquisitions. In those cases where the owner of the land and of the trees that grow on it is not one and the same person, the subterranean part of plants is said to belong to the proprietor of the field, while the aboveground portions pertain to the owner of the trees. But the rule is not applicable to palm trees, whose "owner does not receive any of the wood because the trunk of a palm tree does not bring forth shoots."[4] What is the justification for this reasoning? Bereft of generative power in their trunks, palm trees are nothing but extensions of their roots and, as such, legally belong to the owner of the land. In addition to being—like all other plants—deprived of life, they are poor in the distinctively vegetable capacity of growth. Doubly marginalized, the palm is, for Maimonides, a deficient tree, barely reminiscent of the miracle of Creation, the memory of which is preserved in the generative power of vegetation, time and again, renewing and reaffirming this singular event.

It is this power, in fact, that converts plants from appropriated objects into the means of appropriation. Like classical Liberals after him, Maimonides believes that the act of possession is not sealed until the possessor's labor is mixed with the property: a field is plowed, seeds are sowed, fruits are gathered, and so on.[5] But the activity of nature itself *(natura naturans)* is equally admissible as grounds for appropriation. So how and when do trees act as justifications for legitimate land claims? And does this usage mitigate their objectification?

Consider the following two stipulations: (1) When a vendee purchases three trees, he receives, along with them, the ground necessary for them to grow.[6] (2) When the titleholder of a plot sells it excluding the trees that grow there, he thereby retains half of the land.[7] The foundation for these judgments is a simple form of appropriation by occupation,[8] where the occupying agent may be a plant, not a human subject. But the agency of this agent is perplexing, as it is denied the status of a living being and thus rendered uprootable either unconditionally, as in the case of a palm tree, or provided that minimal conditions are satisfied, as in the case of an olive tree.

The exceptionality of *arbor sacra* extends so far as to absolve a potential violator of the Sabbath of responsibility and deflect accusations of wrongdoing. In *The Book of Seasons (Zemanim)*, Maimonides states that "if one hurls a stone or shoots an arrow, intending to kill another human or an animal, and the missile does not kill but instead uproots a tree in the course of its flight, he is exempt."[9] Although he does not specify what happens when, aiming to uproot a tree, one actually kills a human or an animal, it is not hard to guess that the exemption would not apply. If the unintended nature of the outcome frees the shooter of liability, it is because the "victim" of the action is not a victim at all, but *arbor sacra* prone to unrestrained violence. In contrast to Christianity, intentions are not as weighty as the unintended practical outcomes of human behavior that, only seemingly arbitrary, emanate from God's sovereign and recondite will. One uprooted tree is a small price to pay for absolving a potential violator of the Sabbath through a direct (and sovereign) divine intervention in the sublunary realm.

Any residual doubts on the value of plant life in the work of Maimonides immediately dissipate when we chance upon the other law of the Sabbath, prohibiting work to "promote the growth of plants." Whether one "sows seeds, or plants trees, or layers trees, or grafts or prunes them,"[10] one shows disregard not only for the day of rest itself but also for the divine act of Creation it reminds us of. What is salient in the juxtaposition of the two laws is that the unintended termination of a plant's existence does not break the Sabbath, but the intended care for plants does. (The case of the intentional uprooting of a plant during the Sabbath is more nuanced: such activity is sternly prohibited and classified with other instances of "gathering.") This is a perfect example of what, centuries later, Nietzsche would consider as the inverted, "life-stunting values" of both Judaism and Christianity, consistent with their overall nihilistic weltanschauung. Were a virtual dialogue to ensue between the two thinkers, Maimonides would have certainly contended that plants did not really live and, therefore, that, *stricto sensu*, there was no plant life to be either valued or violated. But this rejoinder does not change the fact that a theological-metaphysical hierarchy, which takes shape in the Code, prioritizes God's sovereign will over human intention (*kavanah*)—and human intention over the rest of the world. A palm tree, much like all other trees and plants, can be demoted to the condition of *arbor sacra* thanks to its identification with mere matter, whereupon human intentions and divine will are stamped.

The Maimonidean palm, indeed, betokens the destructible materiality of everything in the sublunary world, as opposed to the indestructibility of heavens:

> There are no contraries in heaven. That thesis is correct. However, we have not claimed that the heavens have been generated as the horse and palm tree are. Nor have we claimed that their being composite renders necessary their passing-away as is the case with plants and animals because of the contraries that subsist in them.[11]

The tree may be destroyed with impunity because it is thoroughly destructible—to do so is to bring out its finite nature and to activate the clash of the contraries it contains in nuce, the contraries ready to erupt at some point in time, rendering the tree's existence no longer logically possible. The composite nature of plants and animals, represented by the palm and the horse, is radically distinct from the metaphysical simplicity of heavens. It matters, of course, in which context we facilitate the passing away of plants and animals, that is, whether this is done in a ritually correct way and at an appropriate time (i.e., not on the Sabbath). But from the ethical standpoint informed by the thought of Maimonides, there is nothing inherently wrong in terminating the existence of a given plant or animal, seeing that this possibility is anticipated in their genesis, the mode of their generation. Harboring contraries, they contain the seeds of their own destruction.

At the same time, it is misleading to talk about the place of "plants and animals" in the philosophy of Maimonides. Exemplary of the plant as such, the palm tree grows in the space of a permanent exception from the ethical order of being. Within this order, if "the Universe does not exist for man's sake, but . . . each being exists for its own sake, and not because of some other thing,"[12] it would be reasonable to assume that plants, too, have an intrinsic value and an inherent worth. This ethical principle is a part of the admirable vein in Maimonidean thought that resists the immaturity of anthropocentrism and anthropomorphism, both when it comes to the contemplation of God's essence and to our relation to the world around us.[13] His statement "man has an erroneous idea of himself, and believes the whole world exists only for his sake"[14] could very well be the rallying cry in today's struggles against human domination of nature.

The problem is that "each being," deserving of life and respect in its own right, does not include plants! Already on the next page of the same text, Maimonides emphasizes that "God gave the plants to man and other living beings" and that "plants exist only for the benefit of the animals, since the latter cannot live without food."[15] Far from a logical contradiction, the exclusion of plants from the ethical base of Creation is tantamount to their exclusion from the realm of being. Assuming that "each being exists for its own sake," the plant, which exists only for the sake of animals and humans, does not exist for its own sake and, therefore, is not a being. As *arbor sacra*, it is suspended between being and nothingness, in yet another Agambenian "zone of indistinction." The ban on vegetable ontology and on plant ethics, legible between these lines, is further reinforced by the negation of plant vitality. Whether Maimonides can, in practice, sustain the scandalous argument that plants are not exactly alive remains to be seen.

"A PLANT OR A MINERAL" OR GOD

The Guide for the Perplexed, Maimonides' major philosophical work, composed in Arabic as a three-volume letter to his student Rabbi Joseph ben Judah of Ceuta, is both clear and austere on the subject of plants. Rather than group them together with animals, the author of *The Guide* prefers to lump plants together with inorganic matter. Explaining the idea of "negative attributes" that characterize a thing as what it is not, he suggests those who see a living being from a distance first grasp "that the object is not a plant or a mineral."[16] Whence this categorical denial of plant vitality? What is the reason for the plant's closer proximity to minerals than to the animal kingdom?

In the first instance, departing from the Aristotelian tradition, Maimonides associates the Hebrew terms *nefesh* (soul) and *khai* (living) with sentience. He particularly emphasizes the homonymy of soul and blood, which is also denoted by the word *nefesh* in Deuteronomy.[17] Evidently, then, since plants are insentient and bloodless, they cannot be said to live. Second, locomotion is "one of the distinguishing characteristics of living beings, and is indispensable or them in their progress toward perfection."[18] In consequence of this assertion, the plants' immobility disqualifies them from participating in the realm of the living as well. The Maimonidean verdict sounds irreversible. But is it really so? To get a full picture, let us take a closer look at some of the wrinkles and ambivalences in this ostensibly smooth theoretical narrative.[19]

Maimonides is adamant about the absolute difference between the life of sentient creatures and that of God. Ordinary language fails us; we take it upon ourselves to describe the existence of God based on our own measure and, in so doing, commit a series of blunders when we attribute to Him an enormous body, all-detecting perception, and the aptitude for moving voluntarily from place to place. Counseling his readers on the sense of biblical anthropomorphisms, Maimonides warns them against the insidious prejudices that creep into a common conception of life. In contrast to the "ordinary man's"[20] idea of life, which would certainly be inapplicable to divine existence, he recommends resorting to the negative attributes of God's vitality, namely, the insight that "God exists without possessing the attribute of existence." "Similarly," Maimonides continues, "He lives, without possessing the attribute of life; knows, without possessing the attribute of knowledge."[21] His life is not an accident superadded to His essence, but is this very essence, and the same holds for His oneness, knowledge, and power. The issue is that humans are rarely, if ever, contented with empty and abstract negative descriptions alone, which is why they help themselves to an analogical understanding of God's movement, organs of perception, and bodily extension. But what if our epistemic relation to plants were comparable to that of God? What if, in other words, we made a basic error when we tried to comprehend their life through the lens of animal (and human) existence?

It is imperative today to decouple plant life from animal vitality and to reiterate the critique Maimonides launched against those who understood biblical anthropomorphisms literally, this time with regard to plant existence and intelligence. For plants, too, know otherwise, insofar as they "see," "smell," "feel" pressure, and perhaps "hear" in the absence of readily recognizable organs of perception. They also move differently: not by dislocating themselves in space, but by reaching out with their roots to the mineral resources in the soil and with their branches and leaves turned to the light of the sun. Maimonides is correct in his assessment of locomotion, which, he observes, allows animals "to approach that which is good for them and in harmony with their nature, and to escape from what is injurious and contrary to their nature."[22] The claim that God moves in space is as absurd as the assertion that He requires food and drink for His sustenance, given that all three modes of behavior are the results of a certain need or lack. Animal perfection, transposed onto divinity, mutates into "the highest degree of imperfection."[23] And the same goes for plants: they approach what is good for them in a manner different from animal motion and, though they are unable to flee, react to dangerous stimuli by changing their physiological states. Maimonides did not pursue to the full extent the implications of his critique of this narrow-minded view of life. But he did supply us with a formidable rule of thumb, namely, to keep in mind the relevance of each activity and mode of behavior to the being that acts.

Still, the Aristotelian heritage of medieval philosophy is too weighty for the notion of plant soul, *tō threptikon*, to fall by the wayside in the writings of Maimonides. In *Eight Chapters*, included in his *Commentary on the Mishnah*, the Jewish thinker objects to the ascription of the same nutritive soul to everything that lives. Consistent with his relativizing of "perfections," this faculty of the soul varies along with the kind of being it animates, such that "the man's nutritive part, for example, is not the same as the nutritive part belonging to a donkey or a horse."[24] Plants are absent from this discussion, albeit not for long. Already in the next sentence, a palm tree makes an appearance alongside animals and humans. And this time it is not entirely soulless: "For man is nourished by the nutritive part of the human soul, a donkey is nourished by a nutritive part of the donkey's soul, and a palm tree is nourished by the nutritive part of its soul."[25] The point is that the faculties of the soul do not find exact equivalents in other species and are not divisible as parts of the body are. What Aristotle treated as the most common, "shared" kind of psyche is, in Maimonides, a soul specific to each creature. The question is why Maimonides is so invested in proving that Aristotle went astray on this point. My hypothesis is that, lurking behind this laudable avowal of difference by the medieval thinker, is the general rule of noncontamination—avoiding mixes of the pure and the impure, as well as one class of beings and another—which is the ontological and ethical lynchpin for the entirety of Maimonidean philosophy and theology.

The indivisibility of the soul, unaffected by its specialization into individual faculties, is, for Maimonides, the ground for all phenomena of life. He grasps life as the property of the whole organism, buttressed by the fact that "when parts of a living being are cut off they cease to live."[26] Plants, on the other hand, disprove this proposition, in that their shoots continue to live when they are detached from a loose assemblage that constitutes the "whole" plant. It is, most likely, this transgression of the borders that separate part and whole (not to mention life and death) that prompted Maimonides to divorce the concept of the plant from that of life. But if plants do not properly live, then what is the alternative principle of their existence? What motivates their growth?

To grasp the logic guiding the exclusion of plants from the realm of the living in the Maimonidean system, it is necessary to touch upon his "theory of spheres." The unity of the universe is a simple fourfold of spheres that (1) effect "the mixture and the composition of the elements," (2) supply "every growing thing with its vegetative functions," (3) give "each living being its vitality," and (4) endow "rational beings with intellect."[27] The movements of the spheres trigger the motions of the souls that correspond to them. It is noteworthy, for our purposes, that the vegetative force is distinguished from the power that imparts vitality to the living. Plants are animated by the first two spheres, without attaining to the life of sentient beings, let alone to the intellect of the rational ones. Humans, conversely, combine all four spheres in their existence and thus microcosmically embody the entire universe, the unity of which reflects the Oneness of its Creator.[28] In this scheme of things, plant-thinking is an abomination, as it mixes the elements of the second and the fourth spheres.

Even so, Maimonides is not unaware of the biblical and Talmudic passages where the nutritive appears to be conflated with the rational. He does not condemn these texts, but vindicates them as "figurative." (Let it be said, in passing, that, despite all appearances, the hermeneutical stance of Maimonides is quite different from that of Augustine, who did his best to spiritualize meaning as a part of a larger process of transitioning from the literalness of Jewish Law to the inwardness of Christian Love. Maimonides, in turn, is more pragmatic: he terms those meanings figurative that do not accord either with the insights of reason or with the articles of faith that prohibit the attribution of a physical, or human, body to God.) The Guide's section devoted to a scrupulous analysis of homonyms in the Bible, for example, clarifies why the verb "to eat" may be linked to "acquisition of wisdom" and "learning." Intellectual perceptions, Maimonides states, "preserve the human form (intellect) constantly in the most perfect manner, in the same way as food preserves the body in its best condition."[29] Nutrition is the all-important vegetative function, reluctantly admitted as a template for the assimilation of knowledge.

The semantic contamination of thinking with the intake of food does not violate the principle of nutritive souls unique to each class of beings or species. If pressed for a further explanation, Maimonides would argue that the association of eating with the acquisition of wisdom is attributable to the peculiar makeup of the human nutritive soul, which is a biological capacity in a being gifted with intellect. This unstated premise works as the invisible prosthesis propping up the parallel between the preservation of intellectual and bodily forms through the incorporation of knowledge and food, respectively.

Now, the sphere regulating vegetative functions was, like all the others, set into motion by God. That, Maimonides corroborates, was the first cause of the growth of plants: "Our Sages have already explained that the herbs and trees, which God caused to spring forth from the ground, were caused by God to grow, after He had sent down rain upon them. . . ."[30] Whenever seeds germinate and sprout, we are reminded about the act of Creation. The Maimonidean plant may not live as animals do, but each time it returns to the earth as a seed or reconnects with the soil through its roots, it renews and reaffirms the Creator's will. So much so that the plant's bond to the earth, while still unbroken, immunizes it against any sort of uncleanness or impurity. Replaying the exceptional time of Creation on the mundane timescale of the seasons, plants restore the judgment of God about the result of His work, "that it was good."

RITUALS OF PURIFICATION: THE PLANT, THE GROUND, AND A PERFORATED POT

On several occasions, *The Book of Cleanness (Taharah)* praises the purifying properties of the ground, or, more precisely, of the plant's undisturbed attachment to the soil. Paragraph 19 in the chapter on "Uncleanness of Foodstuffs" reads, "If unclean seeds are sown, what sprouts from them is clean, even if it is something whose seed does not perish, provided that the seed has sent out roots; but if they have not yet sent out roots, they remain unclean, even if it is something whose seed perishes."[31] Along the same lines, "roots which are left in the ground . . . and all roots usually chopped off whenever they are pulled up with the edible part" do not "contract uncleanness nor convey uncleanness."[32] And, finally, "foodstuffs which grow from the ground can contract uncleanness only after they are uprooted: so long as they are attached to the ground by but the smallest root from which they are able to live, they cannot contract uncleanness."[33] What is behind this quasi-miraculous, purifying influence of the soil? What does it dispense to the plant, in addition to the water, minerals, and physical support they draw from it?

Their reversion back to the earth retrieves not just the biological but also the theometaphysical origin of plants in the act of Creation. The genesis of creatures, of course, must be pure; to hold otherwise is to teeter dangerously on the precipice of blasphemy, blaming imperfection and impurity on God. So the defect does not lie in the plant itself, which is why even the weakest of the root's attachment to the soil exonerates the entire lettuce rooted in it. The flaws and blemishes are in how humans handle produce, rendering it impure by bringing it into proximity with a dead body, for instance. Regardless of seed contamination, their sprouts are purified, once they give off roots, reviving their primordial connection to the divine origin of existence. Humans who transgress the Law are impotent to undo the work of Creation, which is vigorously repeated in each germinating seed.

As always, Maimonides stays attentive to the nitty-gritty details of everyday life that complicate the unconditional purity of natural growth. What if a plant is grown in a pot? Although rooted in the soil, would it not be closer to a product of human industry than to a spontaneously sprouting thing of nature? This question reverberates across the entire Maimonidean legal corpus. In *The Book of Seasons*, where to "pick something growing is a species of reaping" and is thus prohibited on the Sabbath, an exemption from liability is granted to anyone who "picks a plant from a pot without a hole . . . because the plant is not in its natural place of growth." "On the other hand," Maimonides adds, "a pot with a hole large enough for a small root is subject to the same rule as the ground, and if one plucks a plant from it, he is liable."[34] The Book of Acquisitions relates that seeds planted in a perforated pot no longer fall under the category "movables"—these seeds are, rather, deemed to be "planted in the ground, and whatever is attached to the land is like the land."[35] The Book of Cleanness validates this idea: "If a plant pot has a hole big enough for a small root to come out through it, it counts as the ground, and what is planted is not susceptible to uncleanness."[36]

Anxiety about such seemingly meaningless details is symptomatic of a deeper source of worry for Maimonides. The plants' uncontrollable growth, above and below ground level, threatens to destabilize the rigid boundaries set by the Law. Rootlets growing through the perforation of a pot muddle the difference between natural and artificial environments. The roots of a tree in a field disrespect private property lines and extend to neighboring territory (in this case, if, while digging a well, one encounters the roots of a neighbor's tree, one is legally allowed to cut through them).[37] Giving rise to new plants, contaminated seeds cause an upheaval in the distinction between the pure and the impure. What plant growth thus compromises is the very integrity of the Law, which is built on the premise that the boundaries it has drawn would ensure, with the greatest precision possible, the conceptual, categorial, and practical segregation of various types of beings, spheres, and activities. In traversing distinct fields—both agricultural and ontological—plants thwart nothing less than the spirit or the animus of the Law. The philosopher's worry about them is, at bottom, a worry about the limits of the Law and its finite capacity to institute a perfectly immutable world-system (or, better yet, to reiterate and subscribe to the one already created by God).

The philosophical dimension of this anxiety is discernable in the Maimonidean ratiocination that the nutritive and imaginative faculties of the soul are completely unrelated to the Law. Besides their incapacity to follow the commandments, they are powerless even to transgress legal precepts because "there is no obedience or disobedience in the nutritive or imaginative parts."[38] While it is not a carbon copy of the vegetal soul in Aristotle, the nutritive part of our soul is equally heedless to the voice of reason crystallized in the Law. Along with imagination, it cannot act otherwise than it does, being totally oblivious to the distinctions spelled out in *Mishneh Torah* and elsewhere. As a result, the nutritive and the imaginative parts of the soul potentially imperil the entire systematic project of Maimonides.

Since legal frames cannot contain the activity of the nutritive soul within and outside of us, Maimonides resorts to the purity of the species in order to keep the vegetal excess in check. He prohibits grafting, which violates species boundaries and rouses idolatry and raw sexuality, the two crucial components of fertility rituals. Maimonides actually singles out grafting for its orgiastic and ritualistic connotations. Appalled by the rites of the Sabaeans, who in the beginning of the first millennium BC founded a kingdom in the area of contemporary Yemen and the southern tip of the Arabian Peninsula, he describes how "when one species is grafted [by the Sabaeans] upon another, the branch which is to be grafted must be in the hand of a beautiful damsel, whilst a male person has disgraceful and unnatural sexual intercourse with her; during that intercourse the woman grafts the branch into the tree."[39] To Maimonides, grafting is offensive both for its public display of raw vegetal and human sexuality and for the mixing of species. But, above all, it is a perversion of Creation, where the divine decree caused plants to spring forth from the ground, not from other plants. Whereas the return of the seed to the soil purifies the shoots that germinate from it, the technical operation of grafting, imbricated with the "unnatural" sexual intercourse prominently featured in the ritual, is a sign of heresy and contamination.

It bears repeating that the plants themselves are not blameworthy, as they are a priori freed from responsibility for their activity. Without further ado, Maimonides assumes that their growth is indifferent to the outcome, whether it reconnects the plant with the ground from which it is separated by a perforated pot or fastens it to another tree as a graft. It is up to humans to prevent vegetable miscegenation by taking precautions, for example, not to "sow any two kinds of seed together or near each other."[40] The Law is entrusted with the mission of policing the conceptual and physical borders between species, domains, and categories. The proscription of growing different crops together is but the tip of the iceberg in the *Book of Agriculture*, with its detailed prohibitions of seed *(zeraim)* mixtures. Here, the root ceases to play a purifying role; au contraire, "mixed" grains and fruit become hallowed when sowing is successful and when they take root.[41] For all intents and purposes, seed mixtures and grafts are indistinguishable in their negative effect on the legally instituted order.

So extreme is the demand for noncontamination—and, at times, so foreign to the modern sensibility—that it prescribes the purification of urban spaces of trees that do not properly belong in the city. "A tree," Maimonides writes, "may not be grown within a distance of twenty-five cubits [about eleven meters or thirty-eight feet] from the town, or fifty cubits if it is a carob or a sycamore tree, in order to preserve the beauty of a town."[42] After we get a chance to catch our collective breath upon reading this admittedly outlandish rule, its logic becomes relatively clear. The beauty of urban space lies in its purity—a formal purity, in Kantian vernacular—that does not tolerate any admixtures of elements drawn from the natural environment. The ban on planting trees within and immediately outside the city limits resurrects the figure of *arbor sacra* for aesthetic reasons, themselves deeply rooted in the concerns with what is sacred, that is, separated and set apart. From the perspective of a city dweller, the tree is relegated to a permanent state of exception, which is congruent with our alienation from nature.

AGAINST A TALKING TREE, OR THE UNFINISHED WORK OF DISENCHANTMENT

Vis-à-vis polytheism and idol worship, the nonmystical strands of Judaism present themselves as the champions of disenchantment. Despite operating within a religious context, "rational" Judaism ridicules those who see wondrous, if not miraculous, features in the creaturely existence of animals, plants, and certain aspects of inorganic nature. The ban on grafting needs to be set within this broader context, much like Maimonides' scathing critique of fertility cults that mention "a tree which in its root resembles a human being, utters a loud sound, and speaks a word or words."[43] The fables about the wonders of plants are just that—mere fables. But they carry a grain of truth, which we are only now beginning to discover in plant signaling and communication studies. Certainly, plants do not speak in a human voice, but they do send complex biochemical messages to other plants and insects. The roots of corn seedlings, for instance, produce acoustic emissions, for a yet unknown reason.[44] What Maimonides pejoratively dubs "those days of darkness" might well be more in tune with the future of botany than the reductionist view of plants to which the Jewish sage adhered.

With his unwavering commitment to science and to a reconciliation of faith and reason, Maimonides conducted his own botanical researches, assembled in his treatise Medicinal Plants, a book that falls within the tradition of Aristotle and Dioscorides.[45] In the context of this commitment, his denial of plant vitality is itself an effect of his earnest desire to "disenchant the world," as Max Weber once put it. To speculate a little, Maimonides must have thought that to grant plants the status of the living is to indulge in the excesses of animism, separated by a hair's breadth from the myths of talking trees and other fabular, fabulous, wondrous things. Determined to purge the Bible of anything reminiscent of the premonotheistic worldview, he advances a figurative reading of those sacred textual fragments that are ostensibly inconsistent with the precepts of reason. The rational form of religion demands this sacrifice of literalness; only on the condition that the text announce something other than what it actually says does the holy writ gain the right of admission into a "reconciled" conglomeration of faith and reason.

Along these lines, the Maimonidean hermeneutical machine processes two striking passages from Isaiah: "The mountains and the hills shall break forth in song before you, and all the trees of the wood clap their hands" and "The fir-trees rejoice at thee." Animated or emotive vegetation is, on this reading, "clearly and evidently" a rhetorical device.[46] With a great dose of sobriety, Maimonides insinuates that anthropomorphic descriptions of nonhuman beings and of God are symptomatic of the immaturity of mythic thinking. He holds that myths are much more than childish stories; they are also the narrative dressing of our hubris, which begins by placing the human at the center of the universe and culminates with anthropomorphizing the entire world—and, alongside the world, its Creator. Read without the patience they deserve, prophetic visions can pass for mythic fragments in an otherwise rationally defensible text. So what differentiates them from myth? Why are Isaiah's rejoicing fir trees admissible while the talking roots of the Sabaeans aren't?

Maimonides perceives the glaring difference between mythic thinking and prophetic allegory as dependent not on the usual contrast between dream and reality, but on a distinction between a dream that does not know itself as such and a dream conscious of itself. Psychoanalytically speaking, prophesies are procured from unconscious material already elevated to the level of conscious analysis. As such, they are aware of their indirect meaning and dreamlike, associational structure.[47] Prophets yearn for the interpretation of the vision (*khazon:* also meaning "dream"), the deep meaning of which is often foreclosed to them at the beginning. Myths, conversely, are entirely submerged in unconscious life, where ideas are not represented but embodied in objects, both animate and inanimate. They do not move past the belief that a talking tree, qua tree, is the dwelling place of a spirit that communicates to us. Abstractly put, myths do not contend with the meaning of meaning, starting with a metarealization that, in addition to being itself, the tree is a cipher for something else.

There is much to be said in defense of literalness, which, to be sure, is not as entrenched in mythic thinking as Maimonides makes it out to be. A literal reading may, in effect, be more ethical than its allegorical counterpart. Prophetic visions see past the trees themselves but myopically miss the forest; myths give vegetal life its due, in that they do not ask (at least, not openly so) whatever else this life signifies. However contrived it may be, the literalness of myth resonates with the literal meaning spatially expressed by the plants themselves and contained in their every shoot, branch, and leaf.

For a proponent of allegorical sense, the plant itself, in the bareness of its existence, is meaningless. This axiom is the cornerstone of the paradoxical hermeneutic construction of *arbor sacra*. Nowhere is this meaninglessness as pronounced as in the processes of vegetal decay, because what does not truly live cannot really die. Whereas germination is a symbol reaffirming the continuity of Creation, the death of plants and the loss of their parts are downright inconsequential. As mere chance occurrences in nature, they are too paltry to be subject to God's decision-making power ("For I do not believe that it is through the interference of Divine Providence that a certain leaf drops [from a tree]"),[48] which judges humans alone the epicenters of free will.[49] The nonmechanistic complexity of humans plays itself out at the expense of the machine-like simplicity of nature. It is this complexity that gives us depth and makes us interesting, perhaps even for God Himself. In the great *theatrum mundi*, God and, in a different sense, the humans are actors; the rest is a series of props and decorations. Worse still, the plants' exclusion from the category "living beings" in Maimonides relegates them to the background of the background, the mostly unobtrusive green milieu, a stage set for a stage set.

Forlorn by the ideally omnipotent God, the plant is entrusted to the blind routines of mechanical causality and chance. But in this state of abandon lies the promise of freedom. Plants are trivial and, therefore, unworthy of divine interest—that is how they manage to slip away from God's untiring vigilance and potency. They delineate the edges of direct divine engagement in the world and drop off the radar of God's (and "the great eagle's") totalizing, panoramic gaze. A chain reaction ensues: plants are neglected, left to their own devices, and subsequently grow all the more mysterious. Their freedom is still more radical than that inherent in human free will. Incidentally, this last notion is a metaphysical fiction that creeps into Maimonides' dream of a disenchanted, purely rational religion. The work of disenchantment is unfinished and will remain so until the last tree is uprooted and the final bit of unconscious material taken up in conscious analysis.

NOTES

1. Moses Maimonides, *The Code of Maimonides, Book Twelve: The Book of Acquisitions*, trans. Isaac Klein (New Haven, CT: Yale University Press, 1951), 86.
2. Giorgio Agamben, *Homo Sacer*, trans. Daniel Heller-Roazen (Stanford, CA: Stanford University Press, 1998), 10.
3. Agamben, *Homo Sacer*, 21.
4. Maimonides, *Acquisitions*, 88.
5. Maimonides, *Acquisitions*, 7.
6. Maimonides, *Acquisitions*, 87.
7. Maimonides, *Acquisitions*, 88.
8. Compare with "Whoever takes possession of ownerless property acquires title to it. Thus also in the case of deserts, rivers, and streams, the law is that whatever is in them, as for example, plants, trees, and the fruits of the trees of the woods, has the status of ownerless property, and whoever is first to take possession of them acquires title to them." Maimonides, *Acquisitions*, 110.

9. Moses Maimonides, *The Code of Maimonides, Book Three: The Book of Seasons*, trans. Solomon Gandz and Hyman Klein (New Haven, CT: Yale University Press, 1961), 7.
10. Maimonides, *Seasons*, 41.
11. Moses Maimonides, *The Guide for the Perplexed*, trans. M. Friedländer (New York: Dover, 1956), 180, translation modified.
12. Maimonides, *Guide*, 274.
13. See Eric Silverman, "Anthropocentrism and the Medieval Problem of Religious Language," in *Anthropocentrism: Humans, Animals, Environment*, ed. Rob Boddice (Leiden: Brill, 2011), especially the section "Maimonides' Via Negativa," 121–126.
14. Maimonides, *Guide*, 309.
15. Maimonides, *Guide*, 275.
16. Maimonides, *Guide*, 81.
17. Maimonides, *Guide*, 56.
18. Maimonides, *Guide*, 35.
19. On the irreducibility of ambivalence in Maimonides, see Idit Dobbs-Weinstein, "The Ambiguity of the Imagination and the Ambivalence of Language in Maimonides and Spinoza," in *Maimonides and His Heritage*, ed. Idit Dobbs-Weinstein et al. (Albany: SUNY Press, 2009), 95–112.
20. Maimonides, *Guide*, 60.
21. Maimonides, *Guide*, 80.
22. Maimonides, *Guide*, 35.
23. Maimonides, *Guide*, 35.
24. Moses Maimonides, *The Ethical Writings of Maimonides*, ed. Raymond Weiss and Charles Butterworth (New York: New York University Press, 1975), 61. See also Jehuda Melber, *The Universality of Maimonides* (New York: Jonathan David, 1968), 76ff.
25. Maimonides, *The Ethical Writings*, 61–62.
26. Maimonides, *Guide*, 124.
27. Maimonides, *Guide*, 115.
28. Maimonides, *Guide*, 115.
29. Maimonides, *Guide*, 140.
30. Maimonides, *Guide*, 215.
31. Moses Maimonides, *The Code of Maimonides, Book Ten: The Book of Cleanness*, trans. Herbert Danby (New Haven, CT: Yale University Press, 1954), 339.
32. Maimonides, *Cleanness*, 352.
33. Maimonides, *Cleanness*, 336.
34. Maimonides, *Seasons*, 43.
35. Maimonides, *Acquisitions*, 15.
36. Maimonides, *Cleanness*, 338.

37. Maimonides, *Acquisitions*, 193.

38. Maimonides, *Ethical Writings*, 64.

39. Maimonides, *Guide*, 337.

40. Maimonides, *Guide*, 337.

41. See Moses Maimonides, *The Code of Maimonides, Book Seven: The Book of Agriculture*, trans. Isaac Klein (New Haven, CT: Yale University Press, 1979), esp. Kilayim 5:13.

42. Maimonides, *Acquisitions*, 191.

43. Maimonides, *Guide*, 318.

44. See Monica Gagliano, Stefano Mancuso, and Daniel Robert, "Towards Understanding Plant Bioacoustics," *Trends in Plant Science* 17, no. 6 (2012): 323–325.

45. Sherwin Nuland, *Maimonides* (New York: Schocken, 2005), 94.

46. Maimonides, *Guide*, 248.

47. Maimonides, *Guide*, 238–239.

48. Maimonides, *Guide*, 286.

49. Even then the "prophets . . . express their surprise that God should take notice of man, who is too little and too unimportant to be worthy of the attention of the Creator; how, then, should other living creatures be considered as proper objects of Divine Providence!"

Main Pathway: Cross-Pollination

Subthemes

Proceed to Transcending, p. 43
Proceed to Decolonization, p. 43

3

HERMENEUTICS OF TREES IN AN AFRICAN CONTEXT: ENRICHING THE UNDERSTANDING OF THE ENVIRONMENT "FOR THE COMMON HERITAGE OF HUMANKIND"

Angela Roothaan

INTRODUCTION

In this chapter, I will look into case studies of the relations of human communities to trees, especially in West-African traditions, and ask how these contribute to a richer understanding of the environment. In traditional cultures all over the world, trees have been important to humans as "natural symbols" of the central values of communal life, as sources of food and medicine, and as signs of spiritual realities. African traditional relations to trees are of special interest, as they are contested in present-day clashes between modernization movements, religious conversion movements, secular conservationalist movements, and traditionalist movements. Looking into the content of the contested—a rich hermeneutics of trees—is not only of historical interest. It can also contribute to an understanding of the environment that can help create more sustainable relations of humans to their environment for the future.

Originally published as "Hermeneutics of Trees in an African Context," in *African Philosophy and Environmental Conservation*, ed. Jonathan Chimakonam (London: Routledge, 2018). Reprinted with permission of the Licensor through PLSclear

In the first section, I will outline which different frameworks determine the human relationship to the environment, especially in the West-African context. The frameworks described are those of secularization, of monotheistic theology, and of traditionalism. Whilst conservationalists might work together with Christians, Muslims, or those practicing traditional religions, their basic presuppositions will be scientific and secular. All the same, Muslims and Christians have their own spiritual understanding of the relation of humans to nature, in the frame of a theology of creation, religious morality and the afterlife, which can conflict with secular as well as traditionalist outlooks. All parties mentioned will also try to negotiate their interests within the framework of the global economy, "selling" sacred forests as places of touristic interest or of rare plant life, for instance, or using religious fervor to promote economic progress.

After presenting the intersections of frameworks for understanding the meaning of trees, I will discuss, in the second section, two examples of cases of the cutting of trees which show conflicting meanings attributed to trees. Here I will show how the frameworks clash into each other and make a shared discourse on what is of common human interest a complex issue. To view trees as a place of contested meaning, it is important to understand them as bearers of symbolism and signification—something which has been described in the work on trees in public and religious discourse in Senegal by geographer and Islamologist Eric Ross. In the third section, I will go deeper into his work on the holy city of Touba, the capital of Mouride Sufism, which represents *tuba*, the tree of paradise. This work shows us how neoplatonic understandings of (spiritual) reality play their role in Sufi theology, and how an ontology can be seen to be at work in it (as it is in Christian traditions that value worship of holy places, moments, and persons), which I will call "shamanistic."[1] Ross has thus shown that religious ascription of meaning to trees is not to be understood in a simple, one-dimensional manner, but that here, as in other frameworks, complex historico-cultural developments have shaped understandings and practices.

In the final section, I will then return to a more general discussion of how different contexts and discourses lead to contested meanings of trees. I will present here also a more specific philosophical account of African views of nature, as it is given in an article by Michael Onyebuchi Eze on eco-humanism.[2] In the tradition of writers such as Tempels and Mbiti, he proposes to adopt a holistic view of nature understood as life force, which leads to viewing human beings as an element in the whole of nature., As much as such an account helps to explain the spiritual meaning of trees, it suppresses the difficulties described in my earlier sections, arising from the clashing of frameworks. Therefore, I make a plea for a multidimensional approach which brings the varying positions and views into dialogue after first having disentangled and understood their differences and conflicts.

INTERSECTING FRAMEWORKS

When we study the subject of trees in an African context, several frameworks of action have to be taken into account. There is, first, the framework of modernization, with its separate streams of secularization, the growth of an autonomous economic sphere and technological development. These streams are often taken to be identical, but although they have been going hand in hand for the most part of European history since the 17th century, they never have been simple, and their relations are certainly more complex in other regions and times. In the United States, for instance, for a long time one of the world's driving nations with respect to economic and technological developments, society and politics remained largely determined by the Christian religion.

On the African continent, things have been still more complex, and historiographies which are not biased by the colonial outlook are still in the process of being written. Although secularization is a force in present developments, the processes of Christianization and Islamization are also an important force, although in a different manner in different parts of the continent. Economic and technological developments often also are driven by these religious developments, as well through migrant worker networks as in transformations on local levels. Further, the potential of different religious groups to impact society again depends on economic and political factualities that in themselves are not religious. The rise of societal influence of the Sufi-Islamic Mouride brotherhood in Senegal, e.g., could take place only in the political voids left by colonialism in their destruction of traditional kingdoms and nobility, as well as in the frame of economic opportunities created by the colonial trading system, and the new global trading networks that came after decolonization (cf. Barry, 1988; Ross, 2006).

Taken from their own perspective, movements which focus on the purification of monotheistic religion, and/or the conversion of people may coincide with the modern secular outlook which values technological and economic progress, overruling traditional practices based on the belief in the sacredness of nature. An example can be seen in how the Mouride brotherhood in Senegal, valuing prayer and work as central values, has played a pivotal role in cutting down several forests (which are traditionally seen as sacred places) in Senegal for purposes of peanut production.[3] All the same, whereas the Islamic theology in principle robs trees from the protection by guarding spirits (because the might of God/Allah will always be greater than that of any spiritual being), it still lends a spiritual meaning to nature in general, and to trees in particular, as the symbol of heavenly paradise that Allah holds for his believers[4] (Ross, 2006).

A framework that is also of importance for understanding the plural meanings of trees is the modern-secular framework that drives the work of many international environmentalist and conservationalist organizations working on the African continent. Such a framework will make us see religious movements, as well as traditional beliefs and practices, only as having a positive or negative effect on the thriving of the environment, without valuing their normative viewpoints in their own right. The environmentalist/conservationalist framework has its own normative views, of course, of which sustainability is a key one. Our ways to live in the world should be sustainable, that is, the human race should not use up resources, looking only for short-term profit, and creating long-term death and destruction. All the same, propagators of this framework never ask about the perspective expressed in the word *environment*. Environment for whom? For the human race, in the end. Although striving for a sustainable environment for humans will probably have the effect that animals and trees and other living beings also have better chances than if we strive only for profit and domination of nature, the perspective of secularism cannot ask about the meaning of nature—or of trees, for that matter—in a wider frame than that of humanity. Humanity cannot be understood, by secularists, from an angle in which non-human or supra-human values count.

Finally, there are also traditionalist movements, which, in an attempt to counter the negative influences of the colonial era, aim for a return to old religious beliefs and traditional social customs. An example is to be found in Benin, where Vodun religion has been reinstalled on a national level. Traditionalist movements have for their aim to preserve (or, if necessary, to reconstruct or reinvent) traditional knowledges and practices in which the relation of humans to their environment is considered from a perspective in which the spiritual aspect of all beings is taken into account. Humans in that perspective can live healthy and prosperous lives only if they know how to address the spiritual world that transcends their strictly human aims. In the present situation, where the forces of global economies and nation-based politics reign, traditionalism will have to negotiate its values with those of, most notably, international tourism and national culture (cf. Juhe-Beaulaton and Roussel, 2003) and, through these, also with conservationalism. We see this happening where the traditionalists' view of certain forests as sacred has now been taken up by the international conservation efforts of the UN by declaring those forests cultural heritage, naming them ICCAs: Indigenous Peoples' and Community Conserved Territories and Areas (www.cbd.int/pa/doc/ts64-case-studies/senegal-en.pdf). These negotiations, however, may have the effect that the return to traditional spirituality will transform into a matter of cultural folklore.

When we zoom in on the subject of trees as bearers of meaning in an African context, the different frameworks mentioned above overlap, interact, and come into conflict. For my purposes, I want to question not only how these different frameworks prestructure any possible hermeneutics of trees, but also how the different meanings given to trees can enter into dialogue with each other. The meaning of trees should not be understood one-dimensionally, but we should carefully disentangle the different meanings bestowed by different groups in societies, and thus take their frameworks of reference into account.

RELIGION AND THE SYMBOLISM OF TREES

A first example of trees' contested meaning is provided in the case of the cutting of the Mbegue' forest (Khelkom in Senegal), described by Schoonmaker Freudenberger (1991), where deforestation was carried out for economic and religious reasons (to provide opportunities for the agricultural labor through which salvation is supposed to be reached). In this case, we see how monotheistic religion can suspend possible cultural or spiritual inhibitions against felling old trees whilst at the same time stressing their symbolic religious meaning (i.e., the "right" religious meaning). Schoonmaker Freudenberger has described in a passionate tone how in 1991 Mouride faithful, following a call of their religious leadership on the radio, cleared a whole forest in just a few weeks:

> From village and city, the faithful flocked to Mbegue, bringing axes and saws to clearcut 173 square miles of one of the last remaining forests in Senegal's degraded heartland. In three weekends, they felled more than five million Sahelian trees and shrubs. [...] For his part, the Khalifa-General (supreme head) of the powerful Mouride Islamic brotherhood was well

on the way to meeting his goal: 45,000 hectares of newly cleared and fertile land would soon be put into peanut production. (Schoonmaker Freudenberger, 1991, p. 1)

In this example, we see a conflict of meaning given to trees by the secular environmentalist author (who wants to ward off desertification and uphold a livable human habitat) and the religious Mourides, who negotiated economic opportunities and a theology of the good religious life, resulting in ending the life of the forest. Underneath these conflicting views there is also a conflict between two peoples/cultures: the Wolof Mouride faithful and title Fulhe herders who traditionally lived in the forest, and who were displaced by the (legal) cutting of the trees. The Fulbe possibly also hold more traditionalist views of the spiritual meaning of trees, although they just as well consider themselves Muslims.

A second example of the contested meaning of trees is from a story narrated to me by Michael Onyebuchi Eze on the tree called Uvuru, which was dominating the central square of his native village in the present day Enugu state of Nigeria. Ukwu Uvuru may have been more than 1,000 years old, according to reports, and had served from time immemorial as a place for public assemblies, as a source of fruits for children sitting in its shade, and it was ascribed a status of sacredness. It was cut down in 2002 by young Christians, who had been motivated to do so by their pastor. The motivation given was that the tree not just symbolized, but actually embodied evil forces which would explain the social and economic problems of the locals. It supposedly held the people chained to the past and would hinder progress—so chopping it down was expected to solve that.

Although I don't know more details of the case, it seems a clear example of what happens when Christianity claims its ground by opposing traditional (folk) beliefs and practices. The idea is that ancient sacred places (or the opposite—places of evil), be they a water source, a magnificent tree, or a crossing of roads, should either be Christianized or be removed. In many places in Europe, you see images of the Christian cross, or road altars for certain saints, where there used to be places of ancient taboos, or of worship—like under an oak, at a well, or at a crossing.[5] Surveying the literature makes clear that traditional spirituality, which often survives in folk beliefs and practices, is seen as a problem in the eyes of many Christian leaders. In the example of Ukwu Uvuru, the loyalty of people towards anything traditional, even if there might not be an attitude involved that would contradict Christianity, is seen as a sign of lack of religious trust.

In religious studies, a sociological and anthropological point of view is predominant—leading to the explanation of the resurgence of traditional beliefs as a consequence of problems of modernization (cf. Juhe-Beaulaton, 2008, p. 8, and Ter Haar, 1992, p. 111). Economic difficulties, or the alienation resulting from urbanization, would be the main factor in seeking help in the spiritual realm of traditional deities. Christian theological discussions of the matter sometimes harmonize with these views in describing traditional spiritual practices as disturbing the order in society. One final example of this approach in a recent thesis on the tensions between belief in deities and Christianity in contemporary Igbo culture. The author, Christopher Okwor, writes as a recommendation that

> the church should as a matter of necessity adopt a holistic approach to evangelisation. Christianity must be ready to feed the deep spiritual and material quests of the Igbo *in order to control them and be able to divert their attention from deities* (italics are mine). [. . .] Shrines are valuable heritage of our past. Burning of shrines should be treated as a very serious offence. [. . .] Shrines should be developed into tourist centres. They are homes for endangered species of plants and animals and some have beautiful caves and springs. (Okwor, 2012, pp. 134–135)

The central problem with traditional practices of worship of deities seems to be that they escape the dominant morality and legality and are therefore "beyond control." Here we see the secularist framework, with its two main interests, tourism and sustainability, join hands with a Christianizing interest: the striving for a moral life according to biblical prescriptions for the good life. We see the same effect in the work of Juhe-Beaulaton, a historian, who directs attention to issues concerning law and order surrounding sacred forests and shrines. Like Okwor, she sees a harmonization between conservationalist, traditionalist, and the legal and economic interests of the state as a solution to preserve the "beautiful" places of worship whilst pacifying the spiritual needs of the people (Juhe-Beaulaton, 2008). In these approaches, however, the inherent value of the spiritual meaning of these shrines, often part of small forests, and therefore of the trees that mark and localize them, is lost, thus excluding the other mentioned framework which claims certain meanings for the environment in general, and trees in particular, namely the framework of a more spiritual outlook on things, in monotheist as well as in traditional religions. More apprehension for this aspect is found in the work of geographer and Islamologist Eric Ross, who has studied the symbolic meanings and usage of trees in West Africa, especially in Senegal, in their own right. While in non-African contexts the central tree in an African community has become known as "palaver tree" (from the Portuguese word for "speech" or "discussion"), Ross indicates that this name is too narrow:

> [it] designates what is in reality a number of different phenomena which make political, social or religious use of individualized trees. [. . .] Rather than a single "palaver tree" serving as locus of public debate, polities were marked by a number of different trees, of various species, which served a variety of public and collective functions, only one of which was the "palaver" process. (Ross, 2008, p. 136)

Through field research, Ross has located and described many ancient trees in Senegal, which often have survived the royal palaces or the villages of which they at one time were the center. He has opened up a new branch of research, combining the locating on Google maps of the individual trees, photographing them, and describing the oral histories that are told by the people living there. Thus, he has made a beginning to make local knowledge accessible to the wider world: the knowledge that distinguishes between the public, social, political, and religious functions of trees. The ancient, hollow, baobabs are known to have been used as shrines, altars, and tombs for the griots (court singers, like the medieval European jesters or troubadours). Trees are also mentioned where a battle took place, or a boundary existed (Ross, 2008, pp. 136–137). In their function as the embodiment of political legitimacy, they can be compared with the obelisks, triumphal arches, and other symbolic structures in Europe. In addition, trees could be the places where justice was rendered. In these public functions, they were and are seen as "places of power" and places of memory (Ross, 2008, pp. 139, 144). Trees thus function as

> markers, as memorials and as monuments. These functions are spatial in that they contribute meaning to the landscape, but they are also social and political, in that they "fix" identities while also articulating a spiritual worldview. (Ross, 2008, p. 146)

TREES AS ARCHETYPE

In his work on the sacred city of Touba (an elaborated and reworked version of his dissertation), the urban place which is the center of worship in Senegalese Mouride Islam,

Ross explains the mystical and symbolic understanding of trees. Mouride mysticism is a modern branch (defying the conflict between modern and traditional) of neoplatonic Sufi understanding of the world in relation to God as creator and provider of grace for human beings. The city of Touba, in the inner land of Senegal, was founded in 1887, by Shaykh Ahmadou Bamba Mbacke (1853–1927), on the authority of a revelation from God about the locality of this sacred place. According to a local legend:

> After a patient search his [of the Shaykh] attention was drawn, one day, to a tree which stood out dearly from the others by its size, its importance and its peculiar location. The tree [. . .] stood on a plateau on the spot where the dome of Touba Mosque now stands. Ahmadou Bamba prayed in the shade of the tree, and that is where he had his long awaited revelation. (Cited in Ross, 2006, p. 28)

The sacredness of Touba is experienced and reinforced in the yearly pilgrimage believers make to the city, where they offer prayers in its grandiose mosque, longing to be buried within the city when they die, which for them symbolizes the closest connection to heavenly paradise. Touba, the name of the city, originally comes from the word *tuba*, which means "the Tree of Paradise" in Islamic tradition. It stands for the bliss of the heavenly state of the righteous after death.

As trees often play a critical role in foundation legends of places of human habitation as well as of religious movements (think of Buddha, who also received a revelation under a tree, and the symbolic "tree" of the Christian cross), Ross explores the specifics of this role in the case of Touba within the context of Sufi neoplatonic understanding. Here Touba is seen as "a qutb, a 'pole' or axis mundi. [. . .] The concept of qutb is primarily an astronomical one. It designates the 'celestial pole,' a hypothetical spot in the sky around which the heavens revolve" (Ross, 2006, p. I 8). In neoplatonism, the cosmos is understood as an unfolding of reality in layers of being, emanating from God, which are closer or farther removed from his, so to speak, ontological and spiritual gravity center. According to Ross,

> Sufism has invested this astronomical term with several related spiritual meanings. The term qutb is used to describe *transcendence*. It can be applied to any being, moment, event, or place which connects various layers of reality to each other. (Ross, 2006, p. 18)

It can be a moment, which thus should be remembered with reverence—like the moment of revelation of an individual. It can also be a special, rare and beautiful place such as a river, a grove, a high mountain, or a city (cf. Jerusalem, which is understood as a place where the divine can be almost 'touched' by Jews, Christians, and Muslims). It can also be, according to Sufism, a person—which then leads to taking, for instance, the grave of this person as a place for pilgrimage. Touching the grave or some other act of dedication can then help the believer on his/her spiritual path. Ross further explains this in more philosophical language by citing Mircea Eliade:

> A sacred place constitutes a break in the homogeneity of space; this break is symbolised by an opening by which passage from one cosmic region to another is made possible (from heaven to earth and vice versa; from earth to the underworld); communication with heaven is expressed by one or another of certain images, all of which refer to the axis mundi, pillar [. . .], ladder (cf. Jacob's ladder), mountain, tree, vine, etc.; around this cosmic axis lies the world (= our world), hence the axis is located "in the middle", at the "navel of the earth"; it is the Center of the World. (Cited in Ross, 2006, p. 20)

The qutb, the axis, can therefore also be a tree, and it often is. To make things more clear for modern readers, Ross introduces the term *archetype*, coined by Carl Gustav Jung in his psychology of the collective subconscious. He makes clear that one does not have to accept Jungian drive-psychology to use this concept, which just indicates what Sufi theosophism means by fixed essences, the forms which "hold," or refer to, the divine presence of God. Although, as is clear from the above, designating trees as archetype of the relation of humanity to the spiritual realm is in no way restricted to an African context, trees play an important role in African spiritual symbolism (next to all kinds of other signs, of course, such as water, certain animals, fire, etc.).

As Ross's research into the *palaver* trees has made clear, the central tree of a village or royal courtyard often survives the mud-structures of the human habitats themselves. The trees thus serve as memorials of human deeds and experiences in the past. In the specific instance of Touba, the belief in the spiritual tree, symbolizing the entrance of paradise, is considered as the "celestial register upon which the names and deeds of individuals are recorded" (Ross, 2006, p. 31). The symbolism of the tree is even more elaborate, as the words of Cheickh Tidiane Sy make clear:

> In Islamic tradition, Touba also designates a tree of Paradise on whose leaves are inscribed each human's good and evil acts. Each leaf, as it falls, inexorably provokes the death of the

individual whose acts have been recorded. The leaf is then preserved for the Day of Judgment. (Cited in Ross, 2006, p. 32)

To inscribe themselves on this divine spiritual record, Mouride believers scratch their names and those of their loved ones on an actual baobab tree in the city of Touba. In this religious practice, there is thus no sharp distinction between a material act (taking out a knife and carving letters into the bark of a tree, like lovers do in modern Europe, and perhaps all over the world, to pledge the eternity of their bond); and a spiritual act of faith (believing in or hoping for the saving grace of paradise, which is just another metaphor for the nearness of God).

This "mixing" of matter and mind, of belief and practice, shows how "shamanistic"[6] spiritual ontologies are present in monotheistic religion, even if full shamanistic ontologies do not focus so much on unity, as in the unity of God, but see all phenomena as potential manifestations of spirit, or as vehicles to reach the spiritual realm. Moving in the spaces of such "hybrid" (to borrow a concept of Bruno Latour) realities is contrary to the protestant (modern Christian) idea that only belief can save souls, for which reason much of traditional ritual behavior then should be considered irrational, and even banned. In this respect radical Protestantism reflects the same spirit as secular modernism (although I would not want to make a historical claim as to one inspiring the other). And since this secularism forms the actual (although not the necessary) framework of most modern philosophy, it has become hard in philosophy to understand archetypal relations of humans to trees as something more than irrationality.

The relation to ancient mysticism, which is so central in Mouride Sufism, can be put in a wider framework, as Ross has done in an article from 1994. He there tries to understand present day Islam from an Afrocentric perspective. In Afrocentric research into the origins of African civilizations (originating in the work of Cheikh Anta Diop and leading up to present day writers such as Sarwat Anis Al-Assiouty), the link with ancient Egyptian cosmology is more and more researched, as well as its influencing role in Greek, Semitic, and, in the end, European and modern African science and religion. From a more philosophical perspective, this relation resonates in the seminal work by V. Y. Mudimbe, *The Invention of Africa*, which, in a productive dialogue with the philosophy of the French philosopher Foucault, develops the understanding of African philosophy as *gnosis*, the neoplatonic word for higher wisdom, which can be sought by means of the secret training of the initiated. This concept of gnosis, then, according to Mudimbe, is also a vehicle to transcend the cultural-anthropological concept of "Africa" as a special place or to transcend the localizing concept without leaving the place. Even to transcend the discipline and overcoming its colonialist preconditions by making it into "a more credible anthropou-logos, that is a discourse on a human being" (Mudimbe, 1988, p. 186).

TREES—CONTESTED MEANINGS

After outlining the attitude towards the meanings of trees in the crossroads of conversion movements, traditionalism, and modernization, we still have to take a closer look at the secularist point of view before we can try to show how the different frameworks might be brought into dialogue with each other.

The secular perspective, which is central to most environmentalism as well as to the investigation undergirding it, shows very clearly in the reports of Schoonmaker Freudenberger cited above, in the second section. In her account of the cutting of the Mbegue forest we see a shrill contrast with the tree-friendly mysticism of the Mouride brotherhood described by Ross. Schoonmaker Freudenberger shows that she has a more positive idea about the Fulbe pastoralists who were displaced by the cutting of the forest and who have been in conflict with agriculturalists in West Africa several times. This choice is based not on a more favorable view on one group's spiritual outlook or way of life, but on insights from environmental science and prospective expectations of which lifestyle in the Sahelian landscape might be more sustainable.

It is of importance here to underline the positive aim of secularist environmentalism—to preserve the earth for future generations of human beings, as a beautiful and healthy place to live, among a wealth of other species—plants and animals. From this aim for the future, environmentalism lends its legitimacy to critically question the behavior of human groups, peoples, but also governments and the corporate world. Its voice is an important one in the shared human efforts to live a good life, and its adherence to planning on the basis of scientific research (objective data) provides an indispensable complementary discourse to the religious conversion movements described above. All the same, one has to be critical towards its accounts too—firstly, because of the provisionality of all scientific results, which often rest on researching a limited amount of factors, leaving others in the dark, and, secondly, because it fails to grasp the role symbolism and spiritual meanings may play in motivating human behavior. If we put this second point to work with respect to the double-edged sword of Mouride theology—respecting individual trees as representative of the spiritual tree of paradise; whilst also stimulating agriculture as a good way of life for believers, even though it kills actual trees—we might be able to not just criticize the role of the Mouride leadership, as Schoonmaker Freudenberger does, for having too much power in a relatively weak state, but we might criticize it on a theological level itself.

What would such a theological criticism look like? It should direct itself at the level of understanding the relationship between the visible/material world and the religiously understood spiritual world (the paradise of God, the afterworld). In Senegalese Mouridism, there might be a conflict at work between a "shamanistic" ontology, which considers matter and ontology of heaven and earth being separate places. This kind of conflict is not specific to this branch of Islam, but can be seen in monotheistic traditions in general, and even in modern secularist worldviews where they deal with the relationships of human beings to things. Whereas shamanistic ontologies recognize each (living) being as an expression of (divine) spirit, monotheist ontologies attribute a unique meaning to the human being as the servant of God, playing a role in his plans with the cosmos. The role the human being plays in monotheism is understood to take place in two realms simultaneously: s/he can live a moral life in the visible/material world, actually helping others or making the world a better place to live in, but the real meaning of these actions lies in the "other" world, the world of eschatological issues concerning the spiritual salvation of the human and/or of everything created.

We find an example of this monotheistic approach in the Mouride felling of the Mbegue' forest, as it lets the aims of spreading the faith and the striving of humans to deserve heavenly bliss in the afterlife prevail over the life of the trees concerned. All the same, we saw the meaning of trees not to be absent in Mouride theology—as it is preserved symbolically in the reverence for certain exemplary individuals in specific holy places.[7] Here we see a reminder of how shamanistic ontology can live in monotheistic religions, not as a strange element to be rooted out (like reformation movements such as radical Protestantism or Salafism aim to do), but providing ways for religiosity to be experienced and acted out in human lives. Would this shamanistic element be more explicitly acknowledged, it might be used to criticize and correct violent acts of religions against our natural surroundings, harmonizing traditionalism and modern religiosity. In such an acknowledgement, we can see an alternative to the strictly secularist discourse of environmentalism, while creating the terms for a dialogue on the religious interpretation of our environment.

CONCLUSION

To conclude, I discuss a philosophical attempt to take the spiritual and the material wellbeing of human beings in relation to trees simultaneously into account, as presented in an article by Michael Onyebuchi Eze,[8] which aims to provide an Africanist theory of environmental ethics. His holistic viewpoint aligns with descriptions of "African" ontologies as given by the Belgian Franciscan Tempels and Kenyan theologian/philosopher John Mbiti. Both authors worked to present a view of African religion, ontology, and ethics in general, in reaction to ethnographic work from the colonial age that provided descriptions of so many different African cultures as local and exotic—over and against (Western) universal religion and ontology. (cf. ter Haar and Ellis, 2009, 404) In Tempels' work, the concept of life force is especially important. Tempels summarizes the "Bantu" metaphysics as an ontology that encompasses all being and understands it as interdependent. Whereas *Bantu Philosophy* claims to reconstruct reality as it is, it admits this reality to be accessible through different cultural frames in different ways. Following Tempels, Eze coins an understanding of ontology as dependent on cultural frames, on the one hand, but as simultaneously providing a *true* description of things, on the other, even if it may be mythological.

> It does not matter whether the exploits of Api or Uhere (river deities who were considered to protect the people, AR) during the Nigerian civil war is true or false. As a myth or legend however, what it does convey are certain philosophical truths [. . .] of the people's cosmology and understanding of their environment. Their understanding and relationship to it is adapted through this socio-cultural mindset (2017).

Eze also quotes Ramose in this context:

> According to Ramose, this idea of community includes "the greater environing wholeness in the sense of both the encompassing physical and metaphysical universe, together with the human universe in the sense of community." This community is not just a collective of humans, it is a fluid habitation of interactive forces, beings, elements, animate and inanimate matters of the environment (2017).

For our purpose, to understand the meaning of trees, the most important conclusion of Eze's article is that "environment" cannot be understood as the counterpart of an independent humanity. Nor can the aim of religion be taken to be opposed to a nature devoid of spirit. "The sacredness of nature is because all elements have vital force" (Eze, 2017). This leads then to the insight that "The environment is not just inconsequential, it is part of life and constitutive of humanity" (Eze, 2017). In this view, then, our relationship to trees should be caring and nurturing rather than economic, as the trees, together with all of nature, deserve of a respect as bearing the possibility of human life. Here we have a view that reconciles philosophically the aims of environmentalism and a certain spirituality which encompasses respect and prudence in human–nature relations.

Although I agree with the ideals as worded by Eze, his philosophical underpinning of them fails to disentangle the practical difficulties which arise out of the misunderstandings between the factual and different frameworks indicated in this work. It is my conviction that only by articulating the frameworks, highlighting their loci of conflict and internal paradoxicality, can we work towards a richer hermeneutics of trees (and the environment in general) that can form the basis for the dialogue humanity has to carry out—a dialogue that will try to reconcile the insights from science, from religious theology, and from spiritual practice, and bring them to fruition for a better cohabitation of different species on this earth. In my view, we need a multi-dimensional understanding of the meaning of trees, which alone will be able to provide a sustainable basis for conservationist policies—an understanding that will take a) scientific research, b) religious movements and theologies, and c) traditional spirituality and healing rituals serious. African philosophy as well as historical, geographical, and religious knowledge developed on the African continent provide, as I have shown, important sources for such an understanding, as well as for the envisioned dialogue from which, first, African regions and cultures, but, in the second instance, also those beyond Africa, might benefit.

NOTES

1. In Roothaan (2015), I have argued against restricting the concepts "shamanism" and "shamanistic" to the (practices of) Siberian spiritual mediators from whom they originally stem . . . and for following I. M. Lewis where he states: "I prefer to see shamanism as a general, cross-cultural phenomenon based on the shaman's mastery of spirits and the practice of this art with the aid of spirits." When we broaden his wording by substituting "the spiritual" for "spirits," it is clear that the concept also covers certain monotheistic, Buddhist and agnostic practices.

2. I want to express my gratitude to Michael Onyebuchi Eze for letting me read and make reference to an article which is still in press as well as for commenting to the first version of this paper.
3. A branch of agriculture originally stimulated by the colonial trading possibilities, although later colonial authorities worried about the desertification that might be the result—cf. Schoonmaker Freudenberger (1991, pp. 7–8; Schoonmaker Freudenberger and Schoonmaker Freudenberger, 1993, p. 15).
4. As several authors have shown, however, monotheistic conversion or purification movements also often vilify traditional spiritualism by calling its practices immoral or amoral (cf. ter Haar, 1992; ter Haar and Ellis, 2009).
5. The oak is almost the only tree that is still known to the public in Europe as symbolizing a sacred place in pre-Christian times. But of course, the pre-Christian peoples knew all the trees for their specific natural and spiritual goods and evils. Similarly to the pre-Christian traditions of Europe (of which some living practices can still be found in remote rural areas), traditional African societies know or knew the different species of trees for their medicinal usage, their food, and attribute(d) them also religious or public functions.
6. For a discussion of the word *shamanistic* and why I choose to use it, see Roothaan (2015) and note 1 above.
7. In Roothaan (2015), I have shown how monotheist founding narratives are rooted in shamanistic imagination—which might put in question whether the new religions in fact replaced the old ones, as is commonly thought, or rather adapted them to new lifestyles.
8. Since this article is still in production, no page references can be given.

REFERENCES

Barry, B. 1998 (1988). *Senegambia and the Atlantic Slave Trade*. Cambridge: Cambridge University Press.

Cabral, A. 2007 (1979). *Unity & Struggle. Speeches and Writings.* 2nd ed. Pretoria, South Africa: Unisa Press and Tsehai Publishers.

Eze, M. O. 2017. "Humanitatis-Eco (Eco-Humanism): An African Environmental Theory." In *Handbook on African Philosophy*, edited by Adeshina Afolayan and Toyin Falola, 621–632. New York: Palgrave Macmillan.

Juhe-Beaulaton, D. 2008. "Sacred Forests and the Global Challenge of Biodiversity Conservation: The Case of Benin and Togo." *Journal for the Study of Religion, Nature and Culture* 2, no. 3: 351–372.

Juhe-Beautaton, D., and B. Roussel. 2003. "May Vodun Sacred Spaces Be Considered as a Natural Patrimony?" In *Creating and Representing Sacred Spaces*, edited by T. Gardner and D. Moritz, 33–56. Göttingen: Peust & Gutschmidt Verlag.

Mudimbe. V.-Y. 1988. *The Invention of Africa: Gnosis, Philosophy and the Order of Knowledge*. Bloomington: Indiana University Press.

Okwor, C. O. 2012. "The Significance of Deities in the Contemporary Nsukka Northern Igboland." Master's thesis, University of Nigeria, Nsukka.

Roothaan, A. 2015. "The 'Shamanic' Travels of Jesus and Muhammad: Cross-Cultural and Transcultural Understandings of Religious Experience." *American Journal of Theology and Philosophy* 36, no. 2: 140–153.

Ross, E. S. 2006. *Sufi City: Urban Design and Archetypes in Touba*. Rochester, NY: University of Rochester Press.

Ross, E. S. 2008. "Palaver Trees Reconsidered in the Senegalese Landscape." In M. J. Sheridan and C. Nyamweru (Eds.), *African Sacred Groves: Ecological Dynamics & Social Change*. Athens: Ohio University Press.

Schoonmaker Freudenberger, K. (1991. "Mbegue: The Disingenuous Destruction of a Sahelian Forest." Paper No. 29. London: International Institution for Environment and Development.

Schoonmaker Freudenberger, M., and K. Schoonmaker Freudenberger. 1993. "Pastoralism in Peril: Pressures on Grazing Land in Senegal." Drylands Program: Pastoral Land Tenure Series No. 4. London: International Institution for Environment and Development.

ter Haar, G. 1992. "Spirit of Africa: The Healing Ministry of Archbishop Milingo of Zambia." *Journal of Religion in Africa* 22, no. 4: 381–384.

ter Haar, G., and S. Ellis. 2009. "The Occult Does Not Exist: A Response to Terence Ranger." *Africa* 79, no. 3: 399–411.

Main Pathway: Cross-Pollination

Subthemes

Proceed to Transcending, p. 107
Proceed to Decolonization, p. 277

4

A WEED IS A PLANT OUT OF PLACE

Allegra Pesenti

I was alone, exploring some derelict outhouse [. . .] In one, which was roofless as well as derelict, I suddenly came upon the plant. But it wasn't a plant, in my sense of the word, it was a shrub, almost a tree, and as tall as I was. It looked the picture of evil and also the picture of health, it was so glossy and strong and juicy-looking: I could almost see the sap rising to nourish it. It seemed to have found the place in the world that suited it best.
—L. P. Hartley, *The Go-Between*

There are two principal definitions of a *weed* in the Oxford English dictionary. The first relates to nature as "a wild plant growing where it is not wanted and in competition with cultivated plants" (this includes any wild plant growing in salt or fresh water, and cannabis.) The second belongs to the British informal manner of speech and relates instead to a human characteristic as "a contemptibly feeble person."[1] I have never understood how the voracious and aggressive attributes of one could be aligned by name with the meek essence of the other. I have, however, thought a lot about the ties between weeds and humankind, particularly in relation to the movement and nomadic nature of both. These perusals form the basis of this exhibition at Lismore Castle and link the flora and foliage of its gardens to the installations in the gallery and in one of the castle towers. It is fitting to remember the words of L. P.

Originally published by Lismore Castle Arts on the occasion of the exhibition *A Weed Is a Plant Out of Place*, April 3–September 30, 2016. Introduction by Eamonn Maxwell. Allegra Pesenti, "A Weed Is a Plant Out of Place," 11–29. Reprinted with permission.

Hartley, the British writer who turned the dangerous and seductive qualities of the weed known as deadly nightshade, or *Atropa belladonna*, into the leitmotifs of his most acclaimed novel, *The Go-Between*. Hartley, who had himself stayed at Lismore Castle, evokes the humane properties of the plant and places them at a par with the provocative exploits of his heroine.

PARALLEL LIVES

One is tempted to say that the most human plants, after all, are the weeds.
—John Burroughs (American naturalist, 1837–1931), *Pepacton*

The first time I considered the wider associations of weeds was after a discussion with artist Michael Landy about a series of etchings he focused on in 2002, following the radical eradication of all his possessions in *Break Down*, a notorious piece of performance and destruction commissioned by Artangel in 2001.[2] I was intrigued by his turn to the more insular practice of draftsmanship and manual dexterity during this period of calm after the storm, and by his quest to describe plants that survive no matter what, and wherever most other forms of life have been annihilated and uprooted by man. "I just saw the plants as really optimistic things," says Landy, "they'll find little patches of ground to germinate in and flourish. [. . .] That analogy really," he continues, "where they're constantly moving on and they are just really adaptable to their changing surroundings. It's like people have to be, so it's [. . .] an analogy of that, a reflection of time."[3] During the course of nine months, Landy drew and etched thirty-one types of weeds in what could be described as a monumental herbarium of the pavements and gutters of East London. The placement of the image at the center of the sheet, the carefully distinguished details of each species, the individuality of their names, and the square format of the paper liken them to portraits of people (and to the artist's own portrayals in pencil of the people around him).

I was reminded of this conversation with Landy on my return to America a few days later, as I was sitting soberly and sour-faced in the room where those of us subjected to "secondary inspection" are sent to on entering the country (or attempting to enter it). In this territory of transience and immigration at LAX airport, I also likened myself to a weed of sorts—of Italian birth, raised in Paris and London, and working in Los Angeles, where I stubbornly returned to, despite the difficulties that daunted me at each landing. My fellow captives in the room, I thought, are not that different from Landy's *Smooth Hawk's Beard*, his *Fat Hen*, or *Shepherd's Purse*. They, too, are eager to go where they are not wanted. It was these thoughts, and not any particular affinity with botany, that took me to the world of untamed and lawless vegetation. They prompted me to delve into a subject that, I soon found out, has been the source of study and fascination since Antiquity. From the scientific observations of Pliny the Elder in the 1st century AD, to Shakespeare's knowledge of the fatal and resuscitating effects of weeds and wildflowers, to John Ruskin's alternating lure and repudiation of them, and more recently to the contemporary author Richard Mabey's recent bestseller *Weeds: In Defense of Nature's Most Unloved Plants*,[4] this type of "unmanned" vegetation has long had a special place in the visual arts as well. The dandelion, for instance, is a common symbol of grief in Christian iconography; and the poppy is a symbol of fertility, sleep, ignorance, extravagance, and indifference, but it also alludes to the Passion of Christ in Renaissance paintings.[5] The landscape in Giovanni Bellini's *St. Francis in Ecstasy* is barren but for a panoply of grasses and flowers that stem from the rocks of the saint's cave. Rudimentary life is made monumental in what is undoubtedly among the most breathtaking scenes of the fifteenth century. Here, too, weeds echo human nature and represent life amidst desolation.

The jagged, awkward form of a thistle in the foreground of one of Lucian Freud's early self-portraits is a poignant evocation of the artist's perception of place in terms of his own position both as an artist and a Jewish émigré in London. Man and thistle are adjoined as diffident outcasts. They conjure the metaphor Robert Lowell uses for his bleak state of mind in the poem "Home after Three Months Away," which he wrote after being treated in hospital for mental illness in 1958: "Just twelve months ago, / these flowers were pedigreed / imported Dutchmen; now no one need / distinguish them from weed."[6] Georgia O'Keefe's *Jimson Weed* of 1936 is of a different nature, but its large and fleshy flower head also incites a parallel with figurative portraits. O'Keefe is known to have been immensely fond of jimson weed and to have allowed it to flourish around her patio despite its seeds' toxicity.[7] She became somewhat of an outsider herself when she elected to live in self-appointed exile in Abiquiù, New Mexico. Other women who chose to work in the wilderness in the early part of the twentieth century include the Canadian painter Emily Carr and Henrietta Shore from California. Later on in the century, Agnes Martin also sought an isolated existence when she relocated from New York to New Mexico, and found the solace and serenity that sourced her abstract compositions, and ultimately her true identity:

I believe in reincarnation, and every time you're born you're different. . . . and you see you have to live according to what you were born to do and be. When there's a bare place on the ground, the best possible weed grows there, and it was the same with us, we were born to a purpose. And it took me 20 years to find my vision and do exactly what I was born to do, and I've finally found it. Everybody should study that up, what they are like and what they like and what they want to do, and be.[8]

Martin's association with disparate growth on bare ground may well have been on her mind when she titled a small work on paper of 1963 *Weeds*.

Today more than ever, artists are drawn to the depiction of weeds for their intrinsic physical traits and as viaducts to more intangible issues. Mat Collishaw resuscitates the untamed grasses of Albrecht Dürer's *The Great Piece of Turf* of 1503 in an animated piece that has the emotional quality of a portrait. A close look at Dorothy Cross's bronze *Foxglove* reveals casts of her own fingertips in lieu of the tubular flowers that flop from its tall bent stem. It is a most sensuous and elegant plant, yet the cutting edges of its leaves fend the onlooker from its more dangerous properties: extracts of digitalis, as it is otherwise known, are used in the treatment for heart conditions but can be toxic if taken in large doses. At once alluring and repulsive, these are the twofold characteristics of *Atropa belladonna* that underlie the drama of Hartley's *The Go-Between*:

I knew that every part of it was poisonous, I knew that it was beautiful, for did not my mother's botany book say so? . . . I felt that the plant could poison me, even if I didn't touch it, and that if I didn't eat it, it would eat me, it looked so hungry, in spite of all the nourishment it was getting.[9]

The glass bricks in Pae White's *June Gloom* have the silver flicker and ephemeral quality of stalactite, as perceived within one of the Lismore Castle watchtowers on the outer perimeter of the garden. Like weeds, they come from afar and attempt to weave their way into the contained and cultivated space of the castle grounds, but these non-natives pause on the cusp of the property. The pallets they sit on denote their mobility, as they could slip out of sight at the bat of an eyelid or through a gush of water. Rachel Whiteread's Hackney weeds (aka buddleia) also occupy a periphery, that of the façade of Whitechapel Art Gallery in East London. Buddleia was introduced to the United Kingdom from China in 1890 and was some of the first greenery to grow in bombsites following the Blitz. Now, its leaves are fossilized in gold and as entrenched in the fabric of Whitechapel as the communities of Southeast Asians that occupy the neighborhood.

MISE EN PAGE

The field of herbariums and illustrations of the natural world is a unique and extraordinary genre that bridges art and science.[10] It is perhaps not a coincidence that many of the great botanical artists of the past were women. Historically barred from the profession of medical and natural sciences, women have specialized in the scientific illustration of flora and the natural world since at least the seventeenth century. The German artist Maria Sibylla Merian, born in Frankfurt in 1647 to a family of Swiss printmakers and publishers, devoted a lifetime to perfecting this particular combined expertise of scientific observation and draftsmanship.[11] In 1699, at the age of 52, after selling most of her belongings, she and her daughter Dorothea Maria set sail for the Dutch colony of Suriname on the northeastern coast of South America. The life-size studies she made of indigenous insects and plants during the course of two years in the country's tropical terrain were to form the nucleus of her most important publication, *The Metamorphosis of the Insects of Suriname* (1705). Merian does not merely record specimens, she incorporates them into a wondrous journey through the magic and threats of nature. For each plate, finely framed in red, she configures a layout of elements, or *mise en page*, with remarkable equilibrium and vibrancy in line and color. It is hard to fathom that she died a pauper in Amsterdam in 1717.

Elizabeth Blackwell might have described herself as an illustrator rather than an artist, but her story is worthy of mention within the context of plants (and figures) out of place. In 1737, she embarked on the ambitious production of a new herbal based on her findings at London's Chelsea Physic Garden, which had been established in 1673 as a garden for teaching apprentice apothecaries to identify plants. *A Curious Herbal . . .* contains 500 plates in two volumes and was produced with the intent to bail her husband from prison with the proceeds of its sale. While less adventurous than Merian in her draftsmanship, Blackwell did have a flair for composition and endowed her subjects, such as *The Female Hemp* and *Red Poppy*, with elegance and vitality. Her efforts were in vain, however, as Alexander Blackwell, a practicing physician himself, was released from prison but continued to incur debts and eventually left for Sweden, where he was hanged for treason and political conspiracy.

Technical prowess and visual acuity are impressively conjoined in the work of Anna Atkins. She trained as a botanist and became one of the earliest practitioners of photography as a means to record specimens. She learned the cyanotype printing method through its inventor, the astronomer and scientist Sir John Herschel, and in 1843 she began the publication of one of the most important contributions in the history of photography: *Photographs of British Algae: Cyanotype Impressions*.[12] Generally accepted as the first book to use photographic illustrations, it is as ambitious in scope, with all known species of algae in the British Isles reproduced in three separate volumes, as it is in design. Atkins made the plates by placing wet algae directly onto light-sensitized paper and exposing the paper to sunlight (each identifying label is also reproduced in this camera-less technique). The variegated silhouettes of her findings against the signature blue tone of the cyanotype are compellingly composed and transporting. *Photographs of British Algae* is perhaps the most coveted book of weeds to date, with fewer than twenty copies known to exist in current times.

Atkins is reported to have visited Chatsworth, which makes her place in this exhibition particularly pertinent and aligns her with a long tradition of patronage in the arts of landscaping and botany on behalf of the Dukes of Devonshire. The legacy of the gardens at Lismore and Chatsworth includes the commissions of Capability Brown from 1755 and of Sir Joseph Paxton from 1826, a heritage kept alive by the family and their head gardeners today. Specimen books of ferns assembled during the nineteenth-century, like the one dedicated to the 6th duke by botanist Margaretta Riley in 1840, are reminiscent of the collecting passions and connoisseurship nurtured on the estates. While weeds may generally have been considered undesirable aliens in such sophisticated terrain, head gardener Darren Topps has identified around 50 species of them within the inner gardens of Lismore Castle—some of which are contained and welcome parts of its diversified landscape. Many of the "family" weeds and wildflowers have been carefully portrayed by Emma Tennant, who brings her own scientific and historical knowledge of plants and expert draftsmanship to this important legacy.

New York–based artist Susan Hartnett makes regular visits to the Hudson River to follow the life cycle of several grass species: if the world of weeds were a kingdom,

Hartnett would be the *grande dame* of grasses.[13] An email she wrote on 23 February 2016 reflects the depth and sincerity of her practice:

> rainy; asia witch hazels bloom by hudson river.
>
> i'm 75 years old and time seems short and the earth a wreck.
>
> weeds are something i know about. i worked in 2 botanical gardens. This is literally a life-long pursuit of mine, as conservationist and artist. wild flora is called weeds by ignoramuses: tragedy to native americans and land-based people everywhere. goddamn gardens and lawns.

Hartnett draws from life, and her delineations in charcoal on pristine paper embody the zest of nature. They are not sketches, as one might surmise on first encounter, but rather represent the all-encompassing yet elemental character of which drawing is capable. Her loose and confident hand is reminiscent of that of a Chinese or Japanese calligrapher: "Like jazz, one has to get it done right on the first go," she explains.[14] Contrary to the anonymity and abundance we may associate to grasses, each one of Hartnett's drawings has its own identity, marked on the verso with the botanical and English name of the species and the date it was made, and as a group they represent the larger and less tangible scope of nature: "Grass is the hair of mother earth, it keeps the ground together and covers the place where humans are buried."[15]

THE RAVAGES OF TIME

Weeds are often associated with death. Michael John Whelan muses on the passing of an era in his series of pressings of wild flowers collected from the mountain where the last Irish wolf was killed in 1786. Each plant has been removed, and what remains on the paper is essentially its ghost. The pressings are themselves reminiscent of the herbariums traditionally assembled during the age of Enlightenment like the ones discussed above, but, like footsteps in the snow, they are traces of enduring life amidst barrenness too. A sense of resurgence is also felt in the scenes of children weeding out a cemetery and liberating its stone tombs from years of neglect in Adrian Paci's film *The Guardians* of 2015. Set in Shkodra, the artist's hometown and the center of Roman Catholicism in Albania, it can be read as an attempt to clear the ravages of time in a country devastated by the curtails of Communism after World War II. A stone cross, masked by an overgrowth of rambles, is emblematic of the ban imposed on all forms of worship during that period.

Burdock, whose giant clubfoot leaves hog a garden's sunlight, holds the earth in a death grip.
—Michael Pollan, "Weeds Are Us"

The dark configuration of skulls intertwined with foliage in Philip Taaffe's *Sea of Timor* of 2007 invokes the metaphors of a memento mori ("remember that you must die"). Like the decaying fruits and flowers of a Dutch still life, weeds that thrive on burial sites, or on grounds disturbed by the bombing and shelling of war, like the Rosebay willow herb that proliferated in London after World War II, can be a reflection of immortality and the afterlife. Shakespeare summons these more somber associations when the ghost warns Hamlet: "Duller shouldst thou be than the fat weed / That roots itself in ease on Lethe wharf, / Wouldst thou not stir in this" (I. 5. 32–34). In Greek Mythology, Lethe is a river whose waters induce forgetfulness.

There is also a sense of melancholia in the plants that flourish in ruins, or ruderals as they are otherwise known. The British medical doctor Richard Deakin recorded 420 species in the Colosseum in Rome in 1855.[16] These are the weeds that John Ruskin contemplates in his recollections of Rome in a letter to Charles Eliot Norton of December 1856:

Still, I can quite understand how—coming from a fresh, pure and very ugly country like America, there may be a kind of thirst upon you for ruins and shadows which nothing can easily assuage: that after the scraped cleanliness and business and fussiness of it mildew and mould may be meat and drink to you—and langour the best sort of life—and weeds a bewitchment—(I mean the unnatural sort of weed that only grows on old bricks and mortar and out of cracks in mosaic—all the campagna used to look at me as if its grass were grown over a floor-) and the very sense of despair which there is about Rome. [17]

In Pierpaolo Campanini's luscious portrayals of overgrown garden bushes, large low-headed leaves slump from their stems: time passes slowly, decadence prevails, but sometimes life doesn't seem to know where to stop. Colombian artist Mateo Lopez's small paper weed visible through an inflated wastepaper bag is more discreet but no less vocal in its message. Where there is death there has to be hope.

WEEDS ARE US

When an alien lives with you in your land, do not mistreat him. The alien living with you must be treated as one of your native-born. Love him as yourself, for you were aliens in Egypt.
—Leviticus, 19:33–34

Accounts of the plight of populations can be traced back to biblical times and earlier. History has long seen the forced displacement of civilians under the strain of political and religious strife, war and famine, and with it the difficult integration of people and their cultures as aliens in foreign lands. Writing in 1984 in his "Reflections on Exile," Edward Said stated that the difference between now and then is scale: "Our age—with its modern warfare, imperialism and the quasi-theological ambitions of totalitarian rulers—is indeed the age of the refugee, the displaced person, mass immigration."[18] Thirty-two years on, his statement is more poignant than ever as we witness the desperate escape of victims of the crisis in the Middle East in unprecedented magnitude. Exodus for survival is just as real for the many minors who attempt to reach America through Mexico, as it is in other parts of the world. With this in mind, weeds can be interpreted as visual metaphors for the uprooted and as symbols of dispossession. The multitude of miniature heads that file through Luisa Rabbia's deployable painted-paper book resemble the now too familiar scenes of rows of migrants on their long walk across Europe. They carry with them their families, languages, traditions, myths, and more, and will attempt to reintegrate the sinuous roots that fall from them. Theirs are the lines that defy borders and that attempt to tie countries together as common land rather than as isolated terrains.

The strange feeling of being out of place permeates the work of Latifa Echakhch—an artist, born in Morocco in 1974, who moved to France with her family as a young child and now lives in Switzerland. Her tumbleweeds, iconic of the Wild West, are adrift and out of context on the floors of a medieval castle in County Waterford, Ireland: "[My work] is about all these possible slips and slides of meaning."[19] A further twist in the scope of shifting identities is the fact that tumbleweed itself is not native of the American deserts either. It came from the steppes of the Ukraine with a group of Russian immigrants who settled in Bon Homme County, South Dakota, in the 1870s.[20] Regardless of how entrenched a migrant may be in his or her new home, a person's origins can never be buried. The words of the Jewish Holocaust survivor from Munich who established himself in Manchester in W. G. Sebald's *The Emigrants* are a vivid expression of this:

> I succeeded sometimes in maintaining a certain equability by my self-imposed seclusion; but the fact is that that tragedy in my youth struck such deep roots within me that it later shot up again, put forth evil flowers, and spread the poisonous canopy over me which has kept me so much in the shade and dark in recent years.[21]

No verbal or visual records can replace the reality of the migrant, nor can they truly render the atrocities of persecution. But artists can and do find ways to message those realities and to make them tangible. Art is a necessary platform for expression when no other means are possible: its need is as urgent as a weed's stubbornness to stay. This was made particularly evident recently by the performances held under the dome of the Good Chance Theater in the center of the refugee camp formerly known as the Jungle on the outskirts of Calais, France. The dome was a haven of freedom and a place of no reprimand, a home away from home amidst a self-appointed league of displaced nations: Syria, Iraq, Iran, Kurdistan, Pakistan, Afghanistan, Sudan, Eritrea, Ethiopia, Egypt, Kuwait.[22] The camp has now been dismantled, but its residents will weave themselves into other terrains and communities, and with them their stories and identities will follow, for "though we may be the earth's gardeners, we are also its weeds."[23]

> Far from being dead that past has remained embedded in its time fully alive like a seed in the soil, awaiting the season of warmth and growth to bring it to germination. As such, what has been is nothing other than a potentiality ready to be fertilized and redeployed.
> —Ranajit Guha, "The Migrant's Time"

NOTES

This essay was written with the kind and intelligent assistance of Rosabella Brown.

1. "Weed," *Lexico Online Dictionary* (n.d.), http://www.oxforddictionaries.com/definition/english/weed.
2. See *Contemporary Art in Print: The Publications of Charles Booth-Clibborn and His Imprint the Paragon Press 2001–2006*, ed. Etienne Lullin and Florian-Oliver Simm (London: Paragon

Press, 2006); and *Michael Landy: Break Down*, with an interview between the artist and Julian Stallabrass (London: Artangel, 2001).

3. Lullin and Simm, *Contemporary Art in Print*, 318.

4. Richard Mabey, *Weeds: In Defense of Nature's Most Unloved Plants* (London, Profile Books, 2010). On Ruskin's attitude toward weeds, see Nina Edwards, *Weeds* (London: Reaktion Books, 2015), 31, 80–81.

5. George Ferguson, *Signs and Symbols in Christian Art* (New York: Oxford University Press, 1954), 37. A dandelion appears on a rock near Raphael's signature in *The Entombment* of 1507 (Rome: Galleria Borghese). See Roger Jones and Nicholas Penny, *Raphael* (New Haven: Yale University Press, 1983), 44.

6. Robert Lowell, "Home after Three Months Away," in *The Anthology of Contemporary American Poetry*, ed. Helen Vendler (London: I. B. Tauris, 2003), 97.

7. Hunter, *Drohojowska-Philp, Full Bloom: The Art and Life of Georgia O'Keeffe* (New York: W. W. Norton, 2004), 376.

8. Jenny Attiyeh, "Interview with Taos Artist Agnes Martin," *Scribd* (2001), https://www.scribd.com/doc/221427944/Interview-with-Taos-artist-Agnes-Martin.

9. L. P. Hartley, *The Go-Between* (London: Penguin Classics, 2000), 33; first published by Hamish Hamilton, 1953.

10. See *Of Green Leaf and Flower, Artists' Books and the Natural World*, ed. Elisabeth R. Fairman (New Haven: Yale University Press, 2014); and Catherine de Zegher and Carol Armstrong *Ocean Flowers, Impressions from Nature* (New York: The Drawing Center, 2004).

11. See Ella Reitsma, *Maria Sibylla Merian and Daughters: Women of Art and Science* (Los Angeles: Getty Publications, 2008); and David Brafman and Stephanie Schrader, *Insects and Flowers: The Art of Maria Sibylla Merian*, (Los Angeles: Getty Publications, 2008).

12. See Fairman, *Of Green Leaf and Flower*, 42–44.

13. See Susan Hartnett *(Richard Serra für Susan Hartnett)*, Uwe Rüth, Ausgestellt-Vorgestellt IV (Skulpturenmuseum, Glaskasten Marl, 1999).

14. Hartnett *(Richard Serra für Susan Hartnett)*.

15. Artist statement, shared by Frank Demaegd, Zeno X Gallery, Antwerp, on October 15, 2013.

16. Richard Deakin, *Flora of the Colosseum of Rome* (London, Groombridge, 1855). See Christopher Woodward, "Rooted in the Past: The Plants That Flourish in Ruins," *Financial Times*, June 5, 2015, https://www.ft.com/content/66319312-0559-11e5-8612-00144feabdco. I thank Léonie Booth-Clibborn for this reference.

17. *The Correspondence of John Ruskin and Charles Eliot Norton*, ed. John Lewis Bradley and Ian Ousby (Cambridge: Cambridge University Press, 1987), 31.

18. Edward Said, "Reflections on Exile," in *Reflections on Exile and Other Essays* (Cambridge, MA: Harvard University Press, 2002), 174.

19. Anne Ellegood, Hammer Project Brochure, Los Angeles, Hammer Museum, 2013. See also "HuffPost Arts Interviews Latifa Echakhch on Her Upcoming Exhibition 'Currents,'" *Huffington Post*, February 6, 2012, http://www.huffingtonpost.com/2012/02/02/latifa-echakhch-interview_n_1250639.html.

20. Michael Pollan, "Weeds Are Us," *New York Times*, November 5, 1989.
21. W. G. Sebald, *The Emigrants* (London: Random House, 2002), 191. First published in German in 1992.
22. My thanks to Joe Robertson and Joe Murphy, the founders of Good Chance Theatre, for their invitation to attend the perfomances.
23. Pollan, "Weeds Are Us."

Main Pathway: Orientations

Subthemes

Proceed to Politics, p. 73
Proceed to Ethics, p. 73
Proceed to Place, p. 73

5

NUUČAAŃUŁ PLANTS AND HABITATS AS REFLECTED IN ORAL TRADITIONS: SINCE RAVEN AND THUNDERBIRD ROAMED

Marlene Atleo (ʔeh ʔeh nah tuu kʷiss)

When Quʔušinmit (Son of Raven) flew over the dark waters, he was looking for the light. All over the world he flew. As the story of the Northwest Coast is told, Son of Raven saw a *haw'ił* (chief)[1] keeping the light in a *huupakwan'um* (bentwood box) in which the *haw'ił* kept his treasures. The *haw'ił* would open the chest now and again to admire his greatest prize, the light. As he admired it, some light leaked out. Quʔušinmit, keen-sighted and possibly the smartest bird on the coast, caught a glimpse and vowed to get it at any cost.
—Based on E. R. Atleo, *Tsawalk: A Nuu-chah-nulth Worldview*

OVERVIEW

This chapter provides an intimate account of people–plant relationships from my perspective as a member of the Nuučaańuł (Nuu-chah-nulth) community of Ahousaht. As my contribution to this volume, it focuses on the role of botanical and environmental knowledge in considering First Nations' land rights and title. This reflection takes a storywork approach to learning about plants and their role in the everyday life and culture of the Nuučaańuł (Archibald, 1997, 2008; M. R. Atleo, 2001)

Originally published as "Nuučaan'uł Plants and Habitats as Reflected in Oral Traditions: Since Raven and Thunderbird Roamed," in *Plants, People, and Places: The Roles of Ethnobotany and Ethnoecology in Indigenous Peoples' Land Rights in Canada and Beyond*, ed. Nancy Turner (Montreal: MQUP, 2020).

and is based on some of the learnings from over half a century of participating in lifeways, relations, and ceremonial living in the Ahousaht community. It is about my experience of how the Ahousaht elders welcomed me into the lineage of the House of Klaaq-ish-peethl/ ƛaaq-iš-piił by socializing me into the *tsawalk/čawaak* (oneness) of relationships in which the people, the plants, the animals, and the territory exist in the indivisible unity of story over time.

Ahousaht First Nation is located on Flores Island at the ancient site of Maaqtusiis, a remote Nuučaańuł community on the west coast of Vancouver Island. I married E. Richard Atleo (Umeek), the elder descendant of the Atleo lineage and the third chief of Ahousaht, becoming "Mrs. Richard," who needed schooling in her role as wife, mother, sister, cousin, aunt, grandmother, granddaughter, and friend. Fresh off the plane from Vancouver with my four-month-old son, Shawn, I stepped onto Mark Atleo's troller, the *Shamrock*, at the dock in Tofino for the two-hour ride to Maaqtusiis. In many ways, I was just another woman coming into the community from afar who needed to be schooled in the local knowledge. As we moved into a house on stilts with Nan (Grace) Margaret Atleo, the matriarch of the family, and Teddy George, a prominent Kelsemaht chief, it was clear from the beginning that I was expected to be able to learn how to fit in—initially in their home and then in the larger community—and so I did. The focus of this chapter is the role of specific plants in the life to which I was introduced in the territory where Nuučaańuł women have lived for millennia. It is my version of the story as it was shared with me so that I would be able to nourish and nurture my family through the sacred teachings of family, community, and mythos, which emphasize the riches of the surrounding life. Thus, my schooling is grounded in the kinship into which I married and in the relations that I have developed in Ahousaht over a lifetime. In this context, I need to acknowledge the relational logic of the training. This storywork is based on the knowledge embedded in the human and territorial relationships in which plants are embedded, which is often a vehicle for what Turner (1979) calls "Indian technology." The storywork is anchored by my experience as a person who has long been expected to actively participate in narrating the story of the lineage to which I belong. In fact, the storywork is a complex of epistemology, ontology, and axiology manifest in lineage, time, territory, social roles, positions, and the stories that weave culture into lived experience (Archibald, 1997, 2008; M. R. Atleo, 2001, 2008a). The Nuučaańuł elders oriented me (M. R. Atleo, 2009) to engagement with the living world, the intimacy of which Armstrong (2008, 2009) so effectively articulates and Bourdieu (1990) characterizes sociologically as habitus. In this habitus, cultural capital is developed. It may be embodied (e.g., knowing how to recognize basket materials, where to pick them, and how to physically manage their production), objectified (e.g., creating a basket to give), and institutionalized (e.g., being known as the best cedar hat weaver on the coast or being able to lead others in the development of aspects of cultural capital). In this case, it reflects my education about the relationships between Ahousaht people and plants, which are regarded as companions in the territory, providers of medicine, food, shelter, clothing, transportation, and names, and sources of cultural meaning.

This work has augmented the cultural and social capital of the lineage and has become a part of the treasures of the *huupakwan'um*. Knowledge is recognized as a special treasure that reproduces the social and cultural capital of the lineage, which is celebrated in designs, songs, stories, dances, landmarks in the territories, or amulets, all of which serve as memory aides or heuristics. Thus my perspective is positioned in the House of ƛaaq-iš-piił (liquid fat all over the floor), Hiimix ƛaaq (tallow), and Humiis (western red cedar). Because this house is the steward of three resource domains, it has three names and, with its many seats, overflows with the riches, or "fat," of the sea life, the land mammals, and red cedar, respectively. This house thus also overflows with people who are socialized and dedicated to developing competencies needed to manage such riches for their community. As the wife of the head of the house, I was expected by Nan Margaret Atleo to learn all that was needed to support the many people in the house and to aid in managing its riches. It was the role of the grandmothers to teach me so that I might fulfil their expectation that I should embody enstoried living (M. R. Atleo, 2009) through my role as an educator.

These women were my premier models for familial engagement in the everyday and ritual lives of the Atleo family. They were the matriarchs of the Atleo and Little families respectively. Nan Margaret Atleo came from a chiefly family in Kelsemaht and had married George Atleo (Shamuck George), who was the third chief of Ahousaht, the father of Eugene, and a grandfather of Richard. Mary Hamilton Little's father was Chief Dick of Manhousaht. She was an only child who had five children. She was proud because her grandchildren and great-grandchildren were many who had come from one. She was a consummate basket weaver. Their combined perspective framed the curriculum that shaped the lens through which I entered into knowledge of the Ahousaht territory and its history.

Thus my life lens is shaped by my experience as a German toddler in my paternal grandparents' extended family and semi-rural household, by my Canada-wide experience of living in more than two dozen homes in Ontario, Alberta, and British Columbia, and then by my immersion in Ahousaht teachings as a teenaged wife and mother. Through the embrace and teachings of the elders, lineage, and community, Ahousaht became my heartfelt and official home.

I recall canoe trolling with my husband on my birthday that first summer in Ahousaht. My new husband rowed me out across the wide channel in front of the village. We landed the canoe on a small pebble beach with a grove of fruit trees. Someone's apple and plum trees, planted within sight of the village, were decades old and scraggly. Now, they provided food to share with the bears that had marked the trees and deposited scat around them. It was a little scary for this city girl but also exciting since it was a new, fresh experience. The sight of abandoned cultivation was familiar to me. I had lived in remote areas of British Columbia where the "plant people" had swiftly reclaimed spaces abandoned by humans. In that grove across the channel, the wild *milk'iw̓um* (gooseberries, *Ribes divaricatum*) and *y̓am̓a* (salal, *Gaultheria shallon*) that were reclaiming the space were still green in early August. There was detritus at the tidal zone, promising good things to come, which were still invisibly embedded in the territory, to be embodied in experience and enstoried in memory. We were enjoined by the elders to "watch until it becomes clear to you" (M. R. Atleo, 2008b).

Umeek speaks of the concept of *hišukiš čawaak* ("everything is one") (E. R. Atleo, 2004, p. 117), and so it is when experience, memory, territory, and kinships are relationally understood in cultural context. Thus oral knowing is narrative knowing (Polkinghorne 1988) that results in narrative explanations, converts "congeries of events into concatenations, and emphasizes and increases the scope of synoptic judgment in our reflection on experience" (Mink, 1968, p. 191, quoted in Ricoeur, 1990, p. 157). In short, narrative is a powerful cognitive instrument with which to create meaningful wholeness. We make sense of a jumble of events by turning them into a narratology in story in order to create meaning (Fludernik, 2002). This chapter follows suit, as it offers a narrativizing of my life in relation to the plants in the ecology of the Nuučaań̓ul people. To do so in English, I also need to acknowledge that I am operating within a cross-paradigmatic/cross-cultural logic, akin to what might be identified as the logic displayed on a two-row wampum belt, except that mine has three strands of history rather than just two (M. R. Atleo, 2012). Kuhn (1962) claims that operating within logics across paradigms is not possible because they are incommensurable, but people do it every day as they externalize their inner worlds. How do they do it? They do it through relational logic, which moves toward or away from oneself in some way—in my case, through a triple cycle of knowing (M. R. Atleo, 2012). Thus, my story proceeds by moving through the annual cycle of the West Coast to illustrate how Nuučaańuł plant teachings and use entered into my life story in the Ahousaht territories.

HUMIIS/WESTERN RED CEDAR

The annual round starts by acknowledging the Atleo lineage house named Humiis—named for the western red cedar *(Thuja plicata)*, the life-giving tree that makes possible the culture of winter feasts (Stewart, 1984). The red cedar is acknowledged as the life-giver because it allows its transformation into the *čapac* (canoe) for travelling far and wide on the highways of the sea; provides the *pits'up* (inner bark) that is woven into mats for eating and sleeping on and that is worked into all manner of woven textiles, including capes, hats, dancing shawls, and soft pounded fibers for diapers; is used for the carved welcome figures on the beach and in the feast halls; and furnishes the very boards of the halls themselves, which are built with a uniquely West Coast architecture anchored in the mighty stands of *humiis*. So important is *humiis* that it is one of the names of the Atleo lineage house.

After the feasting, in the winter when the salmon are scarce, the *ƛusmit* (herring) becomes the life-giver, being smoked, boiled, and dried. Girls coming of age are taught not to despise eating herring because they are bony and so labor-intensive to preserve, but to rejoice in the gift of their flesh, which is able to feed the family in winter. The shape of the head of the deer's ulna bone provides the perfect handgrip for extended herring gutting, making it possible to fill the rows of cedar or alder *(Alnus rubra)* sticks used in the smokehouse. I gave my granddaughters such *čiimaak* (knives), along with the story that cultivates the love of Xusmit, for their *ʔiičt'uuta* (female coming of age) ceremony, as a reminder of the vital importance to their families of herring during winter scarcity. Herring is a hedge against starvation.

K'ʷaqmis (herring spawn) announces the early spring, when the shoals of fish begin to surface in the bays. At the first sign of the herring, young *qʷiƛ'aqmapt* (hemlock) trees *(Tsuga heterophylla)* on which they can lay their spawn are anchored in the bays. Schooling herring release milt that creates milky shoals as the eggs are fertilized to create spawn, dressing the trees in a creamy icing-like layer of goodness. Families take up the trees to strip the spawn, which are plump and sound crunchy: *"kʷaq, kʷaq, kʷaq."* Today, *kʷaqmis* is salted, bagged in plastic, and often frozen. In the past, it was dried in the March winds and sunshine on hemlock branches stripped from the trunk. Sometimes it was gathered on long ribbon-like leaves of *ćaay̓imc* (seagrass, *Zostera marina*) or surfgrass *(Phyllospadix* spp.). In days gone by, when steamed, it may have been dressed with *ƛ'iiňa* (oolichan grease) or *ƛaaq* (whale oil) stored in bulbs of *husmin* (bull kelp, *Nereocystis luetkeana*). Today, it may be dressed with butter or perhaps Yamasa soy sauce. It is a singular treat!

Spring usually comes early to the West Coast, announcing itself in the greening of the landscape. Bracken ferns *(šiƛmapt, Pteridium aquilinum)* spring up, their fiddleheads unfurling. Shoots of skunk cabbage *(tima't, Lysichiton americanus)* burst into broad leaves, providing plenty of fronds for the pit cooking, berry drying, and food preparation of the year. Possibly, because of their waxy coating, they function like parchment paper in baking and cooking. Today, the leaves are usually replaced by less hygienically offensive brown cardboard, gunny sacks, Handi Wipes, newspaper, parchment paper, or other wraps and fiber products that are imported, sometimes incidentally, to the community.

These other materials do not have the anti-microbial qualities of the fern fronds (Lee and Shin, 2011), which had inhibited spoilage when they were used to wipe the mucus and dirt off the many species of salmon processed during the year.

Teddy George helped me to fashion my *č'it'aqƛ* from a piece of Swede-saw blade, using a scrap of red cedar for the handle. In this case, it was a Somass River sockeye, donated by Wilma Keitlah for the North Island College Barbecue in Port Alberni, British Columbia, in the late spring of 2003, that permitted this demonstration of traditional salmon processing, complete with the teachings that follow.

For the most part, the canon of Victorian hygiene instilled in residential school operations and training (Kelm, 1999) robbed community members of their cultural confidence in using local plants and processing knowledge. That canon required food to be processed by washing everything with fresh water, which was contra the traditional food-processing technology. The oral tradition that fresh water should never touch salmon was observed quiring the processing of the fish for smoking and drying. In our family, this tradition continues to be observed. The mucous film encasing the salmon is scraped off with the *č'it'aqƛ* (D-shaped fish knife) and wiped away with paper, whereas traditionally fronds of *šiƛmapt* (bracken fern, *Pteridium aquilinum*) would be used. Because salmon is a saltwater fish, fresh water was never consumed with ocean-caught salmon. According to custom, doing so would have been disrespectful to the spirit of the salmon. The cultural norms that were instilled by such teachings created a foundation for interaction between species based on mutual survival and sustainability. The mucus that covers salmon protects the fish physically and immunologically, whereas fresh water degrades the mucus. Merely scraping the mucus off meant that some would remain for the smoking and drying process, possibly as a protection against spoilage. In the early 1980s, I was working in the shipping department of a major BC fishing company when commercial trollers were encouraged not to wash their salmon catch but to retain the mucous film encasing the whole fish because it preserved the freshness longer for air shipments to markets. Science had caught up with oral tradition!

QAAWII/BERRIES

The greening of spring brought with it new growth on the *qaawii* (berry) bushes. *Qaawii* were highly prized and anticipated by all. Of interest, first, were the tender *m̓aayi* (shoots) of salmonberry *(Rubus spectabilis)*. I remember the young children who came to sit on Nan Margaret Atleo's porch peeling the outer layer from the shoots to expose the tender inner core and asking her for sugar to dip them into. Ah, bliss! Tender *m̓aayi* were so highly desirable that when Raven was attempting to get into the chief's house to steal the light, he disguised himself as a giant *m̓aayi* to tempt the chief's daughter to eat it—so that she might become pregnant with him—but that is another story! Of course, *m̓aayi* are usually thin and delicate. Raven gave himself away! The chief's daughter saw through the ploy and did not eat the fat *m̓aayi*.

M̓aayi heralds the berry-growing season. There are many desirable berries that yield their nutritional bounty, including *qawii* (salmonberries)l *tł'aachʔaał* (thimbleberries, *Rubus parviflorus*); *kałkintapiih.* (strawberries, *Fragaria* spp.); *hisʔinwa* (red huckleberries, *Vaccinium parvifolium*), *situp* (blueberries, *V. alaskaense, V. ovalifolium*), *hisshitł* (blackberries, *R. ursinus*); *y̓am̓a* (salal); *quʔušinamapt* (Oregon-grape, *Mahonia aquifolium*); *p'ap'aʔis* (bog cranberries, *V. oxycoccos*); and, late in the fall, *siinamuxsʔits* (evergreen huckleberries, *V. ovatum*). Almost six months or more of nutritious, ripe berries are available in the territory.

Traditionally, berries would be dried and formed into cakes to be consumed over the winter as a bountiful source of vitamins A and C. In my day, cases of blackberries and cranberries were jarred for use in sweet desserts, and salal and blackberries were made into jam. Even today, the value of the "sweet," called *chumas*, starts with berries and other fruit. Especially after a feed of seafood, some *chumas* is always served.

In late August, a week-long gathering of Nuučaańuł *hawii* (chiefs) at Friendly Cove was an occasion for Umeek and me to be invited for a dip in the deep-brown, tannin-rich depths of the ritual pool of the Muwač'ath Yuquot Whaling Shrine (Jonaitis and Inglis, 1999). Along the well-trodden path above the beach, I spied a veritable hedge of *siinamuxsʔits* (evergreen huckleberries), the like of which I had never seen because they are usually lone-growing plants. The ripening berries were also larger than any I had ever seen. The hedge has been clearly cultivated over years. Even today, the huckleberry plants that line the pathway grow tall and thick in the face of the winds in the area; indeed, Yuquot (windy place) derives its name from the word *yuiʔiʔis* (windy).

PLANT MATERIALS IN NUUČAAŃUŁ TECHNOLOGY

Whether wood, sedges, roots, withes, or reeds, both fibrous and nonfibrous plants have provided the raw materials for fashioning the goods needed for daily life. The embodied knowledge of the Nuučaańuł brings the territory alive as a storehouse of materials that are culturally encoded to be recognizable as required. The yew, or "ironwood," tree—referred to as *ƛatmapt* ("wedge plant," *Taxus brevifolia*)—once provided wood for digging sticks, hailers, and wedges. Ceremonial implements were also fashioned from the wood to last, and the leaves were part of the medicine storehouse. Even today, extracts from yew bark have become part of modern oncological medicinary, of which Taxol is one such brand (Bryan, 2011). The rhizomes of *hihit'a* (licorice fern, *Polypodium glycyrrhiza*), readily available growing in the moss patches on the trees, provided an important appetite suppressant. All manner of kelps are available on the shoreline. The beach keeper in Ahousaht, the second chief, manages the shoreline. I have witnessed children fashioning toys from the *husmin* (bull kelp, *Nereocystis luetkeana*) on the beach, including dolls with the leafy fronds braided like hair and puppets with the bulbs shaped into heads. To make cars and trucks, the round, hollow stems can be used as "wheels," and races have taken place on the front beach, where children play at life, practicing for adulthood and using the resources at hand.

The relational networks of cultural logics are expressed in the relationship between people's names and the world to which their names refer. Atl-iu (Atleo) is the name of the *takumlth* (group) to which members of the lineage of the third chief of the Ahousaht people belong. *Atl-iu* also refers to a technology, a three-stranded lanyard made of cedar withes whose enormous tensile strength is capable of towing whales to shore. This tradition is about 4,500 years old (McMillan, 2015). The originator of this ancient economic activity of whaling, the first Umeek, got his insight during *ʔuusumč* (ritual bathing) from a Friendly Stranger. *Iiychtuup* (whale) means "something big/valuable"—a reasonable observation because, previous to the economic shift to whaling, the hunt was by twos for seals. A single whale is the equivalent of about 3,000 seals in nutritional value (M. R. Atleo, 2001). The whaling harpoon and spear were made of California mussel shell, yew wood, and pitch. But, as one Ahousaht woman told me (Charlie, 1975), it was so much more than those raw materials because it required know-how, ritualized physical and mental strengthening, as well as a deep understanding of whales and the environment in which they came to the West Coast. While others waited for drift whales to wash ashore, the first Umeek learned how to call in and catch whales, converting a stick into a weapon with mussel shells and pitch. The twisted cedar withe was tested and found to have a tensile strength of almost 10,000 pounds per square inch (Stewart, 1984, p. 161). The whaling harpoon is clearly a Nuučaańuł technological "secret"—a weapon that goes far beyond its mere constituent parts of "mussel shells and pitch" (Charlie, 1975; E. R. Atleo, 2004, 2006; M. R. Atleo, 1990). The Nuučaańuł *atl-iu* provided an incredibly strong, flexible, and long extension of the shaft with which to "shake hands" with the whale since the flex and spring-back action of the launcher were of paramount importance. This device evolved into bow and arrows for some applications, but the *atl-iu*, decontextualized and decultured, may be seen as culminating in the perfected firepower of the harpoons used in the whaling industry.

CONCLUSION

In this account, I have provided some illustrations of the integrated knowledge conveyed to me as I learned to live in the *hahuulthi*—or hereditary system of ownership and management of Nuučaańuł territories (M. R. Atleo, 2006)—of the lineage into which I married and wherein our sons and grandchildren were raised. These are illustrations of the elders' teachings, which wove me into the integrative wholeness—the oneness—of the relationships between Nuučaańuł and the flora and fauna that share the world of the land, the sea, and the air. These relationships between Nuuchah-nulth and the plants that share the world they both inhabit have existed for millennia—at least since the start of whaling 4,500 years ago (Marshall, 1993; M. R.

Atleo, 2008a). This time period is extended back much further by newly discovered evidence of habitation on the West Coast, such as the Triquet Island discovery dated to 14,000 years ago and based on Heiltsuk oral tradition in collaboration with the University of Victoria and the Hakai Institute (Nair, 2017), and it may even extend back as much as 130,000 years (Holen et al., 2017).

The Nuučaańuł assimilated the knowledge of their coastal territory, which has in turn been shaping them since time immemorial as they have culturally modified the landscape. In an ancient context of territorial sovereignty, when Raven and Thunderbird roamed the heavens and the earth, Raven brought the light so that the people might see by gaining a bird's-eye perspective on life, or a spiritual view. Thunderbird was defeated in the contest for the whale through the prayers of the people who acknowledge the Creator: the Wakashan-speaking Nuučaańuł (M. R. Atleo, 2011). It is no wonder that the women decorate the very baskets they weave with the good news of such a victory!

Increasingly, traditional ecological knowledge, cultural teachings and usage, as well as language are being revived and practiced in the community (Atleo and Fitzner, 2010), supported by the assertions of the Truth and Reconciliation Commission of Canada (2015), the Royal Commission on Aboriginal Peoples (1996), and of course the United Nations Declaration on the Rights of Indigenous Peoples (2007). In 1998, when I attended the UNESCO symposium on the biodiversity of sacred sites (see M. R. Atleo, 1998), the attendees codified the criteria for sacred sites. From the front beach of Maaqtusiis, the Atleo family has a clear view and is within earshot of the sacred sites that circumscribe the family's multimillennial history. It is time that Canada recognized this Indigenous history and Canada's legal obligation by co-scripting with the Ahousaht people the fulfilment of the recognition of Aboriginal rights articulated in section 35 of the Constitution Act, 1982, rather than continuing to attempt to thwart such serious dialogic reconciliation through contentious court cases and spurious legislation. True reconciliation can be achieved only if Indigenous and non-Indigenous Canadians collaborate in rewriting an inclusive Canadian history.

NOTE

1 Throughout the chapter, Nuu-chah-nulth *t'aat'aaqsapa* (words) are from Powell (1991), the Scientific Panel for Sustainable Forest Practices in Clayoquot Sound (1995), and Stonham (2005).

REFERENCES

Archibald, J. 1997. "Coyote Learns to Make a Storybasket: The Place of First Nations Stories in Education." PhD diss., Simon Fraser University.

Archibald, J. 2008. *Indigenous Storywork: Educating the Heart, Mind, Body, and Spirit*. Vancouver: University of British Columbia Press.

Armstrong, J. C. 2008. "Indigeneity: Situating the Tribal and the Local in the Global." In *North America in the 21st Century: Tribal, Local, and Global*, edited by Kerstin Knopf, 111–129. Trier, Germany: Wissenschaftlicher Verlag.

Armstrong, J. C. 2009. "Constructing Indigeneity: Syilx Okanagan Oraliture and tmixwcentrism." PhD diss. University of Greifswald, Germany. https://d-nb.info/1027188737/, 34.

Atleo, E. R. 2004. *Tsawalk: A Nuu-chah-nulth Worldview*. Vancouver: University of British Columbia Press.

Atleo, E. R. 2006. *Principles of Tsawalk: An Indigenous Approach to Global Crisis*. Vancouver: University of British Columbia Press.

Atleo, M. R. 1990. "Studying Canadian Indigenous Families: A Special Case of Ethnicity in a Multicultural Nation." In *Western Region Home Management and Family Economics Educators Research Conference Papers of the Western Region Home Management and Family Economics Educators*, vol. 5, edited by J. M. Hilton, 35–54. Reno, NV: University of Nevada.

Atleo, M. R. 1998. "Hishuk-ish-ts'awalk: The Role of Sacred Sites in the Embodiment of the Territories of Nuu-chah-nulth First Nations." In *"Natural" Sacred Sites: Cultural Diversity and Biological Diversity*, 7. Symposium abstracts. https://unesdoc.unesco.org/ark:/48223/pf0000113456.

Atleo, M. R. 2001. "Learning Models in the Umeek Narratives: Identifying an Educational Framework through Storywork with First Nations Elders." PhD diss., University of British Columbia.

Atleo, M. R. 2006. "The Ancient Nuu-chah-nulth Strategy of Hahuulthi: Education for Indigenous Cultural Survivance." *International Journal of Environmental, Cultural, Economic and Social Sustainability* 2, no. 1: 153–162.

Atleo, M. R. 2008a. "Indigenous Learning Models in the Context of Socio-Economic Change: A Storywork Approach." In *Indigenous Education: Asia/Pacific*, edited by W. Heber, 21–32. Regina, SK: Indigenous Studies Research Center, First Nations University.

Atleo, M. R. 2008b. "Watching to See until It Becomes Clear to You: Metaphorical Mapping—A Method for Emergence." *International Journal of Qualitative Studies in Education* 21, no. 3: 221–233.

Atleo, M. R. 2009. "Understanding Aboriginal Learning Ideology through Storywork with Elders." *Alberta Journal of Educational Research* 55, no. 4: 453–67.

Atleo, M. R. 2011. "Red Griffin and Thunderbird Nests—Indigenous and Academic Knowledge: Re-Localizing the Global-Glocal." In *North America* in *the 21st Century: Tribal, Local, and Global—Festschrift fiir Hartmut Lutz*, edited by K. Knopf, 29–40. Trier, Germany: Wissenschaftlicher Verlag.

Atleo, M. R. 2012. "Adult Health Education and Practice: Working with Aboriginal People." In *Health and Adult Leaming, Section 2: Adult Education and Health Professionals in Practice*, edited by Leona English, 90–106. Toronto: University of Toronto Press.

Atleo, M. R., and L. Fitznor. 2010. "Aboriginal Educators Discuss Recognizing, Reclaiming and Revitalizing Their Multi-Competences in Heritage/English Language Usage." *Canadian Journal of Native Education* 32: 13–34, 154.

Bourdieu, P. 1990. *The Logic of Practice*. Translated by R. Nice. Stanford, CA: Stanford University Press.

Bryan, J. 2011. "How Bark from the Pacific Yew Tree Improved the Treatment of Breast Cancer." *Pharmaceutical Journal*, September 21. https://www.pharmaceutical-journal.com/news-and-analysis/news/how-barkfrom-the-padfic-yew-tree-improved-the-treatment-of-breast-cancer/11084729.article.

Charlie, G. M. 1975. Personal communication with author.

Fludernik, M. 2002. *Towards a "Natural" Narratology*. London: Routledge.

Holen, S. R., T. A. Demere, D. C. Fisher, R. Fullagar, J. B. Paces, G. T. Jefferson, J. E. Beeton, R. A. Cerutti, A. N. Rountry, L. Vescera, and K. A. Holen. 2017. "A 130,000-Year-Old Archaeological Site in Southern California, USA." *Nature*, April 27, 479–483. https://www.nature.com/articles/nature22065.

Jonaitis, A., and R. Inglis. 1999. *The Yuquot Whalers' Shrine*. Seattle: University of Washington Press.

Kelm, M.-E. 1999. *Colonizing Bodies: Aboriginal Health and Healing in British Columbia*, 1900–50. Vancouver: University of British Columbia Press.

Kuhn, T. 1962. *The Structure of Scientific Revolutions*. Chicago: University of Chicago Press.

Lee, C. H., and S. L. Shin. 2011. "Functional Activities of Ferns." In *Working with Ferns: Issues and Applications*, edited by H. Fernandez, A. Kumar, and M. A. Revilla, 347–359. New York: Springer.

Marshall, Y. M. 1993. "A Political History of the Nuu-chah-nulth People: A Case Study of the Mowachaht and Muchalaht Tribes." PhD diss. Simon Fraser University.

McMillan, A. D. 2015. "Whales and Whalers in Nuu-chah-nulth Archaeology." *BC Studies*, no. 187: 229–261.

Mink, L. O. 1968. "The Autonomy of Historical Understanding." In *Philosophical Analysis and History*, edited by William H. Dray, 160–192. New York: Harper and Row.

Nair, Roshini. 2017. "Archeological Find Affirms Heiltsuk Nation's Oral History: Settlement on B.C.'s Central Coast Dated back to 14,000 Years." *CBC News*, March 30. http://www.cbc.ca/news/canada/british-columbia/archeological-find-affirms-heiltsuk-nation-s-oral-history-1.4046088.

Polkinghorne, D. E. 1988. *Narrative Knowing and the Human Sciences*. New York: SUNY Press.

Powell, J., ed. 1991. *Our World—Our Ways: T'aat'aaqsapa Cultural Dictionary*. Port Alberni, BC: Nuuchahnulth Tribal Council.

Ricoeur, P. 1990. *Time and Narrative*. Vol. 1. Translated by K. McLaughlin and D. Pellauer. Chicago: University of Chicago Press.

Royal Commission on Aboriginal Peoples. 1996. *Report of the Royal Commission on Aboriginal Peoples.* Ottawa: Indigenous and Northern Affairs Canada. https://www.bac-la.c.gc.ca/eng/discover/aboriginal-heritage/royal-commission-aboriginal-peoples/Pages/final-report.aspx.

Scientific Panel for Sustainable Forest Practices in Clayoquot Sound. 1995. *First Nations' Perspectives Relating to Forest Practices Standards in Clayoquot Sound.* Victoria: Cortex Consulting.

Stewart, H. 1984. *Cedar: Tree of Life to the Northwest Coast Indians.* Seattle: University of Washington Press.

Stonham, J. 2005. *A Concise Dictionary of the Nuuchahnulth Language of Vancouver Island.* New York: Edwin Mellen.

Truth and Reconciliation Commission of Canada. 2015. *Honouring the Truth, Reconciling for the Future: Summary of the Final Report of the Truth and Reconciliation Commission of Canada.* Ottawa: Truth and Reconciliation Commission of Canada. http://publications.gc.ca/site/eng/9.800288/publication.html.

Turner, N. J. 1979. *Plants in British Columbia Indian Technology.* Victoria: British Columbia Provincial Museum.

United Nations. 2007. *United Nations Declaration on the Rights of Indigenous Peoples.* https://www.un.org/development/desa/indigenouspeoples/declaration-on-the-rights-of-indigenous-peoples.html.

Main Pathway: Orientations

Subthemes

Proceed to Politics, p. 205
Proceed to Ethics, p. 159
Proceed to Place, p. 145

6

INTERVIEW WITH MARK DION

How do you identify the species of plants you decide to work with? What parameters guide your selection process and why?

MARK DION: There are three principal ways I represent the vegetal world in my work:

1. Actual living organism—thriving plants existing in nurturing conditions
2. Plant specimens—dried plants, wet preparations, herbarium vouchers, seed, fruits, seed pods
3. Watercolors, drawings, or prints made from the observation of living plants

So many factors go into the selection of particular plant species based on the unique conditions of each project. For example, when making the *Seattle Vivarium*, I needed to find and relocate a massive nurse log from the forests outside the city, back into the heart of the town, and into a vast purpose-built greenhouse. When one thinks "tree" in the Pacific Northwest, one has to think big, at least 150 years old, and there are only a handful of species in the region large enough to make productive nurse logs. I identified about six target species. But I still had to find a tree accessible for removal without destroying any forest. In the end, I located a Western hemlock (the state tree of Washington) that had fallen some years before and was close enough to a road that we could take it without overly disrupting the rest of the vegetation and soil.

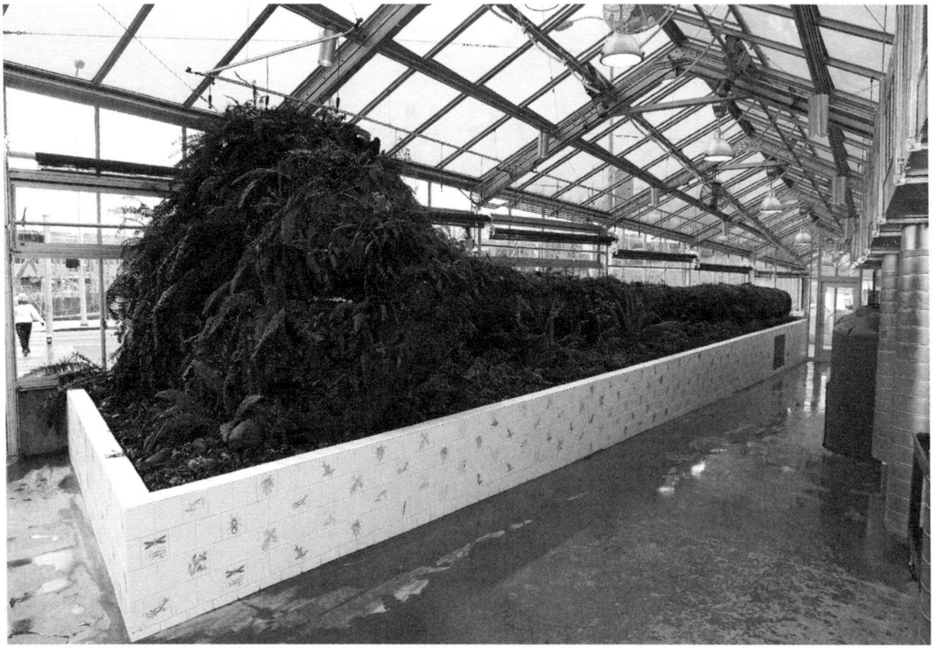

I have also worked on other projects that have required building herbara or carrying out field illustrations of plants. For example, in 2017, for the Istanbul Biennial, my team and I collected hardy weeds emerging from tarmac and buildings in urban spaces. We took clippings of them back to our studio, where we produced watercolor illustrations. In this case, I was keen to use plants as a metaphor for resilience or resistance.

Do you ever consider plants as subjects in your work, and how does that change your approach to them?

MD: In the *Seattle Vivarium* and other Vivarium projects, the structures are built around the host tree trunk, to foster the life of the next generation of plants and other organisms. In a sense, the entire work is made to encourage the growth of other plants. I feel that I am rooting for the plants to thrive. They are collaborators.

Vivarium, 2012. Mark Dion.

In your artistic practice, what have you learned from the plants themselves? In which ways does your art follow their movements, metamorphoses, and modes of being in the world? How does it interact with these vegetal processes?

MD: Anyone who works with plants learns one important lesson: patience. There is a lot of tension between the schedule of art exhibitions, the art world, and the schedule of plant lives. I have worked on many large-scale garden projects, like *The Tasting Garden* in Lancaster (1997), which was designed to emphasize heritage fruit trees, no longer commercially grown varieties. Needless to say, it takes years for fruit trees such as these to produce in such a way that fulfills the promise of the work. You have to imagine in tree-time.

What ethical or political considerations inform your work with plants? What are the ethical and political implications of this work?

MD: In much of my work that employs plants, I want to project the possibility that human interactions with other living beings need not always be destructive, objectifying, and degrading. We can choose to foster life, to enhance diversity, to restore damage, rather than merely promote a culture of Thanatos and pernicious destruction. I know no greater political concern than this.

What, if any, are the aspects of your work with plants related to the current global environmental and mass extinction crises?

MD: Needless to say, over the past 30 years or so, extinction and biodiversity have been central aspects and thematics of my artistic practice. Part of my focus on these notions has been a commitment to trying to understand the impossibility of representing the natural world, in part because nature is a process rather than a thing or place. For the ecosystems I care about the most—tropical rainforests, coral reefs, oceans, and also organisms like corals or birds—there has been very little positive news over the past three decades. It is hard not to become melancholic about these issues when the situation merely continues to worsen.

Which pressing challenge, or challenges, has working with plants presented to you?

MD: Working and thinking about plants always puts me in the orbit of biodiversity concerns. Well, we are used to thinking about the loss of biodiversity as related to issues like pollution, habitat loss, overcutting, invasive species, and other issues related to the legacy of colonialism and capitalism. Mostly, it seemed that species loss was the thoughtless collateral damage of the extremes of resource extraction. However, it seems that more recently living beings are casualties of information wars, ideology, and a highly polarized extremist public, willing to burn the planet to the core.

Trumping the past ecological concerns, of course, is global warming, which puts all extinction and biodiversity issues in stark relief.

How is the interaction between your artistic practice and theoretical endeavors shaped by vegetal life?

MD: In many ways, I am very much an artist of the 1990s. My interest and the fulcrum of my practice is a critique of representation around questions of the culture of nature. Plants have a special place in the history of natural history, since they are vital elements in the colonial endeavor. Whether we look at timber, spices, agricultural products, medicines, or new genomic prospecting, plants are central to understanding the history of the West's relationship with the biotic world. This is true in terms not only of resource extraction but also in the conceptual ordering and establishing of hierarchies. Linnaeus was a botanist. I think of plants as the decoder ring to the human ecological history of the world.

In terms of my being a student of actual plants, there is so much I have learned from my relationship with them: patience, complexity, the interconnectedness of things, fragility, and resilience. Plants are masterful in reminding me how little I actually know.

Mark Dion was born in 1961 in New Bedford, Massachusetts. His work examines the ways in which dominant ideologies and public institutions shape our understanding of history, knowledge, and the natural world. Appropriating archaeological; field ecology; and other scientific methods of collecting, ordering, and exhibiting objects, Dion creates works that question the distinctions between "objective" ("rational") scientific methods and "subjective" ("irrational") influences. He is the codirector of Mildred's Lane an innovative visual art education and residency program in Beach Lake, Pennsylvania. Dion lives with his wife, and frequent collaborator, artist Dana Sherwood in Copake, New York, and has been exhibited worldwide in some of the most prestigious institutions.

7

INTERVIEW WITH ZAYAAN KHAN

How do you identify the species of plants you decide to work with? What parameters guide your selection process and why?

ZAYAAN KHAN: My parameters generally are land (including sea), space, and place. It is also about need, harvesting or planting according to my own needs (or community of practice, including family) or the needs of the plants.

Do you ever consider plants as subjects in your work, and how does that change your approach to them?

ZK: Always. I often refer to plants as subjective within the collective, as "us" or "everyone," meaning myself, the plants, the soils, and so on. Pronouns are a very difficult space for a lot of English speakers, so I navigate this. I regard my work as "working with" instead of against, or as an extractive nature.

In your artistic practice, what have you learned from the plants themselves? In which ways does your art follow their movements, metamorphoses, and modes of being in the world? How does it interact with these vegetal processes?

What ethical or political considerations inform your work with plants? What are the ethical and political implications of this work?

ZK: The longer I work with plants, the more I know that I am interested beyond the human—all those who engage with plants because plants are more ancient than most of us. This is an ethical practice to always consciously de-center myself as a knowledge carrier. But a lot of work with plants (and particularly the microbial community through fermentation) has also helped me to see through knowledge extinction or knowledge birthing. Knowledge comes from the land and working and being with plants is a portal to that. Indigenous peoples around the world faced and face persecution, genocide, and erasure, and it is my duty to carry that knowledge and highlight that plight and call out extractive approaches. Of course, my work sees colonial implication and inherited violence and works to bring it forth. It aims to identify pathways through which healing can be the first step. There are so many laws and economical parameters around plants and land; I remain aware of these and continue to work at my subversive duty.

Other considerations are around biological functioning and sustainability, not harvesting too much, harvesting correctly, approaching plants in a specific way, and so on, to not be too disruptive unless general health leaves no other alternative.

What, if any, are the aspects of your work with plants related to the current global environmental and mass extinction crises?

ZK: All of it, as per the answer above, but also to say I use the fluid nature of time as a theme and theory. My work starts with care and healing wherever it finds itself. I really work from an "ancient futures" perspective. It helps me move away from that anthropocentric space but also helps me to recenter within myself—a gentle vortex, I guess.

Which pressing challenge, or challenges, has working with plants presented to you?

ZK: It has helped me to rethink communication breaking down and, through silo thinking, being interdisciplinary by nature, thinking through egos, learning how to grieve. My PhD is currently thinking through the global seed laws and patenting acts (as inherited from imperial and neoliberal systems) and how this affects our relationship with plants.

How is the interaction between your artistic practice and theoretical endeavors shaped by vegetal life?

ZK: I think by listening, by soft awareness, and gentle practice. By the constant and never-ending learning and the realization that through this work, the more I know,

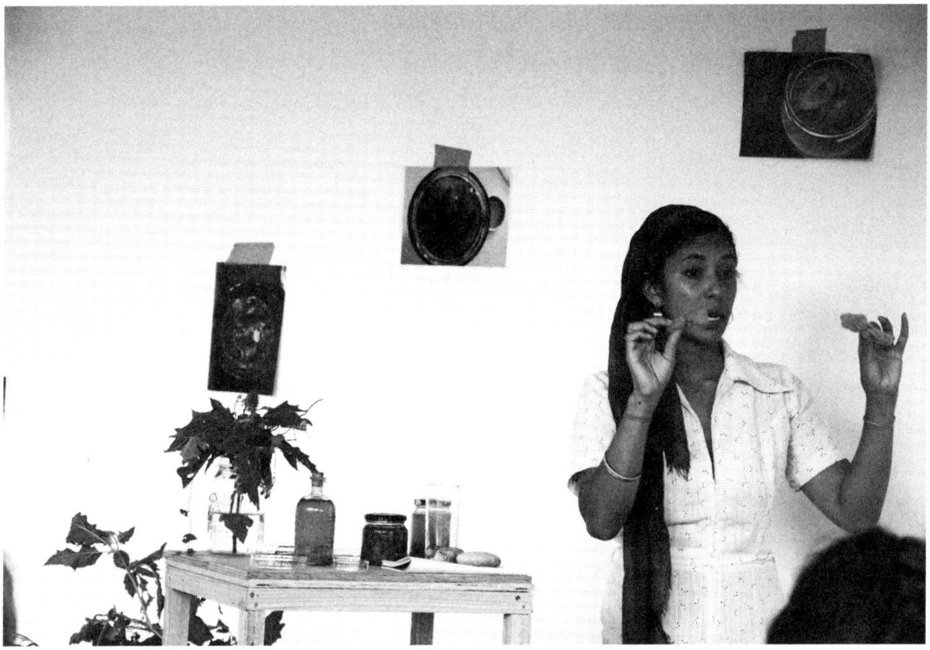

the more I know I don't know. Thus, the creative process and potential are ever greater. The same with nonvegetal work such as other foods or ceramic, those that live in the same spaces as us, whether water or clay or animal or microbial. It's all a lesson in humility, especially for me, who subscribes to evolutionary thinking.

Zayaan Khan is an artist and cultural worker from a sociopolitical platform to understand truer meanings of transformation and expressing solutions through the ways in which we consume. The local urban ecological environments and their interchangeable relationship intrigue Zayaan, and through curiosity, research, experimentation, and engagement, her work found a resting place through food as a means of understanding the world, particularly land and our collective heritage.

A workshop moment with wild fermentation explaining plant dyes, here oxalis pes-caprae flowers used to dye wool and also used as food. March 30, 2019, Zayaan Khan. POOLSpace, Johannesburg.

II

METHODOLOGIES

8

THE HUMAN BUMBLEBEE

Michael Pollan

The seeds of this book were first planted in my garden—while I was planting seeds, as a matter of fact. Sowing seed is pleasant, desultory, not terribly challenging work; there's plenty of space left over for thinking about other things while you're doing it. On this particular May afternoon, I happened to be sowing rows in the neighborhood of a flowering apple tree that was fairly vibrating with bees. And what I found myself thinking about was this: What existential difference is there between the human being's role in this (or any) garden and the bumblebee's?

If this sounds like a laughable comparison, consider what it was I was doing in the garden that afternoon: disseminating the genes of one species and not another, in this case a fingerling potato instead of, let's say, a leek. Gardeners like me tend to think such choices are our sovereign prerogative: in the space of this garden, I tell myself, I alone determine which species will thrive and which will disappear. I'm in charge here, in other words, and behind me stand other humans still more in charge: the long chain of gardeners and botanists, plant breeders, and, these days, genetic engineers who "selected," "developed," or "bred" the particular potato that I decided to plant. Even our grammar makes the terms of this relationship perfectly clear: *I choose the plants, I pull the weeds, I harvest the crops*. We divide the world into subjects and objects, and here in the garden, as in nature generally, we humans are the subjects.

But that afternoon in the garden I found myself wondering: What if that grammar is all wrong? What if it's really nothing more than a self-serving conceit? A bumblebee would probably also regard himself as a subject in the garden and the bloom he's plundering for its drop of nectar as an object. But we know that this is just a failure of his imagination. The truth of the matter is that the flower has cleverly manipulated the bee into hauling its pollen from blossom to blossom.

The ancient relationship between bees and flowers is a classic example of what is known as "coevolution." In a coevolutionary bargain like the one struck by the bee and the apple tree, the two parties act on each other to advance their individual interests but wind up trading favors: food for the bee, transportation for the apple genes. Consciousness needn't enter into it on either side, and the traditional distinction between subject and object is meaningless.

Matters between me and the spud I was planting, I realized, really aren't much different; we, too, are partners in a coevolutionary relationship, as indeed we have been ever since the birth of agriculture more than ten thousand years ago. Like the apple blossom, whose form and scent have been selected by bees over countless generations, the size and taste of the potato have been selected over countless generations by us—by Incas and Irishmen, even by people like me ordering French fries at McDonald's. Bees and humans alike have their criteria for selection: symmetry and sweetness in the case of the bee; heft and nutritional value in the case of the potato-eating human. The fact that one of us has evolved to become intermittently aware of its desires makes no difference whatsoever to the flower or the potato taking part in this arrangement. All those plants care about is what every being cares about on the most basic genetic level: making more copies of itself. Through trial and error these plant species have found that the best way to do that is to induce animals—bees or people, it hardly matters—to spread their genes. How? By playing on the animals' desires, conscious and otherwise. The flowers and spuds that manage to do this most effectively are the ones that get to be fruitful and multiply.

So the question arose in my mind that day: Did I choose to plant these potatoes, or did the potato make me do it? In fact, both statements are true. I can remember the exact moment that spud seduced me, showing off its knobby charms in the pages of a seed catalog. I think it was the tasty-sounding "buttery yellow flesh" that did it. This was a trivial, semiconscious event; it never occurred to me that our catalog encounter was of any evolutionary consequence whatsoever. Yet evolution consists of an infinitude of trivial, unconscious events, and in the evolution of the potato, my reading of a particular seed catalog on a particular January evening counts as one of them.

That May afternoon, the garden suddenly appeared before me in a whole new light, the manifold delights it offered to the eye and nose and tongue no longer quite so innocent or passive. All these plants, which I'd always regarded as the objects of my desire, were also, I realized, subjects, acting on me, getting me to do things for them they couldn't do for themselves.

And that's when I had the idea: What would happen if we looked at the world beyond the garden this way, regarded our place in nature from the same upside-down perspective?

This book attempts to do just that, by telling the story of four familiar plants—the apple, the tulip, cannabis, and the potato—and the human desires that link their destinies to our own. Its broader subject is the complex reciprocal relationship between the human and natural world, which I approach from a somewhat unconventional angle: I take seriously the plant's point of view.

The four plants whose stories this book tells are what we call "domesticated species," a rather one-sided term—that grammar again—that leaves the erroneous impression that we're in charge. We automatically think of domestication as something we do to other species, but it makes just as much sense to think of it as something certain plants and animals have done to us, a clever evolutionary strategy for advancing their own interests. The species that have spent the last ten thousand or so years figuring out how best to feed, heal, clothe, intoxicate, and otherwise delight us have made themselves some of nature's greatest success stories.

The surprising thing is, we don't ordinarily regard species like the cow and the potato, the tulip and the dog, as nature's more extraordinary creatures. Domesticated species don't command our respect the way their wild cousins often do. Evolution may reward interdependence, but our thinking selves continue to prize self-reliance. The wolf is somehow more impressive to us than the dog.

Yet there are fifty million dogs in America today, only ten thousand wolves. So, what does the dog know about getting along in this world that its wild ancestor doesn't? The big thing the dog knows about—the subject it has mastered in the ten thousand years it has been evolving at our side—is us: our needs and desires, our emotions and values, all of which it has folded into its genes as part of a sophisticated strategy for survival. If you could read the genome of the dog like a book, you would learn a great deal about who we are and what makes us tick. We don't ordinarily give plants as much credit as animals, but the same would be true of the genetic books of the apple, the tulip, cannabis, and the potato. We could read volumes about ourselves in their pages, in the ingenious sets of instructions they've developed for turning people into bees.

After ten thousand years of coevolution, their genes are rich archives of cultural as well as natural information. The DNA of that tulip there, the ivory one with the petals attenuated like sabers, contains detailed instructions on how best to catch the eye not of a bee but of an Ottoman Turk; it has something to tell us about that age's idea of beauty. Likewise, every Russet Burbank potato holds within it a treatise about our industrial food chain—and our taste for long, perfectly golden french fries. That's because we have spent the last few thousand years remaking these species through artificial selection, transforming a tiny, toxic root node into a fat, nourishing potato and a short, unprepossessing wildflower into a tall, ravishing tulip. What is much less obvious, at least to us, is that these plants have, at the same time, been going about the business of remaking us.

I call this book *The Botany of Desire* because it is as much about the human desires that connect us to these plants as it is about the plants themselves. My premise is that these human desires form a part of natural history in the same way the hummingbird's love of red does, or the ant's taste for the aphid's honeydew. I think of them as the human equivalent of nectar. So while the book explores the social history of these plants, weaving them into our story, it is at the same time a natural history of the four human desires these plants evolved to stir and gratify.

I'm interested not only in how the potato altered the course of European history or how cannabis helped fire the romantic revolution in the West, but also in the way notions in the minds of men and women transformed the appearance, taste, and mental effects of these plants. Through the process of coevolution human ideas find their way into natural facts: the contours of a tulip's petals, say, or the precise tang of a Jonagold apple.

The four desires I explore here are *sweetness*, broadly defined, in the story of the apple; *beauty* in the tulip's; *intoxication* in the story of cannabis; and *control* in the story of the potato—specifically, in the story of a genetically altered potato I grew in my garden to see where the ancient arts of domestication may now be headed. These four plants have something important to teach us about these four desires—that is, about what makes us tick. For instance, I don't think we can begin to understand beauty's gravitational pull without first understanding the flower, since it was the flower that first ushered the idea of beauty into the world the moment, long ago, when floral attraction emerged as an evolutionary strategy. By the same token, intoxication is a human desire we might never have cultivated had it not been for a handful of plants that manage to manufacture chemicals with the precise molecular key needed to unlock the mechanisms in our brain governing pleasure, memory, and maybe even transcendence.

Domestication is about a whole lot more than fat tubers and docile sheep; the offspring of the ancient marriage of plants and people are far stranger and more marvelous than we realize. There is a natural history of the human imagination, of beauty, religion, and possibly philosophy too. One of my aims in this book is to shed some light on the part in that history these ordinary plants have played.

Plants are so unlike people that it's very difficult for us to appreciate fully their complexity and sophistication. Yet plants have been evolving much, much longer than we have, have been inventing new strategies for survival and perfecting their designs for so long that to say that one of us is the more "advanced" really depends on how you define that term, on what "advances" you value. Naturally we value abilities such as consciousness, toolmaking, and language, if only because these have been the destinations of our own evolutionary journey thus far. Plants have traveled all that distance and then some—they've just traveled in a different direction.

Plants are nature's alchemists, expert at transforming water, soil, and sunlight into an array of precious substances, many of them beyond the ability of human beings to conceive, much less manufacture. While we were nailing down consciousness and learning to walk on two feet, they were, by the same process of natural selection, inventing photosynthesis (the astonishing trick of converting sunlight into food) and perfecting organic chemistry. As it turns out, many of the plants' discoveries in chemistry and physics have served us well. From plants come chemical compounds that nourish and heal and poison and delight the senses, others that rouse and put to sleep and intoxicate, and a few with the astounding power to alter consciousness—even to plant dreams in the brains of awake humans.

Why would they go to all this trouble? Why should plants bother to devise the recipes for so many complex molecules and then expend the energy needed to manufacture them? One important reason is defense. A great many of the chemicals plants produce are designed, by natural selection, to compel other creatures to leave them alone: deadly poisons, foul flavors, toxins to confound the minds of predators. But many other of the substances plants make have exactly the opposite effect, drawing other creatures to them by stirring and gratifying their desires.

The same great existential fact of plant life explains why plants make chemicals to both repel and attract other species: immobility. The one big thing plants can't do is move, or, to be more precise, locomote. Plants can't escape the creatures that prey on them; they also can't change location or extend their range without help.

And so about a hundred million years ago plants stumbled on a way—actually a few thousand different ways—of getting animals to carry them, and their genes, here and there. This was the evolutionary watershed associated with the advent of the angiosperms, an extraordinary new class of plants that made showy flowers and formed large seeds that other species were induced to disseminate. Plants began evolving burrs that attach to animal fur like Velcro, flowers that seduce honeybees in order to powder their thighs with pollen, and acorns that squirrels obligingly taxi from one forest to another, bury, and then, just often enough, forget to eat.

Even evolution evolves. About ten thousand years ago the world witnessed a second flowering of plant diversity that we would come to call, somewhat self-centeredly, "the invention of agriculture." A group of angiosperms refined their basic put-the-animals-to-work strategy to take advantage of one particular animal that had evolved not only to move freely around the earth, but to think and trade complicated thoughts. These plants hit on a remarkably clever strategy: getting us to move and think for them. Now came edible grasses (such as wheat and corn) that incited humans to cut down vast forests to make more room for them; flowers whose beauty would transfix whole cultures; plants so compelling and useful and tasty they would inspire human beings to seed, transport, extol, and even write books about them. This is one of those books.

So am I suggesting that the plants made me do it? Only in the sense that the flower "makes" the bee pay it a visit. Evolution doesn't depend on will or intention to work; it is, almost by definition, an unconscious, unwilled process. All it requires are beings compelled, as all plants and animals are, to make more of themselves by whatever means trial and error present. Sometimes an adaptive trait is so clever it appears purposeful: the ant that "cultivates" its own gardens of edible fungus, for instance, or the pitcher plant that "convinces" a fly it's a piece of rotting meat. But such traits are clever only in retrospect. Design in nature is but a concatenation of accidents, culled by natural selection until the result is so beautiful or effective as to seem a miracle of purpose.

By the same token, we're prone to overestimate our own agency in nature. Many of the activities humans like to think they undertake for their own good purposes—inventing agriculture, outlawing certain plants, writing books in praise of others—are mere contingencies as far as nature is concerned. Our desires are simply more grist for evolution's mill, no different from a change in the weather: a peril for some species, an opportunity for others. Our grammar might teach us to divide the world into active subjects and passive objects, but in a coevolutionary relationship every subject is also an object, every object a subject. That's why it makes just as much sense to think of agriculture as something the grasses did to people as a way to conquer the trees.

When Charles Darwin was writing *The Origin of Species*, deciding how best to spring his outlandish idea of natural selection on the world, he settled on a curious rhetorical strategy. Rather than open the book with an account of his new theory, he began with a side subject he judged people (and perhaps English gardeners in particular) would have an easier time getting their heads around. Darwin devoted the first chapter of *The Origin of Species* to a special case of natural selection called "artificial selection"—his term for the process by which domesticated species come into the world. Darwin was using the word "artificial" not as in fake but as in artifact: a thing reflecting human will. There's nothing fake about a hybrid rose or a butter pear, a cocker spaniel or a show pigeon.

These were a few of the domesticated species Darwin wrote about in his opening chapter, demonstrating how in each case the species proposes a wealth of variation from which humans then select the traits that will be passed down to future generations. In the special realm of domestication, Darwin explained, human desire (sometimes consciously, sometimes not) plays the same role that blind nature does everywhere else, determining what constitutes "fitness" and thereby leading, over time, to the emergence of new forms of life. The evolutionary rules are the same ("modification by descent"), but Darwin understood that they'd be easier to follow in the story of the tea rose than the sea turtle, in the setting of the garden than the Galápagos.

In the years since Darwin published *The Origin of Species*, the crisp conceptual line that divided artificial from natural selection has blurred. Whereas once humankind exerted its will in the relatively small arena of artificial selection (the arena I think of, metaphorically, as a garden) and nature held sway everywhere else, today the force of our presence is felt everywhere. It has become much harder, in the past century, to tell where the garden leaves off and pure nature begins. We are shaping the evolutionary weather in ways Darwin could never have foreseen; indeed, even the weather itself is in some sense an artifact now, its temperatures and storms the reflection of our actions. For a great many species today, "fitness" means the ability to get along in a world in which humankind has become the most powerful evolutionary force. Artificial selection has become a much more important chapter in natural history as it has moved into the space once ruled exclusively by natural selection.

That space, which is the one we often call "the wild," was never quite as innocent of our influence as we like to think; the Mohawks and Delawares had left their marks on the Ohio wilderness long before John Chapman (aka Johnny Appleseed) showed up and began planting apple trees. Yet even the dream of such a space has become hard to sustain in a time of global warming, ozone holes, and technologies that allow us to modify life at the genetic level—one of the wild's last redoubts. Partly by default, partly by design, all of nature is now in the process of being domesticated—of coming, or finding itself, under the (somewhat leaky) roof of civilization. Indeed, even the wild now depends on civilization for its survival.

Nature's success stories from now on are probably going to look a lot more like the apple's than the panda's or white leopard's. If those last two species have a future, it will be because of human desire; strangely enough, their survival now depends on what amounts to a form of artificial selection. This is the world in which we, along with Earth's other creatures, now must make our uncharted way.

This book takes place in that world; consider it a set of dispatches from Darwin's ever-expanding garden of artificial selection. Its main characters are four of that world's success stories. The dogs, cats, and horses of the plant world, these domesticated species are familiar to everyone, so deeply woven into the fabric of our everyday lives that we scarcely think of them as "species" or parts of "nature" at all. But why is that? I suspect it's at least partly the fault of the word. "Domestic" implies that these species have come in or been brought under civilization's roof, which is true enough; yet the house-y metaphor encourages us to think that by doing so they have, like us, somehow *left* nature, as if nature were something that only happens outside.

This is simply another failure of imagination: nature is not only to be found "out there"; it is also "in here," in the apple and the potato, in the garden and the kitchen, even in the brain of a man beholding the beauty of a tulip or inhaling the smoke from a burning cannabis flower. My wager is that when we can find nature in these sorts of places as readily as we now find it in the wild, we'll have traveled a considerable distance toward understanding our place in the world in the fullness of its complexity and ambiguity.

I've chosen the apple, the tulip, cannabis, and the potato for several logical-sounding reasons. One is that they represent four important classes of domesticated plants (a fruit, a flower, a drug plant, and a staple food). Also, having grown these four plants at one time or another in my own garden, I'm on fairly intimate terms with them. But the real reason I chose these plants and not another four is simpler than that: they have great stories to tell.

Each of the chapters that follows takes the form of a journey that either starts out, stops by, or ends up in my garden but along the way ventures far afield, both in space and historical time: to seventeenth-century Amsterdam, where, for a brief, perverse moment, the tulip became more precious than gold; to a corporate campus in St. Louis, where genetic engineers are reinventing the potato; and back to Amsterdam, where another, far less lovely flower has made itself, again, more precious than gold. I also travel to potato farms in Idaho; follow my species' passion for intoxicating plants down through history and into contemporary neuroscience; and paddle a canoe down a river in central Ohio in search of the real Johnny Appleseed. Hoping to render our relationships with these four species in all their complexity, I look at them, by turns, through a variety of lenses: social and natural history, science, journalism, biography, mythology, philosophy, and memoir.

These are stories, then, about Man and Nature. We've been telling ourselves such stories forever, as a way of making sense of what we call our "relationship to nature"—to borrow that curious, revealing phrase. (What other species can even be said to have a "relationship" to nature?) For a long time now, the Man in these stories has gazed at Nature across a gulf of awe or mystery or shame. Even when the tenor of these narratives changes, as it has over time, the gulf remains. There's the old heroic story, where Man is at war with Nature; the romantic version, where Man merges spiritually with Nature (usually with some help from the pathetic fallacy); and, more recently, the environmental morality tale, in which Nature pays Man back for his transgressions, usually in the coin of disaster—three different narratives (at least), yet all of them share a premise we know to be false but can't seem to shake: that we somehow stand outside, or apart from, nature.

This book tells a different kind of story about Man and Nature, one that aims to put us back in the great reciprocal web that is life on Earth. My hope is that by the time you close its covers, things outside (and inside) will look a little different, so that when you see an apple tree across a road or a tulip across a table, it won't appear quite so alien, so Other. Seeing these plants instead as willing partners in an intimate and reciprocal relationship with us means looking at ourselves a little differently, too: as the objects of other species' designs and desires, as one of the newer bees in Darwin's garden—ingenious, sometimes reckless, and remarkably unself-conscious. Think of this book as that bee's mirror.

Main Pathway: Cross-Pollination

Subthemes

Proceed to Experience, p. 263
Proceed to Place, p. 569

9

COSMOLOGIES: PERSPECTIVISM

Eudardo Viveiros de Castro

Can the anthropological theorist justifiably deny theoretical insight to his subjects?
—Irving Goldman, *The Mouth of Heaven*

The subject of these lectures is that aspect of Amerindian thought, which has been called its "perspectival quality" (Århem, 1993) or "perspectival relativity" (Gray, 1996): the conception, common to many peoples of the continent, according to which the world is inhabited by different sorts of subjects or persons, human and non-human, which apprehend reality from distinct points of view. I shall try to persuade you that this idea cannot be reduced to our current concept of relativism (Lima, 1996a, 1996b), which at first it seems to call to mind. In fact, it is at right angles, so to speak, to the opposition between relativism and universalism. Such resistance by Amerindian perspectivism to the terms of our epistemological debates casts suspicion on the robustness and transportability of the ontological partitions which they presuppose. In particular, as many anthropologists have already concluded (albeit for other reasons), the classic distinction between nature and culture cannot be used to describe domains internal to non-Western cosmologies without first undergoing a rigorous ethnographic critique. That critique, in the present case, implies a dissociation and redistribution of the predicates subsumed within the two paradigmatic sets that traditionally oppose one another under the headings of "Nature" and "Culture":

Originally published as selections from *Cosmological Perspectivism in Amazonia and Elsewhere* (HAU Books [Creative Commons], 1998), 47–60. Reprinted with permission.

universal and particular, objective and subjective, physical and social, fact and value, the given and the instituted, necessity and spontaneity, immanence and transcendence, body and mind, animality and humanity, among many more.[1]

Such an ethnographically based reshuffling of our conceptual schemes leads me to suggest the expression "multinaturalism" to designate one of the contrastive features of Amerindian thought in relation to modern "multiculturalist" cosmologies. Where the latter are founded on the mutual implication of the unity of nature and the multiplicity of cultures—the first guaranteed by the objective universality of body and substance, the second generated by the subjective particularity of spirit and meaning—the Amerindian conception would suppose a spiritual unity and a corporeal diversity.[2] Here, culture or the subject would be the form of the universal, whilst nature or the object would be the form of the particular.

This inversion, perhaps too symmetrical to be more than a speculative fiction,[3] must be developed by means of an analysis of Amerindian cosmological categories enabling us to determine the contexts we can call "nature" and "culture." The dissociation and redistribution of the predicates subsumed by such categories, therefore, is not enough: the latter must be desubstantialized as well, for in Amerindian thought, it is not simply that the categories of nature and culture have other contents to their Western counterparts, they also have a different status. They are not ontological provinces, but rather refer to exchangeable perspectives and relational-positional contexts; in brief, points of view.

Clearly, then, I think that the distinction between nature and culture must be subjected to critique, but not in order to reach the conclusion that such a thing does not exist. There are already far too many things which do not exist. The flourishing industry of criticisms of the Westernizing character of all dualisms has called for the abandonment of our conceptually dichotomous heritage, but to date the alternatives have not quite gone beyond the stage of wishful unthinking. I would prefer to gain a perspective on our own contrasts, contrasting them with the distinctions actually operating in Amerindian perspectivist cosmologies.

PERSPECTIVISM IN AMAZONIA AND ELSEWHERE

The initial stimulus for the present reflections were the numerous references in Amazonian ethnography to an Indigenous theory according to which the way humans perceive animals and other subjectivities that inhabit the world—gods, spirits, the dead, inhabitants of other cosmic levels, meteorological phenomena, plants, occasionally even objects and artefacts—differs profoundly from the way in which these beings see humans and see themselves.

Typically, in normal conditions, humans see humans as humans, and animals as animals; as to spirits, to see these usually invisible beings is a sure sign that the "conditions" are not normal. Animals (predators) and spirits, however, see humans as animals (as prey), to the same extent that animals (as prey) see humans as spirits or as animals (predators). By the same token, animals and spirits see themselves as humans: they perceive themselves as (or become) anthropomorphic beings when they are in their own houses or villages, and they experience their own habits and characteristics in the form of culture—they see their food as human food (jaguars see blood as manioc beer, vultures see the maggots in rotting meat as grilled fish, etc.), they see their bodily attributes (fur, feathers, claws, beaks) as body decorations or cultural instruments, they see their social system as organized in the same way as human institutions are (with chiefs, shamans, ceremonies, exogamous moieties, etc.). This "to see as" refers literally to percepts and not analogically to concepts, although in some cases the emphasis is placed more on the categorical rather than on the sensory aspect of the phenomenon; in any case, the shamans, masters of cosmic schematism (Taussig, 1987, 462–463) and dedicated to communicating and administering these cross-perspectives, are always there to make concepts tangible and intuitions intelligible.

In sum, animals are people, or see themselves as persons. Such a notion is virtually always associated with the idea that the manifest form of each species is a mere envelope (a "clothing") which conceals an internal human form, usually only visible to the eyes of the particular species or to certain trans-specific beings such as shamans. This internal form is the soul or spirit of the animal: an intentionality or subjectivity formally identical to human consciousness, materializable, let us say, in a human bodily schema concealed behind an animal mask.

At first glance then, we would have a distinction between an anthropomorphic essence of a spiritual type, common to animate beings, and a variable bodily appearance, characteristic of each individual species but which rather than being a fixed attribute is instead a changeable and removable clothing. This notion of clothing is one of the privileged expressions of metamorphosis—spirits, the dead and shamans who assume animal form, beasts that turn into other beasts, humans that are inadvertently turned into animals—an omnipresent process in the "highly transformational world" (Rivière, 1994) proposed by Amazonian ontologies.[4]

This perspectivism and cosmological transformism can be seen in various South American ethnographies, but in general it is only the object of short commentaries, and seems to be quite unevenly elaborated. In South America, the cosmologies of the Vaupés area are in this respect highly developed (see Århem, 1993, 1996; Reichel-Dolmatoff, 1985; Hugh-Jones, 1996a), but other Amazonian societies also give equal emphasis to the theme, such as the Wari' of Rondônia (Vilaça, 1992) and the Yudjá of the Middle Xingu (Lima, 1996a). It can also be found, and maybe with even greater generative value, in the far north of North America and Asia, as well as amongst a few hunter-gatherer populations of other parts of the world.[5] Outside these areas, the theme of perspectivism seems to be absent or inchoate. An exception could be the Kaluli of Papua New Guinea's Southern Highlands, who have a cosmology quite similar in this respect to the Amerindian ones. Schieffelin (1976, chapter 5) and Sahlins (1996, p. 403) reminded me of this parallel. Interestingly, Wagner (1977, p. 404) characterized Kaluli cosmology as "bizarre"—by Melanesian standards of course, for it would sit rather comfortably in Amazonia.[6]

Perspectivism in the Literature: Some Examples

The notes and quotations below are an aleatory sample of the ethnographic record about our subject (other references will be given as the argument unfolds).

(1) François Grenand (1980, pp. 41–42), on the Wayãpi of French Guiana: a man who falls in the subterranean world is seen by its denizens, who are giant sloths, as a kinkajou. "For humans, animals are animals; for animals [who are humans for themselves, presumably], humans are animals." But for the Sun and the Moon, both humans and animals are animals (humans are monkeys).

(2) Fabíola Jara (1996, pp. 68–74), on the Akuryió of Surinam: vultures go "fishing" on earth; the maggots on rotten meat are their fish. For the spirits living on the river bottom, fishes are forest animals; land animals are seen by them as birds. The "banana" of the tapir is an inedible fruit of the forest; the forest floor is the hammock of tapirs; in the village of tapirs, identical to a human one, "manioc" can be seen (the leaves tapirs eat), etc. These Akuryió myths, like many other references to animal perspectivism (e.g., Hallowell. 1960, p. 63; Lévi-Strauss, 1985, p. 151), can be read as lessons in natural history, presenting a detailed account of the ethnogram of different species. The motif of human–animal

parallelisms suggests, furthermore, that Amerindians conceive of something like an abstract, pan-specific behavioral schema which includes humans: culture is human nature, just as animal nature is culture. However, perspectivism cannot be reduced to—even if it may be derived from—a sort of generalized analogical ethology (with more than a grain of Western-scientific truth in it, by the way). It applies to other beings besides animals, like the dead, spirits, chthonian and celestial races, plants, artefacts and so on. It often has important cosmographic connotations, as noted in items 3, 5, and 8 below. And in many cases the theme has no obvious naturalistic references, as in the long Matsiguenga myth analyzed by Renard-Casevitz (1991, pp. 16–27).

(3) Gerald Weiss (1972, p. 170) on the Campa of Peru:

And what is the nature of the universe in which the Campa find themselves? It is a world of semblances; for example, what to us is the solid earth is airy sky to the beings inhabiting the strata below us, and what to us is airy sky is solid ground to those who inhabit the strata above. It is a world of relative semblances, where different kinds of beings see the same things differently; thus humans eyes can normally see good spirits only in the form of lightning flashes or birds whereas they see themselves in their true human form, and similarly in the eyes of jaguars human beings look like peccaries to be hunted.

(4) Aparecida Vilaça (1998, p. 4) on the Wari' of Rondônia (Brazil):

Humanity is defined by the possession of a spirit or soul. Animals endowed with spirit are considered as "people," "human." They have a human body that shamans can see; they live in houses, drink maize beer and eat their food roasted and boiled. All "human" animals have culture, the same culture of the Wari'. That is why they hunt, kill enemies, use fire to prepare their food, cultivate maize etc. This, however, is the way they [the animals] see things. The Wari' know the jaguar kills its prey with tooth and claw, and eats it raw. But for the jaguar, or rather, from the jaguar's point of view (shared by shamans, but not by the rest of the Wari'), he kills his prey with arrows like the Wari' do; he takes the prey home, gives it to his wife and tells her to cook it.

(5) Marie-Françoise Guédon (1984a, p. 142), on the Tsimshiam (NW Coast):

There are stories of human beings transformed into salmon, or snails, or mountain goats and living a human-like life with the salmon, snails, or mountain goats . . . and looking at the humans as we look at the supernatural beings, the *naxnoq* So, we are to the animal what the powers of the spirit are to us. For example, consider a hunter shooting a sea lion; from the point of view of the sea lions, who are living in houses with their human-like families, the sea lion which has been struck by the arrow becomes sick; so it needs a shaman, a sea lion shaman to cure a sea lion from the spirit arrow of a *naxnoq*, who is the human hunter.

(6) Robert Brightman (1993, pp. 44–47), on the Rock Cree (Canada). Commenting a myth opposing wolverines' and wolves' behaviors and perceptions, the author sketches a lapidary characterization of perspectivism:

These scenes typify epistemological themes that resonate in other myths, in dreams, and in Cree reflections on the quality of their waking perceptions. Beings or selves of two different species or kinds may have radically different perceptions and understandings of the same events in which both participate. More specifically, individuals or selves of one species or kind experience individuals of other species as different from themselves in appearance and practices. The experience that each "self" has of the "other" may be, however, radically different from the experience that the "other" has of its own appearance and practices. Further, selves of different species or kinds may each experience *themselves* in similar or identical terms: as users of fire, speech, and manufactured objects. . . . Crees speculate that modern animals, whatever they may look like to humans, experience themselves as participating in the same appearances and behaviors that Crees understand themselves to possess.

See also pages 163–185 of Brightman's outstanding monograph, to which I shall be making less mention than it obviously deserves (I still have to give it a closer reading).

(7) Out of America: Signe Howell (1996, p. 139), on the Chewong of Malaysia:

A large number of myths concern deceptive relations between different species of personages. Thus there are stories in which human personages appear in the cloak of animals, and stories where animals, plants or spirits appear in human cloak. An added complication is that non-human personages may appear in human bodies when they are "at home," in "their own land," thus expressing the fundamental equality between all species of personages.

Howell's monograph on the Chewong (1984) is a pioneering study of a perspectivist cosmology remarkably evocative of Amerindian themes.

(8) The *Mythologiques*, of course, include abundant materials relevant to our theme. But it is in *La potière jalouse* that Lévi-Strauss deals more directly with it. It appears there in connection with the notion of *"le monde à l'envers,"* the world as seen by the denizens of other cosmic levels (1985, pp. 134–142, 149–152): for the

red-haired anusless chthonian dwarves who feed on the smell of foods, wasps are enemy Indians, hares are jaguars; their day or summer is our night or winter and vice-versa. (Lévi-Strauss takes the chthonian dwarves, present in many Amerindian mythologies, to be a spatial translation of the arboreal fauna). In Arapaho mythology, the dwarves speak the same language as humans, but with the meaning of words systematically inverted, a theme that reappears in the Chinook idea (1985, p. 152) that the language of the dead is to that of the living as figurative is to literal. (Compare this to the "twisted language" used by Yaminahua shamans when dealing with the spirit world, see Townsley [1993].) More generally, Lévi-Strauss observes the connection between perspectivistic themes and the many-layered universes so common in native America, and identifies the "reciprocity of perspectives" as a characteristic of Amerindian myths: *"la réciprocité de perspectives où j'ai vu le caractère propre de la pensée mythique"* (1985, p. 268).[7]

(9) The most insightful exploration of a perspectivist cosmology is to be found in Tânia S. Lima's thesis on the Yudjá (Juruna) of Eastern Amazonia (1996a, 1996b). The richness and complexity of Lima's analyses makes any summary mention of her data inappropriate. I can only refer the reader to her work; it was one of my major inspirations, even if my extrapolations would not necessarily meet her approval.[8]

ETHNOGRAPHIC CONTEXT

Some general observations are necessary. In the first place, perspectivism does not usually involve all animal species (besides covering sundry other beings), or does not involve them to the same extent. The emphasis seems to be on those species which perform a key symbolic and practical role such as the great predators, the rivals and enemies of human beings, and the main species of prey for humans: one of the central dimensions, possibly even the fundamental dimension, of perspectival inversions refers to the relative and relational statuses of predator and prey (Vilaça, 1992, pp. 49–51; Århem, 1993, pp. 11–12; see also Howell, 1996, p. 133).

Personhood and "perspectivity"—the capacity to occupy a point of view—is then a question of degree and/or context (Hugh-Jones, 1996a; Gray, 1996, pp. 141–44; see also Howell, 1996, p. 136), rather than an absolute, diacritical property of some species and not of others. Some non-human beings evince this attribute in a more consequential manner than others; as a matter of fact, many of them have powers of agency far superior to humans and in this sense are "more persons" than the latter (Hallowell, 1960, p. 69). On the other hand, the question of non-human personhood has an essential a posteriori dimension: the possibility that a thus far insignificant type of being turns out to be a prosopomorphic agent capable of affecting humans is always open—context and personal experience are decisive here.

In the second place, to affirm that non-human beings are persons capable of a point of view is not the same as affirming that they are "always" persons, that is, that humans' interactions with them are always predicated on a shared personhood. I am not referring here to any "dual attitude" to animals or nature in general, that is, to a distinction between practical cognition and religious ideology.[9] If there is any duality—and there is indeed—it belongs primarily to persons themselves (human and non-human), not to the attitudes towards them, for these are but a consequence of the two-sided nature of persons. It has nothing to do with reality vs. illusion, economy vs. ideology, or practice vs. theory: it derives from a distinction between visible and invisible, objective and subjective, affects and percepts. The personhood of animals (and of humans) is in effect a question of context; but contexts cannot be imported ready-made from our own intellectual context—they must be defined in Amerindian terms.

Finally, it is not always clear whether spirits or subjectivities are being attributed to each individual animal, and there are examples of cosmologies which deny consciousness to post-mythical animals (Overing, 1985, pp. 249 ff; 1986, pp. 245–246) or some other spiritual distinctiveness (Viveiros de Castro, 1992, pp. 73–74; Baer, 1994, p. 89)—but it is also far from clear whether this constitutes "animality" as a unified domain opposed to "humanity." (I believe it does not; see below.)[10] Be that as it may, the notion of animal spirit "masters" ("mothers of the game," "master of the white-lipped peccaries," etc.) is widely spread throughout the continent. These spirit masters, clearly endowed with a type of intentionality-based agency analogous to that of humans, function as hypostases of the animal species with which they are associated, thereby creating an intersubjective field for human–animal relations even where empirical animals are not spiritualized.

We must remember, above all, that if there is a virtually universal Amerindian notion, it is that of an original state of undifferentiation or "undifference" (don't mistake this for "indifference" or "sameness") between humans and animals, described in mythology:

> [What is a myth?] If you were to ask an American Indian it is extremely likely that he would answer: it is a story from the time when humans and animals did not distinguish themselves from one another. This definition seems to me to be very profound. (Lévi-Strauss and Eribon 1988, p. 193)

Myths are filled with beings whose form, name, and behavior inextricably mix human and animal attributes in a common context of intercommunicability, identical to that which defines the present-day intrahuman world. Myth is thus the vanishing point of Amerindian perspectivism, where the differences between points of view are at the same time annulled and exacerbated: this gives it the character of an absolute discourse. In myth, every species of being appears to others as it appears to itself (as human), while acting towards others as if already showing its distinctive and definitive nature (as animal, plant or spirit). All the beings which people mythology, manifest this ontological entanglement or cross-specific quality which makes them akin to shamans (an analogy which is explicitly made by some Amazonian cultures).[11] Myth speaks of a state of being where bodies and names, souls and affects, the I and the Other interpenetrate, submerged in the same immanent pre-subjective and pre-objective milieu, the demise of which (ever incomplete, always undone) is precisely what the mythology sets out to tell.

The "end" of this primordial immanence is, of course, the well-known separation of culture and nature which Lévi-Strauss showed to be the central theme of Amerindian mythology. But such separation was not brought out by a process of differentiating the human from the animal, as in our own evolutionist mythology. *The original common condition of both humans and animals is not animality, but rather humanity*. The great separation reveals not so much culture distinguishing itself from nature, but rather nature distancing itself from culture: the myths tell how animals lost the qualities inherited or retained by humans. Humans are those who continue as they have always been: animals are ex-humans, not humans ex-animals.[12] As Father Tastevin tersely remarked with regard to the Cashinahua: "Contrary to Spencer, they deem animals to have descended from man and not man from animals" (in Lévi-Strauss, 1985, p. 14). In the cosmology of the Campa, humankind is the substance of the primordial plenum or the original form of virtually everything, not just animals:

> Campa mythology is largely the story of how, one by one, the primal Campa became irreversibly transformed into the first representatives of various species of animals and plants,

as well as astronomical bodies or features of the terrain. The development of the universe, then, has been primarily a process of diversification, with mankind as the primal substance out of which many if not all of the categories of beings and things in the universe arose, the Campa of today being the descendants of those ancestral Campa who escaped being transformed. (Weiss, 1972, pp. 169–170).[13]

In sum, "the common point of reference for all beings of nature is not humans as a species but rather humanity as a condition" (Descola, 1986, p. 120). This distinction between the human species and the human condition—analogous to that between "humankind" and "humanity" made by Ingold (1994)—should be retained. It has an evident connection with the idea of animal clothing hiding a common spiritual "essence" and with the issue of the general meaning of perspectivism.

There is one further well-known aspect of Amazonian mythologies which deserves to be mentioned. I am thinking of the rarity of the idea of creation *ex nihilo* in Amazonian cosmogonies. Things and beings usually originate as a transformation of something else (a *trans*-formation, not an *in*-formation, by which I mean the creative imposition of mental form over passive and inert matter)—in the case of animals, as I have noticed, as the transformation of a primordial, universal humanity.[14] Wherever we do find notions of creation—almost never *ex nihilo* anyway, but as the fashioning of some prior substance into a new type of being—it seems to me that what is stressed is the imperfection of the end product; the typical Amerindian demiurge (often because of the misdeeds of his trickster twin brother) always fail to deliver the goods.

In like manner to this transformed rather than created nature, culture is not a matter of invention, but of transference (of "tradition," then). In Amerindian mythology, the origin of cultural implements or institutions is canonically explained as a borrowing, a transfer (violent or friendly, by stealing or by learning, as a trophy or as a gift) of prototypes of these institutions or implements such as already possessed by animals, spirits, or enemies. The origin and thereby the essence of culture is acculturation.

I would like to call your attention to the difference between the idea of creation-invention and the idea of transformation-transference, and to associate the creation idea to the metaphor of *production*: of production as a kind of weak version of creation, but at the same time as its model, as the archetypal mode of action in—or rather, upon and against—the world. I borrowed this contrast from François Jullien (1989, 1997), but I am using the notion of transformation in a sense very different from

Jullien's, who is concerned with Chinese ideas of efficaciousness. I am referring to production as the imposition of mental design over formless matter. By the same token, I would associate the idea of transformation to the metaphor of *exchange*. An exchange event is always a transformation of a prior exchange event; there is no absolute beginning, no absolute initial act of exchange—every act is a response, that is, a transformation of an anterior token of the same type. Now, creation-production is our archetypal model of action—the heroic or epic model of action, as Jullien observes, which dates from the Greeks and which is still very much alive: let us recall our current obsession with "agency" and "creativity"—while transformation-exchange would probably fit better the Amerindian and other non-modern worlds.[15] The exchange model of action supposes that the other of the subject is another subject, not an object; and this, of course, is what perspectivism is all about (Strathern, 1992, pp. 9–10). In the creation paradigm, production is causally primary, and exchange its encompassed consequence; exchange is a "moment" of production (it "realizes" value) and the means of *re*-production. In the transformation paradigm, exchange is the condition for production (without the proper social relations with the non-human world, no production is possible: production is a type or mode of exchange), and production the means of "re-exchange"—a word we certainly do not need, for exchange is by definition re-exchange. Production creates, exchange changes.[16]

I would venture a further remark on this contrast: the idiom of production applied to what lies without the source domain of material production—like when we speak of the production of persons, of social reproduction, of "consumptive production" as if it meant the production of subjects rather than simply of humans organisms, etc.—is necessarily "metaphorical"; it is as metaphorical, at least, as the idiom of exchange when applied to the engagement between human and non-human beings. To speak of the production of social life makes as much, or as little, sense as to speak of the exchange between humans and animals. Historical materialism is on the same plane as structural perspectivism, if not at a further remove from "the native's point of view."

It is also worth pointing out that Amerindian perspectivism has an essential relation with shamanism, and with the valorization of hunting as the archetypal mode of practical interaction with the non-human world. The association between shamanism and this "venatic ideology" is a classic question (for Amazonia, see Chaumeil, 1983, pp. 231–32; Crocker, 1985, pp. 17–25). I stress that this is a matter of symbolic importance, not ecological necessity: full-blown horticulturists such as the Tukano or the Yudjá, who couldn't have less of a "hunter-gatherer" disposition (and who in any case fish more than they hunt), do not differ much from circumpolar hunters in respect of the cosmological weight conferred on animal predation, spiritual subjectivation of animals, and the theory according to which the universe is populated by extra-human intentionalities endowed with their own perspectives. In this sense, the spiritualization of plants, meteorological phenomena, or artefacts seems to me to be secondary or derivative in comparison with the spiritualization of animals: the animal is the extra-human prototype of the Other, maintaining privileged relations with other prototypical figures of alterity, such as affines (Erikson, 1984, pp. 110–112; Descola, 1986, pp. 317–30; Århem, 1996).[17] This hunting ideology, as I said, is also and above all an ideology of shamans, insofar as it is shamans who administer the relations between humans and the spiritual component of the extra-humans, since they alone are capable of assuming the point of view of such beings and, in particular, are capable of returning to tell the tale.[18]

THEORETICAL CONTEXT

Before we proceed to examine the ethnography, I should address some likely disputable points. I am prompted to this by an awareness that substantive arguments about "how 'natives' think" (as opposed to arguments about how other anthropologists think), and especially arguments that appeal explicitly to a contrast with Western intellectual traditions as an expository device (as opposed to those wherein such contrast is willy-nilly left embedded in the very process of describing and analyzing), are mandatorily prefaced by a wealth of qualifications, apologies, and disavowals. I suppose I have to abide by the current protocol, on pain of being convicted of uncouthness or worse—of naiveté. The major qualm I must do my best to appease concerns the nature and purpose of this overall contrast between Amerindian and modern Western cosmologies. But I would also like to say something about the relation between what I shall be doing here and contemporary theories of human cognition.

Cosmology

By applying the labels "perspectivism" or "multinaturalism" to "Amerindian cosmologies" and contrasting it to a "Western cosmology," I am bound to be accused of two complementary faults (among others). It might be said that I am over-differentiating these two poles, and perhaps even essentializing them, that is, of proposing yet another Great Divide theory, and that I am under-differentiating each of them internally—the Amerindian one by treating, say, the Kayapó and the Tsimshian as birds of a feather who flocked together just yesterday from Siberia, and the Western one by lumping under this label an ungodly bricolage of histories, languages, cultures, intellectual traditions, discursive practices, genres, and what have you.

Great Divide theories, i.e., polarities and other "othering" comparative devices, have had a bad press lately. The place of the other, however, can never remain vacant for too long. As far as contemporary anthropology is concerned, the most popular candidate for the position appears to be anthropology itself. Firstly, in its formative phase (never completely outgrown), anthropology's main task was to explain how and why the primitive or traditional other was wrong: savages mistook ideal connections for real ones and animistically projected social relations onto nature. Secondly, in the discipline's classical phase (which lingers on), the other is Western society/culture. Somewhere along the line—with the Greeks? Christianity? the Reformation? the Enlightenment? Capitalism?—the West got everything wrong, positing substances, individuals, separations, and oppositions wherever all other societies/cultures rightly see relations, totalities, connections, and embeddednesses. Because it is both anthropologically anomalous and ontologically mistaken, it is the West, rather than "primitive" cultures that requires explanation: the Occident was an Accident. And, thirdly, in the postpositivist (still very much desiderative) phase of anthropology, first Orientalism, then Occidentalism, is shunned: the West and the Rest are no longer seen as so different from each other. On the one hand, we have never been modern (this is true) and, on the other, no society has ever been primitive (this is very true as well). Then who is wrong, what needs explanation? (Someone *must* be wrong, something *has* to be explained.) Our anthropological forebears, who made us believe in tradition and modernity, were wrong—and so the great polarity now is between anthropology and the real practical/embodied life of everyone, Western or otherwise. In brief: formerly, savages mistook (their) representations for (our) reality; now, we mistake (our) representations for (other peoples') reality. Rumor has it we have even been mistaking (our) representations for (our) reality when we "Occidentalize."

But once the blame games and guilt trips are over, what is left? The present writer, probably because he is stuck in anthropology's second stage, does believe there are striking differences between our modern official, hegemonic ontology—a precipitate of the Cartesian, Lockian, and Kantian reformations (i.e., epistemologisations) of previous ontologies—and the cosmologies of many "traditional" peoples, such as those I am most familiar with: Amazonian Indians. I take it this belief is not contradictory with the idea that "we have never been modern"; for the belief that we have been, or still are, modern (a belief that created, among many other things, the very category of "belief") is distinctive of modernity, and as such is related to a number of epistemo-political consequences, as shown by Latour (1991, 1996b).[19] (I should also remark that some of the most forceful deconstructors of Great Divides show a propensity to rebuild them along different fault lines. Goody (1996) is the most obvious example. Showing himself very much in phase with recent geopolitical realignments, he duly chastises orientalisms, sneers at the "hot/cold" contrast, etc., but quickly replaces these "othering" devices by a number of coincident divides—the hoe and the plough, bridewealth and dowry, the oral and the written, etc.—which simply transform the East/West polarity into a North–South one.)[20]

I have to say in my defense that the decision to concentrate on some similarities internal to (but not exclusive to) the Amerindian domain and on an overall contrast with the modern West is mostly a question of choice of level of generality; it has no "essentialist" value. Had I chosen instead to emphasize the commonality of human thought processes—about which I would not have much to talk about—or, conversely, the uniqueness of each Amerindian culture—in which case there would be no reason to stop talking—I would have to deliver a very different series of lectures. Let me just observe that these options I have not followed are actually far more liable to carry essentialist presuppositions.

The word "Amerindian" refers here to a limited number of native cultures from Lowland South America (mainly from Western Amazonia) and from septentrional North America (Northwest Coast, N. Athapaskan, N. Algonquian, Eskimo). These limits are the limits of my ignorance: I am not conversant with the ethnology of other, more southerly parts of North America. I am not including the Mesoamerican and Andean regions in my synecdoche, either. Generally speaking, I am at a quite unsafe remove from the ethnographic realities discussed here. My own fieldwork with the Araweté of Eastern Amazonia was certainly a crucial inspiration for the pages that follow, but these are based on the work of other ethnographers, sometimes on secondary sources already of an analytical and interpretive nature; more often than not, I shall be commenting on comments rather than on Indigenous statements and narratives.

It should be quite obvious that the Kwakiutl and the Cree are not "the same thing," let alone the Kwakiutl and the Tukanoans. Both of the major regions from which I take my examples exhibit marked internal differences in social morphology, economic and political structure, ceremonial life, religion, and so on. As with many of my colleagues, I have been much intrigued by some Amazonian contrasts, and have even been suspected of "reifying" some of them (between central Brazil and Amazonia, for example).[21] Be that as it may, with the present lectures I shall be moving up in the reification scale. They are an effort to tackle themes and problems that would allow me to make sense of some of these differences by identifying a sort of cosmological background from which they could be shown to emerge (as opposed to a cosmological horizon into which they should be resorbed). In this I am simply following the lead of Lévi-Strauss, who in his *Mythologiques* provided a forceful demonstration of the historical unity of Indigenous America. The ethnographic and thematic grounds I shall be covering are a small subset of the *Mythologiques*' universe.

I must also stress that there is not a hint of comparison in the present endeavor; there is only generalization. The materials I refer to, culled from a small sample of texts (I did not engage in a collation of different sources on the same groups—no internal, "critical" comparison as well), are used as a springboard for a thought-experiment consisting in abstracting and generalizing a set of ideas about subjects and objects, bodies and souls, humans and animals, and then sketching what could be called the "virtual ontology" underlying these abstracted generalizations.

Lévi-Strauss famously described Indigenous America as *"un Moyen âge auquel aurait manqué sa Rome"* (1964, p. 16).[22] He might have added: and a Greece as well, were it not for the fact that his own work shows the remarkable unity of the Amerindian world when we leave the socio-political for the mythico-philosophical plane. There was no Greece of course, and no identifiable Plato or Aristotle: there was no one, in particular, to oppose "myth" and "philosophy." But the thought-experiment that follows may be read as outlining a sort of imaginary identikit picture of an Amerindian philosophy who would stand to Indigenous mythopoeisis as Cartesian or Kantian ideas, say, stand to what I am calling the "modern West." If the analogy strikes you as too far-fetched, then what about this one?

> I have not authored a "perspective" on Melanesian society and culture; I have hoped to show the difference that perspective makes . . . I have not presented Melanesian ideas but an analysis from the point of view of Western anthropological and feminist preoccupations of what Melanesian ideas might look like if they were to appear in the form of those preoccupations. (Strathern, 1988, p. 309)

Now, it would very likely be argued—after Bourdieu (1972) and his strictures against the "theoricist" misrepresentation of the practical-embodied life of all peoples, Westerners included—that such an endeavor is meaningless, for people do not act out philosophical systems or cosmologies: the first belong to a very specialized type of discourse characteristic of higher civilizations, and the second are fanciful constructs of anthropologists unduly modelled on the former. The peoples of the world live through practice, in practice, and for practice. Any "plausible" anthropological theory must begin with this principle: that the phenomena that it studies differ radically from itself, not only in their contents, but also in their form and even in their reason for being. All anthropological theory must be a theory of practice. And practice and its behavioral pre-conditions (which go by various names—schemata, presuppositions, premises, scripts, habitus, relational configurations, etc.—the important criterion here being that the name must *not* be a word that resembles "culture" or "structure") are quintessentially non-propositional.[23] What "goes without saying" (Bloch, 1992) is the stuff social life is made of. We study the opposite of our study; nothing is more different from an anthropological theory than the practice of a native.

Thus anthropologists find themselves sometimes obliged to make embarrassing compromises in order to be able to say anything at all about this stuff that goes without saying. Take, for example, the brilliant analysis of Yaminahua shamanic knowledge carried out by Graham Townsley (1993). The paper's thesis is that

> Yaminahua shamanism cannot be defined by a clearly constituted discourse of beliefs, symbols or meanings. It is not a system of knowledge or facts known, but rather an ensemble of techniques for knowing. It is not a constituted discourse but a way of constituting one. (Townsley, 1993, p. 452)

In other words, the author stands against the traditional anthropological understanding of shamanism—shamanism as the expression of a traditional indigenous cosmology (Townsley, 1993, p. 450). At the same time, however, he admits that, to account for this "constituting discourse" that constructs meaning from the actual experience of ritual (practice, practice), "it will *first* be necessary to discuss some of the basic Yaminhaua *ideas* about the *constitution of the world* which provide the *framework* for shamanism . . ." (Townsley, 1993, p. 452, emphasis mine). Such ideas involve concepts like *yoshi*, i.e., "spirit, or animate essence," and certain subtle native theories (my word) of language that seem to me fairly explicit. On the whole, all of this, these "basic ideas" about the "constitution of the world," are quite similar to that which once got called, in the bad old days, "cosmology," "ontology," or even "culture."

It seems to me, all in all, that we have to resolve our highly ambivalent attitude concerning the propositional content of knowledge. Contemporary anthropology, both in its phenomenological-constructionist and in its cognitive-instructionist guises, has proven notable for insisting on the severe limitations of this model when it comes to dealing with intellectual economies of non-modern, nonwritten, non-theoretical, non-doctrinal—in short, non-Western type. Anthropological discourse has embroiled itself in the paradoxical pastime of heaping propositions on top of propositions arguing for the fundamentally non-propositional nature of other peoples' discourses. We count ourselves lucky when our natives display a blissful disdain for the practice of self-interpretation, and even less interest in cosmology and system. We're probably right, since the lack of native interpretation has the great advantage of allowing the proliferation of anthropological interpretations of this lack. Simultaneously, the native's disinterest in cosmological order fosters the production of neat anthropological cosmologies in which societies are ordered according to their greater or lesser inclination towards systematicity (or doctrinality, or whatever). In sum, the more practical the native, the more theoretical the anthropologist. Let us also not forget that the non-propositional mode is held to be characterized by a constitutive dependency on its "context" of transmission and circulation. This makes it the exact opposite (supposedly, it goes without saying) of scientific discourse—a discourse whose aim is precisely universalization. All of us are context-bound, but some are so much more context-bound than others.

My issue here isn't with the thesis of the quintessential nonpropositionality of untamed thought, but with the underlying idea that the proposition is in any sense a good model of conceptuality in general. The proposition continues to serve as the prototype of rational statements and the atom of theoretical discourse. The nonpropositional is seen as essentially primitive, as non-conceptual or even anti-conceptual. Naturally, such a state of affairs can be used both "for" and "against" this non-conceptual Other: the absence of rational-propositional concepts may be held to correspond to a superpresence of sensibility, emotion, sociability, intimacy, relational-cum-meaningful engagement in/with the world, and what not. For or against, though, all this concedes way too much to the proposition, and reflects a totally archaic concept of the concept, one which continues to define it as the subsumption of the particular by the universal, that is, as essentially a movement towards classification and abstraction. Now, rather than simply divorcing, for better or worse, the concept from "cognition in practice" (Lave, 1988), I believe we need to discover the infra-philosophical, i.e., the vital, within the concept, and likewise (perhaps more importantly) the virtual conceptuality within the infra-philosophical. What kind (or "form") of life, in other words, is virtually projected by ideas such as the Cartesian Cogito or the Kantian synthetic a priori? (Recall Wittgenstein's indignation against the petty spiritual life presumed by Frazer's interpretations of primitive rites.) And in like manner, what sort of virtual conceptuality pulsates within Amazonian shamanic narratives, Melanesian initiation rituals, African hunting traps, or Euro-American kinship usages? (Think of the ludicrously stunted conceptual imagination presumed by many an anthropological expatiation upon wild thought.) We need a little less by way of context and much more by way of concept.

Cognition

The style of analysis instanced in these lectures has been repeatedly assailed by anthropologists who favor so-called cognitive approaches. I will not examine their arguments in detail. Let me just say I think the materials presented here have little to expect from, and little to contribute to, cognitivist theories and concerns. Cognitivism belongs to my field of objects, not tools. It is something I shall be contrasting (more or less explicitly) with Amerindian ideas, not the standard of evaluation of these ideas or the instrument for their analysis. In other words, my problem is not that of Bloch (1989), i.e., that of showing how humans move (upwards and backwards, so to speak) "from cognition to ideology"—and how anthropology followed, historically, the inverse direction, leaving the dark ages of ideology to enter the enlightened era of cognition—but rather that of treating cognition *as* "ideology," the Western ideology of cognition.

Let me resort to an analogy to illustrate my contention that the materials presented here have little to do with cognitivist preoccupations. Consider the following trenchant remarks by Pascal Boyer on structuralism. (I am using Boyer as a target because, if we are to refer to anthropological cognitivism, we must go for the real McCoy, not some recent convert—and because I greatly admire his work.) These are his words:

> Structuralist descriptions of cultural realities are generally based on strong assumptions about supposedly universal patterns of thinking. From a psychological viewpoint, however, such claims are generally unconvincing. . . . For instance, structuralism assumes that the most

important aspect of conceptual structure is binary opposition. . . . Psychological research, however, has never found anything of the sort in the mental representations of concepts and categories. . . . Binary oppositions . . . play virtually no part in these representations In the same way, a central tenet of the Lévi-Straussian analysis of myth is that these same binary oppositions are crucial to the memorisation and transmission of stories. Again, however, empirical research in this domain has uncovered many complex processes to do with the reorganisation of stories in memory . . . none of which have anything to do with structuralist oppositions. In so far as it is making claims about the "human mind," structuralism seems to be pointing to realities which elude any psychological description. (1993, pp. 16–17)

Now, in the same article whence this dismissal of the psychological substance of binary opposition was extracted, we can also behold a dichotomous tree, used by Pascal to demarcate his own theoretical tribe from the rest of anthropology (figure 9.1).

I do not know about the human mind in general, but Boyer's manifestly has some sort of commerce with binary oppositions, and his mental representations of concepts and categories do seem to resort to this type of device after all. As for myself, and contrary to whatever empirical research has uncovered, I must say I found the binary tree above quite useful for memorizing Boyer's place in the cast of characters of his theoretical mythology. (There would be other things to observe about this tree, like the nobly pure vertical line connecting directly the "explanation" root above down to the branch on which Pascal is perched.)

My point here, let me be very clear about it, is *not* to prove that Boyer is wrong about structuralism, and that the human mind does feature binary opposition as its central conceptual mechanism. For all I know, he is probably right. But it is also a fact that some of his thought *contents*—his thoughts about cognitive anthropology, its relationships to other anthropological styles, the encompassing dualism of "interpretation" and "explanation," etc.—if not his thought *processes*, seem definitely to have been cast into a binary mold, as shown by the tree above. Nothing strange about that. Our intellectual tradition abounds in dichotomies. Boyer's tree, for example, has solid roots in both Plato and Aristotle, and we are certainly not an exception: from the Chinese *yin/yang* to the Bororo *aroe/bope*—both dualities, it should be remarked, very different from any Western construct—any anthropologist could recall dozens of examples to the effect that we are not alone in imagining dual principles and using them as master schemes for ontology-building.[24] So the human *mind* may not have binary opposition as the basic building material of its "mental representations" . . . But many human *cultures*, or if you wish, many

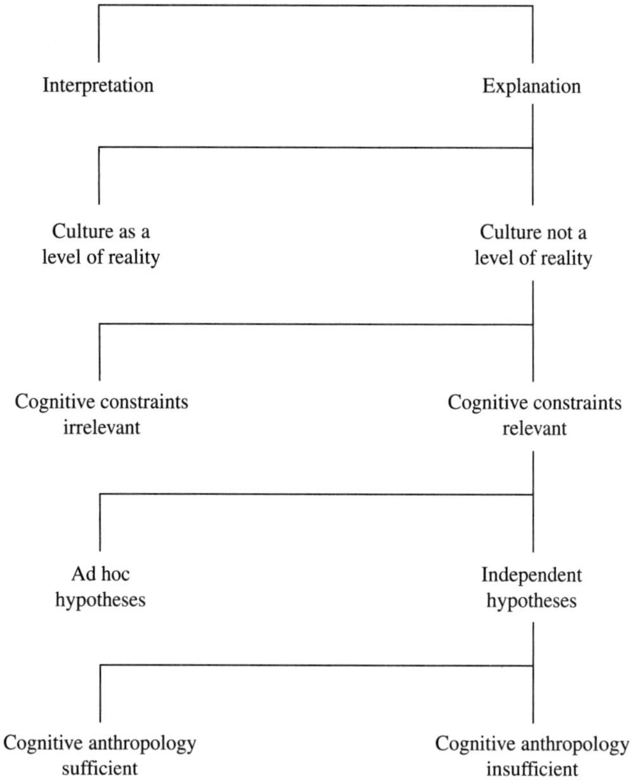

9.1

Five choices in the study of religious symbolism. (From Boyer, 1993, p. 7.)

historically specific intellectual traditions, obviously use dualistic schemes as their conceptual skeleton key.

What can we conclude from that? At the very least, that cognitive psychology cannot tell us much—certainly not the whole story—about higher-level, collective "mental" constructs such as cosmologies or philosophical systems. Conversely, we are led to suspect that the anthropological analysis of these objects may have little to tell us about the human mind—in this respect, the ambitions of structuralism, and indeed of much of classical anthropology, may have been a bit too grand—and still less about the ultimate nature of reality (Gell, 1992). In short, I believe that there is a gap here, which, far from having been bridged by neo-cognitive anthropology, has only been made wider.[25]

My real problem with cognitivism, however, concerns its central concept, that of "mental representation." It is of course perfectly feasible to account for the perspectivist cosmologies of Amerindians with the help of the concept of mental representation. But one of the contentions in what follows is that a representationalist account of these cosmologies seriously misrepresents, if one may say so, the Amerindian point of view. My aim here, anyway, is not to *explain* this point of view, that is, to find its causes (cognitive, economic, and what have you); it is rather to *explicate* it: to explore its consequences and follow its implications.

WORDS

I would like to close this general introduction to our subject with some miscellaneous remarks on my use of certain words or concepts. I shall proceed from the more "abstract" or merely definitional to the more "concrete" and substantial.

Subject and Object

These dangerous words are used here in a purely—but metaphorically—pragmatic, indexical, or pronominal sense. "Subject" is the semiotic position correlated with the capacity to say "I" in a real or virtual *cosmological* discourse. "Object," by the same token, is that which is "talked" about. As will become clear in the following lectures, I am relying essentially on Benveniste's seminal work on "subjectivity in language" as expressed in the pronominal set (1966a, 1966b). I use "person" as a synonym of "subject," when wishing to mark the fact that persons are "objects" capable of acting as "subjects." This notion of "person" is equally pronominal, and can also be derived from Benveniste. My metaphors come, therefore, from semiosis, not production or desire: there is no dialectics of "self" and "other" intended, for there is no synthesis and co-production, but rather alternation and disjunction, that is, exchange (of perspectives). The possible connections of my "subject" and "object" to the concepts of "objectification," "personification," and "reification," such as developed, for instance, by Strathern (1988), are left open for further exploration.

Body and Soul

I shall be here using the words "soul" and "spirit" as partial synonyms to refer to the subjective, volitional-intentional invisible component of persons associated to, but detachable from, the visible bodily forms that characterize each species. I shall also be calling "spirits" some entities of Amerindian worlds that do not have a stable, normally visible bodily form, evincing in a superlative manner the metamorphic capacity proper to all persons (Hallowell, 1960, p. 69): spirits are, in a sense, more-than-human persons, or meta-persons.

I am aware that the words "soul" and "spirit" have quite distinct connotations in our tradition, especially in their more philosophical usages. Also, an exact inter-lingual translation of these two words, even between closely related languages, is a very difficult task (Wierzbicka, 1989).[26] Be that as it may, my somewhat loose usage of "soul" and "spirit" is based on the sentiment that these words span a continuous semantic space (as suggested, for instance, by the fact that the adjectival form associated to "soul" is "spiritual"). This common space is separated by a marked discontinuity from the one covered by notions such as "body," "matter," and (in its modern, non-philosophical usages) "substance."

As to "body" versus "soul," let me firstly observe that there is a curious asymmetry in anthropological attitudes towards them. When we translate the indigenous words that correspond to our notions of "soul," "spirit," "vital principle," etc., we usually spend whole pages to comment on their glosses, cushioning these in warnings about the inadequacy of the available notions in the target-language. On the other hand, our "mind" seems perfectly at ease when translating the words that correspond to "body"—sometimes we do not even bother to write the relevant word in the source-language. It is as if the concept of body were evident, because universal, whilst the concepts of "soul," "spirit," etc., were supremely culture-specific, and therefore ultimately non-translatable. This asymmetry when dealing with the semantic aspect of "body" and "soul" is a symptom of their asymmetric status in our ontology: the body is common, is what connects us to the rest of reality, whilst the soul is what separates and distinguishes. Solipsism (a standard "modernist" philosophical obsession), therefore, is not only *caused* by the soul—by its absolute singularity—but *affects* first and foremost the concept of soul. Another source of this difficulty in translating the words for "soul" may be this: How does one translate what "does not exist"? One must not only translate, but explain and justify—two things "body" would supposedly not need.

In the wake of the pervasive dichotomy between a dichotomous West and a non-dichotomous Rest, the notorious "mind–body dualism" (Pauline, Augustinian, or Cartesian—but also Kantian and Durkheimian, of course: cf. the *Homo duplex*) became the sitting duck of anthropologists as well, who thus belatedly joined the antidualist sentiment of post-Kantian philosophy (Lovejoy, 1960). It is now de rigueur to state that Amerindians (or Melanesians, Africans, non-modernist, non-modernist cultures, non-academic Westerners) do not "have" such a thing. Very well—I am an anti-dualist myself. But a conceptual duality needs not imply a metaphysical dualism. It is one thing to argue that Amerindians do not separate body and spirit the way "we" do, and quite another that they make no distinction whatever between body and spirit. To take the first argument (which is quite true) as entailing the second (which is patently false) is unfortunately a very common rhetorical practice nowadays. All the available ethnographic evidence indicates that the distinction between body and spirit (or analogue qualities and states) plays a central role in Amerindian cosmologies, and indeed in all shamanic cosmologies. The whole problem, of course, consists in determining the nature of this distinction, and the referents of "body" and "spirit" in the Amerindian context.

This same analytico-rhetorical non sequitur, this slippage from "not like here" to "not at all there," afflicts all the other conceptual pairs I shall be concerned with: humans/animals, nature/culture, subject/object, etc.[27] For it will not do simply to argue that "body" and "soul" (especially "soul," for today we all love "body") and their opposition are modernist or Western constructs and accordingly should be shunned. This is linguistic "fetishism," a typical Western disease (modern and post-), incidentally: the prison-house of language, etc.[28] This is, in fact, simple-minded linguistic-cultural relativism. It is better to follow here the lead of Amerindian perspectivism and be aware that the same signs may stand for entirely different things: the dictionary of the jaguar also contains the concept of "manioc beer," and it has the same signification as in a human dictionary (a tasty and nutritious liquid substance that makes you drunk)—but jaguars use it to refer to what we call "blood." Why not treat "body" and "soul" (and "nature," "culture," etc.) in like manner, in our analytical language?

Perspective

Considering all that has been written about the visual bias of our philosophical tradition, it might seem hazardous to lay such stress upon the notion of perspective, this hyper-Western, supremely modernist, "sightist" metaphor. But then, "what . . . does the anthropologist do in the face of deliberate provocations to vision?" (Strathern, 1994, p. 243).[29] All I can do here is observe that most Amerindian cultures evince a visual bias of their own: vision is the model of perception and knowledge (Mentore, 1993); many indigenous languages feature evidentials that distinguish between direct knowledge (obtained by sight) from hearsay knowledge; shamanism is laden with visual concepts (Gallois, 1984–1985; Townsley, 1993); in many parts of Amazonia, hallucinogenic drugs are used as a "deliberate provocation" *of* visions; more generally, the distinction between the visible and the invisible (Kensinger, 1995, p. 207; Gray 1996, pp. 115, 177) seems to play a major ontological role; we might also recall the emphasis on the decoration and exhibition of bodily and object surfaces, the use of masks, etc. (See Gow, 1997, for a detailed and insightful analysis of vision in an Amazonian culture.)

In some cases, the notion of "perspective" or "point of view" is literally and indigenously expressed. Consider this passage by Guédon:

> One of the first Tsimshian women I have met who is still involved today in shamanism has explained to me that it is not the *atiasxw* [the healer's helper, the embodiment of his gift: an object that serves as the shaman's tool] as object that matters but the methods used to place the power in proper focus with the help of the *atiasxw*. In her case, her power is the rope. One may think that a rope can be used to tie or to pull, but hers is not a material rope, it is an *atiasxw*, that is, as she explains it, a *"point of view."* If she is looking at a sick person in a normal way, she knows she cannot get through (not only to the sick person but also to herself), that there is nothing she can do to help the person. Her idea is to shift the point of view: she would imagine herself as a rope, "a big rope of light going from way, way back to way, way in the future. As a rope I can do something. I can be there as a rope and there would be that other rope (the patient) with a big knot (the disease). . . ." We may note that she is not actually transformed into a rope The *atiasxw* is simply used as a point of view. (1984b, p. 204)

It might be argued that this woman had been "exposed" to Western idioms and concepts, is probably literate, and a very sophisticated person. Perhaps. Be that as it may, she chose this particular notion of a point of view; she did not say the rope was a metaphor, a symbol, or a manner of speaking. Indeed, the rope was definitely *not* a manner of speaking.

The Wari' of Brazilian Amazonia, who are very likely unaware of what "point of view" means in Portuguese, also emphasize sight, and here directly in the context of human/animal perspectival differences:

Shamans possess two simultaneous bodies, one human, the other animal. They can alternate their points of view by manipulating their sense of sight. When he wishes to change his vision, a shaman rubs his eyes for a few seconds: if he was seeing humans as animals—this being the point of view of his animal body—then he starts seeing them as humans; if he was seeing some particular animal as a person, then he will start seeing it as an animal and will then feel free to kill and eat it.[30] The problem, as Topa explained to me, is that these different points of view alternate too quickly, and a shaman always runs the risk of suddenly realizing that the animal he had just killed was actually some relative of his.

. . . Orowan, who is a shaman, told me he made this "mistake" once, while he was in his jaguar body: he killed and ate a man because he saw him from the jaguar's point of view, as an enemy or game. (Vilaça, 1998, pp. 25–26)

This same emphasis on the eyes and sight is clearly expressed in the most developed non-Amerindian example of perspectivism, the Chewong of Malaysia:

Much of Chewong morality is expressed through directives involving food which in turn are predicated upon how each species actually sees reality. This is directly attributable to the quality of their eyes, which are subtly different in each case. The way one species sees another is dependent upon what constitutes food for them. Thus, when human beings see a monkey's body they see it as meat; when a tiger sees a human body it sees it as meat. A *bas* (a group of harmful spirits) upon seeing human *ruwai* perceive it as meat, and so on. (Howell, 1996, p. 133)[31]

In those Amazonian cultures where one finds the notion of multiple personal souls, the eyes are usually endowed with a soul of their own, and this eye soul is often the "true soul." This is what Mentore says of the Waiwai (Caribs of Guiana):

Besides the body as a whole, only the eye possesses a distinct soul. At death, when detached from their corporeal self, the body soul remains on the earthly plane, while the eye soul rises to the first ascending plane of *kaup* (the celestial spirit world) to know, that is, to be human, is "to see" in all its various forms. (1993, p. 31)

The same idea can be found among the Peruvian Aguaruna (Jívaro): there are two human souls, an eye soul residing in the pupil—this is the one that goes to the celestial world after death—and the demon-shadow *iwanch* that remains on earth under various animal guises (Brown, 1993, p. 55).

Among the Panoans, these ideas are present in a rather more elaborated form (Kensinger, 1995; Townsley, 1993; McCallum, 1996). In a nice prefiguration of the theory of cognitive modularity, the Cashinahua assign different modes of knowledge to different organs: skin, ears, eyes, liver, hands, genitals, etc. (see Kensinger, 1995, chap. 22). This modular knowledge is associated with different souls: thus skin knowledge, an attribute of the skin soul, has as its object "the natural world," it is knowledge of "the jungle's body spirit," the visible, sensory aspect of things; hand knowledge refers to bodily skills, ear knowledge to social behavior, the genitals are the source and the site of knowledge of mortality and immortality, and so on. These different bodily-based types of knowledge appear to be subsumed by a generalized "body spirit" which encases the person as an outer skin (so skin-knowledge would be the dominant synecdoche). To this body knowledge the Cashinahua oppose eye knowledge, an attribute of the eye-soul, also called the "true soul" or "real spirit." This is the module which allows one to see "the true nature of people and things that make up the natural world"; it is "knowledge of the supernatural" (Kensinger, 1995, p. 233). The eye soul is the immortal part of the person; it is the agent in dreams and drug-induced hallucinatory experiences. McCallum (1996, p. 32) describes the eye soul as "a kind of person within the person"—a metaphoric or iconical double then, as opposed to the metonymical and indexical partial souls of the other organs.

This may suffice as evidence for the importance of vision in Amerindian cosmologies and justify my appeal to the notion of "perspective." I must stress, however, that the salience of these visual idioms should not make us disregard the fact that there is more to the concept of perspective than meets the eye, and that Amerindian perspectivism uses perceptual differences to express conceptual ones: the epistemological language of "seeing/knowing" the world is at the service of an ontology. What is at stake there is the relation between different ontological, not epistemological, perspectives. These differences may be expressed in visual terms, but differences are not visual as such: they are relational. (You do not "see a difference"—a difference is what makes you see.) The point, in short, is that perspectives do not consist in representations (visual or otherwise) of objects by subjects, but in relations of subjects to subjects. When jaguars see "blood" as "manioc beer," the terms of the perspectival relation are jaguars and humans: blood/beer is the "thing" which relates (separates) jaguar and human "persons." As Strathern (1988, 1992) has shown, the exchange of perspectives or points of view need not be cast in visual language, or concern vision as such. And perspectives are "about" exchange, for they relate subjects or persons.

Animal

In what follows, "animal" is to be understood in the distributive, not the collective sense: each and any (non-human) animal species, not the animal kingdom, let alone animality as opposed to humanity. The available ethnographic evidence suggests that Amerindian cosmologies do not feature a general, collective concept of "animal" as opposed to "human." Humans are a species among others, and sometimes the differences internal to humanity are on a par with species-specific ones: "The Jívaro view humanity as a collection of natural societies; the biological commonality of man interests them far less than the differences between forms of social existence" (Taylor, 1993, p. 658).

If this is true, then at least one basic meaning of the standard opposition between nature and culture must be discarded when we move to Amerindian contexts: nature is not a domain defined by animality in contrast with culture as the domain of humanity. The real problem with the use of the category of "nature" in these contexts, therefore, lies not so much with the fact that animals also have (or are in) "culture," but rather with the assumption of a *unified* non-human domain (Gray, 1996, p. 114). Our essentialist "non-human" is there a contextual "not-human"; "it" has no overarching, common substantive (even if privative) definition: taxonomical or ethological similarities apart, each non-human species is as different from all the others as it is from humans.

It is indeed rare to find Amerindian languages possessing a concept co-extensive with our concept of "(non-human) animal," although not uncommon to find terms which more or less correspond to one of the informal meanings of "animal" in English: relatively big land animals, typically non-human mammals—as opposed to fish, birds, insects and other life-forms.[32] I suspect that the majority of Indigenous words which have been rendered as "animal" in the ethnographies actually denote something analogous to this. Let me give some examples.

The Gê word *mbru*, which is usually translated as "animal," and sometimes used as a synecdoche for "nature" (Seeger, 1981), is literally neither fish nor fowl, for it does not subsume these life-forms: it refers prototypically to land animals, and has the pragmatic and relational sense of "victim," "prey," or "game," and in *this* latter sense may also be applied to fish, birds, etc.[33] The Wari' (Txapakuran) word applied to "animals," *karawa*, has the basic meaning of "prey," and as such may be applied to human enemies: the contrastive pair *wari'/karawa*, which in most contexts may be translated as "human/animal," has the logically encompassing sense of "predator/prey" or "subject/object"—humans (Wari,' i.e., *wari'*) can be the *karawa* of predators, animal, human, and spiritual, who are in their predatory function or "moment" defined as *wari'* (Vilaça, 1992). In these two cases, then, the words supposedly referring to "animal" as the "non-human" actually appear to have the sense of "prey" or "game" (and are typically applied to land mammals insofar as these are the typical or ideal form of prey for humans). Such concepts of "animal" have a narrower extension than our zoological concept, and a logically more abstract, relational and perspectival, comprehension.

But if what has been called "animal" means first and foremost "prey," "game" or simply "meat," in some other cases it signifies exactly the opposite: inedible spirit.[34] The Yawalapíti (Upper Xingu Arawak) call *apapalutapa-mina* a variety of animals, the majority of them land creatures—and all of them, with one exception, considered unfit to be eaten by Xinguanos.[35] The proper Xinguano diet is fish, and some avian species. The word *apapalutapa-mina*, which is on the same level of contrast as the words for "bird" and "fish," derives from the word *apapalutapa*, "spirit" (meta-person evincing dangerous powers), followed by the modifier *-mina*, which denotes something like "non-prototypical member of a class," "inferior token of a type," but also "of the substance/nature of [the concept modified]" (Viveiros de Castro, 1978). Thus, "land" animals and all mammals are "spirit-like," "quasi-spirits," "sub-spirits."[36] This is quite similar to a Barasana conception (Hugh-Jones, 1996a) according to which game animals are referred to as "old fish"—"old" (or "mature") having here a superlative-excessive connotation. If the Tukanoans think of game as "super-fish," then, implying that these are a particularly potent and dangerous type of fish, the Yawalapiti think of game animals as "sub-spirits": and whilst the Tukanoans are able symbolically to reduce the game they eat to "fish," the Xinguanos, who do not eat game, cannot de-spiritualize these animals and accordingly are empirically reduced to eating (mostly) fish. We may perhaps extend the scope of the Amazonian continuum of edibility (within the meat domain) proposed by Hugh-Jones, then, making it go from fish to spirits, not only to human beings. The Tukanoans start conceptually from the "fish" pole, defining game as a sub-class of it; the Yawalapíti start from the other pole, having game as a sub-class of spirits. This suggests that spirits are the supremely inedible species of being in the cosmos—what makes them the supreme cannibals.

NOTES

1. Each one of these paired predicates plays a role in the syncretic master opposition between nature and culture, but their relative importance in our tradition has varied. There have also been some major inversions of the correlative pairing of the predicates. Thus, as Nietzsche remarked somewhere, in the modern world nature is necessity, culture is freedom; in Classical Greece, on the other hand, nature was freedom (*phusis* is that which grows *sponte sua*), while culture was rule and necessity (*nomos*, "law").
2. This idea is hardly new—it has been variously hinted at by a number of Americanists, as I discovered after having written the first version of my argument. Thus, Goldman, in his brilliant reanalysis of Boas' Kwakiutl materials, sketches the contrast: "Scientific materialism postulates the consubstantiality of matter, primitive religions that of life and the powers of life" (1975, p. 22; see also pp. 182–83, 200, 207). Even closer to my point, as will become clear, is this recently published remark by Andrew Gray on Arakmbut (Peruvian Amazonia) concepts of body and soul: "The physical property of the body separates a person from all others, whereas the soul is a dynamic, invisible substance which is constantly seeking contact outside The effect is a total contrast to the occidental view of the soul as the unique and essential aspect of a person because, for the Arakmbut, whereas the body gives a distinct form to a person, the *nokiren* [soul] reaches out in dreams to others—not just humans but also species and spirits" (Gray, 1997, p. 120). The present lectures are a sustained effort to draw out all the consequences of observations such as these, by connecting them to the theme of perspectivism.
3. Such fictions have their uses, as argued and demonstrated by Strathern (1988).
4. This notion of the body as clothing can be found among the Makuna (Århem, 1993), the Yagua (Chaumeil, 1983, pp. 125–27), the Piro (Gow, pers. comm.), the Trio (Rivière, 1994), and the Upper Xingu societies (Gregor, 1977, p. 322). The notion is very likely pan-American, having considerable symbolic yield, for example, in Northwest Coast cosmologies (see Goldman, 1975; Boelscher, 1989), if not of much wider distribution. I return to this in Lecture 4 of *Cosmological Perspectivism in Amazonia and Elsewhere*.
5. See, for example, Saladin d'Anglure (1990) and Fienup-Riordan (1994) on the Eskimo; Nelson (1983) and McDonnell (1984) on the Koyukon and Kaska; Tanner (1979), Hallowell (1960), Scott (1989), and Brightman (1993) on the Ojibwa and Cree; Goldman (1975) on the Kwakiutl; Guédon (1984a, 1984b) on the Tsimshian; and Boelscher (1989) on the Haida. See also the

following remarkable studies by Howell (1984, 1996) on the Chewong of Malaysia, and Hamayon (1990) on Siberia.

6. Note, however, Wagner's writing on Melanesian notions of the "innate," which has thrown light on Amerindian materials (Brightman, 1993, pp. 177–185; Fienup-Riordan, 1994, pp. 46–50). This suggests that the "perspectivism" found in native America is a possibility in Melanesia, although only (?) actualized by the Kaluli.

7. "The reciprocity of perspectives, where I perceived the singular character of mythical thought." The theme of perspectivism is absent from *Histoire de Lynx*. But we can find there many references (Lévi-Strauss, 1991, pp. 97–100, 113–116, 127, 131, 216) to skin-changing or clothes-changing as inter-specific metamorphosis, and to human–animal marriages as deriving from the "two-sided" nature of mythic animals (part human, part beast). I am far from having completed my survey of Amerindian materials concerning perspectivism; among other interesting Amazonian references not used in the present lectures, see Journet (1995, pp. 193–94) (Curripaco); Nimuendaju (1952, pp. 113, 117–18) (Tukuna); Gallois (1984–1985, p. 188) (Wayãpi); Osborn (1990, p. 151) (U'wa).

8. The notions of "perspective" and "point of view" play a central role in some of my previous work, but there the main focus was on intra-human dynamics (Viveiros de Castro, 1992, pp. 64–66, 68, 343 n. 16, 344 n 22, 248–251, 256–259; see also Viveiros de Castro, 1996). The thesis of Vilaça (1992) and especially that of Lima (1996a) showed me that it was possible to generalize these notions both in terms of extension and comprehension, and made me look deeper into the ethnographic record.

9. For instance, Tanner (1979) and Karim (1981). See Bloch (1989) for a generalization of this argument, which smacks of the classical distinction between "technical" and "expressive" aspects of action.

10. In the Araweté case (Viveiros de Castro, 1992), for example, non-Araweté humans have the same spiritual handicap as animals (their souls do not go to the celestial paradise).

11. "The Earth's present animals are not nearly as powerful as the originals, differing as much from them as ordinary humans are said to differ from shamans. . . . The First people lived just as shamans do today, in a polymorphous state" (Guss, 1989, p. 52).

12. Brightman (1993, pp. 40, 160) and Fienup-Riordan (1994, p. 62) discuss similar ideas in a North American context. For Amazonia, see also Jara (1996, pp. 92–94) (Akuryó) and Guss (1989, p. 40) (Ye'kuana). Schiefflin (1976, pp. 94–95) reports the same for the Kaluli of New Guinea.

13. The notion that the "I" (humans, Indians, my tribe) is the historically stable term in the distinction between the "I" and the "other" (animals, white people, other Indians) appears as much in interspecific differentiation as in intra-specific separations, as can be seen in the various Amerindian myths of origin of white people. The others used to be what we are and are not, as amongst ourselves, what we used to be. Thus it can be perceived how very pertinent the notion of "cold societies" can be: history does indeed exist, but it is something that happens only to others.

14. This point has often been made for other non-Western cosmologies. See, for instance, Gell (1995, p. 23) on Polynesia: "Polynesian thought about the universe differed from Judæo-Christian 'creationist' thought in that it was predicated, not in the creation of the universe *ex nihilo* by God, but on the initial existence of everything in an all-embracing plenum or tightly-bound continuum. The creative epoch occurred as a process of 'differentiation'

within this pre-existing plenum." As I have just observed, the Ameridian plenum, differently from the more "naturalistic" Polynesian cosmogonies, is human: humanity is the form of the primordial continuum. On the relevance of the mythological theme of the continuum in Polynesian cosmologies—a theme originally developed by Lévi-Strauss (1964) precisely in a Polynesian-Amerindian comparative context—see the remarkable book by Schrempp (1992).

15. I do not mean to imply that this obsession is a "mistake," only that we "late Moderns" seem to be particularly haunted by that aspect of Being (though not too willing to extend it to non-human beings).

16. Production is about projection (productive consumption) and introjection (consumptive production). Exchange is about commutation and transmutation (two notions which could perhaps be correlated with the two Strathernian modes of personification, mediated and unmediated exchange). Production has a beginning (creation), but has no end (re-production, the endless dialectics of ablation and sublation); exchange, on the other hand, has no beginning—the "anticipated outcome" as the form of the gift (Strathern, 1988, pp. 221–223) makes any beginning appear as a response—it can, however, have an end (relationships can be terminated).

17. In the cultures of Western Amazonia, however, especially those in which hallucinogens of botanical origin are widely used, the personification of plants seems to be at least as important as that of animals.

18. It is worth noticing that in those Amazonian societies where shamanism as an institution (as opposed to a general cosmological stance) is weakly developed, if present at all, the theme of perspectivism seems barely sketched. The Gê-speaking societies of Central Brazil are a case in point. The basic idea, however, is very much present among some Gê—see the story of Umoro's death in Lecture 4.

19. A tripartition similar to the one proposed above is to be found in Latour (1996a); but my connecting thread is different from Latour's. What makes our three states comparable is their common emphasis on fetishism and reification.

20. "The Munchkins told Dorothy that there were four witches in Oz. The ones from the North and South were good, but those from the East and West were bad." So Orientalism and Occidentalism are politically incorrect in the Land of Oz too—but Goody's "meridionalism" would be quite all right. As an Americanist, I have always found Goody's contrasts between "Eurasia" and "Black Africa" interesting but somewhat arbitrary. In many respects, such as political organization and kinship ideology, Europe and "Black Africa" look quite similar, and quite different from Amazonian forms.

21. See, for instance, Overing (1981, 1983–1984, 1986); Rivière (1984); Viveiros de Castro (1992, 1993); Hugh-Jones (1996b); Descola (1992); Henley (1996a, 1996b); Fausto (1997).

22. "Middle Ages which lacked a Rome."

23. Bourdieu's strictures, of course, did not prevent him from bodying forth that prodigious oxymoron, the "theory of practice," the intended self-irony of which—if any were intended—was entirely lost on the ensuing flock of practice theorists. In like manner, Brunton (1980) and similar expostulations against the anthropological "will to order" in cosmological analyses seem to be slightly deficient in reflexivity. Even as they denounce the socio-professional pressures and rewards leading anthropologists to exaggerate the conceptual

orderliness of non-Western cosmologies, they forget to mention the even more pressing and enticing incentives towards "critical" originality, deconstruction of other analytical styles by using some version of the "ethnocentrism" argument—a fickle weapon, given its intrinsic rebounding potential—and the unveiling of (preferably unconscious) "political" motivations. There is thus more sociological order (and academic calculus) in Brunton's decision to reveal cosmological disorder than he seems prepared to acknowledge.

24. My point here is simply that "binary thought" is not a side effect of the alphabet (see the Bororo; Crocker, 1985), nor dualism an exclusive property of Western theological or philosophical traditions (see Jullien, 1993, on China).

25. *Ideas* like "the mind" or "the ultimate nature of reality," however—in the sense that they are historically constituted, culturally determined, collective intellectual products—are perfect examples of those objects that anthropology *can* claim as falling (among others) within its proper field of study.

26. Portuguese and English vernaculars, for instance, feature a third substantive of the same semantic family—"*mente*" and "mind"—that exists in French only as an adjective, "*mental*." The corresponding substantive, as you know, is "*esprit*."

27. Such slippage sets the stage for those privative oppositions characteristic of "Great Divide" theories.

28. Both the disease *and* the diagnosis are "typically Western."

29. In the face of non-Western cultures that show a visual bias, the anthropologist can, for instance, argue that Western tradition emphasizes the verbal rather than the visual (e.g., Wagner, 1987, p. 57). And indeed, the "mirror of nature" (Rorty, 1980), for all its ocularity, is always cast in writing.

30. A shaman cannot kill or eat the body of the animal species which he shares. Some shamans see *all* soul-endowed animals as people—and are accordingly very poor hunters because the majority of the species hunted by the Wari' are in this category. This reputation of shamans as poor hunters due to their "species-androgyny," is also found among the Cashinahua (Kensinger, 1995, p. 211), and among the Akuryó (Jara, 1996, pp. 92–94), where shamans are not allowed to hunt for this very reason.

31. Shamans and laypersons are also distinguished on the basis of their eyes: the former have cold, the latter hot eyes. This Chewong connection between food and sight, besides illustrating the already mentioned idea that perspectivism is crucially concerned with the relational statuses of predator and prey, brings to mind a remark by Mentore (1993, p. 29) on the Waiwai of Guiana: "the primary dialectics is one between seeing and eating."

32. I am aware that there are such things as "covert categories," i.e., non-lexicalized conceptual forms. But my contention is that in the majority of (possibly all) Amazonian cases there is *no* submerged notion meaning "non-human animal" (in our sense of "animal").

33. I asked Anthony Seeger to check the meaning of *mbru*—which he had translated as "animal" in his books on the Suyá—on a recent visit to this Gê-speaking society of Central Brazil. This is what he wrote to me on his return: "I asked about what the word '*mbru*' means, and was quite surprised by the answer. I was talking with one of the most thoughtful speakers of Portuguese, a man of about 50, and the oldest male Suya, about 65. I asked about what *mbru* was. The response was that it meant animal. I asked, then, if fish were *mbru*, and they said no. They said that everything that swims in the water is '*tep*' (fish), everything that walks or locomotes (as in snakes) on land is *mbru*, and that everything that flies is '*saga*' (bird). I said, then, what about snakes. They said snakes are *mbru kasaga* (bad or ugly game), like frogs and lizards, and other things. I asked about wasps, which they said are *sag-kasaga* (bad or ugly birds). They said in old Suya songs, the *jacaré* (alligator), or *mi*, is called '*te-we-mi-ji*' proving that its classification as a 'fish' or watery animal is an old one. This classification had never occurred to me, so I tried it out on someone else who said 'of course, that's the way it is.' Now, there are some contradictions. One curing chant I collected turns out to call the jacare '*mbru-taw*' or game. There is a word *simbru* (*nyimbru* 'my,' *nimbru* 'your,' *simbru* 'his' . . .) that no one could give me a direct translation for. I believe it means 'my game' in the sense of 'my killed prey.' The word is used to refer to fish, game, and dead birds. It is also used to refer to the cockroaches killed by a wasp (the wasp's '*simbru*'). In this form, the word does mean 'prey' as you suggested when we talked." I am grateful to my teacher Tony Seeger for this detailed explanation.

34. Thus the Araweté word *ha'a*, "meat" or "flesh" (the Araweté have no general word for "animal"), is the cognate of the 16th century Tupinamba word *so'o*, which seems to have meant "game animal." Curiously enough, the Tupinamba word for "deer" is *soo asu*, literally "big game," in a strict analogy to the Anglo/German "deer/tier," and to the Anglo/French "venison/venaison," which derives from the Latin verb for "hunting" (see also Spanish/Portuguese "venado/veado," deer).

35. See Viveiros de Castro (1978) for an analysis of Yawalapíti concepts about "animals" and a tentative explanation of the (apparently paradoxical) dietary exception—*Cebus* monkeys, which are considered fit to be eaten "because they look like humans." All mammals, including aquatic ones, are *apapalutapa-mina*.

36. The prototypical (the "chief" of) *apapalutapa-mina* is the jaguar, which in Xinguano mythology is the ancestor of humans. Upper Xingu mythologies often oppose land, water, and sky domains, making humans and *apapalutapa-mina* share a common origin, as opposed to fish and birds.

REFERENCES

Århem, K. 1993. "Ecosofía Makuna." In *La selva humanizada: Ecología alternativa en el trópico húmedo colombiano*, edited by F. Correa, 109–126. Bogotá: Instituto Colombiano de Antropología, Fondo fen Colombia, Fondo Editorial cerec.

Århem, K. 1996. "The Cosmic Food Web: Human–Nature Relatedness in the Northwest Amazon." In *Nature and Society: Anthropological Perspectives*, edited by P. Descola and G. Pálsson, 185–204. London: Routledge.

Baer, G. 1994. *Cosmología y shamanismo de los Matsiguenga*. Quito: Abya-Yala.

Benveniste, E. 1966a. "La nature des pronoms." In *Problèmes de linguistique générale*, 251–257. Paris: Gallimard.

Benveniste, E. 1966b. "De la subjectivité dans le langage." In *Problèmes de linguistique générale*, 258–266. Paris: Gallimard.

Bloch, M. 1989. "From Cognition to Ideology." In *Ritual, History and Power*, 106–136. London: Athlone. (Originally published in 1985).

Bloch, M. 1992. "What Goes without Saying: The Conceptualization of Zafimaniry Society." In *Conceptualizing Society*, edited by A. Kuper, 127–146. London: Routledge.

Boelscher, M. 1989. *The Curtain Within: Haida Social and Mythical Discourse*. Vancouver: University of British Columbia Press.

Bourdieu, P. 1972. *Esquisse d'une théorie de la pratique: Précédé de trois études d'ethnologie kabyle*. Genève: Droz.

Boyer, P. 1993. Introduction to *Cognitive Aspects of Religious Symbolism*. Cambridge: University of Cambridge Press.

Brightman, R. 1993. *Grateful Prey: Rock Cree Human-Animal Relationships.* Berkeley: University of California Press.

Brown, M. 1993. *Tsewa's Gift*. Washington DC: Smithsonian Institute Press. (Originally published in 1986).

Brunton, R. 1980. "Misconstrued Order in Melanesian Religion." *Man*, n.s., 15, no. 1: 112–128.

Chaumeil, J.-P. 1983. *Voir, savoir, pouvoir: Le chamanisme chez les Yagua du nord-est péruvien*. Paris: École des Hautes Etudes en Sciences Sociales.

Crocker, J. C. 1985. *Vital Souls: Bororo Cosmology, Natural Symbolism, and Shamanism*. Tucson: University of Arizona Press.

Descola, P. 1986. *La nature domestique: Symbolisme et praxis dans l'écologie des Achuar*. Paris: Maison des Sciences de L'Homme.

Descola, P. 1992. "Societies of Nature and the Nature of Society." In *Conceptualizing Society*, edited by A. Kuper, 107–126. London: Routledge.

Erikson, P. 1984. "De l'apprivoisement à l'approvisionnement: Chasse, alliance et familiarisation en Amazonie amérindienne." *Techniques et Cultures* 9: 105–140.

Fausto, C. 1997. "A dialética da predação e familiarização entre os Parakanã da Amazônia oriental." PhD diss., Programa de Pósgraduação em Antropologia Social, Museu Nacional, UFRJ.

Fienup-Riordan, A. 1994. *Boundaries and Passages: Rule and Ritual in Yup'ik Eskimo Oral Tradition.* Norman: University of Oklahoma Press.

Gallois, D. 1984–1985. "O pajé wayãpi e seus espelhos." *Revista de Antropologia* 27–28: 179–196.

Gell, A. 1992. *The Anthropology of Time*. London: Berg.

Gell, A. 1995. "Closure and Multiplication: An Essay on Polynesian Cosmology and Ritual." In *Society and Cosmos in Oceania*, edited by D. de Coppet and A. Iteanu, 21–56. Oxford: Berg.

Goldman, I. 1975. *The Mouth of Heaven: An Introduction to Kwakiutl Religious Thought*. New York: Wiley-Interscience.

Goody, J. 1996. *The East in the West*. Cambridge: Cambridge University Press.

Gow, P. 1997. "A Man Who Was Tired of Living." Unpublished manuscript, July 1997.

Gray, A. 1996. *The Arakmbut of Amazonian Peru, Vol. I: Mythology, Spirituality and History*. Oxford: Berghahn.

Gray, A. 1997. *The Arakmbut of Amazonian Peru, Vol. II: The Last Shaman (Change in an Amazonian Community)*. Oxford: Berghahn.

Gregor, T. 1977. *Mehinaku: The Drama of Daily Life in a Brazilian Indian Village*. Chicago: University of Chicago Press.

Grenand, P. 1980. *Introduction à l'étude de l'univers wayãpi: Ethno-écologie des indiens du Haut-Oyapock: Guyane Française*. Paris: SELAF/CNRS.

Guédon, M.-F. 1984a. "An Introduction to the Tsimshian World View and Its Practitioners." In *The Tsimshian: Images of the Past, Views for the Present*, edited by M. Seguin, 137–159. Vancouver: University of British Columbia Press.

Guédon, M.-F. 1984b. "Tsimshian Shamanic Images." In *The Tsimshian: Images of the Past, Views for the Present*, edited by M. Seguin, 174–211. Vancouver: University of British Columbia Press.

Guss, D. 1989. *To Weave and to Sing: Art, Symbol, and Narrative in the South American Rain Forest*. Berkeley: University of California Press.

Hallowell, A. I. 1960. "Ojibwa Ontology, Behavior, and World View." In *Culture in History: Essays in Honor of Paul Radin*, edited by S. Diamond, 49–82. New York: Columbia University Press.

Hamayon, R. 1990. *La chasse à l'âme. Esquisse d'une théorie du chamanisme sibérien*. Nanterre: Société d'Ethnologie.

Henley, P. 1996a. "Recent Themes in the Anthropology of Amazonia: History, Exchange, Alterity." *Bulletin of Latin American Research* 15 (2): 231–245.

Henley, P. 1996b. "South Indian Models in the Amazonian Lowlands." *Manchester Papers in Social Anthropology 1*.

Howell, S. 1984. *Society and Cosmos: Chewong of Peninsular Malaysia*. Oxford: University of Oxford Press.

Howell, S. 1996. "Nature in Culture or Culture in Nature? Chewong Ideas of 'Humans' and Other Species." In *Nature and Society: Anthropological Perspectives*, edited by P. Descola and G. Pálsson, 127–144. London: Routledge.

Hugh-Jones, S. 1996a. "Bonnes raisons ou mauvaise conscience? De l'ambivalence de certains Amazoniens envers la consommation de viande." *Terrain* 26: 123–148.

Hugh-Jones, S. 1996b. "The Gender of Some Amazonian Gifts: An Experiment with an Experiment." Unpublished manuscript, November 1996. [Published in *Gender in Amazonia and Melanesia: An Exploration of the Comparative Method*, edited by T. Gregor and D. Tuzin, 245–278. Berkeley: University of California Press, 2001.]

Ingold, T. 1994. "Humanity and Animality." In *Companion Encyclopedia of Anthropology: Humanity, Culture and Social Life*, edited by T. Ingold, 14–32. London: Routledge.

Jara, F. 1996. *El camino del kumu: Ecología y ritual entre los Akuriyó de Surinam*. Quito: Abya-Yala.

Journet, N. 1995. *La paix des jardins: Structures sociales des Indiens Curripaco du haut Rio Negro (Colombie).* Paris: Institut d'Ethnologie.

Jullien, F. 1989. *La propension des choses*. Paris: Seuil.

Jullien, F. 1993. *Figures de l'immanence: Pour une lecture philosophique du Yi King, le Classique du changement*. Paris: Grasset and Frasquelle.

Jullien, F. 1997. *Essai sur l'efficacité*. Paris: Grasset.

Karim, W.-J. 1981. *Ma'Betisék Concepts of Living Things*. London: Athlone.

Kensinger, K. 1995. *How Real People Ought to Live: The Cashinahua of Eastern Peru*. Prospect Heights, IL: Waveland.

Latour, B. 1991. *Nous n'avons jamais été modernes*. Paris: La Découverte.

Latour, B. 1996a. "Not the Question." *Anthropology Newsletter* 37, no. 3: 1, 5.

Latour, B. 1996b. *Petite réflexion sur le culte moderne des dieux faitiches*. Paris: Les Empêcheurs de Penser en Rond.

Lave, J. C. 1988. *Cognition in Practice: Mind, Mathematics and Culture in Everyday Life*. Cambridge: Cambridge University Press.

Lévi-Strauss, C. 1964. *Le cru et le cuit*. Paris: Plon.

Lévi-Strauss, C. 1985. *La potière jalouse*. Paris: Plon.

Lévi-Strauss, C. 1991. *Histoire de Lynx*. Paris: Plon.

Lévi-Strauss, C., and D. Eribon. 1988. *De près et de loin*. Paris: Odile Jacob.

Lima, T. S. 1996a. "A parte do cauim: Etnografia juruna." PhD diss., Programa de Pós-graduação em Antropologia Social, Museu Nacional, UFRJ.

Lima, T. S. 1996b. "O dois e seu múltiplo: Reflexões sobre o perspectivismo em uma cosmologia tupi." *Mana* 2, no. 2: 21–47.

Lovejoy, A. 1960. *The Revolt against Dualism: An Inquiry Concerning the Existence of Ideas*. 2nd ed. La Salle, IL: Open Court.

McCallum, C. 1996. "The Body That Knows: From Cashinahua Epistemology to a Medical Anthropology of Lowland South America." *Medical Anthropology Quarterly* 10, no. 3: 1–26.

McDonnell, R. 1984. "Symbolic Orientations and Systematic Turmoil: Centering on the Kaska Symbol of *Dene*." *Canadian Journal of Anthropology* 4, no. 1: 39–56.

Mentore, G. 1993. "Tempering the Social Self: Body Adornment, Vital Substance, and Knowledge among the Waiwai." *Journal of Archaeology and Anthropology* 9: 22–34.

Nelson, R. 1983. *Make Prayers to the Raven*. Chicago: University of Chicago Press.

Nimuendaju, C. 1952. *The Tukuna*. Berkeley: University of California Press.

Osborn, A. 1990. "Eat and Be Eaten: Animals in U'wa (Tunebo) Oral Tradition." In *Signifying Animals: Human Meaning in the Natural World*, edited by R. Willis, 140–158. London: Unwin Hyman.

Overing, J. 1981. "Review Article: Amazonian Anthropology." *Journal of Latin American Studies* 13, no. 1: 151–164.

Overing, J. 1983–84. "Elementary Structures of Reciprocity: A Comparative Note on Guianese, Central Brazilian, and North-West Amazon Socio-Political Thought." *Antropologica* 59–62: 331–348.

Overing, J. 1985. "There Is No End of Evil: The Guilty Innocents and Their Fallible God." In *The Anthropology of Evil*, edited by D. Parkin, 244–278. London: Basil Blackwell.

Overing, J. 1986. "Images of Cannibalism, Death and Domination in a 'Non-Violent' Society." *Journal de la Société des Américanistes* 52: 133–156.

Reichel-Dolmatoff, G. 1985. "Tapir Avoidance in the Colombian Northwest Amazon." In *Animal Myths and Metaphors in South America*, edited by G. Urton, 107–143. Salt Lake City: University of Utah Press.

Renard-Casevitz, F.-M. 1991. *Le banquet masqué: Une mythologie de l'étranger*. Paris: Lierre et Coudrier.

Rivière, P. 1984. *Individual and Society in Guiana*. Cambridge: University of Cambridge Press.

Rivière, P. 1994. "WYSINWYG in Amazonia." *Journal of the Anthropological Society of Oxford* 25, no. 3: 255–262.

Rorty, R. 1980. *Philosophy and the Mirror of Nature*. Princeton, NJ: Princeton University Press.

Sahlins, M. 1996. "The Sadness of Sweetness: The Native Anthropology of Western Cosmology." *Current Anthropology* 37, no. 3: 395–428.

Saladin d'Anglure, B. 1990. "Nanook, Super-Male: The Polar Bear in the Imaginary Space and Social Time of the Inuit of the Canadian Arctic." In *Signifying Animals: Human Meaning in the Natural World*, edited by R. Willis, 178–195. London: Unwin Hyman.

Schieffelin, E. L. 1976. *The Sorrow of the Lonely and the Burning of the Dancers*. New York: St. Martin's Press.

Schrempp, G. 1992. *Magical Arrows: The Maori, the Greeks, and the Folklore of the Universe*. Madison: University of Wisconsin Press.

Scott, C. 1989. "Knowledge Construction among the Cree Hunters: Metaphors and literal understanding." *Journal de la Société des Américanistes* 75: 193–208.

Seeger, A. 1981. *Nature and Society in Central Brazil: The Suyá Indians of Mato Grosso*. Cambridge, MA: Harvard University Press.

Strathern, M. 1988. *The Gender of the Gift*. Berkeley: University of California Press.

Strathern, M. 1992. "Writing Societies, Writing Persons." *History of the Human Sciences* 5, no. 1: 5–16.

Strathern, M. 1994. "One-Legged Gender." In *Visualizing Theory: Selected Essays from V.A.R. 1990–1994*, edited by L. Taylor, 242–250. London: Routledge.

Tanner, A. 1979. *Bringing Home Animals: Religious Ideology and Mode of Production of the Mistassini Cree Hunters*. Saint John: Memorial University of Newfoundland.

Taussig, M. 1987. *Shamanism, Colonialism, and the Wild Man: A Study in Terror and Healing*. Chicago: University of Chicago Press.

Taylor, A.-C. 1993. "Remembering to Forget: Identity, Mourning and Memory among the Jivaro." *Man*, n.s. 28, no. 4: 653–678.

Townsley, G. 1993. "Song Paths: The Ways and Means of Yaminahua Shamanic Knowledge." *L'Homme* 33, no. 126–128: 449–468.

Vernant, J.-P. 1986. "Introduction." In *Corps des dieux: Le Temps de la Réflexion* 7: 19–45.

Vilaça, A. 1992. *Comendo como gente: Formas do canibalismo wari' (pakaa-nova).* Rio de Janeiro: Editora da UFRJ.

Vilaça, A. 1998. "Fazendo corpos: Reflexões sobre morte e canibalismo entre os Wari' à luz do perspectivismo." *Revista de Antropologia* 41, no. 1: 9–67.

Viveiros de Castro, E. 1978. "Alguns aspectos do pensamento yawalapíti (Alto Xingu): Classificações e transformações." *Boletim do Museu Naciona* 26: 1–41.

Viveiros de Castro, E. 1992. "Foreword." In *Comendo como gente: Formas do canibalismo wari*, by A. Vilaça, xi–xxvi. Rio de Janeiro: Editora da UFRJ.

Viveiros de Castro, E. 1993a. "Alguns aspectos da afinidade no dravidianato amazônico." In *Amazônia: Etnologia e história indígena*, by E. Viveiros de Castro and M. Carneiro da Cunha, 150–210. São Paulo: Núcleo de História Indígena e do Indigenismo (Universidade de São Paulo / Fundação de Amparo à Pesquisa do Estado de São Paulo).

Viveiros de Castro, E. 1993b. "Le marbre et le myrte: De l'inconstance de l'âme sauvage." In Mémoire de la tradition, edited by A. Becquelin and A. Molinié, 365–431. Nanterre: Société d'Ethnologie.

Viveiros de Castro, E. 1996. "Le meurtrier et son double chez les Araweté: Un exemple de fusion rituelle." *Systèmes de Pensée en Afrique Noire* 14: 77–104.

Wagner, R. 1977. "Scientific and Indigenous Papuan Conceptualizations of the Innate: A Semiotic Critique of the Ecological Perspective." In *Subsistence and Survival: Rural Ecology in the Pacific*, edited by T. Bayliss-Smith and R. G. Feachem, 385–410. London: Academic Press.

Wagner, R. 1987. "Figure-Ground Reversal among the Barok." In *Assemblage of Spirits: Idea and Image in New Ireland*, edited by L. Lincoln, 56–62. New York: George Braziller.

Weiss, G. 1972. "Campa cosmology." *Ethnology* 11, no. 2: 157–172.

Wierzbicka, A. 1989. "Soul and Mind: Linguistic Evidence for Ethnopsychology and Cultural History." *American Anthropologist* 91, no. 1: 41–58.

Main Pathway: Cross-Pollination

Subthemes

Proceed to Composting, p. 263
Proceed to Transcending, p. 263

10

OF OTHER SPACES: (BRIEF) ENCOUNTERS

Giovanni Aloi

Individual floor plants in their own containers can be quite stunning, particularly in smaller lobbies and reception areas. Plants used this way should be at least 6 to 7 feet tall to make an impact and not get lost in the space. People need to be able to move around the plant, so columnar plants such as those used in corners are your best choice. [. . .] Individual plants are usually used as a focal point or to offset and draw attention to an important design element.
—Kathy Fediw, *The Manual of Interior Plantscaping*

His waiting room contains five chairs, a table in one corner and a potted plant on the table. Above the plant hangs a reproduction of a sunset by Turner. Rather faded. I usually turn up at the appointed time on Tuesday but sometimes Dr. Ellis kindly lets me come later in the day after dusk has fallen, which suits me better.

The first time we spoke, I said I hoped he looked after his patients better than the plant in the waiting room.
—Olaf Olafsson, *A Journey Home*

In the introduction to his 1967 talk titled "Of Other Spaces," Foucault stated that "the present epoch will perhaps be above all the epoch of space." [1] He assessed that, from a phenomenological standpoint, space is not homogeneous and empty, as it

Originally published as "(Brief) Encounters," in *Why Look at Plants?* (Leiden: Brill, 2018), pp. 231–242. Reprinted with permission.

might perceptually appear, but that on the contrary, space is a fragmented and simultaneous entity imbued with quantities that "draw us out of ourselves. [. . .] We do not live inside a void that could be colored with diverse shades of light," Foucault argued, "we live inside a set of relations that delineates sites which are irreducible to one another and absolutely not superimposable on one another."[2] In Foucault's conception space never is an empty vessel—it has specific agential qualities; it is a defining entity with inscribed cultural norms and laws; it is materially as well as relationally specific.[3]

Foucault's focus on the networks of relations developed in and by space was initially outlined through his analysis of the panopticon. Jeremy Bentham's late eighteenth-century design for a prison-system in which the economy of power is dispensed through an architectural configuration imposing visibility for surveillance purposes laid black on white the reflexivity at play between the object of study and what can be said about it.[4] The importance of panopticism in the economies of power and surveillance gain traction through Foucault's comparative, archaeological studies of the medical gaze at work in the hospital and the spatializations of the prison.[5] But mobilizing the ocular metaphor of the panopticon to other spaces, spaces in which humans and plants coexist, for instance, might reveal more nuanced, less polarized, and equally productive biopower relationships.

As it was explained at the beginning, this is the underlining proposal of *Why Look at Plants?* Every chapter has, in different ways, focused on the networks of relations between humans and plants for the purpose of effectively capitalizing on the irreducibility and non-superimposibility of diverse spaces. Within a certain margin of tolerance, every chapter has focused on a more or less delineated space: the forest, the garden, the greenhouse, the gardening center, the supermarket, the house, and the laboratory—all these different spaces have been revealed as specific spatializations that culturally and economically inscribe the blue-prints of biopower relationships between humans and plants. The list I have explored in this book is neither comprehensive, nor exhaustive—I have focused on those everyday spaces that have informed the work of contemporary artists and in which human/plant relations are defined by the livingness and undeniable materiality of both parties—this was the most effective way at my disposal to bring plants forward, to equally put our bodies and theirs at risk, and to engage with ontological derailments in which agency is always distributed rather than centralized. But there are many other spaces in which humans and plants come to contact that have remained unexplored. Many of these, in more than one way, fall into the category of what I have called *(brief) encounters spaces*.

In all honesty, I have developed a difficult relationship with the word "encounter" because it has been substantially abused in human/animal studies arguments—it has generally lost its initial edge, and in time, it has become an abstract cliché stereotyping animal relations under a fictitiously benevolent veneer of reciprocity that can usually only be established with a domesticated animal. My aim was to keep plants as "feral" as possible despite their being potted and rooted. (Brief) encounters, thus emerge as a contingent, relational modalities taking place in spaces where plants are not owned by the human encountering them and where they neither are for sale—to humans, these are public places of transition; to plants, they are spaces of semi-permanence. These usually are loveless spaces for the simple reason that the temporal dimension in which the proximity unravels does not last long enough for love to form. Hotel lobbies, office receptions, restaurants, shopping malls, and hospitals amongst others, are examples of spaces in which human/plant interaction, most regularly, takes place on the level of the silent glance. It goes without saying that in these spaces, plants are more regularly ontologically aligned to decorative objects than living beings. Tellingly, these are the spaces where the distinction between artificial and living plants can sometimes cease to matter—reproductions of very realistic *Ficus benjamina* are extremely popular with low lighting indoor areas—they fool the eye of most people despite their natural propensity to attract dust like few living plants would. Artificial plants are all surface in every sense—the poorly made ones simply look awful as they grossly approximate the morphology of existing species while involuntarily mocking their formal-integrity to the ground. Their fabric leaves and plastic stems metaphorically encapsulate the essence of the plant/human relationship they stage: forever green, in perennial bloom, in full form all year 'round—they aesthetically disavow death while being nothing more than perennially non-living. They exist on the surface of impressions and deeply rooted in the absence of care. But others have been produced by a pseudo-scientific gaze—for a few moments, and from a certain distance, they pass themselves for their live counterpart, thereafter inducing a slight sense of loss in the keen viewer who notices the deceit.

Mark Wallinger explored the nature of this superficial relationship with *Double Still Life* (2009), a pair of almost identical, artificial flower compositions. Placed on two stately looking stands, the lush floral assemblages are too colorful to either suggest a funeral or a wedding—their aesthetic evokes a high-end lawyer's waiting room, a luxury hotel lobby, or a prestigious museum entrance—they are ceremonious but not ceremonial. Their ceremoniousness implies institutional authenticity—they are bold, fresh, ordered, and elegant: all positive qualities which implicitly underline the ethical ethos of the hypothetical institution which presents them. From a few feet away the aesthetic impact equates that of fresh flowers, but nearing closer reveals the bitter truth. Wallinger stages this specific encounter to pose questions related to art and plants alike. Upon noticing the deceit, awe immediately dissipates. But why do we value the composition differently? Why do we desire them to be living flowers when all we are going to do is to pass by and merely glance at them? Wallinger's compositions gesture to the notions of originality and authenticity, which the artifice intrinsic to realistic, classical representations can only flaunt but never truly possesses. Or he might be ironically subverting the memento mori paradigm inscribed in still-life flower paintings from the seventeenth century—the impossibility of death which characterizes these flowers echoing the Hegelian notion that non-human beings cannot truly die as they do not have a grasp of being alive in the first place. But in the case of plants, death becomes a complex problem on both fronts: the ethical and the biological. While it is fair to say that an animal can be clinically declared dead, matters are more nuanced with plants. Is a cut flower dead or still living? When is a plant truly dead considering that an individual one can be splintered apart in multiple cuttings, which can thrive as new independent individuals? Or that even the fragment of roots, leaves, or tendrils can in some species generate a new plant? Plant-life is by nature dispersed and self-perpetuating in a constant form of becoming—with its surrounding space—if the conditions of humidity, heat, and light will support it, the plant will strive to develop within it. Move the plant to another space with different humidity, heat, and light variable, and it might perish.

Here lies the ontological shift necessary in order to conceive plant-life as a compelling non-anthropocentric modality that can enable us to move beyond the binaries of Cartesian thinking. Michael Marder calls this alternative "plant-thinking":

> "Plant-thinking" refers, in the same breath, to (1) the non-cognitive, non-ideational, and non-imagistic mode of thinking proper to plants (hence, what I call "thinking without the head"); (2) our thinking about plants; (3) how human thinking is, to some extent, de-humanized and rendered plantlike, altered by its encounter with the vegetal world; and finally, (4) the ongoing symbiotic relation between this transfigured thinking and the existence of plants.[6]

Marder's theorization of "plant-thinking" essentially constitutes a tool designed to upturn the state of "plant blindness" which has been nurtured by Western philosophy over the past two thousand years. As theorized by biologists Kathryn Williams and Mung Balding of Australia's University of Melbourne, plant blindness essentially is a cultural condition which prevents us to recognize plant-life complexity beyond the realm of curiosity or specialistic knowledge.[7] But most importantly, plant blindness is also harbored in what might seem a tangible awareness of them: aesthetic appreciation—only valuing plants for their aesthetic beauty constitutes a totalizing oversimplification which falls straight into the symbolic limitation of knowledge.

It is for this reason that artist Ethan Breckenridge deliberately compromises their aesthetic beauty (without destroying the plant) in order to induce a sense of empathy that is otherwise hard to experience in the transitional spaces in which many superficial human/plant encounters take place everyday. In his installation titled *Too Soon*, staged in Bolivia (2009) and New York (2010), the artist crammed potted plants into carpeted glass cubes. The gray carpet gestures towards the corporate desire for homologation and functionalism which aesthetically defines the frugality of office environments around the world. The plants are left in the gardening center plastic-pots they grew in—another sign of capitalist frugality—there is no attempt on behalf of the artist to elevate the plant to a metaphor of nature and culture. Despite the elements in this installation that might point towards that direction, the leaves pressing against the glass, pushing into the corners of the cube, and bending downward in the impossibility of continuing upward are simultaneously heart wrenching and outstandingly defiant—the leaves are green, the plant looks healthy—it makes the most of the given environment filling its every corner, not necessarily pushing to break free, but just engaging with space through economies of sustenance and survival that invite us to think beyond anthropomorphism. And this is one of the biggest challenges at stake with plant-thinking. Can anthropomorphism ever be productive in this context? This is a controversial concept in animal studies already. Do we risk obliterating plant alterity once again if we empathize with them on the wrong footing?

Biologically many plants, especially those that have become popular in the transitional spaces of lobbies and waiting rooms, favor continuity of light, humidity, and temperature—that's what seems to make them develop to the best of their domesticated potential. Breckendrige's glassboxes might bring to mind images of medieval torture devices—yet, what constitutes plant torture? Isn't forcing them to grow in accordance to our own aesthetic liking already a form of torture? Isn't dissecting them for propagation a kind of vivisection? Is hybridizing them a form of eugenics? Isn't placing them in the wrong spot of the bedroom or bathroom a lifetime sentence?

Plant-thinking raises these questions not for the purpose of devising an ethical ground upon which human/plants relations should build, but to generate awareness of the concealed forms of violence we inflict upon other non-human beings—forms of violence that fall outside the remit of the law but that nonetheless exist and that in their existence form the essence of human/non-human relations. This should not be intended as an invitation to disregard the suffering of plants—ethical imperatives to treat every living being with respect apply here too. However, plant-blindness is an anthropocentrically induced condition that generates unethicality towards plants—these forms of unethicality can impact plants physically, as just discussed, and also culturally, by relegating them in conveniently objectified conditions.

In this context, the contemporary art gallery is a very specific place—although this might seem a paradox, the heightened regime of the gaze which characterizes imposes upon plants the paradigm of the (brief) encounter, thus flattening them into objectification as long as they are contextualized like paintings and sculptures. The first appearance of plants in the gallery space dates back to 1936, when Edward Steichen's *Delphiniums* exhibit was staged at MoMA for one week only.[8] Steichen, who had an extremely successful career as painter, photographer, modern art promoter, and museum curator, had retired in Connecticut, to focus on his horticultural passion. There he presented his engineered and manipulated new breeds of delphiniums; some gigantified to four feet from their more modest natural height. The artist dosed the delphinium seeds in a chemical bath of colchicine, a toxin that induces polyploidy, resulting in the mutated flowers.[9] The exhibition functioned as a metaphorical take on the Aristotelian view that art perfects nature and inscribed this in a Duchampian-readymade maneuver that implied the reversal of the memento mori stilled aesthetic. Steichen's delphiniums posed questions of originality, authorship, value, and originality. At the time, this proposal was pioneering new artistic territories while engaging in important discursivities with contemporary theories and practices. But contemporary art requires a more engaged relationship with the alterity of plant-being—one that attempts to prevent plant objectification at the least or even to do something that might benefit them, as it will be seen towards the end of this chapter.[10]

How can a gallery space then present a different human/plant relational that differs from the objectification of other spaces in which human/plant contact is time-limited and constrained by the encoded cultural norms which define the space itself? To derail plant blindness in the gallery space, it is necessary to unhinge the cultural framework inscribed in its modality of visual consumption to stage the opportunity for new and productive human/plant interactions. Ontologically, the contemporary gallery has its roots in the spaces of optical experimentation which marked the nineteenth century as a revolutionary time for the history of art and representation more in general. Romantic paintings engaged viewers with a heightened sense of drama, movement, and unbalance. John Martin's sublime paintings were exhibited in theatrical situations that enhanced dramatization through the use of colored lights.[11] Daguerre's diorama exhibits of the 1830s and 1840s incorporated even more complex strategies for the purpose of engaging audiences with new visual narratives.[12] Simultaneously, the reproducibility of the photographic image led to the experimentation with rotating sequences and flickering visions. The salons of the second half of the nineteenth century that took place in Paris and London were exciting because of the spectacle they proposed and the cultural shocks they sometimes caused.[13] The galleries of the Louvre were a place to study classical art, but not one where experimentation could take place. In this panorama, the essential precursor of the contemporary gallery space is not the Louvre, nor any other museum of that kind. It's the commercial gallery space, which emerged during the mid-nineteenth century in its already recognizable modern form: the retail space of a dealer who organized temporary exhibitions of specific genres to attract buying visitors. By 1910, there were hundreds of commercial galleries in London.[14] The Royal Academy of Art and the Louvre were places where the taste and cultural status quo of the establishment were being celebrated and reaffirmed at every step. The commercial gallery was a place where risks, cultural as well as economic, to some extent, could be taken.

However, it is with the irreverent experimentalism of Futurism and Dada that the "ontologically more unstable" space of the commercial gallery was hijacked to become the home of experimental art. Notably, Dada's disdain for bourgeois values led to controversial artistic gestures which questioned the nature of art itself—their interest for time-based media in opposition to the stasis of classical art, their new conceptions of space as a three-dimensional theatrical dimension instead of the wall (painting) and the floor (sculpture), their desire to shutter and break instead of constructing or building, their disrespect for skills and privilege for thinking, and their mistrust for the artist's genius as a mystical entity revolutionized the gallery space so that art could actually happen instead of just being exhibited.[15] After the

Second World War, as the ideologies of modernism became predominant, the gallery became the sacred space of the white cube.

At this point, the art gallery entered a new conceptual dimension based on new experiential potentialities. As art critic Thomas McEvilley argued: "The white cube was a transitional device that attempted to bleach out the past and at the same time control the future by appealing to supposedly transcendental modes of presence and power."[16] Its very essence is that of being a conduit—a passage between the material world and a Platonic dimension of purified ideas in which modernist objects were removed from historical contexts. The relations the gallery space inscribed, its culturally normative forms of consumption enabled implicitly excluded livingness—that of the art object and that of the viewer too. The modernist white cube was a timeless milieu designed to entertain a disembodied eye provoking a fragmentation of the self, ultimately alienating the viewer instead of, as Foucault's would have it, drawing the viewers out of themselves.

The advent of minimalist art changed this paradigm by introducing what Michael Fried negatively connoted as the theatricality of objecthood in the gallery space: an experience proposing a confrontation including the beholder. As Fried argued, "once [the beholder] is in the room the work refuses, obstinately, to let him alone—which is to say, it refuses to stop confronting him.[17] Yet a problem remained—minimalist art also incorporated aesthetics of transcendentalism that had little or no concern with the world outside the white cube. As Brian O'Doherty put it, the gallery space became "unshadowed, white, clean, artificial—the space is devoted to the technology of aesthetics."[18] Its specific agential qualities, inscribed cultural norms and laws, and materiality as well as relational specificities rest on an intrinsic Cartesian paradigm which sanitizes the space and, up until recently, categorically excludes living non-human beings.

Because of these reasons, the white cube is not usually a suitable environment for animals and plants—but most importantly, the encounter which it usually stages in the perimeter of the gallery is more regularly one pre-encoded by the cultural history and materiality of the space itself. Both animals and plants, but more so plants, risk an ontological alignment with objects in ways that are even more counterproductive than the objectification taking place in zoos and botanical gardens. In the context of the gallery space, plants have been superficially associated with the ready-made objects of Marcel Duchamp—to many, they seem to occupy a pop art/realist dimension in which, they claim, the plant symbolizes that which is outside the boundaries of the gallery space—nature. This interpretation is very limited, for it merely situates plant presence as an institutional critique of the Cartesian dimension defining the gallery space—the plant has become a symbol of nature, it is not its own entity, and individualized body—it has become a marker of the nature/culture divide and the disinterest the gallery space has nurtured for connecting with not only the world outside, but the living world more precisely. Understanding a plant in the gallery space as the allusion to nature reassesses the generality and lack of seriousness with which living organisms are regarded within art historical discourses. A cultivar in a plastic pot cannot possibly signify nature. With very few exceptions, the majority of artists involving living plants in their work use cultivars that have been produced in gardening centers—these subtexts cannot be ignored when considering works involving plants. When encountering a ready-made object in the gallery space, art critics take into careful consideration its materiality, its origin, its (original) function, its age—the man-made object is an always charged field of agential potentialities. But a plant is quickly "unpacked" as nature. This hermeneutical (anthropocentric) limitation constitutes a serious obstacle to a more complex consideration of what plants could do in the gallery space.

Part of the reason why plants are clumsily aligned with ready-made objects when in the gallery space is strictly linked to the transitional nature of the white cube itself. Museum displays, as well as the gallery space, have accustomed viewers to a temporally contained consumptive experience inherited from the temporal scales commanded by painting and sculpture. The average person spends 15 to 30 seconds in front of a painting in any museum in the world.[19] The experience is longer in smaller galleries, where the pressure of engaging with an unquantifiable amount art is not incumbent—yet, there is something about the encounter with a plant in the gallery space that just can't be grasped on the time-scale of seconds and minutes—their existence on a different temporal scale from the human one always pushes them back to the background, as symbolic representations, allegories of human anxieties, and decorative expedients. For this very reason, it is important that the contemporary presence of plants in art should prevent brief encounters from being the main relational modality at play.

Beyond the examples explored in this book, many of which entailed a participatory, experiential dimension, artists have been engaging viewers with plants through performative, video, and sound-based scenarios that preclude the brief encounter modality outright. A substantial number of artists, for instance, have staged interactive plant interactions by capitalizing on the applicability of sonic art interfaces. Since 1873, it has been known that plants' electrical signals are the most important intracellular signaling system in plant organisms—they are essential to physiological functions like respiration, water uptake, leaf movement, and biotic stress response.[20] Attaching electrodes to plant leaves and channeling the impulses into a system involving a dedicated software interface and amplification enables us to acoustically encounter plants, thus providing an alternative representational counterpart to their purely aesthetic presence. Mileece Petre produces what she calls organic, electronic music for the purpose of highlighting plants' sentience, as exemplified through the variations in electrical signaling which can be detected in response to different stimuli. In the 1990s, Mileece's father quit a career in the music industry to become a renewable energy entrepreneur. One of the projects father and daughter developed together involved a hydrogen fuel cells system with zero emission that today entirely supports her art installations.

The artist's performances are specifically concerned with bridging the gap we have created between human and non-human beings. As the artist claims:

> We're not really geared, at the moment, to try to take responsibility for things that we feel we don't have any control over, and don't really have a connection with. We're at a loss for how to enable change, especially when dialogue of change is usually baked into the threatening philosophy that we need to move into a kind of austerity in our use of resources, which might effectively reduce or remove our access to technology. Which is very threatening given technology is how we derive our sense of community and communion now.[21]

Mileece's ecocriticist perspective condemns the current ideological attempts being made to mobilize eco-urgency in people. Suggesting that you should care about nature because we are all otherwise going to die is not the way to go, she claims. Her 2013 performance at MoMA's PSA1 series, titled *Speculations: The Future Is* ____, kept the audience's attention focused on the plants' bio-acoustic live composition for an extended period, enabling those present to appreciate plants' electrical responses to being touched by the artist. This human/plant interaction was slowed down and mediated by technological interfaces capable of translating, transforming, and enhancing human/plant perceptibility.[22]

As focusing the attention of audiences on plants and human/plant interaction becomes imperative, Jonathon Keats has also turned his attention to the limitations which the traditional gallery space imposes on human/plant interaction. His preoccupation led to bridging the contrastingly different human/plant sensorial interactions through the use of video—another time-based medium employed to slow the otherwise intrinsically brief encounter in the gallery space. Keats has developed an international profile based on a distinct ability to incorporate sound scientific research with poetics and humor in the production of thought-provoking unconventional artworks.

In 2007, the artist staged the first plant porn cinema screening (Chico, California) for a crowd of about a hundred rhododendrons. Straddling a thin, semi-serious line of argument, Keats inferred that "pollination was the most titillating experience for plants."[23] He then set out to understand how human and plant sensorial could be poetically aligned for the purpose of producing footage the plants might actually enjoy.

> So I spent a couple of days on the ground, seeing how light and shadow were experienced from their perspective. Once I had a very stark black-and-white image—sun up high, bees flying by. I let it run for a month, and let the plants experience vicarious sex. And let people stand at the periphery and giggle nervously.[24]

Plants' sensitivity to light suggested to the artist that cinema would be a perfect medium through which an audience of plants could be effectively drawn into an artistic discourse. Keats came to appreciate the impact of entertainment on non-human audiences while choreographing a ballet for honeybees the year prior. His projects involving performance and non-human beings question the anthropocentric bias according to which only humans are capable of experiencing the non-functionalism of art and entertainment. The black and white footage he produced was optimized for the purpose of being better absorbed by the plants and was projected on their leaves instead of being screened on a wall facing them. Keats made no promise as to the plants' response to the screenings. His intent was not that of either stimulating growth or flowering. In so doing, he deliberately bypassed the notion of cause and effect which governs most of what we do "for plants"—relationships in which we regularly expect something in return.

The success of the first screening led the artist to explore further the potentialities involved in making art for plants, titled *Television for Plants* (2010), which once again was designed to give plants something, expecting nothing in return. Keats thought that

> the subject that would be most interesting to plants is travel. Plants don't get to go anywhere. They're rooted in the ground. But if you're a plant, you're not going to get excited about the Eiffel Tower—instead, you're going to be excited about the sky.[25]

He thus filmed an Italian sky, for over two months, for the purpose of virtually taking plants on a trip of a lifetime. He was aware that both NASA and the Soviet-era agronomy schools were interested in plants' perception of light because of their interest in how to grow plants in space or indoors in Siberia. The artist wanted to use the information gathered, like plants' sensitivity to color, for the purpose of providing for them a unique experience entirely disentangled from an exploitative economy of sort. He thus invited plant owners to bring their houseplants to the gallery space, to share the experience with them. Once again, as it was with *Cinema Botanica*, Keats' approach is semi-serious and yet capable to mobilize viewers and plants from the static pre-encoded, objectifying paradigms which most regularly dominate human/plant relationships in the gallery space. The simple gesture of instilling curiosity about plants' sentience through anthropomorphically grounded paradoxical situation represents a valuable opportunity for different phyto-ontologies to be considered by the general public from a more serious perspective than might initially seem plausible.

Both Mileece and Keats propose new agential registers in which plants are somewhat collaborators or participants and in which their sentient/responsive abilities are emphasized rather than repressed. Both artists slow down the human/plant interaction to a temporality capable of revealing the nuances and complexities of plant-being. They do so through the time-based media of performance, sound art, and video art—these are, perhaps surprisingly, the most productive media through which the ontological objectification of plants can be subverted in contemporary art. But most importantly, both artists simultaneously pose important questions about the synergy of art and science, challenging the stereotypical view that a solid and close discourse between the two might involve a literalism that precludes poetics and humor from playing essential roles in art designed to make us rethink what we thought we already knew about plants.

NOTES

1. M. Foucault and J. Miskowiec, "Of Other Spaces," *Diacritics* 16, no. 1 (Spring 1986): 22–27, quote, 22.
2. Foucault and Miskowiec, "Of Other Spaces," 23.
3. Foucault and Miskowiec, "Of Other Spaces."

4. J. Bentham, *The Works of Jeremy Bentham, Vol. IV* (Edinburgh: William Tait, 1791), 1843.
5. M. Foucault, *Discipline and Punish: The Birth of the Prison*, transl. by Alan Sheridan (London: Penguin, 1975), 1991; and M. Foucault, *The History of Sexuality 1—The Will to Knowledge* (London: Penguin Books, 1998). First published in 1976.
6. M. Marder, "What Is Plant-Thinking?," *Klesis—Revue Philosophique* 25 (2013): 124–143; quote, 124.
7. M. Balding and K. J. H. Williams, "Plant Blindness and the Implication for Plant Conservation," *Conservation Biology* 30, no. 6, December (2016): 1192–1199.
8. G. Gessert, *Green Light: Toward an Art of Evolution* (Cambridge: MIT Press, 2012), 48.
9. F. Stracey, "Bio-Art: The Ethics behind the Aesthetics," *Perspective* 10 (July 2009): 496–500.
10. Of course, it remains difficult if not impossible to determine whether our intentional well-meaning toward plants effectively equates to something they appreciate—yet, there is something interesting in the possibility to explore aesthetics that might bring these questions to the fore without losing the artistic edge.
11. J. Myrone, "John Martin's *Last Judgement* Triptych: The Apocalyptic Sublime in the Age of Spectacle," in *The Art of the Sublime*, ed. Nigel Llewellyn and Christine Riding (London: Tate, 2013).
12. H. Gernsheim and A. Gernsheim, *L. J. M. Daguerre: The History of the Diorama and the Daguerreotype* (Dover, England: Dover, 1968).
13. P. Mainardi, *The End of the Salon* (Cambridge: Cambridge University Press, 1994).
14. P. Fletcher and Anne Helmreich, eds., *The Rise of the Modern Art Market in London, 1850–1939* (Manchester: Manchester UP, 2011).
15. B. O'Doherty, *Inside the White Cube: The Ideology of the Gallery Space* (Berkeley: University of. California Press, 1999).
16. O'Doherty, *Inside the White Cube*, 11.
17. M. Fried, "Art and Objecthood," in *Art and Objecthood: Essays and Reviews* (Evanston, IL: University of Chicago Press, 1967), 148–172; quote, 163.
18. O'Doherty, *Inside the White Cube,* 15.
19. S. Rosenbloom, "The Art of Slowing Down in a Museum," *New York Times*, October 9, https://www.nytimes.com/2014/10/12/travel/the-art-of-slowing-down-in-a-museum.html.
20. A. G. Volkov, *Plant Electrophysiology: Theory and Methods* (Berlin: Springer Science and Business Media, 2007).
21. Mileece quoted in E. Robinsong, "Mileece: Gardening the Future," in *Kadenzeblog*, 2016, https://blog.kadenze.com/2016/10/29/mileece-gardening-the-future/.
22. MoMA PS1 website: http://www.momaps1.org/expo1/image/mileece-lecture/.
23. Jonathon Keats quoted in A. Gopnik, "Plant TV," *The New Yorker*, March 15, 2010, http://www.newyorker.com/magazine/2010/03/15/plant-tv.
24. Keats quoted in Gopnik, "Plant TV."
25. Gopnik, "Plant TV."

Main Pathway: Orientations

Subthemes

Proceed to Experience, p. 159
Proceed to Place, p. 173

11

ADVENTURES IN PHYTOPHENOMENOLOGY

David Wood

Are plants the new animal? Michael Marder's plant books force us to confront this question. I was not initially convinced by his approach, but a major doubt I had about them has dissipated.[1] I was part of the Oxford animal rights movement of the early 1970s. We argued for an ethical extensionism that would continue the process of rights expansion that had over centuries overcome racial and gender prejudice and was now poised to leap the species barrier. Ethics was about rights, and if you could suffer, you deserved protection. Animals yes, rocks no. Lobsters maybe. Plants probably not. The obvious next step would be to argue that plants are the new animals, the new excluded Other, and that our refusal to acknowledge this bears witness to the same self-serving myopic anthropocentrism under which animals still suffer. When philosophers have written about plants, they have not by and large done so in such a way as to justify broader human privilege. Philosophy itself, if there is such a thing, might increasingly come to be seen as an extended riff on the theme: "Why we are so special?," albeit well disguised within the "metaphysical tradition."

Marder writes often about the ethical neglect of plants, or the need to revise their ethical status.[2] And he does argue plausibly for a version of these two strong theses. I will argue, however, that what his treatment of plants most significantly

From *Thinking Plant Animal Human: Encounters with Communities of Difference,* by David Wood (University of Minnesota Press, 2020), 23–34.

raises is the meaning and status of the ethical. I will endorse his broadly phenomenological approach here, but suggest what I will oxymoronically call an Anglo-Heideggerean take on how to understand such an approach. I begin with a series of preliminary remarks by way of orientation.

1. When we talk about plants, we are quickly entangled in the very metaphysical/anthropological machine we have been warned against. Science tells us there are over three hundred thousand species of plants, notwithstanding disagreements about what counts as a plant at all. Linnaeus and Haeckel included fungi and bacteria! If we are not dealing with some sort of natural kind, or plant essence, might not the very idea of a plant be a human construct?[3] Then again, if we consider everyday ways of understanding what a plant is, we need to be happy talking about giant sequoias, front lawns, and buttercups in the same breath. To do that, we have to resort to objective and objectifying characteristics such as immobility, photosynthesis, roots, seed production, and so on. It might be said that we are entitled to do this if all our examples share the same characteristics, but how are such collectivities constituted in the first place? And we have to be happy talking about individual specimens as if they were exhausted by their species or genus membership, which is already a "metaphysical" move. The Goliad Hanging Tree is not just any tree, let alone just any plant, but an individual, an official Texas Historic Landmark.[4] Similarly, the Chandelier giant sequoia, or the Sherman—some 2,100 years old. These issues clearly matter ontologically, and epistemologically, but even more so ethically. Some plants seem to be individuals.

2. Plant ethics seems inextricably entangled with another fundamental question—whether ethics begins with similarity or difference, a question that never quite goes away. Ethical extensionalism understandably draws on the fact that many animals are like us, so much so that it is hard to see how we can exclude them from equal or comparable consideration of interests. The Great Ape Project takes this to the limit. And yet it could be argued that such extensions of consideration require little ethical effort. Fellow feeling or sympathy would have the same effect. Charity begins at home. Mammals suckle like us; it would be mean-spirited not to recognize a certain commonality of maternal feeling. Here, ethical extension has a clear path, if it is needed at all. When we look at a spider in a web, however, things are different. We may see an analog of "home" (or a fishing net, or artistry) in the web, and thence connect with the spider. It

is hard *not* to see something of that. But we may be more struck by just how *different* the spider is (or the snake, or the mollusk). This difference can then operate either as a barrier to ethics, or as a stimulus, a provocation. For we can first notice, and then resist, our own tendency to favor what is like us. White people may "naturally" favor other white people, but recognize that justice demands they set aside color, ethnicity, and so on, in hiring practices and in their own considered responses. There are some exceptionally ugly fish in the sea that, as a fisherman, one might be tempted to treat badly (not throwing them back carefully), but which deserve better. An ethical orientation has to navigate between these two poles of likeness and difference. One obvious consideration is this (echoing Derrida's reading of Levinas's *Violence and Metaphysics*): there has to be *some* basis of similarity for a certain ethical engagement to get going. If a Society for the Ethical Treatment of Clouds found it hard to get as much traction as one for cloud photography, it would be because clouds just don't seem to qualify—not individuals, not stable, not alive, not relationally engaged in interesting ways with their surroundings, and so on. Some would say the same of rocks. We have at best indirect duties (see Kant) to Mount Rushmore, the White Cliffs of Dover, Australia's Uluru, or the North Face of the Eiger. But arguably the issue is not that these rocks are not enough like us, but that they fail to make a quite independent grade as objects of appropriate ethical concern.

The confusion arises only because we humans seem to be exemplary cases of such objects. Plants, if we can speak so generally, seem to straddle this play between sameness and difference, failing to make the grade in one sense, while appealing to us as living beings on the other. They are like us, but only enough for respect—not sympathy, let alone obligation. This situation can then provoke efforts (from Marder, and myself) to show how secretly plantlike humans are, the hidden vegetative side. But this is a fine game in that it accepts the similarity premise. Perhaps the cloud and rock comparisons show why something like this is necessary.

3. I spoke of an Anglo-Heideggerean take on phenomenology. This expression may never have been used before, so what does it mean? Phenomenology, classically speaking (Husserl), involves letting things show themselves as they are in themselves. "Things" here (*Sache*) are not objects, but rather the matter at hand, phenomena, what is experienced. And from a phenomenological point of view, access to this stuff is made possible by resistance to unreflective forms

of objectification (such as science). Husserl uses what he calls an *epoché*, and there are perhaps three ways in which we can draw on Heidegger here. First, there is the Heidegger of *Being and Time*, and things ready-to-hand, things that are essentially, as it were, for us. Bicycles, tools, boats, roads, pencils. Second, there are his expansive fourfold meditations on *The Thing*. Here, to think "a jug" or "a bridge" is to set such things back into dimensions of cosmic and human relevance, hence to draw out layers of engaged meaning. Finally, there is the Heidegger who speaks of *physis*, the creative energy of nature witnessed by the Greeks and lost sight of in contemporary physics. When Sartre speaks of the writhing black root in the park in *Nausea*, he is not simply voicing a mescaline-induced hallucination; he is tapping in to such an upsurge prior to words, prior to the human. These three pathways suggest at least two divergent ways of doing justice to plants. The latter would wage all-out war on any and every human projection, trying to tap into the radically Other represented by the Plant. The second path would accept that the tree or the poppy is typically only glimpsed darkly, and through an all-too-human glass. Do not our human engagements with plants largely instrumentalize them, and largely blind us to their intrinsic veggie or floral or leafy essence? The first is perhaps foreshadowed in Romanticism, the second in a broader attentiveness to the modes of appearance of the plant. The Anglo part of what I have called an Anglo-Heideggerean approach, influenced by Wittgenstein, would take seriously the idea that the detail and metaphysical resistance exhibited in the everyday ways we talk and think about things is worth tapping into. Everydayness, especially drawing on the polyglot English language, would perform a role parallel to Heidegger's deployment of the Greeks—resisting a Latinizing covering-over. Latin (see Roman Britain) is just one of the many layers of English. *Artemisia vulgaris* is better known as mugwort.

Specifically, this calls for a practice of attentiveness to the manifold ways in which we connect with and engage with plants of every stripe. The main body of this chapter is devoted to giving examples of this being-with-plants.

ETHICS AND PHENOMENOLOGY

I agree with Heidegger that we need to trace ethics back to its Greek root *ethos*, and to understand that in terms of dwelling.[5] What this means is that questions of duty, obligation, value, and rights rest ultimately on the coherence of forms of life. But for this insistence on tradition not to turn into a justification of intolerance, bigotry, and provincialism, *dwelling* needs to be understood dynamically and critically. Normative practices we now regard as unduly restrictive or abhorrent (or plain strange) may once have served some vital function that is no longer needed.[6] This approach may seem overly relativistic and naturalistic. Its general justification rests on the observation that ethical practice and the avoidance of impossible dilemmas is enormously facilitated by the lessening of scarcity and the establishment of peace and security. This itself is not just another piece of naturalism. Dire scarcity does not just make selfishness more likely. It creates conditions in which evil can be justified, because it is the lesser evil. (One can justify killing to save lives.) A critical take on forms of dwelling would be able to evaluate whether certain practices were redundant legacies of earlier scarcity or desperation, and open to renegotiation.

With this proviso, the link between phenomenology and ethics would not rest on whether this or that being had a face (à la Levinas, who doubted snakes had a face, and included dogs only indirectly). Nor would it focus on forms of sympathy or empathy à la Scheler. Instead, it would extend the kind of connection between virtue and knowledge that Socrates articulates: "When people make a wrong choice of pleasures and pains—that is, of good and evil—the cause of their mistake is lack of knowledge" (Protagoras, 357e, 358c). Or Jesus: "Father, forgive them, for they know not what they do" (Luke 23:34). The implications for action and choice would flow not just from propositional knowledge, but from a certain attentiveness to detail, to difference, to "All things counter, original, spare, strange."[7] As well as familiar! We cannot respond adequately if we do not look, or if when we look, we do not see. It's true that we will not respond adequately if we do not *care*, but much of caring is tied up with understanding, not least our intimate dependency on plants. So what would a phenomenologically inspired attention to plants involve?

PLANT PROJECTIONS

The permission seemingly given in Genesis for the human domination of Nature (much depends on how we translate *rada*), should caution us about our unreflective thoughts about plants, as well as animals. If God provided them for our nourishment and pleasure, we surely have a license to do with them what we will. But if we do not buy into the biblical creation story, where does that leave us? In an unusual move, I propose a strange variant of the creation story. That story offers a religious ground for a deep relation between humans and plants. But if the theology is suspect, the underlying connection is not. The beings that we are, are essentially dependent on eating plant life, and/or on animals that eat plants, quite as much as we need to breathe air and drink water. If an instrumental relation presupposes the independence of agent and object, this relation—our use of plants—is not fundamentally instrumental. Plants and animals are at some level co-constitutive, even if the animal functions in question need not be provided specifically by humans (pollination, seed dispersal, selective grazing, fertilization). Put another way, we "use" plants to stay alive, for shelter, shade, clothing, and so on. We also "use" our teeth to chew, but when the instrument in question is part of "us," or coevolved with us, concerns about exploitation, or blindness to the intrinsic qualities or value of the object in question, substantially diminish. Consequently, I propose we reserve references to instrumentality for those practices (monoculture, genetic engineering of crops, the use of artificial chemicals, etc.) that transform a necessary relation (we cannot do without plants) into one of highly controlled and myopic subjection. What then is the force of such a restriction? Rice, corn, cotton, sugar, coffee, rape, wheat, grapes, not to mention slash pine, eucalyptus, olives, maple, opium poppies, citrus fruit, avocados, walnuts, bananas are all grown as monoculture plantation crops, supplied by agricultural technology with fertilizer and pesticides. Our relation with these plants—for food, clothing, fuel, drugs, and building materials—is inseparable from the labor markets, the multinational chemical companies, the laboratories, the financial flows, the transport systems that make them possible. We may look at an individual plant and see leaves, stems, flowers, roots, and a whole lot of *physis*, but its invisible conditions of possibility, without which it just would not be, are quite as real. One can trace a series of changes in plant harvesting practices, from gathering wild plants, through informal cultivation, gardening, and farming, to today's Big Ag. Phenomenology is pushed to its limit as our immediate experience of plant products is increasingly cut off from the systems that produce and sustain them.

SCIENCE

What then of the science that studies plants—botany? Is that not intrinsically objectifying and alienating and bound to obscure anything like an attempt to see things from a plant's perspective? If we think of science just as rigid objectification, with domination and control as its ultimate concern, then an ethical orientation to plants would have little to hope for from science. When Heidegger says that "science does not think," he points to the same limitation—science classifies, organizes, generalizes, but in important ways is not open to the phenomena, nor to the limits of its own discourse. Add to this the question of *which* science—botany, ecology, agricultural science, cell biology—each of which has a different take on what we generally call "plants."

These issues are real and not to be casually dismissed. But the link between science and technological objectification and domination is not quite so immediate as it might seem. Two comments here:

1. When we talk of seeing things *from a plant's perspective*, this can look, as Marder admits, like a misplaced attribution of subjectivity. A plant most likely does not have a point of view in anything like a human or animal way. And yet, presence or absence of food, water, sunlight *matter* to a plant—they can be life-and-death issues. Each plant is, in a sense, a focus of such concerns, if not quite what Tom Regan calls the "subject of a life."[8] On the other hand, it might be argued that this mattering, the question of life and death, and then focus, tell us something about what grounds *what we call subjectivity*—vitality, a conatus, will-to-power, and so on—whether or not we go on to think of a plant as lacking something we possess or as having its own style of life.

2. There is much confusion about the idea of science. We too often work with images of a fish out of water (see Merleau-Ponty), or a butterfly pinned to a board, where the living is killed to be studied, and the complexity of its active life is no longer available. Field studies, however, combat that approach, studying living beings in their native habitat, avoiding blindness to constitutive relationality. A serious botanist works in that way and is open to noticing unexpected connections, such as companion plants, new pollinators, climate-change victims. Many an actual scientist (such as Goethe!) begins and is sustained by wonder not just at the beauty of flowers, but at the extraordinary range of forms of leaf, and their climatic and other adaptations. (See Holmes Rolston.) Now it could be argued that we have here a version of the benign dictator issue. Benign dictators do not justify dictatorship as an institution any more than thoughtful scientists show that science thinks. But there is a stronger and better argument. Suppose the study of botany, using microscopes and slides, textbook

illustrations, and collecting expeditions leads us to understand the workings of the stomata on the underside of a leaf opening and closing to allow CO_2 and O_2 in and water vapor and O_2 out (an example from Holmes Rolston). These stomata are possessed by almost all plants and play a vital role in photosynthesis and respiration. We can just treat these as isolated "mechanisms" that we are observing objectively, but equally we can notice the parallels to our own breathing, and the role this management of the exchange of gases plays both in the greater life of the plant and planet: the contribution made by plants to maintaining the earth's atmosphere. Coming to understand "how plants work" through science can itself be a revelation for those who normally get little closer to plants than sitting under a tree, mowing the lawn, or eating lettuce. Objective knowledge is reincorporated into more complex narratives. We do not have to remain transfixed in the objectifying headlights of scientific detachment. There is no better evidence of this than macrophotography and slow-motion film that reveal in astonishing detail the secret lives of plants. Again, it could be said that as mere images or representations, photography and film betray what they depict. But this is a dialectically unimaginative stance. They can teach us to see, notice, attend, and ask more questions.

All this is to say that while there are clear connections between science and technological control and domination, there are equally clear links to wonder and delight and the opening onto the plant world that Marder advocates.

TIME

If modes of temporality and spatiality determine the shapes of possibility for different beings, it is especially interesting that, as part of vegetal existentiality, Marder explores the time of plants. He argues, with more than a glance at Heidegger, that the meaning of vegetal being is time—specifically seasonal change, infinite albeit interruptible growth, and the cyclical temporality of iteration, repetition, and reproduction. He suggests we can learn something (about ourselves) from this "embodied, living, non-conscious intentionality" of plants.[9]

But we need also to plot the shape of our human engagements with plants, as well as their own autonomous existence. And this is especially significant in the case of time. Seasonality, growth, and reproduction are central to gardening and farming. *Old Moore's Almanac* teaches us which phase of the moon to plant. Seed packets tell us days to fruiting or flowering. Our food, building, and clothing supplies, as well as quarterly agricultural profits, are intimately tied to coordination between plant time and human time, and indeed animal times (pollination, insect emergence dates, grain production, and grazing seasons for cattle), and so on.

I have already suggested that we cannot think of plant life simply at the level of the individual plant. From the planetary point of view, there would be no breathable atmosphere without photosynthesis, the production of oxygen, and the absorption of the greenhouse gas CO_2. Animals do not merely eat plants. We are symbiotically dependent on them for the air we breathe and the surface temperature of the planet. Deforestation (as in the Amazon) threatens our survival.

These considerations take us importantly outside any phytophenomenology, although our starting point was paying close attention to the role of leaf stomata and understanding how they contribute to the life of the plant, perhaps a more hermeneutic approach. The planetary role of plants operates below the phenomenological radar, as it were. This is even more so when one thinks about long-dead plants and the energy flows in which they have become the main players. For the fossil fuels we burn—coal, oil, petroleum, gas, and peat—are all derived from ancient highly compressed plant life—the trees, ferns, and algae of the carboniferous period.[10] Our reliance on long-dead plants has fueled civilization, and is destroying the planet. And the hybrid temporality of this practice is quite exceptional. Deposits that took millions of years to lay down are being used up in a flash of history, like taking a chain saw for a few minutes to an ancient tree, but on an unfathomably greater scale. We call these practices "unsustainable" because of the massive gap between rates of consumption and cycles of renewal. And because we would need four earths to absorb the CO_2 generated by burning these fossil fuels. Dead plants figure heavily too in clothing (cotton), in the office and publishing (paper), in building (timber in construction), and last but not least, religion. It is no accident that Christ was crucified on a wooden cross, symbolically capturing Christianity's displacement of the sacred groves of Roman paganism. We do not see "plant" when we put together a new bookcase, but the books are ex-plants, and the shelves are ex-plants. Trees have a special status among plants, and of course one can say a lot more about trees beyond shelter, shipbuilding, and bridges—their place in painting, poetry, philosophy, and fiction.[11] Trees (wood) are plants turned into natural capital, the dead products of past negentropic energy accumulation, dried bound fibers with a myriad human uses.

For Heidegger, Dasein's distinctive being toward death is critical, enabling us each to address our "ownmost possibility," or not, as the case may be. It is hard to know where he would begin to think about plants and death. And yet there is much to be said. With some exceptions (fruit and nuts), we kill them to eat them, and we kill whatever insects and fungi might attack our food crops, and we harvest and preserve the corpses of great plants for our many purposes. We have noted that we use dead plants for fuel, and we are destroying our atmosphere by burning them. Plants are, as it were, at the heart of a giant thanateconomy, a phytobiopolitics. Even as my bamboo chimes sound out their gentle clinking resonances.

POISON AND CURE

Plants fascinate us in other ways. Constitutive coevolution connects our bodies intimately with what is edible in the fields and woods, and what is available for selection. Concern with the destruction of the Amazon rainforest does not end with its role as a terrestrial lung. It is a massive reservoir of actual and potential medicinal plants. Some, to continue the death theme, make excellent poisons. English yew, wolfsbane, castor bean, Quaker button, doll's eyes, water hemlock, white snakeroot—there's a long list of plants that will kill you if ingested. But the highly complex chemicals that plants create for their own purposes—often as defenses of the immobile against insects and grazing animals—often have genuine health benefits for humans. Famously, aspirin, from the willow tree, golden seal, ginger, witch hazel, aloe vera, ginseng, capsicum—the list goes on and on. It was once thought (Paracelsus, Boehme) that plants had signatures indicating the illness they could treat, as if they were God's pharmacy. The botanist William Coles (1626–1662) supposed that God had made "Herbes for the use of men, and hath given them particular Signatures, whereby a man may read . . . the use of them." Regarding Hypericum, he wrote, "The little holes whereof the leaves of Saint John's wort are full, doe resemble all the pores of the skin and therefore it is profitable for all hurts and wounds that can happen thereunto." If that way of thinking has fallen out of favor, we might nonetheless affirm a looser truth—that evolutionary interdependencies and commonalities between plants and animals make it exceedingly likely that the complex organic compounds created by plants for systemic and defensive purposes could actively engage with animal metabolic processes, albeit in ways not preprogrammed. This seems obvious when it comes to food, but no less plausible applied to health.

PSYCHOTROPIC PLANTS

In his *The Marriage of Heaven and Hell*, William Blake wrote, "If the doors of perception were cleansed every thing would appear to man as it is, Infinite. For man has closed himself up, till he sees all things thro' narrow chinks of his cavern." There is, however, one further category of plant effect worth giving special attention to. Plants are often used psychotropically—as stimulants, disinhibitors, and hallucinogens. Our experience with coffee, tea, and tobacco goes without saying. They allow us some measure of deliberate control over energy levels (fatigue), attention, and productivity. This can be a matter of life and death (driving, battle).

But disinhibitors and hallucinogens are perhaps more interesting philosophically. For the first I am thinking primarily of alcoholic products, all fermented plant products (esp. grapes and grain). As for the second, the list begins with cannabis, mescaline (cactus), opium (poppy). And of course, beyond plants, magic mushrooms.

I cannot possibly do justice to the role plants play here. Numerous ancient cultures deployed hallucinogens in shamanic rituals, enabling healing, divination, communication with spirits, and war preparation—practices central to their cultures, in ways in which the symbolic and the material overlap. Arguably, our own society has simply legitimated alcohol as its disinhibiting drug of choice, with marijuana recently making modest inroads. The philosophical interest is also considerable—allow me to make just one observation. Hallucinogens interfere with our normal ways of processing experience, exposing (certainly after reflection, but also viscerally) the hidden normativity of those ways. Sartre's description of the black root (see above) is said to have been influenced by mescaline (peyote). It is tempting to suppose that they lift the phenomenal veil and give us access to the noumenal—to things in themselves. Notwithstanding Blake, that is doubtful. But they do at least enable us to see things differently, and often in highly creative ways. And not just things, but also the boundaries of self, one's relation to one's body, and so on. Arguably they function in a way parallel of Husserl's *epoché*, or reduction, setting aside normal objectifying "theses" about the world.

Plants are not merely the animals of the animals, the newly excluded deserving our compassion. If Marder is right, reflection on plants, and on the categories with which we think them, is a phenomenological/ hermeneutical/deconstructive adventure, which helps us not merely understand plants better but understand ourselves. Hallucinogenic plants, then, would be the plants' plants, offering chemical assistance to a certain deconstructive skepticism about the received ways in which plant-thinking has been trapped.

My broad conclusion, which has been more of a directing presumption, is that attention to plants, along the various dimensions I have outlined, is an ethical enterprise not in requiring us to recognize the rights of plants,[12] but in reanimating wonder, opening our eyes to the unexpected depth, complexity, and dignity of plants, and the extraordinary ways in which our lives are entangled with them. Plant-thinking is inseparable from our being-with-plants.

NOTES

1. Michael Marder, *Plant-Thinking: A Philosophy of Vegetal Life* (New York: Columbia University Press, 2013); Michael Marder, *The Philosopher's Plant: An Intellectual Herbarium* (New York: Columbia University Press, 2014).
2. Marder, *Plant-Thinking*, 3, 90.
3. What we call a plant can vary. Seaweed is not strictly a plant, for example, but an algae.
4. "For 24 years the court trials of Goliad County were held under this big oak tree. Death sentences were carried out promptly, usually within a few minutes, courtesy of the tree's many handy noose-worthy branches. The tree also served as a gallows for a number of impromptu lynchings during the 1857 'Cart War' between Texans and Mexicans." See http://www.roadsideamerica.com/ story/30040.
5. See his "Letter on Humanism" in *Martin Heidegger: Basic Writings* (New York: Harper, 2009).
6. Homosexuality in societies needing to breed ever more bodies for warfare is arguably dysfunctional. In the absence of war, heteronormativity is less compelling. This example is meant purely illustratively. I do not claim this connection actually obtains, though it certainly could, and it might explain the level of passion raised by this issue.
7. G. M. Hopkins, "Pied Beauty" (1877) in *Gerard Manley Hopkins: The Major Works* (Oxford: Oxford University Press, 2009).
8. Tom Regan, *The Case for Animal Rights* (Berkeley: University of California Press, 2004).
9. Marder, *Plant-Thinking*, 95.
10. Some 300–350 million years ago.

11. See chapter 3 in *Thinking Plant Animal Human*: "Trees and Truth: Our Uncanny Arboreality," 12; and Christopher D. Stone, *Should Trees Have Standing? Law, Morality, and the Environment*, 3rd ed. (Oxford: Oxford University Press, 2010).
12. See Christopher D. Stone, *Should Trees Have Standing? Law, Morality, and the Environment*, 3rd ed. (Oxford: Oxford University Press, 2010).

Main Pathway: Orientations

Subthemes

Proceed to Experience, p. 173
Proceed to Ethics, p. 205

12

INTRODUCTION TO PLANT-THINKING

Michael Marder

Of all the beings that are, presumably the most difficult to think about are living creatures, because on the one hand they are in a certain way most closely akin to us, and on the other are at the same time separated from our ek-sistent essence by an abyss.
—Martin Heidegger, "Letter on Humanism," *Being and Time*

Ab herbis igitur que terre radicitus herent, radicem disputationis sumam.
—Adelard of Bath, *Questiones naturales*

The recent explosion of philosophical interest in the "question of the animal"[1] has contributed at the same time to the growing field of environmental ethics (with approaches ranging from Tom Regan's defense of animal rights to Peter Singer's utilitarian argument for animal liberation) and to the decentering of the metaphysical image of the human, who, as we now realize, stands in a constitutive relation to its nonhuman others.

Despite strong tendencies toward the silencing of ontological preoccupations in certain ethical considerations of animality, it would be a mistake to segregate the two sets of contributions into distinct philosophical subfields. Ontological approaches to the question of the animal carry with them significant ethical

Originally published as "Introduction," *Plant-Thinking: A Philosophy of Vegetal Life* (New York: Columbia University Press, 2013), 1–13. Reprinted with permission.

implications as much for our treatment of these non-human "others" as for the human view of and relation to ourselves, while ethical debates on this question unavoidably make basic presuppositions regarding the very being of animals and humans. It is this intersection of ethics and ontology that allows current explorations of animality in philosophy to retain their critical edge, ensuring that they neither slide into a highly speculative metadiscourse on biology nor culminate in a set of normative and, in the last instance, vacuous prescriptions. And it is at the same intersection that new and more daring demands arise: to extend the scope of ethical treatment and to address the diverse modes of being of all living beings, many of them deemed too insignificant and mundane to even deserve the appellation "others."

The above twin demand, however, is yet to be heard. If animals have suffered marginalization throughout the history of Western thought, then non-human, non-animal living beings, such as plants, have populated the margin of the margin, the zone of absolute obscurity undetectable on the radars of our conceptualities. Particularly after the scientific paradigm gained its hard-won independence from theologico-philosophical dogma in early modernity, philosophers, for the most part, refrained from problematizing vegetal life, which they entrusted to the care of botanists and, later on, geneticists, ecologists, and microbiologists. The being of plants was no longer question-worthy; it did not present itself as a problem to those who took the time to contemplate it, let alone to those who made immediate use of the fruit or the flower, the root or parts of the tree-trunk.

But where the questioning impulse is dormant, ontological chimeras and ethical monstrosities rear their heads without delay. In the absence of the will to think through the logic of vegetal life, beyond its biochemical, cellular, or micromolecular processes and ecological patterns, philosophers readily assumed that within the broad evolutionary frame of reference, the existence of plants is less developed or less differentiated than that of their animal and human counterparts and that therefore vegetal beings are unconditionally available for unlimited use and exploitation. Such suppression of the most basic question regarding plants became the breeding ground for their ethical neglect; although—akin to us—they are living creatures, we fail to detect the slightest resemblances to our life in them and, as a consequence of this failure, routinely pass a negative judgment on their worth, as well as on the place they occupy in the modern version of the "Great Chain of Being," from which both the everyday and the scientific ways of thinking have not yet completely emancipated themselves. On the obverse of this unquestioned familiarity, plants are wholly other and foreign to us, so long as we have not yet encountered them, as it were, on their own turf—so long as we have neither let them be, flourish, and appear as they are, nor done justice to them by means of this very onto-phenomenological "letting-be."

Thus formulated, our initial task is twofold: first, to give anew prominence to vegetal life, retracing the paradigm shift that had already taken place between Aristotle's investigations of *animalia* and Theophrastus's studies of plants, and, second, to scrutinize the uncritical assumptions on the basis of which this life has been hitherto explained. And yet, critique is not a panacea here: the indiscriminate dictates of a critical, analytical method and of the reason it shores up might prove to be of little use, since they cannot help but replicate past failures by a priori thematizing and objectifying what invites the inquiry in the first place or, negatively put, by spurning the method that we could adopt from the plants themselves. At a still more fundamental level, therefore, the question is: How is it possible for us to encounter plants? And how can we maintain and nurture, without fetishizing it, their otherness in the course of this encounter?

Human beings have a wide array of possible approaches to the world of vegetation at their disposal. More often than not, we overlook trees, bushes, shrubs, and flowers in our everyday dealings, to the extent that these plants form the inconspicuous backdrop of our lives—especially within the context of "urban landscaping"—much like the melodies and songs that unobtrusively create the desired ambience in cafes and restaurants.[2] In this inconspicuousness, we take plants for granted, so that our practical lack of attention appropriately matches their marginalization within philosophical discourses. Curiously enough, the ab, solute familiarity of plants coincides with their sheer strangeness, the incapacity of humans to recognize elements of ourselves in the form of vegetal being, and, hence, the uncanny-strangely familiar-nature of our relation to them.[3] In other settings, like a farm or a field of cultivated cereals, the plants' inconspicuousness is, to be sure, modified to include the instrumental attitude that sees through and past the plants themselves to what their uses might be and that treats them as nothing but potential fuel: a source of biodiesel or a vital ingredient of human and animal nutrition. When instrumentalizing plants, we do not yet encounter them, even though their outlines become to some extent more determinate thanks to the intentional comportment on the part both of those who tend them and, less so, of those who ultimately consume them. Still, the uses to which we put vegetal beings do not exhaust what (or who) they are but, on the contrary, obfuscate enormous regions of their being.

Are we perhaps in a better position to encounter the plants themselves—for instance, sunflowers—when we do not know what to do with them, are reluctant to interfere with their complex innermost workings, and simply contemplate them as they grow in a field? When we reconstruct their luminous yellowness in memory, in imagination, or on a physical canvas, as Vincent Van Gogh did at the end of the nineteenth century, depicting, more than anything else, the ephemeral nature of the flowers? Or, when we *think* the sunflowers?

The aesthetic attitude, broadly conceived, seems to be more propitious to a nonviolent approach to plants than either their practical instrumentalization or their nominalist, conceptual integration into systems of thought. In the West, nominalism has been the prevalent method of thinking about plants, integrated into ever more detailed classificatory schemas. According to Carl Linnaeus and his famous taxonomic method, I should be satisfied that I know the sunflower if I discover that it belongs to the kingdom Plantae, order Asterales, family Asteracaeae, subfamily Helianthoideae, tribe Heliantheae, and genus *Helianthus*. These names are meant to capture the essence of the plant by assigning to it an exact place in a dead, albeit highly differentiated, system that swallows up the sunflower's singularity and uniqueness. The actual sunflower turns into an example of the genus, tribe, and so forth, to which it belongs and is nothing in itself outside the intricate net of classifications wherein it is caught up.

Conceptualism—particularly that of the Hegelian variety—endeavors, on the other hand, to enliven dead systems of thought, to set them in dialectical motion. But it too loses its authority in the course of considering the living flower to be nothing but a vanishing mediator, a transitory moment in the reproduction of the genus and in the passage from inorganic world to organic life, not to mention a point of transition to the fruit in a grand teleology that justifies the thorough instrumentalization of plants for animal and human purposes. Nominalist classifications and conceptual mediations join forces in violating the flower in a move tantamount to its cognitive plucking, a detachment from the ground of its existence. What they grasp, however, is a plant already dead and dry (as though it, in the first place, germinated on the page of an herbarium), deprived of its distinctiveness, and turned into a museum artifact in the labyrinths of thought.

Needless to say, the extremes of nominalism and conceptualism do not exhaust the possibilities of thinking the sunflower. Closer to the aesthetic attitude, charged with the task of reproducing or recreating the plant in imagination (and thus partaking of the reproductive potential of vegetation itself), the resources of twentieth- and twenty-first-century philosophy have much to offer to the thinking *of* plants that arises from and perpetually returns to vegetal beings. Instead of interposing additional conceptual mediations or more detailed and thorough classifications, the aim of this thinking is to reduce, minimize, put under erasure, bracket, or parenthesize the real and ideal barriers humans have erected between themselves and plants. The resources I am referring to are drawn from hermeneutic phenomenology, deconstruction, and weak thought-all consenting, in various ways, to let beings be, to save singularities from the clasp of generalizing abstraction, and perhaps to put thought in the service of finite life.

Before mining these promising reserves of contemporary philosophy for the methodology of "plant-thinking," it is worth noting that they do not stand alone in their respectful attitude toward vegetation. Non-Western and feminist philosophies contain a wealth of venerable traditions much more attuned to the floral world than any author or mainstream current in the history of Western thought. Plotinus's exceptional theoretical attention to plants and their life (to be explored below) is perhaps itself explicable with reference to his thorough knowledge of Indian philosophy and, especially, Uppanishadic and Advaita Vedantic thought. In the Indian milieu, Jain philosophy ascribed great significance to plants, so much so that it understood them to be the fifth element comprising the universe, alongside the other classical elements: earth, water, fire, and air.[4] And, in a different context altogether, one of the leading feminist philosophers in today's Europe, Luce Irigaray, semi-poetically elaborates the intimate link between a certain version of receptive subjectivity, thinking, and the plant: "The plant will have nourished the mind which contemplates the blooming of its flower."[5]

Although there is much in these heterogeneous sources that is of undeniable value to a coherent philosophy of vegetation, in the current project I limit myself to the history and "after-history" of Western metaphysics. I do so not only because the ideological roots of both the deepening environmental crisis and the exploitation of plants are buried in treatises by some of the most emblematic representatives of this tradition, but also because, on the fringes of Western philosophy and in its aftermath, surprisingly heterodox approaches to the vegetal world have germinated. The import of the external critiques of metaphysics is undeniable. But if a hope for reversing the philosophical neglect of plants in the West and for overcoming the environmental crisis of which this neglect is a part is to stay alive, immanent (internal) criticism of the metaphysical tradition must become a sine qua non of any reflection on vegetal life. This is why, aside from the symptomatic sites in the history of metaphysics itself, three of the most illustrious branches of post-metaphysical thought furnish, through their oft-unintended consequences, the theoretical framework for rethinking the being of plants.

Thus: Hermeneutical phenomenology advocates the kind of description that, going back to the things themselves, interprets them from the ground up and addresses each experience from the standpoint peculiar to it, all the while guarding against any unwarranted presuppositions about its subject matter. Deconstruction exposes metaphysical violence against the material, the singular, the finite; strives to do justice to what metaphysics has suppressed, while admitting that absolute justice—as the utmost attention to singularity—is impossible; and permits us to focus on that which has been otherwise marginalized without converting the margin into a new center. Weak thought resists the tyranny of "objective" factuality and welcomes a multiplicity of interpretations, even as it takes the side of the victims of historical and metaphysical brutality.

In other words, these three traditions put forth an ethical manner of thinking that permits the entity "thought through" to thrive (1) in the way it manifests itself and relates to the world (hermeneutical phenomenology), (2) in its own self-ruination and singularity (deconstruction), and (3) in its essentially incomplete hold on existence (weak thought). Thanks to their quasi-aesthetic receptivity, they leave just enough space for the sunflower to grow without trimming it down to an object readily available for the subject's manipulation, without assigning to it extraneous purposes, and without putting undue emphasis on the knowledge of its genetic makeup or evolutionary adaptational character. Faced with a sunflower, they would resist the easy and obvious generalization of this plant as a unitary organism and would instead joyfully submit thinking itself to the ambivalence of the flower that is both one and many, consisting as it does of a myriad small florets clustered together, yet relatively independent from each other and from the community of beings we know as *a* sunflower. Succinctly put, they create the philosophical infrastructure for our encounter with plants.

In the spirit of the three traditions I have telegraphically summarized above, *Plant-Thinking* envisages the outlines of a method drawn from the plants themselves and of a discourse rooted, as Adelard of Bath has it, in these vegetal beings. By the same token, it formulates the non-transcendental conditions of possibility for encountering plants, instead of confronting them as still-murky objects of knowledge. The participants in any encounter engage in an interactive, if not always symmetrical, relationship; and, conversely, to deny interactivity is to undercut the very prospects of an encounter. The unipolarity of reason, objectifying everything in its path, and the self-proclaimed exclusiveness of the human existential comportment, which according to Martin Heidegger separates us from other living beings "by an abyss," are two salient obstacles on the road to an ontologically and ethically sensitive relation to plants.

It follows that the eventful encounter with plants whereby we find ourselves in the greatest proximity to them without negating their otherness cannot come to pass unless we entertain the hypothesis that vegetal life is coextensive with a distinct subjectivity with which we might engage, and which engages with us more frequently than we imagine. This is not to say that human beings and plants are but examples of the underlying universal agency of Life itself; nor is it to plead for an excessive anthropomorphism, modeling the subjectivity of vegetal being on our personhood. Rather, the point is that plants are capable, in their own fashion, of accessing, influencing, and being influenced by a world that does not overlap the human *Lebenswelt*, but that corresponds to the vegetal modes of dwelling on and in the earth. A counterpoint to both classical and existential idealisms, plant-thinking situates the plant at the fulcrum of its world, the elemental terrain it inhabits without laying claim to or appropriating it. Strictly speaking, Heidegger is correct in arguing that plants, along with the other non-human beings, do not *have* a world, but this not-having or non-possessiveness does not at all signify the sheer absence of what we might call "plant-world," only a different relation of vegetal beings to their environment. Whenever human beings encounter plants, two or more worlds (and temporalities) intersect: to accept this axiom is already to let plants maintain their otherness, respecting the uniqueness of their existence.

Once again, the ontological and the ethical facets of the inquiry have converged at the threshold where the outlines of the vegetal world emerge thanks to our disinclination to conflate plants with complacent things immersed and dissolved in the human environment. At the same time, the task has become more difficult than ever before: we must give prominence to plants, taking care to avoid their objective description, and thereby preserve their alterity. Unlike Jacob von Uexkull, who, in his highly influential A *Foray Into the Worlds of Animals and Humans*, invited the reader to "walk into unknown worlds,"[6] we will not assert an unconditional right of admission into the vegetal world, which is the world *of* and *for* plants, accessible to them. The challenge is to let plants be within the framework of what, from our standpoint, entails profound obscurity, which, throughout the history of Western philosophy, has been the marker of their life. Differently put, the idea is to allow plants to flourish on the edge or at the limit of phenomenality, of visibility, and, in some sense, of "the world."

Of the three theoretical currents at the confluence of which this book stands, phenomenology, with its usual insistence on the coming-to-light and the appearance of beings under the thematizing gaze of the transcendental Ego, may seem particularly suspect when it comes to respecting the obscurity of vegetal existence. Even so, it will prove handy here, provided that it accommodates plants' constitutive subjectivity, drastically different from that of human beings, and describes their world from the hermeneutical perspective of vegetal ontology (i.e., from the standpoint of the plant itself). How does the world appear (or not appear) to a plant? What is its relation to its world? What does it strive to, direct itself toward, or intend?

A skeptic would retort that, assuming a vegetal phenomenology nascent in these questions were even plausible, it would have to be enacted by the plants themselves—an absurd proposition, to say the least. There is little doubt that the sense of the world from the animal, let alone the vegetal, standpoint remains inaccessible to us. Nevertheless, the distance between us and other living creatures loses its static character as soon as the nominal categorial divisions between various "classes" of beings are shaken and muddled, without compromising these beings' differences and commonalities. The gap separating humans from plants may dwindle—though not altogether disappear—thanks to the discovery of traces of the latter in the former, and vice versa. (What kind of traces are these? The human body and subjectivity alike are not pure expressions of Spirit but strange archives, surfaces of inscription for the vestiges of the inorganic world, of plant growth, and of animality—all of which survive and lead a clandestine afterlife in us, as us. Just as well, past and present human intentions and projections are caught up in the fabric of plant existence, reflecting histories of cross-breeding, grafting, agricultural technologies, aesthetic representations of the flora . . .) Cast in Kantian terms, vegetal phenomenology supplies plant-thinking with a normative ideal, the ideal we might approximate but never reach, unable, as it were, to put ourselves entirely in the plants' shoes, or rather roots.

The productive ambiguity haunting the title of this volume further emphasizes the ineluctable paradoxes of vegetal ontology. "Plant-thinking" refers, in the same breath, to (1) the non-cognitive, non-ideational, and non-imagistic mode of thinking *proper to* plants (what I later call "thinking without the head"); (2) the human thinking *about* plants; (3) how human thinking is, to some extent, de-humanized and rendered plant-like, altered by its encounter with the vegetal world; and finally, (4) the ongoing symbiotic relation between this transfigured thinking and the existence of plants. A sound philosophy of vegetal life must rely on the combination of these four senses of "plant-thinking," so as not to dominate (and in dominating, distort) the target of its investigations. The chances of aggravating the abuse of plants by theorizing their existence can be minimized, if the theorists themselves expose their cogitation to the logic of vegetal life and learn from it, to the point where their thinking is ready to melt into this logic, with which admittedly it will never be identical.

No genuine encounter happens without our eventful exposure, unwilled and unplanned, to that which, or the one who, is thus encountered. "Plant-thinking" is in the first place the promise and the name of an encounter, and therefore it may be read as an invitation to abandon the familiar terrain of human and humanist thought and to meet vegetal life, if not in the place where it is, then at least halfway. Part I, "Vegetal Anti-Metaphysics," clears the philosophical ground for this event by putting in question the metaphysical constructions of the plant and of what constitutes "the ground," by showing how in its very being the plant accomplishes a lived destruction of metaphysics, and by carrying out a transvaluation of metaphysical values as they pertain to vegetation. The outcomes of the critique of metaphysics are not entirely negative, given that the contours of plant life come into view as a result of the hermeneutical multiplication of its meanings released from the reductive tendencies of metaphysics that, from Aristotle to Nietzsche, ascribed to it but a single function. Indeed, these contours get redrawn as soon as we turn back to the classical notion of "plant-soul"-a notion that, despite its metaphysical heritage, exceeds the limits of metaphysics from within, to the point of overflowing them-with its countless potentialities, valid, in distinct ways, for plants, animals, and humans.

In discussing plant-soul, it would be unforgivable obdurately to insist on the traditional metaphysical separation between the "soul" and the "body" of the plant, which is only one of the many dichotomies—self and other, depth and surface, life and death, the one and the many, and so forth—practically deconstructed in vegetal existence. The positive dimension of plant-being, as the outcome of the critique of metaphysics, will spell out an inversion of traditional valuations, valorizing the other over the self, surface over depth, and so on. More critically still, it will incorporate the core existential attributes philosophers have tended to reserve for human beings alone. I call the elements of this budding ontology, discussed in part II, "vegetal existentiality."

The intimation that it is high time to approach the existence of plants existentially is surely scandalous within the confines of Heidegger's thought and of post-Heideggerian existentialism, let alone the humanist and anthropocentric traditions of philosophy. In technical terms, its cardinal sin is that it transgresses the boundaries, firmly set in *Being and Time*, between the categorial and the existential analytics, between the categories of readiness-to-hand and presence-at-hand and the *existentiales*, such as the moods or anxiety. The initial shock the transgression may provoke will have been absorbed already in the analysis of the vegetal soul in the preceding part of the study, and it should gradually wear off once I formulate and flesh out the central concern of "Vegetal Existentiality": What are the modes of being-in-the-world appropriate to plants? Among such modes, I concentrate on temporality, freedom, and wisdom.

Just as the soul of the plant is hardly distinguishable from its body, so its time is barely dissociable from space: its outward growth and augmentation, devoid of any final accomplishment, constitutes the "bad infinity" of vegetal temporality. To be more precise, the spatio-temporal movement of plants, nonsynchronous with human time, is directed toward and by the other (light, the changing seasons, etc.) and therefore, unfolding as a hetero-temporality, is governed by the time of the other. Seasonal variation, for its part, imposes cyclical and iterable existence on perennial plants and spells out the finitude of the annual ones.

The indissoluble connection of the plant to the time of the other mirrors its spatial rootedness in the soil, a feature responsible for its coding as the figure of unfreedom. Tragically, occidental thought conflates the most plastic form of existence with the most rigid; not only does this view disregard the ontic exuberance and uncontrollable efflorescence of vegetal life, but it also ignores this life's ontological potentialities, still working themselves out in various guises in animals and human beings—the variations that free it to be otherwise than it is. On the one hand, both colloquial and philosophical discourses associate the rooted mode of being with immobility and captivity, but, on the other, the perceived indifference of plants interlaces their freedom with human liberty in the domains of ethics, aesthetics, and religion. Despite their undeniable embeddedness in the environment, plants embody the kind of detachment human beings dream of in their own transcendent aspiration to the other, Beauty, or divinity.

The living tending of plants toward their other, the tending expressed in growth, the acquisition of nutrients, and procreation, amounts to the non-conscious intentionality of vegetal life, the cornerstone of its "sagacity." In keeping with vegetal ontology, plant-thinking practices an embodied, finite, and material expression; is wholly oriented to the other without establishing either an identity or a self-identity achievable by means of its return to itself; and stands for the impersonal, non-individuated *it thinks* underlying and subverting the ever-present synthesis of *I think*, the accompaniment of all conscious representations.

The uninterrupted connection between plant-thinking and human thought finally becomes apparent when we circle back to the figure of the vegetal soul—from which the animal and human psyches emanate and which is sublimated (and, to a significant extent, dematerialized) in them—and discover the rudiments of a living intelligence in this figure. An encounter with plants awaits us. Far from a head-on confrontation, it will verge on what, in Portuguese, is called *desencontro*—an untranslatable word, which roughly refers either to a narrowly missed meeting, a crossing of paths that was about to happen but ended up not taking place, or to an encounter that is too improbable and was never meant to happen, or, again, to a divergence of two or more (usually human) beings, each of them existing on her or his own wavelength. To meet the plants themselves, the plants as such, is not the goal of this study, if only because, in the absence of identity, they are never "themselves" and because, resistant to idealization, they do not fit within the strict philosophical confines of the "as such." All we can hope for is to brush upon the edges of their being, which is altogether outer and exposed, and in so doing to grow past the fictitious shells of *our* identity and *our* existential ontology. Are we ready to take the initial, timid steps in the anamnesis of the vegetal heritage proper to human beings, the very forgetting of which we have all but forgotten? Whether or not we will be capable of recognizing plants, and especially ourselves, in the wake of the anamnestic encounter-*desencontro* is yet to be seen.

NOTES

Epigraph: "I shall, then, take the root of the disputation from plants, which are fixed in the ground by their roots" (Adelard of Bath, 1998, 93).

1. The recent philosophical literature on this topic is too extensive to allow as much as a representative sampling here. Still, it is worth highlighting the work of the following scholars:

Agamben (2003); Buchana (2008); Calarco (2008); Derrida (2008); Francione (2009); Haraway (2007); Linzey (2009); Oliver (2009); Regan (2006); Singer (2002); Sorabji (1995); Steiner (2010); and Wolfe (2003).

2. For the notion of "plant landscape" see J. Brosse (1958).
3. For the lack of human interest in plants, explained with reference to the difference between human and vegetal beings, see F. Hallé (2002, 17ff).
4. Larson, Bhattacharya, and Potter (2010, p. 165).
5. Irigaray (1992, p. 32).
6. J. Von Uexküll (2010, p. 41).

REFERENCES

Adelard of Bath. 1998. *Conversations with His Nephew: On the Same and the Different; Questions on Natural Science; and On Birds*. Edited and translated by C. Burnett. Cambridge, UK: Cambridge University Press.

Agamben, G. 2003. *The Open: Man and Animal*. Translated by K. Attell. Stanford, CA: Stanford University Press.

Brosse, J. 1958. *L'ordre des choses*. Paris: Plon.

Buchana, B. 2008. *Onto-Ethologies: The Animal Environments of Uexküll, Heidegger, Merleau-Ponty, and Deleuze*. Albany, NY: SUNY Press.

Calarco, M. 2008. *Zoographies: The Question of the Animal from Heidegger to Derrida*. New York: Columbia University Press.

Derrida, J. 2008. *The Animal That Therefore I Am*. Translated by D. Wills. New York: Fordham University Press.

Francione, G. 2009. *Animals as Persons: Essays on the Abolition of Animal Exploitation*. New York: Columbia University Press.

Hallé, F. 2002. *In Praise of Plants*. Cambridge, UK: Timber Press.

Haraway, D. 2007. *When Species Meet*. Minneapolis: University of Minneapolis Press.

Heidegger, M. 1962. *Being and Time*. Translated by J. Macquarrie and E. Robinson. New York: Harper and Row.

Irigaray, L. 1992. *Elemental Passions*. Translated by J. Collie and J. Still. London: Athlone Press.

Larson, G. J., R. Bhattacharya, and K. H. Potter. 2010. *Encyclopedia of Indian Philosophies*, Vol. 4: *Asmkhya, A Dualist Tradition in Indian Philosophy*. Delhi, India: Motilal Banarsidass.

Linzey, A. 2009. *Why Animal Suffering Matters: Philosophy, Theology, and Practical Ethics*. Oxford: Oxford University Press.

Oliver, K. 2009. *Animal Lessons: How They Teach Us to Be Human*. New York: Columbia University Press.

Regan, T. 2006. *Defending Animal Rights*. Urbana: University of Illinois Press.

Singer, P. 2002. *Animal Liberation*. New York: Harper Collins.

Sorabji, R. 1995. *Animal Minds and Human Morals: The Origins of the Western Debate*. Ithaca, NY: Cornell University Press.

Steiner, G. 2010. *Anthropocentrism and Its Discontents: The Moral Status of Animals in the History of Western Philosophy*. Pittsburgh, PA: University of Pittsburgh Press.

von Uexküll, J. 2010. *A Foray into the Worlds of Animals and Humans*. Translated by J. D. O'Neill. Minneapolis: University of Minnesota Press.

Wolfe, C. 2003. *Zoontologies: The Question of the Animal*. Minneapolis: University of Minnesota Press.

Main Pathway: Orientations

Subthemes

Proceed to Experience, p. 205
Proceed to Place, p. 291

13

INTERVIEW WITH JONATHON KEATS

How do you identify the species of plants you decide to work with? What parameters guide your selection process and why?

JONATHON KEATS: My decisions are guided by the physiology of plants and the different ways in which different species grow, reproduce, and experience the world. One of my first works for flora involved the construction of a movie theater where I projected films onto plants' foliage, such that they could absorb the content by photosynthesis. To appeal to my botanical audience, I produced pornography, filming honeybees pollinating flowers from the plants' perspective. For obvious reasons, I had to select an audience in bloom. It would have made no sense to project the porn onto asexual ferns.

Lately, I have begun to collaborate with plants as natural timekeepers, engaging their deep relationship with local and global environmental conditions, and observing how those conditions manifest in phenological traits such as the timing of fluorescence and propagation. My motivation is to provide an alternative to the regular beat of mechanical and electronic clocks, which have been instrumental to human domination of the planet through industrialization. Each species of plant offers a distinctive temporal perspective, which also differs from one place to another. Biodiversity is foundational to my interest in surfacing "chronodiversity," which in turn can provide a pluralistic view of local and global ecology.

Do you ever consider plants as subjects in your work, and how does that change your approach to them?

JK: In many of my early works, plants were my primary subjects, meaning that the works were made for them. Humans were secondary, vicariously experiencing the work by observing the plants experiencing the work directly. My pornography for plants is an example of this, as are my subsequent travel documentaries (which expose houseplants to video documentation of foreign skies) and my photosynthetic restaurant (an outdoor installation that filters sunlight for culinary pleasure).

That said, I was also attentive to how these works were encountered by my fellow humans, striving to make them as accessible as possible, because a secondary motivation was philosophical: by encouraging people to view plants engaged in activities familiar to humans, I sought to close the artificial divide between humans and other species—collapsing dubious anthropocentric hierarchies—while simultaneously engaging plants' manifest otherness to reveal the unnoticed assumptions underlying activities we engage in on an everyday basis. Seeing the familiar in unfamiliar circumstances—and the unfamiliar in familiar circumstances—we no longer take our assumptions for granted.

I have also occasionally approached plants as artists in various genres. For example, back in 2006, I provided 50 Leyland cypress trees with drawing implements and easels, facilitating their self-expression in a vernacular familiar to humans. The gestural abstractions they produced as the wind set their limbs in motion, recorded in strokes particular to their physical structure, were framed and exhibited with full credit given to them as creators. Presented as agrifolk art, the work encouraged people to recognize trees' individuality and the evolutionary intelligence of growth patterns responsive to environmental conditions, including air circulation.

In your artistic practice, what have you learned from the plants themselves? In which ways does your art follow their movements, metamorphoses, and modes of being in the world? How does it interact with these vegetal processes?

JK: Engaging plants as artists and evaluating their artwork, I have become more sensitive to their morphology and dynamics than I was previously. However, I have most seriously and persistently sought instruction from flora by recognizing the authority of plants in domains where humans have presumed to be omniscient or omnipotent.

As mentioned above, I'm currently developing environmentally grounded clocks and calendars that are calibrated by plants. The idea is simple, but the effects are potentially profound. Conceptually I'm developing a system that rejects the conventional human notion that plant growth is variable in relation to technical time; instead, my system acknowledges the seasonal activity and cumulative growth of each and every plant as a valid time standard in relation to which our seconds and minutes and years vary in duration.

For example, I'm working with the Desert Laboratory on Tumamoc Hill at the University of Arizona on annual calendars based on phenology—with the botanical year divided into periods of gestation, fluorescence, propagation, and dormancy—instead of using months of preestablished length. You might plan to meet on the 9th of fluorescence, but you cannot predict when that will occur while the plant is still in the period of gestation.

I'm also working, with the Long Now Foundation and the Center for Art + Environment at the Nevada Museum of Art, on a monumental clock and calendar calibrated by the growth of a bristlecone pine tree over its multi-millennial lifespan. Building on the fact that trees have traditionally been used as calendars by dendrochronologists, who count their rings to calculate the years, and also recognizing the fact that the rings of a tree are thicker or thinner based on environmental factors such as precipitation and carbon dioxide level, I take the current average growth rate as a baseline. The clock runs more quickly or more slowly if growth is faster or slower than this average.

What ethical or political considerations inform your work with plants? What are the ethical and political implications of this work?

JK: Botanical time reckoning is not only an occasion for deeper observation of the natural world. It's also the foundation of a political proposition about temporal authority. Ever since the Industrial Revolution (and arguably earlier than that), humans have sought to control the planet through coordinated action. From railroads to the assembly line, this coordination is based on technical measurement of time. A botanical time standard—or better a multiplicity of botanical time standards representative of planetary chronodiversity—undermines the self-serving human advantage of technical time and respects other life-forms. My clocks and calendars can support an important and heretofore unrecognized right of nature: the right of all beings to live at their own pace.

Another current endeavor addresses ethics and politics even more directly, by seeking political enfranchisement of plants as a practical improvement and an ethical necessity. Based at San José State University, and in partnership with Earth Law Center, my phytodemocracy initiative registers the political will of plants by monitoring their stress level. For instance, increased production of the stress-induced phytohormone ethylene indicates dissatisfaction with the status quo and counts as a vote for change.

Although a Constitutional amendment will be required for the botanical vote to count in elections, polling plants and informing people of the results can influence how people vote and even how politicians behave. Like my botanical clocks, which react to anthropogenic climate change by speeding up or slowing down according to human standards, measurement of plants' well-being in political terms can drive a salubrious feedback loop. However, the proposition is more than merely instrumental. Given that the vast majority of life on Earth is vegetal, we need to recognize the political will of plants if we're to take democracy seriously.

What, if any, are the aspects of your work with plants related to the current global environmental and mass extinction crises?

JK: To survive the Anthropocene—and to prevent it from becoming more than an unfortunate episode in a Greater Holocene—we need the benefit from vegetal insight. For that benefit to affect us sufficiently, plants need greater autonomy. For this reason, my focus has also come to encompass economics. Political power is often a matter of financial clout. Therefore I've been working with Earth Law Center to revise banking law to allow plants to accumulate wealth. Money might accrue in botanical bank accounts through fair compensation for so-called ecosystem services. We might also revise intellectual property law such that biomimetic inventions financially benefit the plants and animals that are the inventors of those biomimetic technologies. In partnership with Earth Law Center, I'm currently building the groundwork for voluntary registration of other species' patent claims through the Interspecies Technology Transfer Consortium.

As always, I see the ethical merits and practical benefits as intertwined. Plants contribute far more to the global economy than humans, and it's only fair that their contribution be compensated according to our economic system (as long as our economic system is in place). The radical redistribution of wealth will moderate human control over the planet and may even address economic problems we have not been able to solve on our own, such as how to manage climate risk. Based on their distributed observation of environmental conditions and their evolved responses to ecological instability, the economic activities of plants can bring greater resilience to the global financial system as a whole. Their investment strategies and approaches to exchange of resources may have even greater impact if adapted by humans. And this systemic biomimicry, if legally recognized as their intellectual property, can be an additional source of income for flora.

Which pressing challenge, or challenges, has working with plants presented to you?

JK: None of the propositions I have mentioned are easily realized. To live on arboreal time, or to participate in a phytodemocracy as a minority species with minimal purchasing power, requires a level of humility that doesn't come easily to *Homo sapiens*. To practice what I preach is almost impossible in the present world, and I struggle with it personally while also working against long odds to achieve it institutionally. More often than not, I am hypocritical. More often than not, I am ineffectual. Yet I must admit that the challenges are exciting in addition to being important. I wouldn't be human if I were wholly altruistic.

How is the interaction between your artistic practice and theoretical endeavors shaped by vegetal life?

JK: My artistic practice is both political and philosophical. I trained in philosophy, and the artworks I create are designed to operate as philosophical instruments supporting open-ended thought experiments. A clock calibrated by a tree, or a voting booth that registers the will of a plant, can provoke questions about who we are as a species and how the world functions. Equally, they are tools that can be enlisted, if we choose, to replace the anthropocentric mechanisms already in place. They facilitate collective self-reflection and stand ready to enact a possible future if the possible future they evoke in the service of collective self-reflection is the future collectively recognized to be most beneficial to all.

Many of my philosophical instruments are vegetal. Vegetal life is at the core of many of my thought experiments. Vegetal life also dominates the possible future that my thought experiments posit. To a great extent, I investigate the world from a vegetal perspective. To a large degree, I want a vegetal perspective to become central to how the world works in the future.

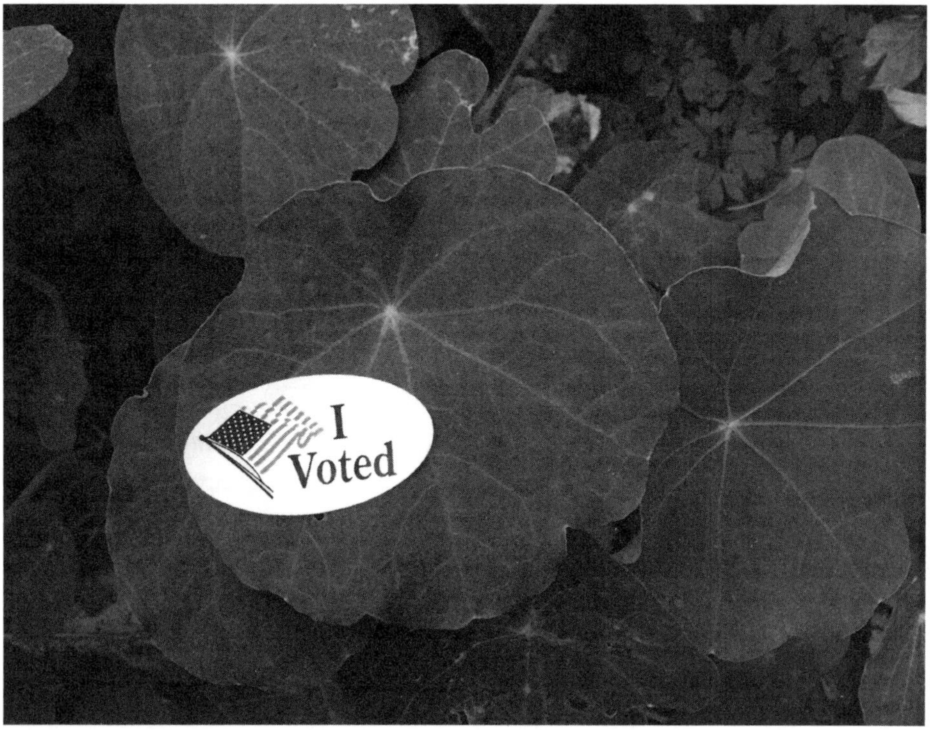

Phytodemocracy (Experiment in Botanical Enfranchisement), 2020, Jonathon Keats.

Jonathon Keats is an artist, writer, and experimental philosopher based in the United States and Europe. His conceptually driven transdisciplinary projects explore all aspects of society, adapting methods from the sciences and the humanities. He is currently a research associate at the University of Arizona's Desert Laboratory on Tumamoc Hill, a visiting scholar at San Jose State University's CADRE Laboratory for New Media, a Polar Lab artist at the Anchorage Museum, and an artist-in-residence at both the SETI Institute and UC San Francisco's Memory and Aging Center. He is the subject of a new monograph titled *Thought Experiments*, published by Hirmer Verlag.

14

INTERVIEW WITH ŠPELA PETRIČ

How do you identify the species of plants you decide to work with? What parameters guide your selection process and why?

ŠPELA PETRIČ: Looking back, the working relationships with particular plant species feel serendipitous, which speaks to the combination of coincidence, convenience, and subsequent attunement folded into what appears as choice; in actuality, it's often a process of trial and error. Sometimes the desires don't align with plant capacities. Sometimes plants that have been the most influential don't even appear in the works!

During the development of the never-realized *Parabiotic Stranger*, I was investigating the possibility of becoming host to a parasitic plant species, the alien-looking *Cuscuta*. This genus of non-photosynthetic plants is used in biotech research to transmit intracellular pathogens as they tap into the sap of different host plants like tomato and pepper, essentially connecting their circulatory systems. I eventually realized that because human serum lacked key molecular signals, which *Cuscuta* needed to form suckers, there wasn't much of a chance they would accept fluids from my body without another plant acting as the intermediary, which undermined the premise. However, while cultivating *Cuscuta* for half a year, I formed an unusual predatory allyship with them, where a visit to the Saturday market always also meant scouting for "fresh blood" I would bring back to the threadlike parasites. It's awkward to say it, but this non-photosynthesizing creature disillusioned me from idealizing plants as exclusively generous; it confronted me with the hard realization that caring for some will involve killing others, and finally that the word "plant" was an unfair generalization for a "green Other" which particular vegetal entities are not. *Cuscuta* thus offered me some of the first vegetal teachings, a bit of which subsequent projects carry.

Another serendipitous choice was garden cress in the 20-hour process of intercognition during the performance *Skotopoises*. I stood still to cast a shadow on the cress, which I chose because of its rapid germination, but unwittingly its pungent smell tapped into the visitors' own experience of vegetal intimacy with the popular sandwich and soup condiment. Being implicated in the plants' consumption, the audience became part of the ethical questions by association.

Finally, the work *Institute for Inconspicuous Languages: Reading Lips* is a tongue-in-cheek insistence on understanding the secret language of plants, where the opening and closing of leaf pores (stomata) observed under the microscope is subsequently interpreted through lip reading. Originally the acting role was meant for *Ficus benjamina*, a houseplant that I had grown up with and so actually spent 18 years with. But upon inspection, I noticed the *Ficus*'s stomata were barely visible and slow to react. I searched the internet for "obvious stomata experiment for schools" and *Tradescantia zebrina* popped up. What a revelation! Not only were the stomata green on a cerise background, but the inchplant is a hardy, invasive species attainable around the world, making it perfectly suited to the demands of exhibition spaces.

Do you ever consider plants as subjects in your work, and how does that change your approach to them?

SP: Purely based on principle I'm inclined to answer no, since concepts of subject/subjectivity/subjectivation were developed in support of, or relation to, human difference, whereas I'm drawn to stranger engagements with plants, questioning the commonsense framings that have colonized the vegetal world with humanistic yardsticks, and through that also uncovering insidious self-colonization practices. To be clear, even if I were only to take into account the current knowledge of plants offered by biological sciences, it would be reason enough for me to consider them fitting a non-anthropocentric, evolutionary definition of subjecthood, mysteriously majestic and respectfully unknowable. The truly intriguing aspect of plant life, however, is that it seems it couldn't care less about aligning with concepts we hold so dear.

I consider the plants involved in artworks as vegetal coworkers, which, like any other partner, have their specific needs and capacities, but also power, since I depend on their performance. I'm not driven to achieve totalizing knowledge about them, which would lend a feeling of control; I wouldn't even consider myself particularly good at caring for plants. But I do obsessively observe and learn from them through the transformations and affects they evoke, both in their material presence as well as the implications they call forth.

I am able to accept the wilting of annuals like cucumbers but am devastated by the ominous brown spots on a slow-growing philodendron. I'm enticed by begonias' revival from apparent death, but envious and alienated from them because my body doesn't possess that kind of plasticity. I enjoy staring at the potted exotics in my apartment because I am attached to the fleeting moments in their genealogy, when they are captured as companions in the cycles of production and consumption. They compel me to time beyond my individual existence. I work with plants precisely because they unsettle me in ambivalent ways, where I am never confident in my moral position.

In your artistic practice, what have you learned from the plants themselves? In which ways does your art follow their movements, metamorphoses, and modes of being in the world? How does it interact with these vegetal processes?

SP: Vegetal principles permeate the conceptual layers of my artistic explorations as I'll outline later, but formal aspects of each work are also defined by plants' needs and particularities, a type of plant-centered design, at least as far as I can grasp it.

To describe it by example, in a recent work titled *PL'AI*, we were exploring manifestations of play as an ontological condition, specifically the possibility that a robot equipped with machine learning and neural networks (aka artificial intelligence) could enter vegetal time to engage in play with the plants. But *where* do plants have the freedom to play? If in the vegetal world growth is movement, and movement behavior, I followed this principle to the tendrils of vining cucumbers, which develop opposite each leaf and search for surfaces to grab onto while the plant stretches toward the light. This evident temporo-morphological expression of environmental inquiry that isn't yet fully explained in science offered the indeterminacy that allows us to suspend our disbelief and accept plant play as a possibility.

To reciprocate the plants' openness, the robot had to approach them with an offering (after all, in spite of its contingent electromechanics and open-ended computational complexity, the "autonomous" robot is still a prosthesis for my desire). Complementing plant architecture, where elements are repeated and segments of the body adopt new tasks as they age, the machine morphology followed the same logic. Thirty-six individually controlled stainless steel wires suspended from above the patch of cucumbers move at a rate of 3 cm an hour, hovering in the space of tendrils' grasp, guessing their location but unable to fully discern them. Once the cucumber catches a wire, another type of signal instructs the neural network to stop moving it, thus transforming the robot tendrils one by one into a cucumber trellis to support their growth. The play between the cucumber and robot leaves morphological traces in the shape of the plants, the steel strings, and the neural network.

In short, being attuned to the vegetal means a deep respect for their material way of being that, as a result, provides me plant teachings that inform the work.

What ethical or political considerations inform your work with plants? What are the ethical and political implications of this work?

SP: What I appreciate most about the ethical uprooting that plants provoke is that it creates a disposition toward strategies and allyship to "make do, generously."

On a very personal and profound level, my investigations of plant otherness led me to connect the recent phenomenon of surveillance capitalism with the constructions that have rendered the vegetal subaltern. In other words, the machine-rendered "statistical human," which has called into question autonomy and individuality in various societal contexts, has finally penetrated and destabilized even the bastions of privilege (as demonstrated by the subtitle of Shoshana Zuboff's seminal work *In the Age of Surveillance Capitalism: A Fight for* the Human *Future . . .* [emphasis mine]). When our financial credit scores are assessed to get a loan, if we wear a smartwatch that tallies steps, cross the border by having our face scanned, send off a sample of our spit to learn our DNA ancestry, use Google Maps to show the quickest route, play Pokemon Go, or swipe a benefit card to rack up points, our person proliferates in the digital realm as innumerable proxies to become the "raw data immaterial" mined by governments and industry to create value. This acceleration of the transmutation of bodies into information creates an economo-biopolitic, in which our ontological opposite is no longer the plant, but the very idea of a self-determining human whose boundaries are delimited by the surface of the skin. In the eyes of algorithms, our cherished interiority is held in leaky vessels so that it appears as flat and superficial as the vegetable kingdom, like a transparent object of tabulation. In the eyes of the algorithm, we become the vegetariat. The vegetariat exists in the conflation of production and reproduction, consumer and commodity, the concrete and its abstraction.

Following this insight, I for the first time experienced plants not as an Other needing to be liberated from human extractivist practices, but as resilient and uncontainable creatures that can inspire us to thrive in totalizing circumstances: how to slip under the radar, to embrace improvised futures, to hang on to the erotics of being together outside of grand narratives, to practice imagining the ecstasy of becoming food, to proliferate to negative infinity in the digital realm, and so forth. This to me presents practices of politics and ethics attuned to vegetal life.

Through these actions that express indebtedness to their alien capacities and that resist debilitating sadness, we wade in the consequences of our species' shortsightedness.

And learn to die like plants.

Which pressing challenge, or challenges, has working with plants presented to you?

SP: There are two points I would like to mention. The first is the realization that to work with living plants in an artistic context, I will risk benevolent intentions that repeat patterns of exploitation. For example, choosing an AI-robot as the interspecies partner to play with plants in the project *PL'AI* is sensible—for one, the robot-as-prosthesis has the capacity to sense and move at plants' paces—but it also echoes mechanization in agricultural contexts whose endless intensification is justified by the equalization of plant and machine. In spite of this, I believe that with our common embeddedness in the logic of the algorithms, we cannot afford to not engage, to not get our hands dirty.

The second is that while I understand how transformative working with plants can be, it requires attention and time to peel back the layers of cultural plant-blindness to get to the juicy center. Making art with plants often feels like trying to stack a pile of things that repel each other. But when the configuration is just right, with a big grin on my face, I turn around to look at the audience and see their curious gaze pointed at something I had long since forgotten. In other words, it's one thing to develop a method that investigates pressing questions, but another to take people along on the journey. Sometimes playfulness and humor help, even when addressing urgent and devastating topics. Since many of us live in urban spaces and experience vegetal liveliness foremost through caring for potted exotics, these can also be familiar points of entry.

How is the interaction between your artistic practice and theoretical endeavors shaped by vegetal life?

SP: Foremost, plants, as the "weeds of metaphysics," radically shifted my attention from questions of "how to understand?" to "what are the *consequences* of a particular understanding?" and "what type of new understanding or attunement is needed to *change the consequences*?" This pragmatism is rooted in the spectrality of plants, whose pure exterior to me appears holographic—its flat dimensionality can paradoxically hold nearly any notion we desire, and I have had to come to terms with this conceptual excess that refracts questions of plant-being back onto us, like the incessant "this is you, but what am I?" rebuttal we would use as kids to annoy each other. The prismatic mirroring they perform in relation to theorizing is one of the things that leads me to think of plants as allies in very human matters, especially since I acknowledge our material interdependency.

That is not to say that plants lack particular and prominent ways of being in the world, but rather that they experience how we *think* of them through the effects and actions arising as a consequence. A question that often comes up in dialogue between critical thinkers and artists is how to avoid the "sin of anthropomorphization." This point beautifully demonstrates the infiltration of scientific epistemology in questions of ethics. The pursuit of objectivity in science, which strictly separates subject (the observer) and object (the observed), reinforces itself through a moral stance framed roughly as "at all cost avoid the violence of thrusting my (human) experience onto nonhumans." This position appears benevolent at first, seemingly defending a de-hierarchization by eliminating the human-as-yardstick. But I would add nuance by asking, "What violence do I risk thrusting upon nonhumans by objectifying them?" When anthropomorphization doesn't come from the disembodied scientific "we," but from a lived experience and situated knowledge, people are invested in relations with imagination and affect, which results in different narratives and different risks.

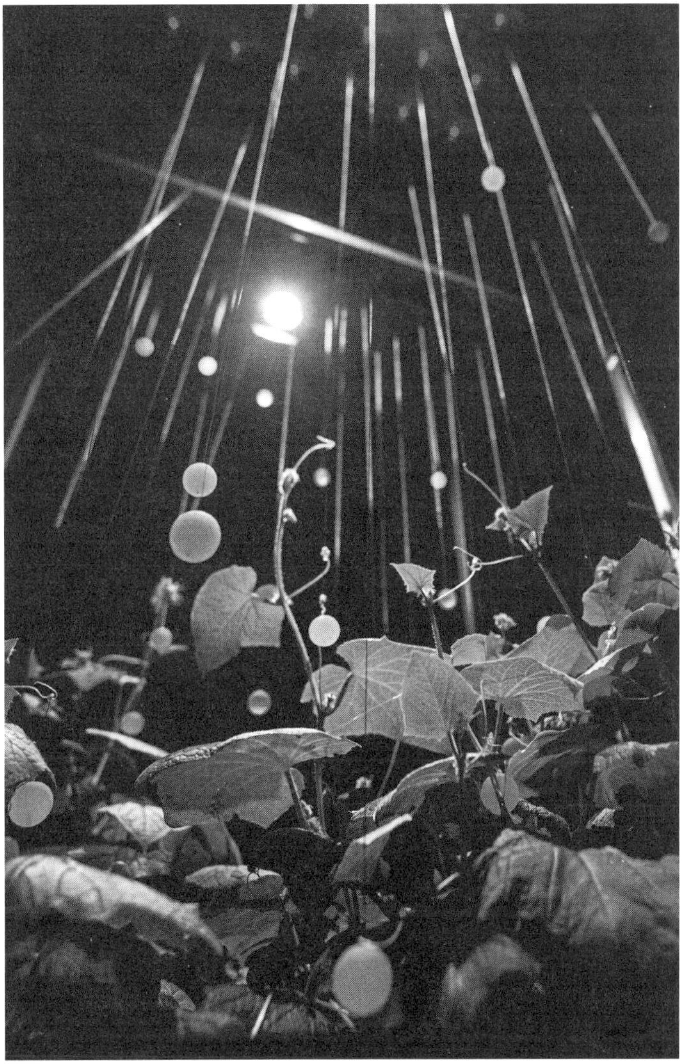

PL'AI, presented at Kapelica Gallery, 2020, corresponding to the work of Špela Petrič: *PL'AI*. (Photo: Hana Josič, courtesy of Špela Petrič and Kersnikova Institute.)

Špela Petrič is a Ljubljana- and Amsterdam-based new media artist who has been trained in the natural sciences and holds a PhD in biology. She is currently working as a post-doc researcher at the Hybrid Forms Lab at Vrije Universiteit Amsterdam. Her artistic practice combines the natural sciences, wet biomedia practices, performance, and critically examines the limits of anthropocentrism via multispecies endeavors. She envisions artistic experiments that enact strange relations to reveal the ontological and epistemological underpinnings of our (bio)technological societies.

III

ENGAGEMENTS

15

SEEDS AND PLANTS AS MY TEACHERS OF ETHICS

Vandana Shiva

I am trained in particle physics and quantum theory, not biology. But seeds, plants, forests have been my teachers of ecology, combining the science of living systems and the ethics of life and living. We are alive because of plants. They give us oxygen by taking carbon dioxide from the atmosphere. They give us food. They give us water. They give us life.

Plants have taught me how the quantum principles of non-separation and potential are the principles of the living world, and the plant world in particular. Separation and mechanistic reductionism, anthropocentrism, and hierarchies have led to violence against plants, the Earth, and humans. This violence has provoked multiple emergencies—a health emergency, a deepening starvation emergency, the climate emergency, and the threat of extinction. Two hundred species are going extinct daily. Humans too are a threatened species.

Plants can be teachers of worldviews and values that help us live in harmony with nature, other species, and each other. From plants we can learn how to stop contributing to existential crises and how we can co-create with plants and biodiversity to address the multiple life-threatening emergencies.

Plants teach us the ethics and epistemology of living systems that help us transcend anthropocentrism and the divisions created by the mechanical mind and its illusions. Plants teach us how to transcend violence against the Earth and her beings, unleashed by the "dead Earth" paradigm. Plants are living and intelligent. They remind us also that intelligence is not unique to humans and that mechanical intelligence is not the only form of intelligence. Plants teach us the ethics of cooperation, mutuality, and interconnectedness, and they can help show the way beyond competition, greed, extractivism.

Plants teach us the economy of abundance through giving and sharing, through diversity and multifunctionality. They teach us how to overcome hunger and scarcity, which are the consequences of a mechanistic, industrial "monoculture of the mind." Plants further teach us equality through diversity, and they can help humans become more conscious of the fact that some humans are not superior to other species and to other humans, based on gender, race, religion, class. Plants teach us rootedness and, through rootedness, the belonging and being of a place. They nourish our identities as Earth Citizens. Plants teach us how to live on the Earth as members of one Earth Family. As our relatives and fellow beings, plants teach democracy, how to live as members of one Earth Community, rich in our diversity.

PLANTS AS TEACHERS OF GENEROSITY AND GIVING: SHOWING THE WAY BEYOND GREED AND EXTRACTIVISM

I grew up in the Himalayan forests and learned the ethics of purity, beauty, bounty from the oak and the rhododendron, the ferns and the mosses. My ecological journey started in the forests of the Himalaya. My father was a forest conservationist, and my mother became a farmer after fleeing the tragic partition of India and Pakistan. It is from the Himalayan forests and ecosystems that I learned most of what I know about ecology. I learned my first lessons of the non-separation between humans and nature from the woods. I learned that soil, water, and plants create a symbiotic system. I learned from plants that diversity is the law of nature, not uniformity and monocultures. The songs and poems our mother composed for us were about trees, forests, and India's forest civilization.

My involvement in the contemporary ecology movement began with Chipko, a nonviolent response to large-scale deforestation that was taking place in the Himalayan region. In 1973, I had gone to visit my favorite forests and swim in my favorite stream before leaving for Canada to do my PhD. But the forests were gone, and the stream was reduced to a trickle. I decided to become a volunteer for the Chipko movement, and I spent every vacation doing pad yatras (walking pilgrimages), documenting deforestation and the work of the forest activists, as well as spreading the message of Chipko.

British colonizers named the commercial extractivism of timber from forests "scientific forestry." The colonial mindset was a commercial mindset, which reduced forests to timber mines and the forest economy to the expansion of plantations of commercially valuable timber. Timber, logged and extracted, led to the "growth" of revenues and profits. The timber extraction introduced by the British during colonialism displaced Aranya Sanskriti, the civilization of the forest, which was the basis of India's Indigenous cultures.

Indigenous forest management by communities that treated forests and trees as sacred gave way to extractivism. The forests were impoverished in their diversity, their abundance, their self-renewal, their ecological functions. Local communities were impoverished to the extent that they were denied their timeless rights to protect and sustainably use the forest as the commons managed by the community. They were denied their basic needs and pushed into ecological and economic poverty.

Logging led to landslides and floods, the scarcity of water, fodder, and fuel. Since women provide these basic needs, the scarcity meant longer walks for collecting water and firewood, as well as a heavier burden. Women knew that the real value of forests was not timber from a dead tree, but water from the springs and streams, or food for their cattle, which gave them organic fertilizer for their fields. The women declared that they would hug the trees, and the loggers would have to kill them before killing the trees. A folk song of that period said: "These beautiful oaks and rhododendrons. They give us cool water. Don't cut these trees! We have to keep them alive."

One of the dramatic Chipko actions took place in the Himalayan village of Adwani in 1977, when a village woman named Bachni Devi led resistance against her own husband, who had obtained a contract to cut trees. When officials arrived at the forest, the women held up lighted lanterns, although it was broad daylight. The forester asked them to explain. The women replied, "We have come to teach you forestry." He retorted, "You foolish women, how can you prevent tree felling by those who know the value of the forest? Do you know what forests bear? They produce profit and resin and timber." The women sang back in chorus: "What do the forests bear? Soil, water, and pure air. Soil, water, and pure air sustain the Earth and all she bears."[1]

From the forests the women had learned the generosity and gifts of the forests. From the forests and Chipko, I learned that there are economies beyond the market, beyond greed and extractivism. I learned that generosity and giving create economies of permanence and abundance. I learned about biodiversity and biodiversity-based living economies; the protection of both has become my life's mission. Plants can teach us how to create economies of giving, how to avert collapse and extinction by transcending greed and the uniformity it imposes on the world. As I described in my book *Monocultures of the Mind*, the failure to understand biodiversity and its many functions is at the root of the impoverishment of nature and culture. The lessons I learned about diversity in the Himalayan forests I then transferred to the protection of biodiversity on our farms.[2]

PLANTS AS TEACHERS OF THE ETHICS OF COOPERATION, MUTUALITY, AND SHARING THAT GENERATES ABUNDANCE: SHOWING THE WAY BEYOND HUNGER AND MALNUTRITION

I did my MSc Hons in particle physics in Punjab. Punjab was peaceful and prosperous in my university days in the late '60s and early '70s. Little did we know that the "Green Revolution" based on war chemicals was being imposed on Punjab at that time, and seeds of debt and discontent were being sown.

In 1984, Punjab erupted in violence. I studied the Green Revolution for the United Nations University Programme on Peace and Global Transformation, where I was involved in research on "Conflicts Over Natural Resources." Based on my research, I wrote my book *The Violence of the Green Revolution* and took a pledge to myself to practice and promote nonviolent, chemical-free farming based on diversity. It is plants that have taught me the ethics of cooperation with each other, with organisms dwelling in the soil, with bees and other pollinators. They also taught me the power of nonviolent non-cooperation with the violence of chemical agriculture.[3]

When the chemicals of the Green Revolution were introduced, the tall, highly productive, multidimensional, and multifunctional plants of native wheat rejected them by "lodging." I call this the *satyagraha* (power of truth) of the plants, their non-cooperation with synthetic chemicals. To deal with the non-cooperation of native plants, Norman Borlaug, who worked for Dupont Defense Labs, was given the task of redesigning the plants and making them "dwarf varieties" to take up more chemicals without "lodging." These were the so-called "miracle wheats" of Borlaug. Borlaug got a Nobel Peace Prize for his work on the Green Revolution in Punjab. From the perspective of the plants, the Green Revolution was based on violence, though, not peace.

The Green Revolution treated straw as waste and reduced it, thus disrupting the nutrient cycle. As Masanobu Fukukua has written in *The One-Straw Revolution*, straw is the part of the plant that goes back to the earth as soil fertility and the potential for future food.[4] No plant is useless. No part of a plant is "waste." Plants share their nourishment with us; with soil bacteria, fungi, and earthworms; with nonhuman animals; and with birds and insects. The food web the plants weave is the web of life.

Organic matter from plants makes living soil, and fertile living soil supports plants and our food system. Living soil is a complex food web, teeming with earthworms, bacteria, and fungi. Its relationships to plants through the nutrient cycle was forgotten for an entire century, with very high costs to nature and society. Soil was defined as an "empty container" into which to pour synthetic fertilizers, which were falsely seen as the source of soil fertility. Explosives that were made by burning fossil fuels at high temperature to fix atmospheric nitrogen were later used to make chemical fertilizers. "Bread from air" was the slogan after the discovery of the Haber Bosch process for fixing atmospheric nitrogen by burning fossil fuels. The illusion grew that we did not need soil.

The arrogance of the militarized mind hid behind the ignorance that peasants had been growing legumes, which fix nitrogen nonviolently. There was the exaggerated claim that artificial fertilizers would increase food production and remove all ecological limits that land puts on agriculture. While Indian peasants knew that leguminous plants (pulses) fix nitrogen nonviolently, the West was industrializing agriculture based on synthetic nitrogen. Today the evidence is growing that ignoring plants as sources of nitrogen has had high ecological costs. Artificial fertilizers have reduced soil fertility and food production, as well as contributed to desertification and dead soils, water scarcity, dead zones in the oceans, greenhouse gases, and climate change.

While we ate a diversity of plants as *dals* in our daily *dal roti*, British colonizers, who had no idea of the nutritional richness of pulses, reduced them to animal food. *Chana* became chickpea; *gahat* became horse gram; *tur* became pigeon pea.

Justus von Liebig, the father of organic chemistry, was the first scientist to explain the role of nitrogen in plants. Liebig's work on nitrogen for plants was appropriated by commercial green. A new industry was created for external inputs of nitrogen called "growth stimulants." In 1861, Liebig wrote a book titled *The Search for Agricultural Recycling*. His was the voice of a true scientist, protecting the truth from the distortions of a pseudo-science created by commercial interests. As he writes,

I thought it would be enough to just announce and spread the truth as is customary in science. I finally came to understand that this wasn't right, and the altars of lies must be destroyed if we wish to give truth a fair chance.[5]

Liebig questioned the false metric of "yield," which merely measures the weight of the nutritionally empty commodity that leaves the farm. It is a measure of farming as an extractive industry, not of real farming. It is an illusionary measure that has displaced biodiversity in favor of a monoculture of commodities based on chemical inputs. It counts neither the total biodiverse output nor the total costs of inputs nor the state of the soil and the farm. "Yield" is not a measure of care for the land. As Liebig stresses, what matters is "not 'yield of harvest' but the state in which the field is left."[6] Leaving the soil in a better condition after the harvest is care for the land. Chemical fertilizers leave the field in worse health, destroying the true productivity of the soil, and hence food productivity. "Yield" as a construct to promote violent farming based on chemical fertilizers artificially projects the reduction of nutrition per acre as an increase in food production. That is why Navdanya, the movement I started to conserve the biodiversity of seeds and plants, has evolved the metric of biodiversity-based productivity and "nutrition per acre" to reflect the contributions of plant biodiversity to abundance, through real farming. When plants cooperate with each other, and we intensify the biodiversity of plants instead of intensifying chemicals and monocultures, we grow more food. Plants show us a path to zero hunger. We merely have to learn from them and respect their self-organization, sentience, and integrity.[7]

The truth that Leibig was defending was that the soil is living, and its life depends on the recycling of organic matter from plants and animals who eat plants. The lie he wanted to destroy was what he called the "chemical hocus pocus," that you can keep extracting nutrients from the soil, giving nothing back, and still have "high yields." Nearly half a century later in *An Agricultural Testament*, Sir Albert Howard called recycling and the circular economy of nutrients "the law of return."[8] Sir Albert Howard, who was sent to India in 1905 to introduce Western systems of farming, found extremely sophisticated systems, which had sustained Indian agriculture over millennia. He decided instead to make the peasants his professors on good farming. *An Agriculture Testament* was the synthesis of that teaching and is now referred to as the bible of modern organic farming.

The key lessons Howard learned were diversity and the law of return. An agriculture of permanence does not grow only one crop, nor does it grow crops alone.

It integrates crops, trees, and animals, and it mixes crops in interspecies diversity—pulses, oilseeds, cereals, vegetables, each in rich diversity. Diverse crops produce diverse nutrients for the soil and for animals and humans, thus continuing the web of life, which is a web of self-organized organisms growing and renewing themselves through interactions with other beings.

The foundations of India's ecological civilization are based on diversity. When you do not grow chemical monocultures with the help of herbicides, plants grow in abundance, including the nutritious uncultivated edibles like bathua (*Chenopodium album*) and chaulai (*Amaranth*); medicinal plants such as bhuiamla (*Phyllanthus niruri*), which heals the liver and is a cure for jaundice and hepatitis; and grass for our animals. All scientific literature shows that biodiversity and mixed cropping has a higher "land equivalence ratio" and that we get more output of produce per acre when we mix crops than when we grow monocultures. Navdanya's metric of nutrition per acre measures biodiversity-based productivity rather than the reductionist "yield" of one commodity from a chemically based monoculture.

Biodiverse mixed cropping is the principle, which Sir Albert Howard learned from Indian farming and spread across the world as organic farming. As he writes in his *An Agricultural Testament*:

> Mixed crops are the rule. In this respect the cultivators of the Orient have followed Nature's method as seen in the primeval forest. Mixed cropping is perhaps most universal when the cereal crop is the main constituent. (Crops like millets, wheat, barley, and maize are mixed with an appropriate subsidiary pulse, sometimes a species that ripens much later than the cereal. The pigeon pea (Cajanus indicus Spreng), perhaps the most important leguminous crop of the Gangetic alluvium, is grown either with millets or with maize). The mixing of cereals and pulses appears to help both crops.[9]

As our report "Health Per Acre" has shown, by conserving biodiversity we can feed two Indias and provide food and health for all.

Sir Albert Howard also found that organic farming promotes mycorrhizal fungi, which are vital to bringing nutrition to plants and to their communication through the root system. That is not to mention that plants offer the pollen of their flowers to bees and pollinators, fertilizing future plants. Navdanya's research has shown that more than 30 percent of the food we eat is produced by bees and pollinators.

When the Green Revolution was imposed on the Third World in the 1960s, we were told that without chemicals and the "miracle seeds" of this revolution, millions would starve. Seeds of "dwarf varieties" were bred to withstand high doses of fertilizers. These were falsely named "high-yielding varieties" (HYVs). As the UN Research Institute for Social Development (UNRISD) pointed out, they were merely "high-response varieties" that responded to chemicals. The illusion of HYVs replaced the diversity of indigenous seeds bred for nutrition, taste, and resilience. The Green Revolution failed because it destroyed soil, water, and biodiversity, on which food production depends. Hunger was not eliminated.

In the 1990s we were again told we would starve without GMOs, genetically modified plants with toxic genes, brought to us by the same poison cartel that had introduced chemicals. GMOs have increased the use of toxic chemicals like Roundup, which kill plants by disrupting the shikimate pathway. It also added new risks, such as cancer. There are more than 125,000 cases against Bayer/Monsanto due to glyphosate/Roundup-related cancer. Furthermore, the exaggerated claim was spread that GMOs would remove all limits of the environment, allowing us to grow food in deserts and toxic dumps. The real reason GMOs were introduced was to claim patents and "intellectual property rights" on seeds and plants, based on the false claim that seeds and plants are machines, invented by chemical companies.

I started the Navdanya movement to defend the integrity and sovereignty of seeds and plants, as well as to resist the false claim that plants and their seeds are invented by Monsanto or any other multinational agribusiness company. Patents on plants and seeds are an attempt to deny them their nature as a renewable, self-organized living system with the right to evolve in freedom. Such patents also undermine the rights of farmers to freely save and share seeds as they have been doing down the ages. These patents transform seeds into a non-renewable, genetically engineered, patented commodity which cannot be saved or shared by farmers, thereby robbing both humans and plants of their right to self-sufficiency.

Today there are only two GMO applications: herbicide resistance and Bt toxins in crops. The first had been claimed to control weeds but has instead created "superweeds." Bt crops had been supposed to control pests but have instead created new pests and superpests. Furthermore, both applications have increased the use of toxic chemicals and water while pushing thousands of Indian and other farmers to suicide because of debt through failed crops, "royalties," and technology fees.

For Monsanto's militaristic, anti-nature mind, biodiversity is a problem: monocultures are fundamental to its profit-at-all-cost policies. And so, biodiversity must be exterminated with their number-one toxic herbicide product, glyphosate. Crops must be genetically engineered to resist glyphosate so that the genetically modified organism survives and everything else dies.

Roundup Ready crops, which have led to an increase of 1,500 percent in Roundup spraying in the United States, failed in their primary objective of weed control. Weeds have evolved resistance to Roundup and have become superweeds, now requiring more and more lethal herbicides. The Palmer amaranth is now a superweed that cannot be exterminated by Roundup. The amaranth is displaying its intelligence and evolutionary potential by becoming resistant to the herbicide that was supposed to kill it. This is another example of the intelligence of plants, the noncooperation and satyagraha of plants against violence and extermination.

Bill Gates and the Defense Advanced Projects Research Agency (DARPA) are even calling for the use of gene drives to exterminate amaranth, a sacred and nutritious food in India, since the Palmer amaranth has become a superweed in the Roundup Ready soya fields of the United States. Thus gene drives to push plants to extinction have become Big Ag's latest tool, not only in a war against biodiversity but also in the extermination of the superweeds they themselves have created.[10]

When I was present at the UN Convention on Biological Diversity negotiations, a Monsanto spokesman said that when they engineer plants to be resistant to Roundup, they "prevent weeds from stealing sunshine." This is violence against plants. No plants are useless. What Monsanto calls weeds are associated crops or uncultivated edibles like amaranth.

Plants create abundance through cooperation with each other, through mutuality and sharing. These are the values we need to learn from plants for the transformation of our food system from one which is spreading diseases, malnutrition, and hunger to one which nourishes all humans and life on Earth.

PLANTS AS TEACHERS OF THE ETHICS OF THE TRUTH OF FOOD AND HEALTH IN TIMES OF POST-TRUTH AND POST-FOOD

Plants are the basis of life on Earth. As Sir Albert Howard writes in *An Agricultural Testament*:

> The energy for the machinery of growth is derived from the sun, the chlorophyll in the green leaf is the mechanism by which this energy is intercepted; the plant is thereby enabled

to manufacture food-to synthesise carbohydrates and proteins from the water and other substances taken up by the roots and the carbon dioxide of the atmosphere. The efficiency of the green leaf is therefore of supreme importance: on it depends the food supply of the planet, our wellbeing, and our activities. There is no alternative source of nutriment. Without sunlight and the green leaf our industries, our trade, our possessions would soon be useless.[11]

With the blessings of the sun, seeds grow into plants that become the green mantle of the Earth, returning parts of plants to the soil as organic matter, to create a living soil, and providing humans and all beings with all their needs for food, clothing, shelter. Plants as the basis of life teach us health and well-being. More than that, they teach us life itself: what is life and how to live (well). However, a profit-driven, mechanistic, industrial food and agriculture system based on the manipulation and objectification of plants has given us disease and hunger.

The latest objectification of plants is the language of "plant-based" food, used for genetically modified, lab-manufactured artificial food. All foods begin in plants. But plant-based food refers to lab-made food using genetically engineered plants as raw material for "carbohydrates" and "proteins." Plants, on the other hand, teach that real food from living plants is itself living and gives us life. The language of "plant-based" is reducing plants to "raw materials": to carbohydrates and proteins to be extracted and assembled in labs. It further devalues and objectifies plants, refusing to recognize them as sentient beings on whom we depend for food. Awareness of the consciousness of plants as living systems with their own integrity creates in us a sense of gratitude and reverence. That is why in Indigenous cultures we hold the plants and seeds as sacred; we thank them for nourishing us; we make a commitment that we will not be violent or greedy. We will not take more than we need to sustain ourselves.

When we talk of something "plant based," plants, with their integrity and diversity, disappear. Biodiversity and fresh vegetables disappear. Real food disappears. Soils and small farmers growing biodiverse crops disappear, and food becomes a genetically engineered manufacture from biotech labs. "Plant based" transforms chemically grown, GMO monocultures into "raw materials." The health of the planet is connected to the health of people through the biodiversity of plants and chemical-free, poison-free, GMO-free systems of production based on the science of agroecology and non-industrial artisanal processing. The epidemics of chronic diseases are rooted in chemical, monoculture diets and industrial processing.

Plants in their integrity give us health. They reconnect us to the ethics of truth, embodying the interconnectedness between the Earth and our bodies, between food and health, between the health of the planet and our health. Violence against the Earth and harm to our health begin with violence against plants manipulated for profits, ignored in their integrity and self-organization. In a period when both the health of the planet and our health are threatened by the "post-truth" claim that the manipulation of plants is necessary for feeding the world, the plants themselves teach us the truth of food, health, and well-being. Conversely, an industrial food system based on the manipulation of plants to increase the use of chemicals for the sake of commodity production is clearly a disease-producing system.

Roundup Ready GMOs have led to an explosion of the use of Roundup, which is a known carcinogen as well as a contributor to chronic disease, including kidney failure and the destruction of gut bacteria, our second brain. To learn the truth of food and health, we need to turn to plants: to their biodiversity, their complex ecological functions which produce more nutrition without the use of chemicals. In this sense, plants teach us about a healthy metabolism, about the maintenance of health by maintaining the self-organizing properties of intelligent, living systems.

The failures repeated at each stage of mechanistic industrial agriculture's violent farming have led to a new spin and a new industry of further manipulating plants rather than learning from plants how to create abundance and health through nonviolence and giving as well as through integrity, co-creation, and co-evolution. Even as more people are shifting to agroecology and organic food as farmers and eaters, and more communities are creating local ecological systems based on diversity, the poison cartel joining hands with Big Tech intends to destroy our living relationship with living and biodiverse plants. It is betting on patented, artificial lab food to create new markets and more profits for industrial agriculture and the digital giants, pushing us further down the dead-end path to a multiplication of ecological emergencies that the greed-driven industrial food system has exacerbated. The big push for one uniform artificial diet came from the EAT Forum, which released the "EAT-Lancet Report."[12] The forum and the resulting report tried to impose a monoculture diet of chemically developed, hyper-industrially processed food on the world while claiming that a "healthy and sustainable (plant-based) diet" protects the health of the planet and of people. The document completely ignored a glaring chronic disease epidemic related to pesticides and toxins used in growing crops and ultra-processed food imposed by chemically intensive industrial agriculture. By not addressing this key reality, the report is actually promoting a diet of hyper-industrially grown and processed food based on monocultures and chemicals.

In writing the report, EAT Forum partnered with FRESH of the junk food industry and Big Ag, including Bayer, BASF, Cargill, Yara, and Pepsico, among others. Bayer became the biggest GMO seed and agrochemical company after it merged with Monsanto, and Yara is the biggest chemical fertilizer corporation in the world. Thus, we could call the report "the poison cartel diet," where real health and sustainability are two alien concepts to its authors and promoters.

FRESH and the poison cartel have together contributed 50 percent of greenhouse gases leading to climate change and 75 percent of chronic diseases related to chemicals in food, loss of diversity in the diet, industrially processed and junk food, and fake food. From feeding the world with fake farming, the rhetoric has shifted to saving the planet and people's health through fake food. The report can be thus seen as an advertisement for industrial food and fake food, with the fig leaf of "plant-based diet."

The report in question is a desperate but failed attempt at "sustaining" agrichemical industry through the unscientific promotion of "sustainable intensification." It reinforces Bayer and the poison cartel's focus on "yield," which, as previously mentioned, is simply a measure evolved for industrial agriculture based on chemicals to produce nutritionally empty toxic commodities. In effect, the report is recommending the destruction of biodiverse small farms that provide 80 percent of the food we eat when it states that

> the current global food system requires a new agricultural revolution that is based on sustainable intensification and driven by sustainability and system innovation. This would entail at least a 75% reduction of yield gaps on current cropland, radical improvements in fertilizer use.[13]

In coming to such conclusions, the report deliberately tries to divert attention from chemical-free agriculture and agroecology, which provide real food through real farming and are recognized as the food paradigm for the future. It ignores the fact that organic farming and regenerative agriculture are the proven paths for rebuilding soil health.

Six months prior to the release of the EAT Report, Navdanya International released a *Manifesto on Food for Health* written by leading health experts and ecologists, who identified toxins as the leading cause of the chronic disease epidemic.[14]

Toxins are the elephant in the planetary and human health room that the EAT Report is totally silent on. More than half a century after Rachel Carson's *Silent Spring*; 37 years after the Bhopal genocide; a year after the UN rapporteur on food put out her report on pesticides 19-; a few months after the Johnson trial firmly established that Roundup is a carcinogen, the EAT Report fails to mention that toxins are driving species to extinction and have led to an epidemic of cancers, neurological problems, endocrine disruption, and infertility.

The use of synthetic fossil fuel–based nitrogen fertilizers is a major contributor to the climate crisis, dead zones in oceans, and the death of soils. Instead of recognizing the role of organic farming and agroecology in providing sustainable ways for repairing the broken nitrogen cycle, the EAT Report recommends "redistribution of global use of nitrogen and phosphorus,"[15] which is in effect saying that chemicals should continue to be spread in the Third World. This is what the GATES Foundation/AGRA are also doing.[16] Those who have contributed to planetary collapse and collapse of our well-being have now joined hands to force-feed us hyper-industrial toxic diets in the name of protecting our health and saving the planet.

We can feed the world and protect the planet by getting rid of fossil fuels and chemicals. The EAT Report is a recipe for sustaining the non-sustainable industrial food system, and not for regenerating the health of the planet or the people. It violates the fundamental tenets and principles of diversity and democracy, on which both freedom and sustainability rest.

THE IMPOSSIBLE BURGER: PRETENDING GMO SOY IS MEAT

In a recent article, "How Our Commitment to Consumers and Our Planet Led Us to Use GM Soy," Pat Brown, CEO and founder of Impossible Foods states that "we sought the safest and most environmentally responsible option that would allow us to scale our production and provide the Impossible Burger to consumers at a reasonable cost."[17] But Roundup-sprayed GMO soy is neither good for the planet nor for human health. It has already caused massive ecological devastation as well as chronic worldwide health problems.

Although Monsanto's glyphosate-based Roundup herbicide was first classified a Class C carcinogen by the Environmental Protection Agency (EPA) in 1985, this did not stop its continued widespread use throughout the world. More recently, in 2015, the World Health Organization's (WHO) International Agency on Cancer

Research conducted a study that showed that glyphosate, the main active ingredient in Roundup, is probably carcinogenic to humans (Group 2A). The WHO study has led to a spate of lawsuits against Monsanto and Bayer after the German pharmaceutical behemoth bought Monsanto in 2018. All of these lawsuits were brought by people who, through the use of Roundup, have developed cancer. Courts have ruled in favor of the first three plaintiffs, with millions of dollars in awards, and there are some 18,000 other plaintiffs waiting in line.[18]

The "Impossible Burger," based on vast GMO monocultures and Roundup-sprayed soy cannot be considered a "safe" option, both because of its high levels of glyphosate and its effect on our gut microbiome. As Zen Honeycutt of Moms across America states,

> the levels of glyphosate detected in the Impossible Burger by Health Research Institute Laboratories were 11 times higher than the Beyond Meat Burger. This new product is being marketed as a solution for "healthy" eating, when in fact 11 ppb of glyphosate herbicide consumption can be highly dangerous.[19]

Furthermore, Roundup residues disrupt the all-important biological pathway in our gut bacteria, the shikimate pathway, on which we depend to supply essential nutrients if they are deficient in our food.

Roundup is not just a broad-spectrum weedicide. It is a broad-spectrum biocide that kills beneficial insects, like pollinators, and soil microorganisms. Given that 90 percent of the monarch butterflies have disappeared because of Roundup Ready crops, and we are living through what scientists have called an "insectageddon," using GMO soy is hardly an "environmentally responsible option." By destroying sources of food and fodder, medicine and organic matter, Monsanto steals the livelihoods of millions. Promoting GMO soy "plant-based meat" as both "fake and healthy meat" is misleading the eater in terms of the ontology of the burger and, more importantly, in terms of claims concerning its safety. It also steals our health and our future.

Big Food, Big Ag, and Big Money are driving the artificial food gold rush. They are, in fact, investing millions in the artificial food industry to support the mass proliferation of lab food products such as eggs, dairy, and meat. The promotion of artificial foods seems to have more to do with giving new life to the failing GMO agriculture and junk food industry, in the face of the threat from the raising of consciousness everywhere that organic, local, fresh food is real food that regenerates the planet and our health. As a consequence, investment in "plant-based food companies" soared from nearly 0 in 2009 to $600 million by 2018. And these companies are now looking for more.

Plants as food are being redefined as an "unimprovable technology." Lab foods are, conversely, deemed "improved technologies." Pat Brown of Impossible Foods declared: If there's one thing that we know, it's that when an ancient unimprovable technology counters a better technology that is continuously improvable, it's just a matter of time before the game is over." He added, "I think our investors see this as a $3 trillion opportunity."[20] Among the new players pushing the fake food agenda are companies including Beyond Meat (BYND.O) and Impossible Foods, and even traditional meat producers including Tyson Foods Inc. (TSN.N), Maple Leaf Foods Inc. (MFI.TO), and Perdue Farms.

That said, plants are not "unimprovable technology." They are complex self-organized sentient beings, the bases of the food web for humans and other species. Reducing plants to "raw materials" is the new dimension of violence against plants and humans by an industrial food system based on separation and anthropocentrism. But the main goal is profits and control.

Those jumping on the lab food gold rush have no discernible knowledge, consciousness about, or compassion for living beings, the web of life, or the role of living food in weaving that web or in our health. Their sudden awakening to "plant-based diets," including GMO soy, is an ontological violation of plants and food as a living system that connects us to the ecosystem and other beings. The "awakening" indicates ignorance of the biodiversity of plants and diversity of cultures that have always used diverse plants in their diets. Humans have eaten more than 10,000 plants. Globalized trade reduced food to about 12 globally traded commodities, with a focus on four GMOs: soy, corn, canola, cotton.[21]

Ecological sciences have been based on the recognition of the interconnections and interrelatedness between humans and nature, among diverse organisms, and within all living systems, including the human body. Ecological sciences have thus evolved as a systems science, not a fragmented and reductionist one. Diets have evolved according to climates and the local biodiversity of plants the climate enables. The biodiversity of the soil, of plants, and our gut microbiome is one continuum.

In Indian civilization, technologies are tools. Tools need to be assessed in keeping with ethical, social, and ecological criteria. Tools or technologies have never been viewed as self-referential. They have been evaluated in the context of contributing to the well-being of all. However, through fake food, evolution, biodiversity, and the web of life are being redefined as an "ancient unimprovable technology," a redefinition ignorant of the sophisticated knowledges that have co-evolved with plants in diverse agricultural and food cultures, in different climates and ecosystems, to sustain and renew biodiversity, as well as the health of people and the planet.

Artificial food is thus building on a century and a half of food imperialism and food colonization of our diverse food knowledges and food cultures. These operations involve the colonization of plants and are dismissive of plant biodiversity, as much as the diversity of knowledges and intelligences. We need to decolonize our food cultures and our minds, ridding both of food imperialism.

We stand at a precipice of planetary emergency, aggravated by a health emergency and a crisis of farmers' livelihoods. Artificial food will accelerate the rush to collapse by promoting and sustaining the failed fake farming model of industrial agriculture. Real food gives us a chance to rejuvenate the earth, our food economies, food sovereignty, and food cultures through real farming based on caring for the Earth and for people. Through real food from plants as sentient beings, to whom we relate through reverence, respect, and gratitude, we can decolonize our food cultures and our consciousness. Plants can teach us how to reclaim our food sovereignty and health. They can be the teachers of the truth of food and health in the times of post-truth, post-food, post-health.

PLANTS AS TEACHERS OF THE ETHICS OF EQUALITY, DIVERSITY, AND DEMOCRACY FOR ALL LIFE

Today, at a time of multiple crises intensified by globalization, separation, and monocultures of the mechanical mind, we need to move away from the paradigm of nature as dead matter and of plants as inert objects of manipulation. We need to move to an ecological paradigm, and for this, the best teacher is nature herself—her biodiversity and plants.

Violence against plants and the Earth is rooted in the illusion of separateness, driving objectification, and the assumption that plants and living systems are inert objects to be manipulated and owned in order to extract profits from them. Its contemporary seeds were sown when the living Earth was transformed into dead matter and raw material to facilitate the Industrial Revolution. Monocultures replaced diversity.

This sort of philosophy goes back to Francis Bacon, called the father of modern science, who said that science and the inventions that resulted from it did not "merely exert a gentle guidance over nature's course; they have the power to conquer and subdue her, to shake her to her foundations."[22] Robert Boyle, a famous seventeenth-century chemist and the governor of the Corporation for the Propagation of the Gospel Among the New England Indians, was clear that he wanted to rid native people of their ideas about nature. He attacked their perception of nature "as a kind of goddess" and argued that "the veneration, wherewith men are imbued for what they call nature, has been a discouraging impediment to the empire of man over the inferior creatures of God."[23] The death-of-nature idea allows a war to be unleashed against the Earth. After all, if the Earth is merely dead matter, then nothing is really being killed. As philosopher and historian Carolyn Merchant points out, this shift of perspective—from nature as a living, nurturing mother to inert, dead, and manipulable matter—was well-suited to the activities that would lead to capitalism. The domination images created by Bacon and other leaders of the Scientific Revolution replaced those of the nurturing Earth, removing a cultural constraint on the exploitation of nature. "One does not readily slay a mother, dig into her entrails for gold, or mutilate her body," Merchant wrote.[24]

The "dead Earth" paradigm goes hand in hand with anthropocentrism and the assumed superiority of humans to other biological kingdoms and species, including plants. As the living Earth paradigm re-emerges through the Gaia theory, and as scientists show that plants have intelligence, we can start again learning from plants the ethics of equality. On its obverse, we can see through the illusion of superiority—of humans as superior to other species and of some humans as superior to others on the basis of gender, race, religion, or class. It is from plants that we learn that diversity does not lead to inequality; rather, constructed hierarchies do.

Life is self-organized complexity and intelligence in constant evolution, interaction, change, and emergence. Scientists Maturana and Varela identified living systems as autopoietic systems, organized from within.[25] Machines, on the other hand, are allopoietic systems, assembled and controlled externally. Seeds, like nature and humanity, are, nonetheless, being redefined as auto-allopoietic by global corporate greed. One of the most dramatic ontological shifts in our times is this redefinition of living organisms, especially seeds, as machines, the machines "invented" by corporations. Machines invented by The Machine.

For the last five decades, I have learned the ethics of self-organization from seeds and plants. Seed, uncontaminated seed—*bija, seme, semilla*—is the source of life, of regeneration and abundance. Seed renews and multiples. This is the reason I started Navdanya in 1987. Navdanya, the movement for biodiversity conservation and organic farming, is spreading. So far, we have worked with farmers to set up more than 150 community seed banks across India. We have saved more than 4,000 rice varieties. We also help farmers make a transition from fossil fuel and chemical-based monocultures to biodiverse ecological systems nourished by the sun and the soil. Biodiversity of seeds and plants has been my teacher of abundance and freedom, of cooperation and mutual giving.

This is also the reason I later started The Earth University/Bija Vidyapeeth at Navdanya's Biodiversity Farm, so that plants can continue to be our teachers of equality in diversity, helping us transcend the inequality between plants and people imposed through anthropocentrism. The Earth University is inspired by Rabindranath Tagore, India's national poet and a Nobel Prize laureate. Tagore started a learning center in Shantiniketan, West Bengal, India, as a forest school, both to take inspiration from nature and to create an Indian cultural renaissance. The school became a university in 1921, growing into one of India's most famous centers of learning. Today, just as in Tagore's time, we need to turn to nature and the forest, to plants and biodiversity, for lessons in freedom and democracy.

In "The Religion of the Forest," Tagore wrote about the influence that the forest dwellers of ancient India had on classical Indian literature. The forests are sources of water and the storehouses of biodiversity that can teach us the lessons of democracy—of leaving space for others while drawing sustenance from the common web of life. Tagore saw unity with nature as the highest stage of human evolution. It is this unity in diversity that is the basis of both ecological sustainability and democracy. Diversity without unity becomes the source of conflict and contest. Unity without diversity becomes the ground for external control. This is true of both nature and culture. The forest is a unity in its diversity, and we are united with nature through our relationship with the forest.

In Tagore's writings, the forest was not just the source of knowledge and freedom; it was the source of beauty and joy, of art and aesthetics, of harmony and perfection. It symbolized the universe. In "The Religion of the Forest," the poet says that our frame of mind "guides our attempts to establish relations with the universe either by conquest or by union, either through the cultivation of power or through that of sympathy."[26] The forest teaches us unity and compassion. The forest also teaches us enough-ness: as a principle of equity, it shows us how to enjoy the gifts of nature without exploitation and accumulation. Tagore quotes from the ancient texts written in the forest: "Know all that moves in this moving world as enveloped by God; and find enjoyment through renunciation, not through greed of possession."[27] No species in a forest appropriates the share of another species. Every species sustains itself in cooperation with others. The end of consumerism and accumulation is the beginning of the joy of living. The conflict between greed and compassion, conquest and cooperation, violence and harmony that Tagore wrote about continues today. And it is the forest that can point the way beyond this conflict.

Tagore writes in his essay "Tapovan" [Forest of Purity]:

> Indian civilization has been distinctive in locating its source of regeneration, material and intellectual, in the forest, not the city. India's best ideas have come where man was in communion with trees and rivers and lakes, away from the crowds. The peace of the forest has helped the intellectual evolution of man. The culture of the forest has fueled the culture of Indian society. The culture that has arisen from the forest has been influenced by the diverse processes of renewal of life, which are always at play in the forest, varying from species to species, from season to season, in sight and sound and smell. The unifying principle of life in diversity, of democratic pluralism, thus became the principle of Indian civilization.[28]

At The Earth University, the biodiversity of plants, the soils and food webs they create, along with the insect diversity they support, teach us Earth democracy, which is the freedom for all species to evolve within the web of life, and the freedom and responsibility of humans, as members of the Earth family, to recognize, protect, and respect the rights of other species. Earth democracy is a shift from anthropocentrism to ecocentrism, which is vital for life itself.

NOTES

1. Vandana Shiva, *Staying Alive: Women, Ecology and Development* (New York: North Atlantic Books, 2016), 77.
2. Refer to Vandana Shiva, *Monocultures of the Mind: Perspectives on Biodiversity and Biotechnology* (London: Palgrave Macmillan, 1993).
3. Vandana Shiva, *The Violence of the Green Revolution: Third World Agriculture, Ecology, and Politics* (Lexington: University of Kentucky Press, 2015).
4. Masanobu Fukukua, *The One-Straw Revolution: An Introduction to Natural Farming* (New York: NYRB Classics, 2009).

5. Justus von Liebig, *The Search for Agricultural Recycling* (Kollumerzwaag: Mulder Agro).
6. Liebig, *The Search for Agricultural Recycling.*
7. Refer to Vandana Shiva and Vaibhav Singh, *Health Per Acre: Organic Solutions to Hunger and Malnutrition* (Navdanya Research Foundation for Science, Technology & Ecology, 2011).
8. Albert Howard, *An Agricultural Testament* (Oxford: Oxford University Press, 1940).
9. Howard, *An Agricultural Testament*, 13.
10. Vandana Shiva, "Biodiversity, GMOs, and Gene Drives of the Militarised Mind" (New Delhi: Navdanya Research Foundation for Science, Technology & Ecology, 2016), https://navdanyainternational.org/wp-content/uploads/2020/10/BIODIVERSITY-GMOS-GENE-DRIVES-OF-THE-MILITARISED-MIND.pdf.
11. Howard, *An Agricultural Testament*, 23.
12. Walter Willett et al. "Food in the Anthropocene: The EAT–Lancet Commission on healthy diets from sustainable food systems," *The Lancet Commissions* 393, no. 10170 (2019): 447–492.
13. Willett et al., "Food in the Anthropocene."
14. Renata Alleva et al. *Manifesto on Food for Health: Cultivating Biodiversity, Cultivating Health* (New Delhi: Navdanya International, 2019).
15. Willett et al., "Food in the Anthropocene."
16. Vandana Shiva et al., *Gates to a Global Empire . . . over Seeds, Food, Knowledge and the Earth* (New Delhi: Navdanya International, 2020), https://navdanyainternational.org/publications/report-synthesis-gates-to-a-global-empire/.
17. Pat Brown, "How Our Commitment to Consumers and Our Planet Led Us to Use GM Soy," *Medium*, May 16, 2019, https://medium.com/impossible-foods/how-our-commitment-to-consumers-and-our-planet-led-us-to-use-gm-soy-23f880c93408.
18. Guillame Lavallc, "Bayer Says It's Now Targeted in 18,400 Glyphosate Cases in the U.S," *Agence France-Presse*, July 30, 2019, https://www.rappler.com/business/bayer-glyphosate-cases-usa.
19. Zen L. Honeycutt, "GMO Impossible Burger Positive for Cancerogenic Glyphosate," *Moms Across America*, May 16, 2019, https://www.momsacrossamerica.com/gmo_impossible_burger_positive_for_carcinogenic_glyphosate.
20. Zen L. Honeycutt, "Could Plant-Based Meat Be a $3 Trillion Opportunity?," *CNBC*, March 4, 2019, https://www.cnbc.com/video/2019/03/04/could-plant-based-meat-be-a-3-trillion-opportunity.html.
21. See Vandana Shiva, *Who Really Feeds the World? The Failures of Agribusiness and the Promises of Agroecology* (New York: North Atlantic Books, 2016).
22. Quoted in Evelyn Fox Keller, *Reflections on Gender and Science* (New Haven: Yale University Press, 1995), 36.
23. Quoted in Richard Bauckham, "The Modern Domination of Nature: Historical Origins and Biblical Critique," in *Environmental Stewardship: Critical Perspectives, Past and Present*, ed. R. J. Berry (London: Continuum, 2006), 40.
24. Carolyn Merchant, *Radical Ecology: The Search for a Livable World* (New York: Routledge, 1992), 43.

25. See H. R. Maturana and F. J. Varela, *Autopoiesis and Cognition: The Realization of the Living* (Dordrecht: D. Reidel, 1980).

26. Rabindranath Tagore, *Creative Unity* (London: Macmillan, 1922), 59.

27. Tagore, *Creative Unity*, 59.

28. Quoted in Vandana Shiva and Maria Mies, *Ecofeminism* (London: Zed Books, 2014), 265.

Main Pathway: Orientations

Subthemes

Proceed to Experience, p. 377
Proceed to Ethics, p. 335
Proceed to Politics, p. 291

16

CONCEPTS OF ETHNOMEDICINE

Dan Choffnes

Around 60,000 years ago, groups of humans began to venture out of their southern African center of origin and colonize new areas. Consummate explorers, some marched through eastern Africa and onward to Europe, others into Asia and beyond.[1] As they traveled, they encountered new plants and animals, and perhaps new illnesses too. By nature curious, they undoubtedly tasted hundreds of leaves, roots, fruits, and seeds along the way. As they settled into lives in their new homelands, they developed a rich knowledge of which herbs were poisonous and at which times of the year. They learned which plants to gather for sustenance and eventually how to propagate them to support their growing communities. Existence was challenging for these early human explorers and colonizers. Fortunately, wherever they traveled, people discovered plants that fortified their bodies, healed their wounds, eased their pains, and affirmed their faith in the spirits that watched over them.

Communities maintained oral traditions, and in time some developed the ability to document their experiences with medicinal plants in art and writing. Archaeological evidence places the use of medicinal plants to as early as 5700 BCE in Europe and approximately 4100 to 3500 BCE in Asia.[2] Records describing the medicinal properties of plants date to at least 2500 BCE, when ancient medical-religious texts of India describe herbs as components of the "knowledge of life."[3] Around the same time, the Yellow Emperor in China is chronicled in legend as having documented an array of curative plants.[4] In Egypt around 1500 BCE, papyri record that garlic (*Allium sativum*) and juniper (*Juniperus* spp.) were used for their healing abilities.[5] This evidence in written form shadows the tradition linking herbal knowledge across generations in the development of a medicospiritual discipline. In North and South America, Australia, and Africa, people practiced medicine and passed on their expertise, and by the time the Europeans encountered these peoples, elaborate health beliefs and vast herbal resources existed.[6] Indeed, societies from Asia to Europe and the Americas likely independently developed their worldviews and ideas of wellness, philosophies in which plants were integral.

Before the systematic study of anatomy, notions of germs, and the advent of clinics, humans constructed detailed scenarios to explain the circumstances conducive to health and to remedy conditions of illness. In various forms of traditional medicine, people entrusted their physical, mental, and spiritual wellness to a framework of beliefs shared by members of the same community. Interestingly, some of these health-related ideas, while embraced by societies living far apart, share certain elements. For example, one such shared principle in traditional medicine is the belief that human health reflects a balance of forces or energies. When observing the world around them, early societies recognized that natural phenomena can frequently be described by terms in sets of opposites: light and dark, hot and cold, wet and dry, among others. A harmonious natural environment, these observers reasoned, was one in which neither heat nor cold is to an extreme, in which periods of dryness are followed by rain, and they expected a balance of such contrasting forces to promote life and vigor. The human body, being part of the natural world, also expresses such conditions. Thus, when the body loses its balance, illness results, and balance can be restored through spiritual exercises, physical manipulation, and medicinal herbs. This equilibrium must occur in the individual as it does in the world and in the universe, in which the same forces occur and are usually at balance. The idea that health is a function of balance is among the most widespread of the traditional medical beliefs, evident in ancient China, India, the Mediterranean, and the Americas.[7] It also demonstrates that in many societies, medicine was inseparable from philosophy and religion.

As people settled in many different regions of the planet, they harvested native plants for medicinal purposes and cultivated those they brought from elsewhere or acquired in trade. The combination of locally sourced flora, particular landscapes and physical challenges, distinctive languages, cosmologies, and social structures together imparted unique characteristics to the world's many types of

Indigenous medicines. Rather than look at any region as uniform in terms of medical culture, it is worthwhile to consider the diversity in health-related beliefs and practices along several dimensions.

First, numerous ways of treating health can exist at the same time among a group of people—that is, medical plurality. For instance, different practitioners living in a single community may have vastly divergent approaches to addressing a patient's condition, and individuals may address medical concerns with a combination of professional assistance and self-care. Second, health-related ideas evolve over time, adapting to new illnesses, accommodating changing philosophies, and incorporating innovations. Therefore, a regional medicine as practiced now or in the past, though it may be dubbed "traditional," is not a static entity, but rather dynamic. Third, cultural borrowing can lead to a synthesis between local medical knowledge and that appropriated from other people. While some forms of medicine have developed in isolated communities, many Indigenous medical practices bear witness to years of commerce and exchange. Many of the world's major traditional medicines are complex amalgamations of beliefs and techniques, employing pharmaceuticals having originated in different places.

The following sections provide an overview of some of the traditional medical beliefs and practices of East Asia, South Asia, Africa, and the Americas, and demonstrate the diverse ways that people have conceptualized health and the role of plant-based treatments in influencing it. The remainder of the discussion follows the European experience in medicine, where, as elsewhere, health was considered to be the product of a balanced physical, mental, and spiritual state. In recent centuries, an approach to medicine emerged in Europe in which the scientific testing of herbs offered new ways to gauge therapeutic activity while rejecting many previous ideas about disease causation. Now widespread, particularly in the industrialized world, this biomedical system of health care coexists with numerous traditional medical systems and countless informal and folk practices that also employ plants as medicines.

TRADITIONAL MEDICINE IN EAST ASIA

Many of the world's medical traditions developed concepts of health that viewed the person in the context of society, the local environment, and the universe as a whole. In these systems, the body is the beneficiary of natural energies (in the form of food and environment) and supernatural forces (such as spirit powers) that promote proper development. In China, people came to believe that the whole organism is healthy when it is in a state of balance and harmony with the world. In this system, health is considered a state of physical and mental well-being.[8]

Chinese traditional medicine[9] views the universe as permeated by the *qi* life force, which constantly flows through heaven, earth, and all living things. Since qi is present in the air, soil, food, and all parts of the environment, it can strongly influence human health. The properties of *qi* are believed to change according to the time of day and the seasons, and they can vary regionally as well. For example, qi has a warmer quality in the summer and a cooler quality in the winter, darker properties at night and lighter properties during the day. According to Chinese medicine, illness results when an individual is unable to adapt to the changing nature of qi.

These ever-fluctuating features of the universe are the foundation of Chinese medical thought. Chinese medicine recognizes that qi and all matter are endowed with two opposing qualities: *yin*, the dark and cool property, and *yang*, the light and warm property. In the body, as in the environment, neither quality should have complete reign. For example, when night falls, the sky becomes quite dark. But in the darkness, there is light in the coming dawn. The cycles of day and night, the four seasons, and the patterns of precipitation and drought are natural processes of a universe at balance. As yin properties increase, yang properties decrease, until the extreme, when yang properties appear again. Because human beings are part of the universe through which qi flows, the yin and yang qualities of the body, changing over time relative to each other, can affect the nature of its qi. As qi is the force for life, so too is it responsible for health and illness.

Chinese medicine views that the body processes qi to derive nutrition and protect itself from illness. Properly extracted from the universe, a type of qi known as orthopathic qi gives the body the means to resist illness. Meanwhile, the illness-causing heteropathic qi assaults the body from the exterior, putting two types of qi in opposition. The ability of orthopathic qi to resist heteropathic qi is considered a state of health. Any overabundance of heteropathic qi activity can lead to illness, as can an excess of orthopathic qi: the healthy state is a balance of these forces. Since *qi* is influenced by its yin and yang properties, illness is thought to emerge from changes in the environment (disrupting a balance by affecting heteropathic qi) and/or changes in the body (affecting orthopathic qi).

To promote the proper qualities of orthopathic qi (and thereby resist illness), practitioners of Chinese medicine are aware that yin and yang qualities in balance promote health. (This does not mean a balance of equal amounts. In Chinese medicine, the yin–yang relationship in a patient is dynamic and responsive to the state of illness and the environment.) To maintain health, they pay close attention to the emotional state, social activities, diet, and exercise regimen, all of which influence the type and movement of qi in their bodies.

Belief in the role of qi in health influences lifestyle by encouraging balance in all activities: maintaining an even emotional keel, striving for social harmony, consuming cuisine with an appropriate representation of "warming" and "cooling" ingredients, and undertaking regular physical and mental pursuits. When illness strikes, however, doctors can identify patterns of colors (of face or tongue), temperatures, pulse profiles, and behaviors that indicate to them whether the patient suffers from an overabundance or deficiency of yin or yang qualities.

Medical interventions are developed to strengthen the patient's internal qi and improve its flow through the body by imparting to it the yin or yang properties that would allow it to promote health and drive out illness.[10] Chinese pharmaceuticals, which are composed of plant material as well as some mineral- and animal-based substances, are commonly given in mixtures of several ingredients, often prepared as soups or pills. When choosing a treatment, doctors look to influence the balance of yin and yang activities. The Chinese herbal pharmacy is extensive, containing thousands of ingredients categorized by their warming or cooling properties and effects on the body's qi.[11] For example, the seed of milkvetch (*Astragalus complanatus*) is thought to support yang, and the stems and leaves of the dendrobium orchid (Dendrobium spp.) to strengthen yin.[12] Chinese medicine also values herbs that serve to reinforce orthopathic *qi* in general, such as ginseng (*Panax* spp.) root.[13] In summary, traditional East Asian medicine considers health to be a condition of balance, in which a person's body and mind are at harmony with universal forces. Medicinal plants, selected according to their yin–yang properties, are thought to reinforce the body's abilities to ward off illness.

TRADITIONAL MEDICINE IN SOUTH ASIA

Among the principal Indigenous medicines of South Asia are *ayurveda*, a form of health care that originated in what is now northern India and Pakistan, and *siddha*, which is more widely practiced in the Tamil-speaking parts of southern India.[14] In ayurvedic medicine, human beings are considered to represent a microcosm consisting of the same energies and substances as the larger universe, and therefore health is fundamentally connected to the state of the macrocosm.[15] The basic matter of the cosmos combines to create the internal forces that govern physiology and behavior, the *doshas*. The *doshas* regulate various bodily functions and are seated in different parts of the head, chest, and abdomen. When they are in balance, a person is healthy.[16] The state of equilibrium is influenced by, and can influence, the physical and mental constitution of the individual, so treatments frequently entail changes in religious or meditative behavior, emotional control, exercise, diet, and sensory experiences in the pursuit of balanced bioenergetic principles.[17]

Ayurvedic medicine recognizes that the flavors of food signal their elemental makeup and, therefore, their effect on the *doshas*. For example, sweet flavors increase one of the *doshas* while decreasing the other two, and pungent flavors raise two of the *doshas* while subduing the third. In total, ayurvedic medicine distinguishes six tastes that can be further classified by their hot–cold, oily–dry, heavy–light, and dull–sharp aspects.[18] Therapeutic approaches in Indian medicine often entail changes in diet and the use of herbal pharmaceuticals with flavor and other properties conducive to the equilibrium of the *doshas*. For instance, the three spices of black pepper (*Piper nigrum*) fruits, long pepper (*Piper longum*) fruits, and the underground stems of ginger (*Zingiber officinale*) are widely employed in South Asia for their culinary, and therefore medical, properties. In addition to taste, color is considered important in its effects on the *doshas*. Because sensory experience plays a role in health and illness, ayurvedic pharmaceuticals draw heavily from fragrant and colorful plant products, including saffron (*Crocus sativus*) and turmeric (*Curcuma longa*).

Drawing on some common sources with ayurvedic medicine and other influences, *siddha* is a prominent form of health care in the state of Tamil Nadu in modern-day southern India.[19] In this system of medicine, properties of the universe are at play in the human body in the form of matter (*shiva*) and energy (*shakti*), and they influence the health of the organs through their connections to the celestial zodiac.[20] In *siddha* medicine, health is a function of five elements that combine in various ways to form three bodily constituents, the *muppini*, whose equilibrium promotes health.[21] In addition to environmental, climatic, and hereditary factors, the diet and a vast array of pharmaceuticals can play a role in the balance of *muppini*. Among many mineral- and metal-based treatments, *siddha* medicine also employs herbal medicines to purify inorganic drugs before use, cleanse the body internally and externally, and treat specific ailments and generally improve health.[22]

TRADITIONAL MEDICINE IN THE AMERICAS

In North America, the Indigenous peoples developed approaches to health care that suited their diverse cultures and geographic settings. It would therefore be impossible to consider them as a bloc. However, a few examples will illustrate that among some American Indian groups, illness and healing has centered on the role of the community and the spiritual world in the well-being of the individual. In these traditions, physical and mental health is seen to be a result of a good relationship with one's community, environment, and deities.[23]

Among the Iroquois (Haudenosaunee) of what is now the northeastern United States, for example, the health of the individual is inseparable from the state of the universe. Human illness is considered a response to harm that has occurred elsewhere in the social group or in nature.[24] The Iroquois generally do not view health in the material (by attributing wellness to the forces, elements, and opposing qualities comprising the universe). Rather, they see health encompassing abstract criteria ranging from physical and mental comfort to the maintenance of life and good luck. Therefore, Native American herbalists integrated medicine into the community-wide sense of fortune, harmony, and spiritual oneness. Plant drugs are chosen to treat the spiritual imbalances in individuals or their surroundings, which reduces the physical manifestations of those conditions.

Because the source of health and illness has often been seen as existing beyond the material world, communities relied on specialists who claimed to mediate and communicate with the intangible, spiritual component of the universe to effect healing. It is often the role of shamans to care for the ill, harnessing their special powers to identify and appease the source of illness. It is also clear that many tribes view health as a community matter, and so healing takes place in ceremonial settings, such as sweat lodges and talking circles, under the supervision of an individual thought to have the power (or skill) to guide the process.[25]

Among the Chippewa (Ojibwe, Anishinaabe) of north-central North America, promotion of health and long life has been thought of as a matter of the spirits as well. Shamans adept at diagnosing and treating illness, sometimes called medicine men, are esteemed in their communities for their ability to identify the appropriate treatment for an ailment, knowledge that they believe they receive in dreams.[26] In addition to remedies of physical ailments, Chippewa medicine men consider the preparation of good-luck charms as part of their healthcare duties. Therefore, they are known to provide patients with substances to attract mates or improve their hunting and fishing success.[27]

The notion that an individual's mental, physical, moral, and spiritual health is interconnected with the well-being of the community is evident in the beliefs of the Lakota people of the North American Great Plains.[28] The Lakota consider that a person comprises "four constituent dimensions of self," including an individual soul or spirit, a divine spirit, a "vital breath" that sets the physical operations of the body in motion, and an intellectual-spiritual presence that guards against evil and helps overcome obstacles in life.[29] In these traditions, medicinal plants serve to not only alter the physiology but also contribute to the fortune and social well-being of an individual or a community.

Thousands of plants serve these roles in Indigenous North American medicine, and they are often used for different purposes in different regions.[30] The big sagebrush (*Artemisia tridentata*) has been employed against respiratory illnesses such as the common cold, as a remedy for stomachache or headache, and as a spiritual cleanser.[31] In what is now the western United States, people turned to native yuccas (*Yucca* spp.) for medicine, and, like many medicinal plants of North America, they are thought to influence physical and spiritual health. The Blackfoot, Cheyenne, and Lakota, for example, harvested the small soapweed (*Yucca glauca*) for use as a hair wash and baldness preventer, among other uses, and the Navajo (Diné) considered it a stimulant and contraceptive.[32] The Hopi prepared extracts of the related narrowleaf yucca (*Yucca angustissima*) in ceremonial purification rituals, in addition to using it as a hair loss–preventing shampoo and laxative.[33]

It is difficult to determine the extent to which Indigenous American medical practices were codified because most groups left no written records. It seems the role of healer or shaman was often a matter of bloodline and special knowledge.[34] Therefore, there are no ancient books describing practices as they occurred in the past and no way to determine the course of development of treatments, such as medicines shared between groups and how medicines may have diverged. Despite the enormous diversity of geographic settings and cultural histories, it is clear that Indigenous Americans employed herbal medicines extensively for a variety of physical, mental, and spiritual conditions. Among many groups, plants served to promote health as a harmonious relationship between the person, his community, nature, and the spiritual universe.

The Aztec (Mexica) civilization, which flourished in present-day Mexico from the fourteenth to sixteenth centuries, left documents and descendants that shed light on its medical beliefs and practices.[35] According to Indigenous mythology, the first humans were created from a divine mixture of material from the heavens and the earth, imbued with opposing properties that must remain in balance to sustain life. Disequilibria of these elements cause illness. The Aztecs viewed the earthly component as the Great Mother, instilled with feminine, cold, wet, and dark qualities. The Great Father was the heavenly contribution, a masculine, hot, dry, and light force.[36] At its core, the Aztec worldview framed a parallel between the organization of the human body and that of the universe, where each bodily function owed something to either the Great Father or the Great Mother.

Aztecs sought balance in their diet, moderation in their emotions and physical activity, and obedience in their relationship with authority as a way to procure the harmonious relationship among the opposing forces that formed their bodies.[37] The ultimate manifestation of harmony between a person, the community, the environment, and the cosmos was the *tonalli*, an energy-laden spirit from the gods that gave a person vigor.[38] Various factors, such as immoderate physical activity, were thought to diminish the *tonalli* and result in illness.

The Aztecs also believed that humans, being made of cosmic material, could influence the fate of heaven and earth. Therefore, they developed means to "give back" to their creators in the form of human sacrifice, which they believed supplied energy to the gods.[39] In addition to the belief that health derives from a balance of opposing properties in the body, the Aztecs held that spirits inhabited the forests, caves, rivers, and other features of the environment. These invisible beings, according to Aztec medicine, had a hunger for *tonalli*.[40]

Among the herbs that could protect the *tonalli* was *tlacopatli* (*Aristolochia anguicida*), "used to treat cold illnesses and to strengthen and revive people."[41] Children wore *tlacopatli* bead necklaces as a remedy, and its roots could be applied to the top of the head to restore *tonalli*.

Some illnesses were caused by, rather than cured by, plants, and the Aztecs harbored beliefs that affronts to plants or their spirits could invoke retribution. For example, people were forbidden to urinate on the *aquiztli* vine (*Paullinia fuscescens*), or else they would be afflicted with blisters all over their bodies.[42] (The same plant was used to treat blisters.) Someone who slept in the shadow of *aquiztli* would lose his or her hair.[43] Furthermore, some plants contained spirits that practitioners could take inside their bodies to derive otherworldly capabilities. For example, herbal drugs that induced visions were thought to function by transferring the god of the plant into the person ingesting it and by directing the user's *tonalli* toward the god's place of residence. Specialists sought such medicines to help them commune with deities and obtain secret knowledge to diagnose and treat patients in their care.[44] Therefore, among the Aztecs, plants (and their spirits) played important roles in both causing and curing illness.

TRADITIONAL MEDICINE IN AFRICA

The many forms of African medicine originated among peoples living throughout a vast continent, maintaining distinctive languages and social customs, practicing different religious traditions, and harvesting medicinal plants particular to their locations. To the West African Akan people of modern-day Ghana, illness results from a combination of social, environmental, and spiritual factors. Poor diet or overindulgence in certain foods can result in sickness, as can the forces of pathogen-laden wind, evil intentions, and the acts of evil people, spirits, and witchcraft.[45] Healers prepare a variety of plants as herbal teas, salves, baths, and so forth, and some have special abilities to communicate with the spirit manifestations of the creator residing in the ocean, rivers, mountains, and plants.[46] In addition, talismans play a role in helping practitioners select medicinal plants for their patients and improve the therapeutic outcome.[47] For instance, the root of a forest tree that goes by a local name signifying "executioner medicine" (*Mareya micrantha*), apparently because of its poisonous effects if prepared incorrectly, is employed in spiritual baths and enemas, and its leaves are used to treat stomach pains and constipation, among other conditions.[48]

Among some southern African groups, such as the Basotho of modern-day Lesotho, health is a product of a body and mind at ease with the environment and spiritual world. Illness can occur when a person is in a state of physical or social disequilibrium, such as having an overabundance of certain substances in the body or having a disturbed social relationship with certain living or deceased people.[49] The state of imbalance presents itself in a number of forms, such as having excess heat (in a figurative sense, rather than fever), which can be treated with cooling drugs "such as ash, water plants, or aquatic animals."[50] Illness and misfortune can often be attributed to malevolent spirits and people with evil will, such as sorcerers, and therefore medical practitioners include herbalists, who are able to diagnose and treat many types of ailments, and diviners and seers, whose special powers to communicate with the spirit world render their diagnoses more accurate and their treatments (including herbal medicines) more effective.[51] The special capacity of medicinal plants to influence a person's luck is evident in the use of lemongrass (*Cymbopogon marginatus*) to procure love, as when a man adds it to his bathwater "while he calls out the name of the desired woman."[52] Other plants are less strongly associated with spiritual powers, such as *lengana* (the wormwood *Artemisia afra*), whose fragrant leaves are used as nasal plugs, in herbal teas, and for steaming in cases of colds, sore throat, and digestive problems, among others.[53]

To the ancient Egyptians, a body "in harmony with the cosmos . . . could serve as a receptacle for the vital forces that created the universe."[54] The Egyptians inhabited a universe composed of both physical matter and immaterial forces overseen by an assemblage of gods with varying responsibilities and powers. Accordingly, they sought to maintain health by regulating both physical aspects of their diet and behavior and by avoiding the ill will of deities who would harm them. Medical treatments commonly invoked the spirits to request relief from the various evils responsible for a person's ailment. Therefore, to the ancient Egyptians, medicine, religion, and magic were deeply intertwined.[55]

Numerous herbal medicines and plant-derived dietary ingredients have been documented in medical papyri and survive as archaeological specimens.[56] Among several hundred pharmaceuticals deciphered in ancient texts are many drugs that act in the bowels, such as the oil of castor seeds (*Ricinus communis*) and the fruits of the fig tree (*Ficus* spp.).[57] To the Egyptians, regularly cleansing the evil toxins that accumulated in food prevented the spread of their harmful properties to the rest of the body. Therefore, castor counts among drugs recorded in the Ebers medical papyrus (ca. 1550 BCE) to "drive out suffering from the belly of a man."[58]

SHARED FEATURES OF MEDICAL SYSTEMS

There are common elements in some of these diverse medical traditions. In many parts of the world, health conceptions tend to link an individual's wellness to the state of the universe. The forces at play in the world also permeate the human body, contributing to vigor and longevity or, oppositely, to illness. Good physical vitality and good fortune represent different aspects of health maintenance. Traditional philosophies stress the importance of balance in physical and mental activities, outlook on life, and choice of foods and spices. They often view psychological and physical health matters as deriving from common causes and sharing treatments. Plant-derived drugs tend to be classified within a scheme in which they serve to influence the vital force or restore equilibrium to the elements operating within a body, the effects of which reduce illness symptoms. In this sense, healers do not always seek to treat the ailment directly with their herbal preparations. Rather, they often treat the underlying imbalances causing the symptoms. In some cases, medicinal plants are used to communicate with and appease the deities or spirits responsible for illness.

The following sections will outline the evolution of the European lineage of medicine, from its origins in the ancient Mediterranean until the modern day.[59] It is clear that traditional European medicine has much in common with other world medical systems, including the classification of life forces or properties into opposing but complementary categories, the idea that physical and mental health are tied together, and the use of herbal substances to promote harmony within the individual and more broadly. During the past several centuries, a new, scientific tradition emerged in Europe that embraced a distinctive methodology for determining effective medical treatments and that now serves as the foundation for practice in much of the world.

TRADITIONAL MEDICINE OF THE MEDITERRANEAN

A group of Greek scholars including Hippocrates (ca. 450–370 BCE) and his followers promoted the idea that the human being, as part of nature, "was subject to the same physical constraints as the rest of the ordered cosmos," and therefore illness could be understood and addressed according to observable phenomena at play in the environment.[60] Over many centuries, their theories were elaborated by doctors working throughout the Mediterranean region and served as the basis of an influential and widespread form of Greek and Roman medicine. To these thinkers, the universe revealed sets of opposing qualities—cold and hot, wet and dry, and so forth—and these principles joined in nature to create matter in the form of earth, air, fire, and water.[61] The relative abundance of these temperature and moisture properties changed over time (such as in the cycling of the seasons), but early physicians believed that the four elements that they produced were fundamentally at balance.[62] The human body generated from the elements a set of substances with properties corresponding to the principles of nature, which they called the humors. In this system, blood (or sanguis) is hot and moist; phlegm is cold and moist; black bile (or melancholer) is cold and dry; and yellow bile (or choler) is hot and dry.[63] These substances were present in the body from conception until death, influenced by diet, seasons, and geography, and affected a person's health and personality.

The four humors of blood, phlegm, black bile, and yellow bile were metaphorical, invisible substances, not actually fluids that could be isolated.[64] The blood humor is not the same as arterial blood, although when red blood emerges from a wound, the blood humor is instrumental. Similarly, phlegm is evident as a force behind watery secretions, black bile perhaps behind clotted blood and accretions in stool, and yellow bile in pus and vomit. People sought to achieve a relative balance among the humors, although individuals tended to be dominated by one of the four. Since the body generated humors from the elements present in the diet, and because the constitution drew influence from lifestyle choices, climate, and other factors, it was possible for imbalances to emerge that threatened the individual's health. Conditions associated with an excess of phlegm, for example, include lack of appetite and thirst, weak brain, miscarriages, dysentery, diarrhea, and chronic fevers.[65] Bronchitis and acute fevers would be rare among individuals with this excess.

The humors also played a role in shaping personality. The mental or psychological constitution of the individual—his or her temperament—could be classified according to the same principles. Someone with an excess of yellow bile was thought to be disposed to anger, particularly in the summer, and a person with too much phlegm might be passive and withdrawn, especially in the winter.[66] Evidence for the classical belief in humors abounds in the modern English language and corresponds to the four temperaments of the ancient Greeks and Romans. Someone with a sanguine disposition is cheerful and optimistic. Phlegmatic means calm and composed. Melancholy is a gloomy or depressed state of mind, and a bilious individual is irritable and cranky.

Although some humoral imbalances were corrected surgically or by lifestyle changes, people often regulated the balance of humors with diet, a practice that includes medicinal herbs.[67] The Greek writers who advanced the humoral system classified all foods and medicines by their fundamental qualities: hot, cold, dry, or moist. Remedies to illness were a matter of matching the personality and symptoms to a therapy with opposite properties.[68] In this view, an excess of black bile, associated with the cold and dry temperament and indicative of conditions such as constipation and depression, could be relieved with the consumption of hot herbs such as senna (*Senna alexandrina*) and hellebore (*Helleborus* spp.).[69] These medicines were thought to function by inducing the body to eliminate feces and, with it, the offending humor.

It is therefore not surprising that many traditional European herbal medicines derive from treatments intended to regulate the humors, with a particular focus on controlling the secretions of the body and the digestive process. Moreover, since excess humors were thought to accumulate poisons, a goal of pharmacy was to remove them from the body. So to purge toxins of the phlegm, yellow bile, or black bile, people sought herbal agents to induce vomiting and defecation. (Even in healthy times, medical wisdom held that frequent vomiting and purgation promoted wellness.)[70] For example, scammony (*Convolvulus scammonia*) was recommended in early Greek texts as a purgative capable of effecting a rapid discharge of the bowels.[71] Scammony remained in use for this purpose in Europe and the United States into the twentieth century.[72]

Medical writers during this period often framed therapies in terms of the humoral system, recognizing that drugs have temperature and moisture properties that could influence the temperament and symptoms of the patient. The Greek physician Pedanius Dioscorides (ca. 40–90 CE) broke with tradition by presenting pharmaceutical knowledge in terms of specific effects on the human body, without interpreting medicine in the theoretical context of the humors.[73] His *De materia medica* (ca. 70 CE), a list of more than 500 herbs describing their names, appearance, and uses in the treatment of illness, was the first of its kind.[74] Such a thorough catalog of medicinal plants was previously unknown in the Mediterranean sphere, and it served as a key medical text for the next 1,500 years throughout Europe and Asia Minor. The value of Dioscorides's work is in its descriptions of medicinal plants, which allowed others to gather the same herbs as he mentioned—an important step toward standardization in medical care—and in his instructions for preparing the medicines, and his inventory of the drugs' uses and risks.

Because most medicinal substances were harvested from plants, and because Dioscorides produced the first book to treat drugs in this way, his influence was long-lasting. A catalog of useful plant medicines became known as an herbal, and many important herbals have since been written. It is now commonplace to call all books listing medicinal plant properties *materia medica* in reference to the title of his work. Dioscorides's *materia medica* also emerged as the first pharmacopeia—a list of all accepted drugs, with their preparation and processing for medical use—in the Western world.[75] Since that time, national and international medical establishments have maintained written inventories of approved medicines. ("Approved" medicines are technically termed "official.") In modern times, approval is often noted on the label of a medicine. For example, "USP" indicates a drug listed in the United States Pharmacopeia.

THE HUMORAL SYSTEM: FIFTEEN CENTURIES OF MEDICAL DOCTRINE

The humoral understanding of health was first described by Greek physicians of the fifth and fourth centuries BCE and elaborated in the writings of many others, including the celebrated physician Galen (129–ca. 216 CE), living in the Roman Empire, on whose authority the practice of medicine in Europe depended for many centuries.[76] Galen's theories on the nature of health satisfied the desire for a rational explanation of illness, and few doctors of his era or of succeeding generations questioned the elegance of the system in which balanced elements ensured health. In the medical tradition that he championed, the role of diet, lifestyle, and environment in health was paramount. In the centuries after Galen, the humoral system that had taken hold throughout Europe was codified into practice in Persia and then later throughout the Muslim world.[77] Even when the glory of Greek and Roman scholarship waned, Muslim doctors preserved Galen's medicine and reintroduced his writings to Europe hundreds of years later.[78] With the revival of classical learning in Europe during the Middle Ages and Renaissance, humoral medicine again became the subject of intensive study, and Galen's works were recopied and widely distributed. The humoral theories held sway in European medical education and practice until the eighteenth and nineteenth centuries, when they gradually began to subside. (It is worth noting that the Hippocratic-Galenic view of health was not the only form of medicine in existence in the classical Mediterranean region. Numerous schools competed for adherents during the era, a phenomenon that resulted in a large critical literature. In addition, many practitioners likely operated without an overarching theoretical framework or advocated religious or magical medicine. Ultimately, however, it was Galen's writings that were elevated to the position of primacy for many centuries.)

UNDERCURRENTS IN EUROPEAN MEDICAL PRACTICE: MYSTICISM AND THE DOCTRINE OF SIGNATURES

With the fall of the Roman Empire in the late fifth century, medical practice in Europe became an amalgam of ancient Greek and Roman tradition, Catholic Church doctrine, and tribal folklore. The emphasis on natural forces and balance in lifestyle and dietary choices that Galen promoted became mixed with beliefs in the healing (or harmful) effects of spirit beings. For example, in the *Leech Book of Bald*, a tenth-century Anglo-Saxon herbal, treatments are described for illnesses caused by a "pagan charm" and "flying venom," a clear departure from the idea that imbalances of body substances were at the core of illness.[79]

In addition to their generally herbal remedies, medical treatises of medieval Europe included prayers and incantations as disease preventatives or treatments. The practice of medicine was closely linked to the Catholic Church: doctors were frequently monks or at least associated with monasteries, the sites of infirmaries. In addition to healing salves, herbal amulets, and surgery, people turned to holy relics such as the bones of saints for their restorative properties.[80]

European medical practice in the Middle Ages was often imbued with mysticism and drew on local folklore. Herbs such as wood betony (*Stachys officinalis*) and peony (*Paeonia officinalis*) saw frequent use for ailments of the skin, bowels, and other complaints. In the medicine of the era, these plants were thought to work in part by warding off evil spirits and through astrological influences whose activities were responsible for illness. For example, an early medieval English herbal from the eleventh century recommends wood betony for eye pain, earache, and constipation, and to protect "a person from dreadful nightmares and from terrifying visions and dreams."[81] Peony root is said to be good for the pain of sciatica when tied onto the body and to cure "lunacy."[82] Some plants were thought to be particularly useful against spirit-borne illnesses and creepy-crawly threats, such as the greater periwinkle (*Vinca major*), whose description in the same eleventh-century herbal claims its utility "for possession by demons, for snakes, wild animals, poisons, for any threats, envy, terror, so you will have grace, so you will be happy and comfortable."[83]

Many people also believed in the evil eye, a curse that penetrated their bodies and souls, bringing them misfortune and poor health.[84] Fear of the evil eye probably goes back millennia, and it has persisted alongside other forms of medical belief.[85] People produced charms from the leaves, stems, and flowers of medicinal plants to repel its malicious powers. Indeed, the same medieval English herbal suggests keeping mugwort (*Artemisia vulgaris*) in one's house, as "it turns away the evil eye."[86]

During the early medieval period, monasteries served as repositories of medical knowledge and centers of practice, where monks and nuns cultivated "physic gardens" of herbs and copied ancient Greek and Latin manuscripts.[87] When medical colleges became established in Europe, they primarily taught the principles of Hippocrates, Galen, and other classical physicians in the context that prayer and divine will were the ultimate source of health.[88] Complementing the church's role in medicine was the oral tradition of folk medicine and home remedies passed down generation to generation and dispensed by spice and herb merchants (apothecaries) and elders.

By the sixteenth century, the European medical practice bore evidence of a complicated mixture of influences, including Galen's humoral theory, Christian belief, and mystical folk traditions.[89] Therefore, medicine encompassed beliefs in the fundamental forces of heat and moisture, whose balance allowed health, alongside divine providence, astrological forces, mystical energies, and curses. It was a complex discipline, and the bold Swiss alchemist-physician Paracelsus (Philippus Theophrastus Bombastus von Hohenheim, 1493–1541) sought to simplify it.

Paracelsus was a pioneering character in many ways. He taught medicine in Switzerland, Germany, and Austria and broke with precedent by writing and lecturing in vernacular German rather than in Latin, as was customary.[90] Considered one of the earliest toxicologists, he was the first physician to record that the dose of a drug can render it either poisonous or therapeutic.[91] Most important, Paracelsus considered that the diversity of medical traditions, overrun by their various humors, spirits, incantations, and the like, obscured humans' ability to perceive the natural healing abilities of plants. The theory of Galen and the superstitions of some religious sects, he thought, stood in the way of matching a medicinal herb to the ailment it treats. Therefore, Paracelsus promoted a simple, folk classification scheme for medicinal plants. Known as the Doctrine of Signatures, this belief held that the Creator designed plants with clues for the ailments they treated.[92] According to the Doctrine of Signatures, a plant growing yellow flowers is expected to cure jaundice, one with red sap would treat blood disorders, and one with fruit shaped like the brain, such as the walnut (*Juglans regia*), should be useful for improving mental abilities.

The long history of the Doctrine of Signatures in European medicine left a legacy in the common names of numerous plants that derive from their medical uses. For example, lungwort (*Pulmonaria officinalis*) grows leaves that bear a resemblance to diseased lungs with whitish spots, and was used to treat lung infections such as bronchitis and tuberculosis.[93] Liverworts (*Marchantiophyta*) produce lobed leaf-like structures and were thought to be effective against disorders of the liver, which is also a lobed organ. The flowers of birthwort (*Aristolochia clematitis*) are reminiscent of a woman's birth canal, and the plant was considered appropriate to treat obstetric concerns.[94] Mandrake (*Mandragora officinarum*), a plant whose root can look vaguely like a virile man, was taken as an aphrodisiac and a fertility drug.[95]

During the sixteenth and seventeenth centuries, medical authority continued to coalesce around major medical universities, where scholars lectured and published in Latin, while a number of rogue physicians published herbals in vernacular. In the English language, some of the most influential herbals of this period were by John Gerard (1597), John Parkinson (1640), and Nicholas Culpeper (1652).[96] The importance of plant medicines is underscored by the prominence of such herbals—catalogs of plants and their uses—as medical texts and field guides for apothecaries and herb gatherers. Because plants figured so prominently in human health, physician training included a thorough study of botany. It was also during this period that multiple new species were appearing in Europe for the first time, brought in from the east by traders and from the New World by conquistadors, missionaries, and natural historian explorers. Many of these plants, too, had valuable medicinal properties. The description and classification of the diversity of plants on earth became a critical component of an advanced medical system.

THE LINNAEAN BIOLOGICAL CLASSIFICATION SCHEME

Although the herbals documented hundreds of medicinal plants and provided doctors and plant collectors a guide to their use, it was not always straightforward for a person to identify the plants described because the field lacked a uniform naming system. The organization of species into clear groups with universally acceptable names, rather than local names that varied regionally, became the life's work of the Swedish botanist-physician Carolus Linnaeus (Carl von Linné, 1707–1778). Among the general population, plants and animals bore local names that were not always geographically consistent, meaning two unrelated organisms could be described by the same name in different towns, and a single type of organism could go by many names. Before Linnaeus, a similar confusion could exist even within the trained botany community: physicians and herbalists sometimes used long Latin descriptions for plants that listed their attributes, but not in a universally standard format. As an example, take the description of the Persian buttercup in Gerard's *Herball, or Generall Historie of Plants*: *Ranunculus Asiaticus grumosa radice flore flavo vario* (Asian crow-foot with lumpy root and yellow striped flowers).[97] Gerard's seven word identifier might just delineate a color variety that he happened to encounter, but not one that applies to all individuals of the same biological type. In any case, the long label is cumbersome. Linnaeus developed a hierarchical system that organized all the specimens he studied by similarities and differences in structure and resulted in each unique type being assigned a single, simple Latin descriptor.

This advance, first published in *Systema Naturae* (1735) and elaborated in the monumental two-volume *Species Plantarum* (1753), gave all unique plant types two names: a genus name, a broad category encompassing many physically related varieties, and a species name, a precise name delineating just one type of organism.[98] This name, composed of a genus and species, is known as the Linnaean binomial, and it is the standard format by which scientists identify and distinguish organisms and varieties with precision.

Over the centuries, new knowledge has been applied to Linnaeus's classification scheme, and systematists (specialists in biological classification) refined the original hierarchies and species assignments. In particular, recent advances in molecular biology have allowed biologists to study the DNA of plants and ascertain evolutionary relationships not apparent to previous generations of researchers examining only the outward appearance of specimens. In some cases, molecular data have helped rewrite the classification of species by placing them among their closest genetic kin, despite differences in morphology.[99]

The binomial system pioneered by Linnaeus remains the only accepted way to identify an organism in the scholarly world. For example, the tomato plant can be properly described by its binomial *Solanum lycopersicum* (note the capitalized genus-name initial, lowercase species-name initial, and italics), which can be shortened to *S. lycopersicum* on subsequent references.[100] There are other members of the genus *Solanum*, relatives of the tomato such as *S. tuberosum*, the potato. Occasionally, distinctions within a species become apparent (sometimes called subspecies), necessitating a special notation, and the binomial is appended. For instance, *Origanum vulgare* refers to oregano, the aromatic perennial herb native to Europe and western Central Asia. *Origanum vulgare* ssp. *gracile* is a particular type of oregano from Central Asia with a distinctive leaf shape and flower color, and *Origanum vulgare* ssp. *hirtum* has been selected for its ease of cultivation and strong flavor.[101]

EMPIRICISM IN MEDICINE

By closely examining plant specimens and systematically describing their similarities and differences, Linnaeus demonstrated that careful observation, coupled with a willingness to break with long-standing intellectual customs, could lead to a new understanding of nature. Whereas much of European medicine sought to treat illness according to the prevailing conceptions of the humors and employed plant drugs chosen by convention or "signature," the European Enlightenment period saw the growth of a movement to question and test medical ideas actively. This movement helped progress medical study from a discipline guided by theological and classical doctrine to one in which physicians refined old medicines and developed new ones by testing drugs and making careful observations of dosage, preparation, and patients' outcomes. To some doctors of this era, no longer were mysterious spirits and invisible substances the primary agents in human health. Rather, they began to see human disease as a manifestation of symptoms with reducible physical causes, and they realized that the constituents of plant medicines could serve as remedies.

During this era, some physicians challenged the spirit-, humor-, and life force–based conceptions of illness and came to regard human health as an essentially mechanical phenomenon that could be influenced by quantifiable medications and interventions, such as specific doses of experimentally tested medicines. An important example of this developing style of medicine is the work of William Withering (1741–1799), an English physician and botanist who pioneered a treatment for the age-old malady known as dropsy.[102] The symptoms of dropsy include the accumulation of fluids in the extremities and lungs, shortness of breath, and a weak pulse. In today's terminology, these conditions indicate congestive heart failure. Prior to Withering, treatment of dropsy frequently entailed piercing the patient's extremities sought to treat illness according to the prevailing conceptions to release the excess fluid.[103] Withering suspected that dropsy could be treated differently and sought to establish a new medical intervention.

To develop a new treatment for this circulatory ailment, Withering turned to the experience of traditional herbal healers in England, who had been producing various plant concoctions for dropsy following folk practices dating back many centuries. He learned that among these treatments was foxglove (*Digitalis purpurea*). "A lady from the western part of Yorkshire assures me, that the people in her country often cure themselves of dropsical complaints by drinking Foxglove tea," Withering wrote, and he set about to examine closely the plant's effects in patients.[104] For ten years (1775–1785), he performed extensive studies to establish the best season in which to harvest the medicine, the most effective part of the plant, the proper preparation of the material, and the effective dose in carefully measured quantities of powdered leaf extracts. As foxglove was known to be poisonous, he needed to establish the drug's therapeutic dose. At the correct dose, the plant's cardiac glycosides work to slow and strengthen the heartbeat, reduce fibrillation, and improve circulation to clear retained fluids. (Through the twentieth century, the foxglove-derived medicine digitalis remained an important treatment for congestive heart disease.)[105] Thus Withering's exacting measurements and reliance on physical, rather than spiritual, evidence for the source and treatment of disease set the stage for a new approach to medicine that took shape after the eighteenth century.

In a break with earlier beliefs, some in the medical community of the nineteenth century began to accept that physical entities, such as germs or chemical toxins, were the cause of disease, rather than harder-to-measure forces such as curses or excesses of yellow bile. The body was viewed in mechanical terms, and advances in anatomy and the understanding of cellular structures encouraged physicians to concentrate their attention on the minutely observable processes of movement, development, and biochemical transformation in human beings. Whereas previous generations of doctors prescribed treatments based on the recommendation of ancient Greek scholars, with diagnoses and dosage never formally tested, some in this era saw prudence in examining the patient for specific symptoms and the drugs for unique active components. Many began to recognize the difference between traditional conjecture and empirical evidence for the efficacy of natural drugs.

While successful herbal medicines have developed—and remain in practice—throughout the world, drawing on ancient philosophies and traditional expertise, a great number of herbs and herb mixtures have not yet been tested in a systematic way.[106] Support for medicinal properties based on measured observation is central to the medical system that grew out of the European Enlightenment. In following practices elaborated during the nineteenth and twentieth centuries, biomedical researchers seek to test the effects on patients of carefully prepared and administered drugs across a broad spectrum of doses (including no drug at all), with data scrupulously recorded and shared with the wider medical community.

THE SCIENTIFIC METHOD

Based on the utility of empirical observation in gathering evidence about natural phenomena, biomedical research has evolved in recent centuries to develop a rigorous methodological platform from which to pose questions about the effectiveness of medicines and to generate answers to advance the discipline. This framework is known as the scientific method, and it serves to establish and support claims of a medicine's value in treating disease. The scientific method consists of a multistep process.

- The first phase of this method is to develop, based on a great deal of prior research, a testable idea (known as a hypothesis) that can be addressed experimentally. For example, the notion that some chemical in foxglove is capable of reducing the symptoms of dropsy could be examined by giving dropsy patients known doses of the foxglove extracts and carefully observing the outcomes. Crucial to this step is the expectation that all measurements would be repeatable by others. That is, no "secret" plant extracts can be promoted, and all characterizations must be precise. Furthermore, all experimental outcomes must be based on natural observations and derive from physical explanations. In this sense, it is not appropriate to assign any biological activities to ghosts, spirits, life forces, hexes, or acts of God, because they cannot be measured or described with existing instruments.

- The second phase of the scientific method is the process of carefully designing and carrying out a controlled experiment. To do this, the researcher must be able to distinguish whether a drug is truly responsible for (that is, causes) a perceived effect. For example, consider another experiment to test the efficacy of purple coneflower (*Echinacea* spp.) extract, an herbal treatment available in many retail drugstores, on the severity of respiratory infections. In this fictional experiment, fifty children suffering common cold symptoms are given daily doses of purple coneflower extracts, perhaps in the form of capsules. On the second day, half the patients report feeling much better, and by the fourth day, nearly all the children feel fine, an assessment supported by objective measurements of their body temperatures and open nasal passages. It might appear that the herbal remedy is effective—after all, most of the children recover, and quickly, it seems. The patients may even report that this herbal treatment seems more potent than alternative treatments taken during previous illnesses. However, biomedical researchers might challenge the evidence for efficacy because of the lack of experimental controls. Without experimental controls, it is not possible to determine whether the patients would have recovered, perhaps just as quickly, even without taking purple coneflower pills.

  How can the researcher determine what the normal progression of the illness would be in the absence of any treatment? To establish this, each experiment can have a negative control treatment, in which a subset of the patients is given a false or mock medication intended to produce in itself no specific effect on the condition being studied. This treatment might consist of a preparation of medically inactive herbs or a sugar pill. The patients, however, are not informed which type of medication ("real" versus "mock") they receive. The treatment not containing active medicine is called the placebo. In this way, the investigator can assess whether the pharmaceutical under consideration has any therapeutic effect distinguishable from the psychological effects in addition to the targeted condition (called side effects), and clinical researchers can employ placebos that cause mild side effects, a way to disguise further the nature of the treatment to the patient. These are known as active placebos.

Use of a placebo group in a clinical study is a key element of modern biomedical research that allows researchers to document the physiological and psychological aspects of treatment in a single experiment. Interestingly, many patients respond symptomatically to the experience of being treated in a medical setting, regardless of taking an active medication. In studies of pain, depression, and numerous other ailments, on average 35 percent of patients experience an improvement in symptoms after taking an inert medicine.[107] This phenomenon, often called the placebo effect, can be traced not to the substance of the medication, which is thought to be biologically inactive, but to the treatment environment and the nature of the interaction between a patient and a caregiver.[108] That is, the patient feels listened to and that his condition is understood, the patient feels concern from others, and the patient feels a sense of control over his own condition. Thus the mental outlook and optimism of a patient can strongly affect the physical sense of health.

Because the placebo effect is such a powerful factor in the manifestations of illness, experiments should account for it. The best clinical studies test a medication of unknown efficacy against a placebo among patients randomly assigned into the two categories. Neither the patients nor the caregivers know whether they are receiving or delivering the medication or the placebo, a design labeled "double-blind." Since the advent of scientific medical practice, countless double-blind, placebo-controlled studies have contributed to a contemporary pharmacopeia of natural and synthetic medications.

- The third phase of the scientific method is the publication and sharing of experimental findings with the broader community. To facilitate this, numerous scholarly journals specialize in printing such medical studies, and their editors and reviewers vet the studies for adherence to scientific guidelines and clarity of conclusions drawn. Published experimental results are then subject to criticism and retesting, a process that strengthens accurate findings and disproves false findings or improperly conducted experiments. Consequently, medical science constantly renews and improves its understanding of human health.

The scientific method, consisting of a carefully composed hypothesis to test, a controlled experimental approach, and the publication of findings, marks an important methodological shift from the practice of traditional medicine in Europe and elsewhere. In recent decades, medical authorities in Europe, the United States, and other parts of the world have emphasized the role of this system, with its clinical trials and statistically determined outcomes, in improving health care in both industrialized and developing nations. Although originating from the European Enlightenment, the scientific medical discipline has spread to many countries, where doctors are trained in its techniques and drugs are studied in certain standardized ways. It is this form of health care, coupled with progress in biochemistry and the strength of recent surgical advances, that is practiced as biomedicine around the world.[109]

PLURALITY, EVOLUTION, AND SYNTHESIS: MEDICAL TRADITIONS IN PERSPECTIVE

The biomedical approach has joined numerous other traditions in offering its own understanding of health and therapy in a diverse and dynamic health-care ecology. In the modern-day United States, for example, patients can seek treatment in hospitals and doctors' offices, where they might be likely to receive pharmaceutical drugs prepared from natural or synthetic sources. Yet the same people may also visit a traditional herbal healer and purchase mixtures of plant products for their health concerns, grow their own herbs to make herbal teas, and follow their grandmothers' dietary advice. In today's China, medical universities train physicians to practice either biomedicine or Chinese traditional medicine, and patients can choose to seek treatment at clinics and hospitals specializing in either.[110] In addition, those same patients might prepare cuisine at home according to traditional and religious principles, whether in terms of the heating and cooling properties of their foods or for their spiritual effects. They may also take medicines deriving from regional folk traditions. As in the past, many ideas about health and, consequently, many forms of herbal medicine coexist in the world's communities.

Medical beliefs and practices evolve, rendering any glimpse of a tradition as written in a text or observed among indigenous people merely a snapshot in time. Among the ancient Greeks, ideas about the humors were vigorously debated. Originally, the Hippocratic system accounted for only three fundamental substances, with black bile added later.[111] As these ideas were elaborated during Galen's time and afterward, differences in interpretation and application of shared concepts abounded. In the Muslim world, Galen's authority was reformulated by a series of influential writers over the course of several centuries, and forms of his teachings took hold in South Asia, Central Asia, and the Middle East, adapting to locally endemic illnesses and incorporating regionally abundant plants in therapy. In medieval and Renaissance Europe, Galen's notions of the humors variously took on astrological and religious inflections. As the voyages of discovery brought back never-before-seen plant specimens to the learned physician-botanists of Europe, these scholars accommodated the novel herbs in the preexisting scheme and assigned to them the qualities of hot, cold, dry, and moist that would enable them to be used alongside a growing number of plants both inherited from the ancients and adopted from folk practitioners. Likewise, biomedicine has gradually developed its robust methodology over the course of more than a century, discovering new treatments and discarding older ones, a process that will continue.

Humanity's many medical traditions have borne witness to significant cultural exchanges that produced new syntheses in various places and times. For instance, South Asian *siddha* medicine is thought to be a fusion of an ancient southeastern Indian folk tradition with theories borrowed from *ayurveda*. Both *ayurveda* and *siddha* probably gained certain diagnostic tools, such as pulse diagnosis and uroscopy, from Greek medicine brought by Muslims.[112] In modern-day China, biomedical concepts of disease have been interpreted according to traditional medical tenets, such that a patient in a traditional medical clinic might be diagnosed in terms of both *yin–yang* imbalance and abnormal hormone levels and be offered an herbal prescription as treatment. After many years of setting aside the spiritual and psychological aspects of therapy, some biomedical practitioners are promoting the approach of "treating the whole person" and "mind–body medicine," the tenets of which clearly resonate with many traditional medical practices.

The medicinal plants of the world are employed in a tremendous variety of human settings. Some are harvested for use in extensive health-care systems grounded in elaborate theory, with specialized hospitals and pharmacies and a worldwide audience, such as those used in biomedicine and Chinese traditional medicine.

Plants such as coffee (*Coffea* spp.) are turned into commodities, sold in markets large and small, and take on importance in locally accented concepts of health and sociability. Still other herbs are used by small communities, by people whose unique understanding of nature may never have been recorded, and whose medical traditions may reside only in the expertise of a dwindling number of practitioners. All these facets of the human experience with medicinal plants, whether found in cosmopolitan parts of the earth or in isolated villages, whether drawn from a large scholarly lineage or a folk custom practiced by few, demonstrate the capacity of medicinal plants to shape our culture.

In many parts of the world, people developed medical traditions that incorporated plants to promote health and treat illness. Among them are schemes where opposing forces or substances find balance in the human body and where plants can help restore disequilibria that develop. Other conceptions involve the intervention of spirit beings in the individual's health. Herbal remedies are employed in diverse therapeutic settings, some of which can be gleaned from ancient texts and others from the numerous peoples who have inherited a medicinal plant legacy. While medicine in Europe experienced many changes across the millennia, it had much in common with other world medical traditions until some of its practitioners developed an empirical and scientific approach during the eighteenth through twentieth centuries. As a result, biomedical researchers test drugs following a prescribed set of expectations in a controlled experiment. In this way, biomedicine has delineated a methodology that approaches disease as the product of physical dysfunction that can be remedied with specific pharmaceutical substances. In a world where numerous traditional medical practices coexist, the diversity of health-related beliefs and the mixture of practices provide a fascinating backdrop for medicinal plants in the modern day.

NOTES

1. Brenna M. Henn, L. L. Cavalli-Sforza, and Marcus W. Feldman, "The Great Human Expansion," *Proceedings of the National Academy of Sciences USA* 109 (2012): 17758–17764.
2. Mark D. Merlin, "Archaeological Evidence for the Tradition of Psychoactive Plant Use in the Old World," *Economic Botany* 57 (2003): 295–323. These dates are for findings of poppy seeds in Italy and hemp-cloth imprints on artifacts in China. Merlin reports earlier dates for a

Neanderthal burial in Iraq in which pollen of an *Ephedra* species was identified (approximately 50,000 BCE) and impressions of hemp rope on pottery in Taiwan (12,000 BCE). Archaeological study of medicinal plant use is complicated by poor preservation of artifacts (including biological material) in many sites, potential contamination of ancient samples with more recent ones, and difficulty in determining the species identity of ancient plant material and in objects designed to represent them. In any case, the absence of artifacts in a region or during an ancient span of time is not an indication that medicinal plants were not used. Furthermore, plants such as poppy and hemp can be used for food and medicine (in the former case) and fiber, food, and medicine (in the latter case). A challenge in such work is that the identification of ancient plant remains does not prove their intended function or use. For an extensive discussion of these matters with regard to the opium poppy and hemp, respectively, see Mark D. Merlin, *On the Trail of the Ancient Opium Poppy* (Rutherford, N.J.: Farleigh Dickinson University Press, 1984); and Robert C. Clarke and Mark D. Merlin, *Cannabis: Evolution and Ethnobotany* (Berkeley: University of California Press, 2013). Undoubtedly, many plant-derived dietary ingredients (grains, fruits, roots, and so on) were considered medicinal beyond their nutritional virtues. Still, investigators are drawn to document early uses of mind-altering plants, whose specific physiological actions imply a particular intention on the part of the ancestral human.

3. From Sanskrit *ayurveda*, which is alternatively translated as "science of life" and "knowledge of longevity." See Hari M. Sharma, "Contemporary Ayurveda," in *Fundamentals of Complementary and Alternative Medicine*, 4th ed., ed. Marc S. Micozzi (St. Louis, MO: Saunders Elsevier, 2011), 495. The text in which this term originates is the *Atharva Veda*. Carlos Lopez places portions of the Atharva Veda as early as approximately 1000 BCE, in "Atharva Veda," in *Oxford Bibliographies: Hinduism* (November 21, 2012), http://www.oxfordbibliographies.com/view/document/obo-9780195399318/obo-9780195399318-0008.xml?rskey=Eag07N&result=12.

4. The *Yellow Emperor's Classic of Internal Medicine* is the first codified text of Chinese medicine, compiled from many sources and attributed to the wisdom of a mythical emperor. Paul U. Unschuld dates the text sources to around the third to first centuries BCE in *Huang Di Nei Jing Su Wen: Nature, Knowledge, Imagery in an Ancient Chinese Medical Text* (Berkeley: University of California Press, 2003), 286. The book includes 224 drugs, of which 106 are of plant origin. Also from this period is a book of pharmaceuticals attributed to a godly author, the *Divine Husbandman's Classic of the Materia Medica*, which includes 365 drug prescriptions. See Paul U. Unschuld, *Medicine in China: A History of Pharmaceutics* (Berkeley: University of California Press, 1986), 17.

5. Cyril Bryan, *Ancient Egyptian Medicine: The Papyrus Ebers* (London: Bles, 1930), 28. The earliest Egyptian medical text, known as the Ebers papyrus, is generally dated to 1550 BCE. It was written in the ninth year of the reign of Amenhotep I (1534 BCE), according to John F. Nunn, *Ancient Egyptian Medicine* (Norman: University of Oklahoma Press, 1996), 30–34.

6. The oral tradition of medicine outside Europe, Asia, and northern Africa is a rich repository of ethnobotanic wisdom. When Europeans first encountered the Aztec and Inca civilizations, they documented Indigenous medical knowledge by asking natives to draw and write descriptions of their medicinal plants. Anthropologists and botanists continue to document medical practices disseminated by the oral tradition, recognizing the valuable resource of traditional, often unwritten, expertise.

7. The notion of balance is integral also to much contemporary medical discourse dealing with biochemical homeostasis, hormone regulation, pH balance, and the like. In many traditional medical settings, the "balance" conducive to health is thought to be influenced by environmental, dietary, social, and spiritual factors in a way not articulated (and sometimes not accepted) by practitioners of mainstream biomedicine.

8. In Chinese medicine, "health is a physiological, emotional, and mental balance, maintained in all three spheres or not at all, for the three are inseparable" (Nathan Sivin, *Traditional Medicine in Contemporary China: A Partial Translation of Revised Outline of Chinese Medicine [1972] with an Introductory Study on Change in Present-Day and Early Medicine* [Ann Arbor: Center for Chinese Studies, University of Michigan, 1987], 4). Medical approaches that view the patient's physical, mental, social, and (sometimes) spiritual health together are called holistic. Holistic beliefs are ancient, but the term is a relatively new one.

9. The practice of medicine in China has evolved over thousands of years. It shares elements with (and probably gave rise to) similar conceptions of health in Japan, Korea, and Southeast Asia. This section addresses the cosmopolitan, widespread form of Indigenous Chinese medicine as taught and practiced in China and elsewhere, but not the many informal health-related practices, integrated Chinese-Western medicine, or the distinctive ethnic medicines of Asia's diverse populations.

10. According to Liu Yanchi, "Chinese medicine contends that disease develops when pathogenic factors disturb the equilibrium of *yin* and *yang* in the human body. Medicinal herbs help to increase body resistance, eliminate pathogenic factors, and restore a relative balance between *yin* and *yang*" (*The Essential Book of Traditional Chinese Medicine*, vol. 2, *Clinical Practice* [New York: Columbia University Press, 1988], 43).

11. The premodern repertory of Chinese pharmaceuticals was very large. The *Grand Materia Medica* (ca. 1596) listed 1,892 drugs, and the *Additions to the Grand Materia Medica* (ca. 1803) added another 716. See Sivin, *Traditional Medicine in Contemporary China*, 180.

12. Dan Bensky, Steven Clavey, and Erich Stöger, *Chinese Herbal Medicine: Materia Medica*, 3rd ed. (Seattle: Eastland, 2004), 830–832.

13. Liu, *Essential Book of Traditional Chinese Medicine*, 2:127; Bensky, Clavey, and Stöger, *Chinese Herbal Medicine*, 710–711, 822–823.

14. *Ayurvedic* medicine's earliest magico-religious Sanskrit texts date to around 2,500 years ago; *siddha*'s origins are less clear. *Siddha* apparently took form beginning in the early centuries CE, with a distinctive literature that emerged during the thirteenth through sixteenth centuries. See Kenneth G. Zysk, "Traditional Medicine of India: Ayurveda and Siddha," in *Fundamentals of Complementary and Alternative Medicine*, ed. Micozzi, 461–462. Another important form of South Asian medicine is *unani*, which came to the Indian subcontinent from the Mediterranean through Muslim scholars.

15. Zysk, "Traditional Medicine of India," 456.

16. According to Dagmar Benner, "Imbalance denotes both a change in quantity as well as the dislocation of a [*dosha*]" ("Traditional Indian Systems of Healing and Medicine: Ayurveda," in *Encyclopedia of Religion*, 2nd ed., ed. Lindsay Jones [New York: Macmillan, 2005], 3854). "The quantity of a [*dosha*] can both increase and decrease, which leads to various symptoms of disease" (p. 3854).

17. Steven Kayne, "Indian Ayurvedic Medicine," in *Traditional Medicine: A Global Perspective*, ed. Steven B. Kayne (London: Pharmaceutical Press, 2010), 195–202.

18. Zysk, "Traditional Medicine of India," 460.

19. Zysk, "Traditional Medicine of India," 461–462.

20. The connection between matter, energy, and the zodiac was a widespread feature of Indian astrology. See Zysk, "Traditional Medicine of India," 462.

21. The five elements and three bodily constituents of *siddha* medicine are similar to those in *ayurvedic* medicine but occur in different proportions. See Zysk, "Traditional Medicine of India," 462–463.

22. According to Zysk, "The Siddha practitioners havea materia medica of at least 108 plants and plant products, some of which are imported from as far away as the Himalayas" ("Traditional Medicine of India," 466).

23. The lineage of many traditional practices was undoubtedly altered during the period of European colonization. The sources reference traditional activities and beliefs surmised from nineteenth- and twentieth-century anthropological study.

24. James W. Herrick summarizes Iroquois health concepts: "Bad health, illness, or disease must be understood in a general sense as a disturbance of balance in the power or life force of some person, place, thing, or event" (*Iroquois Medical Botany* [Syracuse, N.Y.: Syracuse University Press, 1997], 33).

25. John K. Crellin considers these to be "magico-religious/spiritual practices" ("Aboriginal/Traditional Medicine in North America: A Practical Approach for Practitioners," in *Traditional Medicine*, ed. Kayne, 55). The word "shaman" can refer to a person with special access to the spiritual world in many traditional settings.

26. Frances Densmore, "Uses of Plants by the Chippewa Indians," *Smithsonian Institution–Bureau of American Ethnology Annual Report* 44 (1928): 322.

27. Densmore, "Uses of Plants by the Chippewa Indians," 328.

28. According to Richard W. Voss, "Mental health and physical health were viewed as inseparable from spiritual and moral health. The good balance of the one's life in harmony with the wo'ope, or natural law of creation, brought about wicozani, or good health, which was both individual and communal" ("Native American Healing," in *Fundamentals of Complementary and Alternative Medicine*, ed. Micozzi, 540).

29. Voss, "Native American Healing," 540.

30. Daniel E. Moerman identifies over 2800 medicinal plants used by North American native people in *Native American Ethnobotany* (Portland, OR: Timber Press, 1998), 11.

31. Moerman, *Native American Ethnobotany*, 101–102.

32. Moerman, *Native American Ethnobotany*, 607. The "stimulant" use is attributed to the Navajo and the "contraceptive" use to the Ramah.

33. Moerman, *Native American Ethnobotany*, 603.

34. The Chippewa medicine men were part of a *midewiwin*, a religious-medical sect whose teachings were secret.

35. The Aztecs, Toltecs, and other groups comprise a larger Nahuatl-speaking people that inhabit parts of modern-day Mexico and El Salvador.

36. Alfredo López Austin, *The Human Body and Ideology Concepts of the Ancient Nahuas*, trans. Thelma Ortiz de Montellano and Bernard Ortiz de Montellano (Salt Lake City: University of Utah Press, 1988), 1:52–53.

37. López Austin, *Ancient Nahuas*, 1:255–264.

38. López Austin, *Ancient Nahuas*, 1:204–222.

39. Bernard Ortiz de Montellano, *Aztec Medicine, Health, and Nutrition* (New Brunswick, NJ: Rutgers University Press, 1990). According to López Austin, "Just as the force of the sacrificial victims could revitalize the gods, so their representatives on earth . . . participated in order to strengthen and prolong their own lives" (*Ancient Nahuas*, 1:377).

40. López Austin, *Ancient Nahuas*, 1:225–226.

41. Synonym *A. mexicana*. López Austin, *Ancient Nahuas*, 1:219.

42. Bernardino de Sahagún, *Florentine Codex: General History of the Things of New Spain*, book 11, *Earthly Things*, trans. Charles E. Dibble and Arthur J. O. Anderson (Santa Fe, NM: School of American Research, 1963), 131.

43. Francisco Hernández, *Historia natural de Nueva España*, vol. 1 (Mexico City: Universidad Nacional de México, 1959), cited in Ortiz de Montellano, *Aztec Medicine*, 141.

44. López Austin, *Ancient Nahuas*, 1:356, 358.

45. Kwasi Konadu, *Indigenous Medicine and Knowledge in African Society* (New York: Routledge, 2007), 66–68, 85–86.

46. Konadu, *Indigenous Medicine and Knowledge*, 52–55.

47. Konadu, *Indigenous Medicine and Knowledge*, xxi, 53.

48. Konadu, *Indigenous Medicine and Knowledge*, 95–96.

49. Mariana G. Hewson, "Indigenous Knowledge Systems: Southern African Healing," in *Fundamentals of Complementary and Alternative Medicine*, ed. Micozzi, 523. Another articulation of this idea is discussed by A. Moteetee and B.-E. Van Wyk: "The Basotho believe that good health is not only physical but also spiritual; therefore ancestral spirits (*balimo*) form an integral part of their lives. If a person experiences bad luck and misfortune, then this is most likely ascribed to the fact that they have neglected their ancestors and are therefore being punished" ("The Medical Ethnobotany of Lesotho: A Review," *Bothalia* 41 [2011]: 210).

50. Hewson, "Indigenous Knowledge Systems," 523.

51. Moteetee and Van Wyk, "Medical Ethnobotany of Lesotho."

52. Moteetee and Van Wyk, "Medical Ethnobotany of Lesotho," 210.

53. Moteetee and Van Wyk, "Medical Ethnobotany of Lesotho," 211.

54. Bruno Halioula and Bernard Ziskind, *Medicine in theDays of the Pharaohs*, trans. M. B. DeBevoise (Cambridge, MA: Harvard University Press, 2005), 8.

55. Halioula and Ziskind, *Medicine in the Days of the Pharaohs*, 8–10. Nunn notes that the earliest Egyptian medical documents (ca. nineteenth to sixteenth centuries BCE) have less magical content than later ones, in *Ancient Egyptian Medicine*, 96.

56. Nunn, *Ancient Egyptian Medicine*, 24–41; Halioula and Ziskind, *Medicine in the Days of the Pharaohs*; Lise Manniche, *An Ancient Egyptian Herbal*, rev. ed. (London: British Museum Press, 2006); J. R. Campbell and A. R. David, "The Application of Archaeobotany, Phytogeography, and Phamacognosy to Confirm the Pharmacopeia of Ancient Egypt 1850–1200 b.c.," in *Pharmacy and Medicine in Ancient Egypt: Proceedings of the Conferences Held in Cairo (2007) and Manchester (2008)*, ed. Jenefer Cockitt and Rosalie David, BAR International Series 2141 (Oxford: Archaeopress, 2010), 20–29.

57. Halioula and Ziskind, *Medicine in the Days of the Pharaohs*, 31, 33. Nunn relates that identifying herbs in Egyptian hieroglyphic texts has been challenging, citing an estimate of 20 percent of the 160 plant products in papyri having reliable translations, in *Ancient Egyptian Medicine*, 151.

58. Translation of Ebers 25, in Nunn, *Ancient Egyptian Medicine*, 159.

59. The European lineage is set apart from other world medical traditions because it gave rise to the predominant form of healthcare in the United States, Europe, and much of the world, known as biomedicine. Its evolution provides context to the changing roles of medicinal plants highlighted in the text.

60. Vivian Nutton, "Medicine in the Greek World, 800–50 b.c.," in *The Western Medical Tradition 800 b.c. to 1800*, by Lawrence I. Conrad et al. (Cambridge: Cambridge University Press, 1995), 23. The authors of the Hippocratic Corpus lived around 420 to 350 BCE.

61. The notions of opposing qualities, elements, and humors might have originated in India. See Noga Arikha, *Passions and Tempers: A History of the Humours* (New York: HarperCollins, 2007), 4.

62. The Hippocratic authors wrote that health was a function of balance but differed on how imbalance led to illness: "The author of *On regimen* thought that the whole body was in a perpetual state of flux, and health consisted in keeping this flux within certain limits. By contrast, the author of *On the Nature of Man* argued that the body remained in a stable balance until something, external or internal, occurred to overturn it" (Nutton, "Medicine in the Greek World," 24).

63. Black bile was not considered a cardinal humor in the earliest Hippocratic writings. See Nutton, "Medicine in the Greek World," 24–25.

64. The humors "did not need to be observable to have explanatory power. In fact, none of the humors needed to be visible to exert their hold on the imagination, and to provide a credible, at times effective physiological account of the unseen operations within the body" (Arikha, *Passions and Tempers*, 9). Yet physicians recognized that the humors had some connection to actual substances, fluids that on occasion emanated from the body. For example, blood was both a humor in the metaphorical sense and a red liquid that emerged from wounds: "Bile and phlegm were visible only when excreted during illness, and hence might be considered permanently dangerous [but] other fluids were more ambiguous" (Nutton, "Medicine in the Greek World," 24).

65. Arikha, *Passions and Tempers*, 13.

66. Arikha, *Passions and Tempers*, 40.

67. Excess of blood, stagnant blood, or bad blood were treated by slicing the patient (phlebotomy or venesection) or applying bloodsucking leeches. Bloodletting was common medical practice in Europe until the nineteenth century.

68. Jerry Stannard, "Hippocratic Pharmacology," *Bulletin of the History of Medicine* 35 (1961): 497–518.

69. The reference to black hellebore is from Pliny the Elder, *Natural History* 25.22; *The Natural History of Pliny*, trans. John Bostock and H. T. Riley (London: Bohn, 1856), 5:98–99. *Helleborus niger* is black hellebore, although the ancients may have referred to other *Helleborus* spp. or *Veratrum album*, known today as white hellebore or false hellebore. Both plants are medicinal and highly toxic in overdose; *V. album* is the more effective purgative.

70. This belief held sway for many centuries. Edward Shorter describes European medicine of a later era: "The aim of traditional therapeutics was getting the bowels open. One treated fever with laxatives, getting those bad humours out by procuring an 'opening.'" ("Primary Care," in *The Cambridge History of Medicine*, ed. Roy Porter [Cambridge: Cambridge University Press, 2006], 108).

71. Stannard traces the first mention of scammony to the Hippocratic text *Diseases of Women*, in "Hippocratic Pharmacology," 503.

72. John Uri Lloyd, "History of the Vegetable Drugs of the Pharmacopeia of the United States," *Bulletin of the Lloyd Library of Botany, Pharmacy, and Materia Medica* 18, no. 4 (1911): 78–79; H. C. Wood, Joseph P. Remington, and Samuel P. Sadtler, *The Dispensatory of the United States of America*, 19th ed. (Philadelphia: Lippincott, 1907).

73. John Riddle, *Dioscorides on Pharmacy and Medicine* (Austin: University of Texas Press, 1985), xix, 11–13. Dioscorides assigned hot–cold and dry–moist properties to herbs, but generally did not reference the humors.

74. *De materia medica* is the better-known Latin name of a work written in Greek, sometime between 60 and 78 CE. See Riddle, *Dioscorides*, 13–14. The number of medicinal substances described is subject to some discussion because the author may have made distinctions in naming that modern experts do not, and vice versa. The five-book treatise contained over 1,000 listings of plant-, animal-, and mineral-based pharmaceuticals; today's scholars itemize roughly 500 to 600 unique plant entries. See Jerry Stannard, "The Herbal as a Medical Document," *Bulletin of the History of Medicine* 43 (1969): 212–220; and Riddle, *Dioscorides*, xiii, xivn.2.

75. In *Medicine in China*, Unschuld considers *De materiamedica* the world's first pharmacopeia. Although Chinese medical books of the era included descriptions of medicinal plants and their uses, they did not provide instructions for their standard preparation as in Dioscorides.

76. Susan P. Mattern, *The Prince of Medicine: Galen in the Roman Empire* (Oxford: Oxford University Press, 2013), 233–234.

77. A detailed account can be found in Owsei Temkin, *Galenism: Rise and Decline of a Medical Philosophy* (Ithaca, NY: Cornell University Press, 1973).

78. A form of Galenic medicine is still practiced in the Muslim world under the name of *unani*.

79. Oswald Cockayne, ed., *Leechdoms, Wortcunning, and Starcraft of Early England* (London: Longman, Green, Longman, Roberts, and Green, 1863), 2:15, 113, 291; Audrey Meaney, "The Practice of Medicine in England About the Year 1000," *Social History of Medicine* 13, no. 2 (2000): 230.

80. Meaney, "Practice of Medicine in England," 222, 232–235.

81. Anne Van Arsdall, *Medieval Herbal Remedies: The* Old English Herbarium *and Anglo-Saxon Medicine* (New York: Routledge, 2002), 138–139. The original Old English, literally translated, diagnoses "evil night spirits."

82. Van Arsdall notes that at the time, "the moon was believed to cause 'lunacy,' and the Old English word for it is 'month-sickness,' months being measured in moons" (*Medieval Herbal Remedies*, 178).

83. Van Arsdall, *Medieval Herbal Remedies*, 138, 227. The herbal instructs the practitioner to pluck the plant while enunciating a special Latin incantation, helpfully provided.

84. Belief in the destructive potential of a malevolent gaze, or evil eye, is a pre-Christian idea that maintains currency in many parts of Europe and the Near East. A recent study of plants protective against the evil eye in Spain is José Antonio González et al., "Plant Remedies Against Witches and the Evil Eye in a Spanish 'Witches' Village," *Economic Botany* 66 (2012): 35–45.

85. Frederick Thomas Elworthy, *The Evil Eye: An Account of This Ancient and Widespread Superstition* (London: Murray, 1895).

86. Van Arsdall, *Medieval Herbal Remedies*, 152.

87. Percy Flemming, "The Medical Aspects of the Medieval Monastery in England," *Proceedings of the Royal Society of Medicine* 22 (1929): 771–782; Lucia Tongiorgio Tomasi, "The Renaissance Herbal," in *The Renaissance Herbal* (Bronx: New York Botanical Garden, 2013), 11.

88. Roy Porter, *The Greatest Benefit to Mankind: A Medical History of Humanity* (New York: Norton, 1997), 106–112.

89. Jerry Stannard, "The Theoretical Bases of Medieval Herbalism," *Medical Heritage* 1 (1985): 186–198.

90. Charles Webster, *Paracelsus: Medicine, Magic, and Mission at the End of Time* (New Haven, Conn.: Yale University Press, 2008), 15–19, 56–57. In addition to his unconventional beliefs about medicine and chemistry, Paracelsus wrote inflammatory tracts on theology.

91. Webster, *Paracelsus*, 150.

92. The Doctrine of Signatures touted by Paracelsus draws from a long line of folk practices in Europe. Nor is it unique to Europe: many world folk practices have beliefs intreating disease with "similars" or "like-cures-like." Bradley C. Bennett considers the practice "ubiquitous" and argues that the Doctrine of Signatures serves as a mnemonic to help people in nonliterate societies teach and recall the uses of medicinal plants, in "Doctrine of Signatures: An Explanation of Medicinal Plant Discovery or Dissemination of Knowledge?," *Economic Botany* 61, no. 3 (2007): 246–255. See also Michael J. Balick, *Rodale's Twenty-First-Century Herbal: A Practical Guide for Healthy Living Using Nature's Most Powerful Plants* (New York: Rodale, 2014), 22–23.

93. There are also lungworts in the genus Mertensia and others.

94. R. C. A. Prior, *On the Popular Names of British Plants*, 2nd ed. (London: Williams and Norgate, 1870), 22, 136, 140. *A. clematitis* is a common European species of a widespread genus.

95. Mandrake was well known in antiquity and emerges in many ethnobotanic contexts through history.

96. These are John Gerard's (1545–1611?) *Herball or Generall Historie of Plantes* (1597, revised 1633); John Parkinson's (1567–1650) *Theatrum Botanicum*; and Nicholas Culpeper's (1616–1654) *The English Physitian* (1652). See Graeme Tobyn, Alison Denham, and Margaret Whiteleg, *The Western Herbal Tradition: Two Thousand Years of Medicinal Plant Knowledge* (Edinburgh: Churchill Livingstone/Elsevier, 2011), 13–15.

97. John Gerard, *The Herball, or Generall Historie of Plants* (London, 1597), 960.

98. For the significance of Linnaeus's contribution to simplifying nomenclature in a botanical community awash in impractical Latin names, see James L. Reveal, "What's in a Name: Identifying Plants in Pre-Linnaean Botanical Literature," in *Prospecting for Drugs in Ancient and Medieval European Texts: A Scientific Approach*, ed. Bart K. Holland (Amsterdam: Harwood, 1996), 57–90. Linnaeus's scheme for classifying biological specimens based on morphological features (in plants, flowers were deemed especially useful) came first, in 1735, and then his binomial was introduced in publications beginning in the 1740s, culminating in the grand *Species Plantarum* of 1753.

99. For a concise explanation of modern botanical classification, see Balick, *Twenty-First-Century Herbal*, 42–49. See also P. F. Stevens, the Angiosperm Phylogeny website, Version 14, July 2017, http://www.mobot.org/MOBOT/research/APweb/.

100. Botanical convention expects that plants be identified by genus, species, and the authority (botanist or botanists) credited with the formal description of the organism in the scholarly literature. Therefore, the pumpkin is most properly identified as *Cucurbita pepo* L. The genus and species names are followed by L., which means Linnaeus was the first to describe this plant. Similarly, lavender (*Lavandula angustifolia* Mill.) bears the added name of the eighteenth-century botanist Philip Miller. This text will omit the authority in species names, although the precision of using the full botanic identifier is preferable in technical and scientific publications. See Bradley C. Bennett and Michael J. Balick, "Phytomedicine 101: Plant Taxonomy for Preclinical and Clinical Medicinal Plant Researchers," *Journal of the Society for Integrative Oncology* 6 (2008): 150–157.

101. Systematists frequently reevaluate the taxonomic placement of species as new information about biological relationships become available in morphological and genetic studies. Up-to-date botanical name databases are maintained by the U.S. government (Integrated Taxonomic Information System, www.itis.gov), the Missouri Botanical Garden (www.tropicos.org), and the Plant List, an international consortium (www.theplantlist.org).

102. William Withering, *An Account of the Foxglove and Some of Its Medical Uses* (Birmingham, 1785).

103. Empirical evidence for a pharmaceutical's positive effects generally cannot be demonstrated without a carefully constructed experiment. Empirical evidence for negative outcomes might be deduced from folk experience. For example, surveying the hundreds of plant-derived treatments available to modern-day practitioners of Indigenous medicine in the Peruvian rain forest, the Amazonian herbalist Justo Renquifo Guevara noted, "In the past, many of our brothers and sisters died so that we can have these medicines" (personal communication, 2009). He refers to the countless people who overdosed on medicinal plants or made poor combinations of herbs and whose experience served as warning to herbalists who followed them. Such lessons are passed along through the generations, helping shape a practice that seeks to maximize possible benefit and reduce risk.

104. The mainstream or predominant health-care practice in North America and Europe, among other places, goes by many names among comparative medical scholars, including Western medicine, biomedicine, and orthodox medicine.

105. Chinese traditional medical training incorporates coursework in biomedical anatomy, pharmacology, and so forth.

106. Nutton, "Medicine in the Greek World," 24–25.

107. Among the first analyses of this phenomenon was in Henry K. Beecher, "The Powerful Placebo," *Journal of the American Medical Association* 159 (1955): 98–109. The placebo effect in various clinical settings is reviewed in Howard Brody, "The Placebo Response: Recent Research and Implications for Family Medicine," *Journal of Family Practice* 49, no. 7 (2000): 649–654; F. Benedetti, "Placebo Analgesia," Neurological Science 27 (2006): S100–S102; and Damian G. Finniss et al., "Placebo Effects: Biological, Clinical and Ethical Advances," *Lancet* 375 (2010): 686–695. Despite the common vocabulary of the clinical research field that designates such treatments as "inactive," "mock," and "sham," the placebo effect is associated with quantifiable, replicable neurobiological-systemic changes in patients.

108. A shorthand for the therapeutic setting is the "doctor–patient relationship." For a reevaluation of the "placebo effect" phenomenon as a response to the "meaning of medicine," see Daniel E. Moerman, *Meaning, Medicine, and the "Placebo Effect"* (Cambridge: Cambridge University Press, 2002).

109. The mainstream or predominant health-care practice in North America and Europe, among other places, goes by many names among comparative medical scholars, including Western medicine, biomedicine, and orthodox medicine.

110. Chinese traditional medical training incorporates coursework in biomedical anatomy, pharmacology, and so forth.

111. Nutton, "Medicine in the Greek World," 24–25.

112. Zysk, "Traditional Medicine of India."

Main Pathway: Ecologies

Subthemes

Proceed to Experience, p. 407
End of Healing
End of Transcending

17

BLOSSOMING SEX: FLORAL TRANSPOSITIONS IN THE WORKS OF NATALIA LL AND ZOFIA KULIK

Monika Bakke

The sensuality of flowers, perceived as a display of colours, scents, or flavours, seems obvious to people, though, as Richard M. Doyle rightly notes, "It is . . . not human fascination toward which the (wild) flower is evolutionarily tuned."[1] Flowers are in fact the genitals of plants, whose bodies and lives have a sexual dimension too. The numerousness of plants' sexual strategies and the anatomic diversity of their sexual organs are unmatched among any other group of organisms, and their bodies and lifestyles are completely different from those of animals, and especially people. Although flowers' seductive abilities are geared towards animals—pollinating insects in particular—and plants' survival depends on success in this regard, human ritual preoccupation with flowers dates back to the oldest manifestations of culture, e.g. burials. The origins of Western botanical knowledge can be found in the writings of Aristotle and his disciple, Theophrastus, but the first treatise on the sexuality of plants[2] was published only in the late 17th century. A real breakthrough, however, occurred with the sexual system of plant classification presented half a century later by Carl Linnaeus, so it was only modern botany that developed knowledge about the sexual life of plants, even though in its early period it became embroiled in erroneous analogies between plant sexuality and the normative sexuality of humans, as it was understood at the time. Contemporary studies of plants don't look

Originally published in the exhibition catalog *Natalia LL.—Consumer Art and Beyond*, ed. Agata Jakubowska (Warsaw: Ujazdowski Castle Centre for Contemporary Art, 2017), 68–83. Reprinted with permission.

at plant lives for analogies with the human condition, but rather as inspiration for rethinking the way plants function in nature cultures. Both botanical sex and the diversity of plant forms can stimulate human fantasies and inspire non-normative sexual practices. Today, when people know much more about the plant kingdom, thanks to rapid advances in biology, the question of how plants can actually inspire us becomes increasingly urgent.

Not only insects but humans too are attracted by the charm of flowers; people see in them aesthetic values, erotic power as well as transient nature; therefore, flowers have been omnipresent in Western philosophy, both metaphorically and metonymically.[3] In this essay I wish to analyse the presence of floral representations and their semantic productivity in selected works of two Polish women artists: Natalia LL (*Fidgety Flower*, video, 1994; and *Hortus Eroticus*, installation 2003) and Zofia Kulik (works from the *Garden (Libera and Flowers)* series, 1996–2004). In these artworks, plants are not just good-looking props, but their images represent flowers themselves, i.e. plants' sexual organs, introducing a broader perspective on sexuality and gender. In order to highlight this aspect of the art works, I will resort to metonymy[4] in its cognitive sense, which I construe as a "force of conceptual spreading (inside and across adjacent conceptual domains)."[5] Based on relationships of adjacency and tangency, metonymy doesn't consist in simply replacing one element (source domain) with another (target domain), but in a conceptual condensation achieved by integrating both. Flowers, therefore, lead us metonymically towards male and female genitals, and towards masculinity, femininity, and androgyny existing beyond the world of plants—among living organisms in general—as well as towards all kinds of reproductive strategies and sexual strategies. But Western culture's dominant tendency to anthropomorphise non-human bodies and lifestyles—an effect of anthropocentrism or zoocentrism in sexual research—means that what people see reflected in the "plant mirror" is above all themselves, as in flowers as metaphors of human bodies with their sexual organs, practices, and desires. Such instrumentalisation of plants, informed by a metaphorical relationship of similarity, obscures, or even invalidates, the flower itself with its complex, non-heteronormative sexuality. Therefore, if we don't stop at a metaphorical interpretation of floral representations and broaden our perspective to include the plant/flower considered metonymically, we will see the plants themselves, with their corporeal specificity, in the context of sexuality and corporeality in general. We will also be able to discover in the works of Natalia LL and Zofia Kulik the possibility of going beyond anthropocentric and phallocentric interpretations of sexuality and gender. On the one hand, the dynamics of plant life and a trans-species sexual energy will emerge, horrifying in its negation of individuality, in the repetition of sexual-physiological compulsion that both human and non-human bodies are subject to, while, on the other hand, we will be able to acknowledge floral sexuality in all its diversity, uninhibitedness and non-normativity.

FLORAL VERTIGO

The vegetative soul, a concept present in the Western imagination since Aristotle's *On the Soul*, has been associated with growth and reproduction, and hence with irrationality and femininity. As Elaine Miller argues in *The Vegetative Soul: From Philosophy of Nature to Subjectivity in the Feminine*, "Western philosophers from Aristotle to Hegel have repeated the analogy of men to animals and women to plants by virtue of their (perceived) respective characteristics of activity and rationality, on the one hand, and passivity and lack of rationality, on the other."[6] The common association of women with flowers, as a matter of both linguistic convention and an ontological conviction, connects femininity to a decorative function rather than practical or political power. Hence passivity, chastity, and fragility have for centuries been praised as female virtues, while women-as-flowers have been considered as objects of male desire, appearing in the role of lovers, but also mothers. The representation of women as flowers reduced them ultimately to an aesthetically pleasing object equipped with reproductive functions, a perfect illustration of which is Odoardo Fialetti's famous 17th-century engraving of the *Petal Venus*.[7] Showing a woman with her belly open, the skin unfolded in the semblance of flower petals, with the foetus centrally placed, such images of women-as-flowers consolidated normative models of sexual behaviour: male activity and female passivity.

Fidgety Flower is a video piece by Natalia LL showing the anthurium flower—with its characteristic spadix and large red-coloured spathe—in movement, trotting out its morphology in considerable detail. While the flower doesn't move about like a rootless plant blown by the wind, the character of its movement is complex, dynamic, and at times actually aggressive. It can also be misleading for the viewer, for not only does the flower not move on its own, being moved around instead, but at times it only appears to be mobile; in fact, it is an immobile object moved towards and away from the camera, appearing closer to or farther from the viewer. The "fidgety flower" thus owes its dynamics to an external rather than internal principle; its movement doesn't originate in the flower itself.

For centuries, the idea of a plant moving by itself contradicted traditional dichotomies such as activity/passivity, animal/plant or, for that matter, man/woman. Since Aristotle's times, the ability to move has been considered as one of the key distinctions between flora and fauna. Hence the introduction to Europe of the touch-me-not (*Mimosa pudica*), a plant able to rapidly fold its leaves inward, as well as the discovery of the Venus flytrap (*Dionaea muscipula*), which closes its leaves to trap and digest insects, came as something of a shock. We know today that all plants are capable of movement, but it is usually so slow as to be imperceptible to the human eye. Plants move for various reasons: growth in a specific direction results from the need to access light, water, and mineral nutrients, or to gain support; the movement of leaves and flowers as they follow the sun helps maximise solar exposure; the opening and closing of flowers is an element of sexual strategy, usually supported by external movement, as flowering plants commonly take avail of wind energy, but also of the movement of water or animals. But the trope evoked by Natalia LL's *Fidgety Flower* is not that of an active plant, capable of autonomous movement and—as plant biologist Daniel Chamovitz calls it in his book *What a Plant Knows*[8]—aware of the surrounding world. Even though it appears mobile, it is in fact moved by an unidentified external force, its purpose unknown.

Presenting a performative approach to materiality and subjectivity, Elizabeth Grosz stresses the operation of forces rather than subjects, and it is precisely this theme that is most evident in *Fidgety Flower*, where the source and purpose of the flower's movement remain obscure. Forces, Grosz believes, precede the emergence of subjectivity against the tradition connecting force with will, and the imposition of one's will on others in particular, that is with oppression and exploitation, which have been associated with a male model of power.[9] The philosopher stresses however that "this manoeuvre of identifying force with the masculine is already to humanize force (which in effect is to masculinize it, in a phallocentric logos), to anthropomorphize it."[10] Similarly in *Fidgety Flower*, if we assume that the movement is caused by a human being or a non-human animal, their action should be described as aggressive, even mortally dangerous. Plant biologists point out that touching or shaking a plant arrests its growth and can even kill it. It seems, however, that in *Fidgety Flower* we can discern a suggestion to construe force as non-human, impersonal and subjectivity-preceding, for it doesn't reveal itself there—neither as an active plant nor an external mover. Strong subjectivity and stable identity are therefore an effect, not a cause, yielding to action, becoming, changeability and openness. From this perspective the "fidgety flower" is neither a source nor a purpose, but a temporary and transient effect of that force.

FLOWER, SEX, DEATH

"Sexuality is an open system," Grosz argues, explaining that its "future is not necessarily contained in and constrained by its past and present."[11] Given the work's formal and semantic aspects, this is precisely the image of sexuality that is conveyed by Natalia LL's installation *Hortus Eroticus* and its other versions known as *Calamitas Erotica*[12] and *Allusive Space*.[13] *Hortus Eroticus* is an installation consisting of two spatially separated series of multiplied black-and-white photographs. The first series, displayed on the wall, shows a human skull with a banana between its jaws, surrounded by five anthurium flowers; the second one, which is presented as an undulating roll of paper, comprises various images of a single anthurium flower.

What is striking here in the first place is a stubborn, even compulsive repetition of images of floral sexual organs. Rather than building tension, however, this repetition, like the repetition of the sexual act, reduces the force of sexual energy to inner compulsion. Another important facet of this stream of (images of) flowers, fruits, and bones is the absence of a distinct beginning or end, which in turn suggests infiniteness, processuality, and becoming, connected with biological life in its totalising aspect. The artist herself believes that "we are driven by reproductive energy rooted in eroticism,"[14] which is connected with vital force construed as *zoe*, something that Rosi Braidotti describes as the "generative vitality of non- or pre-human or animal life,"[15] in which human-animals are included too. It is precisely this egalitarian force, repressed by the humanist tradition, that returns with a critique of anthropocentrism.

Zoe, as an unbridled force operating through the material bodies of plants and animals, as a force that individual organisms experience as not only generative but also destructive, goes beyond individual needs and desires, beyond individual lives, opening up to life itself. In this context, *Hortus Eroticus* appears on one of its levels as a traditional memento mori, a *vanitas*-type still life with flowers, a fruit, and a skull, while Natalia LL states point-blank that "this eroticism is catastrophic, not to say tragic."[16] Despair and horror remain within the bounds of sexual, generative energy inasmuch as individual lives reach their end so that life itself in its irrepressible force can go on. Rather than a dominant motif in this installation, the human skull is but one of the many corporeal elements inscribed in the natural order, where death goes hand in hand with sex, the latter ensuring evolutionary variety and diversity, and thus the perpetuation of life.

Hortus Eroticus offers sexual excessiveness not only by repeating the floral motif, but also by featuring a bisexual, or "perfect," flower that has both male (stamen) and female (carpel) sexual organs, tightly packed, with one carpel surrounded by four stamens. Plant sexuality was perceived as excessive since its exposition by Linnaeus in the mid-18th century. The Swedish botanist proposed the so called *Systema Sexuale* ("sexual system"), classifying plants according to the structure of their flowers, or more precisely, the number of their stamens and carpels. As botany developed, there emerged the uncomfortable truth that flowers can be not only male or female but also hermaphroditic. From the very beginning, a classification based on sexual organs proved highly controversial among naturalists, and Linnaeus, not daring to propose a third sex—something that the flowers would suggest—insisted on heterosexual allegories, using matrimonial terminology, e.g. in the description of hermaphroditic flowers. In his writings, the petals were referred to as the conjugal bed; the stamens as husbands, bridegrooms, and escorts; and the carpels as wives, virgins, concubines, or brides. But that didn't solve the problem because bisexual flowers, such as anthurium, contain one female organ and multiple male ones, "residing in the same bed." So not just correct identification but, above all, the acceptance of the sexual distinctness and complexity of flowers created within botany the possibility of moving beyond ideologically charged norms based on the heterosexual model.

SEX OF (MY) FLOWER

Whereas in Natalia LL's *Hortus Eroticus* the human element (the skull) has no obvious sex, in Zofia Kulik's photographic series *Garden (Libera and Flowers)* (figure 17.1), the human body has distinct male characteristics, being usually shown with the genitals exposed, and the male model's last name is mentioned in the work's title. In the foreground, however, are carefully posed plants—usually just the flowers of various unnamed species—conveying a message concerning not so much sexual energy in general, but rather the diversity of its manifestations, while constituting an affirmation of individual, specific sexuality built in a relationship of a specific human body with the body, each time different, of a plant.

The series *Garden (Libera and Flowers)* consists of eleven colour photographs, each showing the same male figure accompanied by a different floral motif. The nude model has been captured in a pose that mockingly imitates the Vetruvian man, with the legs slightly bent and the hands wide open. Multiplication means that his image becomes a sign, a template, contrasting with the organic features of the plant bodies, always different and individually arranged. The compositional effect has been achieved by superimposing images of various flowers, e.g. rose, acacia, or poppy, on the black-and-white image of the model, and photographing the resulting montage in colour. As the artist says herself, "Flowers are photographed here, and the figure is reproduced, so you can say it is an image of an image."[17] This gesture means that the human body becomes more "distant," while the flowers, due to their full-colour organicness and scale—they are much enlarged compared with the human figure—visually dominate. It is them that constitute the main critically active element here, impacting on the caricaturally mocked matrix of the anthropocentrically construed human body, the body of the Vetruvian man.

The whole series resembles a herbarium—a form of plant preservation identified, to an extent, with a dry or winter garden—but only resembles because it doesn't include actual plant bodies. From the very beginning herbaria were about "suspending and then restoring at least the appearance of life."[18] Their special character is that they offer various levels of mediation at the same time. Representation and presentation go hand in hand here, and the actual presence of plant bodies means that it is possible, to a greater or lesser degree, to restore their three-dimensional shape, that is, actual embodiment. Traditionally the dried plant specimens were re-embodied by immersing them in water. Today, when research on bodies has largely moved to the molecular level due to advances in biotechnology, herbaria serve as an important source of DNA, allowing detailed study of rare or extinct species. As Leah Knight suggests, "Herbaria are thus notable for their unusual ability to narrow the gap between a representation and the thing represented, and they could therefore be said to problematize the broader gap between those overarching categories, art and nature."[19] In Kulik's works, the male/human intimate co-presence with plant bodies is staged similarly as in herbaria, the artist achieving the effect through colour and scale variation. As a result, key elements of the composition—such as the human and plant bodies—seem to have a completely different ontological status, the human body appearing as only represented, while flowers enjoy real presence.

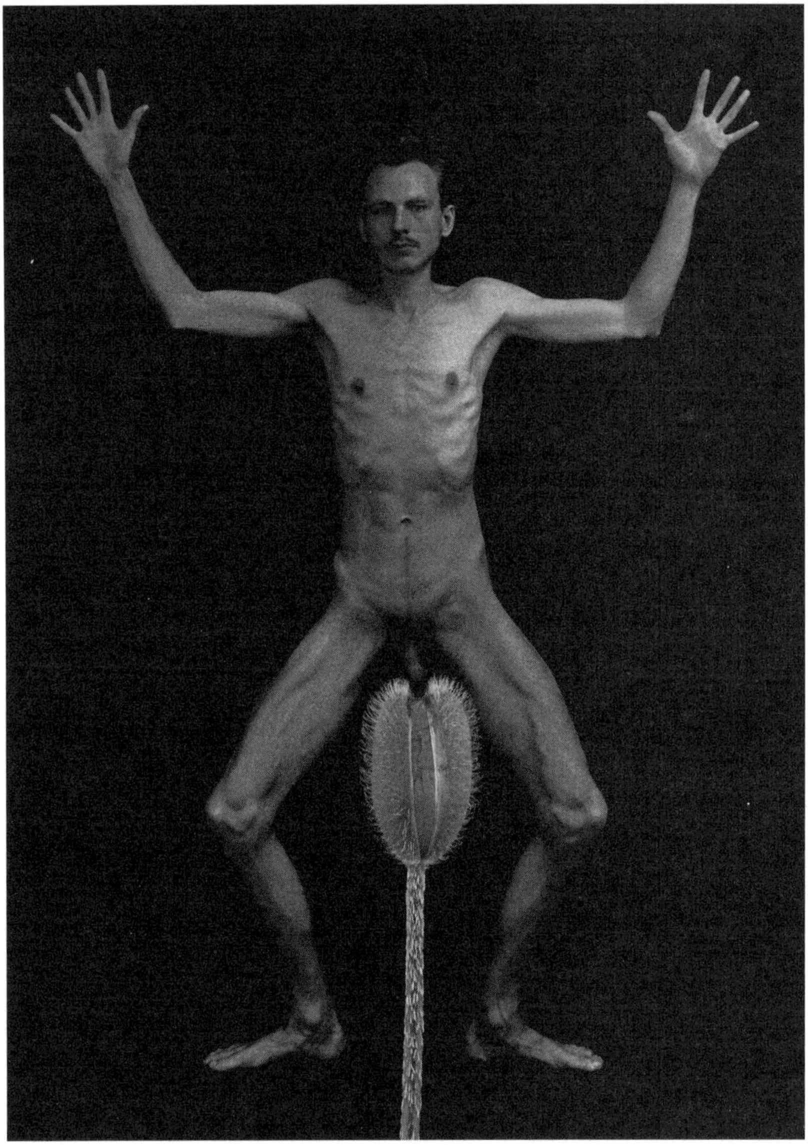

17.1

Zofia Kulik, *Garden (Libera and Flowers) 1996–2004*, photographs, part of a series, courtesy of the artist and Kulik-KwieKulik Foundation.

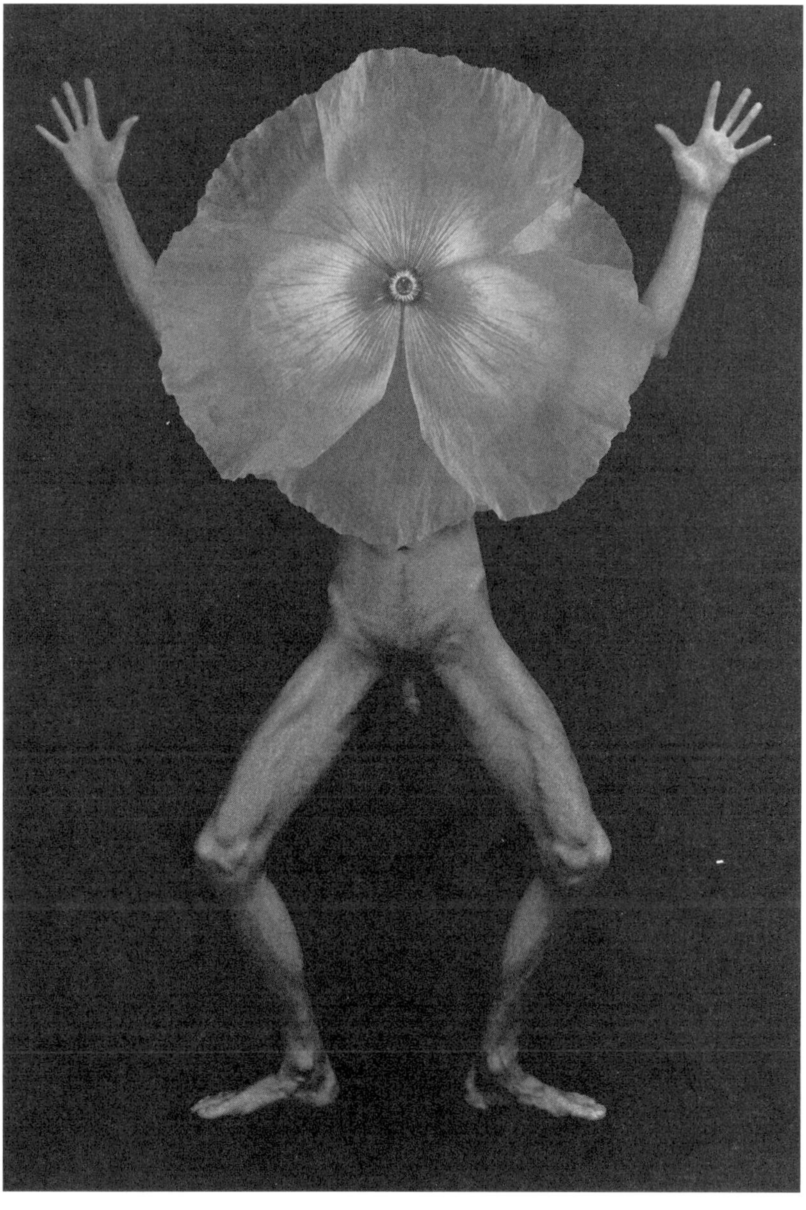

Zofia Kulik's *Garden* series makes also an interesting reference to the 18th-century origins of botany as a modern science based on Linnaeus's sexual taxonomy.[20] The ease of use of his sexual system contributed to the rapid popularisation of botany in the West, for now virtually everyone, with just a little bit of effort, was able to discover never-before-described species. Women, until then excluded from naturalistic studies, took up the botanic challenge most enthusiastically, but only outside the established academic framework, which they still had no access to at the time. As amateur botany afficionados they were able to spend a lot of time outdoors collecting plants in order to create herbaria and make botanical drawings. The fact that women were drawing sexual organs, even if that meant flowers, was objected to by many men, who openly expressed concern with their moral condition.[21] Anthropomorphic interpretations of botanical sex were always in the first place a current diagnosis of social relationships and of the notion of human sexuality. To this day flowers have been associated with sex, as confirmed by Zofia Kulik, who says that the "poppy flower is incredible in its beauty, with its delicate, fragile petals, velvety and wrinkled. When the red petals break out of the hairy green [stalk], this is an immensely erotic moment."[22] In Kulik's herbarium, the eroticism of flowers overshadows male nudity while raising questions about gender and sex. Answers to those questions can be sought in *Garden* in many ways, not least by following Luce Irigaray's suggestion and following the "trope of efflorescence."

Critically analysing the ontological and political status of the woman-as-flower figure in her *Elemental Passions*, Irigaray makes an attempt to reformulate it in more affirmative terms. She identifies the flower with lips, since both allude to the female subject and female intimacy. Both lips and labia, like flower petals, meet in an act of caressing, and therefore both the mouth and the flower represent the female subject. Yet the flower figure is ambiguous in Irigaray's interpretation, for the author distinguishes between becoming a flower as an act of will and as an act of coercion. The latter case involves adapting to male expectations and the normalisation of femininity, and connects to a metaphorical reading of the woman as a flower. In a dialogue with a male subject, the woman asks: "You want to make me into a flower? . . . Before I knew you, already I was a flower. Must I forget that, to become your flower? The one which is your destiny for me."[23] Irigaray suggests therefore that the woman has her own ways of becoming herself, just as the flower has its own roots, allowing it to grow and blossom. Thus the woman-as-flower dissociates herself from the male ways of imposing traditional social roles on women, while not renouncing them altogether as long as they stem from "her own roots." Elaine P. Miller believes that Irigaray departs from the metaphorical interpretation of the woman-as-flower on behalf of a metonymical meaning of the figure; in other words, the woman is not *as a flower* constructed by and for men, but rather she *is a flower*, with her own growth dynamics, roots, and lush sexuality.[24]

Whereas the flower in its sexuality is always different, the man remains a fixed and immutable element of Kulik's *Garden*. But even if we assume that the flower is metonymically connected with the woman, female sexuality, as Grosz notes, eludes classification, refusing to be framed in norms and mechanisms.

> What we can say about female sexuality—its fluidity, its contiguity with the non-sexual, its indeterminacy of organs and sensations, its tactility, formlessness, open-endedness—means that any attempt to know the sexuality of all women will lose the specificity of each particular woman rather than indicate in probabilistic terms her general features.[25]

In each specific situation, in relation to another—or her own—body, the woman always becomes anew.

Elizabeth Grosz says that "we await, no longer a science of sexuality, its formalization and abstraction, but an art of sexuality, not its analysis but its celebration as diverse becoming, not knowing and thereby containing it, but elaborating and extending it."[26] If she is right, then are we willing to turn towards plants—their genital flowers and sexual strategies—in a quest for inspiration for ourselves? Botanical sexuality free from heteronormative assumptions ("botanical queerness"[27]) makes it possible to move away from anthropomorphic projections, such as the association of the anthurius stamen with the phallus, for it is actually something far more complex—a cluster of numerous sexual organs comprising hermaphroditic flowers. In the field of plant sexuality, nothing can be determined according to the human sexual specificities, for as Richard M. Doyle notes,

> Plant sex is perhaps unusual for its object of seduction and not its methodology. Instead of beguiling or otherwise manoeuvring a partner to exchange genetic information, flowers make themselves sensitive to the wind and resonant with the bee perceptual system.[28]

With their sexuality, plant bodies open the possibility of unthought fantasies and unknown practices, for sexuality, including human sexuality, is never determined;

it is "contained in the next sexual encounter, rather than in the synthesis of all one's past sexual activities."[29]

Translated by Marcin Wawrzyńczak

NOTES

1. Richard M. Doyle, *Darwin's Pharmacy: Sex, Plants, and the Evolution of the Noösphere* (Washington: University of Washington Press, 2011), 70.
2. *De Sexu Plantarum Epistola*, by the German botanist and doctor Rudolf Jakob Camerarius, published in 1694.
3. In Western art, flowers have appeared directly since the 1930s, meaning they are presented rather than represented.
4. The metaphorical trope in the reading of flowers in the works of Natalia LL and other artists leads to different, anthropocentric, interpretative propositions (cf., e.g. Jakub Piwowarski, "Aroids (*Araceae* Juss) in the Art of Natalia LL," in *Natalia LL: Secretum et tremor*, ed. Ewa Toniak (Warszawa: CSW Zamek Ujazdowski, 2015), 106–109.
5. Brigitte Nerlich and David D. Clarke, "Serial Metonymy: A Study of Reference-Based Polysemisation," *Journal of Historical Pragmatics* 2, no. 2 (2011): 245.
6. Elaine P. Miller, *The Vegetative Soul: From Philosophy of Nature to Subjectivity in the Feminine* (Albany: SUNY Press, 2002), 188.
7. Cf. copperplate engraving by Giulio Casserio (anatomist) and Odarado Fialetti (artist), in Adriaan van Spiegel, *De formato foetu liber singularis* (Frankfurt, 1631), reprinted in Michael Sappol, ed., *Dream Anatomy* exhibit catalog (Bethesda, MD: National Institutes of Health, 2006), https://www.nlm.nih.gov/exhibition/dreamanatomy/da_g_I-D-4-01.html.
8. Cf. Daniel Chamovitz, *What a Plant Knows: A Field Guide to the Senses of Your Garden—and Beyond* (Oxford: Oneworld, 2012), 167–175.
9. Cf. Elizabeth Grosz, *Time Travels: Feminism, Nature, Power* (Durham, NC: Duke University Press, 2005), 186–187.
10. Elizabeth Grosz, *Time Travels*, 187.
11. Elizabeth Grosz, *Time Travels*, 213.
12. *Calamitas Erotica*, presented in the exhibition *Kobieta o kobiecie* [Woman about Woman], Galeria Bielska, Bielsko-Biała, 1996.
13. *Allusive Space*, shown at the Frauen Museum, Bonn, 1995.
14. Natalia LL, "Calamitas erotica," in *Natalia LL. Texty. Teksty Natalii LL. O twórczości Natalii LL*, ed. Natalia LL (Bielsko-Biała: Galeria Bielska BWA, 2004), 182.
15. Rosi Braidotti, *Transpositions* (Cambridge: Polity Press, 2006), 37.
16. *Calamitas Erotica*, 182.

17. "Autoportrety. Ja to jednak nie ktoś inny. Z Zofią Kulik rozmawia Bożena Czubak," in *Autoportrety i ogród*, ed. Bożena Czubak (Warszawa: Galeria Le Guern, 2004), 70.
18. Leah Knight, *Of Books and Botany in Early Modern England: Sixteenth-Century Plants and Print Culture* (Farnham, UK: Ashgate, 2009), 32.
19. Knight, *Of Books and Botany.*
20. Cf. Elizabeth Heckendorn Cook, "'Perfect' Flowers, Monstrous Women: Eighteenth-Century Botany and the Modern Gendered Subject," in *Defects: Engendering the Modern Body*, ed. Helen Deutsch and Felicity Nussbaum (University of Michigan Press, 2000).
21. Cf. George Sam and Alison E. Martin, eds., "Botanising Women: Transmission, Translation and European Exchange," *Journal of Literature and Science* 4, no. 1 (2011).
22. *Autoportrety i ogród*, 68.
23. Luce Irigaray, *Elemental Passions*, trans. Joanne Collie and Judith Still (New York: Routledge, 2013), 34.
24. Miller, *The Vegetative Soul*, 192.
25. Grosz, *Time Travels*, 213.
26. Grosz, *Time Travels*, 214.
27. A term coined by Catriona Sandilands.
28. Doyle, *Darwin's Pharmacy*, 68.
29. Grosz, *Time Travels*, 213.

Main Pathway: Cross-Pollination

Subthemes

Proceed to Experience, p. 329
Proceed to Composting, p. 329
Proceed to Transcending, p. 541

18

BOTANICAL DECOLONIZATION: IN DEFENSE OF CULTIVARS

Giovanni Aloi

Wouldn't a more cosmopolitan garden, one that borrowed freely from all the world's styles and floras, that made something of history rather than trying to escape it—wouldn't such a garden be more in keeping with the American experience?
—Michael Pollan, "Against Nativism"

"Natives" are only those organisms that first happened to gain and keep a footing.
—Stephen J. Gould, "An Evolutionary Perspective on Strengths, Fallacies, and Confusions in the Concept of Native Plants"

It looked like a massive fish tank of the kind seen in corporate lobbies—perfectly clean, vibrantly colorful, and expertly arranged. But its waters were uncunningly still and deserted of fish. Instead, over a thousand plants at the peak of their aesthetic glory filled the space with baroque pomp. Perfectly formed and harmoniously arranged to dazzle, the plants looked otherworldly and yet vividly real.

Marc Quinn's *Garden* was a quintessential utopia made possible by the intricate synergy of art, nature, and technology. What at first glance looked like water was revealed by the accompanying exhibition text to be 25 tons of low-viscosity silicon kept at -20°C.[1] The plants were frozen solid, preserved in an impossible diorama—a postmodern interpretation of the Garden of Eden. The many varieties obtained

Originally published as "Botanical Decolonization: In Defense of Cultivars," in *Beyond Plant Blindness* (Berlin: Green Box Publications), 23–30. Reprinted with permission.

from around the world required a powerful set of generators and a cold-lighting system to appropriately preserve the artist's vision. *Garden* incarnated man's desire to control nature, to select and organize what we find beautiful, to make this beauty visible, and most importantly to prevent it from ever fading. But in its dioramic stasis, Quinn's *Garden* was more than a sophisticated tableau. As a beautiful provocation, it asked viewers to consider the contradicting narratives of human and nature co-evolutions through the geo-cultural delimitations of the garden: a space heavily burdened by symbolism, defined by specific power/knowledge relationships, and driven by often implicit and problematic aesthetic desires for purity and perfection.

In Judeo-Christian beliefs, the garden appears as the quintessential place of otherworldly harmony—an island of peace man ruined when Adam and Eve ate the forbidden fruit from the Tree of Knowledge. That moment coincided with the destruction of the perfect balance in God's creation. The awareness of nakedness and the experience of an irreconcilable separateness from nature followed. This world-forming narrative has, at least in the West, tinged gardens with a sense of nostalgia. It is not an understatement to say that many Renaissance and Enlightenment gardens, implicitly attempted to restore the Garden of Eden on Earth. As the systematic study of animals and plants emerged from the religious tales of the *Bestiarium*, Renaissance botanic gardens found their cultural roots firmly planted in Biblical interpretations.[2] To recreate Edenic utopias was, therefore, an attempt to praise the greatness of God's work in an ultimately futile bid for salvation. As Marc Quinn explains:

> People thought that when Adam and Eve were expelled from the Garden of Eden, all the plants in it were scattered all over the world. The idea [. . .] was that, if they could bring them all together again in one place, then it would be possible to recreate the Garden of Eden and the wisdom of God.[3]

Quinn's installation gestured towards the spiritual narrative of separateness between man and nature that still dominates today's thinking. It essentially presented a conflation of the beloved representational devices that made Victorian natural history iconic: the diorama, the fish tank, and the greenhouse. These spaces of the impossible employed glass for practical purposes. But the transparency of the material also reassessed our exclusion from the natural world. For better or worse, this cultural background has shaped our modern understanding of nature: stilling, boxing, dividing, and categorizing have been the tools we have always used to wade through the bio-flux of this world, its unpredictability, and unwillingness to comply with our expectations and desires.

Quinn's *Garden* was a haunting ground of Platonic perfection—the installation invited a comparison with the world outside. Its heavenly purity revealed as a device designed to unmask the politics of the material world we live in, its messiness, and its inexorable proclivity to change. The bottom line was clear: despite their harmonious aesthetic, gardens of any kind have always been sites of struggle in which humanity works hard at repairing, envisioning, and maintaining an ideal. In the garden, nature is artifice, and therefore culture. As a result, the pleasure one can derive from gardening is complexly woven in connected layers of desire, memory, hope, and care. The process is endless, the drive compulsive.

Once, over a casual conversation at Goldsmiths during my graduate studies, someone said: "Gardening is an extremely violent activity." Those swords struck a chord—they changed the way I looked at what I do in the garden forever. There was blatant truth in the paradox. Gardening was marketed to my generation as a female hobby, a gentile pastime for delicate hands and flower-patterned rubbery kneepads. Yet, it is all about ripping up, cutting, and digging. But it is all done in the name of love; for the good of the plants we admire, and primarily for our own good, of course.

More than fragments of heaven on Earth, gardens are political battlegrounds. The foliage and flowers in our gardens emerge from underground histories we might sometimes not be aware of. And perhaps more importantly, plants define our identities in ways we sometimes don't even suspect. This is, at least in part, why for the past thirty years, gardeners, scholars, and plant nurseries have animatedly discussed the representational and biological values of our gardens. The topics have been varied, but much of the conversation has focused on the controversial subject of *botanical decolonization*.[4] In a nutshell, plant-native supporters understand their philosophical position as "a strategic location for ethical action in the Anthropocene," and they vehemently object those on the other side, who link their ideology to anti-immigrant "nativism."[5]

Decolonization is currently very fashionable in academia. The term lends an ethical edge to scholars in a desperate need to reaffirm their relevance amid a fast-changing world besotted by online entertainment. "Decolonizing" sounds aware and agentially charged. Academia can no longer afford to be seen purely thinking about the world. It has to been seen changing it and, ideally, quite quickly too. Politicized views seem to overshadow research well before scholars have seriously pondered the value and nature of the change they propose.

But let's be clear, not everything is wrong about the ideas defining cultural decolonization and botanical decolonization more specifically: science tells us that biodiversity is generally good for ecosystems. But, I argue that we need to think harder and longer about the chains of inference linking our thinking between plants to animals, peoples, and territories starting from the meaning and agency of the word "native."

Concerns about the term's application to the natural world have grown for years.[6] In the mid-1990s, Michael Pollan published an inflammatory article in *The New York Times* titled "Against Nativism," which condemned the "natural garden movement" for implicitly promoting purist ideologies that worryingly echoed the rise of a natural-gardening movement "founded on nationalistic and racist ideas" in pre–World War II Germany. Inspired by the study of "plant sociology," a group of landscape designers set out to give the German people its characteristic garden and to help guard it from unwholesome alien influences, including foreign plants and landscape formality, which they condemned as both anthropocentric and apt to weaken the "Nordic races."[7]

Pollan's quotes from articles published in the 1930s are blood-chilling. Four years later, evolutionary biologist Stephen Jay Gould published a compelling essay titled "An Evolutionary Perspective on Strengths, Fallacies, and Confusions in the Concept of Native Plants," in which he quoted the equally worrying views of Danish-American landscape architect Jens Jensen's "Our Native Landscape," published in 1937.[8] Jensen proudly proclaimed:

> The gardens that I created myself shall . . . be in harmony with their landscape environment and the racial characteristics of its inhabitants. They shall express the spirit of America and therefore shall be free of foreign character as far as possible. The Latin and the Oriental crept and creeps more and more over our land, coming from the South, which is settled by Latin people, and also from other centers of mixed masses of immigrants. The Germanic character of our cities and settlements was overgrown . . . Latin spirit has spoiled a lot and still spoils things every day.[9]

It seems clear that by definition, gardens are ideological islands. Perimeters, boundaries, fences, walls—a garden is a miniature state: a self-contained nation inhabited by plants whose biological origins are often difficult to clearly identify or ascertain. Jens Jensen's ideology is truly troublesome. His sentiments were clearly linked to mass deportation and Hitler's concentration camps. That the "undesirable non-native plants" could far too easily be turned into symbols of peoples from different cultures constitutes an alarming historical precedent. Yet, it is also an important symptomatic aspect of the ways in which some of us conceive national identity and the complexity of its construction processes in relation to otherness.

In my recently published essay "Sorely Visible: Plants, Roots, and National Identity,"[10] I have mapped the ideological currents that led right-wing political exponents to protest and burn palm and banana trees in Milan's Piazza del Duomo. How we think about plants is an important index of our relationships with other humans—this is also why we should take plants very seriously. The opening of Hugh Ruffle's "Mother Nature's Melting Pot" from 2011 worryingly sounds as it could have been written yesterday:

> The anti-immigrant sentiment sweeping the country, from draconian laws in Arizona to armed militias along the Mexican border, has taken many Americans by surprise. It shouldn't—nativism runs deep in the United States. Just ask our non-native animals and plants: they too are commonly labeled as aliens, even though they also provide significant benefits to their new home.[11]

A more recent essay from 2014, titled "Botanical Decolonization: Rethinking Native Plants," penned by social scientists, provides an interesting summarization of the ideals that have shaped the botanical decolonizing movement, but ignores these evident ideological links in order to rewrite a different and more ennobling "academic activist" narrative in support of cultural and environmental decolonization. In the essay, the authors reduce the shared history of humans and plants to the colonization of America, with a focus on California. As someone who has migrated from Europe to the USA only a few years ago, I have had the opportunity to notice that very frequently, to American cultural politics, colonialism is the beginning and end point of pretty much anything. In this myopic historical framework, millennia of global human–plant *naturecultures* that have substantially changed the biological history of this planet can go willfully overlooked. The authors firmly believe in an Edenic notion according to which native plants have "evolved in a given area or that arrived there by natural means . . . without the intentional or accidental intervention of humans."[12] And they furthermore believe that "This emphasis on the absence or mediating presence of human action provides a useful point of analytical departure."[13]

These statements are troublesome for they erroneously support the mistaken notion that Western colonizers were the only agents who (negatively) impacted the ecosystems of this and other lands. These views implicitly cast native peoples as passive and "natural." They presuppose that native people always lived in harmony with a nurturing natural world they had no need to tame or manage, to survive. It goes without saying that this vision is extremely patronizing to Indigenous people since it also erases their cultural and technical range of skills required to support their civilizations. This view also contradicts knowledge that Indigenous people regularly "practiced tilling, sowing, weeding, pruning, burning, and selective harvesting to manage plant populations and shape their natural environments,"[14] and that, as Gould argues:

> Preindustrial people have been just as rapacious (though not so quickly perhaps, for lack of tools) as the worst modern clear-cutters. The Maori people of New Zealand wiped out a rich fauna of some twenty moa species within a few hundred years. The "native" Polynesians of Easter Island wiped out everything edible or usable (and, in the end, had no logs to build boats or to raise their famous statues), and finally turned to self-destruction.[15]

Yet, to the "botanical decolonization" movement, the real problem is that "we still live in a *colonial* environment."[16] Some, therefore, advocate the removal of non-native plants from gardens and parklands in order to completely erase colonial legacy.[17] The movement's invitation shows no consideration for the value of individual plant lives, for the local histories that have led to the existence of these plants today, and for the ecosystems that might have developed around and through them. This problematic relationship with history seems to pervade the cultural politics of the United States to the point that very few productive conversations about the past and its legacy can emerge. More and more Americans seem to be coming to terms with the fact that their country was not built on virgin lands, as they were told, by the wit, knowledge, ambition, and strength of the founding fathers. My undergraduate students are angry at their primary school teachers for not telling them the truth about the genocide, the slavery, the environmental destruction. It's all happening now, as white people are told to "check their privilege" and the crumbling of metanarratives begins to reveal the inconvenient truth behind the American Dream—and it hurts; it hurts badly. So, in a bid for salvation, scholars are rushing to decolonize without having devised methodologies or frameworks that might allow those whose lives and histories have been most negatively impacted by colonialism to lead the decolonization.[18]

Worryingly, this desire to cleanse our gardens of non-native plants is pervaded by some of the most dangerous forces in our cultural makeup: purity and redemption. Yes, we are back to Marc Quinn's *Garden* and the spiritual voices ventriloquized by social scientists. This ultimately is the real issue with the line of thinking of decolonizing anything in the USA. The need to remediate the past most often equates to erasing it in the hope that scars might disappear with it. So, purging the land from the invasive plants brought to the continent by white settlers is representationally perceived as a productive political reversal.

But this simplistic line of thinking is very flawed. It wasn't just European settlers who brought non-native species to the USA. The advocates of the botanical decolonization claim that "when new lands are occupied, the deep place connection idea is dispensed with, and new lands are made appropriate by changing the flora to make it like the homeland."[19] But isn't this what all immigrants do when they relocate elsewhere? Haven't we all craved to see a bloom that smells of our childhood or that reminds us of faraway family members? What can be said in this context of the Little Italies, French Quarters, Chinatowns, and Little Tokyos around the world? Immigrants of all colors and creeds have always brought some of their foods, plants, customs, and architecture to their new homes. This is what, up until now, we have celebrated as cultural diversity. But this is also at risk in the ideological musing of those who in academia crave purity and decolonization.

The essential issue is one of representation. In our ever-faster world of online communication and social media entertainment, we seem to have developed a proclivity to read symbols in very superficial ways. The semantic polysemy highlighted by semiotic theories at the end of the last century has been oversimplified by a poststructuralist righteousness. The scale has tilted too far towards validating the individual's perception of objects and events over the historical and the contextual background. While poststructural critique rightly emphasized the interpretative importance of the subject over the authorial vision, we now seem to have come to a point where the subject's personal proclivity conveniently restricts the semantic bandwidth of symbols, leading to a troublesome rewriting of history and science.

Native plants are the construct of dangerous fictions that implicitly supports the nature/culture divide that has led us to the ecological crisis and sixth mass extinction we are currently experiencing. These notions of nativeness reassess the separateness between us and a sublime and distant nature from which we have been expelled. They thus prevent us from productively building on past ecological histories. Decolonizing should not equate to dismantling or erasing, and living plants should not be seen as monuments to white supremacy either. At this point, we need to focus on the nuances of representation and its entanglements with multiple historical and scientific milieus.

Cultivars, the type of plants Marc Quinn selected for his *Garden* installation, are more than non-native species. They inscribe the "natureculture coevolutions" of many peoples and cultures over time. They are varieties selectively bred and manipulated to fulfill our desire for a different world that can only be achieved with the complicity of plants. Cultivars are the result of centuries (sometimes millennia) of naturecultural processes designed to obtain bigger flowers, deeper colorations, and more intense fragrances. Simultaneously, by biologically allowing certain changes to happen, and forbidding others, plants have shaped our aesthetic taste and our economies, along with our senses. I see cultivars as the result of important, creative/cultural conversations between humans and lands, and humans and plants. Those who insist on reading cultivars as a form of subjugation of plant-life do so because they have never tried to cross-breed and select a vegetal species themselves. The process is extremely laborious, expensive, frustrating, and riddled with failure—plants don't simply do what we want. They say "no" through their biological definitions. They resist. This is why I look at cultivars as an undervalued collaborative artform.

Ultimately, the first appearance of plants in the gallery space in 1936 was, for good reasons, Edward Steichen's *Delphiniums* exhibit at MoMA.[20] Steichen, who had an extremely successful career as a painter, photographer, modern art promoter, and museum curator, had retired in Connecticut to focus on his horticultural passion. At MoMA he presented his engineered new breeds of delphiniums; some gigantified to four feet. The artist doused delphinium seeds in a chemical bath of colchicine, a toxin that induces polyploidy, resulting in mutated flowers.[21] The exhibition functioned as a metaphorical take on the Aristotelian view that art perfects nature, and it delivered this idea to the artworld as a decaying Duchampian-inspired readymade, thus also problematizing the Dutch Golden Age memento mori stilled aesthetic. Steichen's delphiniums also posed important questions of originality, authorship, and value while challenging the very essence of what we call "natural."

Conceptions of rarity, eroticization, and exoticism all come into play, of course. But while these can all be traced back to our colonialist past, they are by no means its invention, and neither are they exclusively white values. How long should a plant have settled in its environment for it to count as native? As far as we can remember?

According to Gould, "'Natives,' in short, are the species that happened to find their way (or evolve in situ), not the best conceivable for a spot."[22] At least in part, the problem is one of timescale. The concept of the Anthropocene is applying productive pressure on our consideration of deep-time and the relativity between the biological history of this planet and our extremely short presence upon its surface.

The history of plant cultivars spans the globe. Over millennia, from oranges to cherries, and cabbages to basil, we have selected, cross-bred, manipulated, grafted, exported, and imported. Throughout it all, plants have made us human. They have seduced us and colonized us. They have invaded our homes and have provided emotional reference points for our memories, grieving, and joy, along with food and materials.

We regularly look at our gardens as retreats from capitalist economies of exploitation that dictate the frantic rhythms of our everyday lives spent in polluted urban environments. Yet any garden actually is the result of multiple capitalist transactions, from the land to the tools, from the shingles and pebbles to fertilizers and pesticides, and the plants purchased from the gardening center—nothing in the garden is ever "pure" or "native," especially when those supporting the botanical decolonizing movement flock to garden centers to buy *nativars*: manipulated cultivars of "native" species that have been molded by botanical experts to fit the garden market with illusive realness. These plants are not the same as the wild varieties they impersonate, and as such, they do not perform the same biological functions of their wild counterparts. Pollinators don't seem to like them as much,[23] and the industry pumps these plants with neonicotinoids (powerful antiparasitic poisons) that will kill butterflies and bees that feed on them.[24] It is important to come to terms with the fact that there is no true way back to purity because purity only exists in our mind. And what can decolonization accomplish if it is governed by the capitalist systems that have emerged from colonialism anyway?

Cultivars have been selected to thrive and withstand the reckless conditions of capitalist mass production and sale. Real wild plants cannot survive the transportation and storage cultivars have been selected to endure—we have made them evolve into "hyper plants" addicted to regular fertilization, lighting, and watering. Their life-cycles are self-contained and regulated within the artificiality of the system which produces them and sells them—a wild plant is a differently adapted organism. Furthermore, experts have also pointed out that since nativars are cloned plants, the genetic variation loss they imply makes them vulnerable to devastating blights. It seems clear that a genuine botanical decolonization would require substantial research and means that are not within everyone's reach, rather than the quick swap over at the Home Depot that the natural garden movement implicitly promotes.

In 1994, Michael Pollan argued that a "cosmopolitan garden, one that borrowed freely from all the world's styles and floras, that made something of history rather than trying to escape it" would be more in "keeping with the American experience."[25] Over twenty years later his sentiment seems even more topical for different reasons. Beyond providing a positive representational model for diversity, the cosmopolitan garden can also adequately support local wildlife in a more unpredictable and changing climate. The staggered flowering of cultivars in early spring, like tulips and daffodils, provides sustenance for bumblebees and other pollinators that prematurely wake up because of the milder winters we have been recently experiencing. The key to botanical decolonization would therefore not be a dismantling of cultivars from our gardens and parks based exclusively on representational values, but a calibrated promotion of biodiversity capable of sustaining local ecosystems regardless of their origin. A botanical decolonization would entail once and for all getting over ourselves and our desire to control and regulate. We desperately need to prioritize the survivals of ecosystems. We should be focusing on interconnectedness and sustainability instead of chasing dreams of purity that, as we know from past histories, only lead to the irreparable traumas upon which we have no choice but to build our future.

Art might not necessarily lead us down the appropriate biological path every time. But it might nonetheless help us think about our relationship with plants in new and productive ways. An interesting and hopefully useful metaphor through which to reframe the representational value of plants beyond the simplistic nationalisms of botanical decolonization is provided by the recent work of African American artist Rashid Johnson, whose gridline-architectural structures usually incorporate a variety of exotic potted plants forming a hanging garden at the center of which a pianist performs. The artist deliberately employs a range of different plants from all over the world to symbolize diversity and organicity. Furthermore, as he explained, in a cultivated setting, plants are utterly dependent on us for watering, nourishment, and light; remembering to water a plant calls us back to reality and to our surroundings—it is an invitation to be present, in the moment, and to be aware. The plants in Johnson's work represent a sign of care, a reminder to tend to the least vocal, and perhaps more vulnerable individuals in our families and communities, or to the facets of our lives we take for granted and most regularly overlook. But on another level, to Johnson, the plants also represent a destabilization of institutional power—a peaceful objection to the rules and restrictions placed on artists by the museums and the art market alike. This is a form of true botanical decolonization—the ability to conceive plants beyond the semantic strictures of nationalistic and xenophobic paradigms in order to envision a different future that makes something of history rather than trying to erase it.

NOTES

1. Miuccia Prada, Germano Celant, Darian Leader, and Marc Quinn, *Marc Quinn* (Milano: Fondazione Prada, 2000), 286.
2. Richard Drayton, *Nature's Government: Science, Imperial Britain, and the 'Improvement' of the World* (New Haven: Yale University Press, 2000); and John M. Prest, *The Garden of Eden: The Botanic Garden and the Re-Creation of Paradise* (New Haven: Yale University Press, 1981).
3. Prada et al., *Marc Quinn*, 214.
4. Tomaz Mastnak, Julia Elyachar, and Tom Boellstorff, "Botanical Decolonization: Rethinking Native Plants." *Environment and Planning D: Society and Space* 32, no. 2 (2014): 363–380.
5. Mastnak et al., "Botanical Decolonization," 363.
6. Nancy Shackelford, Richard Hobbs, N. E. Heller, L. M. Hallett, and T. R. Seastedt, "Finding a Middle-Ground: The Native/Non-Native Debate," *Biological Conservation* 158 (2013): 55–62; Daniel Simberloff, Daniel "Confronting Introduced Species: A Form of Xenophobia?," *Biological Invasions* 5, no. 3 (2013): 179–192; Paul Robbins and Sarah Moore, "Ecological Anxiety Disorder: Diagnosing the Politics of the Anthropocene," *Cultural Geographies* 20, no. 1 (2013): 3–19.
7. Michael Pollan, "Against Nativism," *New York Times Magazine*, May 15, 1994, 52–55.
8. Stephen Jay Gould, "An Evolutionary Perspective on Strengths, Fallacies, and Confusions in the Concept of Native Plants." *Arnoldia* 58, no. 1 (Spring 1998): 3–10.
9. Quoted in Joachim Wolschke-Bulmahn, "Political Landscapes and Technologies: Nazi Germany and the Landscape Design of the Reichsautobahnen (Reich Motor Highways)," in *Council of Educators in Landscape Architecture (CELA) Annual Conference Papers VII* (1995): 157–170; quote, 159.
10. Giovanni Aloi, "Sorely Visible: Plants, Roots, and National Identity," *Plants, People, Planet* 1, no. 3 (2019): 204–211.
11. Hughes Ruffles, "Mother Nature's Melting Pot," *New York Times*, April 2, 2011, 12.
12. Mastnak et al., "Botanical Decolonization," 364.
13. Mastnak et al., "Botanical Decolonization," 364.
14. Marjorie G. Schmidt and Katherine L. Greenberg, *Growing California Native Plants* (Berkeley: University of California Press, 2012), 50.
15. Gould, "Evolutionary Perspective," 9–10.

16. Mastnak et al., "Botanical Decolonization," 370.

17. J. L. Lowry, "Native Plants for Coastal Gardens," in *Symposium Proceedings: Out of the Wild and Into the Garden II. California's Horticulturally Significant Plants*, ed. B. O'Brien, L. Fuentes, and L. Newcome (Rancho Santa Ana Botanic Garden, Claremont, CA, 1997), 104–111.

18. An example: *Decolonizing Nature*, the academic book sensation of 2013 was written by T. J. Demos, a graduate of Columbia University and professor of history of art at the University of Santa Cruz, who is neither black nor native American. T. J. Demos, *Decolonizing Nature: Contemporary Art and the Politics of Ecology* (Berlin: Sternberg Press, 2013).

19. Isis Brook, "Making Here Like There: Place Attachment, displacement and the Urge to Garden," *Ethics, Place, and Environment* 6, no. 3 (2013): 227–234; quote, 230.

20. George Gessert, *Green Light: Toward an Art of Evolution* (Cambridge: MIT Press, 2012), 48.

21. Frances Stracey, "Bio-Art: The Ethics behind the Aesthetics," *Perspective* 10, no. 7 (July 2009): 496–500.

22. Gould, "Evolutionary Perspective," 8.

23. Annie S. White, "From Nursery to Nature: Are Native Cultivars as Valuable to Pollinators as Native Species?," *Pollinatorgardens*, February 8, 2013, https://pollinatorgardens.org/2013/02/08/my-research/.

24. Daniel Raichel, "10 Things You Always Wanted to Know about Neonics," *NRDC*, May 25, 2022, https://www.nrdc.org/experts/daniel-raichel/ten-things-you-always-wanted-know-about-neonics

25. Pollan, "Against Nativism," 55.

REFERENCES

Aloi, Giovanni. "Sorely Visible: Plants, Roots, and National Identity," in *Plants, People, Planet 1*, no. 3 (2019): 204–211.

Brook, Isis. "Making Here Like There: Place Attachment, Displacement and the Urge to Garden." *Ethics, Place, and Environment* 6, no. 3 (2003): 227–234.

Demos, T .J. *Decolonizing Nature: Contemporary Art and the Politics of Ecology*. Berlin: Sternberg Press, 2013.

Drayton, Richard. *Nature's Government: Science, Imperial Britain, and the 'Improvement' of the World*. London: Yale University Press, 2000.

Gessert, George. *Green Light: Toward an Art of Evolution*. Cambridge: MIT Press, 2012.

Gould, Stephen Jay. "An Evolutionary Perspective on Strengths, Fallacies, and Confusions in the Concept of Native Plants." *Arnoldia* 58, no. 1 (Spring 1998): 3–10.

Lowry, J. L., "Native Plants for Coastal Gardens." In *Symposium Proceedings: Out of the Wild and Into the Garden II. California's Horticulturally Significant Plants*, edited by B. O'Brien, L. Fuentes, and L. Newcome, 104–111. Rancho Santa Ana Botanic Garden, Claremont, CA, 1997.

Mastnak, Tomaz, Julia Elyachar, and Tom Boellstorff. "Botanical Decolonization: Rethinking Native Plants." *Environment and Planning D: Society and Space* 32, no. 2 (2014): 363–380.

Pollan, Michael. "Against Nativism." *New York Times Magazine*, May 15, 1994, 52–55.

Prada, Miuccia, Germano Celant, Darian Leader, and Marc Quinn. *Marc Quinn*. Milano: Fondazione Prada, 2000.

Prest, John M. *The Garden of Eden: The Botanic Garden and the Re-Creation of Paradise*. New Haven: Yale University Press, 1981.

Raichel, Daniel. "10 Things You Always Wanted to Know about Neonics." *NRDC*, May 25, 2022. https://www.nrdc.org/experts/daniel-raichel/ten-things-you-always-wanted-know-about-neonics.

Robbins, Paul, and Sarah Moore. "Ecological Anxiety Disorder: Diagnosing the Politics of the Anthropocene." *Cultural Geographies* 20, no. 1 (2013): 3–19.

Ruffles, Hughes. "Mother Nature's Melting Pot." *New York Times*, April 2, 2011, 12.

Schmidt, Marjorie G., and Katherine L. Greenberg. *Growing California Native Plants*. Berkeley: University of California Press, 2012.

Shackelford, Nancy, Richard Hobbs, N. E. Heller, L. M. Hallett, and T. R. Seastedt. "Finding a Middle-Ground: The Native/Non-Native Debate." *Biological Conservation* 158 (2012): 55–62.

Simberloff, Daniel. "Confronting Introduced Species: A Form of Xenophobia?" *Biological Invasions* 5, no. 3 (2003): 179–192.

Stracey, Frances. "Bio-Art: The Ethics behind the Aesthetics." *Perspective* 10, no. 7 (July 2009): 496–500.

White, Annie S. "From Nursery to Nature: Are Native Cultivars as Valuable to Pollinators as Native Species?" *Pollinatorgardens*, February 8, 2013. https://pollinatorgardens.org/2013/02/08/my-research/.

Wolschke-Bulmahn, Joachim. "Political Landscapes and Technologies: Nazi Germany and the Landscape Design of the Reichsautobahnen (Reich Motor Highways)." *Council of Educators in Landscape Architecture (CELA) Annual Conference Papers VII* (1995), 157–170.

Main Pathway: Ecologies

Subthemes

Proceed to Decolonization, p. 407
Proceed to Diasporas, p. 517
End of Politics
Proceed to Ethics, p. 407

19

INVASIVE SPECIES, INDIGENOUS STEWARDS, AND VULNERABILITY DISCOURSE

Nicholas J. Reo, Kyle Whyte, Darren Ranco, Jodi Brandt, Emily Blackmer, and Braden Elliott

North American Indigenous nations are confronting various forms of rapid environmental change, ranging from climate-induced sea-level rise on the Gulf Coast, to melting permafrost and shifting sea ice patterns in the Arctic, to invasive species–induced trophic cascades in the Great Lakes.[1] These changes are all evidence used to justify calling our current geologic era the "Anthropocene," viewed as the period during which human activity has been the dominant influence on climate and the environment.[2]

Invasive species can cause dramatic changes to ecosystems, including shifts in species composition, species mortality, biodiversity, disturbance regimes, and ecosystem-level nutrient dynamics. Globally, the impacts of invasive species cost billions of dollars annually.[3] Land managers and policy makers in the United States and Canada try to minimize these ecological and economic impacts through a range of management strategies, including prediction, prevention, preparedness, education, eradication, containment, monitoring, and research/development.

Indigenous peoples in the United States and Canada have a long history of dealing with environmental changes. They are acutely aware of invasive species in their territories and are actively responding in various ways as well. Indigenous nations' invasive species work is generally underreported in the literature but includes communication and education initiatives, scientific research that tests new

Originally published as "Invasive Species, Indigenous Stewards, and Vulnerability Discourse," *American Indian Quarterly* 41, no. 3 (Summer 2017): 201–223. Reprinted with permission.

stewardship strategies, ecosystem restoration through Indigenous knowledge, and adaptation of cultural practices to account for changing conditions, including incorporating introduced species into Indigenous food systems.[4] Thus, Indigenous nations' responses to invasive species include all of the generalized steps taken by settler governments and NGOs plus some unique, culturally informed strategies reported in the literature; we describe these below.

Despite this range of activities, Indigenous peoples are rarely mentioned in the literature on human dimensions of invasive species, and most of the publications that do discuss Indigenous peoples' experiences with invasive species focus on sociocultural impacts. For example, Jeanine Pfeiffer and Elizabeth Huerta Ortiz document the effects of invasive species on culturally important plants, landscapes, livelihoods, and traditions.[5] In their case study of sudden oak death on the Hoopa and Yurok reservations in California, Janice Alexander and Christopher Lee note the cultural significance of the affected tanoak trees and reference the deep personal connections that frame tribal involvement in ta-noak mortality and efforts to combat it.[6] Importantly, these and related papers highlight the unique cultural dimensions of Indigenous peoples' experiences with invasive species.[7]

The key messages in these and related papers are about cultural impacts and Indigenous peoples' vulnerability to invasive species. Native American and Indigenous studies scholars have increasingly problematized the vulnerability narratives used to characterize Indigenous peoples' experiences with rapid environmental change.[8] One reason is that vulnerability narratives obscure the actions, strategies, resources, and knowledge that Indigenous groups mobilize to navigate environmental change. Vulnerability narratives are criticized for portraying Indigenous groups as passive or helpless, hiding the agency of very active Indigenous groups. Vulnerability narratives can portray Indigenous nations as dependent on settler colonial nation-states and other non-Indigenous parties for relief from environmental problems, which could lead to policymakers drafting climate change or invasive species policies that interfere with Indigenous nations' aspirations of self-determination.[9]

Benedict Colombi's studies about the Nez Perce (Niimiipu) are noteworthy because they show dimensions of the tribe's response to the degradation of salmon habitat that do not arise out of a vulnerability or help narrative.[10] His studies reconceptualize the current habitat issues the tribe faces from the tribe's own history of having to adapt to multiple habitat changes before and after US colonization. Colombi found that the Nez Perce developed important strategies for adaptation, or adaptive capacities, that included proactive approaches to strengthening and continuing Nez Perce leadership models and knowledge systems. Far from being passive recipients of salmon habitat degradation, the Nez Perce draw on their own history and culture to develop strategies that are both innovative and ancient for exercising self-determination in the face of risky changes. Colombi's work highlights how, for the Nez Perce, culture is not a passive victim to the degradation of salmon habitat; instead, culture itself is an essential adaptive capacity that supports Indigenous self-determination.

In the same spirit as Colombi and others, our article seeks to contribute to a shift toward recognizing Indigenous agency in environmental change research. We contribute to this transition through our exploratory research, which characterizes the range of ways Indigenous natural resource managers and practitioners are responding to invasive species. We ask how and why Indigenous people in the United States and Canada are preparing for, responding to, and adapting to invasive species in their respective territories. This investigation will lead to a better understanding of (1) how Indigenous knowledge, perspectives, and values guide Indigenous nations' environmental governance in relation to invasive species; (2) the motivations and goals behind Indigenous peoples' approaches to invasive species; and (3) the tools and methods Indigenous people use to carry out planning, adaptation, and mitigation measures.

METHODS

We collected data on Indigenous peoples' responses to invasive species through an online survey of staff from natural resource, environmental, and cultural departments from Indigenous nations across the United States and Canada.[11] We used a combination of purposive and snowball sampling to identify hard-to-find respondents with expert knowledge.[12] We chose a nonprobabilistic (i.e., nonrandom) sampling strategy, which means that we cannot quantitatively estimate the odds that we have represented the population well. This approach was appropriate given the dearth of published information about Indigenous peoples' approach to invasive species management in the United States and Canada. Given the exploratory nature of this research, our goal was to cast as wide a net as possible. The survey was sent via email to contacts within our professional networks; these contacts then forwarded the survey to Indigenous nations' staff from the contacts' own networks and to staff identified through publicly available contact lists for Indigenous nations. We sent one follow-up email to each potential respondent to increase our response rate. We informed respondents that their participation was voluntary, that they could skip any of the questions, and that they could exit the survey at any time. The survey was posted from July 2013 through June 2014.

The survey consisted of fourteen questions, including multiple-choice, open-ended, and Likert scale questions. Survey questions were structured based on findings and questions posed in the literature and our own experiences working with Indigenous nations in and outside of research settings. The survey instrument was designed following Jelke Bethlehem and Silvia Biffignandi. A draft of the survey instrument was pretested with representatives from one tribe in the United States and one First Nation in Canada and modified based on their feedback.[13]

Once data collection was complete, we used the survey software (SurveyMonkey Gold) to remove forty-five respondents who exited the survey before reaching the end. Descriptive statistics were calculated primarily as percentages to identify notable trends and anomalies. Open-ended questions/comments were qualitatively analyzed through an iterative coding process to further understand the context and nuances of invasive species management by Indigenous peoples.

Respondent concerns, rated from 0 to 5 on a Likert scale, were quantitatively analyzed with Cronbach's α, which allows multiple questions to be combined into an indirect measure of an underlying concept. Cronbach's α scores range from 0 to 1, with 0 indicating a set of questions that measure unrelated concepts and 1 indicating a set of questions that measure the same concept. Therefore, any particular response to one question perfectly predicts a particular response to another question in the set. An α score of 0.7 or higher is considered sufficient to group questions together as an aggregate measure of an underlying concept. When an α score greater than 0.7 was found for a group of specific concerns, a mean score is reported for the whole category of concern in addition to the mean score for each specific concern. Cronbach's α scores were calculated with the "ltm" package in R (version 3.2.2).

RESULTS

Demographic Summary

We numerically analyzed the data from all complete responses to the survey ($n = 107$, table 19.1). Sixty-three percent of respondents identified as citizens or descendants

Table 19.1. Demographics of survey respondents and summary of responses

Variables	All respondents ($n=106$) %[a]
Female	50
Age in years (mean ± SD)	45 ± 12
Indigenous nation citizen	63
Harvester	79
Employed by Indigenous nation[b]	88
Position within nation	
Natural resources	88
Research and education	16
Cultural resources	13
Planning	6
Official	2
Health services	2
Other	15
Prevention	
Increasing resilience	82
Cooperating with non-Indigenous government agencies	81
Creating education programs	70
Cooperating with an NGO	58
Cooperating with other Indigenous nations	55
Cooperating with a university	50
Developing policies with non-Indigenous entities	44
Developing emergency response	25
Creating Indigenous nation policies	24
Mitigation	
Hand pulling	83
Educational programs	76
Mechanical removal	64
Chemical application	50
Fire	37
Hunting	36
Biocontrol	36
Ceremony	21
Grazing	20
Adaptation	
Documenting traditional ecological knowledge	53
Saving native seed	47
Sharing strategies with other Indigenous nations	47
Traveling farther to harvest native species	46
Ceremony	38
Transplanting native species	27
Shifting from native to introduced species	16
Using alternative materials	14

[a] Percent of respondents who are employed by an Indigenous nation ($n=94$); multiple responses permitted per individual.
[b] Except where noted.

of Indigenous nations, and 94 percent were employed by an Indigenous nation. The largest majority (88%) of Indigenous nation employees described natural resource and environmental management as their primary work roles.

In total, through enrollment, descent, and employment, respondents represent 144 unique Indigenous nations in 17 US states and 4 Canadian provinces. The final number of respondents is higher than our sample size of 106 because several respondents were citizens of one Indigenous nation and worked for a separate nation.

Prevention

Indigenous nations commonly draw on partnerships in their work to prevent invasive species on their lands. Most (81%) respondents indicated that their communities have worked with non-Indigenous governments, including local, state, provincial, and federal government bodies and agencies, to prevent new invasive species. Indigenous nations have also partnered with nongovernmental or nonprofit organizations, including lake associations, numerous intertribal councils, and conservation organizations. Despite all the partnerships that Indigenous groups appear to be participating in, they can be left out of the loop or informed too late about new invasive species populations, compromising early response strategies. As a representative from the Caldwell First Nation in Ontario indicated, "We are [often] not informed that a new species has taken root until it is already too late and then we are dealing with damage control."

Efforts directed at educating the public and increasing the resiliency of lands and waters are important components of invasive species prevention. Seventy percent of respondents' Indigenous nations have given or currently give education programs to recruit public participation in prevention efforts. Tribal nations in the Great Lakes region, including the Lac Vieux Desert Band of Lake Superior Chippewa, Fond du Lac Band of Lake Superior Chippewa, and Little Traverse Bay Bands of Odawa, give harvesters maps of areas with invasive species and instructions on how to prevent spreading, and they have established prevention services such as free boat washes.

Nearly a quarter (24%) of respondents noted having established code or formal Indigenous governmental policies intended to prevent the spread of invasive species. In several cases, Indigenous nation policies that formally target invasive species include protocols for nation citizens and employees who work regularly in the field and may encounter invasive species, as well as broader protocols governing community responses to invasive species.

Mitigation

Hand pulling is the most commonly used means of invasive species removal; 83 percent of respondents indicated that their nation had removed invasive species by hand. Mowing is the second most commonly used means (64%). Other possible methods, including chemical treatments (50%), fire (37%), hunting (36%), biological controls (36%), ceremonies to support native species (21%), and grazing (20%), were less common.

While the Stockbridge-Munsee Band of Mohican Indians and other nations treat up to several hundred acres a year with chemicals and other controls, many other Indigenous nations lack the funding to use many mitigation methods and the knowledge of how to implement removal methods. For instance, a representative from the Menominee Nation considered using fire but was unsure "whether it would help reduce the invasive, or prepare the area to be invaded." This response and others show a wariness over potential negative outcomes, and these concerns are warranted. The Nanwalek IRA Council in Alaska used bacterial treatments designed to control geometrid moths on berry bushes, but this action wound up negatively affecting berry harvest for their communities. Concern for the cultural impacts of removal treatments has also halted potential action.

Education remains a primary tool in combating unwanted invasive species. Seventy-six percent of respondents and their communities have used education programs, including brochures, public service announcements, and public presentations, to limit the spread of established invasive species. Indigenous nations are also actively engaged in improving their own understanding of invasive species and how to treat them. Several Indigenous nations have looked to Western science to mitigate the impact of invasive species. The Walpole Island First Nation noted that their community had conducted a small trial of comparative methods in controlling invasive *Phragmites australis* (common reed). Chugachmiut, a Native organization that serves the seven tribes in the Chugach region of Alaska, is modeling areas where berry bushes will be most resistant to moth defoliation, and plans to use the data to "implement silvicultural berry improvement treatment in areas most likely to resist future defoliation."

Adaptation

Data suggest that no single adaptation measure is more commonly used than others. More than half (53%) of respondents have documented traditional knowledge and practices about threatened native species. Almost half have shared adaptive strategies with other Indigenous nations (47%), saved seeds from threatened native species (47%), and/or traveled farther than normal for harvest (46%). Twenty-seven percent have transplanted plants or animals to new locations to protect them from invasive species.

Even though, broadly, respondents tended to be very concerned about the sociocultural impacts of invasive species and less so about cultural adaptations, their responses to the latter are noteworthy. Following impacts by invasive species, 16 percent have shifted their reliance to alternative species. This includes forgoing more traditional foods that are less abundant or more at risk, as well as harvesting edible invasive plants. Fifteen percent have maintained skills or expertise following invasive species impacts by using alternative materials (e.g., basket makers using alternative materials). A representative from the Hiawatha First Nation noted, "We frequently harvest European purging buckthorn instead of native varieties of dogwood and willow for basketmaking. We've begun to harvest garlic mustard as a food source, while leaving [culturally valued] wild leeks and wild ginger alone." An Aleut community from the Pribilof Islands of Alaska employed a more symbolic measure by renaming an island after invasive species were removed.

Traditional Ecological Knowledge

Survey responses provided some insights into the ways traditional ecological knowledge (TEK) factors into Indigenous groups' interactions with invasive species. For instance, 54 percent of respondents indicated that their nation is actively documenting their community's TEK about native plants and animals (or human–animal and human–plant relationships) threatened by invasive species. For example, in the northeastern United States, Indigenous nations reported documenting their knowledge about ash trees given the likely arrival of the emerald ash borer in the future. In this case, documentation would include knowledge concerning the role of ash in creation stories as well as use-specific or artisan-specific knowledge and skills like those held by ash basket makers.

Documenting TEK often means documenting the knowledge held by a community's elders. The Nanwalek IRA Council in Alaska indicated that they are gathering information from their elders about ways to enhance berry populations impacted by invasive species. In Maine and Michigan, ash tree gathering methods are being documented to show not only methods of locating and harvesting appropriate trees but also family and tribal stories associated with traditional gathering areas. For the Wabanaki Nations of Maine, the urgency of this documentation ties back to their creation story of Gluskabe shooting an arrow into the ash tree, the spot from which all Wabanaki people emerge, singing and dancing.

Traditional ceremonies are one form of TEK. Thirty-nine percent of respondents use ceremonies to honor Indigenous plant and animal population, and 21 percent of respondents said their Indigenous nation has used ceremonies specifically to help native species impacted by introduced species. Some of these same respondents indicated that they factor in elders' perspectives and TEK when determining their invasive species response strategies, like the Sokaogon or Mole Lake Band of the Lake Superior Chippewa:

> We have to be real careful how we combat the invasives because our elders won't allow us to use herbicides in some areas so we have to hand pull those protected areas. Which is fine with us because we respect their wishes.

Indigenous Concerns

Though it was not the focus of our survey, we also asked respondents about their concerns over invasive species. We distinguish concerns from goals and motivations in the following way: goals are aspirational statements for desired future conditions or actions; motivations are underlying reasons or inspirations behind a group's actions or decisions; concerns are the current phenomena or future conditions groups are worried about. In this way, "concerns" are often about impacts. Emphasizing goals and motivations over concerns was our way of acting as a counterbalance to the large body of work on Indigenous experiences with global change emphasizing impacts.

Respondents were most concerned about environmental impacts, then cultural impacts, then economic impacts (table 19.2). A substantive majority (83%) of respondents reported that they were "very concerned" about the impacts to overall

Table 19.2. Mean ratings and Cronbach's alpha scores for invasive species concerns

Concern	A	Mean
Ecological	0.754	3.68
Overall ecosystem		3.73
Indigenous species		3.64
Cultural	0.824	3.32
Communal TEK		3.41
Tribal food systems		3.37
Cultural identity		3.19
Economic	0.855	2.79
Regional economy		2.94
Respondent's finances		2.77
Tribal economy		2.63

Note: Mean scores are based on responses to a Likert scale question indicating 1, not concerned; 2, neutral or unsure; 3, somewhat concerned; or 4, very concerned.

health of ecosystems, while 76 percent were "very concerned" about impacts to specific populations of indigenous plants and animals. Respondents noted that invasive species reduce the overall availability of essential resources, including water in semiarid environments and flora and fauna populations that have traditionally been staples in food and material cultures. One person from the Hopi Tribe explained their concerns over impacts to water availability, describing how reduced water availability affects plants, animals, and humans alike:

> In a semi-arid environment, water is of the utmost concern, with invasive species such as salt-cedar and Russian olive overtaking drainage systems/ecosystems that were havens for water, plant and animal species utilized by our people devastated, the ecosystems have been drastically altered with no means of controlling or stabilizing the situation.

A representative from the Quinault Indian Nation described how invasive species are impacting the habitat of cultural keystone species:

> The large river floodplains are severely degraded due to dense populations of invasive species. Riparian Habitat for native salmon is threatened by extensive knotweed infestations which will negatively impact Quinault salmon fisheries and elk populations.

These concerns are intimately related to concerns about the impacts on culture and traditions. Sixty-two percent of respondents were "very concerned" about the impacts of invasive species on both local food systems and communal traditional ecological knowledge, and 53 percent were "very concerned" about impacts on cultural identity. A representative from the Ketchikan Indian Community commented that "hardly anyone collects our [medicinal plants] for medication and that knowledge is being lost." One Akwesasne Mohawk respondent noted that the loss of native species and subsequent decreased use has resulted in loss of their native language associated with those species.

Overall, respondents were less worried about the potential economic consequences of invasive species. Responses averaged just below "somewhat concerned" (2.74) on a four-point Likert scale. The impact on an Indigenous nation business's ability to generate revenue was of least concern. However, individuals still do have their livelihoods on the line. One Mississauga respondent worried, "If emerald ash borer gets in here, we'll lose good basket and bow wood. I depend on bow making and basketry to make an income."

DISCUSSION

Indeed, invasive species are an important type of environmental change, but to suggest that such change is unprecedented, as is implied with the idea of the Anthropocene, is problematic for several reasons. First, the concept of the Anthropocene assumes that invasive species are a "problem" for Indigenous peoples. Whatever Indigenous peoples are doing today to approach invasive species flows out of their own histories with environmental change and how these histories shape their assumptions today about the meaning or significance of their current interactions with novel species. These histories and assumptions—which do not flow out of nonindigenous frameworks such as "the Anthropocene"—shape what Indigenous peoples view as appropriate approaches to invasive species. Without losing sight of the reality of Indigenous vulnerabilities and Indigenous suffering, our focus is on what Indigenous peoples' agency will hopefully disclose about Indigenous strategies, knowledge, and capacities for stewardship and policy responses to invasive species. Such a focus is committed to how Indigenous peoples exercise self-determination (a term that itself is nuanced and culturally and politically specific) and recognizes Indigenous creativity, which tends to get marginalized or washed out by the concept of the Anthropocene, too often defined by what others assume about Indigenous peoples.[14]

Climate change literatures and media coverage of Indigenous peoples' experiences with environmental change are dominated by characterizations of Native peoples as vulnerable, "endangered others."[15] This rhetorical trend has potentially serious implications for Indigenous nations and their citizens. Our primary concerns about this trend are the power dynamics at play and the political implications of these power dynamics. Focusing on an Indigenous group's impacts or vulnerability obscures and glosses over the relationship between Indigenous nations and settler colonial governments that seek to balance Indigenous autonomy and the responsibilities settler states have to address underlying territorial rights and land claims issues; assure Indigenous free, prior, and informed consent; respect Indigenous knowledges; and work to ensure that Indigenous groups have the freedom to build their own self-determining governance capacities to address environmental issues.

For instance, existing scholarship details the ways that pervasive vulnerability messaging is influencing policy and directing, if not limiting, options for Indigenous nations without their full participation in policy-making processes. In locations where Indigenous homelands are threatened by rising sea levels and coastal erosion, community relocation planning has become a disenfranchising process for Indigenous nations in instances where they have not been centrally involved in planning or determining appropriate new locations for their own communities.[16] Such disenfranchisement is occurring in the case of small Pacific Island nations, where climate change discourse focuses on ecological impacts of climate change, often ignoring the presence of islanders altogether and very rarely seeing the relevancy of Indigenous knowledge systems and adaptive capacities of Indigenous Pacific Islander societies for understanding and responding to climatic change.[17]

From an ethical or human rights perspective, Indigenous nations need to be directly involved in developing any environmental change policies that aim to generate, or happen to constrain, future options for their societies. As legal scholar Sarah Krakoff says concerning the disenfranchisement of Indigenous peoples in climate change adaptation initiatives, "We should support governance structures that will allow indigenous peoples to chart their own path in a world that has no precedents."[18] Our results indicate that Indigenous nations in the United States and Canada have ample experience with different forms of environmental change policy making, including drafting invasive species policies within their nations and partnering with non-Indigenous governments from local to federal levels to codetermine invasive species policy. Considering these results alongside the various US and Canadian laws that require meaningful consultation with Indigenous nations, it is difficult to imagine a convincing rationale for *not* involving Indigenous nations in environmental change policy making.[19]

As Bethany Haalboom and David Natcher point out, these vulnerability-focused characterizations also have the potential to shape the ways Indigenous peoples view themselves. As Native peoples continually shape their own identities, pervasive endangerment messages could prompt feelings of vulnerability among Indigenous community members, interfering with their goals of autonomy and self-determination.[20] This outcome is of concern to Indigenous leaders. For example, in a recent lecture, Indigenous leader and author Sheila Watt-Cloutier explained why she wrote her book *The Right to Be Cold*:

> Inuit are not victims of globalization. [W]e have a powerful history of strength, of wisdom, that can be offered back by integrating that kind of wisdom into the new institutions. But what's happened is that these institutions have taken over the role of parents, the role of the provider, and have even helped to make it worse in many cases.[21]

Thus, she wrote this book specifically to help empower Inuit youth and to intervene against any tendencies to see themselves as victims.

Elizabeth Hall and Todd Sanders refer to what they call the "endangered other" trope, which leads to fear for loss of tradition: "Faced with rapid climate change, [the endangered other's] traditional survival strategies are in peril, and likely at any moment to collapse."[22] James Ford posits that the climate change impacts facing Inuit peoples occur within a backdrop of "acculturative stress" following recent and historic socioeconomic shifts in Inuit communities.[23] Henning Pedersen describes increased access to Western pop culture as a form of cultural pollution that, with the added stress of climate change, puts "Arctic cultures and societies . . . at major risk of extinction."[24] These contentions expose authors' assumptions about what constitutes "culture" and "tradition" vis-à-vis Indigenous peoples and exemplify the ways many social scientist and humanities scholars who work on climate change are thinking about Indigenous experiences.

While our results confirm that Indigenous nation citizens are concerned about the cultural impacts of invasive species (table 19.2), open-ended responses to our survey indicate that Indigenous citizens regard their cultures as more or less resilient to environmental change. For instance, one Anishinaabe respondent stated, "At this point the problem isn't so bad as to affect tribal identity or traditional knowledge." We certainly recognize the potential impacts climate change and invasive species could have on Indigenous sociocultural and economic systems. The strong linkages between land/environment and Indigenous ways of knowing and being are undoubtedly affected by rapid environmental or biological changes.[25] But there are important elements of Indigenous cultures and traditions that are understudied and often ignored by researchers and journalists. For instance, traditional values, morality, and spirituality, important elements of Indigenous knowledge and lifeways, are woven into subsistence systems in complex and subtle ways.[26] And these elements of Indigenous sociocultural systems are more persistent, or change very slowly, even while outward expressions of culture undergo rapid evolution. Thus, in our view the threats to Indigenous peoples and their cultures posed by invasive species and other forms of rapid environmental change are not as dire as they are often made out to be.

Furthermore, regardless of the extent of cultural impacts, our study supports the idea that Indigenous nations and their citizens are focused on active response strategies, deemphasizing impacts and emphasizing actionable responses. Our results show that Indigenous groups in the United States and Canada are actively preparing for and responding to introduced species using a wide range of practices and leveraging both Indigenous knowledge systems and Western science and resource management tools. Respondents removed invasive species by hand and via other mechanical measures and used chemical responses, fire, grazing, and biocontrols. In addition to all these approaches used by their non-Indigenous counterparts, more than half of respondents reported using Indigenous knowledge directly in their invasive species work. For instance, Indigenous nations are documenting traditional knowledge and practices about threatened native species and using ceremonies to care for lands, plants, and animals. In response to introduced species, Indigenous peoples also use ceremonies that honor and enact reciprocal moral responsibilities between humans and nonhumans.

North American Indigenous nations have embraced Western science not as a new worldview that supplants their preexisting ways of knowing and being but as a tool useful in meeting community objectives and priorities. Just as Indigenous peoples have adopted new technologies and enfolded them into their subsistence and socioeconomic systems, they are using Western science to support important community activities, including traditional land- and marine-based activities.[27] Our study indicates that invasive species management is one area where Indigenous groups are utilizing Western science alongside Indigenous knowledge approaches to protect culturally significant Indigenous plants and animals as well as places. This approach to using non-Indigenous tools is also reflected in the creative ways in which Indigenous nations are building resilient systems of governance. The high percentage of Indigenous nations partnering with other sovereign and nongovernmental entities (81%) in managing invasive species shows a strategic use of Western modes of governance, as well as reinscription of Indigenous modes of governance.[28] For the Wabanaki Nations in Maine, the cooperative governance issues for detection and response to the anticipated arrival of the emerald ash borer, present in multiple Memoranda of Understanding with USDA-APHIS, reflect communication processes and respect for different forms of knowledge reflective of multinational partnership principles in the Wabanaki Confederacy.[29]

Our results indicate that Indigenous groups in the United States and Canada clearly see the value of partnering with Indigenous and non-Indigenous neighbors in preparation for and response to invasive species. Two obvious rationales for partnering in these contexts are that (1) invasive species pay no attention to property lines or treaty boundaries and therefore require cross-boundary coordination, and (2) sharing equipment, human resources, knowledge, and data tends to increase the effectiveness and longevity of partnerships.[30] However, not all partnerships achieve their potential, or even get off the ground. One reason is that misperceptions and stereotypes can create obstacles to cross-cultural partnerships.[31] We hope that by providing a more accurate picture of the various ways Indigenous nations and organizations are thinking about, preparing for, and responding to invasive species, this chapter can help set the stage for more land management and community research partnerships in the future.

For many of the Indigenous groups whose staff or members responded to the survey, their approaches to invasive species are perceived as opportunities to exercise self-determination in several respects. First, they are building relationships with non-Indigenous parties, which can strengthen the diplomatic and cooperative potential of Indigenous peoples to negotiate invasive species and other changes. Second, they are finding ways to build self-determining capacities by harnessing Western science, connecting this form of science to Indigenous knowledge and including Indigenous forms of science where appropriate. Third, Indigenous responses to and interactions with invasive species provide opportunities to renew and expand Indigenous knowledges, including determining the nature of novel relationships between Indigenous peoples and invasive species.

Responses to our survey question about the impacts of invasive species raise important follow-up questions. Because our study was intended to assess the current response to invasive species, and the survey tool was advertised as such, it may have biased participation from people who are already aware of and concerned about invasive species. We also purposively sampled natural resource and cultural agency staff from Indigenous nations along with subsistence practitioners and artisans such as basket makers. What remains unexplored is whether other Indigenous North Americans who are less involved in subsistence activities, as well as staff from departments in Indigenous nations other than environmental and cultural programs, care one way or another about invasive species. Our survey was not set up to address this question, and future research is necessary to understand perceptions of invasive species in Indigenous communities more generally. Another critical area for future work includes studies that help us see how introduced species fit into Indigenous cosmologies. In Indigenous communities where local plants and animals are thought of as part of your extended family, how do you respond to newly introduced species, especially if they somewhat aggressively take over habitat of the long-standing plant and animal members of your community? In other words, to borrow a term from Rarámuri (Tarahumara) scholar Enrique Salmón, what does a "kincentric ecology" of invasive species look like, or if none exists, how could such an understanding be cultivated?[32]

NOTES

1. J. K. Maldonado, C. Shearer, R. Bronen, K. Peterson, and H. Lazrus, "The Impact of Climate Change on Tribal Communities in the US: Displacement, Relocation, and Human Rights," *Climatic Change* 120, no. 3 (2013): 601–614, doi: 10.1007/ s10584-013-0746-z; ACIA, *Arctic Climate Impact Assessment* (Cambridge: Cambridge University Press, 2005); IPCC, *Impacts, Adaptation and Vulnerability: Contribution of Working Group II to the Fourth Assessment Report of the Intergovernmental Panel on Climate Change* (Cambridge: Cambridge University Press, 2007); B. K. Ellis, J. A. Stanford, D. Goodman, C. P. Stafford, D. L. Gustafson, D. A. Beauchamp, D. W. Chess, et al., "Long-Term Effects of a Trophic Cascade in a Large Lake Ecosystem," *Proceedings of the National Academy of Sciences* 108, no. 3 (2011): 1070–1075, doi: 10.1073/pnas.1013006108.
2. L. Head, B. M. H. Larson, R. Hobbs, J. Atchison, N. Gill, C. Kull, and H. Rangan, "Living with Invasive Plants in the Anthropocene: The Importance of Understanding Practice and Experience," *Conservation and Society* 13, no. 3 (2015): 311, doi: 10.4103/0972–4923.170411. While for some people the climatic changes of the Anthropocene are unprecedented, Indigenous groups have historically faced and persevered through related forms of environmental change, and from Indigenous community perspectives, the rapid change characteristic of the Anthropocene is not entirely novel. Rather, our contemporary climate destabilization is experienced additively, as a current form of change occurring on top of the history of preexisting anthropogenic environmental change caused by settler and other types of colonialism. See K. G. Lightfoot, L. M. Panich, T. D. Schneider, and S. L. Gonzalez,

"European Colonialism and the Anthropocene: A View from the Pacific Coast of North America," *Anthropocene* 4 (2013): 101–115; and K. P. Whyte, "Our Ancestors' Dystopia Now: Indigenous Conservation and the Anthropocene," in *Routledge Companion to the Environmental Humanities*, ed. U. Heise, J. Christensen, and M. Niemann, 222–231 (London: Routledge, 2017), https://www.routledge.com/The-Routledge-Companion-to-the-Environmental-Humanities/Heise-Christensen-Niemann/p/book/9781138786745.

3. D. Pimentel, R. Zuniga, and D. Morrison, "Update on the Environmental and Economic Costs Associated with Alien-Invasive Species in the United States," *Ecological Economics* 52 (2005): 273–288.
4. A. J. Willow, "Indigenizing Invasive Species Management: Native North Americans and the Emerald Ash Borer (EAB) Beetle," *Culture, Agriculture, Food and Environment* 33, no. 2 (2011): 70–82, doi: 10.1111/j.2153-9561.2011.01051.x; T. M. Poland, T. M. Ciaramitaro, M. R. Emery, D. J. Crook, E. Pigeon, and A. Pigeon, "Submergence of Black Ash Logs to Control Emerald Ash Borer and Preserve Wood for American Indian Basketmaking," *Agricultural and Forest Entomology* 17, no. 4 (2015): 412–420, doi: 10.1111/afe.12122; D. Douterlungne, S. I. Levy-Tacher, D. J. Golicher, and F. R. Dañobeytia, "Applying Indigenous Knowledge to the Restoration of Degraded Tropical Rain Forest Clearings Dominated by Bracken Fern," *Restoration Ecology* 18, no. 3 (2010): 322–329, doi: 10.1111/j.1526-100X.2008.00459.x; J. M. Pfeiffer and R. A. Voeks, "Biological Invasions and Biocultural Diversity: Linking Ecological and Cultural Systems," *Environmental Conservation* 35, no. 4 (2008): 281–293, doi: 10.1017/ S0376892908005146.
5. J. M. Pfeiffer and E. H. Ortiz, "Invasive Plants Impact California Native Plants Used in Traditional Basketry," *Fremontia* 35 (2007): 7–13, http://www.cnps.org/cnps/publications/fremontia/Fremontia_Vol35-No1.pdf#page=9.
6. J. Alexander and C. A. Lee, "Lessons Learned from a Decade of Sudden Oak Death in California: Evaluating Local Management," *Environmental Management* 46, no. 3 (2010): 315–328, doi: 10.1007/s00267-010-9512-4.
7. T. Jevon and C. M. Shackleton, "Integrating Local Knowledge and Forest Surveys to Assess *Lantana camara* Impacts on Indigenous Species Recruitment in Mazeppa Bay, South Africa," *Human Ecology* 43, no. 2 (2015): 247–254, doi: 10.1007/ s10745-015-9748-y; B. Sundaram, S. Krishnan, A. J. Hiremath, and G. Joseph, "Ecology and Impacts of the Invasive Species, *Lantana camara*, in a Social-Ecological System in South India: Perspectives from Local Knowledge," *Human Ecology* 40, no. 6 (2012): 931–942, doi: 10.1007/s10745-012-9532-1; D. S. Turner and M. D. List, "Habitat Mapping and Conservation Analysis to Identify Critical Streams for Arizona's Native Fish," *Aquatic Conservation: Marine and Freshwater Ecosystems* 17, no. 7 (2007): 737–748, doi: 10.1002/aqc.802; Pfeiffer and Voeks, "Biological Invasions."
8. B. J. Colombi, "Salmon and the Adaptive Capacity of Nimiipuu (Nez Perce) Culture to Cope with Change," *American Indian Quarterly* 36, no. 1 (2012): 75–97, doi: 10.5250/amerindiquar.36.1.0075; N. Ferris, *The Archaeology of Native-Lived Colonialism: Challenging History in the Great Lakes* (Tucson: University of Arizona Press, 2009); R. White, *The Middle Ground: Indians, Empires, and Republics in the Great Lakes Region, 1650–1815* (Cambridge: Cambridge University Press, 1991); E. F. Hall and T. Sanders, "Accountability and the Academy: Producing Knowledge about the Human Dimensions of Climate Change," *Journal of the Royal Anthropological Institute* 21, no. 2 (2015): 438–461, doi: 10.1111/1467-9655.12162; B. Haalboom and D. C. Natcher, "The Power and Peril of 'Vulnerability': Approaching Community Labels

with Caution in Climate Change Research," *Arctic* 65, no. 3 (2012): 319–327, http://hdl.handle.net/10515/sy5ccov84.

9. Haalboom and Natcher, "The Power and Peril." To clarify our use of the term "self-determination," the "selves" we speak of are individual Indigenous nations; thus, we are discussing self-determining collectives, not individuals. Self-determination is an aspirational term that describes Indigenous nations' ability to serve their own interests and enact their values through various forms of political autonomy. See A. E. Buchanan, "The Right to Self-Determination: Analytical and Moral Foundations," *Arizona Journal of International and Comparative Law* 8 (1991): 41.

10. Colombi, "Salmon." See also Colombi's 2009 chapter entitled "Salmon Nation: Tribal Sovereignty and Climate Change," in *Anthropology and Climate Change: From Encounters to Actions*, ed. S. Crate and M. Nuttall (Walnut Creek, CA: Left Coast Press), 186–196.

11. By Indigenous nations, we mean federally recognized tribes, unrecognized tribes, and Alaska Native corporations in the United States, as well as First Nations and Inuit nations in Canada. We use this term throughout and occasionally use the term "community" because Indigenous nations are simultaneously governments and communities.

12. H. R. Bernard, *Research Methods in Anthropology: Qualitative and Quantitative Approaches* (Lanham, MD: Rowman Altamira, 2011).

13. J. Bethlehem and S. Biffignandi, *Handbook of Web Surveys*, vol. 567 (New York: John Wiley and Sons, 2011).

14. F. S. Chapin III, M. Sommerkorn, M. D. Robards, and K. Hillmer-Pegram, "Ecosystem Stewardship: A Resilience Framework for Arctic Conservation," *Global Environmental Change* 34 (2015): 207–217, doi: 10.1016/j.gloenvcha.2015.07.003; Head et al., "Living with Invasive Plants."

15. Hall and Sanders, "Accountability and the Academy."

16. Hall and Sanders, "Accountability and the Academy."

17. J. Barnett and J. Campbell, *Climate Change and Small Island States: Power, Knowledge, and the South Pacific* (New York: Routledge, 2010).

18. S. Krakoff, "Radical Adaptation, Justice, and American Indian Nations," *Environmental Justice* 4, no. 4 (2012): 207–212, doi: 10.1089/env.2010.0034.

19. The government of Canada's duty to consult with Aboriginal groups was affirmed by the Supreme Court of Canada in several Supreme Court rulings, including *Haida Nation v. British Columbia*, 2004 (2004 SCC 73). The government of Canada departments and agencies are responsible for understanding how and when their activities could have an adverse impact on Aboriginal and treaty rights, and this responsibility is coordinated by Indigenous and Northern Affairs Canada. In the United States, federal responsibility to coordinate and consult with tribal governments as they develop policy on issues that impact tribal communities is encoded in numerous policy documents, including Executive Order 13175 (2000) and President Obama's 2009 Memorandum on Tribal Consultation.

20. Haalboom and Natcher, "The Power and Peril."

21. S. Watt-Cloutier, "Voices from COP21: Changing Climate and the Health of the Arctic," public lecture, Dartmouth College, NH, January 2016, https://www.youtube.com/watch?v=mPpoOKqusXg.

22. Hall and Sanders, "Accountability and the Academy."

23. J. D. Ford, "Dangerous Climate Change and the Importance of Adaptation for the Arctic's Inuit Population," *Environmental Research Letters* 4, no. 2 (2009): 1–9, doi: 10.1088/1748–9326/4/2/024006.

24. H. S. Pedersen, "Health in the Arctic and Climate Change," *Polar Research* 26, no. 2 (2007): 104–106, doi: 10.1111/j.1751–8369.2007.00026.x.

25. L. R. Simpson, "Anticolonial Strategies for the Recovery and Maintenance of Indigenous Knowledge," *American Indian Quarterly* 28, no. 3 (2004): 373–384, https://muse.jhu.edu/article/181506/; M. Battiste and J. Youngblood, *Protecting Indigenous Knowledge and Heritage: A Global Challenge* (Vancouver: University of British Columbia Press, 2000).

26. N. J. Reo and K. P. Whyte, "Hunting and Morality as Elements of Traditional Ecological Knowledge," *Human Ecology* 40, no. 1 (2012): 15–27, doi: 10.1007/ s10745-011-9448-1.

27. G. Wenzel, *Animal Rights, Human Rights: Ecology, Economy, and Ideology in the Canadian Arctic* (London: Belhaven Press, 1991); Reo and Whyte, "Hunting and Morality."

28. D. J. Ranco, "Wabanaki Diplomacy," *Communities and Banking* 27, no. 1 (2016): 23–35, https://www.bostonfed.org/publications/communities-and-banking/2016/winter.aspx; J. Ford and E. Giles, "Climate Change Adaptation in Indian Country: Tribal Regulation of Reservation Lands and Natural Resources," *William Mitchell Law Review* 41, no. 2 (2015): 519–551, http://open.mitchellhamline.edu/wmlr/vol41/iss2/3.

29. D. J. Ranco, "Wabanaki Diplomacy," *Communities and Banking* 27, no. 1 (2016): 23–35, https://www.bostonfed.org/publications/communities-and-banking/2016/winter.aspx

30. L. A. Schulte, M. Rickenbach, and L. Merrick, "Ecological and Economic Benefits of Cross-Boundary Coordination among Private Forest Landowners," *Landscape Ecology* 23, no. 4 (2008): 481–496, doi: 10.1007/s10980-008-9207-x; J. Pretty, "Social Capital and the Collective Management of Resources," *Science* 302, no. 5,652 (2003): 1912–1914, doi: 10.1126/science.1090847.

31. J. M. Wondolleck and S. L. Yaffee, *Making Collaboration Work: Lessons from Innovation in Natural Resource Management* (Washington, DC: Island Press, 2000).

32. E. Salmon, "Kincentric Ecology: Indigenous Perceptions of the Human–Nature Relationship," *Ecological Applications* 10, no. 5 (2000): 1327–1332, https://www.sciencebase.gov/catalog/item/50541aa1e4b097cd4fcfde85.

Main Pathway: Orientations

Subthemes

Proceed to Decolonization, p. 25
Proceed to Politics, p. 479
Proceed to Place, p. 97

20

INTERVIEW WITH URIEL ORLOW

How do you identify the species of plants you decide to work with? What parameters guide your selection process and why?

URIEL ORLOW: When I was doing research in South Africa about the entanglements between Europe and its former colonies—which often took different forms of non-reciprocal relations of control, domination, exploitation, and appropriation—I came across a number of trees that can be considered "witnesses": A wild almond tree hedge in Cape Town, planted in 1660 by the first Dutch settlers to keep the indigenous Khoikhoi and their grazing cattle out of the vegetable gardens set up to replenish the passing ships of the Dutch East India Company; the planting of this wild almond can be considered as one of the first botanical expressions of colonial violence. Or a specific Lombardy poplar tree in Johannesburg that literally saved lives by serving as a landmark for fugitives from the apartheid security forces, to find the safe house of the anti-apartheid activist Ruth Fischer. I didn't set out to work with almond trees or poplars; rather, they presented themselves as inadvertent and unmarked monuments to a violent history. Nevertheless, these plant encounters are, of course, framed and guided by the necessity to engage with the entwinements of history and politics with the vegetal world.

Do you ever consider plants as subjects in your work, and how does that change your approach to them?

UO: The larger project that came out of the work in South Africa is called *Theatrum Botanicum* (2015–2018), after John Parkinson's eponymous herbal lexicon from 1640, which alludes to the natural world as a stage upon which humans act. But the title can also imply that the actors themselves are botanical: plants acting on the stage of history, subjects rather than merely being passive objectives, vegetal agents as opposed to a botanical backdrop for human action.

A few years into their 18-year-long incarceration, Nelson Mandela and his fellow Rivonia trial prison inmates set up a garden in the courtyard of Robben Island prison, off the Cape Town Coast. It started informally with a few tomato seeds given to them by well-meaning prison guards. On their way to the quarry where they were forced to do hard labor, the political prisoners collected ostrich droppings as fertilizer. In time they also planted chilies and other vegetables to complement their meager prison diet. Later, as Mandela was writing the manuscript for what became his autobiography, *Long Walk to Freedom*, the completed pages would be buried in cocoa tins in the garden to hide them from the prison authorities. As such, the seemingly benign activity of gardening, of tending to plants, became a highly politicized gesture—that of claiming and cultivating a patch of land and using it subversively to undermine an oppressive regime and grow the ideas of liberation. As a consequence, the garden itself became entangled in historical events, and the plants played an active role rather than merely being bystanders. But there is a further plant protagonist in this story: in the late 1960s, rare yellow flowering bird of paradise flowers (*Strelitzia reginae*) were found at Kirstenbosch, the South African National Botanical Gardens in Cape Town. Because these native flowers are usually orange, a process of selective breeding was started, pollinating yellow flowers with each other by hand. It took almost 20 years to build up stock of the highly prized yellow *Strelitzia*—roughly coinciding with the time Mandela was in prison in Robben Island. In 1994, after Mandela became the first democratically elected Black president of South Africa, the flower was named after him: Mandela's Gold. However, there is a twist: the grounds of the botanical garden were bequeathed by the colonialist Cecil Rhodes, who, out of nostalgia, had previously introduced the gray squirrel from England. The naturalized squirrel now consumes the entire capsule of the Strelitzia seeds if unchecked. So, in a haunting of history, in order to protect Mandela's Gold's seeds from its European "predator" each fertilized flower is enclosed in fine-mesh metal chicken wire. These intertwining plant stories and their plant protagonists were the subject of my work *Grey, Green, Gold* (2016–2017). What interested me is how processes of botanical cultivation, modification, and representation can be the means of oppression, discrimination, and dispossession—and, conversely, also agents of resistance, sustainability, and self-determination.

In your artistic practice, what have you learned from the plants themselves? In which ways does your art follow their movements, metamorphoses, and modes of being in the world? How does it interact with these vegetal processes?

UO: In 2019, I was invited to do a project in the DRC for the Lubumbashi Biennale and began working with *Artemisia afra*, an indigenous plant that effectively treats and prevents malaria and can be taken as an infusion (*Learning from Artemisia*, 2019–2020). Despite studies that show its effectiveness and the simplicity of its administration and sustainability of its local production, it is not recommended as a treatment by the World Health Organization (WHO), which favors the pharmaceutical industry. I worked closely with a women's cooperative in the south of the country that is cultivating *Artemisia afra* to sell locally—but because of the lack of official support, word of *Artemisia afra*'s simple anti-malaria powers is hard to spread. So we decided to plant an *Artemisia afra* garden in Lubumbashi which would be part of my work for the biennale—a place to let people know about *Artemisia afra* in the city, as well as a way to promote its propagation through cuttings. In practical terms, we had to follow the rhythm of the seasons and the cycle of the plant itself. But what became most important for me conceptually were the medical vegetal processes. How do plants do medicine? Conventional medicine looks for the so-called active ingredient or compound in a plant and then extracts or replicates it. Medicine's deep roots in an extractive colonial logic became starkly clear in the Congo, one of the most mined and exploited places on the planet, where the specters of colonial capitalism and its contemporary, extractive afterlife haunt the landscape through fissures and lesions. *Artemisia afra* escapes the extractive logic. Its sister plant *Artemisia annua*, which had been used in China against fevers for centuries, is already known for the active ingredient artemisinin that is used in the last line of drugs against malaria. (This, and the difficulty of precise dosing of traditional medicine are among the reasons why the WHO does not support its use, because of the fear that it could create resistance to the artemisinin-based medicines). However, the partial use of a plant through extraction of a single compound is what allows parasites to adapt and become resistant to it. *Artemisia afra* does not contain artemisinin, yet many studies have demonstrated it is still highly effective against malaria when taken as a simple infusion. So how does it work? Perhaps it is because the cocktail of minerals (including Congo's much mined copper) the plant gets from the soil in Katanga produces a synergy of different components to which the parasite is much less likely to adapt and that works with the plant to resist resistance.

What ethical or political considerations inform your work with plants? What are the ethical and political implications of this work?

UO: Plants—as food, medicine, and the foundation of our world's ecosystem—are essential to our life on this planet. However, Western modernity, the capitalocene, the plantationocene, or whatever one might call it, has developed a fundamentally instrumental relationship with plants, as with all other natural resources. It views plants as things and asks how such things are best exploited for profit and our benefit. In my work, alongside many others, I rethink this relationship and shift from our focus on control, domination, and extraction to emphasizing the complex entanglement of living processes. How can plants "teach" us to unlearn and discard set patterns of thought, ways of doing, and structures that are based on nonreciprocal relations of control and exploitation? How can engaging with the vegetal world allow us to go beyond our present-day mediatized spectacle of environmental catastrophe, the destruction of natural environments and human–nonhuman relations, which involves violations of both human and nonhuman rights that reach deeply into the past? So for me a large part of this work has been connected to what one might call plant hauntology: becoming attentive to plant ghosts, vegetal specters from the past that live on in the present and remind us of colonial and other injustices; unfinished business from the past that haunts the Western idea of progress that inherently incorporates violence and domination over human and nonhuman others. Plant ghosts can remind us that the consequences of this history have not yet been reckoned with, and so we must foster a sense of responsibility, of being-with, as acts of concern and care for the past as well as the present.

What, if any, are the aspects of your work with plants related to the current global environmental and mass extinction crises?

UO: The current environmental crisis is inseparable from and stems from other, overlapping events of dispossession and violence that produce ongoing forms of coloniality, not least the system of classification and naming the natural world set in place during colonial conquests that has led to the suppression and loss of older forms of knowledge and being with the vegetal world.

The warming climate is causing many changes in our environment and ecosystems that affect biodiversity. Some of these changes and effects are happening quite fast and are already very visible and get a fair amount of attention. However, there are others that take much longer to manifest and often elude our attention. Mountain ecosystems present an interesting contradiction: the climate is warming at a higher pace than the global average, yet the vegetation response is slower than might be expected. Nevertheless, plants—often thought of as unmoving—are shifting their habitat ranges in order to follow the conditions they are adapted to. Moreover, there are interesting correspondences of changes in plant communities in unconnected sites such as the Swiss Alps and the Himalayas. In tracing these (*Free Climbing*, 2020–ongoing) I continue to be mindful of what environmental humanities scholar Rob Nixon refers to as "slow violence," that is, a violence of delayed effects that escapes the spectacle-driven media images as well as our own diminished attention spans and is therefore generally not even perceived as violence. It's literally outside the frame.[1]

Which pressing challenge, or challenges, has working with plants presented to you?

UO: One of the biggest challenges—or even aporias—lies at the heart of considering plants as active subjects or agents while also trying to avoid anthropomorphizing them by ascribing the vegetal being human qualities or agencies. And connected to this is the challenge of working with plants without falling back into an extractivisit logic that instrumentalizes plants. So, for example, how to engage with vegetal life as witness (as in the above mentioned series *The Memory of Trees*, 2016–2017) without making trees "speak" in order to testify to what they have witnessed over the centuries? How to allow plants to be silent witnesses that bear witness through their vegetal still-being-there, which is both a persistent presence and a haunting? In this I am guided by the notions of complicity and dialogue: living and being among plants, becoming familiar with their context, their specificities, their histories, their vegetal being; trying not to speak *for* plants, but rather conversing *with* plants without making them speak our language. But of course the challenges of cutting across human–vegetal relations always remains; and also the challenge of finding a visual, artistic form for this vegetal witnessing. Echoing Nixon again, the challenge is "How are we to act ethically toward human and biotic communities [i.e., including the vegetal world] that lie beyond our sensory kern?" As an artist, the challenge then is how to find forms, images, sounds for what is not immediately visible and be attentive to the invisible or inaudible entwinements of different life-forms and ways of knowing.

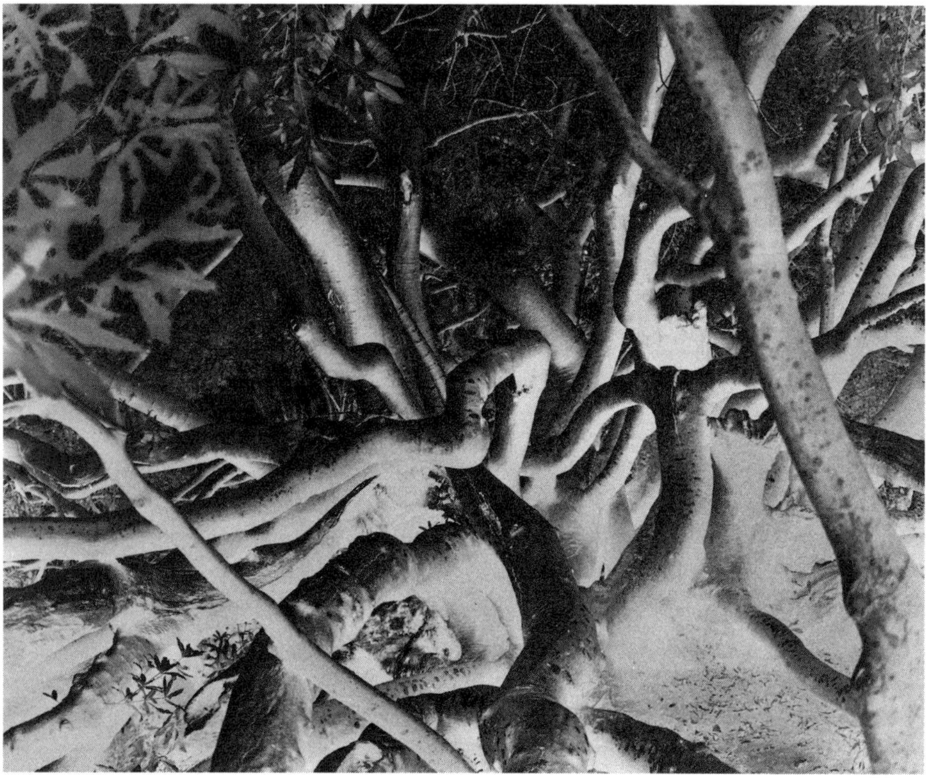

Wild Almond (Capetown), 2016, Uriel Orlow. (Image © 2022 Artists Rights Society [ARS], New York/DACS, London. Reprinted with permission.)

Uriel Orlow is a Swiss-born artist who lives and works in London and Zurich. He studied fine art at Central Saint Martins College of Art & Design and The Slade School of Art, London and Philosophy at University of Geneva. He was the recipient of a prestigious Swiss Art Award in both 2008 and 2009.

NOTE

1. Rob Nixon, *Slow Violence and the Environmentalism of the Poor* (Cambridge: Harvard University Press, 2011); see esp. 1–44. See also Shela Sheikh's entry on "Violence" in *The Posthuman Glossary*, ed. Rosi Braidotti and Maria Hlavajova (London: Bloomsbury, 2017), 448–452; and Shela Sheikh: "Conversing With," in *Uriel Orlow: Conversing with Leaves*, ed. Stefanie Böttcher (Berlin: Archive Books, 2020).

21

INTERVIEW WITH D. DENENGE DUYST-AKPEM

How do you identify the species of plants you decide to work with? What parameters guide your selection process and why?

D. DENENGE DUYST-AKPEM: I am most drawn to plants that have a historic cultural connection to African art traditions, such as the kola nut, a caffeinated plant that is used both as a caffeinated snack and as part of ritual. I share the kola nut—sometimes to be eaten, other times as an oil-anointed hand-modeled clay form—when opening African art–focused class sessions, for ritual performances, and in the limited-edition velvet box set of my book *AFRIFUTURI 02022020*.

In my home, an extension of my Afro-Futurist design practice as a self-defined "space sculptor," I currently have mostly *Pachira aquatica*, aka "money trees," each started from a tiny plant or cutting, now growing past room height. They bring me so much joy and abundance. I let my heart guide me as to which plants will share my space and attentions. My baby Meyer lemon tree was a birthday gift to myself last year, and the tiny boxwood shrubs on the balcony were chosen for their greenery and hardiness in a very windy location.

I always like to say, I'm the granddaughter of a peach farmer—that's why I'm so sweet. Whether that's true or not may vary on what I have to deal with that day! Mainly, it's a legacy that brings me joy, for the difficulty of the labor, in honor of the work that produced such sweetness. I remember the taste of a California peach fresh off the tree in the warmth of summer, enjoyed under a cool tree, sitting in the grass behind the farmhouse, peach juice dripping down your arm into a pool that makes the ants dance, the sound of crickets in evening's hush.

I also grew up as a teenager in the era of Prince at the height of his purple power. It felt like "Peach" was written just for me. His songs were contraband for the cloistered wild child I was. And they were everything. Validation. Awakening.

The heritage of plants, watching my father and families tending our farms cross-continentally, the way Mom would grab cuttings when we traveled, so our yard became a story in plants of all of the places we'd been, an ever-growing, ever-morphing map of our family history over time. Plants are legacy, documentation, and archive, shifting and remaking the original mnemonic spaces.

Do you ever consider plants as subjects in your work, and how does that change your approach to them?

DDD-A: *The Osanyin Commemorative Portrait Series* and *The Camo Coat Collection* comprise a two-part project that remixes camouflage as a point of agency, taking its cue from the Yoruba *orisa* Osanyin, god of healing, leaves, and forest wisdom, often depicted as half tree, half human, traversing the visible/invisible as shape-shifter through time, space, and place. The project's inception lies in a portrait series of the 2014 National Endowment for the Humanities Fellows in the Institute of Black Aesthetics and Sacred Systems taken at individually selected locations around Emory University, Atlanta, in a commemoration of the historic institute, documenting fleeting moments, representation in collaboration, and site as an archive.

Companion leaf drawings also developed as an Institute Fellow were later made into textile and wall coverings and were included in the Camo Coat capsule collection for which I developed additional commemorative textiles such as the Chicago-specific camo, which utilizes photographs of a rapidly changing cityscape and nature preserves (as viewed from the historic Bronzeville lakefront on the city's south side) as well as details of flowers and bees from Lurie Garden in Millennium Park downtown.

Plants have always been subjects in my work, largely as symbols and representations based on real plants but transformed into larger, imaginary creations, sensual grotesque forms like in the Luscious Garden series exhibited as part of the *Warm Kitty, Soft Kitty* exhibition at Chicago's Hyde Park Art Center and in activated multisite installations. Many of my earlier works looked at disease as an aberration and a fact of nature. Each sculptural construction investigates the human relationship to this dis-ease with objects that are simultaneously titillating and repellent, as with the large-scale installation *Rapunzel Revisited: An Afri-Sci-Fi Space Sea Siren Tale* (2006, Museum of Contemporary Art, Chicago), which flirts with representations and perceptions of Black femininity.

The African yam is a recurring theme—not a sweet potato, but the large tuber found in tropical climates in West Africa and specifically farmed by my father's people, the Tiv, in Benue State, southeastern Nigeria, an area known for its fertile soil. The yam is a staple and much beloved by the Tiv for making what we call "ruam," also known more generically across the country as "fufu," served pounded, boiled in hunks, and fried, with a variety of stews and toppings, depending upon one's cultural background.

A sculpted yam was a central piece of *Wan Chuku and the Mystical Yam Farm*, arranged with clay fruits such as peaches, plum, strawberries, cashew fruits, and more, all referencing my Dutch-American farming family in California and Tiv-Nigerian farming family in Nigeria. This cross-cultural representation plays a big part in the inspiration for my artistic practice. The 10-foot black-and-white striped "trees" growing from yam mounds in the *Wan Chuku* installation marked the four directions and formed a kind of mystical grove in the vein of legendary Nigerian writer Amos Tutuola's *My Life in the Bush of Ghosts*, with dazzle camouflage effects and Strass crystal droplets raining down onto the fruit as I painted in collaboration with a projection of the Akire Mothers shrine painters, creating a cross-temporal activation. The stripe references *a'nger*, a Tiv-Nigerian traditional black-and-white-striped loom-woven textile that represents being clothed in the essence of Tiv.

In your artistic practice, what have you learned from the plants themselves? In which ways does your art follow their movements, metamorphoses, and modes of being in the world? How does it interact with these vegetal processes?

DDD-A: In my home, which doubles as a studio, plants have taught me patience. They teach me to stay hydrated. We all drink water together, and I talk with them, letting them know how much I appreciate them, how sweet they are to me. They remind me that growth is possible since they are continually sprouting new leaves, even through a Chicago winter. They keep me grounded, especially living in a high-rise during the pandemic, where access to the outside world has been severely limited.

In working with plants in the imaginary, much of my work is currently in textiles. I utilize an ankara wax print from Nigeria that has vegetal representations, and I play with the patterns in combination with other materials, organic and synthetic; sometimes recycled, sometimes new. I reference *àṣẹ*—specifically defined as the catalytic life force by African art historian Dr. Rowland Abiodun—the central Yoruba spiritual and aesthetic energy, how it is contained in the textiles, and the ritual encrustation of an object for use in manifestation or divination, how an object contains power.[1]

Luscious Garden soft sculptures are embellished and accented with golden barbs, highly faceted crystals, pearls, and other materials that highlight a kind of uncontrolled growth, seductive and dangerous, a sculpture that draws you in but may take out an eye if you lean too close and are not careful. Perhaps there is a bit of my Scorpio Moon at work there in the obsession with the cycle of life and death, the dark, sexy parts that are an exquisite and terrible pain. The work has to speak to the danger of living. The dis-ease. The rebalancing. Dead growth fertilizing the new. The cycle. I'm not afraid of such processes, but it can hurt going through it. This goes back to the theme of *Rapunzel Revisited*, the interplay between extremes of experience and emotion, between who one is and how one is perceived by larger sociocultural structures, a kind of push-me-pull-you.

What ethical or political considerations inform your work with plants? What are the ethical and political implications of this work?

DDD-A: All of my practice is deeply informed by the writings of and divination with Elder Malidoma Patrice Somé from Burkina Faso, whose name, "Malidoma," foretold his destiny before his birth: "he who befriends the stranger/enemy," one who would bridge cultures to bring the healing of Dagara Ancestral traditions to the fractured dis-eased West. Elder Malidoma writes in his critically acclaimed book *Of Water and the Spirit: Ritual, Magic and Initiation in the Life of an African Shaman*:

> Nature, in fact, is such a complex organism that only the intelligence of Spirit can manage it . . . The Dagara people . . . believe that if there is a problem with the physical, one must look to the spiritual for a solution.

This work is life work, elemental, concerning the deepest depths and the farthest universes and day-to-day survival, how we build toward a sustainable future for all members of society, especially those who've been traditionally and systemically disenfranchised. I create objects as totems, signifiers, and activators. The installations are an invitation to both rest and to be excited, a design framework that places comfort, pleasure, and love at the forefront through my In The Luscious Garden initiative.[2]

What, if any, are the aspects of your work with plants related to the current global environmental and mass extinction crises?

DDD-A: The multifaceted *Osanyin Portrait and Camo Coat Project* explores uses of camouflage in everyday life and within formalized ritual practice, highlighting methodologies of conceptual, spiritual, and physical protection in pattern and textile. With Chicago-specific prints, *The Camo Coat Collection* considers what it means to survive and to thrive in the urban landscape,[3] addressing self-presentation, garment-based strategies to confront the consumption of the gaze, invisibility and hyper-visibility, and pattern as signifier.

The body becomes a vessel of liberation[4] that can be mobilized to effect shapeshifting transformation with garment as device in an alchemic dance of body and landscape. "Vessels of Liberation" is a concept I introduce in "Afro-Futurism: Pathways to Black Liberation" courses—one of the first cross-disciplinary courses in the then-early field of Afro-Futurism that I root specifically in Black Arts Movement tenets of the 1960s–1970s—which investigates the activation of site, environment, and body through installation, material, and performed gesture, further developed in studio practice and courses "Afro-Futurist Ecologies" and "Take Root Among the Stars: The Legacy of Octavia Butler, Surviving the 21st Century & Beyond."

The latter was based upon *Parable of the Sower*, Butler's prophetic novel that foretold the current times, for which students created and exhibited conceptual survival packs. Chapter 9 contains a journal entry about leadership and power in a book that protagonist Lauren Oya Olamina titles *Earthseed: The Books of the Living*:

All struggles
Are essentially
power struggles.
Who will rule,
Who will lead,
Who will define,
refine,
confine,
design,
Who will dominate.[5]

Butler's narratives take us from visions of utopia to realities of dystopia; through fear, loss and abandonment to the creation of new communities, webs, and patterns

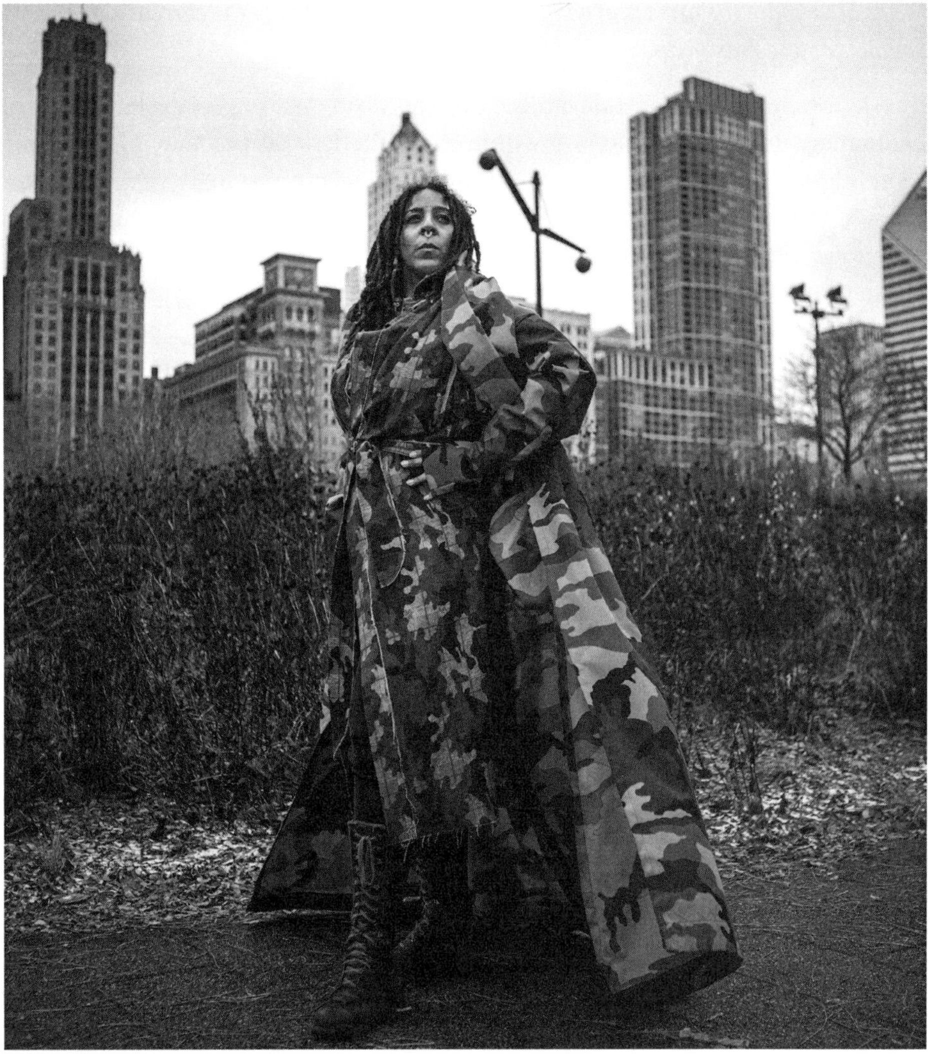

D. Denenge Duyst-Akpem in Lurie Garden, Millennium Park, Chicago, 2018. (Photo: Hilary Higgins/Chicago Tribune. Reprinted with permission.)

informed by resistance to the progression of climate destruction and the rise of fascism. From hyper-empathy to time travel, human nature and hierarchy, migration and enslavement, fundamentalism and apocalypse: Butler's writings serve as tools of survival and strength as we create and move forward to hopefully brighter futures. Olamina founds the new Earthseed group based on her theory of change, writing, "All that you touch / you Change. All that you Change / Changes you . . . God is Change."[6]

Which pressing challenge, or challenges, has working with plants presented to you?

DDD-A: One of the most pressing and immediate challenges is quite practical: living and working in an old mid-century high-rise with an antiquated heating system that tends to cook every living being (including me) in the space with an intense dry heat. I've noticed the changes in my own skin and how it affects the plants. So I've simply given over to plants that can best survive this atmosphere.

How is the interaction between your artistic practice and theoretical endeavors shaped by vegetal life?

DDD-A: The energy informing my theory of Afro-Futurist ecologies reorients "the center" outside of marginalization[7] and in resistance of the label "underrepresented," working to decolonize the canon and privileging African aesthetic systems rooted in the explication of internally derived frameworks as called for by African art historian Dr. Rowland Abiodun.[8]

Vegetal life and its relationship with humans, to the body and design and to the pursuit of joy and pleasure—all of this continues to inform my sculptural and ritual work.

D. Denenge Duyst-Akpem is a space sculptor whose award-winning teaching, art, and writing bridge disciplines of ritual, design, ecology, and Afrofuturity. Her fantastical interactive environments and performances interrogate, titillate, decolonize, and empower, asking: "Who controls the future?" She is associate professor, Adjunct, School of the Art Institute of Chicago, and founder of Denenge Design and In the Luscious Garden, focused on holistic and conceptual approaches to human-centered design.

NOTES

1. Rowland Abiodun, "Understanding Yoruba Art and Aesthetics: The Concept of *Ase*," *African Arts* 27, no. 3 (1994): 68–103.
2. See OCAD-U Dean Dori Tunstall's keynote speech for the Helsinki Futures Conference, where she speaks of the use of the Native American Grandfather Principles as foundation for a new design pedagogy based on seven principles, including "love."
3. This is inspired, in part, by architect and visionary Amanda Williams's term "thrival," a combination of survival and thriving, which speaks directly to the Black experience and Black Radical Imagination traditions presented through sculptural form in *Thrival Geographies (In My Mind I See a Line)* with Andres Hernandez and Shani Crowe for the 2018 Venice Architecture Biennale.
4. "Vessels of liberation" is a concept that I developed for my first course on Afro-Futurism in 2010, to discuss the concept of a vessel that can be activated as a pathway to liberation and which is featured within Black aesthetic systems referencing this liberatory theory, including George Clinton's P-Funk Mothership, Lee "Scratch" Perry's Black Ark Studios and Sun Ra's Arkestra, a combination of the biblical Noah's ark that saved human and animal life, and the orchestra with music as the teleportation device.
5. Octavia Butler, *Parable of the Sower* (New York: Warner Books, 1993), 94.
6. Butler, *Parable of the Sower*, 79.
7. bell hooks, "Choosing the Margin as a Space of Radial Openness," in *Yearnings: Race, Gender and Cultural Politics* (Boston: South End Press, 1990), 203–209.
8. Rowland Abiodun, "Preface," in *A History of Art in Africa*, 2nd ed., ed. Monica Blackmun Visonà, Robin Poynor, and Herbert M. Cole (London: Pearson Prentice Hall, 2008), 10.

IV

SUBJECTIVITIES

22

ESTADO VEGETAL

Manuela Infante and Marcela Salinas

NORA

You're very pale, you need more light, my sweetie, I'm going to put you here. Do you feel better there, hon? Great. And you, my dear, are too big, I'm going to have to do something about you, you're drinking too much water. Hey! Look at you. You keep getting blonder. You're in your prime, love. You know I'm going to have to move you to another pot. This flowerpot doesn't suit you anymore . . . No. Of course, a bigger flowerpot, that's what I was telling you. What? No, I am not running off. Of course, love, I can get closer . . . tell me . . . What? Are you threatening me? What do you mean I'm not understanding your problem? . . . of space. That's what I'm saying. No! Don't shout at me, darling, I have my device turned on.

Now what, my love? But, all of you? . . . On the floor? How? Yes, my sweetie, but you see the problem is that the earth is under the floor . . . What do you mean lift? The floor? You want me to lift the floor so I can bury you? Forgive me for laughing, my love, but it seems to me like "the cherry on top." But, why would you want me to tear up the floor of my house? What do you mean it's not my house? What do you mean you were here before me? What's that smell? Love, what's that smell?

Okay then, let's get the job done But I don't know if I can do it alone. Who? Joselino? Yes, yes, the boy who comes and helps me take care of you. But he doesn't get here until later.

Extract from *Estado Vegetal* playscript. Reprinted with permission.

What . . . ? A pen and a piece of paper? Of course, I must have a pen and paper, my love.

Who? Me? Of course, I know how to write, my love. Don't call me any more names, please.

Ok, who is going to tell me what to write first?

What? What a beautiful image, that image seems so biblical to me . . . What? Okay, I'll shut up.

JOSELINO

Audio: "Joselino! Joselino!" I heard someone say, barely, like a . . . when . . . I was just coming in the house and there was the ma'am calling "Joselino! Joselino!" Her voice was worn out, she had but a hint of voice, who knows how long, how long she was there with the . . . crying out . . . you can feel it when words get tired.

The lady was like . . . How can I explain, she was like, because she stayed, literally . . . how can I say . . . literally the lady was . . . planted. She had her legs buried in the ground, like this, up to the height of her thigh, more or less. She was buried like . . . right there in the earth sir! She had raised all the floorboards like . . . she had taken all the plants of the house, and I am talking about a huge amount of plants, sir!

I remember that in the room inside she had taken out the whole floor and had buried them in the ground below. She had taken them out of all their pots, which were . . . pff! There was a tower of flowerpots, in a corner. I remember clearly that I thought the plants had kind of rebelled against the pots. You see flowerpots were an invention of humans to do what they will, and move . . . how could I say . . . the immovable, you see; there's a reason plants grow roots, you know.

It couldn't fit inside my mind . . . how on Earth had the lady raised the floor alone? She was more than eighty years old.

She had all her clothes, like, they were broken, they were ripped. She had . . . all of—all of her parts exposed. It made me nervous because I was a kid, and at that time she was like . . . like my mother. I went over and I wanted to take her like . . . She had her hands, where there was . . . in order to pull the . . . she had her hands with her fingernails pulled back because of all of the force she had . . . Her knees were all scratched, and when the firemen came and they had to uproot her, you could even see the bones, because, you see, she had very thin skin.

Her hair was all tangled. She cried, she looked like . . . She cried like a little animal, the lady cried.

Me, I never went back to that house . . . I don't dare to pass by, it scares me. It's just . . . you can feel something there. The property is still there. The house is there but no one ever pimped it. The plants ate up the house, it's all covered up. The vines covered the doors, you can't enter or leave anymore. The house is barely visible. The thing looks like the Garden of Eden, that thing . . . It's been over twenty years already. That day the lady said to me in a voice like a whisper: "Joselino, they say they want to reclaim the territory." I remember clearly that she asked me to take a wrinkled piece of paper she had in her hand, stained with blood. A letter, what do I know, that I later took for a poem . . . well, I took that paper, and I saved it.

When I heard about the accident of this kid with the tree—the fireman that crashed with his bike and everything, against the tree . . . Ironic right? Having been in so many fires, saving so many trees, to end up crashing into one—Look, I know I have nothing to do with all of this, but I wanted to bring the paper because I think it can be of use to you. You are interrogating the wrong people, sir. Look, officer, you could see this coming, but this is such a slow coming, that you don't see it, do you understand me? They are up to something, Maybe in 500 years the world will be nothing but a green ball, pure vegetation, just like the lady's house, like the Garden of Eden . . . do you understand me?

It's written in the poem left by the lady, I brought the paper so you can understand.

Well . . . this wasn't the piece of paper, this is like going back in the lifetime of the paper, but I'll read it to you anyway, and we go back in time.

MANUEL

Forgive me. Forgive me. Good Heavens, forgive me. Stubborn are the times in which I try to make do with this. Injured I am, by the times in which I open my eyes to find this landscape. I am an animal. I am novice in the practice of inhabiting, novice in surviving. Thou wert all here before I was, nevertheless it is me who survives with limited understanding, guilty reverse of a mystery, that you understand, however, better than I do. Because you live within time, not against it.

I am animal. My response to the world was to flee, my condemnation then, was movement. When you stay, I move forward. Where you settle, I evade. In the face of difficulty, I avoid. Where you establish, I invade. I am animal. I hold my head with my two hands because in it wallows the question I ask of myself. Because my will is distributed in the absurd hierarchy of animal anatomy, in which the brain makes decisions for the hands, for the legs, for the kidneys.

Oh, noble vegetal dispersion! Noble and marvelous branched democracy. God, I beg of you: absolve me of the animal kingdom's forms! Give me something of theirs! May my lungs beat instead. May the tips of my fingers breathe, may my stomach think! May I feed with my skin, so that eating is more like touching than devouring. May the ever-changing forms of my body be my only language, so I become incapable of lying. May death be something that occurs in my chest, while my back, in turn, is born, so I never get the absurd idea that we are moving forward. May the passage of time be nothing more than a new ring in my trunk, every memory a layer of bark that covers me, so that I may touch my rugged memory.

Teach me this day, here, now, with what is left of you and what is left of me, how to speak in chemicals. Open for me your chemical recitation. Teach me how to speak in combinations of bromine and water, rather than in highs and lows. I want to use signifiers that taste of iodine. Signs that can only be deciphered with touch. Sentences that if exposed to the sun, refract into mineral spectrums of blues and greens. I want to deliver speeches of poison. Let us recite poems whose lines only rhyme their levels of acidity.

What would it be like to grow without returning to the center, without ever regrouping, always moving outwards? Never being able to close oneself upon oneself, never reaching the full circle of "This is I." To be, to grow, always, further out. So that, that thing called I is only the memory of a seed. To be oneself, to be just one-self, is only a seasonal event. They tried to tell us all this, to cover the whole world with their varied words, but all they managed to say was: leaf. Always the same leaf. It´s not possible to escape planthood by means of plants. Nor to escape humanity by human means.

I am the last animal. Sitting at the site of the final catastrophe.

This forest was Hell, ladies and gentlemen, even before the flames. This forest was made up of only pine trees. Imagine a city made up only of shoemakers. Only bakers, only nurses. All the pine trees planted in this forest were the same age—because this is how humans found it more efficient to plant. Imagine, if you will, a city of only children. Children alone. Here, ladies and gentlemen, it's as if a kindergarten had been burnt down. "The wind is blowing, the wind is blowing hard, Mom!" The wind sounds of beauty in the forest until there's a spark. Until the earth dries up so much that he who softly whistled his friction with the vertices of the leaves, suddenly no longer whistles, but screams in a voice that is not his own, but the voice of fire.

There are not four elements, there are three: water, air, and earth. Fire is not an element. Fire is a force that transforms one element into another. It transforms water into steam and wood into ash. By way of fire, we can all become "other."

Hear me, Zeus: I know we can be other. How much other can we be? Must we burn to come to see? To God I ask: Is there something in me that could become them? Given the green in my eyes perhaps? Or if when I speak I always use the same words as if the words themselves were leaves, citations of other leaves, my words like foliage of alternate repetitions, perhaps?

And if those words were only flavors? Not an accumulation of signs that represent ideas . . . And if memory, then, was only body that is added onto body and not a series of images that represent events . . . We could then argue: No more representation! May nothing represent anything. May no one speak on behalf of anyone.

The hand thinks for itself, breathes for itself. Every limb has its own brain, its own lungs, its own eyes, its own ambitions, its own deities. Autonomy. The hand is not represented by ideas of the brain, nor by the needs of the eyes. No! It is only from political animal physiologies that tyrants could arise, or representative democracy which is the same. Let us no longer continue down the immature route of the animal.

May the world once more become one big green ball. A sovereign vegetal state. Make landscape painters of those who in some near future wish to paint it.

I am the last animal. Come. Let me do what animals do and what plants do not: let me die.

Translation: British Council, Chile Bruce, Gibbons Fell, Alex Ripp

Main Pathway: Cross-Pollination

Subthemes

Proceed to Experience, p. 495
Proceed to Time, p. 385
End of Composting

23

DISSEMINATION, RHIZOMES, EFFLORESCENCE: THE LEGACY OF THE VEGETATIVE SOUL IN TWENTIETH-CENTURY THOUGHT

Elaine Miller

The rose is without why, it blooms because it blooms
It pays no attention to itself, asks not whether it is seen.
—Angelus Silesius

Nineteenth-century German literary and philosophical thought sowed the seeds of the displacement of binary metaphysical oppositions and the questioning of the atomistic conception of the subject that became such important focal points for twentieth-century Continental philosophy. The twentieth-century critique of subjectivity, which starts explicitly with Nietzsche and continues through the philosophical schools of phenomenology, genealogy, deconstruction, and French feminism, among others, builds indirectly on Kant's critique and the massive reworking of metaphysics into an organic, living growth by German Idealism. The concern that links these movements is a search for the assumptions or presuppositions that underlie classical metaphysical tenets, particularly modern metaphysics, which grounds truth in the rational self-transparent subject. Martin Heidegger, for example, using a plant metaphor, writes:

Descartes, writing to Picot, who translated the *Principia Philosophiae* into French, observed: "Thus the whole of philosophy is like a tree: the roots are metaphysics, the trunk is physics,

Originally published as "Dissemination, Rhizomes, Efflorescence: The Legacy of the Vegetative Soul in Twentieth-Century Thought," in *The Vegetative Soul: From Philosophy of Nature to Subjectivity in the Feminine* (Albany, NY: SUNY Press, 2002), 181–200. Reprinted with permission.

and the branches that issue from the trunk are all the other sciences." Sticking to this image, we ask: In what soil do the roots of the tree have their hold? Out of what ground do the roots—and through them the whole tree—receive their nourishing juices and strength? What element, concealed in the ground, enters and lives in the roots that support and nourish the tree? What is the basis and element of metaphysics? What is metaphysics, viewed from its ground?[1]

Here, a tree, a form of plant, is likened to an individual, to philosophy considered in its entirety. Clearly there is no one model for plant growth, and clearly one might challenge the metaphor of plant growth on the basis of the tree, which appears, especially as Descartes describes it, to be a self-sufficient individual in the same way that an animal is. Yet Heidegger's point is to ask about the surrounding environment upon which the tree is dependent and in which it is fixed. The roots of a plant in this image, which must remain enclosed by a concealed ground in order to allow the rest of the plant to flourish, reflect the silent ground that metaphysics rarely questions, the unspoken assumptions that make it possible. The aspect of modern metaphysics that Heidegger, Foucault, Derrida, Irigaray, and others question is the assumption that this ground can be found in the metaphysics of presence, and in particular in the animal-like configurations of the thinking "I," the rational subject, whose boundaries are known to itself and defensible. This is certainly where Descartes found the roots of metaphysics to be securely grounded. At the same time that they trace the assumptions that metaphysics makes, however, the critiques of these thinkers do not seek an alternative univocal origin; displacing the fiction of this origin is one of the things the plant-like reading seeks to achieve. Heidegger speaks of the "groundless ground" of Being with reference to the rose, which is "without why," in the words of the seventeenth-century mystic and poet Angelus Silesius.[2] Heidegger's interest in this line from a poem occurs in the context of his study of Leibniz's principle of sufficient reason, which states that nothing is without a why, without grounds. Heidegger considers how a rose can simultaneously be grounded—insofar as it becomes an object for human cognition, as we can deduce the causal mechanism at the origin of its blooming—and be without why—insofar as it does not explicitly take itself into consideration, does not "insert itself in between its blooming and the grounds for blooming, thanks to which grounds could first be *as* grounds."[3] Heidegger goes on to interpret the fragment as saying that "humans, in the concealed ground of their essential being, first truly are when in their own way they are like the rose—without why."[4] For Heidegger, heeding and uncovering this concealed ground of human essential being, that which is prior to calculative thinking, causal determination, and human action considered in terms of explicit conscious agency, is philosophy's task in confronting the hegemony of the modern subject which has been characterized in just such ways.

To trace a linear history of influence between the thinkers whose work we have been considering and what has been called postmodern critique would be to configure the history of thought in the manner we have called animal lineage, as a straightforward heritage linking bodies of work. The thought of Kant, Hegel, and Nietzsche, and to a lesser extent Goethe and Hölderlin, has been disseminated in twentieth-century Continental philosophy and feminist theory in a manner that more resembles vegetable growth, as political intervention and transformative interpretation. As Jacques Derrida writes in "Otobiographies," his reading of Nietzsche:

> We are not, I believe, bound to decide. An interpretive decision does not have to draw a line between two intents or two political contents. Our interpretations will not be readings of a hermeneutic or exegetic sort, but rather political interventions in the political rewriting of the text and its destination. This is the way it has always been—and always in a singular manner.[5]

Here Derrida refers to the appropriation of Nietzsche's work for both fascist and anti-fascist purposes, and the same argument might apply to his own appropriation and transformation of Heideggerian critique. A straightforwardly hermeneutical reading seeks to uncover univocal roots of meaning of a work, to analyze its origins and codify its meaning. Such a reading would kill a plant, if indeed a text is a plant-like growth. The transformative style of thinkers like Derrida, Luce Irigaray, and Gilles Deleuze and Félix Guattari, by contrast, envisions texts and interpretations as vegetative growth, untraceable to singular or determinate origins, disseminating and productive rather than reducibly polysemic and analytic. Derrida's notion of dissemination, Deleuze and Guattari's articulation of the rhizome, and Irigaray's trope of efflorescence all explicitly perform what we have called a plant-like reading. A disseminating reading of texts recognizes that interpretation is always productive or fecund rather than simply investigative and analytical. It resists totalization and subverts any attempt to master a reading definitively. A rhizomatic reading emphasizes nonlinearity and a genealogical refusal of unique unified sources or meanings. Efflorescence complicates the notion of the atomistic subject and the singular, phallic reading, while subverting and transforming the tradition with a metamorphic, ivy-like growth.

In the preface to *Dissemination*, Derrida draws our attention to the metaphorical register in the history of philosophy that encompasses Nature conceived as a book, the notion of *logos spermatikos*, and the equation, most explicitly articulated by Plato, of writing with strewing seed, speech with animal insemination. Dissemination, understood as the multiple, antisystematic fecundity that occurs when seed is blown to the wind rather than the reductive, purposive insemination of animals, is described by Derrida as "the heterogeneity and absolute exteriority of the seed" which "constitute[s] itself into a program, but . . . a program that cannot be formalized . . . [which] does not take a form saturated with self-presence in the encyclopedic circle."[6] Aligning itself most explicitly against Hegel, but also against the onto-theological project of the history of metaphysics in general, Derrida calls dissemination a resistance to the "effacement of seminal difference through which the leftoverness of the outwork gets internalized and domesticated into the onto-theology of the great Book."[7]

The "great Book" is Nature, conceived by medieval thinkers to be God's book, written in such a way that it is representative and true, an ordered totality that gives the reader a structured idea of the seemingly chaotic logos scattered like seed among its forms, articulated retroactively as the origin of all its diverse forms. Derrida then turns to Novalis, who, in his philosophical fragments entitled "Pollen" (*Blüthenstaub*) envisioned an Encyclopedia that would "complete" Nature as it inscribed it. Derrida asks how one can think the identification of Nature with a Book if the book is what *completes* it, and what is signified about completedness as such by the fact that Novalis never finished this Encyclopedia.[8] True to the vision of the nineteenth-century vegetative soul we have been considering, Derrida speculates that the Novalisian Encyclopedia signifies that which goes beyond the "always-already-constitutedness of meaning and of truth within the theo-logico-encyclopedic space, of self-fertilization with no limen."[9]

Deleuze and Guattari expand upon the various kinds of "plant structures" that different kinds of philosophical and literary efforts employ. In "Rhizome," the introduction to *A Thousand Plateaus*, Deleuze and Guattari sketch three general figures of a book: the root-book, the radicle-system or fascicular root-book, and the rhizome-book.[10] The root-book, exemplified in the world of plants by the tree, traces the image of the world, the roots of the book imitating the "world-tree." Deleuze and Guattari ask, "How could the law of the book reside in nature, when it is what presides over the very division between world and book, nature and art?"[11] The root-book or tree-book constitutes itself as the reflection of nature, as the One that becomes two. We might add that this root-structure, explicitly seen in Descartes' analogy of metaphysics to the roots of a tree, is the method of individuation based on the animal body as well. Deleuze and Guattari argue that "in nature, roots are taproots with a more multiple, lateral, and circular system of ramification, rather than a dichotomous one."[12] The root-book opens upon all classification according to binary logic: nature and culture, natural reality and spiritual reality, literature and philosophy, annual and perennial plant. This system of classification lay at the heart of botanical research, epitomized by the Swedish botanist Carl von Linné (Linnaeus), in the time of Goethe. Think of the family tree, the charts of families of languages, which begin at point X and proceed by dichotomy. Binary logic rules the classical book, according to Deleuze and Guattari, and still dominates psychoanalysis, linguistics, structuralism, and, of course, computer technology and information science.

The second figure of the book, in Deleuze and Guattari's introduction, is that of the fascicular root, or radicle system. When the principal root of a plant has been aborted or its tip destroyed, an indefinite multiplicity of secondary roots appear on it, and the plant as a result undergoes an intensified growth. This description parallels an experiment performed by Linnaeus that Goethe describes in *The Metamorphosis of Plants*, in which a young tree was placed in a pot that was too small for it. Obviously the smaller pot would not allow the primary roots to expand to their normal degree, and so secondary, smaller roots took over the process of nourishing the plant. Linnaeus based his theory of prolepsis on the immediate flourishing of the plant that resulted as the tree bore blossoms and fruit very quickly, long before its usual six years of development. The theory posits that the plant anticipates many years of development at once by compressing the successive stages through time. This phenomenon also resembles the gardens of Adonis described in Plato's *Phaedrus*. In Deleuze and Guattari's terms, in this case the primary root's unity still subsists in the form of potentiality: its past or future may be unified, or at least the promise of unity remains since its structure is a fragmentation of a former whole. They give the examples of William Burroughs's cut-up method (folding one text into another), Joyce's shattering of the linear unity of language, and Nietzsche's aphorisms. Such a structure does not really break with the root: "The world has become chaos, but the book remains the image of the world: radicle-chaosmos rather than root-cosmos."[13]

The third book-type, and also plant-type, is that of the rhizome. Rhizomes grow horizontally rather than vertically, putting out a multiplicity of small roots and shoots without any one central root or stem. Rhizomes connect any point to any other point, and have no identifiable beginning or end, but are always in the middle, on the way: "When a multiplicity of this kind changes dimension, it necessarily changes in nature as well, undergoes a metamorphosis."[14] Rhizomes have no territory; they may spread with the wind and cover any amount of ground, since they grow outward rather than upward. They are acentered, nonhierarchical, nonsignifying, "all manner of beginnings."[15] Deleuze and Guattari cite the diary of Franz Kafka, who wrote, "Things . . . occur to me . . . not from the root up but rather only from somewhere in their middle. Let someone then attempt to seize them, let someone attempt to seize a blade of grass and hold fast to it when it begins to grow only from the middle."[16]

Deleuze and Guattari, like Goethe and Hölderlin, emphasize the adaptability of the transplanted shoot of a plant, the fact that a broken-off part can reattach itself and from the point of adaptation take up further stages of metamorphosis: "[A] new rhizome may form in the heart of a tree, the hollow of a root, the crook of a branch."[17] Hegel calls this ability of the plant a kind of monstrosity, but Goethe counters that such an adaptation manifests flexibility, not monstrosity. Goethe's observation seeks to refute the metaphor of the seed as self-enclosed and purposive, a metaphor that plays into the depiction of the plant as homologous to an animal, and thus a deficient animal.

Deleuze and Guattari also connect the arboreal structures of technical production with the West, and rhizomatic growth patterns with the East: "The East presents a different figure: a relation to the steppe and the garden (or in some cases, the desert and the oasis), rather than forest and field; cultivation of tubers by fragmentation of the individual; a casting aside or bracketing of animal raising, which is confined to closed spaces or pushed out onto the steppes of the nomads."[18] This account is a reversal, in terms of approbation, of the traditional binary oppositions Detienne traces in *The Gardens of Adonis* between "superficial, lightweight plants" with no roots and no fruit, and "serious, solemn, rooted" plants, the former associated with women and the East, the latter with men and the West. Goethe was deeply interested in the plant culture of the East, and his *West-Oestlicher Divan* (1819) has much to say on this theme. In Europe in the nineteenth century, the Turkish "language of flowers," used to pass secret messages between lovers,[19] seized the popular imagination. The "language of flowers" came to signify any secret code of writing that did not follow the rules of ordinary discourse, in precisely the sense of the multiple significations and nonlinear branchings-out described by Deleuze and Guattari.

In spite of the fascinating analogies Deleuze and Guattari draw between the different kinds of plant growth and various styles of writing, and in spite of the obvious value of challenging the received understanding of the proper way of writing, it seems necessary to question any pairing that relies—as Deleuze and Guattari's account ultimately does—on the traditional definition of metaphor as a lively description that illuminates the structure of another reality that lies behind it, in this case, the description of plants that stands in for the description of writing.

Instead, here metaphor might be understood as an intertwining that reads two things in terms of one another in such a way that no priority can be drawn, no implication that one figure represents, or stands in for, the other.

While a productive metaphor brings two things together, it does so in such a way as to still remind one of the provisionality of such a juxtaposition and the space between the terms of the juxtaposition. As Sarah Kofman puts it in her study of Nietzsche and metaphor:

> On the one hand there is no metaphor without a stripping away of individuality, without masquerade and metamorphosis. To be able to transpose, one must be able to transpose oneself and one must have conquered the limits of individuality: the same must partake in the other, must be the other. At this level metaphor is founded on the ontological unity of life represented by Dionysos. But if there is metaphor it is because this unity is always already in pieces and can only be reconstituted when symbolically transposed into art. Beyond individual separation, symbolized by the dismemberment of Dionysos, metaphor allows for the reconstitution of the originary unity of all beings, symbolized by the resurrection of the god. On the other hand metaphor is linked to the loss of the proper understood as the essence of the world, which is indecipherable and of which man can have only representations which are quite improper.[20]

This understanding of metaphor allows the possibilities of representation *itself*, the hiatus between the terms, rather than one particular reading or representation, to come to presence. The "loss of the proper" is an absolute loss, without the possibility of recuperation, rather than being a plenitude which, though unknown, supplements and fulfills the provisionality of the metaphorical bond. The difference between a "living" and a "dead" metaphor would lie in the fact that one still experiences the rhythm of the new metaphor, creating the impression of living growth *(physis)* that Aristotle declared to be the quality of the best metaphors.[21]

For Aristotle, of course, metaphorical speech supplements nonmetaphorical discourse, adding interest and liveliness rather than content. Irigaray uncovers a less generous reading of plant growth in Aristotle's theory of the soul. In *De Anima* Aristotle introduces the notion of the vegetative soul as one component of the irrational part of the soul, namely that component responsible for simple growth and alteration. This soul, unlike the sentient soul (the other part of the irrational soul), is shared by both plants and animals, hence its name. The nutritive or vegetative soul is also associated with reproduction, particularly with the womb and fetation. The vegetative soul reappears in discussions in the *Nicomachean Ethics*, *Generation of Animals*, and *Politics* to indirectly bolster, among other things, claims about the role of women in political life.[22] The explanation of the Aristotelian vegetative soul—which gained force in its adoption by medieval Scholasticism—contributes to an argument dispersed through various works of Aristotle justifying the inferior political status of women. The part of the argument that concerns us here rests on the claim that since the vegetative soul predominates over the rational soul in women by virtue of their capacity for bearing children, women by nature are not suited to rule. Irrationality is thus directly linked to the perceived primacy of the reproductive capacity in women via the vegetative soul. Western philosophers from Aristotle to Hegel have repeated the analogy of men to animals and women to plants by virtue of their (perceived) respective characteristics of activity and rationality, on the one hand, and passivity and lack of rationality, on the other.

In works spanning her intellectual career, Irigaray takes up the metaphor of the plant again and again, both to criticize the negative way in which it has traditionally been used to characterize the ontological status of woman, and, increasingly, to subvert the traditional metaphor in the productive notion of efflorescence. In doing so, Irigaray gives an indication as to the language in which a feminine subject, as opposed to a "concept of femininity," might be couched. In "How to Conceive of a Girl," Irigaray considers Aristotle's analogy of women to plants. She writes:

> The substance of the plant, like that of any (female) being, cannot move, or move beyond, the ontological status assigned to it. Once and for all. It is not capable of any less or any more.[23]

Woman is supposed to have an essence that defines her as woman, once and for all. She is relegated to the status of nature or matter, and in this sense can do no more than assist or ground man in the actualization of his subjectivity.

Irigaray's project of performing a subversion of a traditional metaphor such that it turns into a productive metonymical structure takes the German nineteenth-century discourse on vegetable genius as its productive ground. Critique does not exhaust the philosophical scope of Irigaray's effort; she attempts to move beyond simple historical critique, as important as this activity is, toward a positive feminist philosophy. In *The Forgetting of Air in Martin Heidegger*, and even more explicitly in *Elemental Passions*, Irigaray uses the rhetorical configuration of "efflorescence" to designate a blossoming or blooming forth that cannot be enclosed within the traditional boundaries of embodiment and philosophical discourse. Efflorescence—a figure that implies metamorphosis and indefinite individuation—forms the positive facet of Irigaray's critique of Aristotle and of the history of metaphysics. This critique can be read as aimed at the primacy of traditionally "animalistic" metaphors that emphasize self-enclosedness, self-preservation, and strict identity over time, qualities that, among other philosophical constructs, could be predicated of the fiction of the (masculine) subject.

Among other contemporary feminist critics of the articulation of subjectivity in the history of metaphysics, Irigaray stands out in her attempt to reconsider the Enlightenment conception of the atomistic subject (the Hobbesian man) through her use of specifically natural, yet nonhuman and even non-animalistic forms to think sexual difference and feminine subjectivity. Irigaray's use of the trope of efflorescence reminds us that the flowering subject is always a sexed subject, a multiple subject, and a subject-in-becoming. Irigaray's work stands out among other twentieth-century critics of the history of the way in which subjectivity has been configured in that she envisions the possibility of another kind of subjectivity. She does not assume, as others upon whose work she builds do, that the subject qua subject necessarily is constituted according to the model of the animal, and thus must be left behind. Her politics of subjectivity, motivated by an interest in the ethical and political empowerment of women, does not rest content with dissecting and critiquing the history of metaphysics, but grafts a positive vision onto the destructive insights of psychoanalysis, phenomenology, and deconstruction. Irigaray proposes a feminine model of subjectivity, one that returns to a close connection to the philosophy of nature, and in particular to the figure of the plant. In doing so

Irigaray is not suggesting that a return to unmediated nature—in itself an impossible task—would bring about a meaningful change for women. Rather, she implies that a return to and reworking of the symbolics of nature might be a place from within the social or symbolic order from which to retroactively restructure the ways in which women's embodiment, natural role, and passage into subjectivity are thought, and thereby to effect a real change for women in the cultural order. By "real change" I mean that such a restructuring would not merely manipulate the existing conception of subjectivity in order to make room for women, thereby leaving its implicit masculinity intact, but would make room for sexual difference. This distinguishes her philosophy and makes her the heir to nineteenth-century *Naturphilosophie*, a title we must recognize that she might well not wish to claim, especially given her critique of Hegel's philosophy of nature and its link to his treatment of the feminine.

Yet Irigaray herself explicitly links women to the vegetable world. Irigaray transforms the negative association of woman with plant into a positive possibility, first by recalling pre-patriarchal cultures where goddesses were associated with the vegetable world:

> One might well wonder if women are closer to the vegetable world than to the animal world, as was claimed by certain ancient philosophers, and particularly by female cultures, although, it is true, in different ways. Could it be that in this proximity there lies an accurate explanation of her relation to passivity? Woman's receptivity would not be restricted to her relation to man alone but would extend to the natural economy, especially the cosmic one, with which her equilibrium and growth are more closely associated. Her so-called passivity would not then be part of an active/passive pair of opposites but would signify a different economy, a different relation to nature and to the self that would amount to attentiveness and to *fidelity* rather than *passivity*. A matter, therefore, not of pure receptivity but of a movement of growth that never ultimately estranges itself from corporeal existence in a natural milieu. In which case, becoming is not cut off from life or its placing. It is not extrapolated from the living nor founded in a dead character. It remains attentive to growth: physiological, spiritual, relational.[24]

Irigaray associates plantlike growth and the feminine with nature, much in the way these figures have traditionally been linked, but with a different agenda. For Irigaray, there is a grave danger in the fact that nature has been appropriated by an approach that seeks to harness and utilize it without recognizing the loss such a process involves. This loss, in her view, includes an occlusion of the bodily and its intimate relationship to the spiritual, the forgetting of the rich ground of possibility in favor of the certainty of the actual and the conceptual. The narrowly scientific and technological world view leaves no room for nature as excess, as that from which human beings arise and over which they ultimately have no absolute control, an excess that guarantees the possibility of change in the depiction of sexual difference. As Margaret Whitford analyzes it, nature, for Irigaray, is that which is symbolized as nature (as opposed to culture or the symbolic), but, more explicitly, it is "those parts of himself that the male imaginary has split off and projected—into the world, on to women."[25] Nature, as we have emphasized in other contexts, is not a pre-symbolic, untouched realm to which one can retreat, from which one flees, or which one can symbolize at will. For Irigaray, one might add, nature is not an essentialized, fixed nature attached to a sex, but is part of a hierarchized system (as we have seen most clearly in Hegel's philosophy of nature) that is legitimized by virtue of being presented as natural and inevitable. At the same time, however, I would argue that for Irigaray "nature" also represents the possibility of transformation of that order through a restructuring of the feminine imaginary (thereby effecting the possibility of a feminine subjectivity) by way of reworking the symbols of nature.[26] Whitford quotes Irigaray in saying that according to Hegel, women remain in the plant world rather than acceding to the animal, as part of the "in itself" rather than "for itself," interpreting this as merely a claim that women need to move beyond the "natural" into the "social." However, in other places Whitford shows how Irigaray uses existing symbols of femininity to transform the symbolic order, which I believe is precisely what she is doing with vegetal figures as well. "Nature," then, signifies the exhilarating possibility that ideas and traditions may be either recouped or transformed. Irigaray writes in *Sexes and Genealogies:* "Once the natural, familial, female, or, if you like, nocturnal spirit, is sacrificed, the dark rootedness of nature is rejected in favor of a *sightless era of concepts*. This sightlessness seems to consist in the unconsidered, unconscious destruction of our senses."[27]

A tendency toward metonymical profusion (itself characteristic of vegetative growth) rather than either blind conceptual language or metaphorical substitution characterizes Irigaray's strategy of transformative mimesis. Rather than simply pointing out the flaws of traditional philosophy's linkage of the feminine with the earth or nature, Irigaray focuses on the redemptive possibilities inherent in the very metaphors that have been used to reduce the feminine to the silent, concealed ground of Being, just as a "plantlike" reading transforms its textual object in a metamorphic growth. Plant growth provides one of the most striking and pervasive examples of such a guiding principle in Irigaray's work. The figure of efflorescence functions not simply as one of many poetic figures, but as a privileged figure in Irigaray's work, as the metaphor, as it were, for metonymy, the underlying structure of language that metaphor presupposes. A metaphor for metonymy would repeat its displacing function endlessly, so that, in spite of its privilege, the very nature of plant metamorphosis would make it impossible for this figure for femininity to take over as a metaphor for woman in a substitutive logic that would simply replace the phallus with veiled lips, or the measured and autonomous animal with the interconnected and vulnerable plant. Rather, the figure of efflorescence provides support for Irigaray's imagining of a feminine subject through an open-ended inquiry into and transformation of thinking about language, becoming, and individuation.

Irigaray criticizes Aristotle for allowing everything he says about nature to be "already co-opted by prescriptions that direct or interpret his findings."[28] But in a stranger turn, she goes on to write:

> The plant may indeed conform to her own purpose, but an other has to certify this. And that other must speak, and speak, moreover, as a philosopher. She may be fully herself, and in herself, but an other has to declare that this is the case. Thus, her development is subject to definitions coming from an other.[29]

Without any specific declaration on Irigaray's part, the plant moves from an analogy to woman to a metonym for woman, such that the critique of the philosophy of nature becomes a critique of the architectonic of philosophy, which restricts woman to a prescribed category defined in terms of an other that alone can be actualized and affirm her purpose in her place.

I have repeatedly used the word *metonymy* rather than *metaphor* to characterize Irigaray's use of figurative language, and this shift in vocabulary is significant. In an essay entitled "The 'Mechanics' of Fluids," Irigaray, in the context of critiquing "science" (always placed in scare quotes) for its neglect of fluidity in favor of the study of solids, links this neglect with psychoanalysis' neglect of feminine sexuality, which is fluid. She writes:

> And if anyone objects that the question, put this way, relies too heavily on metaphors, it is easy to reply that the question in fact impugns the privilege granted to metaphor (a quasi solid) over metonymy (which is much more closely allied to fluids).[30]

Irigaray's critique is aimed at Jacques Lacan's discussion of metaphor and metonymy in "The Agency of the Letter,"[31] which, she implies, privileges metaphor over metonymy in much the same way that phallocentrism neglects the feminine. Lacan's understanding of metaphor and metonymy, drawn from Roman Jakobson's linguistic theory, aligns metaphor with the vertical substitution of one signifier for another, and metonymy with horizontal contiguity, in a way that recalls the contrast of tree and rhizome. Jane Gallop suggests a metonymic or "feminine" reading of Lacan which, by "supplying a whole context of associations" that are present in the text, yet not explicitly combined, form an argument in favor of aligning the privilege accorded to metaphor with the hegemony of the masculine in psychoanalytic theory.[32] Gallop warns against the "temptation" of "misreading" Lacan's text as a straightforward neglect of metonymy (and of the feminine), and observes instead, in a very Irigarayan manner, that metonymy functions in the manner of a dark, latent, ground upon which metaphor depends and indeed is grounded. Her argument persuasively shows that although to read the tradition as perpetuating a straightforward neglect of metonymy would be to misread it, nevertheless, metonymy's role has historically functioned in a way that strikingly parallels Irigaray's critique of the role of the feminine in the history of philosophy. Lacan writes, for example, that "metonymy is there from the beginning, and it is what makes metaphor possible."[33]

Irigaray's claim is that the feminine, insofar as it has been a part of philosophical discourse and formulated as part of an ontological structure, has always played the role of ground, of source, of that which is to be contained, but in such a way that a making actual of feminine possibility paradoxically involves its own negation. To the extent that woman is granted an autonomous identity, she receives this status only thanks to an assimilation into a masculine conception of subjectivity, much in the way that the concealed ground feeds the roots of the tree. As Irigaray puts it in *The Forgetting of Air*, "The other is nothing more than the assimilation of the mourning of the other, projected into the 'free.'"[34] By reviving metonymy Irigaray seeks to avoid the substitutive logic of metaphor, refusing to erect feminine metaphors in the place of overturned masculine metaphors of subjectivity.

The mourning of the other Irigaray refers to here resonates with her discussions of Antigone and of the story of Demeter and Kore-Persephone.[35] Both Antigone and Kore are entombed under the earth, relegated to a silent subterranean existence, though both also provide a silent (unacknowledged) propagating force. Antigone's defiance of the law of the state, at least in Hegel's interpretation, upsets the feminine configured as spiritualizing force. She buries her brother to assure his entrance into the public realm of memorial, and thus his subjectivity, if only in memory, but her own transgression results in a burial that has no immediate positive outcome, that seems merely disruptive, but that also signifies the possibility of transformation. Kore's ingestion of pomegranate seeds ensures the necessity of her remaining underground for the winter months of every year, yet it is her very annual appearance at the end of this exile that provides for the blossoming, fruitfulness, and harvest upon which human life depends. The feminine in both cases can be interpreted as a vehicle for blossoming forth who does not herself achieve the liberation and autonomy presupposed of a (Western, masculine) conception of subjectivity, but who nevertheless marks the possibility of another kind of subjectivity.

We recall that Hegel distinguished between the plant and the animal by noting the fact that the plant "cannot retain . . . fluid in itself," so that it is incapable of maintaining a unity between its internal and external world (JI 211). Because of its self-enclosed interior of circulating fluids, the animal carries spiritual liquidity within itself. The universal fluid merely flows through and then out of the plant, whereas the animal holds what Hegel calls the "universal element" within itself as a part of itself (JI 211). This explanation informs Hegel's analogy of woman to plant and man to animal: woman can be, at most, the unconscious vessel of subjectivity, the in-itself and not for-itself, a vessel through which spirit flows and which nourishes the animal, just as the feminine provides the spiritualizing capacity for the masculine, exemplified in Antigone's burial of her brother, Polynices.

Irigaray recognizes the precariousness of her chosen metonymics of vegetative growth, precarious in its very proximity to the tradition it seeks to critique and transform. In her famous discussion of Hegel's Antigone in *Speculum of the Other Woman*, "The Eternal Irony of the Community," Irigaray begins with two epigraphs from Hegel's *Philosophy of Nature*. She consistently draws a connection between the philosophy of nature and Hegel's discussion of Antigone in the *Phenomenology of Spirit*. Such a connection is at first consideration not at all self-evident, but, as we have seen, Hegel clearly draws a connection between the feminine and the vegetative, one that contrasts strikingly with Irigaray's own intertwining of the two, but in which she nevertheless discerns redemptive possibilities:

Clearly, according to Hegel, the dead man is the one who finally finds peace. He is no longer internally split, no longer in constant *polemos*. But it might be possible to have another peace: that of living plant growth. The ensemble of the Hegelian system, apart from a few errors and uprootings, in fact resembles this. Could the secret model for his philosophy overall be *the plant?* But, within the system, as it unfolds on the conscious level, it seems that one can escape from singularness only through the order of death or of the dead man. This idea or conviction seems linked to the *split of body and spirit* that is established following the sacrifice of the female to the State and man's access to citizenship and to a neutered culture.[36]

The difference Irigaray notes between "living plant growth" and the plant that is associated with death recalls the logic of sacrifice according to which Hegelian nature unfolds in its progression from plant to animal. The split between body and spirit that results, epitomized in the discussion of the plant that in laying itself down ferments into communion fare of bread and wine, reminds us that despite his own description of his system as a metamorphosing plant, Hegel's model remains that of Deleuze and Guattari's tree-book, a tree that does not consider its nurturing ground.

Irigaray notes the problematic aspects of the (Hegelian) discourse, yet reads it beyond its intention, in what Elizabeth Grosz calls the "viscosity" or superabundance of the text, its resistance to ownership.[37] Irigaray's implicit argument seems to be that if the very phallogocentricity of the tradition perpetuates itself through concealed metaphorical structures, it is exigent for feminist philosophy not just to reveal and dismantle these metaphors, but also to engage and displace them productively according to the logic of metonymy. The scientific and philosophical tradition has prided itself on being separate from rhetoric, has defined itself in denigrating "literary" language. Irigaray subverts traditional metaphors as a rhetorical weapon against the tradition that has worked to exclude and at the same time to assimilate women. In refusing to simply reject metaphors that have historically been associated with women, Irigaray makes a statement against the politics of assimilation which masks phallogocentrism with the veneer of neutrality. As Patricia Huntington explains in *Ecstatic Subjects*, "Metaphorical transference entails evoking new images of women's autonomy from the 'surplus of meaning' of the metaphor 'Woman' as represented in patriarchy."[38] However, as she is quick to remind us, "The feminine utopian moment, though concerned with the future, does not erect the 'feminine' as a new transcendental signified."[39] It is important to note that the "new" images that are invoked are culled from the "surplus of meaning" of the metaphor "Woman" *as represented in the patriarchy*. This explains why Irigaray chooses a metaphor, that of the plant, that has traditionally been associated with the devalorization of women. Irigaray recognizes that one must not naively believe that it is possible to simply start anew, as if it were easy to reach a vantage point outside of the symbolic order. However, because there is an excess, or surplus of meaning onto which the imaginary opens up, because this excess is that which will always exceed any finite symbolic system, it is possible to subvert traditional metaphors productively while retaining a connection to their source. As Whitford puts it, Irigaray focuses on the imaginary of the history of metaphysics, that is, its repressed, unacknowledged foundation in the unsymbolized maternal-feminine. Yet the imaginary is a structural and not a developmental or chronological stage, so that "symbolic and imaginary form a system, in which we cannot understand one without the other Change in the imaginary *must* bring about change in the symbolic and vice versa."[40] Imaginary and symbolic are contiguous, and Irigaray chooses to strategically address the imaginary by echoing and transforming existing symbols of femininity. Whitford emphasizes that Irigaray's work deliberately takes on male metaphors that describe femininity in order to effect "a possible restructuring of the imaginary by the symbolic which would make a difference to women."[41] This process draws on the rhizomatic displacement of metonymy rather than the substitutive logic of metaphor.

In a continuation of the critique of Hegel in which she contrasts the Hegelian, sacrificial use of plant metaphors with "living plant growth," Irigaray writes, in a way that echoes Goethe, "In fact it is possible to go beyond singularness by obeying growth, by sharing in the universal natural rhythm. This sharing is indeed more universal than a single death. Obviously, the universality of nature is complex, but it is ceaselessly *a figure both complete and changing*, finished and open, globally peaceful in its achievements," a figure like that of the plant. She goes on to critique the Hegelian sacrifice of nature to spirit: "Because it refuses any debt to nature, the return to nature can only be of the order of death."[42]

Not content with a simple destruction of the concept of subjectivity, Irigaray considers the invocation of a feminine transcendental, a feminine universal, or a feminine subjectivity to be a central part of displacing the way in which women's desire as well as interpersonal relationships among each other have been historically mediated through the masculine. However, although the feminine subject is not to be understood in terms of atomistic or self-preservational identity, she is equally not to be associated with a kind of indefinite fusion or chaotic origin. To posit the feminine subject as formless would be to leave the traditional equation of the feminine with matter, with undifferentiated origin, intact. As Irigaray writes in *The Forgetting of Air*:

She, she-of-ever, older and newer than every history, stays within beginning's awakening. Inborn infancy. A passage never completed between inside and outside, night and day, midnight and midday, permanent dawn, she joins these in the portal chink of her awakening. She is never closed, never open. With neither the defined contours of a completed development nor the gaping openness of a chaos from which everything can issue. Ever being born: the living female one.[43]

The opposition of atomistic individual versus undifferentiated exterior itself must be subverted. This is where the individuation characteristic of plant metamorphosis (never completely inside, nor completely outside) becomes important for Irigaray. Irigaray's claim is that the possibility of a different relationship to the transcendental can only emerge if the feminine is granted its own specificity in its relation to language. As Irigaray writes in the preface to the Japanese edition of *Elemental Passions*, "The paradigms of masculine transcendency, which is sometimes considered neutral or bisexual, must be modified in order to establish a feminine transcendency."[44] Such a specificity, like the organism of the plant in contrast to that of the animal, would "reject all closure or circularity in discourse—any constitution of *arche* or of *telos*."[45] The articulation of a feminine subject, likewise, must render any attempt to co-opt it into predetermined structures of "neutral" subjectivity problematic.

In *Elemental Passions*, Irigaray asks a question of a presumably masculine interlocutor:

Do you want the flower to open only once? The unveiling of the opening would then belong to you. The beauty or truth of the opening would be your discovery. Proposed and exposed in one definitive blossoming. The nightly closing of the flower, its flooding back into itself would not take place. Either it would not yet know the sun and would be in the oblivion of sleep, or you would already have unveiled it and it would never return to the shadows. Its becoming would be arrested when you revealed it by day. Growth suspended in ecstasy, the ideal flowering for you.[46]

Here Irigaray seems to be discussing reading and interpretation as much as fixation in an essentialized identity. "Woman," as part of the historical metaphorical register that includes, as we have seen, both "plant" and "nature" in its range, marks that moment that cannot be decided, which always destabilizes in advance the possibility of fixing its ground. Real flowers open and shut, unfold and then withdraw, have a temporal existence. To appropriate this unveiling would be to freeze blossoming into an eternal present, an ideal flowering that reflects the solidity of metaphorical appropriation. The "return to the shadows" is as necessary a facet of the metaphor of growth, metamorphosis, and blossoming as is expansion and disclosure. Here again Irigaray makes a plea for an understanding of nature that does not ultimately refer back to an atomistic subject or self that controls, subdues, and ultimately kills or fixates its natural movement. The flowering must not, in other words, be assimilated into a dialectic that would make it constantly available. At the same time, as Whitford reminds us, for Irigaray, "If multiplicity is to be celebrated, it has to be *after* sexual difference and not . . . by simply bypassing it."[47]

We tend to dismiss flowers as rhetorical flourishes, but Irigaray is doing more than decorating her text. A flower opens up *more than once*. Its "unveiling" is not a definitive, univocal one, but is periodic, episodic. In *The Forgetting of Air*, Irigaray writes:

> Indefinitely open and closed, she unfurls this strange world where outside and inside unite in a light embrace. Never set out, the contours wed each other in overflowing growth that never quits the medium that gives rise to it. That never abandons the body that gives it life. That does not set itself up with the haughty affirmation of a form that draws its vigor from that from which it parts. It rather abides in the delicate entwining of all dimensions: horizontal efflorescences.[48]

The horizontal efflorescences combat the vertical, hermeneutical reading style that seeks to expose the root, a structure that mimics the erect posture of the tree or the animal, in particular the human animal. We have seen that vegetative imagery has been used to connote exactly the contrary of the kind of reading promoted here, through metaphors of grounding and rootedness. This is why Deleuze and Guattari are so careful to distinguish between different kinds of "plant" readings. Thus, at the same time that Irigaray uses positive images of efflorescence to connote what she in other places calls a "sensible transcendental," a kind of Kantian universal in the sense of reflective judgment that arises out of and cannot be separated from the sensuous particular, she also uses the language of "blooming" to indicate a certain masculine usurpation of the feminine ground for the sake of its own fecundity. In *The Forgetting of Air*, she uses the French verb *s'épanouir* to indicate this tumescent, appropriative blooming, and *efflorescence* to refer to a feminine blossoming that overcomes the ontological status assigned to it by the history of metaphysics.

She asks: "Do the installations put into place by man to position himself as man cloak the fact that he makes his own nature bloom only at the price of squaring up and masking nature?"[49] And further: "Must letting-be be understood as letting man's thinking be unfolded/deployed, or as letting nature bloom?"[50] This secondary blooming is a source that conceals the ground from which it arose, the "whole" (gendered feminine).[51] The secondary source comes about only by the masculine appropriation of the feminine into what Irigaray calls a creation of *physis* out of *techne*,[52] which she associates with Heidegger's work. The expansion of the concept of *physis* as bringing-forth, to render the distinction between *physis* and *techne* problematic, is akin to the expansion of masculine subjectivity to make room for the feminine in a process of assimilation. What Irigaray here calls a "forgetting of air" is a forgetfulness of the silent ground out of which all conceptualization arises, the unconscious ground of nature for which Heidegger himself searched fruitlessly, that is, the feminine as it has been figured in the history of metaphysics. "Saving" this ground from oblivion involves not a total rejection of the rhetoric that has structured it, but rather a subversion of that rhetoric's privileged metaphorics in a way that will reveal the strength of the concealed feminine within.

Efflorescence privileges the gesture of an opening at the very source of philosophizing, one that by virtue of its very open-endedness forecloses the possibility of a stable grounding. By using metaphors of plant growth, Irigaray emphasizes the indefiniteness of individuation and the possibility of multiple, simultaneous origins. Efflorescence opens up roots and routes, advocating movement over stasis, temporalizing over eternity or timeless origins. In identifying the purposive with the human mind's interaction with nature, Kant gave the history of philosophy an invaluable means of complicating the simple binary distinction between universal and particular, between conditioning rule and conditioned or determined situation, between necessity and freedom. Irigaray follows the third *Critique* by taking the product of reflective judgment, the figure of the plant conceived out of the observation of metamorphosis, grafting, and perennial fecundity, as the basis for a provisional universal that enunciates the importance of sexual difference for grounding any ethics.

Irigaray reacts against the totalizing, colonizing power of hegemonic philosophical narratives, such as the Hegelian one, that make every outside an inside, every other the same, by proposing, as Hölderlin had, an alternative structure of alterity in metamorphosis and germination. Rather than negating difference, efflorescence is productive of difference. For Irigaray, efflorescence marks the break that inaugurates, but cannot be reduced to, language, symbolics, identity, and order. This break might be seen in Sophocles' tragedy *Antigone*, which, as we have already noted, Irigaray reads through Hegel's appropriation of it in the *Phenomenology of Spirit*. In his discussion of *Antigone*, Hegel aligns the masculine with subjectivity, the polis, and freedom, and the feminine with the family, the private sphere, blind adherence to the divine law, and the repetition of the cyclical time of reproduction. As such, woman is described as acting "unconsciously," in the sense of the genius, whose unconscious channeling of nature's forces makes her unable to articulate the rules for the production of her art. Antigone is unconscious, according to Hegel, because she follows the law of the family, which is also the divine law and hence the law of nature insofar as it pertains to human beings. Her lack of consciousness stems not from her refusal to question the authority of the law of the family, but from her incapacity to articulate her reasons in terms of a decision.

Yet Antigone does not withdraw, unlike the "beautiful soul" criticized by Hegel, or the purely unconscious artist in the tradition of vegetable genius. Her proscribed intervention into the political marks the withdrawing ground of sexual difference. Irigaray critiques Hegel's reading as manifesting Western metaphysics' tendency to reduce the feminine to the unconscious, silent ground, or to a negating force. Antigone's position is somewhat different, and Irigaray focuses on her as a woman who stands between the two laws. Irigaray views Antigone as neither a free citizen who refuses to submit to the law of the state, nor an unconscious vessel for the divine law, but rather as the very moment of the possibility of transformation or displacement rather than dialectical subsumption of this binary opposition. In transgressing Creon's edict, Antigone expresses Kant's reflective judgment, by constituting her purpose from a particular rather than subsuming a particular act under a law. She marks the fragile possibility of a third path between the absolute determinism of law and the unreflective conception of freedom presupposed by the discourse of rights.

Irigaray thus complicates her reading of the place of the feminine configured as silent ground in the history of metaphysics by emphasizing efflorescence as both a non-originary or nondeterminate origin (an origin that withdraws from articulation), and as that which inaugurates subjectivity. As particular, the plant represents the claim that the subject is sexed and finite and thus the impossibility of conflating masculinity with neutrality or universality. As indefinitely individuated and often dually sexed, it resists any possibility of recuperation in a single mode. As such, the metonym works productively to multiply readings and significations. Its signature precludes the temptation to closure, resists an end that will never come.

Books do come to an end eventually, however. What this study has sought to do is both to investigate a facet of nineteenth-century *Naturphilosophie* and its antecedents that has been too little studied except as a literary trope, and to suggest that the figure of vegetable genius transformed into the "vegetative soul" might provide a fruitful alternative to the recently much-denigrated figure of the modern subject. It is interesting to me that the critique of the configuration of the subject was already in place as early as the nineteenth century, and that even though we might want to insist that German Idealism remains a metaphysical system based on the primacy of the subject, we must also concede that the form of that subjectivity has little in common with the atomistic subject found in Descartes and Hobbes, among others. It is appropriate to conclude with a suggestion toward another beginning, another opening, since that is what a plantlike reading does. Contemporary Continental philosophy, with its figures of dissemination, rhizomatic growth, and efflorescence, clearly has discerned the possibilities in the language of vegetative growth.

NOTES

1. In "The Way Back into the Ground of Metaphysics," trans. Walter Kaufmann, in *Existentialism from Dostoevsky to Sartre*, ed. Walter Kaufmann (New York and London: Penguin Books, 1975), 265.
2. Martin Heidegger, *The Principle of Reason*, trans. Reginald Lilly (Bloomington: Indiana University Press, 1991), 35ff.
3. Heidegger, *The Principle of Reason*, 37.
4. Heidegger, *The Principle of Reason*, 38.
5. Jacques Derrida, "Otobiographies: The Teaching of Nietzsche and the Politics of the Proper Name," in *The Ear of the Other: The Teaching of Nietzsche and the Politics of the Proper Name*, 1–40 (Lincoln, Nebraska: 1985); quote, 32.
6. Jacques Derrida, *Dissemination*, trans. Barbara Johnson (Chicago: University of Chicago Press, 1981), 53.
7. Jacques Derrida, *Dissemination*, 45.
8. Jacques Derrida, *Dissemination*, 52.
9. Jacques Derrida, *Dissemination*, 53.
10. My suspicion is that in Goethe's writings on botany and his impatience with the botanical classification system of his time, we can see the glimmerings of the idea of the rhizome

book, the book that would not follow the slow-growing tree with clearly observable stages of growth and clearly distinguishable organs. Gilles Deleuze and Félix Guattari, "Introduction: Rhizome," in *A Thousand Plateaus: Capitalism and Schizophrenia*, trans. Brian Massumi (Minneapolis and London: Minnesota University Press, 1987), 3–25.

11. Deleuze and Guattari, "Introduction: Rhizome," 5.
12. Deleuze and Guattari, "Introduction: Rhizome."
13. Deleuze and Guattari, "Introduction: Rhizome," 6.
14. Deleuze and Guattari, "Introduction: Rhizome," 20.
15. Deleuze and Guattari, "Introduction: Rhizome," 21.
16. *The Diaries of Franz Kafka*, ed. Max Brod, trans. Joseph Kresh (New York: Schocken, 1948), 12. Cited in "Introduction: Rhizome," 23.
17. *Diaries of Franz Kafka*, cited in "Introduction: Rhizome," 15.
18. *Diaries of Franz Kafka*, cited in "Introduction: Rhizome," 18.
19. Different flowers as well as their positions or various other manipulations were assigned meanings, so that a bouquet sent to a lover would have a signification, from invitation ("Come tonight") to question ("Is your husband home?"), to affirmation ("You are beautiful"). In France, in particular, many treatises "explaining" this practice were published in the nineteenth century. Goethe's *West-Oestlicher Divan* includes poems on secret writing using flowers and fruit. See Jack Goody, "The Secret Language of Flowers in France," in *The Culture of Flowers* (Cambridge: Cambridge University Press, 1993).
20. Sarah Kofman, *Nietzsche and Metaphor*, trans. Duncan Large (Stanford: Stanford University Press, 1993), 14.
21. Aristotle, *Rhetoric* 1410b, 12.
22. See *De Anima* (415a 15–416b 30); *Nichomachean Ethics* (1102a 33); *Politics* (1254a 35–1254b 15) and (1260a 5–30); *Generation of Animals* (736a 25–737a, 30) and (787a 26–30).
23. Luce Irigaray, "How to Conceive of a Girl," in *Speculum of the Other Woman*, trans. Gillian C. Gill (Ithaca: Cornell University Press, 1985), 163.
24. Luce Irigaray, *I Love to You: Sketch of a Possible Felicity in History*, trans. Alison Martin (New York: Routledge, 1996), 38–39.
25. Margaret Whitford, *Luce Irigaray: Philosophy in the Feminine* (London: Routledge, 1991), 95.
26. In the final chapter of *Luce Irigaray: Philosophy in the Feminine*, Whitford uses the language of social contract, specifically the philosophy of Rousseau, to clarify an argument she is making about Irigaray's philosophy. She argues that Irigaray's philosophy can be conceptualized as saying that "women are still, symbolically, in the 'state of nature' and need to be brought into the social contract" (p. 170), assimilating social order and symbolic order. Whitford's aim is admittedly to bolster her cogent argument that Irigaray's apparently biologistic remarks about the female body and about nature are in fact statements about the adequacy or inadequacy of the symbolic order and the place allotted therein to women. Indeed, conceptualizing the difficult synthesis of the terminology of Lacanian psychoanalysis and Hegelian dialectic used by Irigaray in terms of social contract theory does render it considerably clearer. I nevertheless find it problematic to describe Irigaray as a contract

theorist, because, as Whitford acknowledges, she draws much more often on Hegel, who is an anti-contract theorist, for good reasons, it seems to me; most prominent among them, the problematic status of the subject and its relation to the social order in social contract theory. I am not sure it is even conceivable to reconcile Irigaray's conception of the feminine subject with social contract theory.

27. Luce Irigaray, *Sexes and Genealogies*, trans. Gillian C. Gill (New York: Columbia University Press, 1993), 113.
28. Irigaray, "How to Conceive of a Girl," 163.
29. Irigaray, "How to Conceive of a Girl," 162–63.
30. Luce Irigaray, "The 'Mechanics of Fluids," in *This Sex Which Is Not One* (Ithaca: Cornell University Press, 1985), 109–110.
31. Jacques Lacan, *Écrits: A Selection*, trans. Alan Sheridan (New York: W.W. Norton, 1977), 146–178.
32. Jane Gallop, *Reading Lacan* (Ithaca: Cornell University Press, 1985), 128 ff.
33. Jacques Lacan, *Le Séminaire III: Les Psychoses* (Paris; Seuil, 1981), 259; cited in Gallop, *Reading Lacan*, 129.
34. Luce Irigaray, *The Forgetting of Air in Martin Heidegger*, trans. Mary Beth Mader (Austin: University of Texas Press, 1999), 23–24.
35. See, for example, *The Marine Lover of Friedrich Nietzsche*, trans. Gillian C. Gill (New York: Columbia University Press, 1991), 110–116; Irigaray, *Sexes and Genealogies*, 110–115; "The Eternal Irony of the Community," in Luce Irigaray, *Speculum of the Other Woman*, 167; and Irigaray, "How to Conceive of a Girl," 214–226.
36. Irigaray, *Sexes and Genealogies*, 112–113.
37. Elizabeth Grosz, "Irigaray and the Divine," in *Transitions in Continental Philosophy*, ed. Arleen B. Dallery, Stephen H. Watson, and E. Marya Bower, 117–128 (Albany: State University of New York Press, 1994), 118.
38. Patricia Huntington, *Ecstatic Subjects, Utopia, and Recognition: Kristeva, Heidegger, Irigaray* (Albany: State University of New York Press, 1998), 127.
39. Huntington, *Ecstatic Subjects, Utopia, and Recognition.*
40. Whitford, *Luce Irigaray*, 76.
41. Whitford, *Luce Irigaray*, 89.
42. Irigaray, *Sexes and Genealogies*, 112–113.
43. Irigaray, *The Forgetting of Air in Martin Heidegger*, 107–108.
44. Luce Irigaray, *Elemental Passions*, trans. Joanne Collie and Judith Still (New York: Routledge, 1992), 4.
45. "Questions," in *This Sex Which Is Not One*, trans. Catherine Porter (Ithaca, NY: Cornell University Press, 1985), 153.
46. Irigaray, *Elemental Passions*, 31–32.
47. Whitford, *Luce Irigaray*, 84.
48. Irigaray, *The Forgetting of Air in Martin Heidegger*, 106.

49. Irigaray, *The Forgetting of Air in Martin Heidegger*, 18.
50. Irigaray, *The Forgetting of Air in Martin Heidegger*.
51. Irigaray, *The Forgetting of Air in Martin Heidegger*, 44.
52. Irigaray, *The Forgetting of Air in Martin Heidegger*, 87.

Main Pathway: Orientations

Subthemes

Proceed to Ethics, p. 359
Proceed to Time, p. 359

24

THE COLOUR GREEN

Prudence Gibson

In the beginning there was green: a chaos of plant cells.
—Stefano Mancuso, *Brilliant Green*

Human representations of nature as green are prolific. The history of the colour—as pigments mixed by artists, as iconic sculptural motifs of green figures, as environmental politics and as more recent philosophies of plant life—has influenced a battle between conventions of nature's expression and changing perceptions of the vegetal world. This chapter addresses the colour green as an aesthetic, cultural, and political tool.

Living cells, capable of performing photosynthesis, first appeared on earth more than three and half billion years ago.[1] Plant life was later charted in the creationist doctrine as the earth sprouted vegetation on the third day, when plants yielded seeds and trees bore fruit . . . and God thought it was good.[2] Conversely, Derek Jarman writes of the Garden of Eden (and of Adam and Eve's eviction from it, post apple-eating) and recalls the angry Adam hacking down the Tree of Knowledge to build the first house.[3] Such terrible irony: as the utopian garden was lost and with that first tree slaughtered by man's hand, as Jarman believed, we began

Originally published as Prudence Gibson, "The Colour Green," in *Covert Plants: Vegetal Consciousness and Agency in an Anthropocentric World*, ed. Prudence Gibson and Baylee Brits (Santa Barbara, CA: Punctum Books, 2018), 163–181. Reproduced with kind permission of the author and publisher.

our environmental demise. Climate change is biting at our heels, and all mythic and philosophical stories of 'green' can now be seen with the eco-eyes of hindsight and reclaimed as a vibrant slice of the colour wheel.

Green, as the vegetal, exists broadly across the surface of the planet as biotic matter: it extends from algae to apple tree, from underground fern to the canopy of a Tasmanian pine, from nori weed to samphires (succulent halophytes). The greens of the sea, the river, the forest, and the grassy plains are the colours we know deeply and in a fundamentally psychological way. These green and natural things affect our mood and our primal urges to strive, to provide, to care. "Green" affects our sense of wonder in the face of life. The fear of losing contact with the natural world is solastalgia, a neologism referring to climate-change-induced stress. How we can build a positive perception of *nature* as a construct of imagination or a material and sensual collective memory is a chronic problem in contemporary society.[4] It is due to the loss of green from our everyday habitats that greenness is more than a hue of nostalgia; it has also become a keen political weapon, an activated and dynamic arena of civic and civil debate. Thinking green is the same as thinking for *the long now*, where plans and concepts need to have longevity and long-distance strategic clout.

THE PHILOSOPHIES OF GREEN

Green has conventionally been relegated to the backdrop of human action. Nature as a wilderness is something "over there" and far away from civilised living. Jeffrey Nealon charts the way plants have been considered in light of their excessive growth, for production, and for further generation. This is what has placed them on the lowest rung of the ontological ladder, following Aristotle's conceptions.[5] In *De Anima*, he asks, "What is the soul of plant, man and beast?" and Nealon qualifies that this question is less about essence and more about differing capacities.[6]

Hearing green, eating green, thinking green, and representing green are all intrinsic to extended philosophies of the vegetal. Prior to any Christian texts, Aristotle spoke of how he believed plants were close to inanimate beings.[7] This lowly status of plants is misleading, however, as the term "inanimate" refers to a lack of mobility rather than a lack of sentience. Aristotle's thinking reflected the ideas of the day that mobility, vast distances, or rapid movement across the surface of the earth was not associated with plants. However, seed passage (via wind) and expansive subterranean movement (via root growth) contradict Aristotle's position. This perception of plant life as less relevant than other species does not constitute the "green thinking" that this essay provokes. The environmental, social, and cultural history of the colour green can be presented as more than a political emblem, more than a representation of nature.

If we think of green in Kantian terms, then we might understand the limits of the concept of the colour. If a leaf is given to us, as Kant explains in *Critique of Pure Reason*, then we understand the form, texture, and colour of a leaf.[8] Green things are described as green so that there is a consensus that the given colour, described as such, is in fact green. When Kant says, "Nature is beautiful because it looks like art,"[9] he is calling our attention to how we fall in love with our human versions of the world in which we live. Kant's suspicion of this recognition of green as a colour is pertinent, as it disrupts the way we assume we understand perceptual experiences as a whole, and in particular how we understand our ocular experience of colour. Our perception of the colour green in nature as a colour of goodness, bounty, sustenance, and moral good is plagued, then, by our conditioning of all experiences as humans. If nature's laws are contingent,[10] as Kant says, then perhaps we need to connect experience with perception. Kant's cautious mistrust of green makes sense, even more so when bearing in mind the current associations of green as pure politics.

Any ocular misgivings regarding colour versus perception of colour are played out in colour blindness. Both my sons have been tested for and diagnosed with red/green colour blindness. The general physician used Dr. Shinobu Isihara's scanned plates of coloured dots which form shapes and numbers. Colour-blind people can distinguish between red and green, but not the same tones as those others see. The discernible features of saturation are different for them. In other words, they literally see the world differently. There are degrees of colour blindness; one end of the spectrum being where my sons sit, where they see different shades of red-green colour from others; and the other end of the spectrum where people only see shades of monochrome brown, a dreary fusion of red and green.

The colour-blind among us learn that the colour they see as grass, for instance, is green. In other words, we are trained to understand and perceive colour. The opportunistic side of me then wonders: if we are so impressionable and so open to forming associations between what we see and how we perceive it, then is there a way to make people understand and perceive our environmental plight more keenly? In other words, can the colour green be used to shift our perceptions of "humans in the world" to "the world in humans"? This requires a dismantling of boundaries of life as lived by humans to include life as lived by all things.

EATING GREEN

Vegans follow an ethical life by not eating any produce from any living animal or insect. They eat a lot of green. What will we do now that new plant science proves that plants have sensory capacities, cognitive-like behaviour, and communication skills? Natalie Angier brings to task the ethical vegans and the moralist vegetarians by reminding us that plants exhibit sensory capacities—hearing, smelling and talking.[11] Discovering that plants have sensory capacities, including being able to sonically "hear" the reverberations of a caterpillar eating their leaves and responsively trying to curl up its leaves, is disturbing.[12] It is also a reality check to discover that acacia trees emit a poisonous chemical during drought times when oxen over-eat their leaves, to warn down-wind acacias of the imminent threat and also to kill the oxen. The problem of discovering these new high-capacity behaviours of plants creates questions regarding the ethics of eating them.

Michael Marder tackles this sticky issue at the very end of *Plant-Thinking* and suggests we eat everything, but with care and ethics. His advice is "if you want to eat ethically, eat like a plant." He suggests that we don't have to eat inorganic minerals, but that what is needed is a "complete and concerted de-commodification of vegetal life."[13] So, this is an effort to eat with a green ontology (in this case a sense of fairness and of equal relevance) and not to homogenise what we eat. The plant replenishes us but it has a greater function in the world than as mere nourishment for us.

Gary Francione, who has written widely on animal rights and proclaims an abolitionist vegan approach to eating, participated in an interesting debate with Michael Marder on this issue.[14] Francione stated that "if plants are not sentient—if they have no subjective awareness—then they have no interests. That is, they cannot desire, or want, or prefer anything. There is simply no reason to believe that plants have any level of perceptual awareness or a mind-like quality that prefers, wants, or desires anything.'[15] This position devalues the rights of any form of life that cannot prove its own sentience. Marder responds to Francione: "It does not make sense to me to advocate something clearly unethical—a total instrumentalization of certain living beings, or plants—in the name of ethics—a complete de-instrumentalization of other kinds of living beings, or animals. In such advocacy, the end does not justify the means, but the means annul the end."[16]

What these discourses highlight is the green methodology of shifting models of ontology away from a human-centred view to a multiple species view. Plants, like humans and animals, engage in non-conscious determination regarding their growth. This does not mean a decision is not made.[17] For Marder this is an elemental and philosophical call for a re-structuring of nature ontology; of the food-chain model of being.

THE COLOUR GREEN

Green, the colour, has facilitated shifts in art history as well as philosophy and geology. It exists as a pigment on paper and as oil paint mixed on canvas since its 19th-century industrial development. Green is taken from below the earth's surface in biotic forms as part of the formations of a deep geology such as the magical malachite. Malachite is a rare semi-precious material that is so mesmerising it incites deep envious desire. Or there are the green-stained stromatolites, rock-like structures that are living fossils. As Bryson says, stromatolites are "living rocks—quietly functioning replicas of the very first organic structures ever to live on earth. You are experiencing the world as it was 3.5 billion years ago."[18]

Likewise, green appears as scientific play: it is conjured in cathode ray experiments where a charged electric impulse (cathode ray) is presented to tubes with slightly varying gas. The lower the gas present, the greener the light fluoresces that is reflected in the glass tube.[19] Fluorescence is naturally green. Green also appears above the earth's surface, high in the atmosphere, in the form of the vibrant hues of the Northern Lights.

"Green" has become an increasingly potent subjectile force in science-centred contemporary "nature art," or bio-art. Think of American artist George Gessart, who bred green plants for art as early as the 1970s,[20] and Brazilian artist Eduardo Kac,[21] whose transgenic co-species experiments changed our understanding of the delineations between human and plant. Both have left a poignant mark on the art-nature scene, blurring the boundaries between the species of plant and human. Land art, plant art, trans-species (human–plant), eco-art: all these praxes follow a green discourse; they participate in a green contract of drawing awareness to tracts of land and also represent themselves in art within the prism of a green or environmental conceptual theory. It is this nexus of all three green elements that makes new iterations of environmental art the colour of political force.

Writer and natural scientist Johann Wolfgang von Goethe (1749–1832) believed there were only two pure colours: blue and yellow, but that magenta had a non-spectral, essential role.[22] If darkness and light interact, and shadowed colour must be added to a full circle, as Goethe proposed, then these two main colours of blue and yellow might meet most obviously at the point of green. Goethe felt the prismatic fringes of any given prism were where all the colours could be derived.[23] His experimental mode of inquiry and his methodology acknowledged the experimental mediation of the subject and the object, that is, the perceiver and the perceived.

The colour green as a field of inquiry, then, can be both a method and a theory of inquiry—the green in art and the green of art, the green in politics and the green of politics, the green in philosophy and the green of philosophy. Goethe's years of observation, poetry, and theoretical writing, sometimes published together, are an example of how experience and perception might correlate somewhere in between the subject and object in art.[24]

Green is a loaded word with extended associations that can't be undone unless we first understand them. An enquiry into its etymology as a colour, a pigment, and a natural material helps to resuscitate the force that has always powered this wondrous colour. Vigorous growth and grass are the associated ideas connected with the word "green." Green is growth; it is the green light of permission (go!); it is the stimulus to change and to move forward, and it is a tender space of the yet-to-ripen. Axioms or clichés surrounding the colour green abound and consistently suggest desirability:

Green is good,
It's not easy being green,
Moving on to greener pastures,
The grass is always greener on the other side,
Oh, she is so green.
(etc.)

Green, as a colour of aesthetically high stakes, achieved newfound interest in 1775 when the Swedish apothecarist Carl Wilhelm Scheele began isolating chlorine and experimenting on chlorine compounds before at last turning his attentions to the chemical properties of arsenic. He soon had a green compound copper arsenite which he manufactured as 'Scheele's green.' The paint colour was used by Turner's

1805 sketch *Guildford from the Banks of the Wey* (1805) and in Edourd Manet's *Music in the Tuileries Gardens* (1862). Manet's was a late use of Scheele's green because it was out-foxed by the better compound, discovered by Wilhelm Sattler, "copper aceto-arsenite, whose brilliant green crystals are made via the reaction of verdigris dissolved in vinegar with white arsenic and sodium carbonate."[25] Otherwise known as emerald green, it became more commercially available by 1822.[26]

Surely life in the nineteenth century had enough mordant troubles, what with its high mortality rates and short life spans, without manufacturing poisonous colours. The arsenic content of these arsenite green colours, used in wallpapers, proved to be gravely hazardous. Naturally, paint releases faint dust particles when brushed or knocked. If exposed to rising damp conditions, the pigments would start to decompose and release an arsenic gas. Napoleon Bonaparte is rumoured to have died from his emerald green paint.[27]

Green also has historical infamy as a mode of coloured room. A room of green! There are Malachite Rooms in Castello Chapultepec, Mexico and in The Hermitage, Moscow. These palatial rooms are designed and constructed using the earthy substance, malachite. Malachite is extracted as a semiprecious geological specimen from deep in the ground. As a mined material, it of course has imperial and economic baggage. Used as decoration for Russian and South American excess, this gives Malachite a quite particular 19th-century colonial imperial power.

This brings to mind the colonial trend of collecting specimens as an expression of imperial power—the attainment of knowledge and the kudos of ownership—and as a way of spreading tentacles of influence into far-flung places. Of course, these trips of botanical collecting were more than a means of obtaining science. They were also a means of reconnoiter, that is, finding plants that had medicinal value that could be harvested for a profit. In more recent post-colonial times, Ayahuasca trips in Peru continue this tradition. Ayahuasca is a natural ceremonial drug, taken to enhance your experience of the world. Its pursuit has started to cause concern for the Peruvian government. This tourist experience offers journeys into the jungle to try out the hallucinatory ayahuasca plant.[28] The ayahuasca hallucinogen is made is by using several species of the genus mixed together. It is believed that local Peruvians could find the appropriate shrub leaf (*chakruna*) to mix with the vine root (*caapi*) by listening to the plants communicate with one another.[29] Recent plant research regarding plant communication by chemical emissions,[30] which looks at the opening and closing of leaf nodes, and the information passed amongst undergrown roots via mycorrhizal communications, make this Peruvian myth believable.

GREEN MYTHOLOGY

If green matter exists beneath the earth's surface, and it can be transformed/created by alchemy as an artist's choice of pigment, so too it has had significance in other, more mythological modalities. Green, in the shape of the Green Man, has a long and apotropaic history. The Green Man is an iconic image that has acted and performed as an important variation of the "wildman," a cautionary symbol, a sign of fertility, virility, and growth, as a warning against the gates of hell. So, the image of the Green Man has been considered in Western and Eastern thought as both benevolent provider and ominous threat. In ecclesiastical and secular buildings alike, the iconic image of the Green Man appears as gargoyles and interior architectural design features. This paradoxical figure entered mythology, pagan worship, and finally the Christian church. Imagery of this interaction reaches back in European history to early architectural gargoyles and to German manuscript illustrations from as early as the 12th century.

As Carolyn Dinshaw writes,

> My ultimate interest in analyzing the Green Man is to explore ideas of interrelations between human and nonhuman that—even as species boundaries are broken and traversed—acknowledge the histories of subjugation and devaluation enabling that human/ non-human distinction in the first place. My goal, then, is not only to trace the afterlife of this medieval imagery but also, and most importantly, to "think with" the Green Man myself in order to develop a framework for understanding human/non-human relations.[31]

The late filmmaker Derek Jarman, who was also renowned for his garden landscaping, refers to the woods being reclaimed via the Green Man: "These woods were the home of the Green Man whose lichen-covered face stares at you from a roof boss in the church. The Green Man moves slowly like the sloth, which is green with algae."[32] He reminds us not to forget that not all green is good. There are poisons in your hedgerow, and deadly agency in your brewed herbs. Green aconite, deadly nightshade, and cuckoo pint will *do you in*.

Norwich Cathedral has a number of leafy heads—nine visages with oak, maple, strawberry, buttercup, or gilded hawthorn leaves. Richard Mabey reads these foliate faces as, in one case, a "gigolo" and in another, a "diablo." He refers to them as "symbolically sinful" and "undoubtedly having a theological status." He cites Kathleen Basford, a scholar who has worked with the history of green men, as creating an admonitory interpretation.[33] Mabey traces Basford's research into 8th-century theologian Rabanus Maurus's interpretation of Green Man's leaves as sins of the flesh from lustful and wicked men, whereas William Anderson sees the Green Man as a more general universal figure of Gaian connection to the earth.[34]

While Anderson's interpretation makes more sense from a contemporary point of view, as it allows for the historical changes from Satan-like terror to more bucolic and wine-guzzling naughtiness to develop, his argument for the leaves emanating from the mouth still needs to be discussed. The attraction of plant imagery in the form of a human-hybrid face (foliate face) began as a seasonal worship. With each new quarter, fruit and berries would arrive, small crops would be harvested, and herbs would be gathered. These gifts were worshipped and mollified. This entered culture through processions, Morris dances (folk music with bells on their shins), and architecture.[35] The pagan worship included both praising and fearing the concept of a green man, a monster that may come out of the woods in spring to rape the women. This leads on from a long history of mythological rapes by the gods. Green Man was a figure of fertility but also of bounty and fecund promise; The Green Man of summer.

They reflect a wish to dominate nature and to guard humanity from evil. Beginning as pagan images, the church soon adopted the Green Man as a means of converting the heathens, appealing to their base framework of belief. The widespread use of these apotropaic symbols is interesting—across Britain, Spain, France, Turkey, etc. The Green Man appears as an emblem on inn signs across Britain by the 16th century. Not just a symbol of fertility and sexual prowess or strength, he was a Bacchus-like figure, a jester, and someone to lead processions and pageants. In the 17th century, the Green Man appeared in association with Distilleries, such as drunk woodmen (wildmen).[36] The Wildman or Green Man became iconic as "sans god"—the necessity of god to keep evil and devils at bay. The Wildman was typically stupid, but the Green Man was pleasantly stupefied by his intoxicating liquors. So there was a linear shift from Wild Man to Green Man of revelry.

The Green Man, as symbol of irrepressible fertility, potential evil, and finally of bacchanalian fun, has an indeterminacy to it. There has been very little documentation of the Green Man image that has existed for over two thousand years, in some churches outnumbering images of Christ. Jarman notes the related green mythology:

But other legends rose out of myth. The Green Knight comes to King Arthur's court, his hair and complexion green, riding a green horse, and carrying an axe of green gold. He commands Gawain to meet him at the Green Chapel at the spring solstice. The Holy Grail was formed from an emerald struck from the crown of Lucifer by the archangel Michael . . . a green chalice.[37]

While the Green Man is a separate entity from Robin Hood or the Green Knight, different from the Swamp Thing or The Hulk, there are some characteristics in common, such as a connection with the wilderness—that which cannot be contained. Green Man is both good and evil.[38] We must be reminded that Green Man is more than a malevolent gargoyle.[39] He is an elusive figure whose mystique provokes our imagination.

THE POLITICS OF GREEN

Have you ever leaned against a paper bark tree and pulled at its papery surface, listening to the sound of the wind shuffling through its leaves, not thinking about whether that tugging of its bark caused a sensory effect in the tree system? Have you ever thoughtlessly snapped off a rose bush branch to smell the intoxicating aroma that sends you into olfactory bliss, not thinking about whether this might elicit a response of chemical activity? I am guilty. Now, with all that we know about communication via chemical emissions in plants as signals, for example, via Suzanne Simard's work,[40] and with all that we know about their sensory capacities via the work of Chamovitz,[41] it is the time to deeply consider or re-orient green politics as a social, cultural, and ethical phenomenon in all its iterations.

There is no possibility of turning back the damage of multiple mining sites, careless logging, overuse of land, and erosion from clearing and fracking. In the 1970s, the Western Australian government had a policy where any owners were allowed to clear native bush land of up to one million acres per year in order to develop more farming land. Called the Iron Ball Taxonomy, these kinds of legislations caused early friction between farmers and "greenies."[42] The tension between green activists and farmers was especially peaky in the 1980s and 1990s, but things have slowly changed.

Val Plumwood reveals the fundamental issues that plague various green political parties around the world:

What might loosely be called "green theory" includes several subcritiques and positions whose relationship has recently been the subject of vigorous and often bitter debate, and which have some common ground but apparently a number of major divergences. The debate seems to have revealed that the green movement still lacks a coherent liberating theory, and raises the question of whether it is and must remain no more than a political alliance of convenience between different interest groups affected differently by the assault on nature.[43]

Plumwood also makes the point that exploitation and disregard for the environment via high technology agriculture, high-yield farming, and sales and licenses for mining to foreign countries not only damages the ecosystems, but also damages its parts. In other words, it's not just the land itself that is left with high levels of toxin, extreme erosion, dirty water runoff, agronomy deterioration, and water table subsidence, etc. These damages are quantifiable, but so are the people that are exploited in the making. The farmers who are forced to sell. The bird life that must leave their habitat. The miners who have to bear the separation from families for months on end. Or the fauna and flora that are completely devastated. Promises of regeneration are hollow, being expensive, finite, and poorly regulated. It's impossible to recreate a thriving ecosystem just by planting some saplings and never returning to check on progress. Waterways are ruined and insects are long gone. Plumwood says, "We die of the product (the destruction of nature) and also of the process (technological brutality alias technological rationality serving the end of commodification)."[44]

Plumwood's idea is that the lack of unity both internationally and within the Greens Party in Australia is caused by a lack of focus about what to do and how to do it. There are economic complexities to mining that make the concept of a domination over nature sound a little precious. There is no strong leadership suggesting alternatives that are powerful enough to make a difference. Perhaps there are too many of us, the deep ecologists, and not enough of them, the social ecologists. We could follow Plumwood's advice and address both the product and the process of ecological assault and create a politics of care that attends to both.

The big question is whether politics can lead the charge for change. Or do we instead need a subtle, sub-political operation of "green" conversion? Although our perceptions of green life may remain intact (most humans care for the greenery in their lives), the experience of anthropocentric human life (the damage humans have caused to nature since industrialisation) suggest the incapacity of humans to stem the flow of neo-liberal decision making and overuse of resources, which leaves only a fetid stench.

Green politics is young. For instance, Australia's Greens party is only 24 years old. Many green political parties are susceptible to the forces of economic and political pressure, and they are under duress to be effective as well as moral, to lead a nation as well as follow more ethical lines of governance. These quandaries make it difficult for green groups to flourish.

There are legal issues surrounding plant (nature) rights, and they are growing in a tumescent way, but there are still no legal precedents in Australia, as there are in Switzerland, New Zealand, Ecuador, et al. The Greens Party is young in Australia yet still one of the earliest protagonists around the world. The United Tasmanian Party was the first to run candidates in 1972 and were the first group to espouse green ideals. The successful fighting of the flooding of the Franklin Dam in Tasmania in 1978–1983 was a landmark event. The German Green Party was established in 1983 and were the first political party based on green politics of social justice environmentalism and non-violence.

More recently in Australia, "wild law" is being discussed in the context of extending current environmental laws away from human actions and to better reflect that the environment has rights. Professor Brendan Mackey, of the Fenner School of Environment and Society at the Australian National University, says that wild law was the "next step in the evolution of environmental law. . . . This is about how law needs to evolve so that it's adequate to meet these big environmental challenges we are facing."[45] Michelle Maloney, a researcher at Griffith University's Socio-Legal Research Centre and advisor of the Australian Earth Laws Alliance, says, "Wild law suggests we look at the world as a community of subjects—that we are only one of many players in the ecological sphere."[46] Her expertise is in earth jurisprudence, or the theory of law, which is a commons-based approach that is centred on the earth and moves her to work towards a governance system that is eco-centric. Cormac Cullinan, influenced by *Should Trees Have Standing* by Christopher Stone, has published *Wild Law: A Manifesto for Earth Justice*,[47] which calls for using systems theory and indigenous systems to build on the small number of wild laws already in place around the world.[48]

A GREEN REMINDER

Earth jurisprudence is slow, but paying attention is always the first step. We can't hear plants and we can't speak to them. Sometimes we don't even notice until someone reminds to look a little harder or tells us to listen with a more attuned ear. The most exciting moment is when we see "green" for what it really is, as something we couldn't see before. The effect is startling.

For instance, one May morning, during the Sydney Writers Festival May 2016, I stood on a bed of mulchy leaves, surrounded by low-slung branches from a huge fig tree. An original creek had been cemented in and straightened, to run from the ridge down to the harbour. By good fortune, there was an incline where Australian poet Eric Avery stood, so the trickle of natural stream water was a constant passage of sonic time.

He read his poem, speaking to the giant fig tree rather than us (a cluster of poetry acolytes). After Bach had danced across his violin to concert standards, there was another poem. And then, Avery began to move his bow in a repetitive allegretto across the strings of his violin. Back and forth, up and over, before joining his instrument with an Aboriginal song learned from his grandfather. This combination of Bach-like reverie and almost moaning of indigenous song which exists on a minimal register with an earthy range created something disruptive. In fact, it was a merging of two cultures, both earthbound, that I had never heard before in tandem. He used his violin like clapping sticks, like a didgeridoo. He found voice from the reverberations of the tree, the rustling of the leaves, and the endless flow of water. The song did not rise to a crescendo, nor did it mimic a narrative arc with repeated choruses. Instead, it existed alongside the tree, winding around its trunk and fluttering around its branches.

The music Avery played was green. He played "to" the tree. He played "for" the tree. In other words, there were flows of energy in Avery's playing that moved beyond the violin and beyond his voice. It was a pattern of green-coloured reverberations that pulsed in the bark, under the fallen leaves, behind the reaching branches. These energies had a colour on this day that was decidedly a deep time green, dark and heavy with the history of aboriginal massacres and stolen land. Yes, Avery's music and singing seemed to offer a redemption. He cooled the red of anger into a green of memorial. He created a sound that matched the glade, in its changed and transfigured form.

But that wasn't the surprising part of the green experience. There was yet something to discover that reminded me to take more care, to peer closely and replace a surface view of nature with a deep ecology view: It was when Avery finished playing music that he told us the place where we stood was a massacre site of Indigenous people. He explained that the grand old fig tree was not the original tree for that spot.

Instead, before white invasion, a paper bark gum tree had been there. *Couldn't we see it?* he asked. *What did he mean?* The poetry lovers looked at each other, bemused, befuddled yet again by our invader whiteness, our inability to see what was in front of us. Patiently, Avery gestured up towards the branching off of the tree and then I saw it.

The limbs of another tree, inside the fig tree, growing out of it. High canopy branches of paper bark were just visible where foliage met bluer skies. The fig had choked the old paper bark and had completely subsumed the entire circumference of its trunk. But still the paper bark had survived. Not symbiotically, the Gardens curator explained, but in tandem, without destroying one another. The metaphor was obvious. Avery sang and played, on an equal ontological footing as his double tree. He sang to it, with it. Not for us.

THE GREEN END

So, to finish, a personal story. When I was small, my mother gave me a full set of Derwent coloured pencils. I loved the waxy touch of the crayon tip; I inhaled the woody smell of the pencil length. I was drawn to several colours such as amethyst, rose, and aqua, but viridian green was my favourite. It was that strange sea green-blue that you never really see in the sea; Close to a dark sage, but more saturated. I used it in my drawings for trees and for grass, for clothes and for walls. I used it for flowers and for cars, for signposts and for dog leashes. It soon became a stub among its tin of giants, too small to grip, left as a reminder of the full colour wheel. Its place in the case stood out as an abused and overused pencil, now no more than a sad little butt of chromium oxide. Handing these pencils down to my daughter, she has all the colours except that viridian green. I used it too much.

My part in a "green contract" is to voice the story of the myriad tales of the colour green, to participate in critical plant studies, and to aid an extension of those studies into aesthetics—visual art, mythology, and philosophy. By thinking green, we may yet discover a connection with the earth we couldn't perceive before.[49]

NOTES

1. Stefano Mancuso, *Brilliant Green: The Surprising History and Science of Plant Intelligence* (Washington, DC: Island Press, 2015), 7.

2. 1. Gen. 1:11 (King James Version).
3. Derek Jarman, *Chroma: A Book of Color* (New York: Overlook Press, 1994), 37.
4. Glenn Albrecht et al., "Solastalgia: The Distress Caused By Environmental Change," *Australasian Psychiatry* 15, Suppl. 1 (February 2007): 41–55, https://doi.org/10.1080/10398560701701288.
5. Jeffrey Nealon, *Plant Theory: Biopower and Vegetal Life* (Stanford: Stanford University Press, 2016), 31.
6. Nealon, *Plant Theory*, 35.
7. Mancuso, *Brilliant Green*, 13.
8. Immanuel Kant, *The Critique of Judgment*, trans. John Bernard (Amherst: Prometheus Books, 2000), 187.
9. Kant, *Critique of Judgment*.
10. Kant, *Critique of Judgment*, 22.
11. Natalie Angier, "Sorry, Vegans, Brussel Sprouts Like to Live, Too," *The New York Times*, December 21, 2009, https://nyti.ms/2mv39up.
12. Daniel Chamovitz, *What a Plant Knows: A Field Guide to the Senses* (New York: Farrar, Straus and Giroux, 2013).
13. Michael Marder, *Plant-Thinking: A Philosophy of Vegetal Life* (New York: Columbia University Press, 2013), 185.
14. Gary L. Francione, "Debate with Professor Michael Marder on Plant Ethics," *Animal Rights: The Abolitionist Approach*, November 3, 2016, http://goo.gl/B41gRL.
15. Francione, "Debate with Professor Michael Marder.
16. Francione, "Debate with Professor Michael Marder.
17. Prudence Gibson, "Pavlov's Plants: New Study Shows that Plants Can Learn from Experience," *The Conversation*, December 6, 2016, https:// theconversation.com/pavlovs-plants-new-study-shows-plants-canlearn-from-experience-69794.
18. Bill Bryson, *Down Under* (New York: Doubleday, 2000), 310.
19. "Crookes Tubes," *The Cathode Ray Tube Site*, December 5, 2016, http://www.crtsite.com/page7.html.
20. George Gessart, *Green Light: Toward an Art of Evolution* (Cambridge: MIT Press, 2012).
21. Eduardo Kac, ed., *Signs of Life: Bio Art and Beyond* (Cambridge: MIT Press, 2006).
22. Neil Ribe and Friedrich Steinle, "Exploratory Experimentation: Goethe, Land and Color Theory," *Physics Today* 55, no. 7 (July 2002): 43–49, at 43, 46, https://doi.org/10.1063/1.1506750.
23. Ribe and Steinle, "Exploratory Experimentation," 44.
24. Johann Wolfgang Von Goethe, *The Metamorphosis of Plants* (Cambridge: MIT Press, 2009).
25. Philip Ball, *Bright Earth: The Invention of Colour* (London: Penguin Books, 2001), 174.
26. Ball, *Bright Earth*.
27. Ball, *Bright Earth*.
28. Ella Damiani, "Deadly Warning on Peru Tea Travel," *Traveler*, August 4, 2013, http://www.traveller.com.au/deadly-warning-on-peru-tea-travel-2r6ga.

29. "Ayahuasca-Plant Spirit Medicine," *Medicine Hunter*, November 3, 2016, http://www.medicinehunter.com/ayahuasca.

30. Monica Gagliano and Michael Renton, "Love Thy Neighbour: Facilitation Through an Alternative Signalling Modality in Plants," *BMC Ecology* 13, no.19 (2013): 1–6, https://doi.org/10.1186/1472-6785-13-19.

31. Carolyn Dinshaw, "Black Skin, Green Masks: Medieval Foliate Heads, Racial Trauma, and Queer World-Making," in *The Middle Ages in the Modern World: Twenty-First-Century Perspectives*, eds. Bettina Bildhauer and Chris Jones (Oxford: Oxford University Press, 2017), 3.

32. Derek Jarman, *Chroma: A Book of Color* (New York: Overlook Press, 1994), 38.

33. Kathleen Basford, *The Green Man* (Suffolk: Boydell and Brewer, 1978).

34. William Anderson, *Green Man: The Archetype of Our Oneness with the Earth* (New York: Harper Collins, 1998).

35. Brandon Centerwall, 'The Name of the Green Man,' *Folklore* 108 (1997): 25–33, at 26.

36. Centerwall, "The Name of the Green Man," 28.

37. Jarman, *Chroma*, 38.

38. Richard Hayman, *The Green Man* (London: Shire Publications, 2015), 11.

39. Hayman, *Green Man*.

40. Monika A. Gorzelak, Amanda K. Asay, Brian J. Pickles, and Suzanne W. Simard, 'Inter-plant Communication through Mycorrhizal Networks Mediates Complex Adaptive Behaviour in Plant Communities,' *Annals of Botany Plants* 7 (2015): plv050, https://doi.org/10.1093/aobpla/plv050.

41. Chamovitz, *What a Plant Knows*.

42. Giovanni Aloi, "Gregory Pryor: Postcolonial Botany," *Antennae: The Journal of Nature in Visual Culture* 18 (2011): 24–36, at 26.

43. Val Plumwood, *Feminism and the Mastery of Nature* (London: Routledge 2003), 13.

44. Plumwood, *Feminism and the Mastery of Nature*, 13.

45. Graham Readfearn, "Calls for Equal Legal Rights for Nature," *The Sydney Morning Herald*, September 16, 2011, http://www.smh.com.au/environment/calls-for-equal-legal-rights-for-nature-20110915-1kbit.html.

46. Brendan Mackey, "Earth Jurisprudence: Building Theory and Practice," paper presentation, 3rd Wildlaw Conference, Brisbane, Queensland, Australia, September 16–18 2011.

47. Cormac Cullinan, *Wild Law: A Manifesto for Earth Justice* (White River Junction: Chelsea Green Books, 2002).

48. Michelle Maloney, "Introduction to Earth Jurisprudence and Rights of Nature," paper presentation, Wildlaw Workshop, Darwin, Northern Territory, Australia, May 17, 2013, http://www.earthlaws.org.au/wp-content/uploads/2013/03/Michelle-Maloney_Introduction-to-Earth-Jurisprudence.pdf.

49. Marder, *Plant-Thinking*, 185.

Main Pathway: Orientations

Subthemes

Proceed to Ethics, p. 377
Proceed to Time, p. 329

25

PREVENTING PLANT BLINDNESS

James H. Wandersee and Elisabeth E. Schussler

Several studies show that U.S. students prefer to study animals rather than plants (Baird, Lazarowitz, and Allman, 1984; Wandersee, 1986). Although this research shows girls are more interested in learning about plants than boys are, even girls report that they prefer animals. A recent cross-age study we conducted with 4th-, 5th-, 6th- and 7th-grade urban, public elementary and middle school students revealed that those students, overall, were twice as interested in animals as they were in plants—with little change as age increased. About 70 percent of the 274 students we queried spontaneously expressed a scientific interest in plants, and of that 7 percent, or about two-thirds, were girls (Wandersee and Schussler, 1998b).

Paradoxically, plants form the basis of most animal habitats and all life on earth (Abbott, 1998). While animals frequently steal the spotlight where extinction is concerned, one in eight plant species worldwide is currently threatened by extinction. Intellectually, we know that you don't get pandas without bamboo plants, but culturally this is often forgotten (Abbott, 1998).

Because plants differ in many important ways from animals, and because biology is taught by members of the animal kingdom, there is a recognized tendency, even for knowledgeable biologists, to overlook, underemphasize, or neglect plants

Originally published as "Preventing Plant Blindness," *The American Biology Teacher* 61, no. 2 (February 1999): 82–86. Reprinted with permission from University of California Press Journals.

when teaching introductory biology courses (Darley, 1990; Hershey, 1993, 1996; Nichols, 1919; Uno, 1994). As two botanists who are concerned about the implications of this imbalance for the nation's science literacy level, we have launched a national campaign to increase public understanding of plants, using these catchwords: "Prevent Plant Blindness."

Those three simple words appear on our full-color classroom poster, which is being distributed to more than 22,000 U.S. science teachers at state and national science teachers' conventions. The poster is designed to be initially puzzling. It shows a tree-lined, riverine environment emblazoned diagonally with the words "Prevent Plant Blindness." Hovering, Magritte-like, in the sky above is a pair of dark-red-tinted spectacles. The implication is that someone wearing these glasses could not see the green plants in the scene below—that if one's vision is "filtered," either physically or conceptually, one may easily miss seeing the plants that appear in one's field of vision.

We consider the current state of underrepresentation as much more than just the result of zoocentrism or zoochauvinism. That's why we decided to introduce a new term, one that emphasizes the perceptual and visual cognition bases of why plants are often overlooked and neglected—not just by biology teachers, but by humans in general. Because we knew people were already linguistically familiar with "blind" as a metaphorical adjective (e.g., blind alley, blind ambition, blind chance, blind copy, blind date, blind landing, blind seam, blind spot, blind trust, snow blindness, need-blind admissions, color blindness), we settled upon plant blindness.

We define plant blindness as (a) the inability to see or notice the plants in one's environment; (b) the inability to recognize the importance of plants in the biosphere and in human affairs; (c) the inability to appreciate the aesthetic and unique biological features of the life forms that belong to the plant kingdom; and (d) the misguided anthropocentric ranking of plants as inferior to animals and thus as unworthy of consideration (Wandersee and Schussler, 1998a).

Those persons afflicted with the condition known as plant blindness exhibit symptoms such as the following: (a) thinking that plants are merely the backdrop for animal life; (b) failing to see, notice, or focus attention on plants in one's daily life; (c) misunderstanding what plants need to stay alive; (d) overlooking the importance of plants to one's daily affairs (Balick and Cox, 1996); (e) failing to distinguish the differing time scales of plant and animal activity; (f) lacking hands-on experiences in growing, observing, and identifying plants in one's own geographic region; (g) failing to explain the basic plant science underlying nearby plant communities, including plant growth, nutrition, reproduction, and relevant ecological considerations; (h) lacking awareness that plants are central to a key biochemical cycle—the carbon cycle; (i) being insensitive to the aesthetic qualities of plants and their structures, especially with respect to their adaptation, coevolution, color, dispersal, diversity, growth, pattern, reproduction, scent, size, sounds, spacing, strength, symmetry, tactility, taste, and texture (Wandersee and Schussler 1998a).

Why do humans overlook plants? Most people think they see all of their surroundings by merely opening their eyes and looking. There is, however, much scientific evidence to the contrary (Cattell, 1895; Nickerson and Adams, 1979). Norretranders (1998) points out that the human eye, during visual perception, generates more than 10 million bits of data every second for visual processing, from which our brain ultimately derives approximately 40 bits per second for our conscious vision to consider; thus, "the bandwidth of our consciousness is far lower than the bandwidth of our sensory perceptors" (p. 125).

In our plant blindness presentation, we demonstrate that this is so by asking our audience members to make a sketch of both sides of a U.S. penny (one-cent coin), using only their unaided memory. After a few minutes of "graphic exasperation," and after generating only a partially correct representation at best, we ask them to examine the (dependably flawed) sketches made by others in the audience as well. Finally, we tell them to compare their drawings to a real penny that they extract from their own pocket or purse. Smiles and consternation are evident throughout the room. Everyone wonders: "How could I possibly fail to recall the details of something I look at and handle almost every day of the year?"

"We . . . tend to be surprisingly bad at recalling details of objects we see or use daily," notes acclaimed memory researcher Alan Baddeley (1982). Just because we looked doesn't mean that we saw everything. Harvard University psychologist Stephen Kosslyn (1993) reminds us that "the mind is not a camera, the brain is not a VCR." Rugg (1998, p. 1151) points out that "all events are not equal; they differ in how they are [initially] encoded into memory." He says that two critical factors determine whether or not we will remember an event: the degree of attention we give to it, and the meaning or importance we ascribe to it.

In seeking a better explanation for plant blindness, we have compiled the following characteristics of human perception and visual cognition to answer the question: Why do humans overlook plants?

1. People typically know less about plants than animals. Persons who have had few meaningful educational experiences involving plants have little basis beyond popular culture for plant recognition. We can only recognize what we know. Psychologists would say that plants have low signal value for most humans today. Once objects have acquired meaning for an observer, they are more likely to be perceived (inattentional blindness). In other words, inattention becomes attention if a stimulus has meaning (Mack and Rock, 1998). Also, the stimulus must actually be present—yet approximately half of the biomass of many plants (the root system) is found underground and rarely seen by most people.

2. When flowering plants are not flowering or have inconspicuous flowers, the homogeneity of their green leaves and stems does not serve to visually label them or make them pop out chromatically from their background. If objects are not sufficiently different from their backgrounds, they blend in with their surroundings, and nothing is perceived. The visual cortex continuously filters out much more of the information the retina sends it than it retains for conscious analysis. Without our intention to preserve it, visual plant-related data is likely to be discarded.

3. Members of plant populations often grow in close proximity to each other (whether cultivated or natural) and appear relatively stationary in contrast to the mobility of most animal population members. Static proximity is a visual cue humans use to group objects (Zakia, 1997), so individual plants and different plant species tend to be de-emphasized, with the totality merely categorized as "plants." This helps to explain the "plants as backdrop" phenomenon. Contrary to the cliche, we are actually more likely to see just the forest, and not the trees.

4. For humans, plants are generally nonthreatening elements of an ecosystem and can usually be ignored without dire consequences. Visual habit and general familiarity diminish the conscious attention we give to objects. If vision operates to minimize expended effort, then low-level attributes may be discarded to make visual processing easier. Note how our visual search is suddenly directed and intensified by the knowledge that poison ivy may be present where we are walking!

5. Visual experiences are structured in the brain by space, time, and color. As a consequence of their different mode of nutrition, plants typically offer fewer spacing-based, time-based, and color-based differentiators for humans to

observe than animals do (Zakia, 1997). The brain is basically a difference detector, and when it finds none, the perceptual field is not perturbed. For example, invasive plants capture our attention because they grow with vigor in places where we don't expect or want to find them.

Couple those facts with these characteristics of nonhuman animal life, and you can understand why the students we queried responded as they did. Animals can move quickly via appendages; have to eat regularly like we do; have eyes for vision; exhibit many interesting behaviors; have dramatic and easily observable life cycles; mate, give birth, and raise their young; and interact with, and sometimes play with, humans (Wandersee, 1986). Beginning in the first six weeks of infantile life, humans develop a propensity to respond first to things in their environment that have faces, and animals best meet this search criterion.

The Botanical Society of America (Niklas, 1995, p. 3), in its turn-of-the-century report titled: *Botany for the Next Millennium*, "situates the importance of plant studies within three major areas of biological inquiry—the evolution and diversity of life, the development of organisms, and the structure and function of ecosystems." It notes, tantalizingly, "In each area, plants offer a wealth of compelling material and systems that have been underexplored or unintegrated with the main questions of biology, largely because of biologists' narrow training."

If we are to escape from the intellectual, perceptual, and visual processing traps that lead to plant blindness, those of us who teach introductory courses must work to expand our students' botanical horizons. While the life sciences may be reorganizing themselves along the line of common themes rather than clusters of organisms studied, plants remain distinctly different life forms that have, historically, rewarded our focused study, observation, and investigation. There are good scientific reasons why botany, like the plants it studies, needs to maintain its visibility and identity.

We have argued that, instead of invoking the bugbear of zoological conspiracy, there is actually a visual-cognitive societal basis for why plants (and the plant sciences) are frequently ignored in everyday life, in the introductory biology curriculum, and as a key component of scientific literacy. Functionally, plants remain "the primary mediators between the physical and biological world" (Niklas, 1995, p. 11). That is certainly no small feat, and it alone is worth modifying introductory biology teaching to "Prevent Plant Blindness!"

REFERENCES

Abbott, C. 1998. "Extinction Threatens 1 in 8 Plants Globally." *Yahoo News*, April 9, 1998.

Baddeley, A. 1982. *Your Memory: A User's Guide*. New York: Macmillan.

Balick, M. J., and P. A. Cox. 1996. *Plants, People, and Culture: The Science of Ethnobotany*. New York: Scientific American Library.

Baird, J. H., R. Lazarowitz, and V. Allman. 1984. "Science Choices and Preferences of Middle and Secondary School Students in Utah." *Journal of Research in Science Teaching* 21, no. 1: 47–54.

Cattell, J. M. 1895. "Measurement of the Accuracy of Recollection." *Science* 2, no. 49: 761–776.

Darley, W. M. 1990. "The Essence of 'Plantness.'" *The American Biology Teacher* 52, no., 6: 354–357.

Hershey, D. R. 1993. "Plant Neglect in Biology Education." *BioScience* 43, no. 7: 418.

Hershey, D. R. 1996. "A Historical Perspective on Problems in Botany Teaching." *The American Biology Teacher* 58, no. 6: 340–347.

Kosslyn, S. M. 1993. "The Mind Is Not a Camera, the Brain Is Not a VCR." *Aldus Magazine (September–October)*: 33–36.

Mack, A., and I. Rock. 1998. *Inattentional blindness*. Cambridge, MA: MIT Press.

Nichols, G. E. 1919. "The General Biology Course and the Teaching of Elementary Botany and Zoology in American Colleges and Universities." *Science* 50, no. 1301: 509–517.

Nickerson, R. S., & Adams, M. J. 1979. "Long-Term Memory for a Common Object." *Cognitive Psychology* 11, no. 3: 287–307.

Niklas, K. J., ed. 1995. *Botany for the Next Millennium*. Columbus, OH: Botanical Society of America.

Norretranders, T. 1998. *The User Illusion*. New York: Viking.

Rugg, M. D. 1998. "Memories Are Made of This." *Science* 281, no. 5380, 1151–1152.

Uno, G. E. 1994. "The State of Precollege Botanical Education." *American Biology Teacher* 56, no. 5, 263–267.

Wandersee, J. H. 1986. "Plants or Animals: Which Do Junior High School Students Prefer to Study?" *Journal of Research in Science Teaching* 23, no. 5, 415–426.

Wandersee, J. H., and E. E. Schussler. 1998a. "A Model of Plant Blindness." Poster-paper presented at the 3rd Annual Associates Meeting of the 15 Degree Laboratory, Louisiana State University, Baton Rouge, LA, April 13.

Wandersee, J. H., and E. E. Schussler. 1998b. "Plants or Animals: Which Do Elementary and Middle Students Prefer to Study?" Unpublished manuscript. Louisiana State University, 15 Degree Laboratory, Baton Rouge, LA.

Zakia, R. D. 1997. *Perception and Imaging.* Boston, MA: Focal Press.

Main Pathway: Orientations

Subthemes

Proceed to Experience, p. 439
Proceed to Ethics, p. 439
Proceed to Healing, p. 541

26

TREES IN SHALLOW TIME

Mark Payne

The form of our relationship with living collectivities of nonhuman beings is arguably no more apprehensible now than it was before the nonhuman turn. The individual encounter has played an important part in animal studies' efforts to extend the face and faciality beyond the human, but faciality is an index of singularity, and efforts to imagine forms of relationality, even with collectivities of animal life, have been relatively unsuccessful by comparison. Donna Haraway's critique of Gilles Deleuze's becoming-wolf as a modality of de-individuation is a critique of the formlessness of this idea of becoming.[1] De-individuation does not lend itself to agent-centered narrative, and conversely, as attention is focused on individual actants, the singular inevitably supervenes upon any vaguer background of collective relationality from which singularity emerges.

The question of time is immediately at issue here. The forms of being in the present, in which living collectivities are vaguely available to us, are non-narrative impressions, whereas narration in the singular enacts conativity in the sharper lines of narrative time. Understanding the form of our relationship with living collectivities of nonhuman beings therefore entails thinking about selfhood outside the constraints of narrative paradigms of the self.[2] The recent movement of critical attention from animals to plants looks promising in this regard. Plant collectivities are regularly available to us in ways that animal collectivities are not, and the

Originally published as "Trees in Shallow Times," in *Imperceptibly and Slowly Opening* (Chicago: GLP, 2016), 76–83. Reprinted with permission.

background plural from which singularity emerges seems to adhere more tenaciously to plants than it does to animals.[3] However, to underscore how attention to the form of our relationality with plants as living collectivities entails renewed attention to non-narrative paradigms of selfhood, I want to point to the close relationship between plant-thinking and the shallow time of lyric poetry.

Jonathan Culler's new book, *Theory of Lyric*, revisits an old question about lyric time in a way that I find stimulating in the context of current discussions about the human being's capacity to rediscover itself in a larger horizon of shared life. Culler notes that the simple present tense of lyric poetry in English is the most obviously marked example of the specialness of the lyric present in the modern languages, because it contrasts with the present progressive, which is the regular tense for events that are unfolding in the present moment of the speaker: "I wander through each chartered street," not "I am wandering." The lyric present offers a unique affordance for sensing our relationship with collectivities of shared life because it vitiates narrativity to the greatest degree possible while remaining recognizable as selfhood in language. Its shallow time disenacts the display of agential conativity and relocates its speaker in forms of shared life beyond the immediate horizon of desire and self-realization.[4]

I will explore this relationship between plant thinking and the shallow time of lyric poetry on two fronts: a poem by John Ashbery that stages the affordance that lyric poetry offers to the vague apprehension of the form of our relationality with living collectivities of nonhuman beings, and the way in which Plotinus works the reading of lyric poetry into his philosophy because of its capacity to resituate the human being in horizons of shared life beyond the human. Here, then, is Ashbery's "Some Trees":

These are amazing: each
Joining a neighbor, as though speech
Were a still performance.
Arranging by chance

To meet as far this morning
From the world as agreeing
With it, you and I
Are suddenly what the trees try

To tell us we are:
That their merely being there
Means something; that soon
We may touch, love, explain.

And glad not to have invented
Such comeliness, we are surrounded:
A silence already filled with noises,
A canvas on which emerges

A chorus of smiles, a winter morning.
Placed in a puzzling light, and moving,
Our days put on such reticence
These accents seem their own defense.[5]

What Ashbery's poem tells us is that the shared life of trees, and our shared life with the shared life of trees, almost has the form of speech. Or rather, it makes us see that an ideal form of speech would have the form of being present to us that trees have: *still performance*. What is to be apprehended would be there in its place, without the need for narration. As Richard Mabey puts it, in his reflection on the site of Wordsworth's daffodils, it is not so much the beauty of plants that moves us, although we are glad not to have invented that too, as a vague apprehension of a distinctive modality of shared life in their being there with us:

In the end it was not so much their good looks that moved me as their presentness. I'm reluctant to say "presence," with its hint of some spiritual aura, and mean just their "being there," at that place and in that moment; present in the sense of "'all present and correct.'" I was touched by the way they belonged to this spot, and that its human inhabitants had been contributors to that persistence-not as hubristic cultivators, managing and force breeding them, but as neighbours and companions.[6]

The expressiveness of their persistence in place is the communicative modality of their merely being there. This is what they communicate to us as hopefulness about our own form of life. Perhaps we will explain ourselves, but only after we have experienced ourselves in the way that the trees give us back to life as a whole, as beings whose self-realization unfolds in the shallow time of persistence, not the peaks and troughs of conativity. And so we come to understand that we have been in the presence of a chorus, as what appears from neighbor joining neighbor, figures of silent care in a different form of life that enacts its individual instances of expressivity as part of a larger horizon of shared life accompanying our own. These forms of life are not fully apprehensible to one another, although some sense of their belonging together in a single shared life is registered when we apprehend the performance as a whole. The apprehension is evanescent, its proper duration appearing and vanishing in the shallow time of the lyric poem.

"Surrounded" and "chorus" name two related modalities of being with shared life, with the nonfactitious beauty of the world—its "comeliness"—being the tipping point between the mere presence of the world, and the sense we have in this presence that it is a world for us: that its merely being here means something. What the shallow time of Ashbery's poem captures, apparatus-like, as still performance, is the momentary apprehension of participation in a larger horizon of shared life that is chorality's gift and chorality's form of life, and what operationalizes this possibility for the poem is the vague apprehension of collective sociality in the trees: the way that they are "some trees," according to the poem's title.

A similar affinity between the shallow time of lyric and our shared life with plants appears in Plotinus' reflections on the way in which the appearance of the natural world affords an experience of chorality. Plants are less obviously arranged as a set of organs in a hierarchical processing arrangement than animals are, and because they have their life and its activity equally in all of their parts, they are a good way of thinking about how we apprehend the presence of life in the cosmos as a whole as dispersed equally throughout it, as opposed to the focused presence of the living activity of what is alive as we encounter it in the eyes of an animal or the face of a human being. We make ourselves at home in the world as insects make themselves at home in the rotten part of a cabbage (*Ennead* 4.3–4). The life of the world is everywhere at once as a signal of its being a home for other organisms. Its homeliness for them does not manifest itself in the modality of an artifact, like a house that has been designed for their use, but rather in the modality of life. Its self-disclosure is the signaling of one living organism to another that it is available to it as a home. The cosmos as plant stands for the ability to recognize the livingness of the life world as home, or to misrecognize it as an aesthetic creation, a disposition of matter that is more or less satisfying as craftwork.

The livingness of the world as our home is what we cannot really get a hold of when we are at home in it, precisely because it is a relationship between the living and the living. It is not seen properly if we think to view it from the outside, as in the contemplation of a purely material, nonliving object.[7] Plotinus likens our awareness of belonging to it to a chorus member's momentary understanding of being part of a chorus when the performer is briefly turned toward the center of its movement (*Ennead* 6.9–4). Our belongingness to the world is evanescent as knowledge because we are at home in it as one living being is at home in another. However, the intermittence of this awareness should not be understood as a crisis for human understanding, but as integral to the experience of the life form that we are when this life form is enacted in a form of life that affords the self-understanding that is proper to it.

That said, there are practices of shared life that bring this self-understanding forward, and one of them is lyric poetry. In the great images of the *Enneads*—the plant that is the same throughout, no matter how far it extends itself (3.8.10; 4.3–8); the sun rising over the horizon, which gives itself to the eyes to see (5.5.8); the spring that empties itself into rivers but is not exhausted by them (3–8.10)—poetic accommodations of the natural world are an analogy for theoretical understanding not just because they avoid the sequential ordering of dialectic and myth,[8] but because the instantaneous, holistic apprehension they allow originates in a subcognitive sense of shared life that lyric captures as the still performance of life.

Sometimes these images are native to lyric, as in Plotinus' frequent turns to Pindar, sometimes they are images sourced from Homer and treated as if they were lyric. Lyric apprehension is a better analogue for contemplation than the sequential cognition of dialectic and narrative because what is to be apprehended in contemplation is that which is prior to multiplicity, and lyric's shallow time affords such apprehension to human beings with respect to the larger horizon of shared life to which they belong. Plotinus' denarrativization of Homer is not violence toward his poems but a recognition of the ways in which the natural forms of attention in reading—the tangency of attention drift with respect to narratives of desire—analogize our capacity to apprehend our belonging to the larger horizon of shared life from inside the self-understanding that is proper to the relentless forward movement of our own conativity. Toggling back to desirous consumption from dreaming by the book, to use Elaine Scarry's term,[9] mimes the switch between the occasions on which we grasp the distant or scientific image of ourselves within the manifest or first personal image of our lives, only to lose it as the story inevitably progresses.

Plotinus evacuates time from his lyric reading, as lyric itself makes time shallow, as an affordance of shared life, precisely with the swarms, collectivities, and intensities—the plants, constellations, rivers, and springs in their more or less intense realization of life itself—that the Gnostics, his self-designated philosophical adversaries,[10] with their flat ontology and human ontic singularity imprisoned in a material universe specially fabricated for its confinement, refuse to acknowledge as living substances in the same way that our bodies are mediations of life itself.

This is a persistent dilemma for Hellenic ecology. Chorality, as the intermittent awareness of belonging to the totality of shared life, has the form of being surrounded that the pre-Socratics call *to apeiron*, in a figuration of the cosmos that draws on the idea of circles, rings, and nets, for which this term is consistently used in Greek poetry. As a "wrapping from which one cannot escape," the poets' sense of living surrounding is consistent with the *apeiron* of Anaximander, for instance, as a "huge inexhaustible mass, stretching away endlessly in every direction," and having the majesty that Earth and Ocean possess for Homer.[11] For both, it is an embrace of the living by the living, but this surrounding embrace of the limitless is always liable to become a mere enfolding, a material frame, setting, or even enclosure of human action.

Indeed, the reflexive narrativity inherent in human conativity is always likely to produce the impression of fully agential being acting upon a world that is present to it as a flat omic frame for its action. This is the impression that lyric is especially good at pushing back on, stilling our depth perception of time such that the world comes into focus as a still performance of its own. Lyric's shallow time militates against the flat ontology of materialism precisely by suppressing our familiar first-person organismic self-understanding in favor of a staging of aliveness as a form of relationality that we might call a value-saturated apprehension of nodality—our awareness of being situated among socialities of the nonhuman that are a reflexive screen for our own, as the chorus is for the performer.

The affinity between plant thinking and the shallow time of lyric reminds us to experience ourselves as the transgenerational mediation of life itself.[12] It opens onto a distinctive experience of the form of our historicity not as ontic singularities, but as the mediation of life that is common to organismic being as a whole. We have something in common with plants other than mere facticity· that we do not have in common with plastic bags, dishwashers, and satellites. We have grown up alongside one another, and we have the powers of expressivity that our form of life allows. Our shared life in shallow time opens on to the historicity of our being as a life form in ways that are not afforded by the being of what is made. Chorality begins in surroundedness, but the surroundedness of chorality is the self-disclosure of what is alive. In the expressivity of individual lives, we sense how their capacity for self-disclosure is enabled by collective life and how this collective life is an enactment of life itself, as what has always already claimed us.

What remains vital about Hellenic ecology is the way it probes the limits of our capacity to apprehend the subcognitive, nonvoluntaristic possession by life to which we are subject. One way in which it does this is to imagine our sympathetic configuration by what else in the world is alive as first philosophy. Heraclitus (DK B62) is exemplary in this regard: "immortals mortals, mortals immortals, living their death, dying their life." Heraclitus iconizes the shared life of mortals and immortals, setting out their being together such that the discovery of livingness as what relates them to one another emerges from an initial formulation in which one is disposed as a choric presence around the other without that presence being articulated in a syntactical formulation. Nonsyntacticality enacts the embrace of what has not yet been named as human beings by what has not yet been named as gods in shallow time. The surroundingness of other life is not a frame for human thinking, but what enables human thinking, and allows it to accommodate itself to other than human thinking in the world at large.

We can contrast the cathexis of the living to the living in Hellenic ecology with the flat ontology of Gnostic ecologies, ancient and modern, if a form of relationality is discoverable in the experience of chorality that is other than the form of our relationality with lifeless objects. Whether an experience with such a special, inner form exists or not is questionable, both in its very possibility and in its limits, but the shallow time of lyric affords us a connection to this questionable possibility as a sense of our belonging to larger living wholes, and so invites us to consider what the limits of belonging to shared life might meaningfully be for us.

NOTES

1. Donna Haraway, *When Species Meet* (Minneapolis: University of Minnesota Press, 2008), 27–30.
2. See also Galen Strawson, "Against Narrativity," in *Real Materialism and Ocher Essays* (Oxford: Oxford University Press, 2008), 189–208.
3. Forms of being together in the plural are a continuous thread in Anna Lowenhaupt Tsing, *The Mushroom at theEnd of the World* (Princeton, NJ: Princeton University Press, 2015).

4. Jonathan Culler, *Theory of the Lyric* (Cambridge, MA: Harvard University Press, 2015), 275–294
5. John Ashbery, *Some Trees* (New York: Corinth Books, 1970), 51.
6. Richard Mabey, *The Cabaret of Planes: Forty Thousand Years of Plane Life and the Human Imagination* (New York: W.W. Norton, 2016), 208.
7. Franz Kafka's "The Burrow" and J. M. Coetzee's rewriting of it in *Life & Times of Michael K* stage the inevitable failure of this effort to see it from the outside.
8. Cf. the discussion of philosophical myth in "On Love" (3.5.9): "Myths, if they are really going to be myths, must separate in time the things of which they tell, and set apart from each other many realities which are together, but distinct in rank or powers, at points where rational discussions, also, make generations of things ungenerated, and themselves, too, separate things which are together."
9. Elaine Scarry, *Dreaming by the Book* (Princeton: Princeton University Press, 2001).
10. See *Ennead* 2.9, "Against the Gnostics."
11. Charles Kahn, *Anaximander and the Origins of Greek Cosmology* (New York: Columbia University Press, 1960), 231–235.
12 See Brooke Holmes's observations on the relationship between the noetic capacities of plants and the vegetality of the basic life functions in the "not so mindless work of living" the Greek medical tradition, in "Pure Life: The Limits of the Vegetal Analogy in the Hippocratics and Galen," in *The Comparable Body: Imagination and Analogy in Ancient Anatomy and Physiology*, ed. John Wee, 358–386 (Leiden: Brill, 2016). For the Greek medical writers, the question was not so much whether human beings are planes, but when, or if, they cease to be them.

Main Pathway: Cross-Pollination

Subthemes

Proceed to Ethics, p. 495
Proceed to Time, p. 569

27

INTERVIEW WITH NATHALIE ANGUEZOMO MBA BIKORO

How do you identify the species of plants you decide to work with? What parameters guide your selection process and why?

NATHALIE ANGUEZOMO MBA BIKORO: It has been imperative to my practice that the methodology of selection should not mimic and perpetuate colonial and institutional violence of theft and erasure; therefore, the narratives I share are based on a process of healing, transformation, and transmission of what has been erased and has not been legitimized as institutional knowledge. I work with plants based on their status as debris left in places and, therefore, as testimonial legacies of the events and architectural landscapes of very difficult histories.

The curation of plants' ecologies is based on the archival remnants of colonial German films from the Weimar Republic to GDR African film productions and botanical research. They are written in poems, such as in the work of Rita Dove and Dionne Brand, and science-fictional writings and tales from the first botanical director in Berlin, Adelbert von Chamisso. The author's work has been reperformed in many German African colonial botanical garden theaters and particularly in the region of Mimbeng, and the author's name transmitted into my mother tongue: Fang culture as a mythical night creature who was particularly feared in the time of World War I. The colonial memories of what he wrote about plants and colonial conditions and Empire requestion the stories of botanical research and the shape of urban cities, and vegetal life as weaponry of war and capital in German cultural industries. The plants that I work with are commonly those in relation to botanical legacies of the African Diaspora through slave trade and those for German scientific usage that became part of the cultural industry's curation of colonial films made in Berlin. These include Boni-udu (for *Maprounea Guianese*, *Discophora guianensis*, and *Banara guianensis*), Matawai nenge (for *Tachigali*), Saramacca dettol (for *Hirtella paniculata*), and Aluku pesi (for *Vigna unguiculata*).

The use of plants and seeds as forms of healing, ritual, and political resistance in African movements and Black liberation during the slave trade Atlantic wars particularly featured in my narratives in thinking about solidarity and white feminist extractivism.

Do you ever consider plants as subjects in your work, and how does that change your approach to them?

NAMB: I consider plants in my stories to hold their own testimonies of events and people that have been purposefully erased from history. They have been the subject of sonic amplifications for lost film scripts, erased Black theater plays, and ghostly Black feminist conversations in immersive installation spaces such as *On the Ruins of Paradise*. Instead of featuring them in the form of objects displayed as herbarium artifacts in botanical museums, they are triggers for emancipatory functions, including wearable warrior attires, underground radio spaces, sonic decolonial disobedience in online and touring performative formats, and testimonial diligences, in particular with regard to the histories of Black African Queer Feminists.

In your artistic practice, what have you learned from the plants themselves? In which ways does your art follow their movements, metamorphoses, and modes of being in the world? How does it interact with these vegetal processes?

NAMB: The plants themselves taught me about the necessity of fiction and the urgency for a decolonial imagination when dealing with the remnants of archives. Their forms should not be taken for their *given* forms, but for the potential for transformation and what they can reveal of the erased stories of our communities. They form part of an Underground Railroad system for liberation if we consider a parallel to the contexts of Black liberation in America and its echoes in the migrational movement between Africa and Europe. Plants can reveal stories and recall the voices of people we were not meant to remember. This process is performative, filled with an urgency of healing and of configuring a different relationship to the place we live. In my opinion this is a botanical legacy that includes our stories too alongside those of plants.

In my work *We Built The Kilimanjaro* and *In Arcadia: How Soldiers Become Mermaids*, the narratives are spoken by the descendants of Black women and former African POWs in Germany. Through their testimonies they speak of the power of botanical memory to decolonize empiricist monuments, based on colonial films of the Weimar Republic, and locate the Halfmoon Camp, one of the biggest colonial camps in Germany, where the remains of plants and water ecosystems in its vicinities reveal the crimes of German governments. Botanical life on its grounds and in the waters holds sonic echoes, through rusted weaponry, garments, and local plants, of the lives that did not survive the atrocities, and forms a testimonial soundtrack. The plants in both performance and film tell stories of who they are, how they reappear, and how they should be remembered through processes of transformation and radio transmissions.

What ethical or political considerations inform your work with plants? What are the ethical and political implications of this work?

NAMB: It helps me to question the very legitimacy of existing technologies and knowledge in museology. It reveals the limitations of curating, science, and historical intentions. It means that it gives the possibility of stories to not be told by the perpetrator. It reveals the fragility and the science of white supremacy through fiction and botanical empiricism as the groundwork exploited by pharmaceutical companies that have criminalized the work of Black farmers on the African continent. It reveals the system of displacement and disparities of farmers, the military research methodologies carried out in Gene Banks (Limbe, Cameroon) that continue the colonial legacies of apartheid-law land divisions, and pharmaceutical and military experimentation with the view to producing weaponry. Those spaces are still withheld and contain a connection between colonial arbitrations and National Socialist traditions.

Such spaces also reveal the importance of plants and farming as places of conflict, division, and political resistance, like the anti-colonial Black women's' resistance movement FREMLINO, when dealing with nineteenth-to-twentieth-century colonies. The ecologies of plants were used by anti-colonial fighters and resisters to foster political fervor in the German contexts, or in writing complaintive letters to its Bismarck government about the genocides and criminal engagements done by the German Schutztruppe (Maji war; Herero–Nama wars). Plants were crucial to the literary works for liberation decolonizing and creolizing German literature and disrupted the very constructs and limitations of modernity and technology. These can be also heard in folkloric stories and testimonies of Black African soldiers, held in German prisoners camps between 1913 and 1944, through phonographic recordings, notably in the Wilhelm Doegen collection at the Humboldt University, which is featured in my work *Black A(n)thena*.

The politics of dealing with the material of plants is its potential to reveal histories that were erased, which is part of their aesthetic and sonority. In my work *A History of Lateness*, plants and gray parrots in Mimbeng reperform the sonic debris of the colonial war of 1914 and mimic intimate conversations held by German troops and settlers of the regions 100 years after their settlements were abandoned. The science is the ecologies of darkness, where the oppressed are no longer the subject, but the oppressor or perpetuator becomes the subject of study (or under trial) and is captured for criminal actions and violations. Plants become a forensic lab for criminal investigation, justice, healing, monumentization and spear-heading fictional potentials outside of white supremacist technologies and narratives.

What, if any, are the aspects of your work with plants related to the current global environmental and mass extinction crises?

NAMB: Crises of migration, displacement, and extinction of local farming have increased through pharmaceutical laws criminalizing Black people on their own land, destroying ancestral heritage and ritual spaces, and poisoning plants by destroying their soils through chemical imports. This in turn affects the food chains, from top to bottom, and continues to legalize apartheid-like laws and the mass displacement and genocide of people.

Which pressing challenge, or challenges, has working with plants presented to you?

NAMB: The ways in which the material changes, appears and disappears, according to place and seasons. The challenge in working through this process with plants is how to disassemble the canonization of what has been given to us as knowledge, which has disempowered future communities to form their own stories. The challenge was and still is to confront, in conversations and in practice, the very work and intention of curating, selecting, and storytelling by white scholarly and scientific premises. That would mean to reclaim our own narratives and technologies if we consider decolonial practice and liberational transitions. The collection of plants in white institutions was based on chains of plantocracy (slave trade).

In my opinion, working with plants revealed a whole history of migrant and trade stories that would not be accessible otherwise. The potential healing elements they can emit emphasize spirituality as an understory technology, which I use in my work through durational ritual performance practices.

How is the interaction between your artistic practice and theoretical endeavors shaped by vegetal life?

NAMB: On the contrary, I feel my artistic practice broke apart the mythology of the imperialistic belief that things start from the theoretical belief. Ecologies of vegetal life proceeded by disassembling theoretical anchors of nature, the idea of "discovery and exploration" and the limitations of colonial projects in curating the world as a North–South divide. According to the nineteenth-century white German feminist and colonialist Frieda von Bülow (whose written works were some of the grounding ideas for Hitler's formation of National Socialism), vegetal life centered the ideas of superiority (entitlement of whiteness to curate, loot, and steal land), the savage (the oppressors' rights to destroy Indigenous heritage to their lands), and nature that had to be tamed (colonies would be owned by European empires).

Much of botanical Western theories can be transmitted full of misinterpretations of the functions of nature according to who creates its narratives.

"There are three stages of scientific discovery: first people deny it is true; then they deny it is important; finally they credit the wrong person."
—Alexander von Humboldt

We read in one of Humboldt's stories, that he acquires two speaking parrots from an Andean tribe. The parrots speak the human language of the community they were stolen from, the community where the tribe Humboldt met had committed the complete destruction of another days prior to his encounter, erasing their existence, beliefs and language. The parrots remained the monument to this community and Humboldt wrote a dictionary of the words the parrots spoke, which, in my point of view, rendered elastic the fiction and amplified the resonance of their existence and its remnants in animal and vegetal life. This principle applies in my artistic process (such as in the work of *A History of Lateness*, *Black A(n)thena*, *Thieves of Echoe,* and *Tropical Fever Letters to My Daughters*) of dealing with archives of vegetal life and how their resonances and echoes are stolen through the destruction

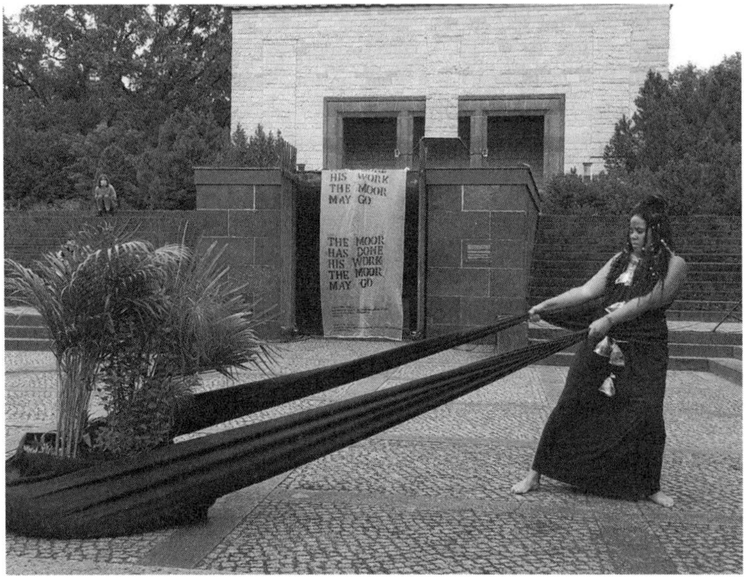

wrought by capitalist functions and gentrifications. This displacement and destruction of the historical echoes of vegetal ecosystems negate the histories of migrant life for the purpose of the white supremacist system. From these forgotten echoes and vibrations of botanical life, or ethnobotany, we can determine the testimonies and traumas that have affected the places of their growth.

Nathalie Anguezomo Mba Bikoro is a French-Gabonese multidisciplinary artist. She studied Fine Arts in Gabon and in England before receiving her master's degree in political philosophy at the University of Greenwich, in London, in 2008. She was awarded a PhD in philosophy, art and postcolonial African studies from the University of Greenwich and Humboldt University, in Berlin in 2013. Her work has been shown in numerous group and solo exhibitions, including the *Fondation Blackère*, in 2013 and the Dak'art Biennial, in Senegal, in 2012.

Black A(n)thena, 2020, Nathalie Anguezomo Mba Bikoro. From A Handful of Dust Series. (Photo: Kathy-Ann Tan.)

28

INTERVIEW WITH MARIA THEREZA ALVES

How do you identify the species of plants you decide to work with? What parameters guide your selection process and why?

MARIA THEREZA ALVES: I have, over the decades, developed works based on varied complex relationships with plants. *Seeds of Change*, begun in 1999, is an ongoing investigation of ballast flora in port cities such as Marseille, Reposaari, Dunkirk, Exeter/Topsham, Liverpool, Bristol, Antwerp, and New York.

Ballast such as stones, earth, sand, wood, bricks, and whatever else was economically expedient was used to stabilize merchant sailing ships so that they could sail efficiently. Along with the ballast, seeds accidentally came. The work investigates where these seeds might be today, where they might come from, and what actions resulted in their arrival in the port.

Wake was originally an investigation of 17 sites in Berlin in 2000, when the city was undergoing intensive urban renewal. With so many construction sites, the city was freed from asphalt—the earth again evident along with the history of its seeds. I removed small samples of earth and potted them, and seeds germinated in the Tiergarten while I researched what events could have potentially contributed to seeds arriving in any one particular site. There have since been iterations in Guangzhou and Dubai.

Wake is an attempt by a resident of a city to create a public forum at an individual level, for active investigations and participation of our place within a space, while considering all its possibilities, which history might limit. Investigations of the history of the earth of the site were conducted based on the vegetal potentials on-site. At the same time, these plant witnesses extended and integrated other possible events and situations, which normally would not be part of a traditional "botanical study."

The research for both these works is based on plants that are non-endemic and that arrived on site in the last hundreds of years. However, in the works *Decolonizing Botany* (2021, in collaboration with Ke´y Rusú Katupyry and Verá Poty Resakã), *This is not an Apricot* (2009), *Bougainvillea* (2009), and *Metaplasmos* (2014), endemic plants are the subject, and the works are concerned with the colonial process of destruction of Indigenous knowledge and relationships of mutual respect.

Do you ever consider plants as subjects in your work, and how does that change your approach to them?

MTA: There are some works I have made about plants that arrived by colonial acts, accidents, or misadventures and not by their own or nonhuman volition. Therefore, they often become by virtue of that simple phenomenon that which is studied. That is to say, it is the often-destructive activities of colonialism that maintain their centrality. The plant themselves, of course, remain subjects and agents in their place.

In your artistic practice, what have you learned from the plants themselves? In which ways does your art follow their movements, metamorphoses, and modes of being in the world? How does it interact with these vegetal processes?

MTA: The plants in *Seeds of Change* and *Wake* are not only the protagonists of these works but are also witnesses of historical narratives that are far more complex than are usually presented by orthodox accounts. For example in the iteration of *Seeds of Change: New York—A Botany of Colonization* (2017), I was very much surprised to discover the vast quantities of earth that was used as ballast in ships from the early days of colonization until the Marshall Plan in 1951. This resulted in much earth being shifted, particularly from the East Coast of the United States to Europe, and vice versa. Hundreds of thousands of tons of ballast arrived in New York City each month. For example, on June 30' 1900, almost 8 million tons of ballast reached the ports of the city from a range of destinations—Colombia, various Caribbean islands, Venezuela, British Guyana, the "Chinese Empire," the Dutch East Indies, Japan, and the British Cape Colony in today's South Africa. The very earth of New York is colonized, and yet that does not signify that what we might term as settler plants are to be acknowledged as the new normality for to do so would make us complicit with colonialism and its violence inflicted on land, plant, and animals.

What ethical or political considerations inform your work with plants? What are the ethical and political implications of this work?

MTA: In *The Return of a Lake*, commissioned for dOCUMENTA(13) an element of the work was the re-creation of a chinampa, a human-made island that is considered the most sustainable agricultural method in Meso-America. However, the re-creation was being carried out in a new situation wherein the water of the lake was salty. We grew various vegetables to see what can survive well within the colonized land and water that no longer respected the relationships between plants and animal. The chinampas of the area had previously all been destroyed when a Spanish colonizer in the early twentieth century unilaterally dried out the lake, which had been a communal resource, and stole the resulting land for nonsustainable monoculture agriculture using the traditional, and for the Americas, destructive European farming method of plowing and irrigation. My work was meant to reiterate the importance of viable Indigenous practices with the land, plants, water, and animals in the current situation, which is still aggressively colonial and dismissive of local traditional knowledge.

Several of my works are based on European colonial practices of destroying languages and thus relationships of Indigenous peoples to land. Tupi-Guarani was the language of the people of the coast of Brazil who inhabited the Atlantic Forest. In Sao Paulo, where I am from, the brutal genocide, along with the prohibition, upon pain of death, by the Portuguese of the use of the language, resulted in the murder of the language. The Indigenous thinking elaborated in conjunction with an intense and millennial relationships with land—murdered. *Metaplasmos* consists of large bronze casts of seeds or fruits from the Atlantic Forest; each is named with Tupi-Guarani words that are difficult to translate into Portuguese as their concepts have no cultural correspondence. Such as *Coigbâcete recou*: strength, as we say, comes from the forest; *Aimõbucu*: to linger in order to postpone as one wishes; and *Aicoabeeng*: to offer something to someone in friendship or as a good upbringing.

And of course, as I previously mentioned: in *Seeds of Change: New York—A Botany of Colonization*, research revealed the extent of the very colonization of the very earth. And that therefore changed my perspective on yet a new level of decolonization that we must work on—the very earth is now from somewhere else. And so much of the earth of New York is in Europe. How do we decolonize? We must begin with the earth.

What, if any, are the aspects of your work with plants related to the current global environmental and mass extinction crises?

MTA: My first on-site installation, *Barra/Barre* (1992, in collaboration with Lynn Lapointe), made by the banks of the Paraguay River in the Pantanal in Mato Grosso, Brazil, questioned the decision process wherein what is considered aesthetically pleasing is worthy of being saved, for example, the Amazon, but not the Pantanal (at that time), which was considered a mere swamp and thus of no interest (to humans).

The installation, *No Soy Su Madre* (*I Am Not Your Mother*) (1990) was my first solo exhibit and was held in the collective gallery space *La Estacion*, founded by Anastacio Acevedo in Cuernavaca, Morelos, in Mexico. The work concerns itself with deforestation and looks at the misogynist language that is then transferred to nature. Such as the concept of the virgin forest, which would have the necessary idea of the rape of the forest attached to it.

To See the Forest Standing (2017) is a 19-channel video installation based on interviews with 34 Indigenous agroforestry agents from the state of Acre in Brazil. They meet once year and discuss their experiments, ideas, and techniques for more efficient agro-forestry methods on Indigenous lands, particularly for areas that have been heavily deforested and destroyed because of cattle ranching by settlers. They are responsible through community consensus for managing reforestation, practicing sustenance farming, overseeing animal life, protecting water sources, providing environmental education programs, and protecting the land from destruction. Some of the reservations, particularly those where major highways were planned to deliberately divide up the lands, have continuous problems, with gold miners, cattle ranchers, hunters, loggers, and settlers. They plant each tree seedling using hand tools and the strength of their bodies—given to the forest. The forest agents are not recognized by the Brazilian government and receive no regular income for their labor and yet they—the makers of our air—are the front line for ensuring the possibility that Brazil and the larger world might have a future. As Poá Katukina, the president of AMAAIAC (Association of the Movement of Indigenous Agroforestry Agents of Acre) says, "We have dedicated ourselves to seeing that the forest stands."

Which pressing challenge, or challenges, has working with plants presented to you?

MTA: My concern with the colonization of plants, land, and animals is the result of my history. The installation *The Flood* (2017) traces human-made actions throughout colonial history until the present, which caused the destruction of a small town my family is from in Brazil. This area had formerly been the Atlantic Forest. Cut down for coffee. Then cut down for sugar cane. Intensive monoculture production resulted in making the nutrients of the earth poor; thus farming was replaced with yet further destruction—cattle ranching. The cattle were imported from Africa, and some seeds attached themselves to their hair. Back in Africa these seeds from the savannas grew quickly after fire had scorched the earth. The favored technique for getting the grasses to grow for cattle in Brazil is to torch the earth. Savanna seeds grew; the rainforest ones did not. A particular plant had arrived, with sharp and spiky leaves. Cattle began dying after eating the spiky leaf, which tore their intestines. The locals then began to grow eucalyptus trees for the production of toilet paper. These trees from water-starved Australia urgently extract water out of the soil and erode the land—crumbling it into heaps. This is where I come from now—how can we love this injured, colonized land? And I do not mean to make peace with the violence inflicted upon it. In 1987, I cofounded the Partido Verde (Green Party) in Sao Paulo and with the help of my cousins was able to register it in this city—hoping that some issues can be raised about the environment. We were able to lobby for the most progressive constitution in regards to the environment in the world at the time. And it would result in hindering the destruction for the Atlantic Forest region. And then the present government came into power, with complete disregard for life.

How is the interaction between your artistic practice and theoretical endeavors shaped by vegetal life?

MTA: I enjoy living in the world which is the entire world. I therefore depend on friends. Sometimes they are different animals, not just humans, and many times they are plants. The terraces in my place in Naples have a great variety of plants which were planted and are maintained by my partner and me. I depend on being with them every day and am grateful for the energy resulting from the connection that is physical, mental, and spiritual. Their modest bounty gives some food to the local birds and provides them with some shelter in this least green of European cities.

It is such a part of life to enjoy whatever fruits and vegetables are seasonal. I am writing this in Berlin, where there is a daily celebration of apples which are so good this year. And sometimes I germinate seeds and give away the seedlings to friends. I have recently been writing about how apple trees and other fruit trees have been

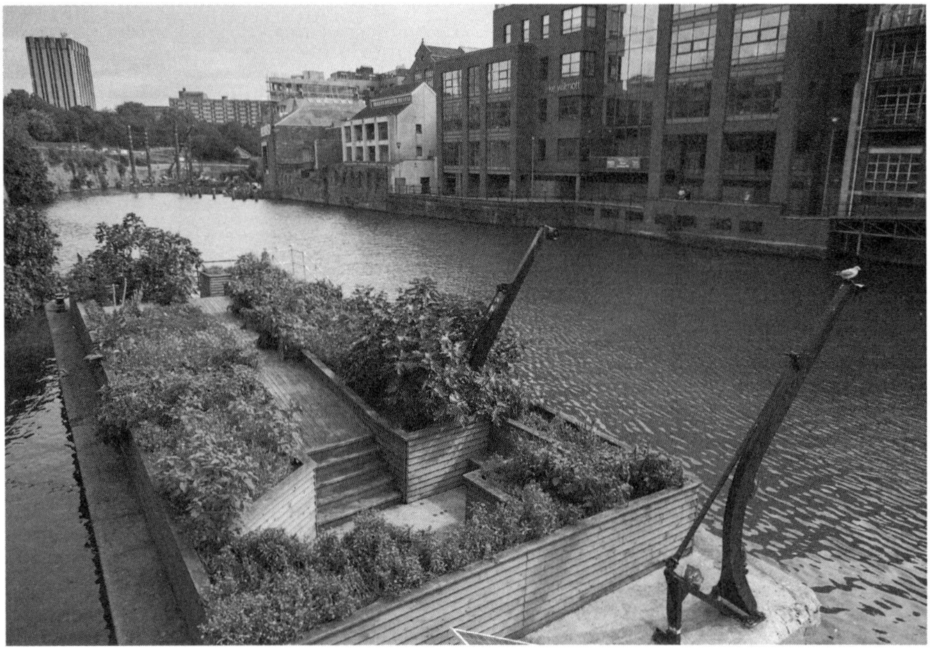

traditionally honored in different parts of the world. People gather around them when they are sickly, and sing to comfort and encourage them. At other times, when there are abundant fruits, people gather and sing to thank them.

Maria Thereza Alves (1961, Brazil) is an artist. Alves was cofounder of the Partido Verde of São Paulo, Brazil in 1987. In 1979, while a member of the International Indian Treaty Council, based in New York, she made an official presentation on the human rights abuses of the indigenous population of Brazil at the UN Human Rights Conference in Geneva. Alves participated in the 2017 Sharjah Biennale, and prior to that in the Bienal de São Paulo of 2016 with a new work, *A Possible Reversal of Missed Opportunities*, which attempts to decolonize the imagination within the Brazilian contemporary context.

Seeds of Change, 1999–, Maria Thereza Alves. (Photography © Max McClure. Reprinted with permission.)

V

INTELLIGENCES

29

THE LIVING THOUGHT

Eduardo Kohn

Funes not only remembered every leaf on every tree of every wood, but even every one of the times he had perceived or imagined it.

I suspect, however, that he wasn't very capable of thinking. Thinking is forgetting differences.

—Jorge Luis Borges, *Funes el Memorioso*

Harvesting fish poison roots[1] in the woody thickets that used to be their gardens, Amériga and Luisa were within earshot when it happened. Back at home, as they talked with Delia over bowls of manioc beer, Luisa imitated how, through the brush, she had heard the family's dogs—Pucaña, or Red Face, their favorite; Cuqui, her aging companion; and Huiqui—barking excitedly, "*hua' hua' hua' hua' hua' hua' hua' hua' hua*," the way they do when they're following game. Then she heard them barking, "*ya ya ya ya*," poised to attack. But then something very disturbing happened. The dogs started yelping, "*aya—i aya—i aya—i*," indicating that now they had been attacked and were in great pain.

"And that," Luisa remarked, "was it. They just fell silent."[2]

Originally published as chapter 2, "The Living Thought," in *How Forests Think? Toward an Anthropology Beyond the Human* (Berkeley: University of California Press, 2013), 71–102. Reprinted with permission.

chun
silence

How could things have changed so suddenly? For the women, the answer turned on imagining how the dogs understood, or, more accurately, failed to understand, the world around them. Reflecting on the first two series of barks, Luisa remarked, "That's what they'd do if they came across something big." That's what they would do, that is, if they came across a big game animal. "Was it a deer they were barking at?" Luisa remembered asking herself. That would make sense. Just a few days before, the dogs had tracked down, attacked, and killed a deer. And we were still eating the meat.

But what creature might look to the dogs like prey but then turn on them? The women concluded that there was only one possible explanation; the dogs must have confused a mountain lion with a red brocket deer. Both have tawny coats and are approximately the same size. Luisa tried to imagine what they were thinking: "It looks like a deer, let's bite it!"

Delia concisely summed up their frustration with the dogs' confusion: "So so stupid." Amériga elaborated: "How is it that they didn't know? How is it that they could even think [of barking], "*yau yau yau*," as if they were going to attack it?"

What each bark meant was clear, for these barks are part of an exhaustive lexicon of canine vocalizations that people in Ávila feel they know. What was less obvious was what, from the dogs' perspectives, prompted them to bark in those ways. To imagine that the dogs might fail to discriminate between a mountain lion and a deer and to trace out the tragic consequences of that confusion—the dogs just saw something big and tawny and attacked it—required thinking beyond what in particular the dogs did, to how it was that what they did was motivated by how they came to understand the world around them. The conversation began to revolve around the question of how dogs think.

This chapter develops the claim that all living beings, and not just humans, think, and explores another closely related claim, that all thoughts are alive. It is about "the living thought."[3] What does it mean to think? What does it mean to be alive? Why are these two questions related, and how does our approach to them, especially when seen in terms of the challenges of relating to other kinds of beings, change our understanding of relationality and "the human"?

If thoughts are alive and if that which lives thinks, then perhaps the living world is enchanted. What I mean is that the world beyond the human is not a meaningless one made meaningful by humans.[4] Rather, meanings—means–ends relations, strivings, purposes, telos, intentions, functions, and significance—emerge in a world of living thoughts beyond the human in ways that are not fully exhausted by our all-too-human attempts to define and control these.[5] More precisely, the forests around Ávila are animate. That is, these forests house other emergent loci of meanings, ones that do not necessarily revolve around, or originate from, humans. This is what I'm getting at when I say that forests think. It is to an examination of such thoughts that this anthropology beyond the human now turns.

If thoughts exist beyond the human, then we humans are not the only selves in this world. We, in short, are not the only kinds of *we*. Animism, the attribution of enchantment to these other-than-human loci, is more than a belief, an embodied practice, or a foil for our critiques of Western mechanistic representations of nature, although it is also all of these as well. We should not, then, just ask how some humans come to represent other beings or entities as animate; we also need to consider more broadly what is it about these that make them animate.

People in Ávila, if they are to successfully penetrate the relational logics that create, connect, and sustain the beings of the forest, must in some way recognize this basic animacy. Runa animism, then, is a way of attending to living thoughts in the world that amplifies and reveals important properties of lives and thoughts. It is a form of thinking about the world that grows out of a specially situated intimate engagement with thoughts-in-the-world in ways that make some of their distinctive attributes visible. Paying attention to these engagements with the living thoughts of the world can help us think anthropology differently. It can help us imagine a set of conceptual tools we can use to attend to the ways in which our lives are shaped by how we live in a world that extends beyond the human.

Dogs, for example, are selves because they think. Counterintuitively, however, proof that they think is that they, in Delia's words, can be "so so stupid"—so indifferent, so dumb. That the dogs in the forest were considered capable of confusing a mountain lion with a deer suggests an important question: How is it that indifference, confusion, and forgetting are so central to the lives of thoughts and the selves that come to house them? The strange and productive power of confusion in the living thought challenges some of our basic assumptions about the roles that difference and otherness, on the one hand, and identity, on the other, play in social theory. This can help us rethink relationality in ways that can take us beyond our tendency to apply our assumptions about the logic of linguistic relationality to all the many possible ways in which selves might relate.

The women certainly felt they were able to interpret the dogs' barks, but that's not what makes them recognize their dogs as selves. What makes their dogs selves is that their barks were manifestations of their interpretations of the world around them. And how those dogs interpreted the world around them, as the women were amply aware, matters vitally. We humans, then, are not the only ones who interpret the world. "Aboutness"—representation, intention, and purpose in their most basic forms—is an intrinsic structuring feature of living dynamics in the biological world. Life is inherently semiotic.[6]

This intrinsically semiotic characteristic applies to all biological processes. Take, for example, the following evolutionary adaptation: the elongated snout and tongue of the giant anteater. The giant anteater, or *tamanuhua*, as it is known in Ávila, can be deadly if cornered. One Ávila man was almost killed by one during my time there, and even jaguars are said to keep well away from them. The giant anteater is also ethereal. I caught a fleeting glimpse of one off in the distance in the forest as Hilario, Lucio, and I were resting on a log on a ridge above the Suno River late one afternoon. Its image still impresses itself on me today: the silhouette of a tapered head, a stocky body, and an enormous, splayed fan of a tail, around whose hairs the late afternoon the sun's rays passed.

Giant anteaters feed exclusively on ants. They do so by inserting their elongated snouts into ant colony tunnels. The specific shape of the anteater's snout and tongue captures certain features of its environment, namely, the shape of ant tunnels. This evolutionary adaptation is a sign to the extent that it is interpreted (in a very bodily way, for there is no consciousness or reflection here) by a subsequent generation with respect to what this sign is about (i.e., the shape of ant tunnels). This interpretation, in turn, is manifested in the development of the subsequent organism's body in a way that incorporates these adaptations. This body (with its adaptations) functions as a new sign representing these features of the environment, insofar as it, in turn, will be interpreted as such by another subsequent generation of anteaters in the eventual development of that generation's body.

Anteater snouts over the generations have come to represent with increasing accuracy something about the geometry of ant colonies because those lineages of "protoanteaters" whose snouts and tongues less accurately captured relevant environmental features (e.g., the shapes of ant tunnels) did not survive as well. Relative to these protoanteaters, then, today's living anteaters have come to exhibit comparatively increasing "fittedness" (Deacon, 2012) to these environmental features. They are more nuanced and exhaustive representations of it.[7] It is in this sense that the logic of evolutionary adaptation is a semiotic one.

Life, then, is a sign process. Any dynamic in which "something . . . stands to somebody, for something in some respect or capacity," as Peirce's (CP 2.228) definition of a sign has it, would be alive. Elongated snouts and tongues *stand to* a future anteater (a "somebody") *for* something about the architecture of an ant colony. One of Peirce's most important contributions to semiotics is to look beyond the classical dyadic understanding of signs as something that stands for something else. Instead, he insisted, we should recognize a crucial third variable as an irreducible component of semiosis: signs stand for something in relation to a "somebody" (Colapietro, 1989, p. 4). As the giant anteater illustrates, this "somebody"—or a self, as I prefer to call it—is not necessarily human, and it need not involve symbolic reference, subjectivity, the sense of interiority, consciousness, or the awareness we often associate with representation for it to count as such (see Deacon, 2012, pp. 465–466).

Furthermore, selfhood is not limited just to animals with brains. Plants are also selves. Nor is it coterminous with a physically bounded organism. That is, selfhood can be distributed over bodies (a seminar, a crowd, or an ant colony can act as a self), or it can be one of many other selves within a body (individual cells have a kind of minimal selfhood).

Self is both the origin and the product of an interpretive process; it is a waypoint in semiosis. A self does not stand outside the semiotic dynamic as "Nature," evolution, watchmaker, homuncular vital spirit, or (human) observer. Rather, selfhood emerges from within this semiotic dynamic as the outcome of a process that produces a new sign that interprets a prior one. It is for this reason that it is appropriate to consider nonhuman organisms as selves and biotic life as a sign process, albeit one that is often highly embodied and nonsymbolic.

MEMORY AND ABSENCE

The giant anteater as a self is a form that selectively "remembers" its own form. That is, a subsequent generation is a likeness of a previous one. It is an iconic representation of its ancestor. But at the same time as such an anteater is a likeness of its forebear (and is thus a sort of memory of it), it also differs from it. For this anteater, with its snout and tongue, can potentially be a relatively more detailed representation of the world around it, insofar (in this case) as its snout, when compared to that of its ancestor, better fits ant tunnels. In sum, the way this anteater remembers or re-presents the generations that came before it is "selective." This is so, in part, thanks to those past protoanteater selves whose snouts didn't "fit" their environments as well and who were thus, in a sense, forgotten.

This play of remembering and forgetting is both unique and central to life; any lineage of living organism—plant or animal—will exhibit this characteristic. Contrast this with, say, a snowflake. Although the particular form that a given snowflake takes is a historically contingent product of the interaction with its environment as it falls to the ground (and this is why we think of snowflakes as exhibiting a sort of individuality; no two are alike), the particular form a snowflake takes is never selectively remembered. That is, once it melts, its form will have no bearing on the form that any subsequent snowflake will take as it begins to fall to the ground.

Living beings differ from snowflakes because life is intrinsically semiotic, and semiosis is always for a self. The form an individual anteater takes comes to represent, for a future instantiation of itself, the environment its lineage has come to fit over evolutionary time. Anteater lineages selectively remember their previous fits to their environments; snowflakes don't.

A self, then, is the outcome of a process, unique to life, of maintaining and perpetuating an individual form, a form that, as it is iterated over the generations, grows to fit the world around it at the same time that it comes to exhibit a certain circular closure that allows it to maintain its selfsame identity, which is forged with respect to that which it is not (Deacon, 2012, p. 471); anteaters re-present previous representations of ant tunnels in their lineage, but they are not themselves ant tunnels. Insofar as it strives to maintain its form, such a self acts for itself. A self, then, whether "skin-bound" or more distributed, is the locus of what we can call agency (pp. 479–480).

Because a giant anteater is a sign, what it is—its particular configuration, the fact, for example, that it has an elongated, as opposed to some other shape of snout—cannot be understood without considering what it is about, namely, the relevant environment that it increasingly comes to fit through the dynamic I've just described. Therefore, although semiosis is embodied, it also always involves something more than bodies. It is about something absent: a semiotically mediated future environment, which is potentially like the environment to which the past generation fit.

A living sign is a prediction of what Peirce calls a habit. That is, it is an expectation of a regularity, something that has not yet come to exist but will likely come to be. Snouts are products of what they are not, namely, the possibility that there will be ant tunnels in the environment into which the snouted anteater will come to live. They are the products of an expectation—of a highly embodied "guess" at what the future will hold.

This is a result of another important absence. As I mentioned earlier, the snouts and the way they fit with the world around them are the result of all the previous wrong "guesses"—the previous generations whose snouts were less like that world of ant tunnels. Because the snouts of these protoanteaters didn't fit the geometry of ant tunnels quite as well as the snouts of others, their forms did not survive into the future.

This way in which selves strive to predict "absent" futures also manifests itself in the purported behavior of Amériga's dogs. The dogs must have barked, the women imagined, at what they expected and trusted was a deer. More accurately, perhaps, they barked at something they saw as big and tawny. Unfortunately, however, mountain lions are also big and tawny. A semiotically mediated future—the possibility of attacking the perceived deer—came to affect the present. It influenced the dogs' decision—"so stupid" in hindsight—to chase the creature they thought was prey.

LIFE AND THOUGHT

A lineage of signs can potentially extend into the future as an emergent habit, insofar as each instantiation will interpret the previous one in a way that can, in turn, be interpreted by a future one. This applies equally to a biological organism, whose progeny may or may not survive into the future, as it does to this book, whose ideas may or may not be taken up in the thinking of a future reader (see Peirce, CP 7.591). Such a process is what constitutes life. That is, any kind of life, be it human, biological, or even, someday, inorganic, will spontaneously exhibit this embodied, localized, representational, future-predicting dynamic that captures, amplifies, and proliferates the tendency toward habit taking in a future instantiation of itself. Another way of saying this is that any entity that stands as a locus of aboutness, within a lineage of such loci that can potentially extend into the future, can be said to be alive. The origins of life—any kind of life, anywhere in the universe—also necessarily mark the origins of semiosis and of self.

It also marks the origins of thought. Life-forms—human and nonhuman alike—because they are intrinsically semiotic, exhibit what Peirce calls a "'scientific' intelligence." By "scientific," he does not mean an intelligence that is human, conscious, or even rational but simply one that is "capable of learning by experience" (CP 2.227). Selves, as opposed to snowflakes, can learn by experience, which is another way of saying that, through the semiotic process I've been describing, they can grow. And this, in turn, is another way of saying that selves think. Such thinking need not happen in the time scale we chauvinistically call real time (see Dennett, 1996, p. 61). It need not happen, that is, within the life of a single skin-bound organism. Biological lineages also think. They too, over the generations, can grow to learn by experience about the world around them, and as such they too demonstrate a "'scientific' intelligence." In sum, because life is semiotic and semiosis is alive, it makes sense to treat both lives and thoughts as "living thoughts." This deepened understanding of the close relationship between life, self, and thought is central to this anthropology beyond the human that I am developing here.

AN ECOLOGY OF SELVES

The semiotic quality of life—the fact that the forms that life takes are the product of how living selves represent the world around them—structures the tropical ecosystem. Although all life is semiotic, this semiotic quality is amplified and made more apparent in the tropical forest, with its unparalleled kinds and quantities of living selves. This is why I want to find ways to attend to how forests think; tropical forests amplify, and thus can make more apparent to us, the ways life thinks.

The worlds that selves represent are not just made up of things. They are also, in large part, made up of other semiotic selves. For this reason, I have come to refer to the web of living thoughts in and around the forests of Ávila as an ecology of selves. This ecology of selves in and around Ávila includes the Runa as well as other humans who interact with them and the forest, and it holds in its configurations not only the many kinds of living beings of the forest but also the spirits and the dead that make us the living beings that we are.

How different kinds of beings represent and are represented by other kinds of beings defines the patterning of life in the forests around Ávila. For example, once a year the colonies of leafcutter ants (*Atta* spp.)—whose presence is normally visible only in the long files of workers carrying to their nests snippets of vegetation they have culled from treetops—change their activity. Over the space of a few minutes, each widely dispersed colony simultaneously disgorges hundreds upon hundreds of plump, winged reproductive ants and sends them flying into the early morning sky to mate with those from other colonies. This event poses, and indeed is structured by, a variety of challenges and opportunities. How do the ants, living in far-flung colonies, manage to coordinate their flights? How can predators tap into this rich but ephemeral cache? And what strategies do the ants use to avoid being eaten? These flying ants, overburdened with fat reserves, are a savory delicacy that people in Ávila, as well as many others who live in the Amazon, covet. Indicative of how much they are valued, they are known simply as *añangu*, ants. Toasted with salt they are a delicacy, and collected by the potful they are an important food source during the limited time they are available. How do people manage to predict the few minutes in each year when these will come out of their underground nests?

The problem of when the ants fly can tell us something about how the rain forest comes to be what it is: an emergent and expanding multilayered cacophonous web of mutually constitutive, living, and growing thoughts. Because in this part of the equatorial tropics there are no marked seasonal changes in sunlight or temperature, and no corresponding spring bloom, there is no one stable cue external to the interactions among forest beings that determines or predicts when ants will fly. The timing of this event is a product of the coordinated prediction of seasonal meteorological regularities as well as an orchestration among different, competing, and interpreting species.

According to people in Ávila the winged ants emerge in the calm that follows a period of heavy rains that includes thunder and lightning and the flooding of rivers. This stormy period brings to a close a relatively drier period that usually occurs around August. People try to predict the emergence of the ants by linking it to a variety of ecological signs associated with fruiting regimes, increases in insect populations, and changes in animal activity.[8] When the various indicators point to the fact that "ant season" (*añangu uras*) is at hand, people go to the various nests around their houses several times throughout the night to check for the telltale signs that the ants will soon take flight. These signs include the presence of guards clearing entrances of debris and sightings of a few slowly emerging and still somewhat lethargic winged ants.

People in Ávila are not the only ones interested in when these ants will fly. Other creatures, such as frogs, snakes, and small felines,[9] are attracted to the ants, as well as to those other animals that are attracted to the ants. They all watch the ants and watch those watching the ants for signs of when the ants will emerge from their nests.

Although the day of the flight is closely linked to meteorological patterns, and this seems to be how the ants coordinate their flights with those from other nests, the precise moment at which the flight will take place on that day is a response, sedimented over evolutionary time, to what it is that potential predators might, or might not, notice. It is no accident that the ants take flight just before daybreak (at exactly 5:10, when I've been able to time it). When they are in their nests the aggressive guards of the colony protect them from snakes, frogs, and other predators. Once they take flight, however, they are on their own, and they can fall prey to the lingering fruit-eating bats still out at twilight who attack them in midflight by biting off their greatly enlarged, fat-filled abdomens. How bats see the world matters vitally to the flying ants. It is no accident that the ants take flight at the time they do. Although some lingering bats are still out, by this time they will only be active for twenty or thirty minutes longer. When the birds come out (not long after a six o'clock sunrise) most of the ants will have already dispersed, and some females will have already copulated and fallen to the ground to establish new colonies. The precise timing of the ant flight is an outcome of a semiotically structured ecology. The ants emerge at twilight—that blurry zone between night and day—when nocturnal and diurnal predators are least likely to notice them.

People attempt to enter some of the logic of the semiotic network that structures ant life in order to capture the ants during those few minutes in the year when they fly out of their nests. One night, as the ants were about to fly, Juanicu asked me for a cigarette so that he could blow tobacco smoke infused with the power of his "life breath" (*samai*) in order to send the impending rain clouds away. If it rained that evening the ants would not emerge. His wife, Olga, however, urged him not to ward off the rain clouds. She feared that their sons, who had gone to market in Loreto, would not return from town until the following day. They would be needed to harvest the ants that would be pouring out of the various nests around the house. To make sure the ants would not fly that night, she went out to all the nearby nests and stomped on them. This, she said, would keep the ants from coming out that evening.

On the night that Juanicu felt sure the ants would finally fly, he urged me, before I went out with his children in the middle of the night to check the nests, not to kick or step heavily around the nest. Then, shortly before five in the morning, at a distance of about four meters from the entrance of the nest closest to the house, Juanicu and I placed some lit kerosene lanterns as well as some of my candles and my flashlight. The winged ants are attracted to light and would be drawn to these sources. The lights were placed far enough away, however, so that the guards would not consider them threatening.

As the ants began to emerge Juanicu spoke only in whispers. Shortly after five o'clock we could hear a buzzing as the winged ants began to come out from the nest and fly off. Many of these were attracted by the light and came to us instead of flying to the sky. Juanicu then began to whistle like a siren alternating between two different pitches. This, he later explained, is something the flying ants understand as the call of their "mothers."[10] As the ants came to us, we singed off their wings with torches made of dry *lisan* leaves.[11] We were then easily able to place them into covered pots.[12]

The leafcutter ants are immersed in an ecology of selves that has shaped their very being; that they emerge just before dawn is an effect of the interpretive propensities of their major predators. People in Ávila also attempt to tap into the communicative universe of the ants and of the many creatures connected to them. Such a strategy has practical effects; people are able to gather vast quantities of ants based on them.

By treating ants as the intentional communicating selves they are, Juanicu was able to arrive at an understanding of the various associations that link ants to the other beings in the forest—an understanding that is surely never absolute, but sufficient to accurately predict the few moments in the year when these ants will fly. He was also able to communicate directly with them, calling them to their deaths. In doing so he was, in effect, entering the logic of how forests think. This is possible because his (and our) thoughts are in important respects like those that structure the relations among those living thoughts that make the forest what it is: a dense, flourishing ecology of selves.

SEMIOTIC DENSITY

The interrelations among so many different semiotic life-forms in this dense ecology of selves result in a relatively more nuanced and exhaustive overall representation of the surrounding environment when compared to the way life represents elsewhere on the planet. That is, the "thoughts" of a tropical forest come to represent the world in a relatively more detailed way. For example, a number of tropical tree species have evolved as specialists that grow only on white-sand soils. Tropical white-sand soils, as contrasted to tropical clay soils, are nutrient-poor, do not hold water well, and have characteristics such as high acidity that can slow plant growth. However, it is not the soil conditions in themselves that account for the fact that there are specialists that live on white-sand soils. Rather, the fact that there are such specialists is the result of their relation to another set of life-forms: plant-eating organisms, or herbivores (Marquis, 2004, p. 619).

Because of the extremely poor conditions of these white-sand soils, plants have difficulty repairing themselves fast enough to sustain the levels of nutrient loss incurred by herbivory. Thus, there is great selective pressure for plants living on such nutrient-poor soils to develop highly specialized toxic compounds and other defenses against herbivory (Marquis, 2004, p. 620).

Interestingly, however, soil differences do not directly affect what kinds of plants can grow where. Fine, Mesones, and Coley (2004) have shown that when herbivores are experimentally removed from poor-soil plots, and rich-soil species experimentally transplanted in, the rich-soil species actually grow better than those adapted to poor soils.

So one could say that tropical plants come to represent something about their soil environments by virtue of their interactions with the herbivores that amplify the differences in soil conditions and thus make these differences important to plants. That is, differences in soil types wouldn't make a difference to the plants if it weren't for these other life-forms. This is why rich-soil plants, not burdened by the need to produce energetically costly toxins, grow better than poor-soil plants in poor-soils plots that have been kept free of herbivores experimentally.[13]

In temperate regions, where insectivorous herbivores are far fewer, there is very little specialization of plants to soil type even in areas where soil heterogeneity (i.e., the juxtaposition of nutrient rich and poor soils) is higher than in tropical regions (Fine, 2004, p. 2). Another way to say this is that plants in the tropics, as opposed to those in temperate regions, come to form relatively more nuanced representations of the characteristics of their environments. They make more differentiations among soil types because of the ways they are caught up in a relatively denser web of living thoughts.

This herbivore-dependent amplification effect of soil differences does not stop with plants but continues to propagate through the ecology of selves. Tannin, for example, is a chemical defense that many Amazonian poor-soil plants have developed against herbivores. Because microorganisms cannot easily break down tannin-rich leaf litter, this compound leaches into rivers, where it is toxic to fish and many other organisms. As a consequence, ecosystems associated with rivers that drain large expanses of white-sand soil are not able to support as much animal life (Janzen, 1974), and historically this has had an important impact on humans living in the

Amazon (Moran, 1993). The various forms that all these ecologically related kinds of life take are not reducible to the characteristics of soil. I'm not making an argument for environmental determinism.[14] And yet this multispecies assemblage captures and amplifies something about the differences in soil conditions precisely as a function of the greater number of relations (relative to other ecosystems) among kinds of selves that exist in this ecology of selves.

RELATIONALITY

Selves, in short, are thoughts, and the modes by which such selves relate to one another stem from their constitutively semiotic nature and the particular associational logics this entails. Considering the logic by which these selves relate in this ecology of selves challenges us to rethink relationality—arguably our field's fundamental concern and central analytic (Strathern, 1995).

If selves are thoughts and the logic through which they interact is semiotic, then relation is representation. That is, the logic that structures relations among selves is the same as that which structures relations among signs. This, in itself, is not a new idea. Whether or not we are explicit about it, we already tend to think of relationality in terms of representation in the ways we theorize society and culture. But we do so based on our assumptions about how human symbolic representation works. Like the words that exist in the conventional relational configurations that make up a language, the relata—be these ideas, roles, or institutions—that make up a culture or a society, do not precede the mutually constitutive relationships these relata have with one another in a system that necessarily comes to exhibit a certain closure by virtue of this fact.

Even posthuman relational concepts, such as Bruno Latour's "actant," the networks of actor-network theory, and Haraway's "constitutive intra-action" (Haraway, 2008, pp. 32, 33), rely on assumptions about relationality that stem from the special kinds of relational properties we find in human language. In fact, in some versions of actor-network theory the relational networks that connect humans and nonhuman entities are explicitly described as language-like (see Law and Mol, 2008, p. 58).[15]

But representation, as I have been arguing, is something both broader than and different from what we expect given how our thinking about it has been linguistically colonized. Extending linguistic relationality to nonhumans narcissistically projects the human onto that which lies beyond it. And along with language comes a host of assumptions about systematicity, context, and difference, which stem from some of the distinctive properties of human symbolic reference and are not necessarily relevant to how living thoughts might more generally relate. In the process, other properties that might permit a more capacious view of relationality are obscured. My claim, in short, is that an anthropology beyond the human can rethink relationality by seeing it as semiotic, but not always and necessarily language-like.

Consider, in this regard, the relation between a wood tick and the mammals it parasitizes, a relation made classic by the early-twentieth-century ethologist Jakob von Uexküll (1982). Ticks, according to von Uexküll, perceive mammals, whose blood they suck, from the smell of butyric acid, warmth, and the ability to detect the bare patches of mammalian skin where they can burrow. According to him, their experiential world, or *umwelt* as he called it, is limited to just these three parameters (Uexküll, 1982, pp. 57, 72). For von Uexküll, and many of those who have picked up on his work, the tick's experiential world is closed and "poor," in the sense that the tick doesn't differentiate among many entities (see Agamben, 2004). But I want to emphasize the productive power of this simplification that is central to living thoughts and to the relations that emerge among the selves that are the products of living thoughts. And I want to highlight the fact that its relational logic is semiotic, but not distinctively symbolic.

Ticks do not distinguish among many kinds of mammals. It makes no difference to ticks that, for example, a dog might be wise to distinguish a predatory mountain lion from potential prey like the red brocket deer. The tick will confuse these two with each other and these with the dogs as well.

Ticks are also vectors for parasites, and because of the ways ticks fail to distinguish among mammals whose blood they indiscriminately suck, these parasites can pass from one species to another. This indiscrimination is a form of confusion, which of course has its limits. If the tick confused everything with everything else, there would be no thinking here and no life; confusion is only productive when it is constrained.

For the tick, one kind of mammal is, in Peircean terms, iconic of another. I want to highlight this view of iconism because it goes against our everyday understandings of the term. When we treat icons (signs that signify through similarity), we usually think of the ways in which we take them to be like some aspect of something else that we already know to be different. We do not, as I mentioned, confuse a stick figure depiction of a man posted on the door of a washroom with the person who might enter through that door. But I'm alluding here to a more fundamental—and often misunderstood—iconic property, one that underlies all semiosis. To the tick, mammals are equivalent, simply because the tick doesn't notice the differences among the beings it parasitizes.

This iconic confusion is productive. It creates "kinds." There emerges a general class of beings whose members are linked to each other because of the ways they are all noticed by ticks, who do not discriminate among them. This emergence of a general class matters to the beings involved. Because the tick confuses these warm-blooded beings, other parasites can travel among them (the "mammals") through the tick. This, in fact, is how Lyme disease is transmitted from deer to humans.

The world of living beings is neither just a continuum nor a collection of disparate singularities waiting to be grouped—according to social convention or innate propensity—by a human mind. It is true that categorization can be socioculturally specific and that it can lead to a form of conceptual violence in that it erases the uniqueness of those categorized. And it is also true that the power of human language lies in its ability to jump out of the local in ways that can result in an increased insensitivity to detail. Speaking of a Japanese insect collector, Hugh Raffles (2002) writes:

> After collecting for so many years, he now has "*mushi*" eye, bug eyes, and sees everything in nature from an insect's point of view. Each tree is its own world, each leaf is different. Insects taught him that general nouns like *insects*, *trees*, *leaves*, and especially *nature* destroy our sensitivity to detail. They make us conceptually as well as physically violent. "Oh, an insect," we say, seeing only the category, not the being itself. (p. 345)

And yet seeing the world with "bug eyes" in many instances actually involves confusing what we might otherwise take as different entities, and this sort of confusion is neither exclusively human nor only destructive.

Borges's character Ireneo Funes, mentioned in this chapter's epigraph, was thrown by a wild horse and suffered a head injury, with the result that he could no longer forget anything. He became "*memorioso*." But living selves are precisely not like Funes, who was incapable of forgetting the distinctive features of "every leaf on every tree of every wood." This, as Borges points out, is not thinking. The life of thoughts depends on confusion—a kind of "forgetting" to notice difference. Generals, such as kinds and classes, emerge from and flourish in the world through a form of relating based on confusion. The real is not just the unique singularity, different from everything else. Generals are also real, and some generals emerge as a product of the relations among living thoughts beyond the human.

How could Amériga, Delia, and Luisa presume to guess at what their dogs were thinking? More generally, how can we ever hope to know these other living selves with whom we relate? Even if we grant that nonhuman lifeforms are selves, doesn't there exist, in Derrida's (2008, p. 30) words, such an "abyssal rupture" separating us from them that theirs might be better thought as an "existence that refuses to be conceptualized" (p. 9)? Might these "absolute other[s]" (p. 11) not be like Wittgenstein's lion; even if they could talk, who would understand them? Thomas Nagel's (1974) answer to the question he posed his fellow philosophers, *What is it like to be a bat?*, was decisive; although there is surely something that it is like to be a bat—that bats, in effect, have some kind of selfhood—we can never know it. We are just too different.

Granted, Amériga, Luisa, and Delia will never know with certainty what their dogs were thinking as they barked at that feline moments before it attacked them, but they could make some good guesses. What, then, might a theory of relating look like that started, not with the search for some secure knowledge of other beings, but with the sorts of provisional guesses that these women were forced to make about the guesses their dogs, in turn, might be making? Such a theory would not begin with what Haraway (2003, p. 49) calls "irreducible difference," nor would it take the refusal to be conceptualized, or its logical opposite, absolute understanding, as inhabitable endpoints.

Absolute otherness, irreducible difference, incommensurablity—these are taken to be the hurdles that our theories of relating must strive to overcome. That there exist differences that are radically inconceivable—differences that are so unimaginable that they are "incognizable" as Peirce (1992b, p. 24) critically calls them—implies an opposite: that knowability is based on intrinsic self-similarity. It implies that there exists such a thing as "being itself" in all its singularity, which we might comprehend if we could just adopt "bug eyes." These poles are taken to define how beings can relate to and know each other.

However, when we consider "the living thought," similarity and difference become interpretive positions (with potential future effects). They are not intrinsic characteristics that are immediately apparent. "All thought and knowledge," writes Peirce, "is by signs" (CP 8.332). That is, all thinking and knowing is mediated in some way.

This has important implications for understanding relating. There is no inherent difference between the associations of living thoughts that constitute the living, thinking, knowing self and those by which different kinds of selves might relate and thereby form associations. Further, because selves are loci of living thoughts—emergent ephemeral waypoints in a dynamic process—there is no unitary self. There is no one thing that one could "be": "[A] person is not absolutely an individual. His thoughts are what he is 'saying to himself,' that is, is saying to that other self that is just coming into life in the flow of time" (Peirce, CP 5.421). Because all experiences and all thoughts, for all selves, are semiotically mediated, introspection, human-to-human intersubjectivity, and even trans-species sympathy and communication are not categorically different. They are all sign processes. For Peirce, the Cartesian *cogito*, the "I think," is not exclusively human, nor is it housed inside the mind, nor does it enjoy any exclusive or unmediated purchase on its most intimate object: the self that we commonly think of as the one doing our thinking.

Peirce illustrates this by asking us to imagine what red looks like to others. Far from being a private phenomenon, he argues, we can be pretty confident that we can have some sense of this. We can even have some idea of what this color is like to a blind person who has never seen red but who gathers from others that it resembles the sound of trumpets: "The fact that I can see a certain analogy, shows me not only that my feeling of redness is something like the feelings of the persons whom he had heard talk, but also his feeling of a trumpet's blare was very much like mine" (CP 1.314).[16] Peirce concludes by suggesting that self-knowledge is ultimately like these processes: "My metaphysical friend who asks whether we can ever enter into one another's feelings . . . might just as well ask me whether I am sure that red looked to me yesterday as it does today" (CP 1.314). Introspection and intersubjectivity are semiotically mediated. We can only come to know ourselves and others through the medium of signs. It makes no difference whether that interpreting self is located in another kind of body or whether it is "that other self"—our own psychological one—"that is just coming into life in the flow of time," as one sign is interpreted by a new one in that semiotic process by which thoughts, minds, and our very being qua self emerge.

Rather than make knowledge of selves impossible, this mediation is the basis for its possibility. Because there is no absolute "incognizable," there is also no absolute incommensurability. We can know something of how red might be experienced by a blind person, what it might be like to be a bat, or what those dogs might have been thinking moments before they were attacked, however mediated, provisional, fallible, and tenuous these understandings may be. Selves relate the way that thoughts relate: we are all living, growing thoughts.

A simple example illustrates this. The Runa make scarecrows, or more accurately "scare-parakeets," in order to scare white-eyed parakeets from their cornfields.

They do so by binding together in a cross two flattened pieces of balsa wood of equal length. They paint these with red and black stripes using *achiote*[17] and charcoal, respectively. They also carve the top part to fashion a head and paint big eyes on it, and they sometimes insert the distinctively barred tail feathers of an actual raptor at the ends of the pieces of wood that will serve to represent the tail and the wings.

The elaborate fashion in which the Runa decorate this scarecrow is not an attempt to "realistically" represent a raptor from the human point of view. Rather, it constitutes an attempt to imagine what from the parakeet's perspective of a raptor looks like. The scarecrow is an icon. It stands for a raptor by virtue of the likeness it has with the raptor for somebody—here, the parakeet. By virtue of stripes, big eyes, and actual tail feathers, the scarecrow captures something of what a raptor is like for a parakeet. This is why parakeets, but not humans, confuse these scarecrows with raptors. Proof of this is that these scarecrows successfully keep parakeets away and are thus made from year to year in Ávila. We can know something of what it is like to be a parakeet, and we know this by the effects that our guesses at how parakeets think can have on them.

ENCHANTMENT

It is very difficult from within our contemporary analytical frameworks to understand the biological world as made up of living thoughts. This, following Max Weber's (1948a, 1948b) diagnosis of the disenchantment of the modern world, is in part an effect of the spread of scientific rationalism. As we come to increasingly see the world in mechanistic terms, we lose sight of the telos, the significance, the means-ends relations—in short, the mean-ings, as I call them, to highlight the close relationship between means and meanings—that were once recognized in the world. The world becomes disenchanted in the sense that ends are no longer to be found in the world. The world becomes literally meaningless. Ends become displaced to a human or spiritual realm that becomes ever smaller and more detached from the mundane world as this vision of science expands to encompass more domains.

If modern forms of knowledge and ways of manipulating the nonhuman world are characterized by an understanding of the world as mechanism, then disenchantment is an obvious consequence. Machines, as material objects, are means to achieve ends that are, by definition and design, external to them. When we contemplate a machine—say, a dishwasher—we bracket out the ends that are actually intrinsic to its being, namely, that it was built for some end by somebody. Applying this logic to the nonhuman living world, seeing nature as a machine, requires a similar bracketing and a subsequent ascription of ends to humans, gods, or Nature. Dualism is one result of this bracketing. Another is that we begin to lose sight of ends altogether. Disenchantment spreads into the realm of the human and the spiritual as we come to suspect that perhaps there simply are no ends and hence no meaning—anywhere.

But ends are not located somewhere outside the world, but constantly flourishing in it. They are intrinsic to the realm of life. Living thoughts "guess" at and thus create futures to which they then shape themselves. Nor is the logic that structures the living world like that of a machine. Unlike machines, living thoughts emerge whole instead of being built from parts by someone bracketed out of the picture. If we attend to Runa engagements with other kinds of beings, as I aim to do here through this anthropology beyond the human, we can come to appreciate selves (both human and nonhuman) as waypoints in the lives of signs—loci of enchantment—and this can help us imagine a different sort of flourishing in this world beyond the human in which we live.

I'm making a claim here about some of the properties of life "itself." Although I recognize how something like life itself can be historically circumscribed—that certain concepts can only become thinkable in specific historical, social, or cultural contexts (Foucault, 1970). Language and the related discursive regimes that condition so much of our thought and action are not closed. Although we must of course be cautious about the ways in which language (and by extension, certain socially stabilized modes of thought and action) naturalizes categories of thought, we can venture to talk about something like life "itself" without being fully constrained by the language that carries this forth.

Nonhuman selves, then, have ontologically unique properties associated with their constitutively semiotic nature. And these are, to a certain extent, knowable to us. These properties differentiate selves from objects or artifacts. Treating nonhumans generically—indiscriminately lumping together things and beings—however, misses this. And this, to my mind, is the biggest shortcoming of STS [science, technology, and society studies], the dominant approach for expanding the social sciences to consider nonhumans.

STS brings nonhumans and humans into the same analytical framework through a form of reductionism that leaves concepts like agency and representation unexamined. As a consequence, the distinctively human instantiations of these become stand-ins for all agency and representation. The result is a form of dualism in which humans and nonhumans acquire mixtures of thinglike and humanlike properties.

Latour (1993, 2004), the main proponent of this approach, for example, attributes agency either to that which can be represented or to that which can resist our attempts at representation (see also Pickering, 1999, pp. 380–381). But these characteristics only capture what, in Peircean terms, would be called the secondness, that is the actuality or brute factuality, of the entity in question—for anything can potentially resist representation or be represented—and this simply reinstates the material/meaning divide STS tries to overcome. We still have, on the one hand, the material (now agentified), and, on the other, those humans (now made a little more obtuse and less certain of their omniscience) who represent or misrepresent things, as the case may be.

But resistance is not agency. Conflating resistance and agency blinds us to the kinds of agency that do in fact exist beyond the human. Because telos, representation, intentionality, and selfhood still need to be accounted for and because the way such processes emerge and operate beyond the human is not theorized, Latourian science studies is forced to fall back on humanlike forms of representation and intentionality as operative in the world beyond the human. These are then applied, if only metaphorically, to entities otherwise understood only in their secondness.

Substances, for example, undergo the "sufferings" of trials (Latour, 1987, p. 88), and they sometimes emerge successfully as "heroes" (p. 89). The piston of an engine is more reliable than a human operator, "since it is, via the cam, *directly interested*, so to speak, in the right timing of steam. Certainly it is more directly interested than any human being" (p. 130; Latour's emphasis). And scientists use "a set of strategies to enlist and interest the human actors, and a second set to enlist and interest the non-human actors so as to hold the first" (p. 132).

This approach to nonhuman agency overlooks the fact that some nonhumans, namely, those that are alive, are selves. As selves, they are not just represented, but they also represent. And they can do so without having to "speak." Nor do they need a "spokesperson" (Latour, 2004, pp. 62–70) because representation exceeds the symbolic, and it therefore exceeds human speech.

Although we humans certainly represent nonhuman living beings in a number of culturally, historically, and linguistically distinct ways, and this surely has its effects, both for us and for those beings thus represented, we also live in worlds in which how these selves represent us can come to matter vitally. Accordingly, my concern is with exploring interactions, not with nonhumans generically—that is, treating objects, artifacts, and lives as equivalent entities—but with nonhuman living beings in terms of those distinctive characteristics that make themselves.

Selves, not things, qualify as agents. Resistance is not the same as agency. Nor, contra Bennett (2010), does materiality confer vitality. Selves are the product of a specific relational dynamic that involves absence, future, and growth, as well as the ability for confusion. And this emerges with and is unique to living thoughts.

ANIMISM

I want to return to the anecdote with which I began this book. Recall that when I was in the forest on a hunting trip, I was told to make sure to sleep faceup. This way if a jaguar were to pass by he would see me as a being capable of looking back and would leave me alone. If I were to sleep facedown, I was warned, that potential passing jaguar might well treat me as prey and attack me. My point was that this anecdote forces us to recognize that how jaguars see us matters to us, and that if this is so, then anthropology cannot limit itself to asking how people see the world. I noted that by returning the feline's gaze, we allow jaguars the possibility of treating us as selves. If, by contrast, we were to look away, they would treat us as, and we may actually become, objects—literally, dead meat, aicha.

The linguist Émile Benveniste (1984) observes that the pronouns *I* and *you* position interlocutors intersubjectively through mutual address, and accordingly he considers these true "person" pronouns. By contrast, the third person is more accurately a "non-person" (Benveniste, 1984, p. 221). It refers to something outside of the discursive interaction. If we extend this reasoning to trans-species encounters, then jaguars and humans, in this act of looking back at each other, would, in a sense, become persons to each other. And in the process, the Runa, in a way, would also become jaguars.

Indeed, as I mentioned in the introduction, the Ávila Runa are renowned—and feared—throughout lowland Runa communities for their ability to become shape-shifting were-jaguars. A person who is treated by a jaguar as prey may well become dead meat. By contrast, one who is treated by a jaguar as a predator becomes another predator. Predator and prey—puma and aicha—are the two kinds of beings that jaguars recognize. As with the tick, how jaguars represent other beings makes beings into kinds. And what kind of a being one thus becomes matters.

Puma in Quichua simply means "predator." For example, in Ávila the name for the crab-eating raccoon,[18] whose diet includes, among other things, crustaceans and mollusks, is *churu puma*, snail predator. Because the jaguar exemplifies the quintessence of predation, it is simply known as puma. Runa who survive encounters with such predators are by definition, then, runa puma, or were-jaguars (the term *Runa* is not only an ethnonym; it also means "person"). One survives, then, by not being noticed as prey by a puma. But in the process one also becomes another kind of being, a puma. And this newfound status translates to other contexts and creates new possibilities.

Puma is a relational category—not, in this respect, unlike the pronouns *I* and *you*. That we can become puma by returning a puma's gaze is a way of saying that we both are kinds of *Is*—that we both are kinds of persons. The Runa, like other Amazonians, treat jaguars and many other nonhuman beings as soul-possessing, signifying, intentional selves. They are (to use a recently resuscitated term) animists; for them, nonhumans are animate. They are persons.

Animism, as it is currently being theorized by people like Descola (2005) and Viveiros de Castro (1998), is quite different from its earlier social evolutionist and sometimes even racist incarnations, and it has provided an important foil for critiquing Western mechanistic representations of nature. And yet such critiques of the ways we in the "West" represent nature only asks how other humans come to treat nonhumans as animate. In this respect these approaches stand in continuity with such classical treatments of animism as Lévy-Bruhl's *How Natives Think* (1926). The case of the jaguar troubles this project; if jaguars also represent us, we cannot just ask how it is that some of us humans happen to represent them as doing so.

Animism, to my mind, gets at something more far reaching about the properties of the world, and this is why thinking with it is central to an anthropology beyond the human. It captures an animation that is emergent with life, hence my title, *How Forests Think*. Runa animism grows out of a need to interact with semiotic selves qua selves in all their diversity. It is grounded in an ontological fact: there exist other kinds of thinking selves beyond the human.

I recognize of course that those we call animists may well attribute animacy to all sorts of entities, such as stones, that I would not, according to the framework laid out here, consider living selves. If I were building an argument from within a particular animistic worldview, if I were routing all my argumentation through what, say, the Runa think, say, or do, this discrepancy might be a problem. But I don't. Part of my attempt to open anthropology to that which lies beyond the human involves finding ways to make general claims about the world. These claims don't necessarily line up with certain situated human viewpoints, like, say, those of animists, or those of biologists, or those of anthropologists.

How Forests Think, not *How Natives Think about Forests* (cf. Sahlins, 1995): if we limit our thinking to thinking through how other people think, we will always end up circumscribing ontology by epistemology. I am making here a general claim about selfhood. This general claim—which is not exactly an ethnographic one in the sense that it is not circumscribed by an ethnographic context, even though it is suggested, explored, and defended, in part, ethnographically—is that living beings are loci of selfhood. I make this claim empirically. It grows out of my attention to Runa relations with nonhuman beings as these reveal themselves ethnographically. These relations amplify certain properties of the world, and this amplification can infect and affect our thinking about the world.

One might say that the animal person is the model of the universe for animists, whereas for us it is the machine. Ontologically speaking, each has its own truth: animals are persons, and there are things about the world that do resemble partible machines (which is a reason why reductionist science is so successful). But my goal here is not to say which one is right or to point out where each fails but rather to see how certain kinds of engagements, based on certain presuppositions that themselves grow out of those engagements, amplify unexpected and real properties of the world that we can harness to think beyond the human as we know it.

Runa animism is pragmatically oriented. The challenge for the Runa, as people who engage intimately with the beings of the forest in order, in large part, to eat them, is to find ways to enter this vast ecology of selves to harness some of its plenty. This requires being attuned to the unexpected affinities we share with other selves while at the same time recognizing the differences that distinguish the many kinds of selves that people the forest.

PERSPECTIVISM

Like many Amazonians, people in Ávila approach this through a way of understanding others that Viveiros de Castro (1998) has described as "perspectival." This stance assumes a fundamental similarity among selves—that all kinds of selves are *I*s. But it also allows for a way to account for the unique qualities that characterize different kinds of beings. It involves two interlocking assumptions. First, all sentient beings, be they spirit, animal, or human, see themselves as persons. That is, their subjective worldview is identical to the way the Runa see themselves. Second, although all beings see themselves as persons, the ways in which they are seen by other beings depends on the kinds of beings observing and being observed. For example, people in Ávila say that what we perceive as the stench of rotting carrion a vulture experiences as the sweet-smelling vapor emanating from a steaming pot of manioc tubers. Vultures, because of their species-specific habits and dispositions, inhabit a different world from that of the Runa. Yet because their subjective point of view is that of persons, they see this *different* world in the same way the Runa see their own world (Viveiros de Castro, 1998, p. 478).[19]

A tendency to see things perspectivally permeates daily life in Ávila.[20] For instance, a myth that explains why the Amazon bamboo rat[21] has such a loud call relates how this creature once asked a fallen log what women's genitals look like from its vantage point. Since such logs constitute the preferred causeways that women use to traverse their gardens, the rat figured that the log was in a privileged position to know this.[22] Alluding to the rat's abundant whiskers, the log responded, "Like your mouth." Hearing this, the rat responded, "Oh stop,"[23] and then exploded in the bawdy laughter that is now associated with its distinctive loud, long, and seemingly uncontrollable staccato call as well as its onomatopoeic name *gunguta*.[24] The humor in this myth for people in Ávila is as much about the sexually explicit reference as it is about the perspectival logic.

Another common form of perspectival joking in Ávila, as well as in other Runa communities, occurs when two people share the same name. Because I share my first name with a man in Ávila the running joke was that his wife was married to me.[25] His older sister jokingly addressed me as *turi* (sister's brother), and I addressed her as *pani* (brother's sister). Similarly, a woman who shares my sister's middle name called me brother, and one with my mother's name called me son. In all these cases shared names allowed us to inhabit a shared perspective. It allowed us to create an affectionate relationship despite the fact that our worlds are so different.

Perspectivism is certainly a historically contingent aesthetic orientation—an orientation that, pace Viveiros de Castro, we might, in this sense, describe as "cultural"—but it is also an ecologically contingent amplificatory effect of the need to understand semiotic selves in a way that simultaneously recognizes their continuity with us as well as their differences. It is a response to the challenges of getting by in an ecology of selves whose relational webs extend well beyond the human, and it emerges from everyday interactions with forest beings.

People in Ávila try to make sense of these various selves that inhabit the forest by trying to see how they see, and by imagining how different perspectives interact. One man took delight in explaining to me how the giant anteater adopts the perspective of ants in order to fool them; when the anteater sticks its tongue into ant nests, the ants see it as a branch and, unsuspecting, climb on. In their interactions with animals, the Runa, in many ways, try to emulate the anteater. They attempt to capture the perspective of another organism as part of a larger whole. This is what is involved in making a scarecrow. It is also employed in certain techniques used to catch fish. Ventura's father used to paint his hands a dark purple with the crushed fruits of *shangu*, a distant ginger relative,[26] so that armored catfish[27] would not notice his attempts to grab them from underneath the rocks and boulders in the river.

Such ecological challenges of understanding how the anteater eats ants, or how to make a scarecrow that will scare parakeets, or how to fish for catfish without being recognized by them requires an attentiveness to the points of view of other organisms. This attentiveness grows out of the fact that ants, parakeets, armored catfish, and indeed all the other life-forms that make up the rain forest, are selves. Who and what they are is, through and through, the product of the ways they represent and interpret the world around them and the ways in which others in that world represent them. They are selves, in short, that have a point of view. This is what makes them animate, and this animation enchants the world.

THE FEELING OF THINKING

People in Ávila take great pleasure in finding a viewpoint that encompasses multiple perspectives. One Ávila myth exquisitely captures this aspect of a perspectival aesthetic. It begins with a hero on top of his roof patching it. When a man-eating jaguar approaches, the hero calls out to him, "Son-in-law, help me find holes in the thatch by poking a stick through them." From the vantage point of someone inside a house, it is quite easy to spot leaks in the thatch because of the sunlight that shines through them. However, because roofs are so high, it is impossible, from this position, to patch these. A person on the roof, on the other hand, can easily patch the holes but cannot see them. For this reason, when a man is patching his roof he will ask someone inside to poke a stick through the holes. This has the effect of aligning inside and outside perspectives in a special way; what can only be seen from the inside suddenly becomes visible to the person on the outside who, seeing these two perspectives as part of something greater, can now do something. Because the hero addresses and "sees" the jaguar as son-in-law, the jaguar thus hailed feels obligated to fulfill the functions incumbent on this role. Once the jaguar is inside, the hero slams the door shut and the structure suddenly turns into a stone cage that traps him.

A perspectival stance is certainly a practical tool, like the stick used to link inside and outside views, but it also affords something else. It allows one to linger in that space where, like a shaman, one can be simultaneously aware of both viewpoints as well as how they are connected by something greater that, like a trap springing shut, suddenly encompasses them. The attention people in Ávila give to such moments of awareness is a signature of Amazonian multinatural perspectivalism. This is lost when multinatural perspectivalism is taken up as a more generic analytic shorn of its shamanistic component (see, e.g., Latour, 2004).

I propose that this perspectival mythic episode, in which the hero comes to unite these divergent perspectives through a vantage that encompasses them, captures, savors, and makes available something about life "itself." It captures something about the logic of the thoughts of the forest. And it captures the feeling of being alive to this living logic in moments of its emergence. It captures, in short, what it feels like to think.

Regarding this experience of coming to see inside and outside perspectives by virtue of something greater that encompasses them, consider Peirce's discussion of the experience of learning to move one's hands simultaneously and in opposite directions such that they trace parallel circular paths in the air: "To learn to do this, it is necessary to attend, first, to the different actions in different parts of the motion, when suddenly a general conception of the action springs up and it becomes perfectly easy" (Peirce, 1992a, p. 328).

Like Peirce's example, the jaguar-trapping myth captures what it feels like when a self "suddenly" comes to see different perspectives as contributing to the more general whole that unites them. As such it calls to mind what Bateson (2002) calls "double description," which he considers central to life and mind. In thinking about double description, I draw on—but simplify—Hui, Cashman, and Deacon's (2008) analysis of the concept. Bateson illustrates what he means by double description through binocular vision. By recognizing the similarities and systematically comparing the differences between what each eye sees, the brain, performing a "double description," comes to interpret each of these inputs as part of something more encompassing at a higher logical level. Something novel emerges: the perception of depth (Bateson, 2002, pp. 64–65).

Bateson asks, "What pattern connects the crab to the lobster and the orchid to the primrose and all the four of them to me? And me to you? And all the six of us to the amoeba in one direction and to the back-ward schizophrenic in another?" (2002, p. 7). His answer: double description is operative in the form-generating dynamics that make these entities what they are and how they are connected. The production of a series of roughly similar legs in a "proto-crab" enabled, over evolutionary time, the adaptive differentiation among these legs (some developing into claws, etc.), which allowed the organism as a whole to better "fit" or represent its environment. Just as depth emerges when the brain compares the differential duplication of ocular perspective, a crab as an organism with an overall form that fits a given niche (enabling it, for example, to walk sideways on the ocean floor) emerges over evolutionary time as an embodied interpretation of the duplication of gradually differing legs. Both involve double descriptions.

The lobster also emerges as a form that is the embodied product of a double description involving the differential duplication of appendages. Via different genetic mechanisms, the distinctive overall shape of the orchid and the primrose flower (each adapted to its respective pollinators) also results, in each case, from a double description involving the differential duplication of petals. When we compare crabs and lobsters, and these to the pair of plants, as Bateson does, we also perform double descriptions; we recognize the similarities and systematically compare the differences among these to reveal the double description that is operative in making each kind of organism what it is. When we then compare the ways we use double description to arrive at this realization with the way double description operates in the emergence of these biological forms, we see that our form of thinking is of and like the biological world; what is more, double description itself emerges as a conceptual object thanks to this higher-order double description.

Developing double description from the double description manifest in the world so that double description as a generative modality of mind becomes apparent gives us, then, the added experience of what it is like to think with the double description that is operative in the world. Or, to put it otherwise: thinking with forests allows us to see how we think like forests in ways that reveal some of the sylvan properties of the living thought itself as well as how we experience these properties.

A shamanistic perspectival aesthetic cultivates and reflects on this process. In the jaguar-trapping myth, a higher-order vantage "suddenly . . . springs up," which connects inside and outside perspectives as elements of something greater. This allows the listener to experience the feeling of a new living thought as it emerges; it captures what it feels like to think. In Ávila this is personified in the figure of the shaman, which is the Amazonian quintessence of a self, for all selves, as selves, are considered shamans (see Viveiros de Castro, 1998), and all selves think like forests.

THE LIVING THOUGHT

Lives and thoughts are not distinct kinds of things. How thoughts grow by association with other thoughts is not categorically different from how selves relate to one another. Selves are signs. Lives are thoughts. Semiosis is alive. And the world is thereby animate. People, like the Ávila Runa, who enter into and try to harness elements of a complex web of living thoughts are inundated by the logic of living thoughts such that their thoughts about life also come to instantiate some of the unique qualities of living thoughts. They come to think with the forest's thoughts, and, at times, they even experience themselves thinking with the forest's thoughts in ways that reveal some of the sylvan properties of thought itself.

To recognize living thoughts, and the ecology of selves to which they give rise, underscores that there is something unique to life: life thinks; stones don't. The goal here is not to name some essential vital force, or to create a new dualism to replace those old ones that severed humans from the rest of life and the world. The goal, rather, is to understand some of the special properties of lives and thoughts, which are obscured when we theorize humans and nonhumans, and their interactions, in terms of materiality or in terms of our assumptions (often hidden) about symbolically based linguistic relationality.

For Bateson, what makes life unique is that it is characterized by the ways in which "a difference" can "make a difference" (2000a, p. 459). Differences in soil can, thanks to layers of living representational relationships, come to make a difference for plants immersed in a complex semiotic ecology. And these differences can make a difference for other life-forms as well. Semiosis clearly involves differences; thoughts and lives grow by capturing differences in the world. And getting certain differences right—dogs need to be able to differentiate between mountain lions and deer—is vital.

But difference, for the living thought, is not everything. A tick doesn't notice the differences between a mountain lion and a deer, and this confusion is productive. Attending to the ways other kinds of selves inhabit and animate the world encourages us to rethink our ideas of relationality built on difference. The way selves relate is not necessarily akin to the ways in which words relate to each other in that system we call language. Relating is based neither on intrinsic difference nor on intrinsic similarity. I have explored here a process prior to what we usually recognize as difference or similarity, which depends on a form of confusion. Understanding the role that confusion (or forgetting, or indifference) plays in the living thought can help us develop an anthropology beyond the human that can attend to those many dynamics central to living and thinking that are not built from quanta of difference.

NOTES

1. Spanish *barbasco;* Latin *Lonchocarpus nicou;* known in Ávila simply as *ambi*, poison.
2. See Kohn (2002, pp. 114–115) for Quichua text.
3. I adopt this phrase from Peirce (CP 1.221) and apply it to a broader range of phenomena.
4. See Roy Rappaport (1999, p. 1) for the position that the human species lives "in terms of meanings it must construct in a world devoid of intrinsic meaning but subject to physical law."
5. That I insist on the centrality of telos as an emergent property inherent to the "enchanted" living world that extends beyond the human puts me at odds with Jane Bennett's (2001) recent reappropriation of enchantment.
6. See Bateson (2000b, 2002); Deacon (1997); Hoffmeyer (2008); Kull et al. (2009).
7. Following Peirce's observations regarding "interpretants" in relation to the thoughts they represent, the organism-as-sign would be "identical . . . though more developed" (CP 5.316) with respect to its progenitor's representation of the world.
8. For a list of some of the organisms that signal to the Runa the coming of the season when the leafcutter ants will fly or, in some cases, more specifically, the exact day when the reproductive ants will emerge, see Kohn (2002, pp. 99–101).
9. For a discussion of the specimens I collected of organisms found in association with leafcutter ants at the time when the winged reproductive ants emerged, see Kohn (2002, pp. 97–98).
10. On the kin terminology the Runa use to describe insects, see Kohn (2002, p. 267).
11. *Carludovica palmata*, Cyclanthaceae (see Kohn, 2002, p. 457, no. 16).
12. People in Ávila continue to try to communicate with the ants and their colonies after they have been trapped (see Kohn, 2002, p. 103, for a discussion).
13. There is actually another layer of interaction among semiotic selves that causes amplification of the differences among soil conditions, which I've left out of the main text for the sake of clarity. Herbivores are themselves preyed upon by a second level of predators. If it weren't for this constraint, herbivore populations would grow unchecked, and the result would be unlimited herbivory on plants living in rich soils. With unlimited herbivory, the differences afforded by different soils would become irrelevant.
14. See Descola (1994) for an eloquent anti-reductionist critique of environmental determinism related to Amazonian soils and the ecological assemblages they sustain.
15. Here is how John Law and Annemarie Mol characterize nonhuman agency in ways that link it specifically to the relationality of human language:

    > Within material semiotics, an entity counts as an actor if it makes a perceptible difference. Active entities are relationally linked with one another in webs. They make a difference to each other: they make each other be. Linguistic semiotics teaches that words give each other meaning. Material semiotics extends this insight beyond the linguistic and claims that entities give each other being: that they enact each other. (Law and Mol, 2008, p. 58)

16. Later in this same passage (CP 1.314), Peirce links this ability to imagine ourselves into the being of another human with our ability to do the same with animals.
17. Quichua *manduru;* Latin *Bixa orellana*, Bixaceae; English annatto (see Kohn, 2002, pp. 272–273, for a discussion of its use in Ávila).

18. *Procyon cancrivorus.*

19. This leads Viveiros de Castro (1998, p. 478) to conclude that there are many natures, each associated with the body-specific interpretive world of a particular kind of being; there is only one culture—in this case, that of the Runa. Accordingly, he refers to this way of thinking as "multinaturalism" and uses it as a critique of the multicultural logic (i.e., many cultures, one nature) typical of contemporary Western folk academic thought, especially in the guise of cultural relativism (cf. Latour, 1993, pp. 106; 2004, p. 48).

20. See Kohn (2002, pp. 108–141) for a more extensive discussion and many more examples of perspectivism in everyday Ávila life.

21. *Dactylomys dactylinus.*

22. For descriptions of these tree causeways, see Descola (1996, p. 157).

23. "*Saqui su.*"

24. For descriptions of this call, see Emmons (1990, p. 225).

25. This woman was already a grandmother, so this form of flirtatious joking was not seen to be threatening. Such jokes would not be made in reference to younger, recently married women.

26. *Renealmia* sp., Zingiberaceae.

27. Quichua *carachama;* Latin *Chaetostoma dermorynchon*, Loricariidae.

REFERENCES

Agamben, G. 2004. *The Open: Man and Animal.* Stanford, CA: Stanford University Press.

Bateson, G. 2000a. "Form, Substance, and Difference." In *Steps to an Ecology of Mind*, 454–471. Chicago: University of Chicago Press.

Bateson, G. 2000b. *Steps to an Ecology of Mind.* Chicago: University of Chicago Press.

Bateson, G. 2002. *Mind and Nature: A Necessary Unity.* Cresskill, NJ: Hampton Press.

Bennett, J. 2001. *The Enchantment of Modern Life: Attachments, Crossings, and Ethics.* Princeton, NJ: Princeton University Press.

Bennett, J. 2010. *Vibrant Matter: A Political Ecology of Things.* Durham, NC: Duke University Press.

Benveniste, É. 1984. "The Nature of Pronouns." In *Problems in General Linguistics*, edited by E. Benveniste, 217–222. Coral Gables, FL: University of Miami Press.

Borges, J. L. 1962. "Funes the Memorious." Translated by J. E. Irby. In *Labyrinths*, 148–154. New York: New Directions.

Colapietro, V. M. 1989. *Peirce's Approach to the Self: A Semiotic Perspective on Human Subjectivity.* Albany: State University of New York Press.

Deacon, T. W. 1997. *The Symbolic Species: The Co-evolution of Language and the Brain.* New York: Norton.

Deacon, T. W. 2012. *Incomplete Nature: How Mind Emerged from Matter*. New York: Norton.

Dennett, D. C. 1996. *Kinds of Minds: Toward an Understanding of Consciousness*. New York: Basic Books.

Derrida, J. 2008. *The Animal That Therefore I Am*. New York: Fordham University Press.

Descola, P. 1994. *In the Society of Nature: A Native Ecology in Amazonia*. Cambridge: Cambridge University Press.

Descola, P. 1996. *The Spears of Twilight: Life and Death in the Amazon Jungle*. New York: New Press.

Descola, P. 2005. *Par-delà nature et culture*. Paris: Gallimard.

Emmons, L. H. 1990. *Neotropical Rainforest Mammals: A Field Guide*. Chicago: University of Chicago Press.

Fine, P. 2004. *Herbivory and Evolution of Habitat Specialization by Trees in Amazonian Forests*. PhD dissertation, University of Utah.

Fine, P. V. A., I. Mesones, and P. D. Coley. 2004. "Herbivores Promote Habitat Specialization by Trees in Amazonian Forests." *Science* 305, no. 5684: 663–665.

Foucault, M. 1970. *The Order of Things: An Archaeology of the Human Sciences*. London: Tavistock.

Haraway, D. 2003. *The Companion Species Manifesto: Dogs, People, and Significant Otherness*. Chicago: Prickly Paradigm Press.

Haraway, D. 2008. *When Species Meet*. Minneapolis: University of Minnesota Press.

Hoffmeyer, J. 2008. *Biosemiotics: An Examination into the Signs of Life and the Life of Signs*. Scranton, PA: University of Scranton Press.

Hui, J., T. Cashman, and T. Deacon. 2008. "Bateson's Method: Double Description. What Is It? What Do We Learn? How Does It Work?" In *A Legacy for Living Systems*, edited by J. Hui, T. Cashman, and T. Deacon, 77–92. Dordrecht: Springer.

Janzen, D. H. 1974. "Tropical Blackwater Rivers, Animals, and Mast Fruiting by the Dipterocarpaceae." *Biotropitca* 6, no. 2: 69–103.

Kohn, E. 2002. *Natural Engagements and Ecological Aesthetics among the Ávila Runa of Amazonian Ecuador*. PhD dissertation, University of Wisconsin.

Kull, K., et al. 2009. "Theses on Biosemiotics: Prolegomena to a Theoretical Biology." *Biological Theory* 4, no. 2: 167–173.

Latour, B. 1987. *Science in Action*. Cambridge, MA: Harvard University Press.

Latour, B. 1993. *We Have Never Been Modern*. New York: Harvester Wheatsheaf.

Latour, B. 2004. *Politics of Nature: How to Bring the Sciences into Democracy*. Cambridge, MA: Harvard University Press.

Law, J., and A. Mol. 2008. "The Actor-Enacted: Cumbrian Sheep in 2001." In *Material Agency*, edited by C. Knappett and M. Lambros, 57–77. Berlin: Springer.

Lévy-Bruhl, L. 1926. *Revival: How Natives Think.* London: Allen & Unwin.

Marquis, R. J. 2004. "Herbivores Rule." *Science* 305, no. 5684: 619–621.

Moran, E. F. 1993. *Through Amazonian Eyes: The Human Ecology of Amazonian Populations.* Iowa City: University of Iowa Press.

Nagel, T. 1974. "What Is It Like to Be a Bat?" *Philosophical Review* 83, no. 4: 435–450.

Peirce, C. S. 1931. *Collected Papers of Charles Sanders Peirce.* Cambridge, MA: Harvard University Press.

Peirce, C. S. 1992a. "The Law of Mind." In *The Essential Peirce: Selected Philosophical Writings, Vol. 1 (1867–1893)*, edited by N. Houser and C. Kloesel, 312–333. Bloomington: Indiana University Press.

Peirce, C. S. 1992b. "Questions Concerning Certain Faculties Claimed for Man." In *The Essential Peirce: Selected Philosophical Writings. Vol. 1 (1867–1893)*, edited by N. Houser and C. Kloesel, 11–27. Bloomington: Indiana University Press.

Pickering, A. 1999. "The Mangle of Practice: Agency and Emergence in the Sociology of Science." In *The Science Studies Reader*, edited by M. Biagioli, 372–393. New York: Routledge.

Raffles, H. 2002. *In Amazonia: A Natural History.* Princeton, NJ: Princeton University Press.

Rappaport, R. A. 1999. *Ritual and Religion in the Making of Humanity.* Cambridge: Cambridge University Press.

Sahlins, M. 1995. *How "Natives" Think: About Captain Cook, for Example.* Chicago: University of Chicago Press.

Strathern, M. 1995. *The Relation: Issues in Complexity and Scale*, vol. 6. Cambridge, UK: Prickly Pear Press.

Viveiros de Castro, E. 1998. "Cosmological Deixis and Amerindian Perspectivism." *Journal of the Royal Anthropological Institute* 4, no. 3: 469–488.

von Uexküll, J. 1982. "The Theory of Meaning." *Semiotica* 42, no. 1: 25–79.

Weber, M. 1948a. "Religious Rejections of the World and Their Directions." In *From Max Weber: Essays in Sociology*, edited by H. H. Gerth and C. W. Mills, 323–359. Oxon, UK: Routledge.

Weber, M. 1948b. In *From Max Weber: Essays in Sociology*, edited by H. H. Gerth and C. W. Mills, 129–156. Oxon, UK: Routledge.

Main Pathway: Ecologies

Subthemes

Proceed to Decolonization, p. 555
Proceed to Experience, p. 555
End of Ethics

30

INTELLIGENCE AND CONSCIOUSNESS

Anthony Trewavas

Not just animals are conscious but every organic being, every autopoietic cell is conscious. In the simplest sense, consciousness is an awareness of the outside world. (Margulis and Sagan, 1995)

INTRODUCTION

The title of this chapter is to be found in an informative book by Lynn Margulis and her son Dorian Sagan (1995). It is an attempt to start the intricate dissection of something often considered to be unique to human beings, consciousness. However, no statement concerning consciousness in any other organism than ourselves is currently open to investigation or refutation by any experimental treatment that is known. Whatever consciousness actually is cannot be established objectively, because it is personal to the individual. The only reason the term exists is because we have this feature of our mental activity, the internal self-referencing, thoughts, images, self-observation, thinking as though one part of the brain is observing another. We convey that process to others by means of language, and it is on that basis that we consider humans are conscious, i.e. they are sentient. Religious attitudes describe it as the soul, but the inadequacy of communication with virtually most other species means we cannot assess whether they are conscious and probably never will. All that can be judged is whether their behaviour is consistent with their being conscious. Only on supposition can we deny it for other species. Trewavas and Baluska (2011) provide evidence that consciousness can be regarded as ubiquitous in all of biology.

AUTOPOIESIS IS A FUNDAMENTAL PROPERTY OF LIVING SYSTEMS

Autopoiesis is a left-over life property from Chapter 3 of *Plant Behavior and Intelligence*. There, I included Jacques Monod's emphasis on teleonomy.

> Teleonomy is that of being objects, endowed with a purpose which they show in their structure and execute through their performances. Rather than reject this idea (as certain biologists try to do), it must be regarded as essential to the very definition of all living being (Monod, 1971, p. 20).

Purposive behaviour in plants was first indicated by Sachs (1887, p. 601): "All those adaptations of the organism are purposeful which contribute to its maintenance and insure its existence." Virtually all plant behaviour comes in that category of being purposeful. Autopoiesis originated because its creators, Maturana and Varela (1980), felt that teleonomy was a programme imposed on the individual by the species during evolution. So they included what they felt was equally crucial to life, the maintenance of organization. Autopoiesis derives from the Greek "auto" as self and "poiesin" as making. The individual acts as a unitary organism and "Through their interactions and transformations, continuously regenerate and realize the network of processes that produced them" (Maturana and Varela 1980, p. 9).

Ninety-eight percent of all the atoms of the human body are replaced within one year. From measurements of average turnover rates of protein and ribosomal RNA in plants, this replacement rate will be similar (Trewavas, 1970, 1972). Again, on average, each cell in the human body repairs about a million bases/day in DNA responding to oxidative damage or external radiation sources, and leaves one uncorrected mutation. The thoughts you have today as images in the brain and your consciousness, and based on molecules, will have been completely replaced next year by equivalent new molecules. How well ordered that process is will determine how much you remember.

TWO KINDS OF CONSCIOUSNESS

Consciousness does indicate intention, it does deal with things or events, it relies on memory and the associated process of learning, but is not a simple copy of experience. There are also the clinical aspects of consciousness, criteria concerned with alertness, motivational behaviour, orientation, and self-awareness.

Edelman (1992) has suggested two kinds of consciousness. Primary consciousness is the familiar properties of heart rate, respiration rate, digestive contractions, hormone release, etc. We are aware of them, but do not control them. Higher order consciousness starts with perception through the sense organs and then control of muscular activities that drives the response. Perception, assessment, response—these are fundamental behaviours for all organisms. Assessment is the issue and perhaps the equivalent of consciousness in all.

Even the simplest organisms perceive their environment through sensory mechanisms and respond accordingly. "The biological self, incorporates . . . facts, experiences, and senses impressions, which may become memories. All living beings perceive their environment, not just animals but plants and microbes too. To survive, an organic being must perceive—it must seek or at least recognize food and avoid environmental danger. . . . Certainly some level of awareness and of responsiveness owing to that awareness, is implied in all autopoietic systems" (Margulis and Sagan, 1995, pp. 32, 122).

"THE CONSCIOUS CELL" (MARGULIS 2001): WHAT IS ASSESSMENT?

Lynn Margulis is famous for her symbiotic theory of life. Mitochondria and chloroplasts were originally free-living bacterial and blue-green algal symbionts that have in the passage of time become critical organelles in eukaryotic cells. Her hypothesis has been well corroborated by DNA analysis. Margulis considers that the evolutionary antecedent of the nervous system is microbial consciousness. Thus, the eukaryotic cell that contains these symbionts is, by definition, conscious too. Her hypothesis also includes a consideration of the origin of neurotubules also acquired through the symbiotic route.

Escherichiacoli, originally isolated from the human gut, swims by means of motors that drive six flagellae by rotation. There are two kinds of swimming—smooth when the flagellae trail uniformly behind the cell, and chaotic tumbling when the direction of rotation is reversed (Sourjik, 2004). Each cell has 10 to 12 receptors in its outer membrane, which sample its surrounding medium for chemicals, usually either food or toxins. The tumbling process is used to comparatively assess the present concentration of a desirable commodity like sugars, amino acids, or toxins, with a previous assessment using the specific receptors. This checking period lasts a few seconds. After assessment, swimming then continues in the direction of food or away from toxins. These few seconds represent its memory that, when accessed, controls behaviour.

Strictly speaking, *E. coli* possesses neither a nervous system nor a brain, but it does have what could be described as a centralised intelligence system. At a simple level it does what bigger brains do. It integrates information from sensory mechanisms that detect salient features of the environment. It has central decision-making machinery that encodes and analyses information about its past and present, and enables it to chart its course into a well-chosen future. And it has the equipment—the behavioural effector systems—to execute the plan (Lacerra and Bingham, 2002, p. 15).

The basis of this intelligent process is derived from a fairly simple system of interconnected proteins and does involve protein modification through phosphorylation and methylation. The connections in this assessment network are transiently modified to adjust the procedures of tumbling and smooth swimming. Phosphorylation is used because rapidity of response is essential. The bacterial cell thus exhibits awareness of its surroundings. Consciousness at its simplest is thus a system, a network property. However, these proteins are embedded in a much larger network of other proteins that create the cell, and its sensing and motors, in the first place.

Eukaryotic cells are an order of magnitude more complex than the common bacterial cell, and the variety of their behaviour increases accordingly. Again, the assessment process depends on a densely connected network of proteins, which are structurally and strategically located inside the cell. However, with many more potential interactions between proteins and numerous post-translational modifications, the complexity of behaviour is greatly increased. These data provide definite clues about the nature of assessing the consciousness equivalent in plants, and complete the consideration of such behaviour in cells. Jennings (1923, p. 336) asks, “Is the behaviour of lower organisms of the character which we should naturally expect and appreciate if they did have conscious states of undifferentiated character and acted under similar conscious states in a way parallel to man?” He concludes they do. When such cells, for example, draw away from unpleasant circumstances, can we conclude they do not experience pain? Our behaviour would be similar. That question has, of course, no answer and never will. Jennings was merely trying to indicate the evolutionary origins of what is called consciousness.

"DO CELLS THINK?"

Ramanathan and Broach (2007) ask this question in a well-argued and provocative paper. They point to a large number of examples of single cells, where genetically identical individuals maintain a range of phenotypes in a uniform environment. Most notable among these are trypanosomes and others that generate antigenic variants in an infection population. *Candida albicans*, a fungus that infects humans, can express a number of phenotypic variants. It can change virulence by altering antigenicity, or alter antifungal resistance or sensitivity to macrophage ingestion. Even *Escherichia coli* can switch into a quiescent state that increases resistance to antibiotics. The optimum switching rate between phenotypes should be proportional to the probability that the environment will change, too.

Slow behavioural changes in plants in response to environmental signals raise an issue here of some importance. When the new phenotype starts to emerge after signalling, it may be unsuitable for the present environment. If the environment changes frequently, then fitter individuals need to maintain a memory of the frequency of changes it has experienced in the past and adjust behavioural responses accordingly. Such a record can be deposited in protein phosphorylation states or epigenetic modifications, and should involve thresholds that are superseded when critical numbers of environmental changes have been recorded. Even *Bacillus subtilis* can manage to remember previous starvation conditions some time after they have been experienced, and changes phenotypic switching accordingly (Suel et al., 2006).

Yeast cells (*Saccharomyces cereviseae*) respond to a number of environmental signals that are interpreted by several well-characterized transduction pathways. Cells can adjust osmolarity in concentrated sugar solutions or respond to mating pheromones for sexual reproduction. The transduction pathways involve well-established cascades of protein kinases and MAP kinase cascades and act like a switch. Some of these critical kinases are shared between the osmolarity and mating transduction pathways. When responding to the mating pheromone, it switches off the osmolarity pathway, and vice versa. In the presence of both signals, some cells switch on the pheromone pathway, while others switch on the osmolarity pathway. The proportion of each type is dependent on the relative strength of the two signals provided. Yeast cells are, in some way, weighing the odds of the signals that are received and adjusting the proportions of each phenotype to better fit the environment. This higher level of information processing "begins to approach the complexity of a true thought process" (Ramanathan and Broach, 2007), something normally identified as cognition. Bear in mind that the cellular system is hierarchical in its construction. This higher order process must work at the pinnacle of the system properties. Again, there is an indication of the mechanisms involved in the process of assessment used during plant behaviour. Systems behaviours become crucial to understanding.

However, the understanding of cognition or thinking may need reassessment. "A cognitive system is a system whose organization defines a domain of interactions in which it can act with relevance to the maintenance of itself. Living systems are cognitive systems and living is a process of cognition. This statement is valid for all organisms with and without a nervous system" (Maturana, 1980, p. 13). This statement had been made before the information above was published, but looks to have predicted it.

THE EVOLUTIONARY CONTINUITY OF CONSCIOUSNESS AND PERCEPTION

From the viewpoint of an evolutionary biologist it is reasonable to assume that the sensitive embodied actions of plants and bacteria are part of the same continuum of perception and action that culminates in our most revered mental attributes. "Mind" may be the result of interacting cells. Mind and body perceiving and living are equally self-referring, self-reflexive processes already present in the earliest bacteria. (Margulis and Sagan, 1995, p. 32)

A greater variety of terms are used to describe the behaviour of more complex organisms, such as motivation, appetite, drive, purposive behaviour (West Eberhard, 2002). Again, these behaviours do describe what we observe in other organisms and about which assumptions are made. They are, of course, nuances of behaviour that we recognize in ourselves, but in essence are equally relevant to all organisms. *Hydra viridis* is a small multicellular coelenterate, and yet both Jennings (1923) and Bray (2009) refer to *Hydra* as sometimes being hungry and at other times full, because in the latter case it then ignores offered food.

Do plants intend to avoid the competition for light? They behave as though they do when they obviously grow away from competition. We do not use the word "hungry" for that circumstance, but is there a real difference in essence between a starving man and an etiolated plant? In both cases, the imperative is to find food or perish. The phenotypic mechanisms used by both to deal with this situation reflect what evolution has given them—movement in one case, growth (a form of movement) in the other—but oddly enough the molecular mechanisms look very similar, since circulating sugar levels may be the crucial signals (Morkunas et al., 2012). A crucial kinase, snf 1 kinase, is activated by starvation and energy-depleting stress conditions in both plants and animals. Once activated, it enables energy homeostasis and thus survival, by up-regulating energy-conserving and energy-producing catabolic processes. It also limits energy-consuming anabolic metabolism. In addition, these enzymes manipulate and control normal growth and development as well as metabolic homeostasis at the organismal level. The plant uses a whole system assessment that is complex and used to change behaviour, mankind uses a more focused assessment to control hungry behaviour, the brain, but who can say one is not conscious and the other is?

West Eberhard (2002) describes the interesting example of salmon feeding, which under the watchful eye of a predator makes many more mistakes. Its behaviour swings between 'fear' and the necessity of feeding. It is an example of the use of the conflict between speed and efficiency. When the slime mould *Physarum* was hurried to make decisions, mistakes increased.

Both organisms are finding their attention is modified by external circumstances. Attention reflects the ability to concentrate on one issue at a time, and if two are present, one will supersede the other, or they may simply alternate. Plant roots get round the issue of two signals by changing the sensing apparatus, which is in continual flux anyway. There have to be choices, perceptions, decisions, and can we add in desire, fear, and hunger? Jennings (1923) uses all these terms for simple organisms, and the obvious answer is whether he was right to do so is that we simply do not know. These characteristics of behaviour are easy to see in our conscious selves and they are terms derived from our experience, but some features of all of these appear in some way or another in single cells and some of them in plants, too. It should be feasible to place a plant under stressful circumstances and see how many errors in behaviour emerge.

The natural world can be divided into human existence, other animals, plants, and then single cells, but such classification hides the general truth that these divisions tend to merge at their boundaries. Animal life with its central direction of a society of cells, plant life with its organized republic of cells and cells with their organized republic of molecules (Whitehead, 1938, p. 157). Like all true republics, plants will assess and vote by the majority view, controlled by a tissue quorum. The whole plant is equivalent to the animal brain.

In conclusion, in this section I agree with Kevin Warwick, artificial intelligence expert. "I believe that dogs and cats are conscious in their own way and bees, ants and spiders are conscious, not as humans but as bees, ants and spiders. I cannot say that a robot with a computer for a brain is not conscious because its brain is not like mine and because it thinks in a different way to me" (Warwick, 2000, p. 184). I will add to Warwick's statement that "plants are conscious in their own way, not as humans but as plants," although there is no obvious way at present in which that can ever be accessed. Assessment, mentioned frequently in this chapter and arising from the connections between cells and molecules, hierarchically arranged in a complex system structure, may represent the plant equivalent of thinking. Those conclusions should hold for any network system sufficiently complex.

IS A SOCIAL INSECT COLONY SUFFICIENTLY COMPLEX TO ACQUIRE A RECOGNIZABLE CONSCIOUSNESS?

Elsewhere, I indicated the distinct analogy in organizational structure between social insect colonies and large plants, such as dicot trees. In this discussion about consciousness, is it possible to conceive that colonies also possess a kind of consciousness? The component individuals through connections with each other form an obvious system whose emergent property is the colony, self-sustaining and self-organizing—that is, swarm intelligence.

Although much of the original investigations on social insects concentrated on bees, ants also construct substantial colonies involving many thousands of workers. Colonies of ants not only gather information, they evaluate, deliberate, consensus build, face choices (and implement one of them), and they are sensitive to context. They hunt for new nest sites, assess their suitability from size and entry ways, and decide its use from quorum sensing. A threshold number must agree to the site after inspection (Franks, 2008). Workers search for food and engage others to follow to this food site. Individual experienced ants teach other, less mature individuals the directions to new nest sites (Franks and Richardson, 2006). More experienced and knowledgeable individuals do the tuition (Stroeymeyt, Franks, and Giurfal, 2011). They communicate all this information by pheromones.

The colony is certainly regarded as behaving intelligently. That is, it has the capacity to solve problems engendered by its environment (Franks, 2008). Perhaps most crucially, the individuals are not credited with intelligence, but it is only the connections between the individuals that give rise to colony intelligence. Ant colonies acquire long-term memories of past experience because frequent movement to different nest sites progressively reduces the total move time (Langridge, Franks, and Sendova-Franks, 2004). The colony seems self-aware because the individual workers do not attack others in the nest, but will raid others nearby of the same or other species. The colony is certainly aware of its environment, as are those of bees and termites, and on that basis has a kind of consciousness, an awareness of the outside world, but it is a form of consciousness that we cannot at present access.

Individual bees in a hive obtain a map of their external circumstances and communicate it to others symbolically. This map is reinforced by repetition of flights. An effective image of the local area is thus slowly constructed, then resides in the colony. A memory of the acquired information presumably lasts as long as the individual workers continue collecting, but must then decline as workers die off. Does this provide a very simple model of how a brain functions?

Central to these concepts of consciousness is recognition of self and non-self. In colonies, members generally do not attack each other, but will do so against other colonies and hive intruders. It is thought that the recognition of non-self, which is what this represents, is the result of exchange of recognition signals between all individuals, using again a chemical, a pheromone. When under attack, other pheromones are released that call other workers to deal with the invasion. Recent work suggests that, in some wasp colonies, facial recognition is also involved (Tibbetts and Lindsay, 2008).

CONCLUSION ON CONSCIOUSNESS

In 1902, Charles Minot stated, in a speech to the American Association for the Advancement of Science, "A frank unbiased study of consciousness must convince every biologist that it is one of the fundamental phenomena of at least all animal life if not, as is quite possible, of all life. Consciousness is a device to regulate the actions of organisms to accomplish purposes which are useful to organisms and are thus teleological" (p. 298). This statement places a different perspective on how we assess plant life.

After a detailed description of insectivorous plant behaviour, Lauder-Lindsay (1876) stated "that unless we re-define the term consciousness we must regard some form of it as occurring in both animals and plants that are destitute not only of brain but of a nervous system . . . to regard mind and all its essential or concomitant phenomena as common in various senses or degrees to plants, the lower animals and man" (p. 520).

THE NERVOUS MECHANISM OF PLANTS

The title of this section is taken from a little-known book by J. C. Bose, published in 1926. Altogether, Bose published about 12 volumes describing his research on plants, at a time (early twentieth century) and place (India) where very little science operated. His research gained recognition with a knighthood and being elected a Fellow of the Royal Society London. Bose is one of those remarkable people that science is often blessed with. Because nervous systems tend to dominate discussion about consciousness and intelligence, I have included reference to his work here. Plants do not have a defined nervous system in terms of neurons and synapses that connect through a central brain. The lack of a defined nervous system does not exclude a complex system built on electrical conduction, something that has given rise to confusion in the past, to some (Alpi et al., 2007).

Bose's extensive experimental information on plant nervous systems also required the construction of highly sensitive equipment, unique for the time, and that enabled so much to be uncovered. His prime experimental material was the touch-sensitive *mimosa*. He was able to demonstrate that the leaf droop after touch excitation was communicated by an action potential through the petiole to motor cells in the pulvinus. A massive efflux of potassium chloride from the vacuoles of these motor cells results in a loss of turgor. Recovery takes about 45 minutes, and during this period, the potassium chloride is actively pumped back into these motor cells, using cellular energy. However, Bose worked on other cells and species than mimosa, so much of what he found can be generalized.

The benefits that animals gain by nerves and brains is speed of connection between sensing system and muscular response. The brain provides for assessment and for awareness. It is part of the animal lifestyle of eat or be eaten that has accelerated the evolution of this apparatus. Predator and prey combined in an evolutionary dance of increasing speed.

SOME OF THE INFORMATION ON THE PLANT NERVOUS SYSTEM THAT BOSE ESTABLISHED

Bose clearly established the details of this nervous system in plants, and he frequently compared the electrical system in plants with that in animals, using the terms freely and rightly, in my mind, of both nerve and nervous system. The prime conductive tissue of action potentials he found to be the phloem, and he identified this vascular tissue as the plant equivalent to a nerve by constructing a delicate voltage-detecting electric probe that penetrated the petiolar tissues to defined depths. He also isolated the nerves (phloem strands) from some plants and demonstrated their conductivity.

Transmission of the action potential is slower than those in defined nerves, but anyone who has observed the touch-induced leaf droop in mimosa will know that the response is over in a very few seconds. A cold ring applied around the conductive tissue slowed the movement of the action potential. Further work established that, as in the animal synapse, conduction works only in one direction at the junction of the nervous tissue with the motor tissue. By careful construction of further highly sensitive equipment, Bose observed the latent period after stimulation to be 0.08 sec and the velocity of transmission of the action potential in thin petioles to be about 400 mm/sec, intermediate between those of higher and lower animals. In the stem it can be as low as 5 mm/sec. In other plants, such as *averrhoa*, indirect stimulation electrically applied or when applied at a distance, led to an increase in turgor in remote tissues.

The pulvinus of mimosa he found to consist of four different effector regions, and stimulation of just one can give rise to torsional movements. There is a definite connection between the nerve end in each quadrant of the pulvinus at its centre and the corresponding subregion of the petiole. When the intensity for peripheral stimulation is adequate, the afferent impulse reaching the pulvinus becomes reflected along a new path and becomes an efferent impulse. A reflex arc is thus formed at the centre. This is considered different to mammals, where the afferent and efferent impulses in a reflex arc are carried by separate nerves. However, Bose contends that there may be two kinds of phloem in mimosa, which may conduct differently, one being afferent, the other efferent, thus mimicking the nervous organization of the reflex arc in animals.

Bose also reported that the heliotropic movements of leaves, in which the leaf blade is positioned at right angles to the direction of light, was brought about by transmission of nervous impulses from the perceptive pulvinar region to the motor tissue of the same organ. Leaf movement was caused by contraction of the proximal and expansion of the distal side of this organ.

Bose (1926) draws several conclusions from his detailed studies.

> Vascular plants possess a well-defined nervous system (p. 218).
>
> Conduction can be modified experimentally in the same way as in animal nerves.
>
> The conducted excitation may, therefore, be justly spoken of as a nervous impulse and the conducting tissue as nerve.
>
> It is possible to distinguish afferent or sensory impulses from efferent or motor impulses just as in animals and to trace the transformation of one into the other to form a reflex arc.

"The observations involve the conception of some kind of nerve centre," but Bose admits no structure corresponding to the nerve ganglion of the animals has ever been detected in Mimosa.

WHY DID BOSE'S RESEARCH LARGELY DISAPPEAR FROM SCIENTIFIC VIEW?

Given the volume of work produced by Bose, it is always surprising that very little of it found its way into textbooks on plant physiology. There are undoubtedly some simple reasons. Mimosa and the Venus flytrap, whose trap was likewise controlled by an action potential, were considered as virtually unique and thus not relevant to most plants. The primary research emphasis in the 1930s was centred instead on crop plants and agriculture. The isolation of auxin in the early 1930s gave rise to a potential for chemical control of plant communication, growth, and thus yield. It is easier to modify plant development by adding a chemical than using complex electrical equipment. So the chemical approaches won out and the electrical ones all but disappeared, but even so Bose indicated, in his enormous compendia of data, that most of his results were applicable to these crop plants, as well. However, another reason was the behaviour of plants themselves. Any reason for electrical conduction was not obvious. Why, it was asked, did plants need rapid responses—they are slow to visibly respond. They don't get up and walk away.

ELECTRICAL FIELDS TOOK OVER THIS AREA OF RESEARCH

However, some took up the challenge in a different way. In the 1930s, there was considerable interest in electrical fields. Could these provide explanation of embryonic fields, particularly in animal embryology or the meristem? Lund and Rosene (1947) provided summaries of several decades of study and measurement on bioelectric potentials in plants. These measurements showed that, for example, potential differences of 100 mV or thereabouts could be detected between the top and bottom of plant organs, such as the coleoptile. When the tissue was laid on its side, the new top and bottom rapidly assumed an equivalent potential difference, the so-called geoelectric effect. Potential differences they found existed everywhere—across plants, across organs—the plant was surrounded by electrical fields. Roots were found to have defined electrical fields around them, and these could oscillate with periodicities in minutes (Scott, 1957; Shabal, Newman, and Morris, 1997).

Any mystery that might have surrounded these was quickly dispelled once it was indicated that these probably reflected no more than the differential accumulation of ions in plant cells across the plasma membrane (Scott, 1967). The difference can be large—up to −200 mV; compare that with a nerve cell at −70 mV. Most research on electrical fields initially identified potassium ions, in particular, as being differentially regulated or accumulated across the plasma membrane.

RECENT UNDERSTANDING HAS IMPROVED THE PERSPECTIVE OF THE PLANT NERVOUS SYSTEM

Part of the reason for the oddity label applied to mimosa was that the only thing affected seemed to be the turgor pressure. The sundew is another plant in which action potentials are used to help catch insect prey and in which relatively rapid movement occurs again using turgor pressure changes. If electrical conduction had greater relevance than just changing turgor pressure, surely some other event should follow—a change in development for example?

APPRECIATION OF THE ROLE OF CYTOSOLIC CA^{2+} IN CONTROLLING MANY ASPECTS OF SIGNAL TRANSDUCTION: THE MISSING LINK?

A slow accumulation of data, starting in the 1980s, indicated that cytosolic calcium was carefully regulated in plant cells at a very low concentration, about 100 nM (Trewavas, 1985). Elevation by two to three orders of magnitude, to a concentration of 10–100 μM, could activate many numerous Ca^{2+}-dependent proteins and kinases in plant cells. Many of these proteins could modify transcription and translation, and change connections within cellular networks. What substantially propelled understanding forward was the development of an entirely simple method of measuring cytosolic calcium in plant cells, using the Ca^{2+}-sensitive luminescent protein aequorin (Knight et al., 1991, 1993). When Ca^{2+} increased, the plants luminesced. Very quickly it was found that numerous signals, such as touch, cold, light, oxidative signals or chemical elicitors of defence, and most signals to which plants respond could induce typical cytosolic Ca^{2+} transients in less than a second and lasting some 20–30 sec. Furthermore, imaging the luminescence, and thus Ca^{2+} dynamics, indicated self-propagating waves of Ca^{2+} elevation from the point of impact to thousands of responsive cells or as small cell clusters.

The speed with which a calcium signal could be induced indicated that, in contrast to the apparently slow response of plants, the initial impact inside cells was equivalent to the speed of response to those in animal cells. Plant cells were far more sensitive to signals than had been appreciated. The reason the response is slow is because it often involves growth. Social insect colonies respond relatively slowly compared with the speed of the workers, because hive change involves slow parameters like honey accumulation. Reproduction, polarity, and circadian processes also used oscillations in cytosolic calcium to control their processes (Trewavas, 2011).

ELECTRICAL SIGNALS, CYTOSOLIC CALCIUM, AND RESPONSES TO HERBIVORES

Herbivory is one of the commonest problems faced by all higher plants. There has been an arms race between insect herbivores and plants for probably 300 million years. In response to herbivore damage, plants synthesize compounds that are toxic, repellent, or anti-digestive, for defence. Many of these chemicals are termed natural pesticides. Some are used by mankind to deal with insect pests.

The activation of at least three resistance pathways occurs after recognition of attack. These involve signal transduction sequences that hinge around the synthesis of jasmonates, salicylate, and ethylene, although these pathways on their own are insufficient to generate resistance. Different herbivores elicit different profiles of expressed proteins from the prey plant, and the kinetics of induction of the known three transduction pathways, which also cross-talk, are often specific to the herbivore (Vos et al., 2005). There can be considerable variation even between individuals of the same species in the resistance mechanisms at the early stages of recognition of herbivore attack (Wu et al., 2008). Specific recognition chemicals that identify the herbivore are recognized through the unique chemical composition of the saliva of the herbivore (Mithöfer and Boland, 2008). The production of specific classes of emitted plant volatiles attracts the attention of parasitoids of the herbivore or act as repellents, but what starts it all off?

When herbivores commence feeding, the initial event, that of wounding, generates action potentials that propagate over considerable distances within the plant, and institute defence mechanisms, including the synthesis of anti-digestive protease inhibitors and jasmonate (Wildon et al., 1992; Fisahn et al., 2004). The action potential results in a transient increase in cytosolic Ca^{2+} some 20–50 msec later. Blockage of the cytosolic Ca^{2+} entry by inhibitors prevented synthesis of specific jasmonate-dependent proteins involved in defence reactions. The subsequent reactions involve induction of protein kinases, including protein kinase cascades and oxidative reactions (Howe and Jander, 2008).

However, the most intriguing is that the action potential can be initially propagated along the surface of leaves to others nearby, and probably also through the phloem. The transmission is primarily through glutamate receptor–like, sensitive channels (Christmann and Grill, 2013; Mousavi et al., 2013). Addition of glutamate to plant cells elicits Ca^{2+} transients and membrane depolarization (Dennison and Spalding, 2000; Vincill et al., 2012). Like animal glutamate receptors, the effect of opening the channel permits the entry of K^+ ions, as well as leading to depolarization.

These unexpected observations intrigue because glutamate is a neurotransmitter in animal brains. Here, glutamate is concentrated in cellular vesicles, and these are localized in the presynaptic region of the neuron. On receipt of an action potential and attendant depolarization in the presynaptic cell, the glutamate is released from vesicles and travels across the synapse to the post-synaptic neuron, where it binds to glutamate receptors in the plasma membrane, inducing cytosolic Ca^{2+}

transients and depolarizing the post-synaptic cell, leading to a further action potential. Glutamate is thus central to brain function involving learning and memory.

The attacks by herbivores on plants result in a learning process called priming, which is remembered for very long periods of time, even beyond reproduction. Its molecular basis is probably epigenetic. The memory can be accessed on future attacks, leading to a quicker and more robust answer to the herbivore (Frost et al., 2008). Volatile chemicals released by plant cells on herbivory can actually have a bigger effect on adjacent undamaged plants (Engelberth et al., 2004).

Glutamate has more specific effects on root systems, causing changes in growth and lateral root formation when applied to the tip (Forde, 2014). Most intriguingly, the transduction pathway involves MAP 3 kinase and probably MEK 1 m as it does in animal cells. There is a clear interaction between nitrate, the nitrate receptor, and the influence of glutamate.

It is extraordinary that the basic elements of signalling and memory events are shared between higher animals and higher plants, the latter in the absence of a defined nervous system.

Action potentials are involved in a variety of processes in plants (Fromm and Lautner, 2007). How many of these involve glutamate and its receptors in plants is not known.

ARE IMMUNE SYSTEMS INTELLIGENT, CONSCIOUS, OR BOTH?

The human immune system depends on both learning and memory. In simple outline, learning starts when the immune system detects a new antigen. Through trial-and-error processes, a kind of Thorndikean learning, the cell with the optimal antibody for this antigen is selected among a number of less optimal possibles and enormously replicated. The memory can last for a lifetime or disappear within a year or less. The immune system involves local contact, cooperation, and direct recognition between several kinds of B- and T-cells, and uses information transfer, feedforward in replication and negative feedback to stabilize active cell populations. There may be epigenetic carry-over of resistance between generations. It is sometimes described as the molecular consciousness of the human body.

There are two kinds of immunity—innate and adaptive—and it is the adaptive form that has all the characteristics of swarm intelligence. It is self-organizing, lacks a central control, is initially imperfect in recognition, which is improved by trial and error, operates in stable overall fashion, adapts to changes in input, giving a diversity of response whose coordinate activity gives rise to evident intelligent behaviour (Timmis, Andrews, and Hart, 2010). The important feature to notice is that the immune system does not directly involve nerve cells. Instead of the collection of social insects in a colony, we now have a colony of interacting cells constructing a highly intelligent system.

PLANTS ALSO HAVE A COMPLEX IMMUNE SYSTEM

Disease pests attacking plants seem to induce unique combinations of proteins that are equally responsible for resistance (Loon et al., 2006). The signalling is highly specific and seems tuned to the individual pest. Once attacked, the learning response is remembered and, again, it is primed for very considerable periods of time. As with herbivory, further attacks are then dealt with more quickly and more robustly (Conrath, 2011). Priming results from:

1. Endogenous elicitors, signals arising from damage per se.
2. Molecular signatures arising from disease microbes.
3. Specific patterns of pathogen-related damage.
4. Colonization by growth-promoting bacteria.
5. Treatment with β-aminobutyric acid.

The initiation of priming is a learning process, and priming can be remembered for years in perennials. The system is very obviously intelligent because it helps solve a problem of continued attack by pests and, in showing such specific awareness, agrees with Margulis's definition of being conscious. The whole organism is involved.

More recent work has shown clearly that the primed state can be passed onto siblings and for several generations, suggesting epigenetic processes, DNA methylation, and siRNAs are likely involved with the learning process that controls specific methylases (Pieterse, 2012).

PRIMING TAKES PLACE AGAINST ABIOTIC STIMULI TOO

Perhaps the most extraordinary aspect of this process is the priming against abiotic stimuli. Treating plants with the amino acid, β-aminobutyric acid, not only primes against disease, but also primes against drought and salt stress—a process involving abscisic acid (Jakab et al., 2005). Large numbers of growth-promoting bacteria are associated with normal root systems and, surprisingly, induce systemic resistance to many fungi, bacteria, and viruses, even in the presence of pathogens (Kloepper, Ryu, and Zhang, 2004; Loon et al., 1998). The growth-promoting bacteria produce a variety of compounds, some of which are volatile, like butane diol. These on their own induce resistance mechanisms, but there is a range of small and large molecular-weight chemicals that do so as well. Most significantly, these rhizosphere bacteria also help plants tolerate abiotic stresses like drought and excess salinity, and thus again alter behaviour (Yang et al., 2009).

REFERENCES

Alpi, A., N. Amrhein, A. Bertl, M. R. Blatt, E. Blumwald, F. Cervone. 2007. "Plant Neurobiology, No Brain, No Gain." *Trends in Plant Science* 12, no. 4: 135–136.

Bose, J. C. 1926. *The Nervous Mechanism of Plants*. London: Longmans, Green.

Bray, D. 2009. *Wetware: A Computer in Every Living Cell*. New Haven, CT: Yale University Press.

Christmann, A., and E. Grill. 2013. Electric Defence. *Nature* 500, no. 7643: 404–405.

Conrath, U. 2011. "Molecular Aspects of Defence Priming." *Trends in Plant Science* 16, no. 10: 524–531.

Dennison, K. L., and E. P. Spalding. 2000. "Glutamate Gated Calcium Channels in *Arabidopsis*." *Plant Physiology* 124, no. 4: 1511–1514.

Edelman, G. M. 1992. *Bright Air, Brilliant Fire: On the Matter of Mind*. London: Penguin Books.

Engelberth, J., H. T. Alborn, E. A. Schmelz, and J. H. Tumlinson. 2004. "Airborne Signals Prime Plants against Herbivore Attack." *Proceedings of the National Academy of Sciences US* 101, no. 6: 1781–1785.

Fisahn, J., O. Herde, L. Willmitzer, and H. Pena-Cortes. 2004. "Analysis of the Transient Increase in Cytosolic Ca^{2+} during the Action Potential of Higher Plants with High Temporal Resolution: Requirement of Ca^{2+} Transients for Induction of Jasmonic Acid Biosynthesis and PINII Gene Expression." *Plant and Cell Physiology* 45, no. 4: 456–459.

Forde, B. G. 2014. "Glutamate Signalling in Roots." *Journal of Experimental Botany* 65, no. 3: 779–787.

Franks, N. R. 2008. “Convergent Evolution, Serendipity and Intelligence.” In *The Deep Structure of Biology*, edited by S. Conway-Morris, 111–126. West Conshohocken, PA: Templeton Foundation Press.

Franks, N. R., and T. Richardson. 2006. “Teaching in Tandem Running Ants.” *Nature* 439, no. 7073: 153.

Fromm, J., and S. Lautner. 2007. “Electrical Signals and Their Physiological Significance in Plants.” *Plant Cell and Environment* 30, no. 3: 249–257.

Frost, C. J., M.C. Mescher, J. E. Carlson, and C. M. de Moraes. 2008. “Plant Defence Priming against Herbivores: Getting Ready for a Different Battle.” *Plant Physiology* 146, no. 3: 818–824.

Howe, G. A., and G. Jander. 2008. “Plant Immunity to Insect Herbivores.” *Annual Review of Plant Biology* 59, no. 1: 41–66.

Jakab, G., J. Ton, V. Flors, L. Zimmerli, J.-P. Metraux, and B. Mauch-Mini. 2005. “Enhancing *Arabidopsis* Salt and Drought Stress Tolerance by Chemical Priming for Its Abscisic Acid Responses.” *Plant Physiology* 139, no. 1: 267–274.

Jennings, H. S. 1923. *Behaviour of the Lower Organisms*. Columbia University Press, New York.

Kloepper, J. W., C.-M. Ryu, and S. Zhang. 2004. “Induced Systemic Resistance and Promotion of Plant Growth by *Bacillus* spp.” *Phytopathology* 94, no. 11: 1259–1266.

Knight, M. R., A. K. Campbell, S. M. Smith, and A. J. Trewavas. 1991. “Transgenic Plant Aequorin Reports the Effects of Touch and Cold-Shock and Elicitors on Cytoplasmic Calcium.” *Nature* 352, no. 6335: 524–526.

Knight, M. R., N. D. Read, A. K. Campbell, and A. J. Trewavas. 1993. “Imaging Calcium Dynamics in Living Plants Using Semi-Synthetic Recombinant Aequorins.” *Journal of Cell Biology* 12, no. 1: 83–90.

Lacerra, P., and R. Bingham. 2002. *The Origin of Minds*. New York: Harmony Books.

Langridge, E. A., N. R. Franks, and A. B. Sendova-Franks. 2004. “Improvement in Collective Performance with Experience in Ants.” *Behavioural Ecology and Sociobiology* 56, no. 6: 523–529.

Lauder-Lindsay, W. 1876. “Mind in Plants.” *British Journal of Psychiatry* 21, no. 96: 513–532.

Loon, L. C. van, P. A. H. M. Bakker, and C. M. J. Pieterse. 1998. “Systemic Resistance Induced by Rhizosphere Bacteria.” *Annual Review of Phytopathology* 36: 453–483.

Loon, L. C. van, M. Rep, and C. M. J. Piertese. 2006. “Significance of Inducible, Defencerelated Proteins in Infected Plants.” *Annual Review of Phytopathology* 44, 135–162.

Lund, E. J., and H. F. Rosene. 1947. *Bioelectric Fields and Growth*. Austin: University of Texas Press.

Margulis, L. 2001. “The Conscious Cell.” *Annals of the New York Academy of Sciences* 929, no. 1: 55–71.

Margulis, L., and D. Sagan. 1995. *What Is Life?* London: Weidenfield and Nicolson.

Maturana, H. R. 1980. “Biology of Cognition.” In *Autopoiesis and Cognition: The Realisation of the Living*, edited by H. R. Maturana and F. J. Varela, 2–58. Dordrecht: Reidel.

Maturana, H. R., and F. J. Varela. 1980. "Autopoiesis. The Organisation of Living." In *Autopoiesis and Cognition*, edited by H. R. Maturana and F. J. Varela, 73–155. Dordrecht: Reidel.

Minot, C. S. 1902. "The Problem of Consciousness in Its Biological Aspects." *Science* 16, no. 392: 1–12.

Mithöfer, A., and W. Boland. 2008. "Recognition of Herbivore-Associated Molecular Patterns." *Plant Physiology* 146, 825–831.

Monod, J. 1971. *Chance and Necessity. An Essay on the Natural Philosophy of Modern Biology*. New York: Alfred A Knopf.

Morkunas, I., S. Borek, M. Formela, and L. Ratajczak. 2012. "Plant Responses to Sugar Starvation." In *Carbohydrates—Comprehensive Studies on Glycobiology and Glycotechnology*, edited by C.-F. Chang, 409–438. Croatia: Intech, Croatia.

Mousavi, S. A. R., A. Chauvin, F. Pascaud, S. Kellenberger, and E. E. Farmer. 2013. "Glutamate Receptor-Like Genes Mediate Leaf-Leaf Wound Signalling." *Nature* 500, no. 7463: 422–426.

Pieterse, C. M. J. 2012. "Prime Time for Transgenerational Defense." *Plant Physiology* 158, no. 2: 545.

Ramanathan, S., and J. R. Broach. 2007. "Do Cells Think?" *Cell and Molecular Life Sciences*, 64, no. 14: 1801–1804.

Sachs, J. V. von. 1887. *Lectures on the Physiology of Plants.* Translated by H. Marshall Ward. Oxford: Clarendon Press.

Scott, B. I. H. 1957. "Electrical Oscillations Generated by Plant Roots and a Possible Feedback Mechanism Responsible for Them." *Australian Journal of Biological Science* 10, no. 2: 164–179.

Scott, B. I. H. 1967. "Electric Fields in Plants." *Annual Review of Plant Physiology* 18, no. 1: 409–418.

Shabal, S. N., I. A. Newman and J. Morris. 1997. "Oscillations in H^+ and Ca^{2+} Ion Fluxes around the Elongation Region of Corn Roots and Effects of External pH." *Plant Physiology* 113, no. 1: 111–118.

Sourjik, V. 2004. "Receptor Clustering and Signal Processing in *E. coli* Chemotaxis." *Trends in Microbiology* 12, no. 12: 569–576.

Stroeymeyt, N., N. R. Franks, and M. Giurfal. 2011. "Knowledgeable Individuals Lead Collective Decisions in Ants." *Journal of Experimental Biology* 214, no. 18: 3046–3054.

Suel, G. M., J. Garcia-Ojalvo, L. M. Lieberman, and M. B. Elowitz. 2006. "An Excitable Gene Regulatory Circuit Induces Transient Cellular Differentiation." *Nature* 440, no. 7083: 545–550.

Tibbetts, E. A., and R. Lindsay. 2008. "Visual Signals of Status and Rival Assessment in *Polistes Dominulus* Paper Wasps." *Biology Letters* 4, no. 3: 237–239.

Timmis, J., P. Andrews, and E. Hart. 2010. "On Artificial Immune Systems and Swarm Intelligence." *Swarm Intelligence* 4, no. 4: 247–273.

Trewavas, A. 1970. "The Turnover of Nucleic Acids in *Lemna Minor*." *Plant Physiology* 45, no. 6: 742–751.

Trewavas, A. 1972. "Determination of the Rates of Protein Synthesis and Degradation in *Lemna minor*." *Plant Physiology* 49, no. 1: 40–46.

Trewavas, A. J. 1985. *Molecular and Cellular Aspects of Calcium in Plant Development*. Berlin: Springer.

Trewavas, A. J. 2011. "Plant Cell Calcium, Past and Future." In *Coding and Decoding of Calcium Signals in Plant Cells*, edited by S. Luan, 1–6. Berlin: Springer-Verlag.

Trewavas, A. J., and F. Baluska. 2011. "The Ubiquity of Consciousness." *EMBO Reports* 12, no. 12: 1221–1225.

Vincill, E. D., A. M. Bieck, and E. P. Spalding. 2012. "Ca^{2+} Conduction by an Amino Acid-Gated Ion Channel Related to Glutamate Receptors." *Plant Physiology* 159, no. 1: 40–46.

Vos, M., de, V. R. van Oesten, R. M. P. van Poecke, J. A. van Pelt, M. J. Pozo, M. J. Mueller, Antony J. Buchalia, et al. 2005. "Signal Signature and Transcriptome Changes of *Arabidopsis* during Pathogen and Insect Attack." *Molecular Plant—Microbe Interactions* 18, no. 9: 923–937.

Warwick, K. 2000. *QI: The Quest for Intelligence*. London: Piatkus.

West Eberhard. M. J. 2002. *Developmental Plasticity and Evolution*. Oxford: Oxford University Press.

Whitehead, A. N. 1938. *Modes of Thought*. New York: Free Press.

Wildon, D. C., J. F. Thain, P. E. H. Minchin, I. R. Gubb, A. J. Reilly, Y. D. Skipper, et al. 1992. "Electrical Signalling and Systemic Protease Inhibitor Induction in the Wounded Plant." *Nature* 360, no. 6399: 62–65.

Wu, J., C. Hettenhausen, M. C., Schuman, and I. T. Baldwin. 2008. A Comparison of Two *Nicotiana Attenuata* Accessions Reveals Large Differences in Signalling Induced by Oral Secretions of the Specialist Herbivore. *Manduca Sexta*. *Plant Physiology* 146, no. 3: 927–939.

Yang, J., J. W. Kloepper, and C.-M. Ryu. 2009. "Rhizosphere Bacteria Help Plants Tolerate Abiotic Stress." *Trends in Plant Science* 14, no. 1: 1–4.

Main Pathway: Orientations

Subthemes

Proceed to Experience, p. 461
Proceed to Ethics, p. 461

31

THE 1970s PLANT CRAZE

Teresa Castro

In his 1972 video *Teaching a Plant the Alphabet*, the late John Baldessari holds up a succession of children's alphabet cards, repeating each letter to a potted banana plant until he has completed the alphabet. Made for presentation at one of his classes at Cal Arts, *Teaching a Plant the Alphabet* is often quoted as a conceptual art parody, a reference to Joseph Beuys's influential performance *How to Explain Pictures to a Dead Hare* (1965). Both points are fair: in his own words, Baldessari found conceptual art of that time "too pedantic" and Beuys's performance was indeed one of the artist's most famous. But as Baldessari himself recalls, "*Teaching a Plant the Alphabet* was done during the hippie times. There were books about how to communicate with your plants. I thought, okay, I guess I'll start with the alphabet, and then we'll talk . . ."[1]

Indeed, the early 1970s were "hippie times," even if the zeitgeist of hippie culture was slowly beginning to wane, and a conservative revolution loomed on the horizon. By 1981, the flower power of the flower children had withered: daffodils and dandelion chains proved harmless against Reagan's doctrine. In the meantime, the seeds of our current infatuation with plant intelligence were sown, for Baldessari's recollection is accurate: in the early 1970s, the belief that plants were sentient and intelligent entities, capable of reacting to human's thoughts and emotions (as well as to animals' pain or music) became widespread, nurturing popular culture's

Originally published as "The 1970s Plant Craze: The Visual (and Audio) Culture of *The Secret Life of Plants*," *Antennae* 52 (2020): 173–192. Reprinted with permission.

flirtation with vegetal beings. Magazine articles on the extraordinary powers of plants were literally everywhere, from the pages of *The Ladies' Home Journal* to those of *Electrotechnology*.[2] As the diktats of interior decoration stipulated it was in good taste to fill one's residence with rattan furniture and all sorts of leafy creatures cascading gracefully from macramé hangers, it became natural to play music to your houseplants. One certain Mrs. Hashimoto took Baldessari's satirical venture seriously, setting herself to teach the Japanese alphabet to a cactus. As a *New Scientist* 1973 article observed, not only "every art school diploma has its share of vegetable sculptures . . . but also several artists are following in the footsteps of scientists by conducting their own experiments with plants and treating these activities as works of art."[3] Echoing other previous fads—tulipomania in the 17th century, the fern fever of Victorian times, etc.—a general *plant craze* emerged in the late 1960s, catching on in visual and popular culture alike. Unlike those earlier fads, which fundamentally cut down the vegetal to the ornamental, the 1970s plant mania came as an eccentric blow to the belief that sentience and intelligence are a human prerogative. Against the background of "hippie times," which celebrated its first Earth Day in the spring of 1970, a different form of relationship between humans and "nature" was slowly taking shape.

The plethora of articles, books, vinyl records, artworks, and films on the subject of plant communication cannot fully be explained by hippie counterculture's love of nature, weed, magic mushrooms, and other mind-altering substances—even though these were important. Cold War paranoia, New Age spirituality, and, more importantly, the flourishing of ecological thinking played their role in an entangled web of sometimes paradoxical tendencies where the zucchini seed that germinates faster to the sound of Mozart and the philodendron that thrives to Indian flutes are as much the proof of plants' mind-blowing sentience as the tacit evidence of rock music's fundamental evilness.[4] Moreover, the 1970s plant craze relied massively on the cybernetic paradigm, systems theory, and electronics. Envisaged as self-regulating biological systems, plants were recognized not only as being able to communicate but as communication systems in themselves. Their electrical and chemical responses to the environment and other stimuli (such as telepathic stimuli) were now understood in terms of inputs and outputs that generated feedbacks. Their intelligence resides in the capacity to learn and self-correct in response to feedback, mirroring the intelligence of other larger and more complex natural systems, among which Gaia itself, as famously advocated by James Lovelock and Lynn Margulis in 1975. In what might appear as a surprise to those who presumed that "plant communication" was merely about hippies hugging trees or passing through the chemical doors of perception, the 1970s plant craze was eminently *technophilic*: even eco-mystical quests to reach the plant-other often depended on the interfacing of electronic extensions, i.e., on "bio-sensing" (conversely, psychedelic experiences were sometimes explained with the language of cybernetics). Perhaps more than ever, the intermediation of different machines proved essential to the plant intelligence argument: *the communicative, sentient plant is a mediated plant*. As a matter of course, the history of science and pseudoscience's encounter with plants' awareness of other plants and of their surroundings has relied, from the nineteenth century onwards, on the mediation of visual and other technologies. Without this visual and audio scaffolding that allows us to tune into the so-many unanticipated possibilities and aspects of vegetal life, our conception of the plant-other in sensitive, intentional, and ultimately intelligent terms would not be the same. In the following pages, I wish to sketch a brief portrait of this complex cultural moment, as visual culture, and in particular film, came to be permeated by references to plant communication, plant sentience, and plant intelligence.

THE SECRET LIFE OF PLANTS

1959. Reverend Franklin Loehr published a book on *The Power of Prayer in Plants*.[5] Based on 700 "experiments" implicating 150 people and 27,000 seeds, the book illustrates how McCarthyism and its deep-rooted fright of communist atheism stirred American piety: in the 1950s, as many as "94% of Americans believ[ed] in the power of prayer."[6] Scientists quickly dismissed Loehr's book, but the idea that the mind could somehow have its way over (vegetal) matter continued to make progress. "Psychic research," whose potential for military and domestic intelligence was apparently evident for more than just the odd science-fiction writer, was to gain momentum from the 1950s onwards, on both sides of the Iron Curtain.[7] A quick search on the CIA's online archives returns an interesting number of declassified reports on the study of "psychic phenomena", sometimes in relation to plants, which the military, in their perpetual war against "the enemy", dreamt of turning into organic-sensors, bio-invaders, green spies.[8]

In 1966, and against all reasonable odds, an inconspicuous event was to shake the very serious world of botanical knowledge. A polygraph expert working for the CIA, Cleve Backster (1924–2013), decided on a whim to hook one of his machines to the leaf of a dracaena. He wanted to see how the plant reacted to being watered. To his astonishment, after a minute or so, the galvanometer registered a surge of electrical activity in the plant, similar to that of an emotional stimulus in a human subject. Backster was intrigued and decided to proceed with his "experiment" by dunking a leaf of the plant in a cup of hot coffee. No reaction. What if he burnt it? And there it happened: as he imagined the dracaena being set on fire, the needles of the polygraph rose again, as if the plant could read his mind. As his hagiographers put it, this was Backster's Eureka moment: he "felt like running into the street and shouting to the world, 'Plants can think!'"[9] In the years to come, he and his collaborators multiplied the experiments, plugging dozens of plants and vegetables into lie detectors and concluding that lettuces, onions, oranges, bananas, and a multitude of ordinary houseplants could perceive and respond telepathically to human thoughts and emotions. As incredible as it sounds, and much to science's dismay, Backster's theses on plants' extrasensory perception and their astounding emotional capacities, shared by the author in the Winter 1968 issue of the *International Journal of Parapsychology*, were to quickly spread worldwide.[10] How was this possible?

"Hippie times" helped. As two concerned scientists were to bitterly acknowledge in the pages of *American Scientist* in 1979: In the troubled years of the late 1960s, a wave of antiintellectualism swept the United States, accompanied by an antiscientism that still persists in some measure. (. . .) Critics were quick to equate science with antihumanism and call for the reliance on alternate ways of arriving at an understanding of the universe about us. This appeal found receptive ears in a world worried about pollution, overpopulation, unemployment, growing crime, and—perhaps most important—a nasty and persistent war in which technology played a major role.[11]

More than "anti-intellectualism," "anti-scientism," or "anti-humanism," it's the "reliance on alternate ways of arriving at an understanding of the universe about us" that interests me. As we will see, the hippie desire to heal the crisis in human/nature relationships overinvested (and sometimes romanticized) the communicative, systemic model behind Backster's theses, according to which "mind" can extend beyond the body into its surroundings. Regarding his theories, they would've probably remained confidential if not for the flare of journalist (and former OSS spy) Peter Tompkins, the author of such celebrated New Age classics as *Secrets of the Great Pyramid* (1971) and *Mysteries of Mexican Pyramids* (1976). With the help of botanist and science vulgarizer Christopher Bird, Tompkins wrote *The Secret Life of Plants*, mainstreaming Backster's findings and rediscovering, along the way, a number of forgotten plant-intelligence champions, such as Bengali biologist Jagadish Chandra Bose. Propelled by a lavish advertising campaign, including a partial pre-publication with a catchy title in the pages of *Harper's Magazine*—"Love Among the Cabbages: Sense and Sensibility in the Realm of Plants"[12]—the book became a bestseller and was quickly translated into many different languages. Taking advantage of the volume's worldwide success, producer Michael Brown adapted it for the screen in 1978: directed by Walon Green, *The Secret Life of Plants* included an original soundtrack by none other than Stevie Wonder.

But *The Secret Life of Plants* was not the only book to get the most out of the untapped powers of plant sensibility and communication. The same year, Dorothy Retallack's *The Sound of Music and Plants* was also to sell well.[13] Like Backster (and Loehr before him), Retallack, a "doctor's wife, housekeeper, bookkeeper, mother, [and] grandmother to fifteen,"[14] had conducted a number of "experiments" in the late 1960s, using the "biotronic control chambers" available at Temple Buell College, Denver. Her thesis: rock music was harmful to plants (and, therefore, to humans too). Retallack was not the first to investigate the effects of classical music on plants' growth rate; she was the first, however, to expose them to a tape of Led Zeppelin, Vanilla Fudge, and Jimi Hendrix. According to her findings, plants seemed to like Bach and Ravi Shankar; much to Retallack's surprise, they even gave positive evidence of enjoying jazz. However, when it came to rock, they leaned away from the music source, displaying smaller leaves and eventually dying. "Some of those plants look like the people who attend rock festivals," confided an appalled Retallack to the pages of the *New York Times*.[15]

Despite Retallack's old-school moral panic about rock, the idea that plants were sensitive to music's soothing capacities resonated with New Age's beliefs in the healing energies of musical melodies. In October 1970, CBS aired "a Rock-versus-Shankar experiment" involving plants (and significantly filmed with time-lapse cameras): Retallack's name became known all across the US. Albums of "music to grow plants" were then making their appearance in record shops, such as the one that Dr. George Milstein produced exactly the same year, complete with a booklet and a packet of coleus seeds.[16] During the 1970s, a few plant music discs were released. Some of them simply compiled chamber and classical music hits; others, such as Baroque Bouquet's *Plant Music* (1975) or Roger Roger's *De la musique et des secrets pour enchanter vos plantes* (1978), offered original compositions for their green audiences.[17] Among these, Mort Garson's *Plantasia* (1976), with its percolating

Moog rhythms, acquired a legendary status.[18] One album, in particular, Molly Roth's *Plant Talk/Sound Advice* (1976), evokes Baldessari's parody, as spoken word artist Roth talks to ivies, ferns, and other plants, wondering if they understand English.[19] At the same time, a few artists became interested in bio-sensing and plant-generative music, among which John Cage who used "amplified plant materials" (i.e., cacti) as musical instruments in pieces like *Child of Tree* (1975) and *Branches* (1976). Others, such as eco-feminist Annea Lockwood, explored the effect of plant growth on musical instruments. But what about film? What role did it play in this peculiar plant craze?

WIRED PLANTS AND CYBERNETICS

Film, I believe, played an important role—and not only during "hippie times." As I've previously hinted at, the mediation of graphic technologies seems to have been a decisive element in the scientific (or para/pseudoscientific) exploration of the richness and complexity of plant life; a sort of epistemological scaffolding opening up theoretical horizons around plants' agency and their potential "awareness," "sentience," "thinking," or even "intelligence."[20] I've argued elsewhere that the sentient plant is in many ways a *mediated plant*: the 1970s plant craze illustrates this remarkably well since it relied massively on polygraph machines' methodical scribblings, photographs of vegetal "energy auras," electronic renditions of plants' signals and films of all sorts.[21] Indeed, if cinema's powers are unique (and I believe they are), when it comes to the mediated plant, film should first of all be placed in the larger landscape of (graphic) technologies allowing for the perception of plants' behavior. Among these, the 20th-century representatives of the more ancient graphic method—polygraphs such as Backster's iconic "lie detector," simpler galvanometers, spectrographs, etc.—are vital. Without these recording apparatuses, the secret life of plants would've remained concealed, imperceptible to the naked eye—and the naked ear. These machines transform plants' electrical and chemical signals into a nonverbal, iconic language: the language of graphs, diagrams, and, ultimately, mathematical formulas. Endowed with an aura of scientificity, these images extend vision into previously unseen (if not unknown) realms (as plant bioacoustics expands audition further). Despite scientists' immediate and continual insistence on Backster's "uncontrolled experiments, random observations, and anecdotal reports,"[22] the theses on plants' extrasensory perception and their astounding emotional capacities progressed, partially pushed by scientific imagery, in particular as embodied by graphs of jagged lines drawn on strips of white scrolling paper. Articles, books, films, and even records' sleeves and booklets all include images of plants wired to these apparatuses as they meticulously generate their machinic self-portrait, giving us access to their inner, secret lives.

Of course, "plants writing themselves" was not a new idea. For the highly influential *The Power of Movement in Plants* (1880), Charles and his son Francis Darwin generated an astounding amount of images, conceived with ingenious devices involving smoked glass plates and beads of wax on glass needles and allowing for plants to record their own motion.[23] Even more suggestively, in 1927, physicist and plant physiologist Sir Jagadish Chandra Bose (1858–1937) published the exquisitely illustrated *Plant Autographs and their Revelations*.[24] Bose was an important pioneer in the study of radio and electromagnetic waves, who later turned his attention towards the movements and electrical responses in plants. In the context of his research, he designed several innovative instruments, such as the "photosynthesis recorder," the "magnetic crescograph" (registering plant growth), the "oscillating recorder" (documenting the ascent of sap), or the "automatic recorder" (recording leaf movements as well as variations of temperature in plants). As Bose puts it in *Plant Autographs*:

> I have been able to make the dumb plant the most eloquent chronicler of its inner life and experiences by making it write down its own history. The self-made records this made show that there is no life-reaction in even the highest animal, which has not been foreshadowed in the life of the plant.[25]

Bose's enterprise encapsulates modern science's aspiration to mechanical objectivity, aptly described by science historians Lorraine Daston and Peter Galison as the "insistent drive to repress the willful intervention of the artist-author, and to put in its stead a set of procedures that would, as it were, move nature to the page through a strict protocol, if not automatically."[26] But when the proud inventor refers to his machines as "artificial organs of extraordinary sensitiveness,"[27] Bose also comes very close to some of Norbert Wiener's famous views. Believing that engineering theories of control and communication could explain behavior in humans, animals, and machines, Wiener coined the term "cybernetics" in 1948, laying the foundations of a new interdisciplinary field that was to become extremely influential during the Cold War.[28] In his attempt to find common elements in the functioning of the human nervous system and automatic machines, Wiener suggested that "every instrument in the repertory of the scientific-instrument maker is a possible sense organ."[29]

Bose's links to cybernetics are not limited to his understanding of rendering apparatuses as artificial sense organs or human sense organs as "antennae, radiating in various directions and picking up messages of many kinds."[30] His insights on vegetal beings as communicating systems that respond to stimulation through electric signaling also foreshadow some of the tenets of the cybernetic model. Bose's devotion to decrypting what he calls the "plant script" is instructive, particularly when he discusses the pulsing movements of the *Desmodium gyrans*, today known as *Codariocalyx motorius*. On this remarkable species, a tropical shrub known for the gyratory self-movements of its leaves, he writes: "the small leaflets move up and down like the semaphore formerly employed for telegraphic signaling," concluding that "there is an evident similarity between the automatic pulsation of the leaflet of the Telegraph-plant and that of the animal heart."[31] Although Bose was by no means the first to refer to this specimen as the "telegraph plant,"[32] the media metaphor is worth stressing. The telegraph in the plant's name refers to the optical semaphore telegraphs made of movable wooden arms which became a privileged means of military communication in Europe in the late eighteenth century and early nineteenth century (in India, semaphore telegraphs were introduced in 1810 and went out of service in 1880). In *Plant Autographs*, Bose refers to the optical telegraph, after which the *Desmodium gyrans* was effectively named but, symptomatically, his discussion of the electromechanical pulses of plants evokes the mechanisms of electrical telegraphy, which uses the coded pulses of electric current to transmit messages. To think about communication in terms of electrical signaling is a portentous affair since the former is no longer thought of in exclusionary, human-centered ways.

Cybernetics was to flourish in the URSS, permeating not only the discourse but also the imagery around plant science, as evidenced by two soviet documentaries shot by the Tsentrnauchfilm (the Moscow Studio of Science Films), *The Voice of Plants* (T. Iovleva, *Golos rastenija*, 1968) and *Are Plants Sentient?* (Leonid A. Panishkin, *Čuvstvujut li rastenija?* 1970).[33] The films' iconography is clearly marked by the overwhelming presence of recording apparatuses, such as the polygraph and their simple, stark graphs, or other electronic instruments. Plant communication was taken very seriously in the Soviet Union, where, by the end of the 1960s, it had become a subject worth studying in the best-equipped science labs. *The Voice of Plants* starts with several shots of three researchers in white coats, gathered around a long strip of scribbled paper: their expert-eye can decipher what the machines themselves have already decoded. The film alternates exterior views of prairies and forests with lab shots, crosscutting the customary time-lapse sequences of flowers blooming and plants spiraling around their tutors. However, the lab shots are more numerous and significant: the quest to hear and understand "the voice" of plants (which Soviet scientists hope will open up perspectives in terms of plant breeding in artificial climates) is presented as an eminently technical enterprise. Superimpositions of plants and polygraph machines, foregrounded against a dark background, rank among the films' most striking images. As a small electronic chip is carefully grafted onto a plant's stem, the cybernetic paradigm becomes evident. Reports in the Soviet press mention transforming plants into "a live electric relay"[34]: already in 1959, the director of the Laboratory of Biocybernetics of the Institute of Agrophysics, Vladimir Grigorievich Karamanov, had published a report on "The Application of Automation and Cybernetics to Plant Husbandry."[35] In the US, the October 1969 number of *Electronics World* includes an article on "Electronics and the Living Plant": inspired by Backster's findings, the author describes the former as an "exceptionally promising field."[36]

Are Plants Sentient?, another Soviet science-propaganda film, evokes the experiments led by Professor Ivan Isidorovich Gunar, head of the Plant Physiology Department at the Timiryazev Academy of Agricultural Sciences in Moscow. The film (which includes a sequence recalling Bose's pioneer experiments) insists massively on the electronic apparatuses available at the Academy. *Are Plants Sentient?* is mentioned by Tompkins and Bird in *The Secret Life of Plants*: shot by Gunar's chief assistant, Leonid A. Panishkin, it was shown to an American delegation in the summer of 1971. According to Tompkins and Bird, one of the American envoys stated in his report that the movie's intriguing part was the method used to record the data. Time-lapse photography made the plants seem to dance as they grew. Flowers opened and closed with the coming of darkness as if they were creatures living in a different time zone. All injury-induced changes were recorded by a sensitive polygraph attached to the plants.[37]

The American delegate's reaction is surprising since time-lapse cinematography was used from at least 1898 onwards to study plant-motion.[38] However, his visual ignorance didn't prevent him from hinting at the exact point raised by film's capacity to manipulate time scale: motion pictures can negotiate a transition from the plant-as-object into the plant-as-subject—what is more, into a subject with intentional movements. By reconciling the temporality of plant life with the temporality of human life, film potentially overturns the basic subject–object dualism, rearranging the frontiers of the living, extending intentionality to a multitude of non-human subjects, sensing other sentiences, and exposing different modes of being alive. As French writer Colette wrote in 1924:

> A time-lapse film documented the germination of a bean . . . At the revelation of the intentional and intelligent movement of the plant, I saw children get up, imitate the extraordinary ascent of the plant climbing in a spiral, avoiding an obstacle, groping over its trellis: "It's looking for something! It's looking for something!" cried a little boy, profoundly affected. He dreamt of a plant that night, and so did I.[39]

As film critics and theoreticians remarked very early on, cinema seems to be "animism's chief apostle"[40]: instead of disenchanting the world, film re-enchanted it, by imputing interiorities to animals, objects, machines, and, naturally, plants. By virtue of cinema's expressive resources (time lapse, the close-up, editing, etc.), films on plant motion seemed to resuscitate what botanical herbaria dried and flattened between their yellowish sheets of paper.[41]

Rekindling with a world full of non-human intentionalities was not, however, the Soviets' goal, even though a reporter from *Pravda* remarked that Professor Gunnar not only "talked about plants as he would about people" as he "appear[ed] to converse with them."[42] Marxist cybernetic science was more preoccupied with discovering computable truths allowing for an even more objective and efficient instrumentalization of the world (in short, with epistemic objectives of prediction and control). While hegemonic, this program had little in common with the New Age agenda of the American screen adaption of Tompkins and Bird's book. Like *The Voice of Plants* and *Are Plants Sentient?*, *The Secret Life of Plants* (1978) features prominently all sorts of recording and sensing instruments; unlike them, however, the film is much more daring in its equally technophilic envisioning of plant beings. Perfectly illustrating New Age's penchant for enlivening perceptions of nature, the picture takes plant sentience and intelligence as a cue to think about the systemic interconnectedness of all life. Towards the end of the film, footage referring to the Dogon's ancient cultural beliefs is crosscut with images from a modern telescope pointed at Sirius, as Stevie Wonder sings, "A seed is a star."[43] Not surprisingly, *The Secret Life of Plants* also makes abundant use of macro-photography and time-lapse sequences: as French filmmaker and theorist Jean Epstein summed up in 1935, "fast motion reveal[s] a world where the kingdoms of nature know no boundaries. Everything lives."[44]

But more original and certainly more epochal than the time-lapse shots is the film's "cybernetic art" sequence, documenting a performance involving artists Richard Lowenberg, John Lifton, Jim Wiseman, and Tom Zahuranec. Reduced to a minimum in the picture's final edit—i.e., to footage from John Lifton's "Green Music" installation at the tropical conservatory of San Francisco's Golden Gate Park—the sequence has since been recalled by Lowenberg.[45] In early 1976, Lowenberg, then an artist in residence at the NASA Ames Research Center, was asked by the film's production team to conceive a number of sequences for the screen version of *The Secret Life of Plants*. Influenced, among others, by cybernetics and the ecological writings of Gregory Bateson, Lowenberg had published in 1972 a small blurb on the concept of "environetic synthesis" in the now historic video magazine *Radical Software*. Accompanied by a suggestive drawing depicting an uncanny "circuited self," made of a joint human head and a television monitor, the text's premise was "that one's environment could be designed to respond to one's own physiology, such as the brain waves (EEG) and muscle potentials (EMG), with video, audio and other sensory devices responding to the person."[46] With the help of John Lifton (who, in 1975, had presented his "Green Music" installation at the Whitechapel Gallery in London),[47] Jim Wiseman (who had built copies of the Paik/Abe video synthesizer and of the Sandin Image Processor), and Tom Zahuranec (who had wired a rhododendron into the oscillators of a Buchla Synthesizer, live on radio in 1972, and invited the audience to telepathically communicate with it),[48] Lowenberg conceived a spectacular media-performance based on the interfacing of plants and different types of synthesizers. In addition to the restaging of Lifton's "Green Music" in San Francisco (an installation based on the bio-electric sensing of plants' reactions to the presence of humans and implicating a battery of monitoring devices), an experiment involving wired plants and six performers connected to bio-telemetric systems was shot in a Hollywood studio. Bioelectric information from humans and plants was inputted to audio and video systems, which outputted glitching, colored videos, and plant noise in a feedback loop connecting plants, humans, and machines: in sum, opening up the doors of perception. The communicative model inherent to Backster's hypothesis reaches here its cybernetic paroxysm. In its embodiment as bio-media performance (as "bio-dis-play," in Lowenberg's terms), *The Secret Life of Plants* is a collaborative venture between organic and non-organic systems, humans and non-humans. Tune in and be(come) aware: electronic mediation is the strategy chosen to counter the deafness and backgrounding to which vegetal beings are usually referred, bringing forth a new "ecology of mind," as Bateson would put it.[49] As video-art pioneer Juan Downey—whose *Vegetal System of Communications for New York State* proposed, in 1972, to transform electromagnetic energy between humans and philodendrons into a navigation tool—had intuited, cybernetic technology bore the portentous promise of closing "the man–nature chasm."[50] Moreover, the images and sounds made under Lowenberg's guidance for *The Secret Life of Plants* embody the idea of the electronic signal as medium; not surprisingly, in the early 1970s, he had worked with Steina and Woody Vasulka. Plant communication was by now more than a simple business of jagged lines drawn on strips of white scrolling paper: John Baldessari might have laughed at it, but plant communication had (also) become video art.

CONCLUSION

By the end of the 1970s, Tompkins and Bird's bestseller had captured popular imagination. References to the book popped up here and there, as in Philipp Kaufmann's remake of *Invasion of the Body Snatchers* (1979), where green plants are played classical music in a mud-bath parlor by an attentive keeper. Also in 1979, a thriller directed by Jonathan Sarno, *The Kirlian Witness* (rereleased recently under the title *The Plants Are Watching*) tells the story of a woman who attempts to telepathically communicate with a philodendron to find out who murdered her plant-loving sister. The film's heroine acquires a copy of *The Secret Life of Plants*, becomes interested in Kirlian photography (a collection of photographic techniques used to capture the phenomenon of electrical coronal discharges and understood by many to be "auras"), and even rents a lie detector. An episode from *Tales of the Unexpected*, "The Sound Machine" (1981), imagines an engine capable of perceiving the ghastly screams of flowers being cut.[51] The same year, in an episode from *Darkroom*, a botanist develops an apparatus able to read daisies' minds. His wife learns from the flowers of his affair with his assistant and shoots him dead.[52] In short, the communicative model quickly became a B-series plot.

From the 1950s onwards, plant agency had become a way for science-fiction and horror films to give voice to communist anxieties (the alien plant spores turn "pod people" in Don Siegel's *Invasion of the Body Snatchers*, 1956), radiation fears (the scowling tree stump from Dan Milner's *From Hell It Came*, 1957), or concerns about genetic manipulation and bio-engineering (the half-human, half carnivorous plant from *Venus Flytrap*, 1970).[53] Since an army of vegetal villains had been feasting on women's flesh for years, an exploitation film such as *Please Don't Eat My Mother* (dir. Carl J. Monson), starring a shy man who befriends a houseplant with unusual appetites (a parody of Roger Corman's 1960 film *The Little Shop of Horrors*, featuring an odd-looking blood-thirsty, consumerist plant), could see the day in 1973. The plant craze of "hippie times" eventually turned plant agency into a spoof, from Baldessari's *Teaching a Plant the Alphabet* to the cult-classic *Attack of the Killer Tomatoes* (1978).

The Secret Life of Plants badly impacted serious scientific research on plants' sensory and perceptual capacities. Widespread press coverage of Backster's pseudo-experiments contributed to this backlash. Work on plant communication and plant signaling "was somewhat stigmatized, and the limited availability of funding and other resources constrained further progress."[54] Indisputably, Backster's theses on the "primary perception" of plants were nonsense. Still, the real baby—the study of plant awareness and its potential challenging of the exclusiveness of both knowing and feeling as human assets—was thrown out with the bathwater. Almost thirty years had to pass before scientific works mainstreaming the perceptual sophistication of plants—such as Chamovitz's *What a Plant Knows: A Field Guide to the Senses* (2012)[55]—were to see the day, as a general "plant turn" sweeps through different fields of knowledge and creation. Plants and their singular life forms, for so long relegated to the margins of conceptual thinking about life itself, finally jut out from the leafy, decorative setting to which they were backgrounded. In our present dire ecological crisis, to acknowledge the richness and complexity of plant-life is an invitation to withdraw from a centric reason that separated humans from "nature," situating human life outside and above it. In what constituted a striking ecological critique of Enlightenment science and its holy dualisms, "hippie times" attempted to tell a different kind of story about "Man" and "Nature" and grappled with a fundamental epistemological shift. Most of all, they experimented widely with alternative modes of engagement with what poet Gary Snyder described as "the most ruthlessly exploited classes": "animals, trees, water, air, grasses."[56] As we emerge shell-shocked from a global pandemic, what are we to do now? Maybe we can learn from the past: instead of imagining that "plants are like people," as suggested by

"America's Master Gardener" in 1971,[57] we can focus instead on what it means to be human on a shared planet.

NOTES

1. J. Morgan, "Somebody to Talk to: John Baldessari," *Tate Etc.*, December 1, 2009, https://www.tate.org.uk/tate-etc/issue-17-autumn-2009/somebody-talk.
2. B. Boulton, "Do Plants Think?," *The Ladie's Home Journal*, May 1971; and G. De La Warr, "Do Plants Feel Emotion?," *Electrotechnology*, April 1969.
3. J. Reichardt, "Art at Large," *New Scientist* 59, no. 858 (August 9, 1973): 347.
4. On ecological thinking, see D. Belgrad, *The Culture of Feedback: Ecological Thinking in Seventies America* (Chicago: 2019).
5. F. Loehr, *The Power of Prayer in Plants* (New York: Signet Books, 1959).
6. J. Michaels, *McCarthyism: The Realities, Delusions, and Politics Behind the 1950s Red Scare* (London: Routledge, 2017), 187.
7. See S. Ostrander and Lynn Schroeder, *Psychic Discoveries Behind the Iron Curtain* (Hoboken, NJ: Prentice Hall, 1970).
8. Cf. https://www.cia.gov/library/readingroom/. Eventually, in 1972, the agency began funding research on parapsychology and "remote viewing," i.e., on the use of extrasensory perception in order to obtain information from a (great) distance. By 1978, a secret army unit had been established: "Stargate" project was on.
9. P. Tompkins and C. Bird, *The Secret Life of Plants* (New York: Avon Books, 1973), 21.
10. C. Backster, C., "Evidence of Primary Perception in Plant Life," *International Journal of Parapsychology* 10, no. 4, (Winter 1968): 329–348.
11. Galston, A. W., and C. L. Slayman, "The Not-So-Secret Life of Plants: In Which the Historical and Experimental Myths about Emotional Communication between Animal and Vegetable Are Put to Rest," *American Scientist* 67, no. 3 (May–June 1979): 337–344.
12. P. Tompkins and C. Bird, "Love Among the Cabbages: Sense and Sensibility in the Realm of Plants," *Harper's Magazine* (November 1972), 90–96.
13. D. Retallack, *The Sound of Music and Plants* (Santa Monica, CA: De Vorss, 1973).
14. Retallack, *The Sound of Music and Plants*, 15.
15. A. Ribley, "Rock or Bach an Issue to Plants, Singer Says," *New York Times*, February 21, 1971, https://www.nytimes.com/1971/02/21/archives/rock-or-bach-an-issue-to-plants-singer-says.html.
16. George Milstein, *Music to Grow Plants*, E.S.C. 121, 1971, Vinyl, LP.
17. Baroque Bouquet, *Plant Music*, Amherst Records, 1976; and Roger Roger, *De la musique et des secrets pour enchanter vos plantes*, Tchou Éditeur, 1978.
18. Mort Garson, *Plantasia*, Homewood Records, 1976.

19. Roth & Bricker, *Plant Talk/Sound Advice*, Plant Talk Productions, 1976.
20. These terms are obviously non-equivalent, referring to different ways of envisaging the richness and complexity of plant life. Symptomatically, they are all used again today, as different fields of knowledge, from biology to philosophy, have taken an interest in plant life. See, among many others, and on biology's side, D. Chamovitz, *What a Plant Knows: A Field Guide to the Senses* (New York: Scientific American Books, Farrar, Straus and Giroux, 2012); A. Trewavas, *Plant Behaviour and Intelligence* (Oxford: Oxford University Press, 2014); S. Mancuso and A. Viol, *Brilliant Green: The Surprising History and Science of Plant Intelligence* (Washington, DC: Island Press, 2015).
21. T. Castro, "The Mediated Plant," *E-flux Journal* (September 2019), https://www.e-flux.com/journal/102/283819/the-mediated-plant/.
22. A. W. Galston, and C. L. Slayman, "The Not-So-Secret Life of Plants: In Which the Historical and Experimental Myths about Emotional Communication between Animal and Vegetable Are Put to Rest," *American Scientist* 67, no. 3 (May–June 1979), 337.
23. C. Darwin, *The Power of Movement in Plants* (London, John Murray, 1880).
24. J. C. Bose, *Plant Autographs and Their Revelations* (London: Longmans, Green, 1927).
25. Bose, *Plant Autographs*, vii.
26. L. Daston and P. Galison, *Objectivity* (New York: Zone Books, 2007), 121.
27. Bose, *Plant Autographs*, viii.
28. R. Wiener, *Cybernetics, or Control and Communication in the Animal and the Machine* (Paris: Hermann & Cie, 1948).
29. R. Wiener, *The Human Use of Human Beings: Cybernetics and Society* (London: Free Association Books, 1989), 23.
30. Bose, *Plant Autographs*, 235.
31. Bose, *Plant Autographs*, 71, 73.
32. In English, the appellation "telegraph plant" goes back, at least, to the mid-nineteenth century. A passage from the American journal *The Horticularist* suggests, in 1856, that the expression originated in Bengal (The Horticulturist and Journal of Rural Art and Rural Taste, *The Horticularist* 11 (1856): 243. "Telegraph plants" were also known as "Semaphore plants": the first use of the word *semaphore* in reference to English use was in 1816. Presumably, the appellation "Telegraph plant" must have appeared between this date and the 1850s, as "semaphoric telegraphs" were built all around Europe and India.
33. Copies of these films are held at the Gaumont Pathé Archives, Paris.
34. As quoted in Tompkins and Bird, *The Secret Life of Plants*, 78.
35. Tompkins and Bird, *The Secret Life of Plants*, 80.
36. L. G. Lawrence, "Electronics and the Living Plant," *Electronics World* (October 1969): 28.
37. Tompkins and Bird, *The Secret Life of Plants*, 79.
38. The German plant physiologist Wilhelm Pfeffer made four time-lapse films between 1898 and 1900, corroborating some of Darwin's contested ideas on plant sensitivity and irritability. On these early plant-motion films, see O. Gaycken, "The Secret Life of Plants:

Visualizing Vegetative Movement 1880–1903," *Early Popular Visual Culture* 10, no. 1 (February 2012): 51–69.

39. Colette, "Cinéma [Magie des films d'enseignement]," in *Colette et le cinéma* (Paris: Fayard, 2004), 369.

40. B. Bilinsky, "Le costume," in *L'Art Cinématographique* (Paris: Félix Alcan, 1929), 56.

41. See T. Castro, "À l'écran, le végétal s'anime: Cinéma, animisme et sentience des plantes," in *Puissance du végétal et cinéma animiste. La vitalité révélée par la technique*, ed. T. Castro, P. Pitrou, and M. Rebecchi, 41-¶3 (Dijon, France: Presses du réel, 2020).

42. Tompkins and Bird, *The Secret Life of Plants*, 78.

43. Tompkins and Bird's book doesn't refer to the Dogon, but in 1976, Robert K. G. Temple had made popular the thesis according to which the latter had been in touch with intelligent extraterrestrial beings from the Sirius star system (cf. R. K. G. Temple, R. K. G., *The Sirius Mystery*, New York: St Martins Press, 1976).

44. J. Epstein, "Photogénie de l'impondérable" (1935), *Écrits sur le cinéma*, vol. 1 (Paris: Seghers, 1974), 250.

45. See "Bio-Sensing art in the 1970s. Data Garden Interviews Bio-Art Pioneer Richard Lowenberg," *Data Garden*, September 20, 2011, https://www.datagarden.org/post/richard-lowenberg-interview (accessed November 1, 2019). Images turned for the sequence have been made available by Lowenberg on https://www.youtube.com/watch?v=OR4ZNV3hU70 (accessed November 1, 2019).

46. Lowenberg, R., "Environetic Synthesis," *Radical Software* 2, no. 1 (Winter 1972): 44.

47. According to a *New Scientist* article from 1973, "Green Music" was also presented at the Edinburgh Festival that same year: Reichardt, *art. cit.*, p. 346–347.

48. The composition and audience reactions are audible at https://archive.org/details/RE_1972_10_18 (accessed November 1, 2019).

49. Bateson, G., *Steps to an Ecology of Mind: Collected Essays in Anthropology, Psychiatry, Evolution, and Epistemology*, Chicago: University of Chicago Press, 1972.

50. J. Downey, "Technology and Beyond," *Radical Software* 2, no. 5 (Winter 1973), 2.

51. Produced by Anglia Television, *Tales of the Unexpected* was aired on British ITV and aired between 1979 and 1988.

52. The episode is called "Daisies." *Darkroom* was produced by Universal Television and aired on ABC in 1981–1982.

53. On such films see A. Knee, "Vegetable Discourses in 1950s Science Fiction Film," in *Plant Horror: Approaches to the Monstrous Vegetal in Fiction and Film*, ed. D. Keetley and A. Tenga, 145–162 (London: Palgrave MacMillan, 2016); A. Howe, "Monstrous Flora: Cinematic Plant Antagonists of the Post-World War II Era," in *The Green Thread: Dialogues with the Vegetal World*, ed. P. Vieira and M. Gagliano , 147–163 (Lanham, MD: Lexington Books, 2016); and J. Adamson and C. Sandilands, "Thinking Plant Politics with *The Day of the Triffids*," in *The Language of Plants*, ed. M. Gagliano, J. C. Ryan, and P. Vieira, 234–252 (Minneapolis: University of Minnesota Press, 2017).

54. M. Mescher and C. De Moraes, "Role of Plant Sensory Perception in Plant-Animal Interactions," *Journal of Experimental Botany* (November 2014), 430.
55. Chamovitz, *What a Plant Knows*.
56. G. Snyder, "Revolution in the Revolution in the Revolution," *Regarding Wave* (New York: New Direction Books, 1967), 39.
57. J. Baker, *Plants Are Like People: How to Grow a Healthier, Happier Garden* (Los Angeles: Nash, 1973).

Main Pathway: Orientations

Subthemes

Proceed to Experience, p. 97
Proceed to Ethics, p. 479

32

FLORAL SENSATIONS: PLANT BIOPOLITICS

Catriona A. H. Sandilands

FROM SENSATIONS TO POLITICS

In her fascinating book *The Flower of Empire*, Tatania Holway traces the ways in which the giant "floral sensation" of the South American water lily *Victoria regia* played a key role tying together colonial botany, bourgeois horticulture, and institutions of Victorian imperial spectacle. The lily, which first came to the attention of the Royal Geographical Society in 1837 (the inaugural year of Queen Victoria's reign), soon became a British obsession. Not only did "the very mention of *Victoria regia* . . . call forth visions of Britain's imperial grandeur . . . [but also] the effort to retrieve this peerless exotic from the equatorial wilds where it grew and to cultivate it in England became an epic quest that captured the world" (2013, pp. 1–2). This plant was a participant in the massive project of colonial botany that saw thousands of exotic species transported to Europe for purposes of taxonomic classification and, often, profitable utilization (Schiebinger, 2004); moreover, it was also a player in the transformation of English gardening from a mostly subsistence practice (except for the elite) to a nationwide preoccupation with horticultural display that gave rise to institutions as diverse as public botanical exhibitions and massed arrangements of bedding plants (Boddy, 2013).[1] Although this chapter is not about the complex role of plants in British imperialism and horticulture, it could be: as Theresa Kelley (2013) demonstrates, for example, exotic species' sensational *differences* from more familiar European plants both cemented their role as a form of colonial currency and facilitated their entry into public debate in the eighteenth and nineteenth centuries because of their overwhelming disruptions of existing systems of botanical understanding.

To continue instead with the larger idea of "sensation" on which this chapter turns, there was recently a line of larger-than-usual bedding plants available at some North American garden centers sold under the brand "Giant Floral Sensations™." The striped purple and white petunias were particularly showy: indeed, like *Victoria regia, Petunia axillaris* and *P. integrifolia* came to European attention from South America, and also became important players in the unfolding of Western garden aesthetics. Unlike giant water lilies, however, petunias are no longer quite so sensational: they are, in some circles, considered horticultural clichés, a status only intensified by their routine appearance in front of suburban corporate headquarters and in mass-produced plastic hanging baskets. Indeed, petunias are no longer really individual specimens; they are design elements, and their value inheres precisely in their *lack* of uniqueness, their regularity and conformity to industrial aesthetic and maintenance demands: season-long bright flowers, uniform height, drought tolerance. Here, the truer sensation of these plants concerns the "™" on the label in each pot: the trademark is followed by the phrase "propagation prohibited by law." Given Monsanto's 2005 purchase of the seed and plant company Seminis—giving it an estimated 85 to 90 percent share of the US nursery market—it is highly likely that those petunias were Monsanto's at some point along the line. What that lineage means is, first, that the plants were likely radically hybridized so as not to be capable of open pollination (as many petunias are) and, second, that a gardener could technically be prosecuted for successfully rooting a cutting.

This consideration of lilies and petunias as botanical sensations indicates the ways in which plants are caught up, in diverse ways, in specific relations of knowledge, power, colonialism, commodification, technology, accumulation, and desire. In other words, plants are subjects of *biopolitics* which, following Foucault, Agamben, and others, refers to the ways *life* is inserted into *power*, perhaps most intensively and invasively at the current neo-liberal/biotechnological conjuncture. For Foucault, power is not simply a question of the sovereign's ability to kill or "make die," but instead involves a diffuse web of institutions and relations—*dispositifs* or *apparatuses*—in which certain bodies and organisms are *made to live* in particular ways through complex relations and practices of power, knowledge, and corporeality. Organized around understandings of population and species, and also identity and desire, biopolitics concerns the simultaneously massive and intimate management of living: everything from environmental policy to personal pleasure. As Foucault puts it, biopolitics consists of "a closely meshed grid of material coercions rather than the physical existence of a sovereign" (2003, p. 36): whereas "for millennia, man remained what he was for Aristotle: a living animal with the additional capacity for a political existence; modern man is an animal whose politics places his existence as a living being in question" (1984, p. 143).

Acknowledging the problem of anthropocentrism that Nicole Shukin identifies as endemic to most biopolitical thought—namely, that it has "been constrained by [its] reluctance to pursue power's effects beyond the production of human social and/or species life" (2009, p. 11)—this chapter argues that understanding plants as part of the complex enmeshments of biopolitics allows us to consider not only the ways in which plants are treated as objects of various forms of extraction, production, consumption, and manipulation, but also the ways in which different plants' specific *capacities* are a crucial part of their diverse involvements in the multispecies relations of, say, imperial display and neo-liberal exchange (giant water lilies and petunias *do* particular things in particular contexts; so do corn, kudzu, and clover). This argument suggests a second gloss on the term "botanical sensation," one in which plants are not simply infinitely manipulable bundles of vegetal resources, but rather complexly embodied and actively *sensate* creatures whose individual and evolutionary lives are deeply intertwined with our own and whose biological abilities have an active influence on the ongoing development of biosocial communities in both evolutionary and everyday relations.

In his book *What a Plant Knows*, biologist Daniel Chamovitz explores the extensive experimental research that currently exists demonstrating that plants see, smell, feel the sensation of touch, know where they are in space (proprioception), and remember, as in storing information for a relatively long period of time.[2] He avoids the contested notion of vegetal intelligence in favor of a strong argument for plant *awareness*: he notes, for example, that "they differentiate between red, blue, far-red and UV lights and respond accordingly[;] they . . . respond to minute quantities of volatile compounds [VOCs] wafting in the air . . . [; they] know when they are being touched and can distinguish different touches[;] . . . they can change their shapes and ensure that shoots grow up and roots grow down[; and they] are aware of their past: they remember past infections and the conditions they've weathered and modify their current physiology based on these memories" (2012, pp. 137–138). Although he is careful to distinguish plant from human awareness, he nonetheless emphasizes that plants respond to their environments in ways that involve constellations of sensation and behavior, not just mechanical unfoldings of genetic potential (there is, of course, considerable debate about this issue). In addition, while plants also have many additional sensory capacities that are not analogous to ours (Pollan, 2013), it is quite interesting to note that in some cases, the precise chemical or physical process that appears to enable a sensory response in a plant is remarkably similar to the one enabling human or other animal response, for example, the fact that the laying down of a short-term memory is a matter of potassium imbalance and the passage of electrical signals in both animal neurons and Venus flytrap leaf cells (Chamovitz, 2012, p. 119).

But it is the issue of plant *communication*—which occurs primarily through the emission and reception of VOCs (i.e., scent)—that is, perhaps, most significant to a biopolitical emphasis on the importance of plant capacities to biosocial organization: plants are not only sensate, but they are also able to broadcast their responses to sensation to insects, to other plants, and even to people, prompting actions by these other organisms even in everyday time, and thereby demonstrating active intervention in the world at the level of the individual plant as well as the species. Of course, exuding scent is an evolutionary adaptation, one of many ways in which particular plant species broadcast their attractiveness to pollinators, either generally or specifically. Pollan (2001) might argue that the fact that humans also like some flower scents over others confers on lavender a potential reproductive advantage over skunk cabbage: note which one of these species has achieved nearly global garden distribution. Likewise, in some cases a plant's *response* to scent also seems to be about reproductive adaptation: as Chamovitz shows us, for example, the ethylene emitted by rotting apples that causes other nearby apples to ripen rapidly "ensures not only that the entire fruit ripens uniformly but that neighboring apples will also ripen, which give off even more ethylene, leading to [a . . .] ripening cascade of McIntoshes. A full display of soft fruits brought on by the ethylene-induced wave guarantees an easily identifiable market for animals, which then disperse the seeds" (2012, p. 31).

But then there is the question of plant *signaling*: since about 1983, there has been a proliferation of research indicating that specific plants respond, *in the moment*, to predation, sending out deterrent chemical signals to predators, sending out warnings to nearby plants (including plants of different species) to do the same, and even sending out signals to insects to come and prey on the predators. To give one example among the hundreds available: wild tobacco plants (*Nicotiana attenuate*) respond to predation in several ways. Their first line of defense is, of course, their general toxicity: nicotine is poisonous. But for some reason, hawkmoth caterpillars are immune to the effects of the nicotine. So the plants have developed several more contextually communicative responses. First, when threatened with an overabundance of caterpillars—which they register chemically through the caterpillars' saliva—the plants send VOCs into the air to attract another insect, the Big-eyed bug (*Geocoris pallens or punctipes*) that feeds voraciously on both hawkmoth eggs and larvae; in one experiment, the bugs arrived within a matter of hours. In addition, when chemically triggered by caterpillar predation, the plants also develop epidermal outgrowths (trichomes) that are specifically *attractive* to the caterpillars but that, when eaten, cause the caterpillars themselves to exude an odor that is attractive to the bugs. And finally, significant predation also causes the plants to dramatically alter their pollinator relations, switching within a matter of days from attracting the nocturnal hawkmoths (which are the main pollinator as well as predator) to attracting diurnal hummingbirds (whose offspring do not eat the plants); in order to do so, the plants come to flower at a different time of day, the shape of the flower changes, and so does the chemical composition of the nectar (Buffie, 2012).

There are several points to be made here. First and most obviously, it seems clear from this research that plants share many registers of sensate and communicative biosocial involvement with human beings. As Elaine Miller (2002), Michael Marder (2013), and Kelley (2013) all point out, in different ways, this observation is not new, and it has troubled Western philosophy at least since Aristotle: plants are clearly alive, sensitive, and responsive (one need only watch a sunflower), and yet they are generally figured as lacking those precise qualities of living that are seen to constitute a fully formed *life*. To put it simply, plants complicate the bifurcation of animacy from inanimacy in obvious ways, which has historically given rise to an array of categorical attempts to devalue, for example, the principle of vegetality as against animality and humanity. As Marder notes, for Aristotle, the fact that plants do not engage in locomotion—their movement inheres in subtle changes of state such as growth and decay—renders them not just differently alive, but less fully so: plants share with humans only "the mere act of living," the proper life of humanity being concerned with something other than nutrition and growth. For Hegel, "plant growth is seen as purposeless because the vegetal soul does not attain to any higher capacities other than those of endless nourishment and propagation. . . .

it may reach completion only from the external standpoint of those who will impose *their* ends onto these essentially goalless living things" (Marder, 2013, p. 25); as Kelley adds, "for Hegel . . . plants [also] looked categorically unreliable: some seemed to move; most seemed to procreate . . . and still others looked like animals" (2013, p. 221). In the context of a philosophy determined that the movement of spirit should prevail over originary nature, suspect botanical life had to be stripped of its unsettling power and placed in the cosmic hierarchy at a level safely below more intelligible modes of being alive. And in different ways for Heidegger and Levinas, for example, because the plant is not fully separate from its environment, it is denied a relation to alterity, reflexivity, and worldliness: what humans may have in common with plants becomes subordinate to some other element that exalts our difference and superiority (Marder, 2013).

There are, of course, important nuances to this history. Miller, for example, traces the figure of "the vegetative soul" through nineteenth-century German philosophy, highlighting the ways in which ideas about plants were key to understandings of organicism in thinking: "the vegetative soul, in contrast to the animated soul, emphasizes rootedness, vulnerability, interdependence, and transformative possibility rather than a separation of soul from body, actualization, and a stance of aggressiveness and self-preservation" (2002, p. 18). Marder discusses Nietzsche and his concept of nutritive desire, which is a faculty that is shared between humans and plants and is also the basic "expression of the overflowing will to power" (2013, p. 39) so central to his work. And as noted earlier, Kelley brilliantly depicts the ways in which the extraordinary burst of "monstrous" plants into European consciousness brought about by colonial botany had a profound effect on both the developing science of taxonomy (which plants continue to confound) and on philosophy, leading Goethe in particular to challenge Hegelian teleology in favor of a view of plant growth "as a series of remarkable, even inventive adaptations and new directions" (2013, p. 229) rather than as an imperfect, incomplete modality of living.

But even with these important botanical fascinations and resistances, plants, like animals, are caught up in the workings of Giorgio Agamben's "anthropological machine," in which one crucial operation of biopolitics consists in the iterative struggle over the distinction between *zoe* and *bios*, "bare life" and "political life," the natural life of nutrition, growth, and decay and what is considered meaningfully human. The struggle with the relation between *zoe* and *bios* lies, in fact, at the center of the always-fraught negotiation of what it means to be human, but the logic of that negotiation is always ex post facto: the idea of the human as a meaningful entity is presupposed on some basis or another, and something else, understood as not-human, is then excluded. Famously, in *The Open*, Agamben shows that the constant redrawing of this line is a key biopolitical moment in which life is brought to the service of power; in Western culture, life is never defined, but rather "ceaselessly articulated and divided" (2004, p. 13). For Agamben, of course, the slippery distinction concerns the one made between humans and "mere" animals; here, the distinctions between vegetality and animality, and vegetality and humanity, are at least equally important. For plants are so clearly identified with *bare life* that the possibility that they might possess something other than what Aristotle referred to as mere "psychic potentiality," that substratum of generalized nutritive liveliness out of which a *life* might eventually emerge, is almost impossible to imagine. Animal lives, for us, generally require something more than mere habitual succession; they require an intelligibly responsive relationship to an external environment, and so it is no accident that end-of-human-life discourses engage the "non-responsive" human body in relation to the vegetative, and not the animal. Animal lives, for us, generally require some kind of rudimentary recognition of self in relation to environment, so it is no accident that Cary Wolfe, in the midst of a nuanced argument about Judith Butler's work on the shared corporeal precarity of humans, animals, and environments, writes that: "not everything included under the rubric of precarious life—*plants, for example*—warrants protection from harm" (2013, p. 19; my emphasis). This fundamental biopolitical distinction is why the research presented above is so important: to say that plants are *aware* of and *responsive* to their environments brings at least one cog in the anthropological machine to a halt. In other words: plants inhabit a biopolitical space in which their lives are not recognized as fully lived because of anthropocentric assumptions about the nature of a "proper" life; contemporary research into plant sensation and behavior underscores both the arbitrariness and the politics of this distinction, and asks us to think differently about plants as parts of our political communities.

Despite his categorical dismissal of the plant kingdom as a whole, Wolfe rightly emphasizes that biopolitics are not only or even primarily a matter of inclusion and exclusion—of the line between human and animal, animal and plant, human and plant—but more a question of the specific *dispositifs* organizing particular bodies in and through particular relations of power. When Foucault writes that humans are now "animals whose politics place our existence as living beings in question," he is moving well beyond the distinction between *zoe* and *bios* and into an examination of the ways in which it is, in fact, our biopolitical relations, our beings as members of species entangled with other species, that are the stuff of the ever-increasingly intimate and pervasive political specifications of modernity. Wolfe's view, of course—like Shukin's—is that animals are not only *one* thing to humans. Contrasting the multibillion-dollar pet insurance industry with factory farming, for example, he demonstrates that some nonhuman animals are incorporated into biopolitical relations as at least quasi-subjects (most famously, those Great Apes to whom formal rights have been granted in New Zealand and several European countries), and others such as broiler chickens and laboratory rats are forced to live under conditions of what Derrida calls "virtually interminable survival, in conditions that previous generations would have judged monstrous, outside of every presumed norm of a life proper to animals" (quoted in Wolfe, 2013, p. 45). Likewise, Shukin's version of this process of specification turns on the idea of "rendering" as a central dynamic of what she calls animal capital: at the same time as animals are rendered *representationally* as part of a spectacular naturalization of capital (cute animals selling cellular technologies), they are also rendered *physically*, en masse, into meat, glue, fertilizer, and most pointedly, pet food. The second large point is, then, that plants are also very much bound up in and organized by these relations: although plants generally share certain qualities as organisms (chlorophyll, photosynthesis, multiple cellulose cell walls, indeterminate growth patterns, etc.), their specific places in biopolitics are not simply a matter of their general, excluded "vegetality," but instead a product of a more complex system of material power relations in which some plants are, in fact, *not* just bare life. This is not to say that plants should be considered biopolitical subjects in the same manner as animals (indeed, we should be as skeptical of the idea of "the plant" as Derrida is of "the animal"); plants simply do different things, both for themselves and for us. The insight does suggest, however, alongside the work of geographers Leslie Head, Jennifer Atchison, and Catherine Phillips, that an understanding of the *agency* of plants is not only important to the formulation of a more ethical relationship with them, but also to a more accurate understanding of what is going on in the biopolitical specification of diverse plant/human relationships (Head, Atchison, and Phillips, 2014). In other words, understanding plants as having certain capacities that are at once prior to, organized by, and responsive to biopolitics requires that we think beyond our generally habitual, knee-jerk mechanization and instrumentalization of plants toward an understanding of the ways in which we are collectively implicated biopolitical subjects.

FROM BIOPOLITICS TO ETHICS

The instant we begin to think about plant–human relations as a plurality rather than a singularity—and people such as foresters, foragers, farmers, gardeners, botanists, and harvesters do so on a daily basis often without the benefit of having read Derrida—we begin to be able to discern something like a constellation that is every bit as complex and contradictory as the one Wolfe describes for animals. Some plants are highly respected and prized as living presences or, at least, as valuable commodities: there is a white oak tree in Athens, Georgia that, because of a deed signed in the 1820s or 1830s, legally "owns itself" and is a valued town citizen with more property rights than many people (Atlas Obscura, n.d.); in a similar vein, California tree-sitting activist Julia Butterfly Hill publicized her intimate relationship with "Luna," a giant redwood, as part of her campaign to prevent logging in the old growth forest in the 1990s (Hill, 2000); and Paul Cloke and Owain Jones describe the ways in which individual trees were key "actants" in conservation politics in a Bristol cemetery (Cloke and Jones, 2004, p. 322). There is such a thing as "orchid tourism," and there are strict national and international regulations prohibiting orchid poaching and smuggling. On the other hand, many plants are treated as raw material for human manipulation: *Phalaenopsis* orchids are artificially propagated on a mass scale and sold in IKEAs and supermarkets worldwide (Sandilands, 2010), and industrial agriculture manipulates plants chemically, physically, and genetically with the sole purpose of producing the highest and most reliable yield in the most profitable manner possible. Potatoes, for example, increasingly grown as sources of high-quality industrial starch rather than directly for food, are subject to intense genetic modification to optimize amylopectin content, and genetic use restriction or "terminator" technologies even propose to remove from certain plants, including but not only potatoes, their capacity to reproduce independently (GMO Compass, 2008).

One highly visible node of plant biopolitics circulates around the opposition of indigenous to "exotic-invasive" species in many current gardening and ecological discourses: certain plants are carefully nurtured and others are carefully exterminated (sometimes very violently, as in Head et al., 2014). In eastern North America, one such invasive plant is dog-strangling vine, or the less menacing DSV for short (*Cynanchum rossicum*); citing the concern that DSV aggressively out-competes desirable, indigenous flora and interferes with the management of timber plantations, the Ontario Invasive Plant Council (OIPC) published a "Best Management Practices" guide that is primarily oriented to evaluating the relative merits of different ways of going about killing the plant: digging, mowing, clipping, tarping, poisoning. While the biopolitics of invasive species are complex, what is particularly striking about DSV is that, in these bio-managerial terms, it is always already killable, a form of life that—unlike indigenous plants—should have no protection *as* a life; for the OIPC, at least, it is necessary to put this being *to death* for the life of the greater ecology or economy (of course, DSV has no apparent value to humans or it might not be so expendable). And yet, DSV—like most weeds—is "invasive" precisely because its outstanding capacities for proliferating in disturbed soils and traveling along roads and railways allow it to take up residence just about anywhere that humans go (Sandilands, 2013). As Richard Mabey documents in his thoughtful book *Weeds*, the tenacity and opportunism of invasive plant species are qualities that one might conceivably find admirable, especially in the human beings among whom DSV so clearly thrives, and especially in the neo-liberal context in which the plant has found such particular purchase. He himself admits to admiring the "insinuation of alien species" as "exquisitely intimate and precise" (2010, p. 256). And yet the infinite killability of invasive species has not only spawned an entire international surveillance and eradication industry, but also demonstrated what happens when plants are rendered purely as examples of bare life: whereas the lively capacities of some plants are admired and encouraged, in the case of invasives, they are always already excessive and detestable.[3]

Of course, thinking about plants' active appearances in these diverse biopolitical relations shows us that the essential nature of their lives is *not* that of bare life or base vegetality. We are so accustomed to thinking about plants as occupying a hierarchical space somewhere between inanimate things and animals that we have few opportunities to consider that plants are actually creatures whose articulations of being alive are simply just stupefyingly *different* from our own. Where both philosophy and biology indicate some important similarities between humans and plants—including common origins, similar electrochemical processes of sensation, and even modalities of movement—the fact is that plants and animals have adapted to their environments in such radically different ways that it is, in some ways, nonsensical to speak about the one as "higher" than the other, even though doing so is of course, biopolitically, probably inevitable. Chamovitz emphasizes the ways in which plants' rooted pursuit of solar energy—as opposed to mobile pursuit of other beings to eat—has given rise to modes of sensitivity and communication that are, in many respects, much more sophisticated than our own. Karen Houle (2011) emphasizes that terrestrial plants are "in" their environments, earth *and* air, in ways that are both quantitatively and qualitatively different from mammalian inhabitations because of their unique sensitivities; even from our perspective, plants are both landscape and *in* the landscape. Marder emphasizes that plants exist with and in a radically different temporality from our own; in addition, a plant is not a unified self in the same manner as a human. As he writes, "the plant is . . . not contemporaneous with itself, in that it is a loose alliance of multiple temporalities of growth—some of its parts sprouting faster, others slower, still others decaying and rotting—and in that it does not relate to itself, does not establish a self-identity" (2013, p. 104).

Depending on the context, biopolitical apparatuses may either accentuate or flatten these differences. To give three mundane, microscopic examples: Germinating tomato seedlings in a sunny late-winter window brings their temporality into closer alignment with specific human desires. Pruning the dead twigs from climbing roses in the spring and deadheading their spent blooms in the summer concentrates their complex being into a more singular identity, one centered on the moment of blooming (and not seeding). Nurturing a bonsai tree (which Pollan thinks cruelly manipulative, 2013) takes advantage of the plant's specifically vegetal sensitivities to its conditions of place in order to create a tree that is as perfectly proportioned in a shallow pot as are its larger, genetically identical kin outdoors. The point is not that we should somehow stop using plants for human ends, especially, for eating; it is, instead, to recognize not only that plants are actively involved in biopolitics because of their unique capacities, but also that our social interactions with these capacities involve multiple encounters with their *difference* that we cannot even begin to fathom as such, even as we routinely harness these differences to our desires. As a result, any more mindful, ethical relation to plants cannot simply involve an anthropomorphic extension of our needs to respond to theirs; plants demand that we pay attention to the fact that life is not a singular force differently arranged in specific bodies to which we can respond as "life," and that the nature of specific bodies transforms the experience and unfolding of living itself, and therefore our responses to plants as living and responsive beings. Plants, then, also seriously challenge forms of ethical and political thinking that are premised on the extension of anthropogenic experiences to those of non-human beings: their lives make very different kinds of demands.

In 2008, the Swiss Federal Ethics Committee on Nonhuman Biotechnology issued a report titled *The Dignity of Living Beings with Regard to Plants: Moral*

Consideration of Plants for Their Own Sake (Willemsen, 2008). This report is quite extraordinary, not least because it involved a legislatively mandated commission, including biologists and philosophers, taking seriously the idea that plants might be morally considerable for reasons other than those concerning basic human utility. The document (which demonstrates more dissensus than anything else) considers the merits of a range of positions on the treatment of plants, ranging from whether or not they merit ethical considerability on the basis of something like sentience, to whether genetic modification is an offense to plant dignity, to whether the proper object of consideration for plants is the individual, the community, or the species. In one example, the report notes that: "two positions represented on the Committee require—with varying justifications—restraint in handling plants. There are also different meanings to 'handling with restraint.' We could understand it to mean that plants may not be arbitrarily impaired or destroyed. Restraint can however also mean a requirement to handle plants carefully and considerately, and to limit their use and exploitation. Handling plants includes the social practice of instrumentalising them in a disproportionate and therefore impermissible way" (p. 10). The majority of the committee supported some version of this argument.

Amazing though it is that the conversation was even had, the Report completely fails to imagine what plants might actually require in the complex of biosocial and political relations in which they are, with us, enmeshed. The only thing that the Committee members agreed upon unanimously was that "an arbitrary harm caused to plants [is] morally impermissible. This kind of treatment would include, [for example], decapitation of wild flowers at the roadside without rational reason" (p. 20). Although it certainly wouldn't hurt for people to think more carefully about what they do to and with individual plants, the facts are that decapitating those flowers—depending on the flower—might help distribute their seeds (in fact, distribution is one of the most important things that humans do for plants); that according to Chamovitz plants don't have the capacity to feel pain as such (stress is a different thing); that they should be not singular beings whose integrity is compromised with the loss of a part; and that whether or not a given human action is arbitrary does not especially matter to the plant, whose being is as affected by being grazed for food as picked for disposal. Simply put, we cannot consider ethical relations to plants without a willingness to engage with their profoundly different articulations of life, in specific contexts, and involving close attention to the ways in which they act in specific biosocial communities.

Thinking about animals, Wolfe is critical of Robert Esposito's ethical insistence on *life* as the basis of a complete normative model, "the principle of unlimited equivalence for every single form of life" (quoted in Wolfe, 2013, p. 56), which we might also roughly ally with both biocentrism in general and the more radical recommendations of the Swiss Committee in particular. The problem with this view, for Wolfe, is that "if all forms of life are taken to be equal, then it can only be because they, as 'the living,' all equally embody and express a positive, substantive principle of 'Life' not contained in any one of them" (p. 56). Ironically, then, the basis of ethics in this position is that individual beings are considered not on the basis of their particular being, but on their abstract affirmation of a larger principle that has little to do with them. As this chapter has argued, plants demand that we understand living not as a singular experience, but as contingent, multiple, changing, and inextricably relational. We cannot understand biopolitics without attending to the ways in which plants are actively involved in their unfolding; likewise, we cannot understand plants without attending to the ways in which their differences are biopolitically articulated in and with their environments, including us. To raise a notion of "plant rights," for example, however politically provocative it might be, is ultimately to bark up the wrong metaphysical tree. In Marder's terms:

> To skirt the pitfalls of efforts aimed at bringing the entire vegetal world into the fold of moral philosophy . . . [we need] to cultivate a way of thinking not only *about* plants, understood as epistemic or moral objects, but also *with* them. What is required therefore is the cultivation of a certain intimacy with plants, which does not border on empathy or on the attribution of the same fundamental substratum to their life and to ours; rather, like all intimacy, it will take place (largely) in the dark, respectful of the obscurity of vegetal life. (2013, p. 181)

As this chapter has argued, such a dark plant intimacy requires a new kind of biopolitical attention to the specific relations in and through which we find ourselves entangled with plants. Although, as biologist Stefano Mancuso suggests, "because plants are sensitive and intelligent beings, we are obliged to treat them with some degree of respect" (quoted in Pollan, 2013, p. 102), it is clearly inadequate to anthropomorphize their capacities and interests in the service of an abstract conception of life or justice. To take plants seriously requires us to attend to the sensational mutuality of our biopolitical co-constitution; to understand biopolitics, in turn, requires that we take plants seriously, sensations and all.

NOTES

1. The lily is also part of a different biopolitical configuration in the Amazon Basin. It plays a role in the origin stories of many indigenous peoples (Galeano, 2009); it appears on the Guyanese coat of arms; its seeds are edible.
2. He acknowledges that, popular wisdom about "talking to plants" notwithstanding, they do not have an experimentally demonstrated capacity to respond to sound per se; Michael Pollan, in his 2013 overview of research on plant intelligence, disagrees.
3. "Invasiveness" is, of course, a discourse that involves plants, animals, and even some humans.

REFERENCES

Agamben, Giorgio. 2004. *The Open: Man and Animal.* Translated by Kevin Attrell Stanford, CA: Stanford University Press).

Atlas Obscura. n.d. "The Tree That Owns Itself." http://www.atlasobscura.com/places/tree-owns-itself

Boddy, Kasia. 2013. *Geranium* (London: Reaktion Books).

Buffie, Erna, dir. 2012. *Smarty Plants: Uncovering the Secret World of Plants.* Canadian Broadcasting Corporation, *The Nature of Things*/Merit Entertainment Inc.

Chamovitz, Daniel. 2012. *What a Plant Knows: A Field Guide to the Senses* (New York: Farrar, Strauss and Giroux).

Cloke, Paul and Jones, Owain. 2004. "Turning in the Graveyard: Trees and the Hybrid Geographies of Dwelling, Monitoring and Resistance in a Bristol Cemetery." *Cultural Geographies* 11: 313–341.

Foucault, Michel. 1984. *The History of Sexuality: Volume I, An Introduction.* Translated by Robert Hurley (Harmondsworth: Vintage Books).

Foucault, Michel. 2003. *"Society Must Be Defended": Lectures at the College de France, 1975–1976.* Edited by Mauro Bertani and Alessandro Fontana. Translated by David Macey (New York: Picador).

Galeano, Juan Carlos. 2009. *Folktales of the Amazon.* Translated by Rebecca Morgan and Kenneth Watson (Westport, CT: Libraries Unlimited).

GMO Compass. 2008. "Potatoes." http://www.gmo-compass.org/eng/grocery_shopping/crops/23.genetically_modified_potato.html.

Head, Leslie, Jennifer Atchison, and Catherine Phillips. 2014. "The Distinctive Capacities of Plants: Re-thinking Difference via Invasive Species." *Transactions of the Institute of British Geographers.* doi:10.1111/tran.12077.

Hill, Julia Butterfly. 2000. *The Legacy of Luna: The Story of a Tree, a Woman, and the Struggle to Save the Redwoods* (New York: Harper Collins).

Holway, Tatania. 2013. *The Flower of Empire: An Amazonian Water Lily, the Quest to Make it Bloom, and the World it Created* (New York: Oxford University Press).

Houle, Karen. 2011. "Animal, Vegetable, Mineral: Ethics as Extension or Becoming? The Case of Becoming-Plant." *Journal for Critical Animal Studies* 9, nos. 1–2: 89–116.

Kelley, Theresa. 2013. *Clandestine Marriage: Botany and Romantic Culture* (Baltimore: Johns Hopkins University Press).

Mabey, Richard. 2010. *Weeds: The Story of Outlaw Plants*. London: Profile.

Marder, Michael. 2012. "Resist Like a Plant! On the Vegetal Life of Political Movements." *Peace Studies Journal* 5, no. 1: 24–32.

Marder, Michael. 2013. *Plant-Thinking: A Philosophy of Vegetal Life* (New York: Columbia University Press).

Miller, Elaine. 2002. *The Vegetative Soul: From Philosophy of Nature to Subjectivity in the Feminine* (Albany: SUNY Press).

Pollan, Michael. 2001. *The Botany of Desire: A Plant's Eye View of the World* (New York: Random House).

Pollan, Michael. 2013. "The Intelligent Plant." *New Yorker*, December 23 & 30: 92–105.

Sandilands, Catriona. 2010. "Calypso Trails: Botanizing Expeditions on the Bruce Peninsula." *Dalhousie Review* 90, no. 1: 5–22.

Sandilands, Catriona. 2013. "Dog Stranglers in the Park? National and Vegetal Politics in Ontario's Rouge Valley." *Journal of Canadian Studies* 47, no. 3: 93–122.

Schiebinger, Londa. 2004. *Plants and Empire: Colonial Bioprospecting in the Atlantic World* (Cambridge, MA: Harvard University Press).

Shukin, Nicole. 2009. *Animal Capital: Rendering Life in Biopolitical Times* (Minneapolis: University of Minnesota Press).

Willemsen, Ariane, ed. 2008. *The Dignity of Living Beings with Regard to Plants: Moral Consideration of Plants for Their Own Sake* (Berne: Federal Ethics Committee on NonHuman Biotechnology).

Wolfe, Cary. 2013. *Before the Law: Humans and Other Animals in a Biopolitical Frame* (Chicago: University of Chicago Press).

Main Pathway: Orientations

Subthemes

Proceed to Politics, p. 277
Proceed to Ethics, p. 385

33

TO HEAR PLANTS SPEAK

Michael Marder

Humans are social beings anxious to communicate well beyond the confines of our own time and place—with future generations, with hypothetical extraterrestrial civilizations, or with other animals, such as dolphins, who interact through sonar media. In each case, the expansion of the linguistic model is faced with the problem of encoding a message intended for others (be they human or not) and deciphering possible messages emitted by them. But only very rarely does language itself become a problem.

Plants have not escaped the human desire for universal communicability. Consider the following, relatively recent, examples. In 2008, a café owner in the Japanese town of Kamakura decided to connect electric sensors to a plant, translating its sensitivity to light, heat, and so forth into Japanese with the help of an algorithm. The result was a widely publicized blog by *Midori-san*, or Mr. Green, the nickname of the *Hoya kerrii* specimen housed in the café and plugged into global telecommunication networks.[1] A more serious instance of the same impulse is evident in seismologists' increasing reliance on trees' sensitivity to changes in ultralow-frequency geomagnetic pulsations in a bid to anticipate earthquakes.[2] In the capacity of biotic measuring devices, trees now serve as the "networking elements of the Internet of Things."[3]

From *The Language of Plants: Science, Philosophy, and Literature*, ed. Patricia Vieira, John Ryan, and Monica Gagliano (University of Minnesota Press, 2017), 103–125.

We want to "hear" plants "speak." What kind of hearing must we resort to and what sort of speech corresponds to it? How to translate the language, or the languages, of plants into terms that are intelligible within the scope of our human languages? What is lost in this transposition, above all when it strives to make everything about the plants' communication with themselves, with other plants, with insects or other animals transparent? What are the conditions of possibility for a cross-kingdoms translation and what is the place of the untranslatable in it? And, in the first place, is the expression "the language of plants" defensible?

From the outset, it should be clear that the word *language*, conjugated with plants, does not *merely* point in the direction of a metaphor, an analogy, or a judgment of nonhuman forms of life based on human phenomena. We are sure not to hear plants speak if we continue to hold onto the anthropocentric prejudice that sees in our intelligence, cogitation, and languages the gold standards of intelligence, cogitation, and language as such. Protagoras's sophistic insight, reported by Sextus Empiricus—"The human is the measure of all things [*pantōn khrematōn einai metron ton anthrōpon*]: of things that are, that they are; of things that are not, that they are not"[4]—still overshadows our thinking millennia after its formulation. While, traditionally, Protagoras has been read as an advocate of extreme relativism in human knowledge (a reading that is not too fanciful, given that the sophist himself insisted on the changeability of truth depending on what appears to each individual), today his statement has an opposite ring to it, if it is heard in a cross-species context. The human (*to anthrōpos*) as human has now become the measure of all things, so every form of life appears to be deficient by comparison with it. Thanks to humanity's alienation from the rest of the natural world, it has turned into an exception that, starting from itself, dictates the rule.

We must, by all means, resist this piece of contemporary sophistry that passes for common sense. A serious consideration of the nature of language cannot afford to ignore the question about its broader meaning, outside a purely human enunciation. This is what Walter Benjamin called "language as such" or "the language of things," to which we shall return. Similarly, in discussing the language of plants, we are invited to reexamine the prevalent and highly impoverished view of language as a tool for transmitting or sharing information. At the very least, it will be necessary to supplement this view with the symbolic dimension of language, the mechanisms of expression and articulation, and the extended material–substantive side of vegetal biosemiotics.

In this chapter, I discuss the question of the language of plants as one of translation into the more or less familiar frameworks of human discourse. I outline four possible modalities of such translation:

(1) the symbolic "language of flowers" that announces itself in writers as diverse as St. Augustine and Sigmund Freud, Novalis and James Joyce;

(2) the figure of "talking trees" that pervades various cultures, from the sacred grove of Dodona in ancient Greece, through vegetalized human beings in Dante's *Inferno*, to the Persian Trees of the Sun and the Moon;

(3) biochemical communication between plants (as well as between plants and animals), quantified in plant sciences; and

(4) the plants' participation in the language of things, with its spatial nexuses and articulations. I argue that to hear plants speak we must learn to listen to the lacunae and silences of language, leaving plenty of room for the untranslatable (and, hence, the unspeakable) in these practices of translation. To the extent that each of the four modalities refuses to impose specifically human voices, categories, and discursive molds onto the vegetal world, it accomplishes this task and gets in touch with the self-expression of plants.

THE SYMBOLISM OF THE "LANGUAGE OF FLOWERS"

When a plant is converted into a symbol, its own language all but disappears underneath a shroud of meanings humans throw over it. It is no longer possible to discern the self-signification of vegetal life, because the symbolic plant does not refer to itself but turns into a token for something else entirely, thrown or cast (*ballein*, "to throw" at the root of *sym-bol*) outside itself. More often than not, the symbolic deployment of vegetation proceeds in the name of spirit—of spirit's separation from the world of matter, which is treated as the substratum for the impression of spiritual marks or signatures. A prevalent strategy in this regard is to locate the ultimate and, indeed, the only source of meaning in nonmaterial reality, divesting existence here below of any inherent sense of its own. Plant life, too, is presumed to be senseless in and of itself, unless it is put in the service of spirit. At the same time, spirit lays heterogeneous claims on various parts of plants; if flowers have been the most symbolic among these, it is because they have been framed, in the history of Western thought, as the closest to the spiritual realm. This is particularly evident in Goethe's botanical theory, according to which the pure colors of petals are the objective embodiments of light. A refined leaf, the petal is the pinnacle of the plant's spiritual ascent toward sexual difference, or "propagation through two genders."[5] Hence, instead of the language of plants, philosophers and poets resort to what they univocally designate as "the language of flowers."

St. Augustine excelled in the symbolic interpretations of texts and phenomena that permitted him to distance his theology and Christianity as a whole from Judaism. He resisted as much the vestiges of paganism (the full title of his 426 CE magnum opus is *The City of God against the Pagans*) as Jewish literalism, with its obedience to the letter of the divine law, rather than its spirit. And plants—particularly, flowers and fruit—were at the forefront of this endeavor. Let me give you an example. When it came to God's commandment to Adam and Eve to "be fruitful and multiply," Augustine refuses to take it literally because physical reproduction is a capacity humans share with plants and animals. For him, it would be absurd to contend that this should be a distinctly human virtue, because other kinds of creatures actually excel in it more than humans. "I might further say," he writes in his *Confessions*, "that this blessing, had I found it bestowed upon trees and plants and land animals, belongs to those kinds which are propagated by reproduction; but for plants and trees and beasts and serpents, there is no mention of 'Increase and multiply.'"[6] The way out of this conundrum is to spiritualize fruitfulness, rendering it symbolic; the true meaning of "fruit" is linked to the "works of mercy"—a spiritual and exclusively human activity that erases its vegetal (and sexual) origin, that is, physical reproduction.

Note that the association of plants with sexuality is the staple feature of "the language of flowers." Where a direct discourse on matters sexual is forbidden, invocations of vegetal sexuality abound as substitutes for the open outpouring of human desire. Thus, in the seventeenth and eighteenth centuries, botany was "the most explicit discourse, in the public domain, on sexuality."[7] In the eyes of Augustine, such connotations of plant life were central to pagan fertility cults, represented by the goddess Flora, who governed everything that bloomed and who was honored in the annual *ludi florales*, or floral games, replete with theatrical performances by naked actresses and prostitutes, some of whom were dramatically transubstantiated into Flora. Augustine calls worship of such deities "wholly wanton, impure, immodest, wicked, and unclean."[8] In order to purify the "shameful propitiation" of paganism, he sublimates plant parts into the spiritual sphere of good works, distancing them from their natural and literal origins. It follows, then, that the Augustinian vegetal symbolism was twice removed from the plants themselves and their languages: while pagan cults already took flowers to be the symbols of sexuality, Augustine recodified this association, making it fit the nascent lexicon of Christian spirituality.

What the author of *The City of God* found especially abhorrent was the flourishing of nonreproductive sexualities, of flowers that did not give rise to fruit. Reacting to the myth of Attis, the Phrygian god of vegetation, who in a temporary frenzy castrated himself, died, and was resurrected, Augustine mocks ancient Greek philosopher Porphyry for thinking that "Attis symbolizes the flowers, and that his mutilation signifies the fact that the flowers must fall before the fruit comes." In a curious inversion of the symbolic operation, whereby a humanized figure (or its organs) betokens a plant (or its parts),

> it is not the man himself, therefore—or the symbolic man whom they call Attis—whom they have compared to flowers, but his male organs. These, indeed, fell while he was still alive; or, rather, they did not fall, nor were they plucked, but were clearly torn off. But when the flower was lost, there was no subsequent fruit; rather, barrenness followed. What, then, is the meaning of this remnant . . . ? Do not the Greeks' fruitless attempts to find an interpretation simply persuade us that what rumor reports and writing records is no more than the tale of a castrated man?[9]

Augustine cannot tolerate a situation whereby a human symbolizes a plant. Nor does he think that flowers have any inherent value unless they give way to fruit or, more precisely, to the products of spiritual activity. Although it appears that his solution to the story of Attis is to take it literally, as "no more than a tale of a castrated man," the ironic metasymbolism of this episode is that Attis denotes the fruitless nature of Greek thought itself, unacquainted with the truth of Christianity.

Centuries later, in *The Interpretation of Dreams* (1900), Freud will avow the symbolic bond uniting the language of flowers to human sexuality and the fabric of the unconscious. Here, Freud's report on his "Dream of the Botanical Monograph" is of special significance: "I had written a monograph on a certain plant. The book lay before me and I was at the moment turning over a folded colored plate. Bound up in each copy there was a dried specimen of the plant, as though it had been taken from a herbarium."[10] Through a variety of unconscious associations, Freud establishes that the words *botanical* and *monograph* "constituted 'nodal points' upon which a great number of the dream-thoughts converged."[11] This, in turn, illustrates his theory of "condensation" and "overdetermination," which, postulating complex, nonlinear, psychic causality, accounts for the emergence of any given dream-image in sleep. Needless to say, the associations Freud records are suffused with sexual innuendo: he reproaches himself for forgetting to bring flowers to his wife; recalls a clinical case, in which Frau L. rightly interpreted her husband's forgetting to give her flowers for her birthday as a sign of his cooling passion; alludes to the "blooming looks" of Professor Gärtner (Gardener) and his wife, and so on.[12]

Even more explicit are the interpretations of dream-images involving live flowers, as opposed to dry ones. When a neurotic young woman reports that in her dream she "arrange[s] the center of a table with flowers for a birthday," Freud hears in that "an expression of her bridal wishes: the table with its floral center-piece symbolized herself and her genitals; she represented her wishes for the future fulfilled, for her thoughts were already occupied with the birth of a baby; so her marriage lay a long way behind her." Once specified, the flowers included in the arrangement were ascribed their precise symbolic functions: the lily of the valley concurred with "its popular sense as a symbol of chastity," while the violet, said and heard in English, conveyed "the dreamer's thoughts on the violence of defloration."[13] We could further multiply these examples, but the conclusion to which they lead us is already obvious: when it comes to the language of flowers, or, perhaps, to the question of symbolism generally construed, psychoanalysis is at its least critical and self-critical. The analytic drive stops at the level of "popular symbolism," accepting the authority of received ideas. Admittedly, this acceptance is partly unavoidable, insofar as it echoes the "truths" held self-evident from the standpoint of the analysand her- or himself. Yet, the analysand's own interpretation should only present materials for psychoanalysis to elaborate upon, not ready-made conclusions for analytic practice.

The formal framework of Freudian associations also appears to be identical to that of Augustine: plants are the symbols for nonvegetal reality, namely, the sphere of human sexuality. Nevertheless, we cannot miss the fact that Freud's "language of flowers" does not translate them into the vocabulary of abstract spirit but into that of the unconscious, the wholly embodied, material, extended part of the psyche. A psychoanalytic *symbol* is a *symptom* of psychic repression or, at least, of sublimation, which analytic dream-work obstinately traces back to its roots. No doubt, his translation of the language of flowers into that of the unconscious fails to respect the inherent meaningfulness of vegetal life, with the plants' own lived interpretations of the world, wherein they grow, orient themselves, and interact. But it is equally certain that Freud's materialism, his resistance to an artificial separation between the mind and the body, or spirit and matter, is more faithful to this life than Augustine's harnessing of flora as an allegory for spiritual reality. Freudian flower symbolism charts the way back to plant life *through* the human psyche, for which sexuality (the classical reproductive faculty that originates in plants and is shared by all living beings) is constitutive. Cast away from itself as a symbol, the plant comes back to itself, having engulfed much of what we consider to be the human. That is why, in *Plant-Thinking*, I pointed out that the "object of *psycho*-analysis, wherein we might detect a vegetal approach to the psyche, is no longer 'a soul of another genus' but an extended psychic thing entwined with the body itself—a somatic, and thus divisible, soul akin to that of a plant."[14]

Across the spectrum of symbolic transcriptions and translations it motivates, the literal plant, the plant itself, remains untranslatable. There are no plants growing on the fields of metaphor, in the gardens of allegory, or in the forests of symbols—except of the metaphorical, allegorical, and symbolic kinds. When I say or write "the plant itself," I do not mean a vegetal version of the Kantian thing-in-itself, foreclosed to human knowledge. I have in mind the language of the plants themselves, irreducible to our superimposition of meanings upon them. Anything but theoretical hairsplitting, this distinction intimates that what we are dealing with is not the classical relation between a signifier—that is, the word *plant*, or the symbolic structure it participates in—and the corresponding signified, prelinguistic concept, but an interchange between two languages: the biosemiotics of vegetal life and human signification. Whether we are mindful of this or not, whatever we know about plants is due to a successful translation from the former to the latter, a translation that never exhausts or depletes but, on the contrary, enriches what it translates (just as no translation, say, from Bulgarian to Swahili, exhausts either the source or the target languages).

Georges Bataille calls psychoanalytic attention, precisely, to the problem of the preanalytic symbolism of plants in his short essay "The Language of Flowers." Rejecting outright the search for a secret meaning of vegetal life, he attacks, without overtly naming Freud, the "fortuitous and superficial character" of this language.[15] Although "love can be posited from the outset as the natural function of the flower," Bataille prefers to shed light on the imperfections, obscene sights, and smells of decay that form the reverse of flower symbolism.[16] "The flower is betrayed by the fragility of its corolla," he writes, and, "thus, far from answering the demands of human ideas, it is the sign of their failure. In fact, after a very short period of glory the marvelous corolla rots indecently in the sun, thus becoming, for the plant, a garish withering. Risen from the stench of the manure pile—even though it seemed for a moment to have escaped it in a flight of angelic and lyrical purity—the flower seems to relapse abruptly into its original squalor: the most ideal is rapidly reduced to a wisp of aerial manure."[17] Bataille couples flower symbolism with the other type of Aristotelian movement, namely, decay, which, alongside growth and metamorphosis, is proper to plants. His flowers bespeak death, the ever-present shadow and source of meaning for earthly existence, be it vegetal or human. With all its gory, unsightly attributes that cannot be easily idealized, the symbolism of decay does not respond to the demands of spirit in its flight from the messiness of matter. It is, therefore, symbolism at the limit of the symbolic, nearly letting a finite life express itself in the language of finitude.

In philosophy and in psychoanalysis, contestations of "the language of flowers" slide on a scale that stretches between idealism and raw materialism; in literature, a corresponding continuum extends between Romanticism and irony. Consider Novalis and Joyce. The hero of Novalis's unfinished novel (1802), Henry von Ofterdingen, embarks on a quest for the idealized and nonexistent "blue flower," *blaue Blume*, which he saw in a dream. In anticipation of its symbolic association with his future beloved, Mathilda, he notices that "the flower leaned towards him and its petals displayed an expanded blue corolla wherein a delicate face hovered."[18] When he finally meets Mathilda, he asks himself: "Do I not feel as I did in that dream when I saw the blue flower? What strange connection is there between Mathilda and that flower?"[19] The connection is, after all, not that strange in the context of Romantic imagination, with its double predilection for the dream, the impossible, the nonexistent, on the one hand, and Goethe's natural language of symbols based on "the symbolic language of nature" itself,[20] on the other. No wonder that Novalis's blue flower grew to be the symbol not only of Mathilda or of metaphysical longing but of the entire German Romantic movement.

The traditional imputations of purity and innocence to the language of flowers that persist in Novalis are a far cry from its utilization by Leopold Bloom, the protagonist of Joyce's *Ulysses* (1922), who adopts the pseudonym "Henry Flower" in the course of an erotic correspondence with his admirer, Martha Clifford. Accompanied by a dry and scentless yellow flower, Martha's letter of longing to meet Bloom implies that he is *her* "blue flower": unreachable and largely indifferent. "Henry Flower" transforms these epistolary yearnings in his stream of consciousness under the heading "the language of flowers," though not before a mocking meditation on such a language, ironically resonating with his pseudonym, which is a synonym of his "real" family name: "Language of flowers. They like it because no-one can hear." His rendition of the letter is even more biting: "Angry tulips with you darling manflower punish your cactus if you don't please poor forgetmenot how I long violets to dear roses when we soon anemone meet all naughty nightstalk wife Martha's perfume."[21] Bloom hints that the muteness of the language of flowers is propitious to launching veiled sexual insinuations under the cloak of civility. He proceeds to unveil the obscenities that lurk in this symbolic language by intermingling real and imaginary flower names with portions of Martha's text. We obtain, consequently, a series of charming phytophallic images, from the sadomasochistically tinged "punish your cactus" to the suggestive "naughty nightstalk."

In the works of Bataille, Joyce, and, to a lesser extent, Freud, the materialist and ironic inversions of the language of flowers internally undermine the spiritual and idealist thrust of symbolic expression. The instability of flower symbolism at the limit of its aspiration to ideality reveals a certain noncoincidence between the symbolizing and the symbolized: reproductive parts of plants can be the signs of purity and innocence *or* obscenity; magnificent growth *or* decay; an unfulfillable yearning *or* sadomasochistic fantasy . . . In other words, this instability indicates that there is much more to the language of plants than meets the eye in the superficiality of its symbolic dimension.

THE ETHICS OF "TALKING TREES"

The figure of "talking trees" traverses different cultures and seems to belong to the Jungian archetypes of the collective unconscious. In India, the rustling of leaves on a pipal tree is thought "to be done by supernatural beings, who speak by that means."[22] Herodotus reports in *The Histories* that the cult of the oracle of Zeus at Dodona in northern Greece, also mentioned in Homer's *Iliad* and by Socrates in Plato's *Phaedrus*, was centered on an oak grove.[23] The rustling of sacred oaks foretold the future, as interpreted by the oracle-priests of the Selli tribe: "The Selli listened to the rustling of the sacred oak and thought they could hear voices. A question spoken with a loud voice in the wind found an answer in the sighing, whispering, and rustling of the oak trees."[24] According to Buddhist traditions, trees that supplied the materials for the statues of Buddha could be observed "speaking, crying, or producing other miraculous signs."[25] Alexander the Great came across prophesying talking trees in Persia; known as Iskandar there, he received predictions about his demise from the male cypress Mithra, the Tree of the Sun, and the female cypress Mao, the Tree of the Moon: "In a letter to his mother, Iskandar describes how the Tree's male heads told him by day that he would soon die, and how the female heads informed him by night that he would not return home."[26] In the fables of Zhuangzi, in Dante's *Inferno*, in Tolkien's *The Lord of the Rings* with its Ents, and the like, plants are endowed with anthropomorphic features, which invariably include the ability to speak.

The very partial list I have compiled above is meant to give but a foretaste of the prevalence of talking plants in world religions and literatures. As a rule, I see in this figure an improvement over the symbolic impositions of human meanings and languages onto plants. Unlike the flowers we have encountered in the previous section of this chapter, the trees themselves speak—for themselves and, usually, with knowledge that is superior to that of human beings. But they do not all speak uniformly, in the same manner, through the same media, or in the same kinds of languages. The crucial difference between their ways of speaking has nothing to do with the (at times forced) divergence between literary and religious representations; rather, it concerns the narrow identification of speech with vocalization, as opposed to its comprehension in terms of giving signs.

The assumption that to have a language is to be able to speak is both erroneous and unethical. Its mistaken premise is thoroughly anthropocentric, insofar as it ties linguistic phenomena to the voice, which only humans possess, and grants other creatures the right to speak only on the condition that they ventriloquize quasi-, proto-, or posthuman voices. When trees converse, as they do in Dante's *Divine Comedy*, the silence of vegetal life, which does not preclude the plants' self-expression, is broken and disrespected. The sentient trees inhabiting his *Inferno* weep, moan, and emit "these loud, unhappy voices."[27] From a broken twig, "words and blood" (*parole e sangue*) gush forth together.[28] And the bush Dante addresses says in response: "Indeed your sweet words break me / Away from silence [*non posso tacere*]: let it not weigh on your ears / If I am enticed to prattle a bit, for your sake."[29] We learn that these infernal talking plants are the souls of those who, having committed suicide, are punished with vegetal incarnations for taking their lives. If these plants are allowed to speak, it is because their bodies are but the vehicles for human spirits, pieces of sentient matter that trap the souls of sinners and cause them pain and suffering: "in the poisoned shade of the bushes we are."[30] Simply put, hell, for Dante, is human thought, speech, and sensation trapped in the body of a plant.

In lieu of translating the language of trees into its anthropic equivalent, we witness a substitution of vegetal communication with the patently logocentric aspects of human behavior. Moreover, this act of substitution does not recognize the origin it has erased: it does not register the existence of plant languages it has automatically denied and replaced with speech. Not every author imagining speaking trees succumbs to such blindness, however. The cult of Dodona inspired James Howell's 1645 *Dendrologia: Dodona's Grove, or The Vocall Forrest*, which narrates the history of England and Continental Europe with the help of talking trees. Howell's poetic opening sentence is worth citing: "It fortun'd not long since that Trees did speake, and locally move, and meet one another: Their ayrie whistlings and soft hollow whispers became articulate sounds, mutually intelligible, as if to the soule of *vegetation* the sensitive faculties and powers of the intellect also had beene co-infused into them."[31] The similarity between trees and people was, in Howell's world, a two-way street. While the former spoke like the latter, early human discourse bore a semblance to the rustling of leaves: "in the nonage of the world, mens voyces were indistinct and confus'd; and sojourning chiefly in the Woods, by a kind of assimulation and frequent impressions in the eare, they resembled those soft susurrations of the Trees wherewith they conversed."[32] The hypothetical convergence of vegetal and human discourses evinces, at the same time, respect for the potentialities of plant language and modesty with regard to the capacities of the early representatives of *Homo sapiens*. Howell does not endeavor to erase the vegetal origin in an act of thoughtless substitution but, on the contrary, attempts to construct a richer and more fluid version of plant existence that reverberates with other forms of life. Still, the markers of intelligence in his account are drawn from a set of largely unquestioned human values, ranging from locomotion to abstract thought and, of course, vocalization. Given the anthropocentric parameters of Howell's world, then, it makes no sense to delve into the difficulties of translating plant languages into their human counterparts, and vice versa, not to mention to care about what remains untranslatable in this carryover.

Although Master Zhuangzi's tale about Carpenter Shi and an oak, dating back to the late Warring States period in China (third century BCE), also puts words in the "mouth" of a tree, it is acutely aware that plants, as well as all other living beings, live in excess of the value systems we thrust upon them. The carpenter's complaint about an old oak he encounters near a village shrine is that it is useless—neither yielding edible fruit nor timber that could stay afloat if used to build a boat. When the oak appears in his dream, it queries him about the value of value, understood in the sense of usefulness. The utility of fructiferous trees, it states, "makes life miserable for them, and so they don't get to finish out the years Heaven gave them but are cut off in mid-journey. . . . As for me, I've been trying for a long time to be of no use If I had been of some use, would I ever have grown this large? Moreover, you and I are both of us things. What's the point of this—things condemning things? You, a worthless man about to die—how do you know I am a worthless tree?"[33] The lesson of the tree is that all existence is worthless from the standpoint of instrumental rationality and that its real worth lies in this absence of utility. More than that, human beings cannot presume to know that their scales of value extend to all creatures, including plants. The thingly nature of the carpenter and the oak implies their finitude, which simultaneously unites and separates them, whether ontologically, epistemologically, or axiologically. Now, all this is said in a speech that, delivered by a tree, subtly undermines the prominence of spoken discourse, which, too, is a disproportionately inflated human value. After all, the determinations of the worth or worthlessness of plant languages must contend with the analogous dilemma of the divergent axiologies, or valuations, corresponding to different modes of life.

Perhaps the most ethically attuned among the narratives of talking trees are those that do not conflate speech with vocalization. When ancient Hindus listened to the rustling of pipal tree leaves, trying to discern the conversations of celestial nymphs (*apsarās*) said to inhabit them, and when ancient Greeks engaged in fortune-telling based on the same sound produced by the wind as it passed through an oak grove, they imbued the interaction of plants and the elements with a secret meaning. To distill meaningful signs from the sounds that leaves, branches, and currents of air emit in concert is not to force a human semantic form onto the language of plants, but to attend to them in the places of their growth. It is also to acknowledge the untranslatable and the indiscernible, what cannot be picked up by the human ear and what exceeds our every interpretative venture, oriented toward the communication (if not the communion) of plants and the elements. Not by chance, the absence of speech from this language parallels the desire to glimpse a temporal absence, namely, the future. Since the future is not a fixed, substantive object of knowledge, a suitable approach to it cannot rely on the rigid mechanisms of comprehension and identification, built into human cognition and speech. We must strain to listen to the inaudible, if we are to be in touch with the future and with the language of plants themselves.

Talking trees are the conduits to another possible relation to plants, perceived no longer as mute objective surfaces for the inscription of meaning that has originated outside them, but as nonhuman subjects in their own right. Does contemporary plant science grasp and elaborate upon this possibility? Does it prepare the ground for an ethics of vegetal life? Or does it provide yet another inflexible method of translating the language of plants into a system of human conceptuality, oblivious to the untranslatable?

THE SCIENCE OF PLANT COMMUNICATION

One virtue of a scientific approach to the language of plants is that it is highly resistant to the groundless attribution of symbolic meanings to vegetal life, on the one hand, and the anthropomorphic temptation pervading stories about talking plants, on the other. Plant scientists work with biochemical substances and electrical signaling that are part and parcel of the plants' life activity. It is from these processes and products of vegetal existence that they deduce the language of plants. A tomato plant, whose leaves have been damaged by a pathogen, can send warning signals concerning the impending attack to nearby undamaged plants through shared mycorrhizal underground networks. Under controlled experimental conditions, the undamaged plants demonstrated a sharp increase in defense enzymes, such as peroxidase, in response to the communication they had received.[34] While the damaged tomato specimen recruits the fungi that symbiotically grow around its roots to transmit this information to its neighbors, the biochemical message it sends is inseparable from its own life, in all its materiality. The only remaining problem seems to be the accuracy of the scientific transcription and interpretation of such communications.

To backtrack a little, it bears mentioning that plant science (like all science, for that matter) is not interested in the materiality of "plant-being," but preoccupied with the information transmitted between plant cells, tissues, specimens, and across biological kingdoms (i.e., between plants and insects). As the word itself shows, information is a very formal notion, quite removed from the life activity of the organisms that share it. In order to arrive at this highly mediated result, scientists must first operationalize their terms and quantify their research, such that whatever they observe would be countable and measurable. Even if plant science does not transform the language of plants into a set of symbols, it does render it in numbers and numeric codes. As I wrote in *Through Vegetal Being*, "More often than not, the scientific codification of reality resorted to numbers, totally indifferent to what they quantified. Sensible qualities dissolved in these empty universals that aimed to supplant, among other things, the elements, within which and thanks to which life unfolded."[35] Quantitative measurements equally apply to a tomato plant and a birch tree, a marigold and a cactus, a chainsaw and the trunk of the pine it is about to cut, a plant and a planet . . . In the universal language of science, the oft-incomparable languages, dialects, and idioms of living beings and extended objects are irretrievably lost. Moreover, convinced that everything in material reality can be, in principle, quantified and operationalized, scientists come to believe in the possibility of a total translation of the world into their code. They lose sight of the untranslatable, the nonquantifiable, and nonoperationalizable—things that, for all intents and purposes, do not exist within the bounds of the scientific worldview. The language of plants is robbed of its specificity, its unique purchase on and expression of life, when it is absorbed without its untranslatable remainder into the research conducted by plant scientists.

Another problem with the scientific construction of the language of plants has to do with the way of operationalizing this concept. For scientists, "language" means "communication," which, in turn, signifies "transfer of information" in the shape of biochemical, electrical, and other kinds of signals. As a result, plants are conceived of as emitters and receivers of information,[36] following the computational standard of intelligence. To be sure, we must be cognizant of the theoretical background for this reductive approach to the language of plants: in the twenty-first century, it is virtually impossible to find scientific formulations of human language and cognition, let alone other-than-human linguistic phenomena, that do not depend upon information exchanges and computational techniques. So entrenched is this paradigm that, nowadays, the untranslatable, in the case of plants, animals, and humans alike, refers to the incommunicable expression and the deep, noninformational stratum of linguistic reality. Martin Heidegger's famous definition of language as "the house of Being"[37] would be a good start for rethinking the alternatives to its current hegemonic operationalization, provided that its scope would extend beyond humans (so that plant languages would be the house of plant being, animal languages the house of animal being, and so forth).

The controversy raging in the scientific community around the idea of plant behavior and intelligence is a moot point, compared to a notion of language that would be qualitatively different from signal emission, processing, and sharing. In 2007, thirty-three plant scientists signed a letter, published in *Trends in Plant Science*, in which they attacked the emerging area of study called "plant neurobiology."[38]

Their chief argument was that, absent the brain and nervous system, plants cannot by any stretch of the imagination be considered intelligent. The signatories to the letter omit the fact that, despite lacking such organs (indeed, any organs whatsoever), computers not only fall under the current category of intelligence but also serve as its prototypes. At its best, science demonstrates the primacy of functions over the organs that execute them, which is why a brain is not absolutely indispensable for intelligence any more than an actual eye is necessary for vision. The presence of photoreceptor cells, detecting light, the direction from which it emanates, and where it fits in the color spectrum, is sufficient to qualify for vision—a capacity that plants also possess. *Arabidopsis* alone has "at least eleven different photoreceptors,"[39] allowing it to see without eyes. The same is true for language: it is not necessary to have the organs for vocalization to exercise this particular function, above all, within the paradigm of communication as a sharing of information.

The tragedy of twenty-first-century plant sciences is that, on the one hand, they prepare the ground for a dispensation to plants of their language and intelligence, while, on the other hand, they make plants, as coherent living beings with their own modes of expression, disappear. Once again, this sleight of hand is typical of all contemporary science, to the extent that it breaks its objects of study down to such minute molecular, atomic, or subatomic components that they are no longer recognizable as entities we experience in everyday life. The primacy of functions over structures has a role to play in this process, which, applied to plants, dissolves them into their chemical components, hormones, or cellular action potentials. Today, there is no more botany, which used to study plants in their integrity, underscoring their morphology and place in systems of classification, itself quite far from the language of the plants themselves. Instead, we have "plant sciences," including an interdisciplinary mix of biochemistry, biophysics, molecular and cell biology, evolutionary theory, and ecology, that happen to converge on the same type of living being.

Curiously enough, the decoupling of language from spoken discourse in the communicative model of Western sciences has much in common with the deconstruction of phonocentrism (that is, of the privilege of speech over writing) in the work of Jacques Derrida. In general, deconstruction may be thought of as a hypercritical deformalization and destabilization of existing meaning clusters. Yet, Derrida also welcomes scientific formalization by means of mathematization, "whose progress is in absolute solidarity with the practice of a nonphonetic inscription."[40] The language of plants is an excellent illustration of "the practice of nonphonetic inscription," a trace or a mark written in biochemical substances and transmitting meaning to other plants and animals. Having said that, Derrida is not ready to give up the legacy of Edmund Husserl, who bemoaned the crisis of the European sciences. According to the founder of phenomenology, this crisis was caused by the separation of formalized and quantified thinking from the "lifeworld." In keeping with Husserl's critical philosophy, meant to accompany scientific research and bring it back to the level of existence obscured underneath layer upon layer of abstraction, he writes: "It seems to me that critical work on 'natural' languages by means of 'natural' languages [travail critique sur les langues 'naturelles' au moyen des langues 'naturelles'], an entire internal transformation of classical notation, a systematic practice of exchanges between 'natural' languages and writing should prepare and accompany such formalization."[41] Akin to phenomenological reduction, deconstructive critique must shadow scientific translation and codification, while nurturing whatever resists this carryover and prevents nonphonetic inscription from lapsing into sheer abstraction. Plant science, even in its most courageous and pioneering instantiations, requires such a deconstructive supplement.

THE PHENOMENOLOGY OF VEGETAL SELF-EXPRESSION

If I were asked to provide a succinct definition of the language of plants, I would characterize it as "an articulation without saying." We would do well to recall that the word *articulation* has two, apparently unrelated, senses: expressing in words and joining two or more things in space. It is one of those rare locutions that combines—indeed, articulates—the ideal and the material strata of language, uniting the Cartesian *res cogitans* and *res extensa*. But what exactly do plants articulate in their language devoid of words?

First of all, themselves: as they proliferate by means of modular growth, reiterating their already existing morphological units, branching out in all directions, they reaffirm vegetal being, which, through them, becomes more spatially pervasive. In other words, plants articulate themselves with themselves, as they join the semiautonomous growths of which they consist. Second, plants articulate the burgeoning emergence, or self-generated appearance, that distinguishes the Greek conception of nature, or *phusis*. Their growth provides a palpable image of nature as a growing whole, encompassing everything that exists. Third, if plants articulate water, air, fire, and earth, it is because they are rooted not only in the earth but in all four elements, including the heat and light of the sun, the atmosphere that they enrich with oxygen, and the moisture they require for their flourishing. Plants are the first living bridges between the elements that, thanks to them, become livable for animals and humans. The connections they forge are nothing short of the language of life itself.

With regard to the first sense of vegetal articulation, we might say that it has much in common with the Benjaminian "language of things," or "the language as such." Still, holding on to the idea of the perfection of human language, compared to that of things, Benjamin argues that "language itself is not perfectly expressed in the things themselves. This proposition has a double meaning, in its metaphorical and literal senses: the languages of things are imperfect, and they are dumb. Things are denied the pure formal principle of language—namely, sound. They can communicate to one another only through a more or less material community. This community is immediate and infinite, like every linguistic communication."[42] The community of things, comparable to that of plants, is created thanks to the environmental articulation of things with other things, plants with other plants and with themselves. Both communities are essentially silent (though "plant bioacoustics" is a cutting-edge area of research, which may still prove this assertion wrong),[43] and it is this muteness that, in Benjamin's view, denies them the perfection of ideal expression, which, since Aristotle, has been tied to the vocal medium, hearing, and sounds. The members of the two communities communicate by contiguity, through the spatial relations they establish with other things, plants, and the elements. Now, things are not merely deposited in empty space; in their mutual articulations, they create a sense of place, a habitable world that accretes around them. This principle is further refined in plants that actively articulate organic and inorganic facets of their milieu, form ecosystems and microclimates, influence the atmosphere, and transform the places of their growth into receptacles for other kinds of life. Their self-affirmation is, simultaneously, the affirmation of their others, be they the classical elements, animals, or humans. And, just as sound is extraneous to the functioning of their language, so their intentionality need not connote a *purposeful* extension of hospitality to the other. Rather, vegetal hospitality is one and the same with the very heteronomous being of plants.

Usually circumspect on the subject of the capacities of plants, Augustine nevertheless admits the possibility of vegetal intentionality, understood as the desire to be known by humans. "In the case of trees," he suggests, "their nourishment and generation have some resemblance to sensation. Yet, though they and all corporeal things have causes which lie hidden in their nature, they do display their forms, which give shape to the visible structure of our world, for perception by our senses; and so it seems that, even though they themselves cannot know, they nonetheless wish to be known."[44] Between the lines of the Augustinian text, we may detect the second level of vegetal articulation and self-expression, related to the ancient notion of *phusis* as a burgeoning emergence. The causes of plants may be hidden, but parts of plants give themselves to our sight and other senses, lending themselves to perception in the course of germination, whereby the seed or the seedling leaves the darkness of the soil, to which it remains attached. The same is true for nature as a whole (particularly according to Plotinus, who exerted enormous intellectual influence on Augustine): in perceivable, natural things, *phusis* silently comes into the light, as the aboveground portion of the plant does, and presents itself to our senses, while remaining rooted in itself. The order of phenomenality—of the surfaces available for perception—and that of nature—of self-generated growth toward the light—blend with each other in vegetal growth. Whereas the human variety of language (*logos*) repeats and formalizes the self-presentation of phenomena, in the languages of things and of plants, a silent *logos* and sunlit phenomenal surfaces (whether they are static in inanimate objects or proliferating in plants) belong together in an uninterrupted unity. Thus, in addition to exemplifying the growth of nature as a whole, plants stand for the principle of a material living expression as such, demonstrating how a being can come into the light, appear, and signify itself.

I have already touched upon the third vegetal articulation of the classical elements and of organic and inorganic worlds. It is crucial to understand that, at this level, the language of plants means that they *form* a world, by which they, themselves, are shaped. The world is neither an empty container for reality nor the seemingly unlimited stuff it contains; rather, its character is deeply relational, dependent on the interconnections between the beings that populate it. The world is what happens in between. To insist, as I am doing here, that plants form a world is simply to emphasize that they institute relations of lived and living significance between things. Take gravitropism: as a result of sensing gravity in the area of root tips, plants are able to send their roots down into the earth and instruct stems to grow upward.[45] "Above" and "below" are spatial determinations that were meaningless and unrelated to each other before their articulation in vegetal growth. Language fosters and develops such meaningful relationality. Although we, humans, habitually enunciate the relations between things (and so form *our* world) in semantic units that we string together in speech, the groundwork of sense lies in the practical articulation and integration of the disparate parts of our environment. The closer we come to actual existence, the more our languages and articulations resemble those of plants.

As for the untranslatable, in the phenomenology of self-expression it entails the tension and the opacity between the two meanings of articulation: the verbal and the spatial. A charitable reading of Benjamin's unwavering commitment to the perfection of human language would reveal that the latter alone manages to synthesize the material and the ideal types of relationality. Unlike plants, humans can signify both by speaking and by altering our bodily positions (i.e., by resorting to "body language"). Granted, meaningful articulations are more varied in our case, but, by and large, we disregard the kind of extended self-expression, which we share with plants, and, by the same token, fail to consider their language qua language. It would be a mistake, however, to conjecture that vegetal self-expression is a less complex, if not a primitive, form of language and, therefore, of being. Everywhere, we are surrounded by plants and even bear a trace of their orientation toward the world in our subjectivities. Nonetheless, the world *of* plants and the language through which it is constructed are opaque to us, because we tend to translate it, without further ado, into the ideal medium of semantic articulation. Besides universal communicability, humans espouse the ideal of an equally universal translatability of all other languages into that "of man." Paradoxically, the greatest opacity stems from the dream of total transparency, which does not permit the dreamers—every single one of us—to encounter other-than-human beings on a nonanthropocentric turf. Only once the languages of things, plants, and animals are given their due, in a mixture of ontological fidelity and justice, will this encounter be possible. It is, perhaps, then that we will finally hear plants speak.

NOTES

1. "Midori-san or the Slightly Potty Blog," *CORDIS*, October 24, 2008, http://cordis.europa.eu/express/20081024/finally_en.html.
2. A. C. Fraser-Smith, "ULF Tree Potential and Geomagnetic Pulsations," *Nature* 271 (1978): 641–642.
3. Francis daCosta, *Rethinking the Internet of Things: A Scalable Approach to Connecting Everything* (New York: Apress, 2013), 109.
4. Sextus Empiricus, *Outlines of Pyrrhonism*, 1.216–19.
5. Johann Wolfgang von Goethe, *The Metamorphosis of Plants* (Cambridge, MA.: MIT Press, 2009), 6.

6. Augustine, *Confessions* 13.24.35.

7. Alan Bewell, "'On the Banks of the South Sea': Botany and Sexual Controversy in the Late Eighteenth Century," in *Visions of Empire: Voyages, Botany, and Representations of Nature*, ed. David Philip Miller and Peter Hanns Reill (Cambridge, UK: Cambridge University Press, 2011), 173–193; quote, 174.

8. Augustine, *The City of God against the Pagans* 2.27.

9. Augustine, *The City of God against the Pagans* 7.25.

10 Sigmund Freud, *The Standard Edition of the Complete Psychological Works of Sigmund Freud*, 24 vols., trans. and ed. James Strachey (London: Vintage, 2001), 4:169.

11. Freud, *Complete Psychological Works*, 283.

12. Freud, *Complete Psychological Works*, 169–71.

13. Freud, *Complete Psychological Works*, 5:374.

14. Michael Marder, *Plant-Thinking: A Philosophy of Vegetal Life* (New York: Columbia University Press, 2013), 44. In continuation of this passage, I write: "Post-metaphysical thought, such as that of psychoanalysis, no longer believes in the fiction of the indivisible and immortal soul 'of another genus.' Psychic divisibility becomes the destiny of humanity that, perhaps without knowing it, sets for itself an infinite task: that of recuperating its vegetal heritage."

15. Georges Bataille, *Visions of Excess: Selected Writings, 1927–1939*, ed. Allan Stoekl (Minneapolis: University of Minnesota Press, 1985), 10.

16. Bataille, *Visions of Excess*, 11.

17. Bataille, *Visions of Excess*, 12.

18. Novalis, *Henry von Ofterdingen: A Novel*, trans. Palmer Hilty (New York: Continuum, 1992), 17.

19. Novalis, *Henry von Ofterdingen*, 104.

20. Brad Prager, *Aesthetic Vision and German Romanticism: Writing Images*, Studies in German Literature, Linguistics, and Culture Series (Rochester, NY: Camden House, 2007), 150.

21. James Joyce, *Ulysses* (London: Wordsworth, 2010), 69.

22. Frederick J. Simoons, *Plants of Life, Plants of Death* (Madison: University of Wisconsin Press, 1998), 47.

23. Herodotus, *The Histories* 2.55–56; Homer, *Iliad* 16.234; Plato, *Phaedrus* 275b.

24. Philipp Vandenberg, *Mysteries of the Oracles: The Last Secrets of Antiquity* (London: I. B. Tauris, 2007), 27.

25. Fabio Rambelli, *Vegetal Buddhas: Ideological Effects of Japanese Buddhist Doctrines on the Salvation of Inanimate Beings* (Kyoto: Scuola Italiana di Studi sull'Asia Orientale, 2001), 52.

26. John Renard, *Islam and the Heroic Image: Themes in Literature and the Visual Arts* (Macon, GA.: Mercer University Press, 1999), 156.

27. Dante Alighieri, *The Divine Comedy*, Northwestern World Classics Edition, trans. Burton Raffel (Evanston, IL: Northwestern University Press, 2010), part 1, *Inferno*, canto 13, lines 25–30.

28. Alighieri, *Divine Comedy*, 40–45.

29. Alighieri, *Divine Comedy*, 55–60.

30. Alighieri, *Divine Comedy*, 105–10.

31. James Howell, *Dendrologia: Dodona's Grove, or The Vocall Forrest*, 3rd ed. (Cambridge, UK: Humphrey Moseley, 1645), i.

32. Howell, *Dendrologia*, ii.

33. Zhuangzi, *The Complete Works of Zhuangzi*, trans. Burton Watson (New York: Columbia University Press, 2013), 30–31.

34. Yuan Yuan Song, Jian Feng Shu, Jun Li, Xiang Shen, and Woldemariam Gebrehiwot Yihdigo, "Interplant Communication of Tomato Plants through Underground Common Mycorrhizal Networks," *PLoS ONE* 5, no. 10 (2010), doi: 10.1371/journal.pone.0013324.

35. Luce Irigaray and Michael Marder, *Through Vegetal Being: Two Philosophical Perspectives* (New York: Columbia University Press, 2016), 191.

36. Refer, for instance, to Hirokazu Ueda, Yukito Kikuta, and Kazuhiko Matsuda, "Plant Communication: Mediated by Individual or Blended VOCs?," *Plant Signaling & Behavior* 7, no. 2 (2012): 222–226.

37. Martin Heidegger, *On the Way to Language*, trans. Peter D. Hertz (New York: Harper & Row, 1971), 22.

38. Amedeo Alpi et al., "Plant Neurobiology: No Brain, No Gain?," *Trends in Plant Science* 12, no. 4 (2007): 135–136.

39. Daniel Chamovitz, *What a Plant Knows: A Field Guide to the Senses* (New York: Scientific American/Farrar, Straus and Giroux, 2012), 22.

40. Jacques Derrida, *Positions*, trans. Alan Bass (Chicago: University of Chicago Press, 1972), 34.

41. Derrida, *Positions*, 34–35; French edition, *Positions* (Paris: Les Éditions de Minuit, 1972), 47.

42. Walter Benjamin, "On Language as Such and on the Language of Man," in *Selected Writings*, vol. 1, *1913–1926*, ed. Marcus Bullock and Michael W. Jennings (Cambridge, MA.: Belknap Press of Harvard University Press, 1996), 62–74; quote, 67.

43. Cf., for instance, Monica Gagliano, "The Flowering of Plant Bioacoustics: How and Why," *Behavioral Ecology* 24, no. 4 (2013): 800–801.

44. Augustine, *City of God* 11.27.

45. Robyn M. Perrin, Li-Sen Young, U. M. Narayana Murthy, Benjamin R. Harrison, Y. A. N. Wang, Jessica L. Will, and Patrick H. Masson, "Gravity Signal Transduction in Primary Roots," *Annals of Botany* 96, no. 5 (2005): 737–743.

Main Pathway: Cross-Pollination

Subthemes

Proceed to Ethics, p. 277

Proceed to Experience, p. 541

34

THE TIME TRAVELERS: IM/POSSIBILITIES OF RETURN

Elaine Gan

H. G. Wells's 1895 novel introduced us to a modernist conception of a time machine, a human-made device that renders time as place, a mode of transport to shuttle back and forth along a track with stops in the past, present, and future. Using this device, Wells's lone Time Traveler, a man of science from Victorian England, witnesses the earth's final destiny: in 30 million years, the planet's rotations will stop. A cold world of crablike creatures, giant butterflies, and lichens mingling on a blood-red beach will end facing a sun that never sets. The scene warns: a world that has no cycles—no returns—has no future.

Wells's conception of time appears as a unilinear sequence marked by distinct periods, ecologies, and protagonists. The Time Traveler leaves a rapidly expanding British society, arrives in distant futures betrayed by the promises of Western civilization, and returns home to tell his stories. He leaves on another journey but never returns. Perhaps he met Walter Benjamin's angel of history, and his time machine was swept away by the storm of unrelenting Progress. Or quite possibly, he collided with Ursula Le Guin's two-faced wall and now burrows somewhere between opposing cosmopolitics of Urras and Anarres. Then again, he may be simply delayed, having slowed down to pick wild matsutake mushrooms with Anna Tsing in the pine forests of the Anthropocene. His journey remains indeterminate and unfinished.

Conceptions of time as a single track, a forward-facing arrow along which individual journeys unfold in fixed intervals such as months, years, and centuries, dominate scientific and social inquiry. Feminist, queer, decolonial, and intersectional thinkers have called for radical reorientations, showing how arrows of time

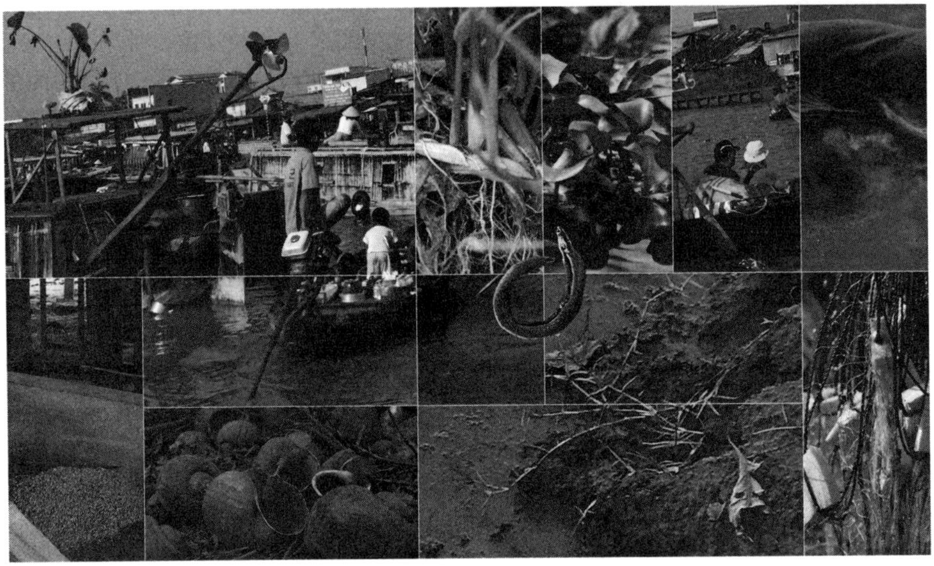

are not neutral registers of events but powerful apparatuses that construct a hierarchy of subjectivities: humans who are modern, purposeful, and innovative versus nonhuman beings who wander timelessly, excluded from technologies of historicity, directionality, and futurity. What might those that have long been tagged as nonhuman—plants in particular—teach us about times otherwise?

This essay plays with Wells's critical figure of the Time Traveler, recomposing its singularity into a dynamic assemblage of more-than-human companions who live and die in various ways along the Mekong, known to mapmakers as the longest river in Southeast Asia and to time travelers as the mother of flows. With this Mekong assemblage, what becomes striking is the importance of return, the possibilities—and impossibilities—for life and continuing existence that depend on a shared capacity to cycle and recur. Each return, each cycle, coordinates the timing of encounters across incommensurable difference. Readers are invited to meet rain, rice, water hyacinths, and animals, and how they experience, involve, and

A manifold of time travelers inhabits the Mekong today. This composition of field photographs from a floating market in Can Tho, Vietnam, brings together fishers, farmers, sand miners, boats, rice grains, catfish, water hyacinths, snails, blood flukes, mud, fishing nets, and a slew of more-than-human beings. (Photos: Elaine Gan, 2010 and 2017.)

enact multiple temporalities in processes of return. These processes are differential and contingent. For time travelers, always and already plural, return is always a relation and never guaranteed.

RAIN

From April to September, monsoon winds blow eastward from Somalia into the Bay of Bengal, moving across the Indian Ocean and bringing rain to the Mekong. Rainfall intensifies into storms and typhoons in the summer months of June and July. From October to March, winds reverse direction and blow westward from the Indonesian archipelago to the Arabian Sea. Rainfall becomes less frequent and the weather becomes dry. For centuries, the oscillation between wet and dry seasons, the presence and absence of rain, has structured a recurring tempo for multispecies ways of life. The Mekong runs for 2,700 miles and crosses six modern nations: it rises in the Himalayas, in a region of Tibet known for its perpetual snow. From there, its waters descend, flowing southward through Yunnan; then between Burma (Myanmar), Laos, and Thailand; and then through Cambodia, before branching out into the floodplains and delta of southern Vietnam. Freshwater meets the tidal pulses of incoming saltwater and sediment as the river flows into the South China Sea.

That's part of the story. The river has also been a site of wave after wave of anthropogenic disturbance, dispossession, and violent extraction. It is shaped by empire, circuits of trade and technology, regimes of taxation and governance. In the eighteenth century, the southward migrations of the Vietnamese displaced lowland Khmer and Cham and introduced wet-rice agriculture to the delta, which has become one of the world's leading rice exporting regions. Scholars have described the credit systems of Chinese and Indian merchants, the ruinations of colonial occupations, the Indochina wars, and the American invasions. Novel trajectories are rapidly emerging. In 2016, China had six megadams in various stages of construction in the upper Mekong. Laos and Cambodia had a dozen underway. Laos intends to build over a hundred more, even as one of its first, in the former Kingdom of Champasak, already collapsed in 2018. The Mekong is hardly static; its flows are agential, making and made by an unruly assemblage of more-than-human capacities for continuity and change.

Rice is the dominant crop along the Mekong. But it is rice entangled with water and soil that coordinates life along the river. High-intensity, long-duration rainfall in April signals the start of the rice planting season. By June, heavy rains overflow riverbanks and lead to floods. By September, the floodwater levels can exceed 20 feet. Many low-lying coastal areas may remain flooded for a few months. To survive the monsoon rains and floods, rice has to either hold its breath or find ways to keep breathing. Over millennia, certain varieties of rice, known as deepwater or floating rice, seem to have done just that.

LIVING WITH FLOODS

There are rice varieties that grow in the wild beyond the management and care of human farmers, and others that are cultivated for subsistence, experimentation, or the sheer delights of novelty. Some varieties respond to flash floods by going dormant. They stop growing and can stay underwater for up to 14 days. When waters recede, they resume growth. Others have evolved more elaborate semiaquatic superpowers. Their seeds can stay dormant in the soil for up to several weeks, waiting for the right signals to germinate. And when they begin to grow, they form internal air tubes, or snorkel-like conduits called aerenchyma, in their stems, roots, and leaves that allow oxygen to circulate into submerged parts. They also have plasticity, a capacity for rapid elongation in direct response to changing water levels; stems can grow by almost 10 inches per day and reach a height of 15 feet to keep their seeds above water. Flowering time coordinates with shorter day lengths, which are tied to the rhythms of the Earth. Grains synchronize, filling and ripening as floodwaters recede. When soils dry in January, the rice is ready for harvest. Farmers use sickles to cut the ripened grain from stems lying on dry ground.

Although millions of people still depend on farming deepwater rice varieties along the Mekong, commercial farmers are increasingly turning to high-yielding, quick-growing varieties that depend on chemical fertilizers and pesticides tied to Green Revolution miracle rice introduced in the 1960s. Since 1975, hydraulic development has intensified. Rather than cultivating long-stemmed deepwater varieties, Vietnam pushed to develop elaborate infrastructures for irrigation. This involved straightening, extending, and deepening canals and waterways in the Mekong Delta. Farmers of *An Giang*, a booming rice province, work three harvests a year, each with yields that can reach 22 tons per hectare (significantly higher than the average two tons per hectare in the 1960s). The annual cycle of rains and floods that used to mix and flush out nutrients and contaminants, groundwater-saltwater-freshwater, became a perennial system of water management. By the 1980s, chemical fertilizers were circulating year-round through irrigation canals and leaching into waterways, causing widespread eutrophication.

These changes benefited two travelers in particular: water hyacinths and snails.

NOVEL COMPANIONS

Like rice, the water hyacinth is a flowering freshwater plant that has become nearly ubiquitous throughout the Mekong. Native to the Amazon, it began crossing into other continents in the late nineteenth century. With its lavender, violet, and pink flowers, the water hyacinth is a beautiful plant, a creature of imperial and colonial expansion that was often given as a gift and planted for aesthetic pleasure. Changes in the twentieth century, however, opened a new chapter in the social life of the water hyacinth. Standing water rich with nitrogen, phosphorous, and potassium—the main ingredients of farm fertilizers and modern water management—are a great boon to water hyacinths. Perennial aquatic plants, water hyacinths negotiate changing conditions by playing with time, producing seeds that can germinate within days or lie dormant in the soil for up to 20 years. Defying popular misconceptions of plants as immobile, water hyacinths are extremely mobile: without roots that anchor them to the ground, they float along the surface of the water, easily carried by currents. They reproduce through stolons—literally, rhizomatic lines of flight that hitch onto boats and just about any kind of water vessel—and they can double their spread every two weeks. Water hyacinths form extremely dense mats so quickly that they end up choking everything else, preventing sunlight from reaching other plants and depleting the oxygen in water. Their speed and density kill fish and other aquatic fauna.

Among the water hyacinth's new companions is a freshwater snail. Endemic to Mekong riverbanks, snails thrive on water hyacinths and on partially submerged rocks—now a perennial condition because of rice irrigation. Snails feed on algae and repopulate every year. They are also the sole intermediate hosts of parasitic blood flukes that cause bilharzia or snail fever. Because of the snails, blood flukes can incubate and reproduce during the dry season. When rains come, the blood flukes release from the snails and work their way through human skin, laying their eggs inside undoubtedly unwilling human hosts. Some eggs are passed back to the river when humans defecate or urinate in the water. Human bodies, thus, are incorporated into the parasite's life cycle—which is now tied to the snail—which now rides the water hyacinth—which is carried by fertilizer-enriched waters that flow from postcolonial water grids that irrigate fast-growth, high-yield rice engineered to feed humans like me who work in 24/7 buildings that are alienated from the cycles of rain and deepwater rice.

COMPETING GIANTS

The parasite first appeared along the Mekong in the 1950s, just as government officials in the north were becoming fascinated with new ways of harnessing the energy of Mekong floodwaters. Dreams of modernization for a new People's Republic of China under Mao Zedong were being yoked onto monumental machines of hydroelectric power—the modern engineering marvels of megadams. In 1986, China, under Deng Xiaopeng, began building a "Mekong Cascade," a series of dams in the upper Mekong to produce electricity and wean the nation off coal and oil. China controls the river's headwaters, which begin high up in Tibet. The geopolitical response from Thailand, Laos, Cambodia, and Vietnam was to form a rival commission to build their own dams. Dams have proliferated, with multiple cascading effects. Here is one example:

There may only be a few hundred left of the largest known freshwater fish in the world: the giant catfish. As the largest bodies in the river, these giants, which can grow up to 10 feet and weigh over 600 pounds, make a difference to the order of things. Through sheer size, their bodies influence the formation of multispecies assemblages, the bioturbation of soil, and the cycling of nutrients. They are herbivores and feed on algae. Like the snail, they feed in the dry season and fast during the wet season—a seasonality that is synchronized with the cycles of algae. Highly migratory, they live out part of their lives at sea, much like the more well-studied salmon. They swim inland from the South China Sea, and travel over 600 miles—that is about a quarter of the length of the river—to spawn in Thailand. The powerful surge of monsoon floods is their signal to head upstream. The signal arrives during their fasting season, which means they need to hitch a ride on river currents, in order to travel quickly, and spawn while there is plenty of oxygen and food. Dams get in their way, cutting off migration routes, sediment flows, and flood surges. Dams silence the signals to which the giant catfish are attuned, violently altering spawning and feeding cycles. The catfish lose their senses of time and place, senses that evolved for survival and play through countless repetitions over millennia.

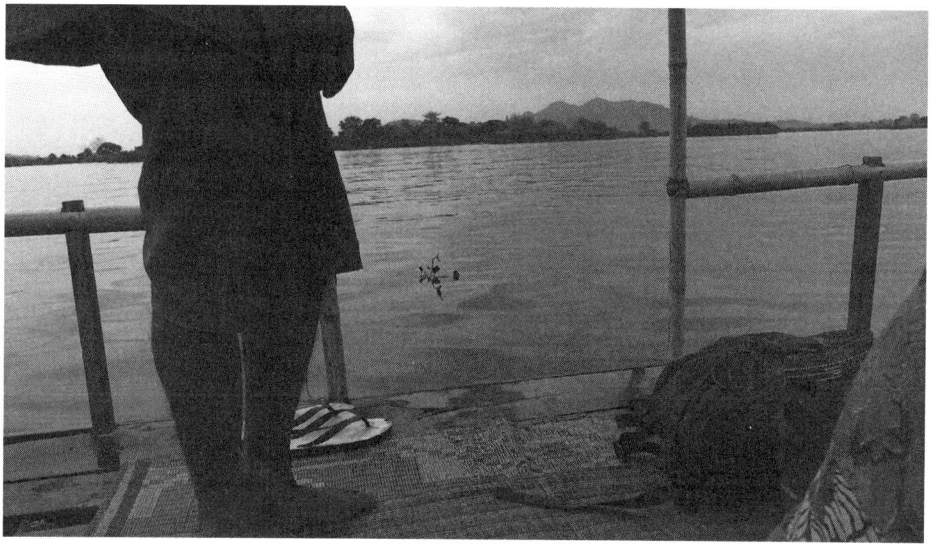

IM/POSSIBILITIES OF RETURN

Commercial fishing along the Mekong has developed alongside commercial rice farming. As larger fish have disappeared, fisheries have turned to smaller and smaller species. Cyprinids (which are common carps, goldfish, and minnows used as bait and aquarium fish) now make up nearly half of the fish catch at Tonlé Sap, the largest freshwater lake in Cambodia and the heart of Mekong fisheries today.

This change cycles through many lives and landscapes in at least two ways. First, cyprinids feed on freshwater snails. This is what scientists call a classic trophic cascade: in the absence of their fish predators, it becomes easier for snails to reproduce and multiply. Snails, as described earlier in this essay, are hosts of blood flukes, the parasites that infect humans as well as dogs, cats, pigs, rodents, and other animals. Second, chemicals persist for a long time, and they never stay put.

I join a rice farmer-fisher on a boat ride at sunset through the waterways of Si Phan Don, an inland archipelago in southern Laos. As we float by, so does another time traveler, the rhizomatic water hyacinth. (Photo: Elaine Gan, 2017.)

Leaching into waterways from farms, chemicals accumulate easily in the bodies of small fish and climb up the food chain. Mekong fisheries are among the largest in the world; they supply a global food network that inherits and metabolizes relations of war and peace, dispossession and sustenance, toxicity and health, with every bite consumed.

This essay began with H. G. Wells's Time Traveler on a blood-red beach, facing a sun that may neither set nor rise. It closes with a photograph of a rice farmer-fisher on a hand-built raft, moving along the Mekong in southern Laos at sunset. At the center of the photograph is a water hyacinth, one of many that are overwhelming waterways and rice fields. Absent are the giant catfish and their companions. This scene exists because of a dynamic more-than-human assemblage whose survival depends on differential capacities for return. The crucial question remains: Who should have the right to return? Vegetal, animal, mineral, aquatic, algal, chemical, human beings—these are just a few of many time travelers, variously composed, haunted, and inscribed into pasts, presents, and futures unfolding simultaneously. Taking them seriously, we might learn to listen for more-than-human possibilities and imagine temporalities otherwise.

ACKNOWLEDGMENTS

The first version of this essay was written for the conference "Cultivation: Vegetal Lives, Global Systems and the Politics of Planting," organized by Matthew Fuller and Sheila Sheikh at Goldsmiths, University of London, in March 2016. It has grown through conversations with Anna Tsing, Karen Barad, and Colin Hoag, to whom I am ever grateful.

Main Pathway: Ecologies

Subthemes

Proceed to Diasporas, p. 593
Proceed to Climate Change, p. 555
Proceed to Time, p. 555

35

INTERVIEW WITH SAMANEH MOAFI

How do you identify the species of plants you decide to work with? What parameters guide your selection process and why?

SAMANEH MOAFI: This is one of the major questions we engage with at the Centre for Contemporary Nature (CCN)—a research division of Forensic Architecture. It was conceived in 2016 as a space for addressing colonial, military, and political forms of violence as they manifest in environmental destruction. Such forms of violence are multiscalar. They occur both in the span of a short few seconds as well as the long durée of a few centuries. They erupt simultaneously at the locality of a small plantation as well as the entirety of the globe.

To address such multiscalar entanglements, we need new investigative techniques and methodologies. I use the word "new," because of the recent shift in the way humans have begun to relate to their environment. Throughout European history, nature was considered a static backdrop against which activities unfolded; a category outside of the civic space of sovereignty. But today, in the era of global pandemics and human-induced climate change, we have finally begun to understand nature as a category closely tied to the law, the economy, and sovereignty. From the Israeli mass killings in occupied Gaza to the ghastly human rights abuses in Indonesian Palm oil plantations, the "Contemporary Nature," we argue, has been both the cause and the consequence of conflicts.

Allow me to explain with an example. One of the investigations that we launched on Israel's human rights violations was centered around leafy crops such as spinach, sabanekh, chard, and peas grown on Palestinian farms along the eastern border of Gaza. Since 2014, these harvests were systematically subjected to unannounced aerial spraying of crop-killing herbicides. The operations were designed to complement the clearing and bulldozing of agricultural and residential lands along the border by the Israel military. In the process of our investigation, we learned that when the Israeli commercial crop dusters performed their aerial spraying, they weaponized the morning breeze for the purpose of border control. In other words, nature was not merely a victim. The leafy crops and the wind were both entangled in the violence, and the latter, the wind, was mobilized by Israel to carry the chemicals across the border and into the Gaza Strip at damaging concentrations.

Do you ever consider plants as subjects in your work, and how does that change your approach to them?

In the example I was just discussing, we approached plants in a particular way. Together with local farmers, FA's dedicated Israeli-Palestine researcher, Dr. Shourideh C. Molavi, who was coordinating the project, had identified the areas along the border where leafy crops were affected. She organized a team to collect samples. To us, the leaves of these crops were sensors. They held memories of environmental violence. Their green biological surface registered an image of an herbicidal attack. We examined each leaf carefully and studied the smallest visible anomalies. A record of each leaf could hold an evidentiary value, and so we saved their photographs.

To investigate the relationship between the sprayed herbicide and the wind, we developed a pioneering methodology: fieldworkers had recorded videos showing events of aerial spraying along the border. Of course, their handheld cameras could only capture the cloud of herbicide close to the crop dusters. The movement of the small particles in the wind could not be captured. We used the videos to reconstruct the paths of spraying with a high-level precision. Together with a scientist from the Imperial College, Dr. Salvador Navaro Martinez, we used our reconstruction of those paths to develop a mathematical, fluid, dynamic simulation of the sprayed chemicals based on the meteorological data of the day, including wind speed, wind direction, and temperature.

Our simulation, grounded in spatial and meteorological data about an actual event of spraying, affirmed that the army protocol of spraying herbicide by air, while wind travels into Gaza, has uncontrollable effects, damaging Palestinian farms hundreds of meters from the border. In CCN, we employ mathematical simulations when the matter in question—here the small particles of herbicide—cannot be or have not been captured by cameras.

In your artistic practice, what have you learned from the plants themselves? In which ways does your art follow their movements, metamorphoses, and modes of being in the world? How does it interact with these vegetal processes?

I should emphasize that CCN is not an artistic practice in the traditional sense. Rather, it is part of a university-based research unit. We socialize the findings of our investigations through a range of legal, cultural, academic, and media forums. Most often, we mobilize each one of our works across many forums. This allows us to raise awareness necessary to address the violence in question. This is crucial for cases of environmental destruction since precedents for legal remedies are limited and the forums that pertain to the field of arts and cultures can play a valuable role.

The example of our casework on palm oil plantations in Indonesia is relevant here. One of the first research projects that we undertook in CCN was on the 2015 fires in Indonesia, which burnt down over 21,000 square kilometers of forest and peatlands. Human rights lawyer Baltasar Garzón—who successfully put an international arrest warrant on former Chilean military dictator Augusto Pinochet—through his organization, Fundación Internacional Baltasar Garzón (FIBGAR), commissioned us to gather evidence regarding the causes and consequences of these fires, with the aim of preparing an international trial. Our investigation revealed that many of the fires originated within the plantations and moved out toward areas under a moratorium, expanding the field that could be cultivated and in turn increasing the possibility for capital gain.

Razing through the plantation borders, the fires violated the livelihood of the species who inhabited the forests, including orangutans. We researched legal precedents where apes received some sort of human rights or "nonhuman rights." This could provide a legal ground for the endangered orangutans to claim a right. Soon we learned that such an approach would have required a total act of individuation. To become subjects of law, the orangutans had to be separated from the forests, from the many species to whom they related, and even from one another. To become subjects of law, they had to lose so much of their shared being in the world.

Indeed, addressing today's extreme forms of environmental violence requires new legal frameworks, tools, and vocabularies. So rather than starting with the court, we chose to begin with the cultural forums. We exhibited evidentiary materials that ranged from remote-sensing and cartographic maps to scientific experiments conducted at the Max Planck Institute, to proceedings of a court in Argentina, to 3-D prints of orangutan nests in Indonesia. We used our case work to engage the public with the possibility of a new legal framework: to extend a kind of collective and environmental "orangutan rights" to humans and with it, in FA's director Professor Eyal Weizman's words, a certain "becoming humanoid" of humanity.[1]

What are the ethical and political implications of this work? Which pressing challenge, or challenges, has working with plants presented to you?

A couple of years afterward, we began socializing our findings on the 2015 forest fires. An environmental organization named Greenpeace commissioned us to take a step further and see if the intentionality in the use of fires could be determined for plantations that were operated by an Indonesian/Korean palm oil agglomerate named Korindo. If the intentional use of fire was part of the operational logic of Korindo, the company was in breach of Indonesian law. What's more, the credibility of international organizations such as the Forest Stewardship Council (FSC), who had awarded their certificate to Korindo, could be questioned.

The plantations we were asked to investigate were in the remote areas of the Indonesian region of West Papua, with little media coverage. Access to the site was militarized, witnesses were few, and footage from fire incidents were almost nonexistent. This posed a great challenge for our investigation. We only had a handful of Greenpeace videos to work with, taken from helicopters flying over the plantations. These precious videos documented tens of fire sources and the thick smoke that rose from them.

We cross-referenced Greenpeace's archival records and the metadata in the videos to confirm their date. The next step was to examine the coordinates of the fires in relation to the borders of the concessions. We used key spatial features such as visible networks of roads to geo-locate the footage and in turn the sources of fire. We then cross-referenced the coordinates of the fires we had detected in video footage with those detected by NASA satellites. Deploying a technique called the normalized burn ratio (NBR) analysis, we revealed the pattern of monthly land clearings inside the concessions. Our research revealed that the pattern of fires, their direction, and the speed with which they moved matched the pattern of land clearing across several months between 2012 and 2016 in many Korindo plantations in the region. This suggested that the fires were set intentionally.

We mobilized our findings on Korindo via an international media outlet, the BBC. The report cross-referenced our findings on the intentional fires with testimonies of laborers and neighboring communities to the company's human rights violations. It was relayed by local news outlets and widely circulated on social media, raising awareness on both national and international scales.

Shortly after our release, another environmental organization named Mighty Earth asked to submit our findings against Korindo for a court case in Germany, to which we agreed. A few days ago, the judge found our evidence of high caliber. Korindo now has to challenge our robust methodology or lose the case. If the court finds Korindo guilty, the implications will have a global impact. Intentional fires have been part of the operational logic of concessions not only in Indonesia but also in the basins of the Amazon and the Congo. The investigative technique that we developed on Korindo can be applied to any of such concessions. This court case can therefore alarm each and every such corporation and maybe help slow down the increasing rate of forest fires that continue to devastate our planet.

What, if any, are the aspects of your work with plants related to the current global environmental and mass extinction crises?

The problem of scale is pertinent. Anna Tsing foregrounds the plantation as an archetype for scalability.[2] European colonial plantations were based on the extermination of local people and plants, preparation of the new emptied land, and the managing of isolated labor (forced or enslaved) and crops for production. Their laborers were replaceable. They were designed to eliminate local histories of companion species and disease relations and hence maximize alienation. They could multiply infinitely, take entire territories and increase economic profit. Alienation, interchangeability, and expansion are for Tsing the formula for scalability. But history is filled with examples where scalability fails, and non-scalable ecological relations erupt.

In 2015, the smoke from the millions of fire sources in and around the palm oil plantations across Indonesia accumulated into a toxic cloud that contained more carbon, methane, ammonium, and cyanide than the entire annual emissions of the German, British, or Japanese industries. As the cloud drifted north and westward, it engulfed a zone that extended from Indonesia across Malaysia and Singapore to southern Thailand and Vietnam. Scientists estimate that this resulted in more than a 100,000 premature deaths and that the fires might have pushed the world beyond

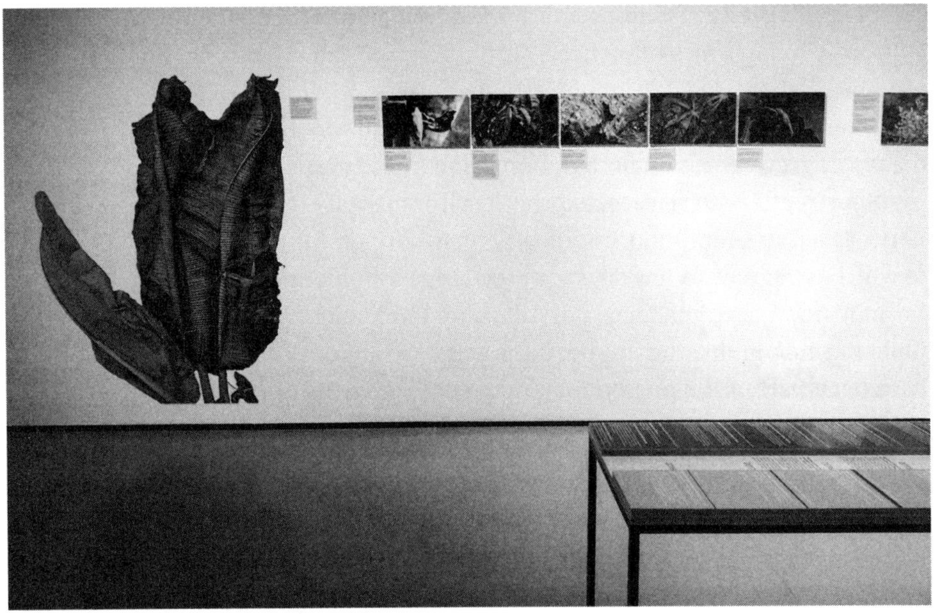

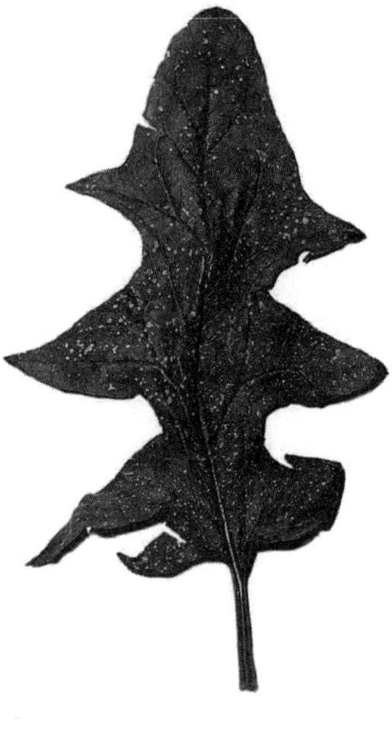

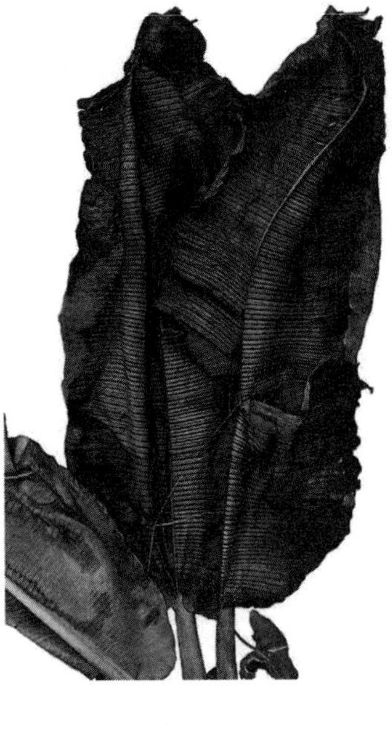

2°C of global warming faster than expected. We understood this vast "carbon cloud" as a harbinger of a new international crime against humanity—ecocide.[3] The Israeli clouds of glyphosate that I mentioned earlier, crossing the border and harming the Palestinian farms, can arguably sit in the same category. If legal practitioners are half-serious about breaking the continuum of military, colonial, and corporate violence in this world that we share with each other, an international law against ecocide is an overdue step.

As Forensic Architecture's senior researcher, **Samaneh Moafi** provides conceptual oversight across projects and oversees the Centre for Contemporary Nature. Her research is focused on developing new evidentiary techniques for environmental violence. She holds a PhD from The Architectural Association (AA), and a BA and an MA in Architecture from the University of Technology, Sydney.

NOTES

1. Eyal Weizman, "Are They Human?" *e-flux: Architecture*, October 10, 2016, https://www.e-flux.com/architecture/superhumanity/68645/are-they-human/.
2. Anna Tsing, *The Mushroom at the End of the World: On the Possibility of Life in Capitalist Ruins* (New Jersey: Princeton University Press, 2015), 37–45.
3. Polly Higgins's proposal for the Rome Statute describes ecocide as "the extensive damage to, destruction of or loss of ecosystem(s) of a given territory, whether by human agency or by other causes, to such an extent that peaceful enjoyment by the inhabitants of that territory has been or will be severely diminished" (*Ecoside Law*, n.d., https://ecocidelaw.com/polly-higgins-ecocide-crime/).

36

INTERVIEW WITH DIANA SCHERER

How do you identify the species of plants you decide to work with? What parameters guide your selection process and why?

DIANA SCHERER: My choice of plants depends on the project. I look at botanical processes with wonder and try to examine them in an intuitive and sometimes scientific way. The work usually starts with an unexplained fascination. For example, the movements of roots or the influence of color changes in light on photosynthesis. It takes a while to find the right plants to work with on specific projects.

For my current work, *Exercises in Rootsystem Domestication*, I use species that are best suited to interweave the roots below ground. To achieve a strong material, it is necessary that the plants do not mind being sown close to each other. This works very well with grasses or cereals such as oats, wheat, or sometimes maize. Root entanglement is essential for the work. Many plants fight for their living space and don't tolerate plants next to them. I am looking for species that like to grow close to each other and support each other underground. I use their natural strength to weave my textiles of plant roots.

At a certain point, I started to approach the root system as if it were yarn.

I studied the movements and the aesthetic qualities of roots. For example, the refined, white root structure of grass reminds me of silk. And I compare the powerful, yellowish strands of the daisy to wool. The structure of the herb verbena is smooth, strong, and has a slight sheen like linen. In my book *Nurture Studies*, I show the results of my first work on the root system.

Do you ever consider plants as subjects in your work, and how does that change your approach to them?

DS: From my collaboration with the root system, I learned about the "magical mind" of plants. Plants are intelligent organisms despite their silent, seemingly passive appearance. They respond to the world, make decisions, and interact. I look at them differently now than I did ten years ago. Every day, I am aware of the strength and wonderfully complex functions they embody. Yes, I often see plants as a subject. I am pleased to see how philosophical thinking on the hierarchical order of nature has changed over time. How plants no longer belong where they were classified by Aristotle: at the bottom of a hierarchy of living nature, passive decor for man and animal. In my research for botanical intelligence, I follow the contemporary ideas of philosophers like Mathew Hall on *Plants as Persons*, Michael Marder's work on *Plant-Thinking* and Bruno Latour's speculative research of *The Parliament of Things*. I am very much interested in these thoughts and their desire to prevent us from seeing nature as a passive resource but as a multitude of agents that co-define our shared existence. Nevertheless, I too use plants in my work. That is a dilemma. My respect is deep, but in my work, I manipulate them to some degree. This contradiction is central to my work. My work is fiction. I make images; images that respond to our relationship with nature.

In your artistic practice, what have you learned from the plants themselves? In which ways does your art follow their movements, metamorphoses, and modes of being in the world? How does it interact with these vegetal processes?

I follow the growing processes and use them to create the work. A root navigates, knows up and down, perceives gravity, and can locate moisture and chemicals. Roots are incredibly strong. In their search for food, they fight for every space they can find. I use this strength to create my work. I expose the subterranean life and how natural networks turns into a textile-like material.

I have learned to deal with the autonomy of nature. Despite my intervention, the outcome is unpredictable every time. The flickering of control and letting go is an important element in my work.

Also growing time is a beautiful addition to my daily work practice. I have learned to adapt to plant-time. That gives me a sort of regularity in my often rather chaotic work practice. It gives me peace. Due to the daily conscious handling of weather, I am also much more aware of the small shifts and changes in the climate.

Today I am much more conscious of the seasons. I have learned to enjoy the winter as a time of rest. I have discovered something vegetable in me.

What ethical or political considerations inform your work with plants? What are the ethical and political implications of this work?

DS: A manipulated root system, presented as a tapestry, a photo, or a living sculpture, shows clear traces of a reckless intervention in a natural system, but also indicates a possible cultivated human–plant path. Through my installations, I examine the boundaries between plant culture and plant nature. What does "natural" mean in the context of the Anthropocene? I want to approach the subject in a poetic way and consider my images as a link between science, art, and the public. I am interested in the beauty, necessity, and at the same time the dangerous, objectifying, side of manipulation.

What, if any, are the aspects of your work with plants related to the current global environmental and mass extinction crises?

DS: In addition to my autonomous work, I also started speculative material research. *Exercises in Root System Domestication* originated as an art project with an intuitive approach. It has also developed into scientific research and a pursuit of possibly new and responsible large-scale production materials. Working on this project, I shift between disciplines, from art and craft to science. To develop this bio-technique, I collaborate with biologists and engineers. For the exhibition *Fashioned from Nature* in the Victoria and Albert Museum, I grew a dress. The dress is a concept and cannot be worn. But it explores an idea that might become viable in a near future.

So far, plant roots have not yet been used for the production of a material. The root system is an overlooked source of natural fiber. Usually, it is discarded as waste after harvesting annual plants.

Roots could also be useful in the context of climate change. Plants absorb CO_2 and fix the carbon in organic compounds. Plant roots in particular have the advantageous ability to store greenhouse gases too.

Which pressing challenge, or challenges, has working with plants presented to you?

DS: My artistic practice is similar to the work of a farmer. That means that I have to deal with the same complications such as bad summers and failed harvests. I regularly need to solve mouse infestations, mold, and plant diseases.

Over the years it has proved challenging to find a strong root that grows fast and that also likes to cooperate. Another challenge has been to control the strength of the root. It took a while for me to find the right materials to guide root growth. Roots grow into every little hole they can find. It often happened in the beginning that the roots would adhere too much to my templates.

The durability of the vegetal material was also part of a learning process for me. We found out that the roots have a fairly high acidity and that they can be preserved without much external assistance as long as they are protected from UV light and moisture—like any other work of art. I know that there are also dried plant roots found in pyramids. It would not surprise me that my roots have a longer shelf life than a drawing or a photo.

How is the interaction between your artistic practice and theoretical endeavors shaped by vegetal life?

DS: When I first became interested in the root system, I came across the experiments of Charles and Francis Darwin. Their research helped me to better understand my own root observations. They described the root apex as a "brain-like" organ. I found that exciting. *The Power of Movements of Plants* was the first body of research to explore the "intelligence" of plants. For contemporary botanists, this matter is still a wondrous land. We now know that an enormous amount of communication takes place underground. The rhizosphere forms a very dynamic environment in which plant roots and many organisms are located. Plants communicate with each other and collaborate with other organisms like fungi and bacteria via their roots.

In my manipulated patterns, I also follow the order of nature. The work starts at the computer, but the real point of departure is provided by the plants. My patterns might look arbitrarily geometrical, but they are based on the structural, ordering principles of nature identified by Pythagoras and Euclid.

The intuitive scientific studies of Johan Wolfgang von Goethe have also been a source of inspiration for me. The confrontation between Goethe's technical and scientific fascination and his romantic background intrigued me.

For example, my installation *Spectrum Crops—Findings in Color* is based on his experiments with light, color, and growth. In this work, I show the development of crops under the influence of manipulated light. It is a search for unknown forms and colors.

I wanted to know whether I could dissect the light spectrum into its various colors or shades in such a way as to create plants with a new shape or length. I was

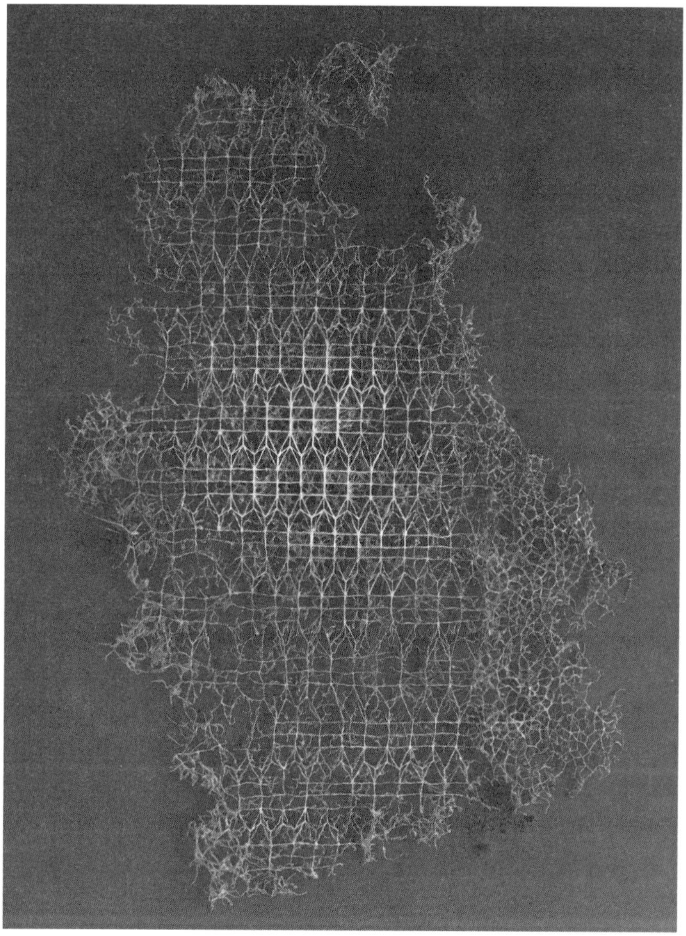

Interwoven #8, 2020, plantrootweaving,
Diana Scherer. (Photo: Diana Scherer
© Diana Scherer.)

curious about the natural process of photosynthesis and whether I could apply the light sensitivity of vegetal life to my work.

Diana Scherer is a visual artist living and working in Amsterdam. She was born in Lauingen Germany in 1971 and studied fine art at the Rietveld Academy in Amsterdam. Her practice encompasses photography, material research, plant root-weaving, and sculpture. Over the past years she has exhibited in several international solo and group shows. She has published two books at Van Zoetendaal Publishers: *Nurture Studies* in 2014 and *Mädchen* in 2016.

VI

AUTOBIOGRAPHIES

37

A . . . MAZING PEA

Monica Gagliano

Gazing in and out of a maze of illuminated landscapes, we travel across the boundless territories of an electrified mind seeking the world. Invisible to the eyes at first, the world emerges out of the formless to make an impression on the canvas of our consciousness with the swirling colors of its dancing photons. Shining outward, brushstrokes of fragmented forms are stitched together into a seamless reality, born out of the mind and seen through the eyes of our imagining. What if we were able to stretch that imagining far beyond our eyes, letting our vision travel far wider than the brushstrokes the mind has learned to comprehend . . . ? But how can we learn the art of seeing that which we cannot yet imagine? Vision is an art, and nature an old master painter teaching us how to see the underlying reality of things to be—before they actually are. Unleash the mind into seeing across invisible territories; then an amazing vision will bring the as-yet-unmanifest world into being.

Landing at Pucallpa's airport felt different from the last time I had come here a few years earlier. The plants had been adamant that I come back to Peru, even if I had no real desire to do so. But there I was again. Later, somewhere in the middle of seemingly nowhere, I was spending my first afternoon back in the Amazon on the banks of the Ucayali River, listening to my new teacher, Don J, as he shared his knowledge on how he used plants to treat illnesses, pointing to a bristly plant down here and a tall and skinny one over there. A strong old man with kind eyes and not many teeth left to his smile, Don J was a Cocama shaman.[1] He had agreed to meet me in Pucallpa for a sort of job interview after a common acquaintance had put us in contact a couple of days earlier. The first thing Don J told me as we sat down for this meeting at a small café was that he had neither interest in nor the intention of teaching Westerners. Then he proceeded to ask me about my reasons for being there. "I am here because the plants have brought me here," I answered. Then, before I knew it, I added, "I need to become a better dreamer." He left without a word, but the next day he came to pick me up and take me to his home in the jungle, where I was going to diet with the plants.

That afternoon, Don J prepared a concoction made from Piñon blanco (*Jatropha curcas*), a drought-resistant shrub[2] also known as "purging nut" because of its cleansing effects on the bowels. By the time darkness descended in the jungle, I had drunk his medicine and entered the dreamscape where the spirit of this maestro was already awaiting to meet me. Wearing a doctor's white coat, Piñon blanco appeared in my dream as a tall, middle-aged man with short black hair and dark eyes.[3] He spoke of many things throughout the night, all the way into the first light of the morning. I paid great attention to his words, but at the same time, I knew that our discussion was somehow bypassing my mind. On the one hand, I knew exactly what he was talking to me about; on the other, my poor brain hadn't really been able to hear the words or understand them.

By the time morning came, I couldn't remember a thing Piñon blanco had said. I spoke with Don J about it. Images and details started flooding my awareness, and abruptly I found myself saying, "He was holding a fruit-like thing in his hand"—my hands were wildly gesturing the "something" I had seen as if I were playing a game of charades. Giving away his childlike delight, Don J's almost toothless smile signaled that he was pleased to hear my description of that which, to me, remained a mysterious "something." "I know what it is!" he said with great satisfaction. "It is a very powerful medicine. You will need to bathe with it and drink it, but only a little." And then he added, "you will diet it once you finish the work with this *doctorcito*."

As Don J had mentioned the day before, while looking at the plants growing around his hut, the plant spirits themselves teach us what to do, including what plants one is ready to diet. By showing me this strange fruit that looked like a cannonball, Piñon blanco had told me about the plant that was waiting to work with me next. And ready she was, the mighty Ayahuma.[4]

"The experiment is pretty simple. Train young plants in a maze, and give them the freedom of choice," Ayahuma declared, inside my head. Then she added, "But you've got to think peas, not sunflowers!" For several months earlier that year, I had tried to design an experiment that would allow me to test plants' ability for associative learning—also known as Pavlovian learning, after the famous experiments of Pavlov and his dogs.[5] The idea was to test whether plants were capable of learning that the occurrence of one event was not only somehow linked to another but also, more importantly, anticipated it. How to actually test this in plants was something that I had stubbornly been thinking about since 2011, as a follow-up to the study with *Mimosa pudica*.

For this purpose, the shed behind my home in Perth had been turned into a carpenter's workshop (and a free-of-charge sauna, courtesy of the scorching Western Australian summer!). Together with Martial—my best friend and long-term collaborator—I had designed and built some "learning boxes," which we had then brought into my lab at the university for testing. Each box was made of plywood, equipped with a timer controlling the activity of a fan, included a light source, and was fitted with a camera taking time-lapse photographs of sunflower seedlings supposedly making their "choices." I was convinced that we had created the perfect system for a Pavlovian learning test in plants, but it simply didn't work! Despite much frustration and time spent mulling over it, I just couldn't figure out why my apparently perfect setup wasn't working! Well, until *she* pointed it out . . .

Ayahuma (*Couroupita guianensis*) is a tree native to the tropical forests of northeastern South America, where is it held in high regard by the shamans of the Amazon Basin region. How this tall, spectacular beauty made it out of the South American jungle and into the Indian subcontinent and Southeast Asia is still a mystery,[6] but there, too, this extraordinary tree holds a special significance in the mythologies of the place and is often found growing at religious sites. In India, for example, the tree is commonly planted as a guardian at the entrance of Shiva temples;[7] in countries like Sri Lanka and Thailand, its evergreen presence stands glorious outside Buddhist temples as a symbol of enlightenment.[8] Away from its Amazonian home, Ayahuma is better known by its English moniker, cannonball tree—and aptly so. Not only are the fruits large, spherical, and as heavy as their namesakes, but also, as they ripen, they come plummeting to the ground with loud and explosive noises. One may be glad to know that signs are often posted near cannonball trees that have been planted in urban settings, warning people to keep at a safe distance to avoid serious head injuries. Ironically, the spirit of Ayahuma was set on that very task—not exactly to crack my head open, but my mind, no doubt. Of course, I had no idea of that at the time, but she did nonetheless. Pragmatic and down-to-earth, Ayahuma intended to unleash a vision that was lying dormant and out of sight in the labyrinth of my mind. Just like her fruits, which do not release their seeds until they fall down to the earth, I was ripening to fall thunderously to the ground of academic science and to burst open and fire my seeds of wild ideas into material existence. But just as her fruits do not continue to ripen if picked prematurely, it was essential that I wait for the right time.

Don J cracked a cannonball fruit open to expose the inner pulp. Inside, the gelatinous and alien-like flesh was peppered by a multitude of black seeds; left exposed to oxygen, the pulp turns bluish-purple. Apparently, these fruits are just about inedible—the pulp is known to cause allergies, and its notorious putrid smell is quite a deterrent for humans.[9] Don J mixed it in water for me to bathe in, so as to begin my *dieta* with her. And later that night I did, standing naked under the loyal watch of a cacao tree, whose reassuring presence gave me the deep inner poise I surely needed in that jungle-raw moment. First I faced the easterly direction of the rising sun as Don J poured the lovely "soup" over my head and shrouded me in the white smoke of his *mapacho*, while I proceeded rubbing my whole body with the foul mixture. Then I faced the westerly direction of the setting sun, and more of the stinky concoction washed over me, and more tobacco smoke enveloped my bare body, which was now shivering in the nocturnal coolness of the jungle. I dried myself off, put some clothes back on, and drank a small glass filled to the rim with the Ayahuma's water. Then I walked back to my bed and went to sleep with fruity tidbits still entangled in my hair, where they remained for the following week, during which time I was not allowed to wash.

Left in complete isolation inside the confines of the mosquito net that hung over my thin mattress, I spent that first day of my *dieta* dry fasting and drifting in and out of sleep. Not put off by the pungent stench of Ayahuma in my hair, the spirits of the plants I had dieted over the years returned within my dreams. Their arrival was accompanied by a warm sense of reassurance—I was glad to retrieve the medicine of my past *dietas* and know that the relationships I had secured with those plant spirits were still there, after all.

That is when she arrived. "There is nothing for you to acquire, only to remember," said Ayahuma. "Watch those false ideas planted inside your mind. Each false idea is a delusion created by a solidified thought pattern, an insane habit that keeps your attention fixed. But nothing is fixed; everything is fluctuating, changing, evolving. . . ." Before I could ask how you get rid of these false ideas, she answered with one simple but enigmatic instruction: "Turn in to find the curse of a false idea within the idea itself." And with that, she disappeared, and I woke up. It has taken me years to start grasping what Ayahuma shared and to begin to recognize the insanity of my delusion. The madness she pointed out truly is the work of a master trickster, a Machiavellian sleight-of-hand pulling the wool over the eyes of the innocent mind. Like a noxious weed planted in the most pristine imaginative ground, the delusion takes hold to fix the mind in place, immobilized into a place of anxious preoccupation. Then, through a socially perpetuated conditioning system, the pure knowing of our infinite nature is squandered in exchange for the penitentiary of a *distorted* awareness. Not long ago, this vertiginous insanity all of a sudden became clear, thanks to my encounter with an extraordinary shaman.[10] To my amusement, I have just found out that in folk medicine, Ayahuma is said to bring someone mad back to sanity. Unquestionably, she had intended to set me on the right track.

Ayahuma is widely recognized as a mighty protector and teacher. Although this tree is typically considered a powerful *maestro*—the gender of the noun implying masculinity—the spirit often also appears as a giant woman and, specifically, one without a head. I never actually glimpsed at her ethereal form (headless or not)—but this wonderfully quirky and buoyant spirit enjoyed playing with my head (in the most benevolent of ways!) and educating my mind. To do so, she made sure I could hear her voice loud and clear when she started prescribing the complete set of instructions for testing Pavlovian learning in plants. I transcribed as she dictated. And literally, this is how the pages of my travel diary filled up with the words she spoke and the diagrams she sketched.

Upon my return home to Australia, those words and sketches started growing, extending their plant-like runners beyond the pages where they had been seeded and out into my lab. There, eventually, they flowered into the pioneering experiments that they had been conceived to be all along.

At the Plant Growth Facilities at the University of Western Australia, I transformed one of the controlled-environment rooms into my plant-learning laboratory. The room was meticulously kept in complete darkness at all times; all light switches were taped over to prevent anyone from accidentally turning the lights on. A thick sheet of black plastic—the kind builders use under concrete—was secured over the entrance to prevent light from coming in when someone opened the door. A sign on the door warned, "Plant learning in progress. Do not enter." This, of course, made some researchers working within the same facility curious about what was going on. Some ventured to ask, but it was never clear to me whether they really heard my answer. "I am trying to teach pea seedlings some tricks," I would say mischievously. I would then wait for puzzlement to creep across their faces before adding, "Yeah, you know, just as you would train your puppy with tasty treats."

The irony was that I was far from joking. In fact, it was by studying his dogs that Ivan Pavlov—in one of the most revealing studies in the history of behavioral research—had demonstrated that behavior could be changed using conditioning. In these experiments, Pavlov's dogs had learned to associate the ringing of a bell with the imminent arrival of dinner, to the point where the sound of the bell alone made the dogs salivate in anticipation of dinner. Would my little peas learn that the position of a small fan—the equivalent to the ringing bell—rightly predicted the time and place for the occurrence of the only light made available to them—their dinner?

As instructed by Ayahuma, I set up a simple series of experiments by placing pea seedlings in individual Y-shaped mazes constructed out of PVC pipes. During training, as each seedling grew inside its maze, I exposed them first to the gentle breeze of a small fan (as a neutral conditioning cue) followed by light (food), a biologically significant cue, which was offered as a kind of reward. For three consecutive days, I repeated this on different arms of the maze, though fan and light always appeared on the same side of the maze in one experimental group and on opposite sides in another group. On the fourth day, I tested their ability to learn by association by turning on the fan alone. Just as in Pavlov's experiment, in which the bell acquired meaning when the dogs learned that it predicted dinner, the fan in my experiment had no meaning to the peas to start with. So the question was whether it would acquire meaning if the peas learned of its significance. It did, though I almost didn't see it.

Two weeks passed. I was in my lab, monitoring peas and setting up mazes, lights, and fans, every single day from the early hours of the morning till late in the afternoon. Technically, the experimental system was working well, and the peas were successfully growing, but their ability to navigate the maze didn't seem to be influenced by the presence of the fan as the cue that would give them the best chance at finding light. The initial data suggested that about half of the seedlings were growing to the left and half to the right of the maze in a random fashion (50–50). In short, they were failing the test.

Head low and tail between my legs, there I was on a sunny Sunday morning, ready to dismantle and pack away the whole setup, dismayed at the outcome.

I left the brightness of the outside world and walked into the dim light of the Plant Growth Facilities' corridor. I opened the door marked "Plant learning in progress. Do not enter," and entered. The controlled-environment room met me with its computerized wave of coolness, which rolled over my skin until I broke into a shiver. The room absorbed me within its undisturbed darkness, where several pea seedlings were quietly waiting inside their mazes. At the flick of one switch, the tiny blue LED lights mounted on each maze glowed like fireflies in the rich blackness of the space, a space where the confinement of walls had become imperceptible.

I glanced around as my inquisitorial mind started the court-martial. How could I have been so daft? Did I seriously believe that a tree in the Amazon—or, to be precise, the *spirit* of a tree in the Amazon—had given me instructions (which, to my credit, I had followed to a T) on how to carry out these experiments? All of a sudden, as the internal assault escalated, my eyes stopped searching. My gaze brushed over a little something that, until that moment, had gone unnoticed.

There in the dark, I had found what I had been looking for.

We believe we see only because of the presence of light, but it is in the dark that light becomes visible. From the encounter of light and darkness we are born, and with us, the world emerges. Constantly molding the world around us with our gaze, we in turn are molded by the gaze the world presses upon us. Unaware of this interplay of luminosities, we rarely recognize that all we see is seeing us. Rarely do we realize that by virtue of its being all around us, the penetrating gaze of the world sees us, at all times and from all sides, in our multidimensionality. We, however, see the world from a one-sided standpoint only: the frontal view. As in single-point perspective drawing, we make the object of our most immediate gaze look realistic and three-dimensional, while most of the world is distorted and lost away to a vanishing point in an illusory distance.

Except on specific occasions, the vegetality of the world seems to be relegated precisely to that distant and imaginary background of our perception. It's perception that—to use the elegant words of philosopher Michael Marder—is the "key passageway for the body's openness to the world and the world's reception by the body."[11] In this openness, as time disappears, our relationship with space is all that matters. No longer separate from the exteriority of our milieu, the world around us ceases to be the *world* in the agreed sense of the word. Effervescing with evanescent and yet endless extemporizations, the world births itself visible in a remarkable fluidity of both composing and decomposing, becoming and undoing. It is in this liminal space of pure possibility, where the being-made meets the coming-undone, where light encounters darkness, that we, too, are conceived. It is here that we wait, not knowing, to encounter the other, to become the other, and—exactly as the *planta maestra* Socoba had susurrated—it is here that we, humans, become them, plants. Can conventional science ever render this *un*knowing knowable, this *in*visible visible? And can we ever unravel our encounters without disrupting the integrity of the other whom we meet? Or is "disruption" a space for mutual transformation, hence a vital element in the encounter? On that Sunday morning, the pea seedlings were waiting in my lab, not to tell me *if*, but show me *how*.

My gaze dawdled over one of the mazes. Time stopped. I found myself simply being—being there with the vegetal presence inside the maze, attending to this presence in the darkness. Suspended in the empty space between expectations, a new configuration of ideas and relations emerged. And in that darkness, I saw it clearly. I was "within the vegetal experience" and able to discern and define that which enabled the green tendril of my young peas to stretch toward the dark in order to find the light. "Holy shit, they are doing it after all!" I squealed. I looked over, inside the maze, once again. I squealed again. My heart was beating furiously, and I started feeling lightheaded. I checked another maze, then another, as an overwhelming exhilaration burst up and outward into luminous tears. The young plants were correctly predicting the imminent arrival of light (*when*) and its direction (*where*) based on the presence and position of the neutral conditioning stimulus, the fan; in response, they were directing their slender vegetal forms into that arm of the maze. In astonishment, I speed-walked right out of the blackness of the controlled-environment room, into the dim light of the Plant Growth Facilities' corridor, and out into the bright sunlight of that Sunday morning, still repeating aloud, "They're doing it! They're doing it!"

The disquieting irony of the whole situation was that the plants had performed their associative task correctly from the word go, and I had not recognized it.

How was it possible I had missed this? I had looked after the young peas in their mazes every single day for a whole two weeks. How could it be that until that moment I had been incapable of seeing how wonderfully they were learning?

The reason for this was pretty straightforward, at least on the surface. The peas were not incompetent at learning; they were simply failing to satisfy the regime of expectations that I (and many other behavioral scientists) had been trained to look out for, that being that a comparison be made using random choice—a hypothetical expectation that, without learning, half of the seedlings would simply grow to the left and half to the right of the maze. According to this expectation, it would be said that the plants had learned to use the fan (conditioned stimulus) as a reliable indicator of future light if a (statistical) majority much greater than 50 percent grew toward the fan. Because the number of seedlings that did grow toward the fan was only slightly more than what one may expect by random chance, I had concluded that they were not able to learn by association. What I had missed, however, was that this hypothetical expectation was incorrect to start with, simply because this is not what *real* pea seedlings that have been exposed to light actually do! It was not their baseline behavior. Their natural behavior is to consistently grow in the direction where light was last experienced. And, in fact, this strong phototropic response of pea seedlings to blue light is well established in the scientific research literature, and my own pilot study had shown me that pea seedlings were never random in how they directed their growth toward light in the first place.

In other words, unless trained to do otherwise (which was the aim of my experiments), pea seedlings successfully grew in the direction where they last experienced light 100 percent of the time, not a random 50 percent of the time. Plants like peas always grow in the direction of sunlight. How could I miss this vital piece of information, which is so obvious as to be forgotten within the complexities of my experimental groups? This meant that one would never expect them to override their innate tendency to continue growing in the direction of that last-presented light and, instead, use the new direction of the fan (conditioned stimulus) as a reliable indicator of future light. This, and not an imaginary random choice with its expectation of 50–50 being the baseline, was the realistic expectation to measure my results against to observe and recognize whether a learned behavior was being expressed. And by switching the location of the fan after it had been associated with the future presence of light during the learning phase, the study had demonstrated that the green tendrils had done exactly what I had been testing for; between 60 and 70 percent of all peas had learned the association and made a rebellious new choice that was unexpected of them—to turn the other way and go against their instinct of growing where they had last experienced light. And while this provided the mechanistic answer to how the experiment unfolded in the first place, it did little to uncover what provoked the perceptual shift in me—how could I have missed this and then, suddenly, have seen the very thing I was testing for?

I thought I had been waiting for something to happen, and instead I was learning to wait without waiting. I understand now that for the something I was waiting for to appear at all, I had to be willing to be surprised. By definition, of course, a surprise can be possible only if it arrives unannounced, unintended, unpremeditated.

The something I was waiting for did appear unanticipated, as the surprise outdid my expectations, based on what I had previously learned.

Paradoxically, the very expectations that, at first, concealed the event I was waiting for also provided the essential backdrop against which the event could be seen. My expectations were the background of my knowing within which a kind of inconsistency could be created; they provided the manured topsoil in which the event could emerge from the background to be recognized, making itself available to the eyes and the mind.

By pointing their green tendrils at that which had obscured the possibility of an alternative view, the young peas had created a profound fissure in my well-sculpted perception of the outer world. So as I tested their learning ability within the Pavlovian conditioning paradigm, the seedlings had tested mine by shining a light on the extent to which the conditioning prescribed by my academic training had bound me to a specific perception of the world—one that restricted what I could see. In an act of volition, they had offered themselves as the substrate through which perceptual conditioning could be expressed so that they could show me where my own conditioning lay.

The advent of this recognition had caused me to appreciate the peas (once more) as brilliant collaborators who, by simply growing into what they chose, overthrew—at least in part—the restrictions regimenting my perceptual freedom. This seeing was truly a gift, one that couldn't be lost—once you see, you cannot unsee. It was from this newly found viewpoint that I also understood that the aggression, derision, or cold indifference some colleagues had expressed toward my work over the years had merely been articulations of their visual boundaries. They were unable to see what was presented because it simply did not exist (yet) in their reality—something that, only a moment earlier, had been the case for me too.

This realization arrived with a wonderful sense of freedom, as a more expanded way to perceive both the world and myself opened. As the groundswell of this realization increased over the weeks and months that followed, my field of view stretched farther to consider the wider context of modern human society. Then the big question surfaced—why do we seem so incapable of taking the steps and actions required to create a world where conflict, poverty, and environmental devastation are things of the past? The simplicity and profound wisdom of the answer moved me deeply as it touched the shores of my awareness.

Throughout human history, we have constructed boundaries to define reality in an attempt to soothe our need to feel safe in our own skin and at home in a world we are, fundamentally, so afraid of. Threatening the very thing they promised to protect—our feeling of being safe—these boundaries are, and always were, fictional walls that restrict our understanding of who we truly are and that replace clear seeing with misconception—the illusion that we need to control a world we have no control over. Our need to feel safe (and, correspondingly, the feeling of *not* being safe) in the world seems inextricably linked to our need to control it. But what if we were to realize that the only reason we feel unsafe in the world is because we *believe* we need to control it?

As the sacred jungle Tobacco would teach me a year later, we have no control over the circumstances that face us *until* we surrender the need to control them. As long as we need to control our circumstances, we also need to feel unsafe and insecure about them, because the two states are bound together in a self-perpetuating and irreconcilable loop that goes something like this: we try to control because we feel unsafe and believe that by controlling our world, we will feel safe in it—and yet we never do, and we cannot feel safe in the world if we keep believing that the world needs controlling because, without our control, there is something unsafe about it.

The greatest insanity of this merry-go-round is that the loop we have invented has no possible internal resolution. The anxious feeling of not being safe is a necessary stipulation within our contract with the need to control; with no loophole to be found, we don't know what to do. As I had experienced in my lab when my experiment didn't seem to be working, what if we accepted that there was actually nothing to do? And once faced with this dead end, what if we stopped and waited in the darkness, like I had to on that Sunday morning? And as we relaxed in the belly of the unknown and handed ourselves over to life, what if we discovered a surprising clarity to *see* what is truly happening and what needs to be done? By dropping our obsession for controlling life, the whole fiction about "being unsafe" drops too. Left with nothing to protect or attack, the loop comes undone!

It seems our society is ready for a perceptual shift capable of undoing this silly loop by overthrowing our conditioned seeing, ready for a disobedient disruption emerging from the tidy background of silent obligations and prepackaged reality that have prevented us from seeing the innovative solutions that could bring planetary well-being and peace into being. The walls that entrap us in the loop are not as impenetrable as we believe. Porous, precarious, and of disputable nature, they were designed to dissolve at the first pure moment of real surrender!

Just like I had experienced with my clever peas in the darkness of my lab, it is when we are willing to let life surprise us that alternatives and unanticipated solutions become visible and accessible. And the best part of this entire process is that once out of our insane loop of control and insecurity, we are effortlessly delivered exactly where we are going. Infused with a sense of awe and deep trust in the life that we are, we wait without waiting to know exactly what to do and when. Free to see clearly, we don't need to find our way out of the maze. We realize there never was a maze.

NOTES

1. Don J was a victim of *brujeria* (witchcraft) and passed away in 2016.
2. This plant is known to be resistant to a high degree of aridity; while dieting with it, Piñon blanco showed me that he bestows the same capacity to endure strenuous conditions on humans by increasing their stamina and supporting their immune system.
3. In my dream, the spirit of this plant had presented himself as a medical doctor, though I was totally unaware at the time that the plant had the genus name *Jatropha,* which is derived from the Greek words *iatrós* (doctor) and *trophé* (food), which implies the traditional medicinal role of this plant across countries. See D. M. R. Prasad, A. Izam, and M. R. Khan, "*Jatropha curcas*: Plant of Medical Benefits," *Journal of Medicinal Plants Research* 6, no. 14 (2012): 2691–2699.
4. Ayahuma refers here to *Couroupita guianensis,* a tree native to the tropical forests of northeastern South America. However, Ayahuma is also the name of one of the main protagonists of the Inti Raymi—the Inca Festival of the Sun, which takes place annually toward the end of June in the Andean villages of Peru, Bolivia, Argentina, and Ecuador. The festival is an occasion for celebrating the life-giving power of the sun, as well as giving thanks for the harvest, hence a perfect time for renewing and strengthening the relationship with Pachamama—Mother Earth. As part of the celebrations, the Ayahuma leads a ritual performance in which a group of dancers go around in circles (representing the equinoxes and solstices) while stamping their feet to encourage Mother Earth to be rejuvenated for the new agricultural cycle. The Ayahuma wears a brightly colored hand-knitted mask, which has become an icon of the Andean folklore. A link between the symbolic and the real (interior–exterior), his two-faced mask represents the duality of the world: past and future, day and night, good and bad. The mask also bears twelve horns (representing the twelve months of the year) and other attachments that look like antennas (representing snakes, an Andean symbol of wisdom). When the Spaniards first encountered it during the colonization of South America, they considered the Ayahuma and his mask as the depiction of a demonic character. However, for the Indigenous people, the Ayahuma is the materialization of the energies of Pachamama (i.e., the vital life forces found in nature) and hence is highly respected.
5. Ivan Pavlov was a Russian physiologist who discovered a new type of learning—associative learning—whereby his dogs learned to associate the sound of a bell to the arrival of food.

For a description of Pavlov's experiment see: S. A. McLeod, "Pavlov's Dogs," *Simply Psychology*, 2013, www.simplypsychology.org/pavlov.html.

6. The tree has been known in India for at least three thousand years. According to some scholars, European traders brought it to the subcontinent; others propose a more ancient migration route. See J. L. Sorenson and C. L. Johannessen, "Scientific Evidence for Pre-Columbian Transoceanic Voyages," *Sino-Platonic Papers* 133 (2004).
7. According to Hindu tradition, the cannonball tree is sacred because the flower petals resemble the hood of the "Naga," a sacred snake protecting the stigma known as the "Shiva lingham"; it symbolizes the sanctified phallus and the serpent protector of elemental sexual energy. The tree's other names, "nagalinga" and "shivalingam," reiterate the tree's symbolism.
8. The cannonball tree is confused with the Sal (*Shorea robusta*), the tree whose flowers supposedly bloomed in unison when Gautama Buddha passed away and under which the previous Buddha Vessabhu attained enlightenment. The Bodhi tree under which Siddhartha Gautama reached enlightenment and became the Buddha is *Ficus religiosa.*
9. In traditional medicine, the plant is used as a disinfectant, a microbicide, and an antidepressant. Said to have antibacterial, antiseptic, and analgesic qualities, the bark supposedly cures colds, the juice from its leaves is good for treating malaria and for skin diseases, chewing young leaves alleviates toothache, and the interior of the fruit can disinfect wounds. The pulp is sometimes fed to pigs and poultry to kill intestinal worms. See M. S. Shekhawat and M. Manokari, "In Vitro Propagation, Micromorphological Studies and Ex Vitro Rooting of Cannon Ball Tree (*Couroupita guianensis* aubl.): A Multipurpose Threatened Species," *Physiology and Molecular Biology of Plants* 22, no. 1 (2016): 131–142.
10. For an introduction to his work, see Lujan Matus's *The Art of Stalking Parallel Perception: The Living Tapestry of Lujan Matus* (CreateSpace Independent Publishing Platform, 2015) and *Whisperings of the Dragon: Shamanic Practices to Awaken Your Primal Power* (CreateSpace Independent Publishing Platform, 2014). See also his website, Parallel Perception, www.parallelperception.com.
11. See M. Marder, "Plant-Perceiving Is Plant-Thinking," *Los Angeles Review of Books Channel Blog*, 2013, http://philosoplant.lareviewofbooks.org/?p=192.

Main Pathway: Cross-Pollination

Subthemes

Proceed to Experience, p. 573
Proceed to Transcending, p. 573
Proceed to Healing, p. 227

38

CONVERSATION: THE INTELLIGENCE OF PLANTS

Robin Wall Kimmerer and Krista Tippett

As a botanist and member of the Citizen Potawatomi Nation, Robin Wall Kimmerer joins science's ability to "polish the art of seeing" with her personal, civilizational lineage of listening to plant life and heeding the languages of the natural world. And she says that as our knowledge about plant life unfolds, human vocabulary and imaginations must adapt.

KRISTA TIPPETT: "Why is the world so beautiful?" This is a question Robin Wall Kimmerer pursues as a botanist and also a member of the Citizen Potawatomi Nation. She's the author of the beloved book *Braiding Sweetgrass*. She's written, "Science polishes the gift of seeing, indigenous traditions work with gifts of listening and language." An expert in moss—a bryologist—she describes mosses as the "coral reefs of the forest." She opens a sense of wonder and humility for the intelligence in all kinds of life we are used to naming and imagining as inanimate.

ROBIN WALL KIMMERER: I can't think of a single scientific study in the last few decades that has demonstrated that plants or animals are dumber than we think. It's always the opposite, right? What we're revealing is the fact that they have a capacity to learn, to have memory, and we're at the edge of a wonderful revolution in really understanding the sentience of other beings.

Originally published as "The Intelligence of Plants," on *On Being* with Krista Tippett. Reprinted with permission.

TIPPETT: Robin Wall Kimmerer is a professor of environmental biology at the State University of New York and the founding director of the Center for Native Peoples and the Environment. She works with tribal nations on environmental problem-solving and sustainability. And part of that work is about recovering lineages of knowledge that were made illegal in the policies of tribal assimilation which did not fully end in the U.S. until the 1970s. Robin Wall Kimmerer's grandfather attended one of the now infamous boarding schools designed to "civilize" Indian youth; and she only began to learn the Anishinaabe language of her people as an adult. We spoke in 2015.

I'm just so intrigued when I look at the way you introduce yourself. It will often include that you're from the Citizen Potawatomi Nation, from the bear clan, adopted into the eagles. I'd love for you to just take us a little bit into that world you're describing that you came from, and ask, also, the question I always ask: what was the spiritual and religious background of that world you grew up in of your childhood?

KIMMERER: I'd like to start with the second part of that question. I was lucky enough to grow up in the fields and the woods of upstate New York. I was lucky in that regard, but disappointed also, in that I grew up away from the Potawatomi people, away from all of our people by virtue of history, the history of removal and the taking of children to the Indian boarding schools. And so, in a sense, the questions that I had about who I was in the world, what the world was like, those are questions that I really wished I'd had a cultural elder to ask, but I didn't, but I had the woods to ask. And there's a way in which just growing up in the woods and the fields, they really became my doorway into culture. In the absence of human elders, I had plant elders instead.

TIPPETT: And it sounds like you did not grow up speaking the language of the Potawatomi nation, which is Anishinaabe, is that right?

KIMMERER: That's right. Yeah, the language is called Anishinaabemowin. And the Potawatomi language is very close to that.

TIPPETT: I was intrigued to see that mention somewhere in your writing that you take part in a Potawatomi language lunchtime class that actually happens in Oklahoma, and you're there via the internet, because I grew up, actually, in Potawatomi County in Oklahoma. And having told you that, I never knew or learned anything about what that word meant, much less the people and the culture it described.

KIMMERER: That is so interesting to live in a place that is named that. This is the ways in which cultures become invisible, and the language becomes invisible. And through history and the reclaiming of that, the making culture visible again, to speak the language in even the tiniest amount so that it's almost as if it feels like the air is waiting to hear this language that had been lost for so long. So it delights me that I can be learning an ancient language by completely modern technologies. Sitting at my office, eating lunch, learning Potawatomi grammar.

TIPPETT: So when you said a minute ago that you spent your childhood, and actually the searching questions of your childhood somehow found expression, and the closest that you came to answers, in the woods. And it seems to me that that's such a wonderful way to fill out something else you've said before, which is that you were born a botanist, which is a way to say this, which was the language you got as you entered college at forestry school at State University of New York.

KIMMERER: Yes. There was no question but that I'd study botany in college. It was my passion. Still is, of course. But the botany that I encountered there was so different than the way that I understood plants. Plants were reduced to object. What was supposedly important about them was the mechanism by which they worked, not what their gifts were, not what their capacities were. They were really thought of as objects, whereas I thought of them as subjects. And that shift in worldview was a big hurdle for me in entering the field of science.

TIPPETT: One way you've said it is that that science was asking different questions, and you had other questions, other language, and other protocol that came from Indigenous culture. There's one place in your writing where you're talking about beauty. You're talking about a question you would have, which is why two flowers are beautiful together. And that that question, for example, would violate the division that is necessary for objectivity. But then, you do this wonderful thing where you actually give a scientific analysis of the statement that beauty is in the eye of the beholder, which would be one of the critiques of a question like that, that it's not really asking a question that is rational or scientific. Do you know what I'm talking about?

KIMMERER: I do. I do exactly.

TIPPETT: Flesh that out, because that's such an interesting juxtaposition of how you actually started to both experience the dissonance between those kinds of questionings and also start to weave them together.

KIMMERER: Yes, it goes back to the story of when I very proudly entered the forestry school as an 18-year-old and telling them that the reason that I wanted to study botany was because I wanted to know why asters and goldenrod looked so beautiful together. There are these amazing displays of this bright, chrome yellow and the deep purple of the New England aster, and they look stunning together. And the two plants so often intermingle rather than living apart from one another, and I wanted to know why that was. I thought that surely in the order and the harmony of the universe, there would be an explanation for why they looked so beautiful together. And I was told that that was not science, that if I was interested in beauty, I should go to art school.

Which was really demoralizing as a freshman, but I came to understand that that question wasn't going to be answered by science, that science, as a way of knowing, explicitly sets aside our emotions, our aesthetic reactions to things. We have to analyze them as if they were just pure material, and not matter and spirit together. And, yes, as it turns out, there's a very good biophysical explanation for why those plants grow together, so it's a matter of aesthetics and it's a matter of ecology. Those complimentary colors of purple and gold together, being opposites on the color wheel, they're so vivid, they actually attract far more pollinators than if those two grew apart from one another.

So each of those plants benefits by combining its beauty with the beauty of the other. And that's a question that science can address, certainly, as well as artists. And I just think that "Why is the world so beautiful?" is a question we all ought to be embracing.

TIPPETT: Now, you did work, for a time, at Bausch & Lomb after college. You went into a more traditional scientific endeavor. I wonder, was there a turning point, a day or a moment where you felt compelled to bring these things together in the way you could, these different ways of knowing and seeing and studying the world?

KIMMERER: Yes. I think the time when it became most important to me to start to bring these ways of knowing back together again is when, as a young PhD botanist, I was invited to a gathering of traditional plant knowledge holders. And I was just there to listen, and it was such an amazing experience. Four days of listening to people whose knowledge of the plant world was so much deeper than my own.

TIPPETT: And were these elders? Were these Indigenous teachers?

KIMMERER: They were. Their education was on the land and with the plants and through the oral tradition. But I just sat there and soaked in this wonderful conversation, which interwove mythic knowledge and scientific knowledge into this beautiful cultural, natural history. And, for me, it was absolutely a watershed moment, because it made me remember those things that starting to walk the science path had made me forget, or attempted to make me forget. And I just saw that their knowledge was so much more whole and rich and nurturing that I wanted to do everything that I could to bring those ways of knowing back into harmony.

TIPPETT: You said at one point that you had gotten to the point where—you were talking about the names of plants. "I was teaching the names and ignoring the songs." What do you mean by that?

KIMMERER: One of the difficulties of moving in the scientific world is that when we name something, often with a scientific name, this name becomes almost an end to inquiry. We sort of say, "Well, we know it now." We're able to systematize it and put a Latin binomial on it, so it's ours. We know what we need to know. But that is only in looking, of course, at the morphology of the organism, at the way that it looks. It ignores all of its relationships. It's such a mechanical, wooden representation of what a plant really is. And we reduce them tremendously if we just think about them as physical elements of the ecosystem.

TIPPETT: So this notion of the earth's animacy, of the animacy of the natural world and everything in it, including plants, is very pivotal to your thinking, and to the way you explore the natural world, even scientifically, and draw conclusions, also, about our relationship to the natural world. So I really want to delve into that some more. You said that there's a grammar of animacy. Talk about that a little bit.

KIMMERER: Yes. This comes back to what I think of as the innocent or childlike way of knowing. Actually, that's a terrible thing to call it. We say it's an innocent way of knowing, and, in fact, it's a very worldly and wise way of knowing. That kind of deep attention that we pay as children is something that I cherish, that I think we all can cherish and reclaim, because attention is that doorway to gratitude, the doorway to wonder, the doorway to reciprocity. And it worries me greatly that today's children can recognize 100 corporate logos and fewer than ten plants. That means they're not paying attention.

In the English language, if we want to speak of that sugar maple or that salamander, the only grammar that we have to do so is to call those beings an "it." And if I called my grandmother or the person sitting across the room from me an "it," that would be so rude, right? And we wouldn't tolerate that for members of our own species, but we not only tolerate it, but it's the only way we have in the English language to speak of other beings, is as "it." In Potawatomi, the cases that we have are animate and inanimate, and it is impossible in our language to speak of other living beings as "its."

TIPPETT: So living beings would all be animate, all living beings, anything that was alive in the Potawatomi language.

KIMMERER: Yes. Absolutely.

TIPPETT: And inanimate would be, what, materials or . . . ?

KIMMERER: You raise a very good question, because the way that, again, Western science would give the criteria for what does it mean to be alive is a little different than what you might find in traditional culture, where we think of water as alive, as rocks as alive. Alive in different ways, but certainly not inanimate. Generally, the inanimate grammar is reserved for those things which humans have created.

TIPPETT: OK. Like the table, something like that?

KIMMERER: Yes, exactly. Right, yes.

TIPPETT: And I have to say—I'm sure you know this, because I'm sure you get this reaction a lot, especially in scientific circles—it's unfamiliar and slightly uncomfortable in Western ears to hear someone refer to plants as persons. It's unfamiliar. Does that happen a lot? Is that kind of a common reaction?

KIMMERER: Sure, sure. Scientists are very eager to say that we oughtn't to personify elements in nature for fear of anthropomorphizing. And what I mean when I talk about the personhood of all beings, plants included, is not that I am attributing human characteristics to them, not at all. I'm attributing plant characteristics to plants. Just as it would be disrespectful to try and put plants in the same category through the lens of anthropomorphism, I think it's also deeply disrespectful to say that they have no consciousness, no awareness, no being-ness at all. And this denial of personhood to all other beings is increasingly being refuted by science itself.

TIPPETT: That's interesting.

KIMMERER: Yeah. I can't think of a single scientific study in the last few decades that has demonstrated that plants or animals are dumber than we think. It's always the opposite, right? What we're revealing is the fact that they have extraordinary capacities, which are so unlike our own, but we dismiss them because, well, if they don't do it like animals do it, then they must not be doing anything, when, in fact, they're sensing their environment, responding to their environment in incredibly sophisticated ways. The science which is showing that plants have capacity to learn, to have memory, we're at the edge of a wonderful revolution in really understanding the sentience of other beings.

TIPPETT: Yeah. Here's something beautiful that you wrote in your book *Gathering Moss*, just as an example. "The rocks are beyond slow, beyond strong, and yet, yielding to a soft, green breath as powerful as a glacier, the mosses wearing away their surfaces grain by grain, bringing them slowly back to sand. There is an ancient conversation going on between mosses and rocks, poetry to be sure. About light and shadow and the drift of continents." That's so beautiful and so amazing to think about, to just read those sentences and think about that conversation, as you say.

KIMMERER: Yes. And it's a conversation that takes place at a pace that we humans, especially we contemporary humans who are rushing about, we can't even grasp the pace at which that conversation takes place. So thinking about plants as persons, indeed, thinking about rocks as persons, forces us to shed our idea of the only pace that we live in is the human pace. It's, I think, very, very exciting to think about these ways of being which happen on completely different scales, and so exciting to think about what we might learn from them.

TIPPETT: You make such an interesting observation that the way you walk through the world and immerse yourself in moss and plant life—you've said you become aware that we have some deficits compared to our companion species. I sense that photosynthesis, that we can't even photosynthesize, that this is a quality you covet in our botanical brothers and sisters. [*laughs*]

KIMMERER: [*laughs*] It's true.

TIPPETT: Take me inside that, because I want to understand that.

KIMMERER: I do. I have photosynthesis envy. The ability to take these non-living elements of the world, air and light and water, and turn them into food that can then be shared with the whole rest of the world—to turn them into medicine that is medicine for people and for trees and for soil, and we cannot even approach the kind of creativity that they have.

TIPPETT: One thing you say that I'd like to understand better is, "Science polishes the gift of seeing, indigenous traditions work with gifts of listening and language." So I'd love an example of something—what are the gifts of seeing that science offers, and then the gifts of listening and language, and how all of that gives you this rounded understanding of something?

KIMMERER: What I mean when I say that "science polishes the gift of seeing" brings us to an intense kind of attention that science allows us to bring to the natural world, and that kind of attention also includes ways of seeing, quite literally, through other lenses—that we might have the hand lens, the magnifying glass in our hands that allows us to look at that moss with an acuity that the human eye doesn't have, so we see more. The microscope that lets us see the gorgeous architecture by which it's put together, the scientific instrumentation in the laboratory that would allow us to look at the miraculous way that water interacts with cellulose, let's say. That's what I mean by "science polishes our ability to see"—it extends our eyes into other realms. But we're, in many cases, looking at the surface. And by the surface, I mean the material being alone.

But in Indigenous ways of knowing, we say that we know a thing when we know it not only with our physical senses, with our intellect, but also when we engage our intuitive ways of knowing, of emotional knowledge and spiritual knowledge. And that's really what I mean by listening. By seeing that traditional knowledge engages us in listening. And what is the story that that being might share with us if we know how to listen as well as we know how to see?

TIPPETT: Let's talk some more about mosses, because you did write this beautiful book about it, and you are a bryologist. And so that's a specialty, even within plant biology.

KIMMERER: Within botany.

TIPPETT: And also, I learned that your work with moss inspired Elizabeth Gilbert's novel *The Signature of All Things*, which is about a botanist. I learned so many things from that book. It's also that I had never thought very deeply about moss, but that moss inhabits nearly every ecosystem on earth, over 22,000 species, that mosses have the ability to clone themselves from broken-off leaves or torn fragments, that they're integral to the functioning of a forest. I mean, just describe some of the things you've heard and understood from moss.

KIMMERER: Thank you for asking that question, because it really gets to this idea of how science asks us to learn about organisms. Traditional knowledge asks us to learn from them. And when I think about mosses, in particular, as the most ancient of land plants, they have been here for a very long time. They've figured out a lot about how to live well on the earth, and, for me, I think they're really good storytellers in the way that they live. An example of what I mean by this is in their simplicity, in the power of being small; mosses become so successful all over the world because they live in these tiny little layers on rocks, on logs, and on trees. They work with the natural forces that lie over every little surface of the world, and to me, they are exemplars of not only surviving, but flourishing by working with natural processes. Mosses are superb teachers about living within your means.

TIPPETT: And you say they take possession of spaces that are too small—other plants are excluded from those spaces, but they thrive there.

KIMMERER: That's right. Mosses have, in the ecological sense, very low competitive ability, because they're small, because they don't grab resources very efficiently, and so this means that they have to live in the interstices. They have to live in places where the dominant competitive plants can't live. But the way that they do this really brings into question the whole premise that competition is what really structures biological evolution and biological success. Because mosses are not good competitors at all, and yet they are the oldest plants on the planet. They have persisted here for 350 million years. They ought to be doing something right here. And one of those somethings, I think, has to do with their ability to cooperate with one another, to share the limited resources that they have, to really give more than they take. Mosses build soil, they purify water, they are like the coral reefs of the forest, they make homes for this myriad of all these very cool little invertebrates who live in there. They are just engines of biodiversity. They do all of these things, and yet, they're only a centimeter tall.

TIPPETT: [*laughs*] Right. Another point that is implied in how you talk about us acknowledging the animacy of plants is that whenever we use the language of "it," whatever we're talking about—well, let's say this. We don't call anything we love and want to protect and would work to protect "it." That language distances us.

KIMMERER: It certainly does. And the language of "it," which distances, disrespects, and objectifies, I can't help but think is at the root of a worldview that allows us to exploit nature. And by exploit, I mean in a way that really seriously degrades the land and the waters, because, in fact, we have to consume. We have to take. We are animals, right? But that, to me, is different than really rampant exploitation. But this is why I've been thinking a lot about: Are there ways to bring this notion of animacy into the English language? Because so many of us that I've talked to about this feel really deeply uncomfortable calling the living world "it," and yet, we don't have an alternative, other than "he" or "she." And I've been thinking about the inspiration that the Anishinaabe language offers in this way, and contemplating new pronouns.

TIPPETT: You've been playing with one or two, haven't you?

KIMMERER: I have. I've been thinking about the word "aki" in our language, which refers to land. And there's a beautiful word—"bimaadiziaki," which one of my elders kindly shared with me. It means "a living being of the earth." But could we be inspired by that little sound at the end of that word, the "ki"? And use "ki" as a pronoun, a respectful pronoun inspired by this language as an alternative to "he," "she," or "it," so that when I'm tapping my maples in the springtime, I can say, "We're going to go hang the bucket on ki. Ki is giving us maple syrup this springtime." This, then, of course, acknowledges the being-ness of that tree, and we don't reduce it to an object. It feels so wrong to say that.

And I have some reservations about using a word inspired from the Anishinaabe language, because I don't, in any way, want to engage in cultural appropriation. But this word, this sound, "ki," is, of course, also the word for "who" in French. It turns out that, of course, it's an alternate pronunciation for "chi," for life force, for life energy. I'm finding lots of examples that people are bringing to me where this word also means a living being of the earth.

TIPPETT: That's really interesting.

KIMMERER: The plural pronoun that I think is perhaps even more powerful is not one that we need to be inspired by another language, because we already have it in English, and that is the word "kin."

TIPPETT: That's the plural of "ki"?

KIMMERER: Yes, "kin" is the plural of "ki." So that when the geese fly overhead, we can say, "Kin are flying south for the winter. Come back soon." So that every time we speak of the living world, we can embody our relatedness to them.

TIPPETT: Sustainability is some language we use about the world we're living into or need to live into. And I sense from your writing and especially from your indigenous tradition that sustainability really is not big enough, and that it might even be a cop-out. You didn't use that language, but you're actually talking about a much more generous and expansive vision of relatedness between humans and the natural worlds and what we want to create.

KIMMERER: I am. I agree with you that the language of sustainability is pretty limited. If something is going to be sustainable, its ability to provide for us will not be compromised into the future. And that's all a good thing. But at its heart, sustainability, the way we think about it, is embedded in this worldview that we, as human beings, have some ownership over these, what we call, resources, and that we want the world to be able to continue to keep—that human beings can keep taking and keep consuming.

The notion of reciprocity is really different from that. It's an expansion from that, because what it says is that our role as human people is not just to take from the earth, and the role of the earth is not just to provide for our single species. So reciprocity actually kind of broadens this notion to say that not only does the earth sustain us, but that we have the capacity and the responsibility to sustain her in return. So it broadens the notion of what it is to be a human person, not just a consumer. And there's such joy in being able to do that, to have it be a mutual flourishing instead of the more narrow definition of sustainability so that we can just keep on taking.

TIPPETT: I keep thinking, as I'm reading you and now as I'm listening to you—a conversation I've had across the years with Christians who are going back to the Bible and seeing how certain translations and readings and interpretations, especially of that language of Genesis about human beings being blessed to have dominion—what is it—"to have dominion and subdue the earth," was read in a certain way and in a certain period of time by human beings, by industrialists and colonizers and even missionaries, so there is language, and there's a mentality about taking that actually seemed to have kind of a religious blessing on it. And now people are reading those same texts differently. Do you ever have those conversations with people? Because the tradition you come from would never, ever have read the text that way. So culturally, we are incrementally moving more towards the worldview that you come from.

KIMMERER: I think that that's true, and I think that that longing and the materiality of the need for redefining our relationship with place is being taught to us by the land, isn't it? We've seen that, in a way, we've been captured by a worldview of dominion that does not serve our species well in the long term, and, moreover, it doesn't serve all the other beings in creation well at all.

So we are attempting a mid-course correction here. And I think that it's really important to recognize, that for most of human history, the evidence suggests that we have lived well and in balance with the living world. And it's, to my way of thinking, almost an eyeblink of time in human history that we have had a truly adversarial relationship with nature.

TIPPETT: It seems to me that this view that you have of the natural world and our place in it, it's a way to think about biodiversity and us as part of that, but reciprocity, again, takes that a step farther, right?

KIMMERER: Yes. The idea of reciprocity, of recognizing that we humans do have gifts that we can give in return for all that has been given to us is, I think, a really generative and creative way to be a human in the world. Some of our oldest teachings are saying, what does it mean to be an educated person? It means that you know what your gift is and how to give it on behalf of the land and of the people, just like every single species has its own gift. And if one of those species and the gifts that it carries is missing in biodiversity, the ecosystem is depauperate, the ecosystem is too simple. It doesn't work as well when that gift is missing.

TIPPETT: Here's something you wrote. You talked about goldenrods and asters a minute ago, and you said, "When I am in their presence, their beauty asks me for reciprocity, to be the complementary color, to make something beautiful in response."

KIMMERER: Yes. And I think of my writing very tangibly as my way of entering into reciprocity with the living world. It's that which I can give and it comes from my years as a scientist, of paying close attention to the living world, and not only to their names, but to their songs. And having heard those songs, I feel a deep responsibility to share them, and to see if, in some way, stories could help people fall in love with the world again.

TIPPETT: You remain a professor of environmental biology at SUNY, and you have also created the Center for Native Peoples and the Environment. So that's also a gift you're bringing. You're bringing these disciplines into conversation with each other. I wonder, what is happening in that conversation? How is that working, and are there things happening that surprise you?

KIMMERER: Yes. What we're trying to do at the Center For Native Peoples and the Environment is to bring together the tools of Western science, but to employ them, or maybe deploy them, in the context of some of the Indigenous philosophy and ethical frameworks about our relationship to the earth. One of the things that I would especially like to highlight about that is I really think of our work as, in a sense, trying to indigenize science education within the academy. Because as a young person, as a student entering into that world, and understanding that the Indigenous ways of knowing, these organic ways of knowing, are really absent from academia, I think that we can train better scientists, train better environmental professionals when there's a plurality of these ways of knowing, when Indigenous knowledge is present in the discussion.

We have created a new minor in Indigenous peoples and the environment, so that when our students leave and when our students graduate, they have an awareness of other ways of knowing, they have this glimpse into a worldview which is really different from the scientific worldview. I think of them as just being stronger and have this ability for what has been called "two-eyed seeing," seeing the world through both of these lenses, and in that way, have a bigger toolset for environmental problem-solving.

So much of what we do as environmental scientists—if we take a strictly scientific approach, we have to exclude values and ethics, right? Because those are not part of the scientific method. There's good reason for that, and much of the power of the scientific method comes from the rationality and the objectivity. But a lot of the problems that we face in terms of sustainability and environment lie at the juncture of nature and culture. So we can't just rely on a single way of knowing that explicitly excludes values and ethics. That's not going to move us forward.

TIPPETT: I know this is a fairly new program, but I wonder, are you seeing results that are interesting about how people are applying this, or where they are taking it?

KIMMERER: Well, it's too early to see it, I think, in those scientific and professional metrics, if you will. But what I see is that the students who have become acquainted with these ways of knowing are the natural disseminators of these ideas. They tell me that when they are taking their other classes in conservation biology or wildlife ecology or fisheries, they now feel like they have the vocabulary and the perspective to speak up and say, "Well, when we're designing this salmon management plan, what is the input of native peoples? How will their traditional knowledge help us do better fisheries management?" The invisible knowledge of traditional knowledge has become visible and has become part of the discourse.

TIPPETT: In your book *Braiding Sweetgrass*, there's this line: "It came to me while picking beans, the secret of happiness." [*laughs*] And you talk about gardening, which is actually something that many people do, and I think more people are doing. So that's a very concrete way of illustrating this.

KIMMERER: It is. In talking with my environment students, they wholeheartedly agree that they love the earth. But when I ask them the question of "Does the earth love you back?," there's a great deal of hesitation and reluctance and eyes cast down, like, "Oh, gosh, I don't know. Are we even allowed to talk about that? That would mean that the earth had agency and that I was not an anonymous little blip on the landscape, that I was known by my home place."

So it's a very challenging notion, but I bring it to the garden and think about the way that when we, as human people, demonstrate our love for one another, it is in ways that I find very much analogous to the way that the earth takes care of us, is when we love somebody, we put their well-being at the top of a list, and we want to feed them well. We want to nurture them. We want to teach them. We want to bring beauty into their lives. We want to make them comfortable and safe and healthy. That's how I demonstrate love, in part, to my family, and that's just what I feel in the garden [*laughs*], as the earth loves us back in beans and corn and strawberries. Food could taste bad. It could be bland and boring, but it isn't. There are these wonderful gifts that the plant beings, to my mind, have shared with us. And it's a really liberating idea to think that the earth could love us back, but it also opens the notion of reciprocity, that with that love and regard from the earth comes a real, deep responsibility.

TIPPETT: Yeah. What is it you say? "The large framework of that is the renewal of the world for the privilege of breath." I think that's right on the edge.

KIMMERER: Yes.

TIPPETT: I'm thinking of how, for all the public debates we have about our relationship with the natural world, and whether it's climate change or not, or man-made, there's also the reality that very few people living anywhere don't have some experience of the natural world. changing in ways that they often don't recognize. And in all kinds of places with all kinds of political cultures, where I see people just getting together and doing the work that needs to be done, and becoming stewards, however they justify that or wherever they fit into the public debates or not, a kind of common denominator is that they have discovered a love for the place they come from. That they share. And they may have these same kinds of political differences that are out there, but there's this love of place, and that creates a different world of action. Are there communities you think of when you think of this kind of communal love of place where you see new models happening?

KIMMERER: There are many, many examples. I think so many of them are rooted in the food movement. I think that's really exciting because there is a place where reciprocity between people and the land is expressed in food, and who doesn't want that? It's good for people. It's good for land. So I think movements from tree planting to community gardens, farm-to-school, local, organic—all of these things are just at the right scale, because the benefits come directly into you and to your family, and the benefits of your relationships to land are manifest right in your community, right in your patch of soil and what you're putting on your plate. Just as the land shares food with us, we share food with each other and then contribute to the flourishing of that place that feeds us.

TIPPETT: I want to read something from *Braiding Sweetgrass*. You wrote, "We are all bound by a covenant of reciprocity. Plant breath for animal breath, winter and summer, predator and prey, grass and fire, night and day, living and dying. Our elders say that ceremony is the way we can remember to remember. In the dance of the giveaway, remember that the earth is a gift we must pass on, just as it came to us. When we forget, the dances we'll need will be for mourning, for the passing of polar bears, the silence of cranes, for the death of rivers, and the memory of snow."

That's one of the hard places this world you straddle brings you to. But, again, all these things you live with and learn, how do they start to shift the way you think about what it means to be human?

KIMMERER: The passage that you just read, and all of the experience, I suppose, that flows into that has, as I've gotten older, brought me to a really acute sense, not only of the beauty of the world, but the grief that we feel for it, for her, for ki. That we can't have an awareness of the beauty of the world without also a tremendous awareness of the wounds. That we see the old-growth forest and we also see the clear-cut. We see the beautiful mountain, and we see it torn open for mountaintop removal. So one of the things that I continue to learn about and need to learn more about is the transformation of love to grief, to even stronger love, and the interplay of love and grief that we feel for the world. And how to harness the power of those related impulses is something that I have had to learn.

Main Pathway: Ecologies

Subthemes

Proceed to Decolonization, p. 583
End of Experience
Proceed to Climate Change, p. 583
Proceed to Time, p. 583

39

RUDERAL SOCIETIES

Lois Weinberger

With the idea of a garden with indigenous wildflowers / belonging to the so-called poor soils / plants / mostly growing in the sphere of neglect / living creatures / owing their survival / to the thoughtless interference / the disturbances by man / dependent / I began in 1988 to work on an area within the city limits of Vienna / gradually increasing it to 500 square meters / here driving or walking across / are replaced / by my thinning out the plants / keeping the garden in a state of turmoil / of movement preventing the overpowering spreading of the stronger ones all the way to a monoculture / the growth of bushes and trees that would overshadow everything else / preparing the ground for the germination of the variety of lower plants.

The concern for nature is based beyond the insight / that we are creatures in an inextricable relationship between nature and culture / since nature manifests itself as a sequence of structural links and is always intact / the concern for nature thus aims at the way we deal with ourselves and those around us / also the fact / that loving nature is not the same as being cultured and that in the final consequence this would demand the disappearance of man.

The attitude of precise carelessness / knowledge need not compel action / might allow the necessary concentration / to make us aware of the change in paradigms from interference to attendance.

From uncertainty
Into apparent certainty
To uncertainty

After years of work / such as collecting seeds / raising seedlings and transferring them to suitable spots in the garden / the plant cover closed upon the poor soil / the plants I had thinned out I began to collect in rows of turf pots / in order to take them ever more often to areas at the periphery of the city / to places / that derive their intensity from the possibility of creation / rather than any certainty. I think—of preserving the significance of the spontaneous vegetation growing on compacted soil / among washed-out rubble / loamy soil compressed by thousands of car tyres and the discarded refuse of civilization / where the metropolis gives way to the open landscape / to the plants growing in marginal zones that move ever further out /—of realizing and recognizing / of an appearance / which helped shape us / of their and my history of them.

The hortus vulgare has turned into a locus amoenus and if it had not simultaneously grown into a pulsating spreading cell / contrary to the usual designation / seeing the garden as a symbol and that as a distrust of the authentic being / of that / which was lost to mankind / one might speak of an area that had become corrupted into a graceful place.

A plant grows out of a non-plant / nature remains incomparable and we will perhaps reappear / this is possible without the mind.

Place of unintentional propagation / no sanctuary of sojourn / of pleasure / nothing special / hills and depressions formed by hand / stones set into soil / above which the soaring indicates / points to elevations / down the summer / nothing is dramatic.

The dazzling hues of a blossom cannot be explained / from the green colour and the dark soil / It is the authentic / torn-away flotsam / that is combined with

Resistance / the stoically vegetal separating from the animal / towards the tranquil / towards the complexity of the indetermined / in the guileless sojourn Herbarium.

Connections—separating us from nature—

Those constructions / which language gives rise to through the possibilities of nature developing by themselves / are aesthetic / if this is understood / as a network of applied culture / that absorbs / and reflects / the connecting

The blossom of the chicory

Open around six in the morning

Closing towards noon

Thus nature and natural life / cannot be idealized in its certain awakening / but wherever / its intactness blossoms into the inevitably conducive dying / it motivates to deeds of glorification and their opposite—autistically in the simile.

“Every weed / that survives the winter in our region / is indigenous / but that does not mean that it must be good for us—it simply exists and is here.”

I remember this statement of my father’s about foreign plants brought in with the seeds / weeds / which has successfully fought for decades as a farmer in the Upper Inn Valley / when in 1993 I introduced into my garden of indigenous wildflowers / the first Greek thistles, *Picnomon acama* and *Ptilostemon afer*, grown from seed and intended as free gift to the place / into which I had been born. In the meantime / after moving twelve metres to the southeast / the neophytes have survived their third winter / I am confident.

Main Pathway: Cross-Pollination

Subthemes

Proceed to Diasporas, p. 277
End of Place
Proceed to Time, p. 517

40

SEEKING REFUGE IN THE VEGETAL WORLD

Luce Irigaray and Michael Marder

From my early infancy, the vegetal world has been my favorite dwelling. Undoubtedly, this is the result of the context of my life at that time, but also of some events and of the way humans behaved toward me.

I was born in a little village of coal mines on the border between Belgium and France. My family occupied a company accommodation, provided by the mine where my father worked. My father was half-Belgian and half-Italian, and my mother was two-thirds Belgian and one-third French. They had in common a love of nature and a mining belonging: my father had studied engineering, and he began to work in the mine, the director of which was my mother's father. Neither of them was very demonstrative, but their love of nature and their admiration for my maternal grandfather were obvious. This latter was, also for me, the hero of the family. He was the son of a miner and he himself became a miner at a really young age, after being expelled from high school for his impertinence. While working in the mine, he secretly prepared the entrance examination for the School of Mining Engineering, and he ended up as the director of a mine.

As I was the third child, I was affectionately adopted by this grandfather, the first two children being the favorites of my mother and my father, respectively. My grandfather, too, loved nature very much, and he often took me along for fishing, visiting the nests of birds, or walking in the garden. It is thanks to him that I could

Originally published as "Seeking Refuge in the Vegetal World," *Through Vegetal Being: Two Philosophical Perspectives* (NY: Columbia UP, 2016), 9–13. Reprinted with permission.

undertake my research work: before dying, he asked my parents to promise to accept my desire to study at the university.

I thus spent my childhood in a context in which nature was really valued. Nature was also our main source of recreational activity. As children, we did not have many toys, and we did not wish for more. On and on, we played in nature with what it provided us with. The only fabricated toy that I received brought me more pain than joy: my godmother gave me a magnificent doll, but it was too big, too cold, too rigid—I may as well say too dead—for me, and this gift plunged me into utter despair, which I tried to soothe by playing with animals, above all with rabbits. I behaved with them as with a doll or a baby: I dressed them; I carried them in a small doll carriage; I bottle-fed them, etc. All that was a little demanding, but I was overjoyed with their movements, with their hearts beating, their jumping out of the carriage, their rebellion against my care. They were living! I also devoted much time to butterflies, to ladybugs, to birds, to lambs, and other animals that populated the garden. Perhaps I rediscovered something of a heaven on earth when I preferred life to death. Moreover, it was in the garden that the religious feasts were celebrated: one fir of the garden was used as a Christmas tree, and we had to find the Easter eggs that were hidden in various plants or bushes.

Unfortunately, I was removed from this Garden of Eden by two events: the beginning of my schooling and the preparation for my first communion. These two things made me ill. I fell into a deep tiredness and continuous anxiety, especially into frequent crises of scruples. The little joyful girl of the garden has become a terrified child, withdrawn into herself and with various sensory problems. Finally, my mother got worried about my condition and took me to a specialist who suggested suppressing my homework and sending me into the garden as soon as I returned from school. It was an excellent prescription that, alas! was not accompanied by banning me from going to confession. Hence I recovered only part of my health, my innocence, and my enjoyment from dwelling in the Garden of Eden.

Two other cataclysms happened in my childhood or adolescence when my parents decided to put me in a boarding school or in a summer camp. Each time this ended with being on a hunger strike, something that corresponded to an instinctual gesture more than a conscious decision. Obviously, everyone imagined that my attitude was the result of the absence of my mother, and also, I, myself, believed that it was the case. However, I am not sure that this was the true reason.

The third time the thing happened, when they finally took me back home, my mother was really angry because I had thwarted the plans of the family. I was weak because I had not eaten for some days, but, instead of stretching out her arms and embracing me, she shouted at me: "Go away into the garden!" Amazingly, her behavior did not affect me too much. In the garden, I felt at home and pacified, and I did not ask for more to recover my health. I was just worrying about the possibility that my parents could send me to the boarding school again.

Once more, a pediatrician was my savior, though it was not the case with all the doctors, and later I had to learn how to cure myself. This wise and loving doctor said to my mother, "The girl suffers from a lack of freedom; she needs to attend a day school and not stay locked up in a boarding school." Luckily, for my mother, this prescription became a gospel truth. My everyday life was very hard, because I had to get up very early, to go to the station, and to travel by train for one hour, then walk for one more hour, to finally reach school; and I had to repeat the same journey to return home in the late afternoon. But I was happy with this style of life, which brought me back to my favorite dwelling each evening.

I would like to add, to be historically rigorous, that the event which led to my last hunger strike was the announcement, by letter, at the time when I was still staying at the boarding school, of the death of Moses, a little rabbit that I had saved after it fell into a great basin full of water. Probably I had the feeling that something went wrong with life when I was far away at the boarding school and I had to go back to the garden to care for life itself.

I could give other examples of my need to seek refuge in the vegetal world and ask for assistance from it. Just a little, but significant, event. One day my mother unfairly and heavily punished me for the howls of my little sister. I was still very young, but I left the family home, and even the garden in which the thing happened, and took refuge in the woods, which were a few miles away from there. My mother sent someone to search for me, and it was not so easy to find me and bring me back home. Already at that time, it was not from humans, but from nature that I asked for help.

I also think that my decision, during my first university years, to opt for defending my feminine identity and values against the neutralization of the individual, of discourse, and of thought took part in the same longing for living, instead of subjecting myself to cultural constructions that paralyzed life, its growing and its sharing. All that did not follow from a completely aware decision, but from a will to live, the conditions of which I instinctively sensed, whereas my culture ignored and even scorned them, preferring constructed values, which had become societal customs, over the care and cultivation of life.

Even when I was writing *Speculum*, though my choices were firm and corresponded to a living and ethical embodiment, their foundation was not yet totally clear for me. But who can imagine, for example, that I wrote *Speculum* while sitting in the woods or near the sea, and not in a library? However, this remained a vital necessity, more than a requirement for my thought, at least on an absolutely conscious level. This book had to cause my expulsion from the university, from the school of psychoanalysis in which I had my training, and from the various scientific circles I frequented and where I had my friends, so that I began to wonder about the truth that I was seeking and upholding. Perhaps, in Heideggerian terms, I could say that a bend or a turn—*ein Kehre*—was necessary, so that I glimpsed something of the horizon that my thinking was opening or reopening.

Luce Irigaray

The controversy began almost one year prior to the publication of *Plant-Thinking*. On 28 April 2012, the *New York Times* featured my opinion piece titled "If Peas Can Talk, Should We Eat Them?" in which I discussed the ethical implications of recent research on the capacities of pea plants to communicate to one another through biochemical substances, released into the soil by the roots. There, I envisioned the ethics of caring for vegetal life that would "not dictate how to treat the specimen of *Pisum sativum*, or any other plant," for that matter, but would, rather, "urge us to respond, each time anew, to the question of how, in thinking and eating, to say 'yes' to plants."[1]

During the weeks and months that followed, my argument was attacked by a wide range of dogmatic opponents, from Christian fundamentalists to vegans and from neuroscientists to humanist rationalists. The heated polemics on the place of plants in our culture turned personal, when I received various pieces of correspondence containing suggestions to commit suicide, wishes for my speedy demise, and the like. The anonymous nature of contemporary communication allowed some readers to spill out their unconscious fantasies and desires, for which the dividing line between someone advocating on behalf of vegetal life and that life itself was quite blurred. In retrospect, it has become evident to me that a small portion of the deadly and nihilistic energy that our culture tends to unleash against life ricocheted in my direction. An affirmation of vegetal existence in its own right was much more than this culture could bear because a long time ago—indeed, at its very *roots*—it swapped a caring cultivation for the productive destruction of plants.

What brought certain scientists, philosophers, and religious fanatics together was their forgetting of diverse lives in favor of Life, whether conceived as otherworldly existence, or as an objectively decipherable DNA code, or, again, as the purified and sterile "life of the mind." (The case of vegans was slightly different: they succumbed to a narrow defense of one kind of life, that of animals, at the expense of other kinds of vitality.) It is this forgetting that stands at the source of the grotesque, upside-down world we inhabit, where life-affirming philosophy is perceived as the height of nihilism. A world where concern for plants passes as a lack of care for animals and humans. One where age-old prejudices about the meaning of life and intelligence wear the mask of "common sense" and are counted among the outcomes of "clear, rational thinking."

When *Plant-Thinking* was finally released in the beginning of 2013, the reception of the book was highly polarized. Some readers thought that it heralded a new era in our relation to nonhuman life, while others went so far as to raise suspicions that the book was an elaborate hoax.[2] What exactly is a hoax? In and of itself, the word is rather telling. Via a not-so-veiled reference to a magical *hocus-pocus* (mock Latin), it harkens back to the key phrase of the Catholic Eucharist, *hoc est corpus meum*—"Here is my body." The liturgical transubstantiation of bread into the body of Christ is the etymological source of the hoax, in which someone (say, an author) announces about a body of writing or another kind of work that it is her or his body, while, in fact, it is not. Such disingenuity is especially dangerous to the bourgeois social and political order, in which the first institution of property necessarily passes through the appropriation of the body: in the first instance, my own and, gradually, that of nature, with which I mix the efforts of my labor. A fraudulent *hoc est corpus meum* thus threatens the entire system of the artificial production and reproduction of life that depends on this first, deadening act of appropriation, itself the biggest fraud the world has ever known.

Why were some convinced that *Plant-Thinking* was a hoax? Precisely because the conversion of everything and everyone, including various living beings, into objects to be possessed has donned the appearance of an unquestioned norm. It seemed ridiculous to assert that plants were the subjects of their world, rather than the more or less impassive growing *things*, the role they have been allotted within the tradition of Western metaphysics. Moreover, it seemed strange that recent achievements in European philosophy could be "mapped" onto the ontology of plants, presumably far removed from such haughty notions as freedom or intelligence. Without giving it a second thought, the proponents of the hoax theory assumed that, if it was not an outright prank, the book executed a magical sleight of hand by anthropomorphizing plants or ascribing to them properly human characteristics. The core argument of *Plant-Thinking*—namely, that humans share intelligence and life with plants, from which much of our own thinking and being derive—remained obscured by their superficial reading.

Of course, the real tricksters are the firm believers in the received wisdom of metaphysics. Their signature hoax, responsible for today's predominant worldview, is the act of transubstantiating all forms of life into lifeless property. The ideally disembodied, presumably gender-neutral (though actually masculine) protagonist of metaphysics has not ceased to pronounce his fraudulent *hoc est corpus meum* upon encountering anything and anyone in his environs. Kant's distinction between appropriable things and appropriating persons did little to silence this magical incantation of "dispassionate reason." On the contrary, Kant strengthened the total logic of appropriation by simply sorting beings into its subjects and objects, not to mention by consenting to the inclusion of animals and plants in the category of appropriable things.

The true mystery of the Eucharist lies in the vegetal constitution of the body of god and of the human. To say, about fermented wheat, "this is my body" and, about fermented grapes, "this is my blood" is not to transform them into one's property, let alone into a purely spiritual shadow of nature, but to discover or rediscover oneself in parts of the plant world. *Plant-Thinking* sought the path of this discovery through philosophy rid of its anthropocentric bias, rather than through religion. If many of my fellow philosophers were unwilling to give thoughtful consideration to this alternative, then at least a few of the vanguard scientists and artists were receptive toward the way of relating to and perceiving the vitality of plants I had only begun to sketch out.

Insofar as the book was concerned, its *hoc est corpus meum* was, at times, interpreted as a hoax, meaning that this body of writing itself was deemed to be somehow insincere. That accusation was supposed to function as a barrier preventing my argument from entering the realm of what could be debated in respectable philosophical circles and, more significantly for me, as a prohibition against stating that my body of writing is truly my "own." But what would it mean to stand by one's text? Would it entail coming out on the digital *agora* of cyberspace with the public disclaimer "For me, this book is the truth, the whole truth, and nothing but the truth"? Or are there more complex issues concerning the ethics of appropriation—above all of bodies, be they living and breathing, corpses, or corpuses—in the hoax accusation?

In a culture built on property relations, withholding the possibility of appropriating one's own body and whatever surrounds it is the most basic form of economic and social oppression. The woman, the worker, the animal, and, certainly, the plant are construed as either incapable or undeserving of self-possession and, therefore, as fit for appropriation by others. Since Aristotle, this list also includes all those who do not follow the ground rules of formal logic and whose bodies of writing and thought are therefore little more than a hoax. In the case of Antigone, Creon disallowed her to claim both her own living body and the corpse of her brother, Polynices. Antigone simply could not say *hoc est corpus meum* about herself or about the body of a close family member she wanted to bury. We would be amiss, however, if we assumed that everything could be resolved peacefully and culminate in a happy end if only Antigone were able to appropriate, as a sovereign and autonomous subject, herself and the remains of her dead brother. This is the point the classical interpretation, stressing a symmetrical conflict between human and divine law, inevitably overlooks.

Faced with the corpse of her brother, Antigone does not wish to claim it for herself, that is to say, for her family, tradition, or even in the name of the law she abides by, the law Creon considers to be a hoax. Rather, she wants to dispense it back to the elements and, in particular, to the element that is most appropriate to it, the earth. Much more than a simple desire to restore the "natural order of things," her care for the dead is care for life itself. For instance, by burying Polynices, she aspires to free the air for the living, which is exactly what Creon denies them, insofar as he locks Antigone up in the cave and lets a putrefying body pollute the atmosphere. He uses the very smell of death and the sight of decomposition as the insignia of his power. She asks nothing for herself; *hoc est corpus meum* is not a gesture of appropriation for her. She claims her brother's corpse in order to pass it on to the larger world around her. We can only surmise, since no one but Antigone herself could confirm or deny this hypothesis, that her self-appropriation, the cultivation of her subjectivity, follows the same route of finding herself without disrespecting the elemental realm to which we all belong. (Need I say that *Plant-Thinking* did not elaborate a model for the appropriation of the vegetal world, but only aimed to restitute the body of the plant back to the soul of plants, as chapter 1 of that book makes clear?)

In turn, Creon's order, his law and his word, are nothing but a hoax. He endeavors to take hold of bodies that do not rightfully belong to him, bodies both living and dead, and, through them, to control organic and inorganic nature as such. His pretense is that these bodies are only moved or not moved (as the case may be) by the grace of his own murderous will, which he has surreptitiously substituted for life's plural directionalities. The same applies to our contemporary nihilism, which perpetuates this hoax on a global, if not on a cosmic, scale. To maintain its power, it must be in a position to convince us that the living are actually dead unless endowed with a sufficient dose of negation and self-negation. On this view, plants are the least alive of creatures because they do not contain as much as a trace of self-negation, will, or subjectivity; in a word, they do not belong to themselves. Completely delivered to external appropriation, their vegetal bodies only become animated when they are chopped down, plucked, or culled. On the other hand, those who take the side of this "unmediated" plant life are seen as naive simpletons or, conversely, as the cunning satirists who intend to make a joke out of the bearishly serious status quo.

In the more pessimistic moments, it appears to me that a dialogue between the nihilistic culture forgetful of life and the culture of caring for and cultivating life is impossible. The truth of the latter is a dangerous hocus-pocus in the eyes of the former. A veritable abyss extends between Creon and Antigone. How to dispel this forgetfulness? Simple reminders wouldn't do here, seeing that contemporary nihilism only makes itself still more rigid and closes off the public sphere of debate as soon as alternative views are sounded. When dialogue fails, however, pure violence ensues. Survival becomes, more so than ever before, a matter of struggle, in the course of which some will give up (or will be forced to give up) and at the end of which all might lose because what is now endangered is not just the existence of an isolated human being but the prospects for the survival of life itself.

Instead of sending persistent but fruitless reminders to a culture forgetful of life, we must cultivate a different culture, starting from a drastically new relation to plants. And what would be a better place to start than by taking a deep breath before beginning again?

Michael Marder

NOTES

1. Michael Marder, *The Philosopher's Plant: An Intellectual Herbarium* (New York: Columbia University Press, 2014).
2. Martin Heidegger, "The Origin of the Work of Art," in *Basic Writings*, rev. ed., ed. David Farrell Krell, (New York: Harper and Row, 1993), 139–212.

Main Pathway: Cross-Pollination

Subthemes

Proceed to Experience, p. 227
Proceed to Transcending, p. 227

41

THE GREEN BELT MOVEMENT

Wangari Maathai

As we entered the twenty-first century, the Green Belt Movement (GBM) was experiencing a rebirth through a new strategic plan. Because this plan significantly reorganized GBM, it was perceived as a milestone. Thus, in order to differentiate the activities of the organization prior to the strategic plan from those that were to follow that planning process, the terms Phase I and Phase II, respectively, were introduced.

This book is a record of the Phase I experience. It mainly focuses on the activities of GBM from its beginning up to 1999—the year that the strategic planning commenced. However, to give readers some insight into what lies ahead for the organization, elements of the Phase II plan will be mentioned.

The Green Belt Movement has been functional in Kenya for nearly three decades, and therefore to clearly understand its operations one needs to have some knowledge of the country. A lot of information has already been published on Kenya and need not be repeated here. However, a brief introduction will suffice to highlight the information that is relevant to understanding GBM.

Kenya is located on the eastern coast of Africa and has a size of 582,644 km^2. The capital city is Nairobi. The equator runs across the country and divides it into two nearly equal parts.

Kenya's relief is varied, with altitudes ranging from sea-level to slightly above 5,000 meters. Its relief features include plateaus, plains, highlands, the lake basin,

Excerpts from Wangari Maathai, *The Green Belt Movement: Sharing the Approach and the Experience* (New York: Lantern Books, 2004) have been used with permission.

and the Rift Valley. The natural vegetation in the country falls into four main categories: heath and moorland, savanna grassland, scrub and semidesert, and forest. Currently, the total forested area in Kenya is less than 2 percent; scrub and semidesert covers the largest area, followed by savanna grassland.

The country has a population of approximately 30 million people, with each belonging to one of the 42 communities; although there are many similarities between those communities, each has its unique culture. These communities include the Luo, Kikuyu, Kamba, Luhya, Maasai, Meru, Embu, Somali, and Turkana.

To the north, Kenya is bordered by Sudan and Ethiopia, to the west by Uganda and Lake Victoria, to the south by Tanzania, and to the east by Somalia and the Indian Ocean. These borders were drawn during the colonial rule that Kenya, and most other African countries, underwent from the late nineteenth century up to the early 1960s. Kenya was colonized and ruled by the British until 1963, when it got independence after an armed struggle known as the Mau Mau Movement.

The system of governance that the British introduced during the colonial period is in many ways still used today in various sectors. For instance, the British colonialists divided Kenya into regions so as to better control the Indigenous people. After independence, the new local government decided to maintain these regions (or administrative units), and it is through these units that the people of Kenya continue to be governed.

The largest of these administrative units are the provinces, which are governed by Provincial Commissioners (PC). The provinces are eight in number as listed below.

Central
Coast
Eastern
Nairobi
Northern-Eastern
Nyanza
Rift Valley
Western

The capital city constitutes Nairobi province. Provinces are in turn divided into districts, districts into divisions, divisions into locations, and locations into sub-locations; a sub-location is therefore the smallest administrative unit. A district is governed by a District Commissioner (DC), a division by a Divisional Officer (DO), a location by a Chief, and a sub-location by a Subchief. As of March 1999, there were 68 districts, 483 divisions, 2,354 locations, and 6,431 sub-locations.

When drawing the boundaries for the administrative units, the British colonialists did not consult with the Indigenous people. In some areas the boundaries cut right through communities so that, today, people residing in neighboring provinces are likely to belong to different communities. The Green Belt Movement recognizes this problem but nevertheless uses the current administrative system in its work, since infrastructure and important development services (e.g., government extension workers) base their work upon it.

Kenya is also divided into constituencies. A constituency is the area that an elected Member of Parliament (MP) represents. Currently there are 210 constituencies, many of which have boundaries similar to those of divisions. In some cases, however, constituencies consist of more than one division.

From the mid-sixties until 1992, all MPs had to belong to the one political party, the Kenya African National Union (KANU). In late 1991, however, the movement for multipartism reached its climax with a constitutional change that re-introduced a multi-party political system. From it, two major political factions emerged: the ruling party, and all the other new political parties, which formed, until the end of 2002, what is now commonly referred to as the Opposition.

Depending on the level of development attained, the country is divided into rural and urban areas. At present, a large majority of Kenyans reside in rural areas, which still require much development if the quality of life in those communities is to be enhanced.

In Kenya, rural development is conducted in several ways. But one very common way is through the formation of government-registered development groups. Members of such groups usually reside in the same sub-location and have some commonality (e.g., they have similar occupations, worship in the same church, etc.). There are various reasons why people form groups. These include the desire to raise capital for self-help projects and socialization, or to strengthen ties between family and/or friends. It is important to note that a large majority of the members in such groups are women; this explains why development groups are also commonly referred to as women's groups.

HOW TO ESTABLISH AND RUN A GREEN BELT TREE-PLANTING CAMPING: THE TEN-STEP PROCEDURE

Over the years, many people have inquired about how to initiate a tree-planting campaign similar to that of the Green Belt Movement. Though it is a good question, it is by no means an easy one to answer because there exists no blueprint for GBM; rather, it achieves its objectives by formulating and revising its strategies until efficiency is achieved and outputs are attained. Because the ability to streamline and fine-tune strategies comes with experience, GBM encourages those interested in establishing similar initiatives to adopt its methodology, modify it as necessary, and then implement it—preferably on a small scale in the initial stages.

THE TEN-STEP PROCEDURE FOR A POTENTIAL INITIATOR

A detailed description of the ten-step procedure is laid out to help you, the initiator, to establish a tree-planting initiative similar to that of the Green Belt Movement.

Step 1: Information Dissemination to Raise Public Awareness and Establish Contact with Groups

If you, the initiator, intend to work at the grassroots level, you may find that many people will be ignorant about issues of environmental degradation and conservation, sustainable development, tree nursery management, and even tree planting. Though a few may be aware of the effects of environmental degradation (e.g., desertification, soil erosion, gullies, malnutrition, disease, etc.), you may still find them ignorant of the linkages between these effects and their causes. The reasons for this are numerous and include the belief that environmental calamities are acts of God.

Therefore, it is important to disseminate information with an aim to raise public awareness on the primary causes of environmental degradation, and on the importance and benefits of conservation. For such campaigns, messages can be spread through popular media such as newspapers, radio and television and through community meetings, seminars and workshops. One should also take advantage of community gatherings such as local administration meetings, church services and so on.

Step 2: Group Formation

In many of the less developed countries, community members usually organize themselves into groups for development purposes. It is important for the initiator to evaluate the ability of the existing systems of organization in a community to conduct the project. It is counterproductive to ask people to form new groups if they have already established other more effective and sustainable ways of organizing themselves. The advantage of working with groups is that a large section of the community (or stakeholders) is mobilized. In addition, such a project stands a greater chance of success when its operations do not heavily rely on a small minority. If it becomes essential to form groups, it is important to allow them to form freely—without coercion—since that is essential for the cohesion and dynamics of groups. When forming groups, members are encouraged to elect their leaders through secret ballot to encourage democratic decision making. If they do not already have a bank account, they are encouraged to establish one and identify signatories, since GBM normally pays groups through checks.

To assist them to focus and also operate efficiently, it is very important to provide group members with enough information about the nature of the project at this stage. This includes the goals of the project, methodology, inputs, risks, expected short- and long-term outputs, and benefits. For the establishment of tree nurseries, groups need to be informed of the preparatory work, which includes searching for seeds and cuttings, transplanting seedlings, supervising work at the nursery site, record-keeping, and carrying out follow-ups.

Providing people with information during group formation avoids misunderstandings that could arise as a result of ignorance on the part of group members or because of greed. The initiator should consider drawing up a constitution, or simply laying down a set of rules to be agreed on and to guide all stakeholders. Language is also important. GBM prefers to use the language that most stakeholders understand. Unless there are restrictions, it is recommended that the initiator adopt the same trend. If the groups still need assistance with communication (e.g., filling out forms), community leaders such as schoolteachers can be very helpful, and indeed they have been helpful in GBM for many years.

Step 3: Locating a Tree-Nursery Site and Registration of Tree-Nursery Groups

Once a group is formed, the members look for an appropriate piece of land to establish their green belt. If they decide to use public land and find themselves in need of assistance, encourage them to seek advice from the local administrators and other leaders, such as councilors, chiefs, and community development officers. GBM prefers to set up nurseries on public land because that way, all members are free to visit the nursery and work on it.

Step 4: Physical Establishment of a Tree Nursery

Preparing the nursery site includes digging trenches, making terraces, laying seedbeds, and building fences. Though groups are able to do much of this work on their own, it is always good to solicit the help of resource persons such as foresters, agricultural extension officers, or experienced members of GBM in neighboring areas. It is very important for groups to learn how to prepare and manage their tree nurseries properly because this determines the success of the entire project.

Without unnecessarily burdening group members with complex procedures and details, these resource persons should teach basic tree-nursery techniques that group members can quickly adopt and practice. For the benefit of conservation of local biological diversity, tree-nursery groups should be encouraged to grow indigenous trees. However, experience has shown that groups will grow seedlings that meet the felt needs of communities even when such seedlings are not appropriate for conservation of local biological diversity. Therefore, it is important to remind the groups and the community at large that conservation is important for the benefit of long-term community goals, including those of future generations.

The nurseries receive plastic bags into which to transplant the seedlings. However, because resources are often limited, methods of improvisation need to be shared with the groups at this stage. For instance, many GBM group members refrain from throwing out suitable polythene bags, tins, and other containers from their homes and instead transplant seedlings into them. This keeps the nursery operational and also helps recycle some of the household "trash."

Step 5: Reporting on the Progress of the Nursery

GBM requires that all groups send in progress reports on a monthly basis. For this reason, each nursery is required to have a tree-nursery attendant to help women to collect data and compile reports. In these reports, the groups indicate the number and types of seedlings (indigenous, exotic, or fruit) that are in the nursery, the number that are ready to be issued to members of the public, and any obstacles that they face at the nursery. Such communications are essential because they maintain the link between the groups and headquarters and inform those at the headquarters on the progress being made by the groups.

Step 6: Promotion of Tree Planting to the Community and Digging of Holes

When tree-nursery groups have sufficient seedlings that are ready for issue to the public, they make announcements in public gatherings such as church services and schools, in barazas (or local administration meetings), and also through house visits; this exercise is called promotion.

During promotion, the tree-nursery group members request those interested in planting trees to dig holes with diameters and depths of about two feet. After the holes are inspected and approved by a member of a given tree nursery, the seedlings are issued. Community members willing to plant trees but unaware of what GBM recommends are instructed by the mini-advisor, nursery attendant, or any group member. The instructions include basic techniques like ensuring that seedlings are removed from plastic containers before planting, containers are recycled, and manure is applied to the holes where soils are poor.

Step 7: Establishment of Public and Private Green Belts

GBM defines a "green belt" as a woodlot established by planting several trees on a piece of land that can either be public or private. To establish a public green belt, one should aim at planting at least one thousand trees, while a private one should aim for at least one hundred trees. The reason for giving these targets was to encourage the groups to plant trees in large numbers. However, some public and private green belts have been established with fewer trees, while others have thousands more.

Public Green Belts

Any public institution that wishes to join the organization can contact any local tree nursery group or GBM field-staff member for details on the procedure.

Those involved in the establishment of green belts are encouraged to form an elected green belt committee to oversee it and to identify a community member, preferably handicapped, to help nurture it; this person is known as a Green Belt Ranger. GBM supports the green belt by providing garden tools and water tanks as a token of appreciation and incentive. These tools are initially used by the ranger but eventually become the property of the public institution. When green belts are established on school compounds, teachers are encouraged to fully involve students in the planting and nurturing processes.

Private Green Belts

Any individual who wishes to establish a private green belt is also requested to contact the local tree-nursery group or field staff in the area for details. Seedlings are issued, free of charge, only after a group member has confirmed that holes have been dug. GBM does not provide tools to facilitate a private green belt since the organization prefers to work with the larger community as opposed to individuals.

In the past, GBM provided seedlings, at no charge, for the establishment of both public and private green belts. Recently, however, it was suggested that GBM encourage the women's groups to sell their seedlings directly to community members as a way of generating income to sustain their nurseries and avoid dependency on the organization. Those who have received free seedlings from GBM nurseries have generally been appreciative of the work of the women and the organization. While recognizing the need for the women to commercialize their tree nurseries, GBM remains apprehensive of the ability of poor rural communities to purchase seedlings from the groups and maintain the tree-planting campaign at the same level and quality of performance.

Step 8: Planting Trees and Follow-Up

During the rainy seasons, farmers flock to the tree-nursery sites to collect seedlings for planting. The group members then do follow-up on the seedlings twice after they are planted. The first follow-up is done after one month, and the second and final one is done after three months. This follow-up exercise is conducted to check on how the seedlings are progressing and to collect data for office records.

Step 9: First Follow-Up for Seedlings

The objective of the first follow-up is to ensure that the seedlings that were issued were indeed planted and that this was properly done. This must be done as soon as possible—even within days—but not later than one month after planting.

Promoters as well as group members are encouraged to follow up their seedlings for up to three months before the first payment is recommended by the monitor.

Step 10: Second Follow-Up and Payment of Groups

The second follow-up was given a minimum of six months to ensure that the seedlings were established and therefore likely to survive. Information gathered in the course of follow-up is forwarded to the headquarters through forms that are used for monitoring the tree-planting campaign. At the headquarters the forms are checked by monitors who, if satisfied with the information provided, approve GBM's purchase of the seedlings through payment by checks to the concerned groups and support staff. GBM pays the groups for only those seedlings that are surviving at the time of the second follow-up because these plants are not as vulnerable and can therefore survive with little or no attention.

Main Pathway: Ecologies

Subthemes

Proceed to Decolonization, p. 593
Proceed to Climate Change, p. 593
End of Time

42

SORELY VISIBLE: PLANTS, ROOTS, AND NATIONAL IDENTITY

Giovanni Aloi

Milan, February 18, 2017—a few minutes after midnight, flames engulfed a cluster of trees in Piazza del Duomo. Committing arson was a group of nationalist protesters, who fled the scene through the semi-deserted piazza, rushing down the Galleria Vittorio Emanuele in the direction of the Scala Theater.

It was all announced a day earlier, on Facebook, by the neo-fascist group Azione Identitaria (Identitarian Action). They describe themselves as a patriotic and militant cultural movement in defense of Italian, regional, and European identity. The post, widely disseminated online by news outlets, clearly connoted the gesture as political. The aim, as they said, was not to hurt the plants, but to send a clear representational statement—a stark sign in opposition to the "Africanization of Italy."

Milan's most common trees are deciduous planes, acers, horse chestnuts, poplars, gingkoes, and magnolias—a varied cohort of versatile and mostly non-native varieties imported and established over centuries of botanical conversation with other parts of the world. But it was palms that Azione Identitaria set alight.

Those familiar with the hustling and bustling northern Italian mini-metropolis might be surprised to hear of palm trees in the first place. Although not indigenous to the Italian peninsula, palm trees have for long been a staple of many southern cityscapes. From Palermo to Naples, and Rome, palms are a common sight on *lungomare* promenades and in public piazzas. But Milan's cold and dark winters badly

Originally published as "Sorely Visible: Plants, Roots, and National Identity," *Plants, People, Planet* 1, no. 3, 204–211. Reprinted with permission.

suit the needs of these monolithic trees. Despite climatic challenges, a few rare palms have been living in the northern metropolis since the end of the 19th century, most often sheltered in the high-society courtyards of the city's historic center. I remember, as a child, peering through a corrugated gate to catch a glimpse of their fronds covered in snow; it was as close as real-life could ever get to Fellinian cinematic magic.

However, the palm trees in Piazza del Duomo are a brand-new addition, part of a marketing campaign orchestrated by Starbucks, the ubiquitous American coffee company founded in Seattle at the beginning of the 1970s and today counting 26,696 locations worldwide (Starbucks, 2017). The 42 palms, along with a grove of 50 banana trees, were intended as a gift to the city: a celebration on the occasion of the opening of their first coffee shop in the country.

As it is well known, in Italy coffee is a very serious business. Sacrosanct rituals and traditions few dare to disrupt make coffee an essential pillar of Italianicity. For many years, the notion of takeaway coffee was deemed heretical, and just the thought of hybridized drinks like the Frappuccino gave espresso purists many caffeine-unaided sleepless nights. But times change. During the early 1980s, fast food seemed an impossible proposition for the country that invented the Mediterranean diet. However, today, Italy boasts 560 McDonald's restaurants, 340 McDrive, and 320 McCafé (McDonald's.it). So, only time will tell if the country will drink the Seattle experience when its much anticipated first store opens in the autumn of 2018.

The exotic grove positioned on the west side of the Piazza del Duomo is the result of a collaboration with Italian architect and urban-green expert Marco Bay. Interviewed soon after the arson, Bay vehemently defended his installation. "The exotic grove was meant to 'surprise, seduce, and disorient' and the installation is not permanent," the architect said. Unless an official renewal is granted by the city, the trees will be removed and relocated by the end of 2019 (Marsala, 2017). But so far, it seems that, the exotic grove might have failed to seduce the city as much as the architect hoped, and it certainly has (not positively) surprised many. The suspicion remains that the provocation was well planned in advance. But what Bay might have underestimated in this case is the ability plants have to ignite heated debate on Italian national identity.

PLANTS, ARCHITECTURE, AND AESTHETIC APPROPRIATENESS

I first learned about these events not from the news, but over a phone call with my parents, who still live in Milan, where I was born. My mother said: "They are planting palm trees in Piazza del Duomo! And bananas too! Everyone's arguing about it." I have to admit that my immediate response was of surprise—I struggled to envision how the tropical lushness of palms and banana trees would come into dialogue with the elegantly cold and chiseled façade of the gothic Duomo and the neoclassical architecture of the surrounding buildings. I immediately searched online to find an image; and there it was. Palms and bananas facing the Duomo, lined up like a silent but resilient army. Nature and culture facing each other: the refined spiritual intricacy of pure pale marble confronted by the raw flourishing of exotic trees. For a few moments, I struggled with the aesthetic incongruity.

It was at that very point that I realized something interesting was happening and that I needed to explore in more depth my own reaction to the images. The news of tree-planting in big cities has always brought me joy. But this instance made me realized that I never lingered too long over questions of supposed appropriateness in relation to species and geographical locations—as an immigrant myself, I find "native" a problematic concept since it is haunted by dangerous contradictions and problematic assumptions. But I realized that my initial surprise to the news wasn't necessarily linked to ecological appropriateness, but *aesthetic appropriateness*, instead. I began to wonder if the vertical solemnity of cypresses, albeit less exuberant, might have been a better fit for the square's history and heritage. The cracks in my thinking began to show. I started to notice how my line of thinking was implicitly frameworked by outdated notions of urbanistic conservation. The feelings were conflicted: I love palm trees and bananas—they remind me of the long summers spent as a child in Calabria, the Italian irredeemable deep south with its bursting flavors, rich traditions, and seemingly insurmountable social problems. So why was I even dwelling over the appropriateness of bananas and palms outside Milan's beloved cathedral? Where was this feeling that "plants might have been put in the wrong place" originating from?

I began to question my aesthetic assumptions further. If an appropriateness of style that binds plants to architecture exists, and if this appropriateness is dictated by our choice to situate plants in specific urban realities, then this aesthetic assumption must be supported by an ideology. After all, curating tree-planting for a national monument is more complex than choosing trees for a trafficked, urban lane—the criteria are different. History and aesthetics intertwine in the conversation established between plant and monument in the production of complex identity paradigm emerging from a perceived continuity between nature and culture. I found the idea intriguing, but I also wondered why this had never occurred to me before.

Today, everything upsets and offends someone, somewhere; and that someone's voice will be heard everywhere through social media. The polarization of politics and cultural discourses pervading the West is inviting closer, sometimes obsessive, scrutiny of representational dimensions in everyday life, not just in the arts. Appropriation, for instance, is more problematic now than it has ever been at the height of postmodernism. Similarly, new constrictions have been placed on the authorial voice—who can say what, and to whom?

But perhaps, and somewhat worryingly, we all seem to be interested in purity like never before. This manifests into a "pseudo-Christian" sense of coherence, guilt, and originality that, I believe, might be at least in part generated by the overwhelming multiplicity of social-media viewpoints and voices that saturate our everyday lives. The constant shifting of cultural parameters, the schizophrenic embracing and rejecting of globalization (we have to equally love "global" and "local"); what my generation experiences today makes idealizations of childhood stronger and vivid. The suspicion that this might be true emerges when, in comparison to today, the 1980s resembles an island of peace, style, and decorum. It is in this context that a dangerous melancholia for a time that never was swells the spirits of those who (from other European countries to the US and the UK) vehemently claim to "want their countries back."

More than ever we are obsessed with our roots, traditions, and ancestry as essentially anchors to ever more fictitious identity emblems. With the recent increase of terrorist attacks across Europe and growing unease with seemingly uncontrollable waves of immigration, it is perhaps no surprise that nationalistic spirits are on the rise. Borders, boundaries, and perimeters thus become even more important when walls are being built not so much to keep someone out but to keep oneself in.

Piazzas are essential historical and political constituents of most cities. In the West, more directly, piazzas also are the contemporary incarnation of the Greek *agora*: the political and commercial heart of the social fabric. In the agora, the athletic, artistic, spiritual, and political life of the city manifested in ways that feed into the formation of a shared social identity. Piazza del Duomo in Milan is no exception. It has a long history of which the city is particularly proud. Its inception dates back to the 14th century and it is intertwined with the prestigious medieval glories of the Visconti dynasty which ruled the city for 170 years (1277–1447). Along with the Sforza, which followed, the Visconti promoted a substantial urban regeneration that promoted the arts to rival the nearby Venice and Florence (Longhi, 1958).

Milan has always suffered from a "second-city" inferiority complex of a sort towards other Italian capitals of culture with deeper histories and more ostentatious artistic beauty. Because of its geographical situation, Milan has always been a functional crossroad and strategic post. And during the last century, it became Italy's most powerful industrial capital, gaining a reputation as one of the least culturally interesting and greyest cities in Italy. Therefore, the Duomo is its jewel—a major historical and architectural accomplishment that characterizes the city's uniqueness in ways that simultaneously separate it from the rest of the peninsula. Because of its geographical situation and the range of northern influences it was exposed to, Milan has always fancied itself as almost-French or/and almost-German rather than seeing itself as linked to Rome and Naples.

The construction of the Duomo began in 1386. Rayonnant Gothic, a markedly French architectural style, was chosen to underline the cultural difference between Milan, Venice, and Florence. French engineers Nicholas de Bonaventure and Jean Mignot were in charge of the early construction stages of a project that will take 579 years to conclude, in 1965. For centuries, the rare pink marble of Candoglia, quarried in Piedmont, was shipped to the heart of Milan aboard large barges. For this purpose, Leonardo da Vinci perfected the city's canal network between 1482 and 1489, designing a complex system of dams and locks which further facilitated commerce (Valentini, 2017).

Towards the end of the 16th century, as a cultural rejection of foreign influences began to emerge, Archbishop Carlo Borromeo turned towards more Renaissance-/Italian-inspired aesthetics (Ackerman, 1949). The eclectic result, which elegantly combines Gothic, Romanic, Renaissance, Baroque, and Neo-Gothic, stands as a testament to a persevering city capable of accomplishing impossible feats through means that victoriously bypass any cultural or technological dependency from Rome, the Italian capital Milan has always rivaled. Given its rich history and pronounced emancipatory cultural value for a city that has always looked at Rome with disdain, it is perhaps no surprise that Piazza del Duomo would easily become a neuralgic point for identity-based issues.

CULTURAL FRAGMENTATION

The negative sentiments revealed by the appearance of palm and banana trees are perhaps best understood in this context, but also in view of the ever-changing cultural shifts that can be mapped around the square itself. As a place for congregation, the piazza has become a point of reference for the many ethnicities that since the late 1970s have arrived in Milan from North Africa, the Philippines, and Eastern Europe. It is not uncommon, especially during the evening hours, to encounter different ethnic groups spending the evening chatting away and drinking in the open air while listening to music. But Italy's relationship to other ethnicities has recently become more complicated, starting from the common use of the legal-bureaucratic and very discriminatory term *extracomunitario*. The word, which literally translates into "extracomunitarian," was originally introduced in the 1980s to designate a subject whose legal standing does not include citizenship to the European Union. However, the term has more generally been used to designate non-white illegal immigrants from Africa and the Middle East. The term has thus become a popular tool of segregation—it's a stamp of shame; a major barrier interfering with any possibility to integrate those who are not yet part of the community.

In this context, it is also important to remember that, despite the history of its famous cities, Italy was only unified in 1861. Its past as a fragmentary conglomeration of regions and city-states characterized by extremely different dialects and traditions still shows its cracks. The cultural unification of Italy has effectively been operated by TV networks—the state-run RAI TV, in the first instance, and Berlusconi's Mediaset, thereafter, during the 1980s. Since the unification, language and customs have erected insurmountable barriers between north and south. The south has been perceived by the north as an underdeveloped and parasitic part of the country. This has led to an internal system of discrimination and hate that eventually produced the Lega Nord political party. Initially ridiculed by many, during the early 1990s, the Lega Nord has relentlessly campaigned for the independence of the North, including economically powerful regions like Piedmont to Tuscany, and has today also become a Eurosceptic leading voice at the government. At the 2018 elections, the right-wing populist party gathered 17.4 percent of the vote, becoming the third largest party in Italy (Brighi, 2018).

Representatives of the Lega Nord have been no strangers to racist statements and other discriminatory controversies. In 2013, Cécile Kashetu Kyenge, the first Black government Minister of Integration (2013–14) was publicly likened to an orangutan by a Lega Nord senator (Jones, 2013). It was therefore not much of a surprise to find delegates of the Lega Nord protesting the palms and bananas with a banner reading "No to the Africanization of Piazza Duomo." With them, also waving banana-inflatables, were representatives of CasaPound, an openly neo-fascist party currently gaining popularity in Italy. Both groups have unequivocally interpreted the exotic trees as an "invitation to African immigrants," a sort of welcome statement (Ema, 2017).

ITALY, COLONIALISM, AND PROPAGANDA

Italy's relationship with immigration has always been complex and contradictory. The waves of emigration that marked the history of the country never seem to play an important cultural role in the contemporary memories of those who object to the arrival of migrants. The Italian diaspora that began with its unification in 1861 has permanently relocated abroad over 25 million citizens, who, in many circumstances, were ghettoized and marginalized in their destination countries (Ben-Ghiat and Malia-Hom But, 2016). It could as well be that the fraught relationship between Italy and immigration has its roots firmly planted in a nearly forgotten, and yet all-important, chapter of the country's history. Could it be that the arrival of the exotic plants in Milan's beloved piazza has awoken uncomfortable memories of the country's short-lived colonialist period? In 1890, Italy conquered its first colony: Eritrea (Murtaza, 1998). Libya was invaded in 1911. In 1936, the conquest of Ethiopia by means of illegal chemical weapons also brought along a set of laws against the "*meticciato*": the bastardization of the Italian race. This preventive measure applied to Italian soldiers and civilians in the colonies of Ethiopia and Somalia (Strazza, 2012). New propagandist messages aimed at de-coupling previously incited notions of colonialist and sexual conquest by casting Black women as disease-ridden undesirables. In this context, preserving the presumed purity of the Italian race entailed dissuading soldiers from entertaining sexual relationships with them or committing rape (Palma, 2002).

It is also at this time that theories on the inherent inferiority of Black people were articulated in Italy by anthropologist Lidio Cipriani. In his book *Ethnical Absurdity: The Ethiopian Empire*, Cipriani overtly likened the "Black race" to the state of sub-human animals. (Cipriani, 1935, p. 181). Meanwhile, on Italian soil, brothels became subject to stricter racial regulations; and abroad, the government actively began recruiting white, Italian prostitutes (referred to in the official paperwork as "secretaries") to entertain soldiers in the colonies (Strazza, 2012). The cultural propaganda that conditioned Italians during the 1930s was by no means an isolated case, and it can be better understood in the context of the broader racial discriminations that impacted other nations involved in much broader and more successful colonialist efforts.

Fast-forward to 2018: Italy finds itself, along with Spain and Greece, at the center of a vulnerable position within the EU. As one of the closest and most accessible ports to waves of immigrants traveling to Europe in search of better futures, Italy has recently received over 100.000 immigrants per year from Mali, Guinea, the Ivory Coast, and Nigeria (BBC, 2018). The loss of life caused by the sinking of overcrowded vessels has made headlines around the world, and the EU continues to deny Italy financial help, or to evenly share immigrant intake. This scenario hardly helps racial integration in a country that, more or less, has been defined by a sequence of political and economic crises for over thirty years.

In 2018, news that a vessel carrying 629 migrants had been refused safe harbor on Italian shore was gaining attention online. This was the first, clear statement of the new populist government stance on immigration (American Free Press [AFP], 2018).

ROOTS AND FIXITY

The fixity of plants has often been metaphorically used to visualize the essence of presumed human-fixity: to truly belong to one or another continent or land. To set roots in one place has for long meant to live and develop a coherent life based on a commitment to ones' own local customs and ideals. However, these rhetorical notions of fixity couldn't be more fictitious when applied to the versatility of real plants; how they can, sometimes very easily, spread across new geographical territories, often adapting to less than congenial climatic conditions. Plants are not static. They travel—in fact, instead of focusing on the fixity of the individual, concentrating on plants' ability to disperse and migrate might allow us to let go of erroneously naturalized conceptions that only really exist in the markedly human fear of the Other. Simply put, plants are the ultimate migrant.

While far-right innuendos of "Let's bring in the monkeys" or "Now the Africanization of Milan is complete: Illegal immigrants will finally feel at home" dominated the news, a left-wing group named Sentinelli di Milano (Milan's Guardians) organized a humorous counter-protest on Palm Sunday. They invited citizens to bring with them "a plant, a fruit, or a vegetable of any form, colour, or provenance to say: we support diversity" (Mattioli, 2017). Let's be clear: never before in Italian history have botanical species functioned as such charged political catalysts. However, as it happens, phyto-histories are never linear, and more often than not their entanglements with transhistorical human–non-human networks produce ambiguously polysemic opportunities.

The original title of Marco Bay's palm and bananas installation was *Milanese Tropical Forest* (Mattioli, 2017). This was revised by the city government to the current *Milanese Garden Between XIX and XX Centuries*. The request for a title change is perhaps indicative of an initial sense of unease with the overtly tropical connotation of the project. Instead, the final title justifies (or perhaps dilutes) Bay's cultural operation as a reference or re-staging of the palm trees that once stood in Piazza del Duomo during the second half of the 19th century.

The ambiguity linked to the title of the installation is further problematized by the complex histories of the species in question. Despite their seemingly naturalized roots, cultural identities can be substantially shaped by rather short but intensely exposed representational constructions. Bananas, for instance, have only become popular in Europe since the 1870s. The plant is not native to Africa, as many might believe, and its long history of domestication spans many ethnic groups from around the world. It is believed that farmers in Papua New Guinea and Southeast Asia first began to select and cultivate banana trees since 600 BCE. Subsequently, Indian traders traveling through Malaysia brought the plant to India, where, in 327 BCE, it was collected by Alexander the Great, who took it back with him to the Western world. Meanwhile, bananas spread to southern regions of China, where different varieties have been selected since 200 BCE. Around 650 CE, Muslim traders important the plant to Africa and crossbred two varieties, *Musa acuminata* and the *Musa baalbisiana*. During the Renaissance, banana trees travelled to Italy for ornamental purposes but were the exclusive possession of the extremely rich; meanwhile, Portuguese sailors discovered bananas in West Africa and established the first banana plantations in the Canary Islands. Thereafter, bananas were exported to Latin America and the Caribbean. The Cavendish variety, which is most commonly available on today's market, is a crossbred variety engineered in the Duke of Devonshire's Victorian hothouse, not in Africa (Bynum and Bynum, 2014, p. 160). The plant is currently grown across the globe in over 150 countries, from the Caribbean to Central America and South America; to West Africa, the Philippines, and Australia. Since the current edible varieties are seedless cultivars, propagation of plants is only possible through side shoots and roots. This long genealogy technically makes bananas a "transhistorical living sedimentation" of many different peoples and geographies.

Despite its rich and deep history, its univocal connection to Africa in the eyes of contemporary Italians may spring from the country's colonialist past. Bananas consumed in Italy between the 1930s and the 1950s came from the colonial Italian-Somalia town of Genale, which vastly strengthen the associated racial and geographical connotation that characterizes the fruit in today's imagery (Houtkamp, 1996).

The distinctive, straight, and unbranched morphology that characterizes over 2,600 species of palms around the world is today universally recognized as a marketing emblem for the leisure-time paradise. Palms thrive in tropical and subtropical climates around the world; therefore, different species can be found in Southern Asia, South America, Northwest Mexico, and the Arabian Peninsula. The history of their domestication does not begin in Africa either, as records show that early cultivation of palms took place in the Middle East 5,000 years ago. From palm oil to dates, coconut, and raffia for rope-making, palms have provided and still provide substantial sustenance and resources.

Only two species of palms indigenous to the Mediterranean area exist: *Chamaerops humilis* and *Phoenix theophrasti*. Other varieties, like *Phoenix dactylifera*, came to Italy during the 19th century. Between the second half of the 18th and 19th centuries, a growth in the interest for exotic plants led to the establishment of climatization gardens in Tuscany, where more varieties of palms could be studied. The Orientalist and Primitivist waves that characterized the nineteenth century and the Italian colonial spell of the 1930s and 1940s both reignited the interest for the cultivation and dissemination of palms in Italy (Moggi, 2012). It is at this time that colonialist ambitions established a more visible cultural connection between palm trees and Africa in the Italian imaginary. The more frequent extraction of palm oil from *Elaeis guineensis*, a species of palm native to west and south-west Africa further popularized the plant as the emblem of an exotic world to conquer, subjugate, and exploit.

But more than that of banana trees, palm's history is also defined by the symbolic values of immortality, triumph, peace, victory, and spirituality—palms are mentioned more than 30 times in the Bible and 22 times in the Quran. In this case, too, the palm is a "transhistorical living sedimentation" of many peoples and geographical realities rather than a specific anchor to a defined notion of national identity.

However, it is likely that the right-wing protesters' conception of palms might conflate multiple alterities. Not only, in their words, has the tree been reduced to a symbolization of the African continent and its people, but the widespread presence of palms in the southern regions from Rome to Palermo makes it the emblem of what right-wing protesters also perceive as an ultimately inferior Italy they would rather separate from. Pejorative comparisons between Italy's South and Africa have been a frequent recurrence through the rise to power of Lega Nord and have been frequently used in order to support their case for secession. At a parliament meeting in 2013, a Lega representative stated: "I believe that Garibaldi has united Italy while at the same time dividing Africa: There are places in our country that resemble Africa where the mentality and economic reality don't match the productivity of the North" (Palma, 2013).

In observing how specific plant species have become a catalyst for racial tensions in the country, it is also important to consider another factor: climate change.

It is now appearing more and more clear that the fixity of plants as a species incarnating the natural essence of a specific geographical area is the result of a persistent myopic perspective on plant evolution and climatic shifts. Plants infiltrate new suitable territories at every opportunity, utterly disrespecting legal or historical borders. Recent research led by Dr. David Greenwood at Brandon University in Canada has, for instance, expanded our understanding of the range and evolutionary speed of palms. Sixty-five-million-year-old fossils of palm leaves found in Alberta demonstrate how different climatic conditions in the Palaeocene enabled palms to thrive much farther north than originally known (Brandon University, 2017).

More than a year after their arrival, the palms and the bananas of Piazza del Duomo are thriving, and the bananas are now bearing fruit (AFP, 2018). The controversy has quieted down, and Chiquita, a well-known, Swiss producer and distributor of bananas, has seized the opportunity to promote the consumption of the fruit through performances and initiatives dotting the square. It remains unclear if the trees will be allowed to remain in place after the end of 2019, when, according to the terms of the original commission, they should be removed. Will public debate reignite once more at that time? Will the right-wing protesters joyfully exult? Regardless, this alleged misplacement of plant species has caused an important short-circuiting of intertwined histories of people and plants. It has demonstrated how important plants can be in the politics of identity construction and how they operate in the context of important conceptions like "native" and "other" lurking beneath notions of cultural and aesthetic appropriateness. But most importantly, instances such as these, in which plants become sorely visible, reveal important chains of inferences that, if untangled, might shed light on our everyday relationship with plants, other peoples, and our past and future histories.

REFERENCES

Ackerman, J. 1949. "'Ars Sine Scientia Nihil Est.' Gothic Theory of Architecture at the Cathedral of Milan." *Art Bulletin* 31, no. 2: 96.

American Free Press. 2018. "Milano, spuntano i primi frutti dei banani in Duomo: Guardare ma non mangiare." *La Repubblica*, May 31, http://milano.repubblica.it/cronaca/2018/05/31/foto/milano_frutto_banani_piazza_duomo-197813513/1/#1.

American Free Press. 2018. "Immigrants in Italy: A Look at the Numbers." *Yahoo News*, June 11, https://www.yahoo.com/news/immigrants-italy-look-numbers-154001793.html.

Azione Identitaria, http://www.azioneidentitaria.it/sample-page/.

BBC News. 2018. "Matteo Salvini: Interior Minister's Claims about Immigration." *BBC News*, https://www.bbc.com/news/world-44397372.

Ben-Ghiat, R., and S. Malia-Hom. 2016. *Italian Mobilities.* London: Routledge.

Brandon University. 2017. "Brandon University Professor Makes Important Canadian Palm Discovery." https://www.brandonu.ca/news/2017/01/12/brandon-university-professor-makes-important-canadian-palm-discovery/.

Brighi, E. 2018. "Do Not Misunderstand the Significance of the Five Star Movement's Electoral Victory." *Huffington Post*, March 6, https://www.huffingtonpost.co.uk/entry/italy-elections_uk_5a9e4f85e4b0a0ba4ad75a8e.

Bynum, H., and W. Bynum. 2014. *Remarkable Plants That Shape Our World*. Chicago: University of Chicago Press.

Cipriani, L. 1935. *Un Assurdo Etnico: l'Impero Etiopico*. Florence: R. Bemporand & Figlio Editori.

Ema, R. S. 2017. "Milano: Le palme che favoriscono l'immigrazione." *Ultima Voce*, https://www.ultimavoce.it/milano-palme-duomo/.

Houtkamp, J. A. 1996. *Tropical Africa's Emergence as a Banana Supplier in the Inter-War Period*. Aldershot, England: Avebury Publishers.

Jones, T. 2013. "Why Is Italy Still So Racist." *The Guardian*, July 30, https://www.theguardian.com/world/shortcuts/2013/jul/30/italy-racism-cecile-kyenge-esterofilia.

Longhi, R. 1958. *Arte Lombarda dai Visconti Agli Sforza.* Milano: Silvana Editore D'Arte.

Marsala, H. 2017. "Le palme di Piazza Duomo? Non una stravaganza a caso. Dietro c'e' l'esperto Marco Bay." *Artribune*, February 20, 2017, http://www.artribune.com/progettazione/architettura/2017/02/le-palme-di-piazza-duomo-non-una-stravaganza-a-caso-dietro-ce-lesperto-marco-bay/.

Mattioli, A. 2017. "Dopo le palme a Milano anche i banani." *La Stampa*, February 24, 2017, http://www.lastampa.it/2017/02/24/cultura/dopo-le-palme-a-milano-anche-i-banani-L4l596BOCv3RgikvRRd4MK/pagina.html.

Moggi, G. 2012. "I Giardini di acclimatazione in Toscana nell'800." *Informatore Botanico Italiano* 44, suppl. 2: 14–15.

Murtaza, N. 1998. *The Pillage of Sustainability in Eritrea, 1600s–1990s: Rural Communities and the Creeping Shadows of Hegemony*. Westport, CT: Greenwood.

Palma, A. 2013. "Leghista Buonanno: La secessione non serve piu', il Sud e' gia' Africa." *Net1News*, http://www.net1news.org/italia-/leghista-buonanno-secessione-gi%C3%A0-in-atto-il-sud-ricorda-lafrica/.

Palma, S. 2002. "Fotografia di una colonia: l'Eritrea di Luigi Naretti (1885–1900)." *Quaderni Storici* 37, no. 1 (April): 104–105.

Starbucks. 2017. "Loxcel Starbucks Map." *Starbucks*. Press release, September 23.

Strazza, M. 2012. "Faccetta Nera dell'Abissinia: Madame e meticci dopo la conquista dell' Etiopia." *Humanities* 1, no. 2 (June): 116–133.

Valentini, G. 2017. *Il Duomo di Milano: L'Ultima delle Grandi Cattedrali Gotiche*. Torino: Lindau.

Main Pathway: Ecologies

Subthemes

End of Decolonization
End of Climate Change
End of Diasporas

43

INTERVIEW WITH LINDA TEGG AND BARACCO + WRIGHT

How do you identify the species of plants you decide to work with? What parameters guide your selection process and why?

LINDA TEGG AND BARACCO + WRIGHT: We came to the grasslands of Victoria's western volcanic plain for different, albeit related, reasons. Linda Tegg was looking to uncover what our state library had replaced in its founding, and came across accounts of a lost, and almost forgotten, grassland. B+W were engaged in thinking about the contemporary condition of this endangered plant community, with its remnants still under threat from industrialization and urbanization, and imagining a role for architecture to be reparative.

A shared interest in this plant community brought our practices together for *Repair*. While plant species were important, it was the plant community as a whole that guided our selection—that they occurred together and were presented as a highly diverse yet crucially connected group.

Do you ever consider plants as subjects in your work, and how does that change your approach to them?

LT AND B+W: The plants that formed *Grasslands Repair* presented themselves in all their vital complexity. And of course, from this complexity comes their perspective, as well as their agency to shape the shared environment. The immediate environment of the Australian Pavilion at the Venice Biennale of Architecture in 2018, sealed off to natural light and engineered to defy the ground plane, typifies the modernist white cube. Adapting the pavilion to meet the needs of living organisms became a key challenge in undoing much of these isolating strategies. We made a direct connection between the gallery and the ground, left the doors open, and installed artificial lights that we called *Skylight* that channeled energy from the Italian grid into the bodies of the plants.

While we hoped that the formal qualities of the pavilion would focus our human visitors' attention on a much overlooked and undervalued plant community, the liveliness of the plants pushed against any sense of stability or enclosure. The artwork became habitat to birds, lizards, insects, and a very well-fed frog, all of which brought their own perspective to the assemblage. As subjects, they depended on human care and this aspect brought a deep knowing. There was no denying the passage of time—some plants withdrew through death or dormancy while others reemerged or continued to flower and grow. There was no sense of mastery from our perspective, but rather a space to be humbled by the capacities of the plant community in this extraordinary circumstance.

B+W: In our architectural work, we try to make space for plants. Over time we have developed our reflection as to how to do this on the plant's terms rather than as another piece of our space-making tools. More recently this has meant exploring scientific studies of plants. But we can't help feeling a tinge of anthropological-style distance and objectification. Working with plants in the way we did in *Grasslands Repair* was new for us as architects. The plants as subjects and the incompatibility of their subjecthood with a building became central to the conceptualizing of the work—how to sustain and support them and their arrangement, which was literally split by the building between inside and outside. Conceptually, it was important to present the plants in *Grasslands, Repair* as a community, and so they were formally mostly grouped literally side by side en mass. But they were actually separated—as well as being split by the building their root systems were separated (in containers). Conceptually this suited us in the field of the artificiality. We've since thought more about the implications of the "plant pot" in that the "site" of the community is as much below as above the ground.

In your artistic practice, what have you learned from the plants themselves? In which ways does your art follow their movements, metamorphoses, and modes of being in the world? How does it interact with these vegetal processes?

B+W: We have more recently focused on the root system, or let's say the ground/underground as the site of the plant. In architecture this is a huge dilemma because architecture usually is in direct conflict—occupying the ground in ways that usually deny most life. Following our work with Linda on *Grasslands Repair* and currently *Grasslands Suspended*, the question of the contained plant is a challenging but fundamental one that may inform our shared practice.

LT: I've noticed how their quiet aliveness pushes against our systems of containment. In the built environment we might see this as a sapling heaving up a footpath. Our work *Grasslands Suspended*, whereby we engaged with a yearlong dialogue with BICON (Australia's biosecurity apparatus) to repatriate indigenous Australian seeds to Australia, demonstrated how a bureaucratic system struggles to deal with entities outside of its known terms. Following plants in this way feels expansive, as if any given framework will be overrun. I sense this openness manifesting in how we look to the field.

My very first work with plants prompted me to look into the background of colonial paintings in an effort to understand something of what our city has replaced. The process revealed to me something of the conditioning of my own vision and how charged figure–ground relationships are in informing what's valued. It's telling that across both our practices we have continued to look to the ground as a space of connection, perhaps placing importance on what's often unrepresented. As you (B+W) are looking to the connectivity of plants through their root systems, I'm reflecting upon how working with plants often fosters a particular kind of openness and generosity in human collaborations. The forms my work takes have become far more externalized, open, and vulnerable—qualities that I recognize in plant life.

What ethical or political considerations inform your work with plants? What are the ethical and political implications of this work?

LT AND B+W: The ethical question of displacing the seeds of the plants that were grown for *Grasslands Repair*, from Australia to Italy, was somewhat the motivation for *Grasslands Suspended*, where their progeny were repatriated so to speak. The seeds themselves were twice removed from their endemic location, and some of those places are incapable of supporting them anymore (now roads). Political boundaries more than natural ones determined the movement of *Grasslands Suspended*.

B+W: We know the world through artificial and political boundaries of land ownership and use. These have to a large extent now defined the physical natural world as much as architecture itself as highly fragmented. To work with plants and their networks requires an unknowing of these frameworks and bringing into your mind large and often invisible systems. Also, in Australia, land ownership and use through these frameworks are unceded and so ethically fraught.

LT: Australia's unceded condition is certainly a powerful motivator, and perhaps one of the reasons why foregrounding endemic plant communities has felt so necessary. It bases our actions in an alternate paradigm. Working with plants, not for our use, but as entities in themselves, radically alters how we see and relate to the collective environment.

What, if any, are the aspects of your work with plants related to the current global environmental and mass extinction crises?

LT AND B+W: The crises created by land clearing were at the core of *Grasslands Repair* and played out in the pragmatics of sourcing seeds: there was not a lot of this plant community left to get seed from and to learn from. The study of temperate native grasslands is a relatively young field. Yet they are still being removed.

The seeds of *Grasslands Suspended* in their turn will support a new plant community. Their novelty is artificial, brought together through *Grasslands Repair*. Although seed migration is a natural phenomenon accommodated through biological processes formed over millions of years, the compressed time frame of movement facilitated by the Anthropocene is part of the crises. The control of biological migration, evident in *Grasslands Suspended*, attempts to expand this compression.

LT: The biodiversity of the plant communities that inspired *Grasslands Repair* and my recent work *Infield* can be seen as an unintended consequence of premodern human and plant interactions. The Australian grassland and European meadow coevolved with human care. Regularly these plant communities were cleared by fire or harvest. These actions prevent any one species from dominating and allow for a greater diversity of life. I hope that there are lessons in how this diversity was maintained so close to human activity, not "out there," but close by within our own patterns of living.

Much of the environmental crisis is articulated in abstract terms, whether it be through data or imagery from elsewhere. The global nature of the crisis can send you spiraling outward, deferring to larger and more complex systems. I'm seeking to register some of these relationships in an intimate way, to create a space to recognize our shared lifetimes and place. My hope is that this may open up alternative perspectives and potentially lead to healthier relationships.

Which pressing challenge, or challenges, has working with plants presented to you?

LT: Increasingly I'm understanding my work as coproduced with plants and the challenges they present. Through encounters between plants, human organizations, images, and the built environment, I access the conditions that produce the work. In a traditional artistic framework, my medium may be understood as the lived tension between anthropocentric structures and vegetal forces. I'm interested in seeing these structures differently; perhaps with plants, we can find hidden capacities and potentials.

B+W: We would say similarly that the challenges plants pose are influencing our work. The connectedness of plants not only with each other but to other organisms presents the challenge of finding forms of human and vegetal coexistence that supports their being "together," or being connected. This is a big challenge given the frameworks architecture typically operates within.

LT AND B+W: Over a six-month period and supported by many different carers, the plants in *Grasslands Repair* changed a lot. The work became its own entity way beyond the original plan for the installation. Considering the context and pressure of a biennale, it was challenging to let it be on its own terms.

How is the interaction between your artistic practice and theoretical endeavors shaped by vegetal life?

LT: To return to B+W's point about unknowing artificial boundaries, it also seems worthwhile to mention how to speak about the presence of scientific knowledge throughout the process of *Grasslands Suspended*. The laboratory became our final threshold. Crucial to the process of securing passage for the seeds was to isolate and articulate each species. As Louise and I were in the lab purifying the seed packets under the magnifying glass, I thought it worthwhile to understand a bit more about how a species is defined. I found that thinkers in biology and the philosophy of science have had a lot to say about this: while there is general agreement about how species exist, criteria and protocol have been the cause of much debate. Our

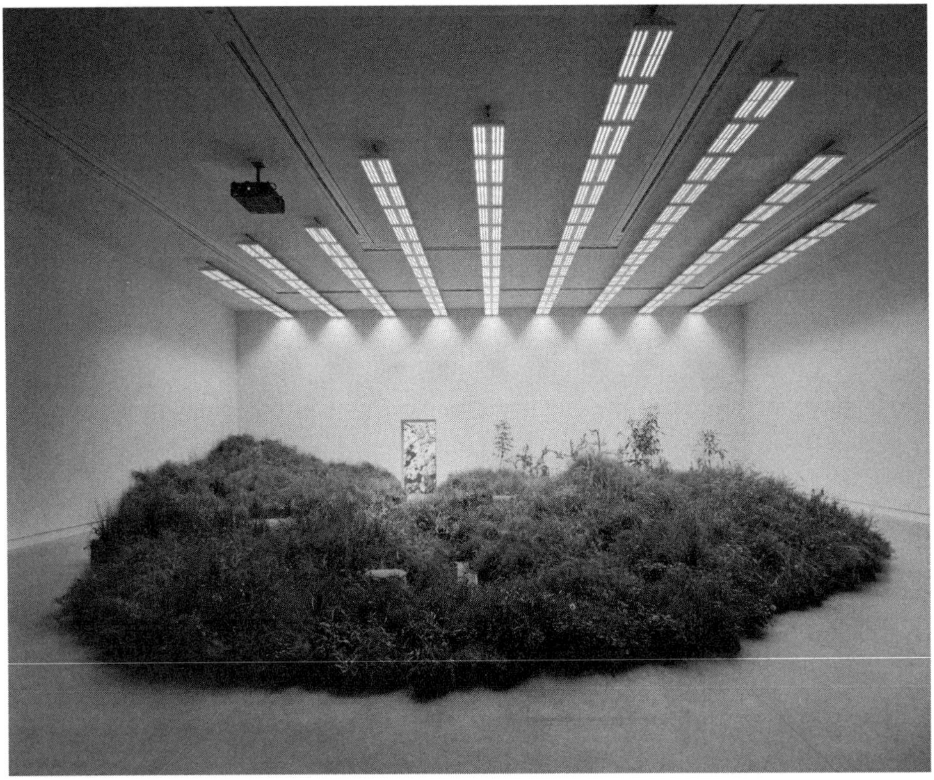

encounter with these knowledges highlighted a disparity between the seeds and the language we use to represent them. Anything that could not be defined would be destroyed!

About half the species we were working with fell outside of BICON's terms, simply listed as "not permitted to sow"—an ironic category for an indigenous plant. We embarked on the processes necessary to draw these plants into the system, actively amassing the information to complete a totally unnecessary weed risk assessment. This process triggered a counter impulse for these plants to be spared the objectifying vision of this system, to remain enigmatic. I sense this impulse carrying over into the relationship between theory and practice in my work. Increasingly I see freedom of expression and biodiversity as cojoined, and hope to find ways of making space for life and art to articulate themselves in their own terms.

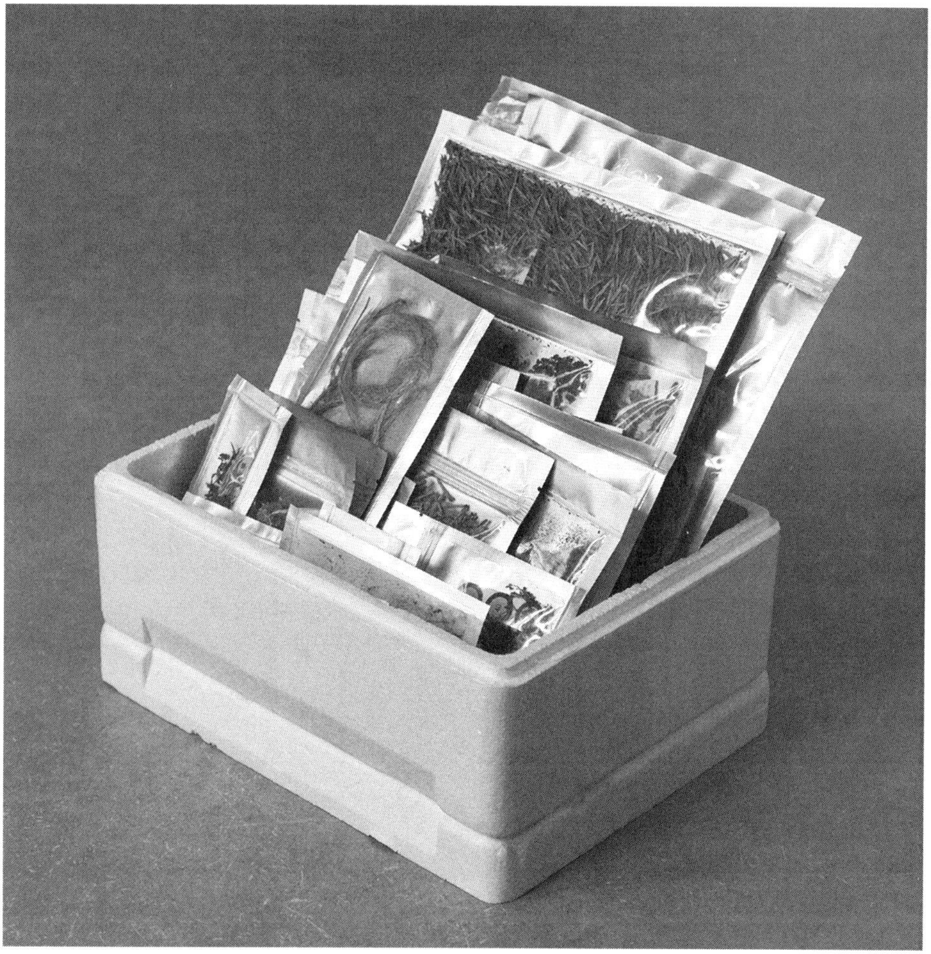

Grasslands Repair, 2018, Linda Tegg with
Baracco+Wright.

B+W: Yes! To similar ends our "thinking" moves between a large (ecosystemic) scale imagining and what this might look like at a small scale, which we can attempt to apply. We are currently imaging an urban pattern that undergoes resistance by underlying ecological forces—geological and hydrological—still largely present under the asphalt, in acts of deurbanization within the wider "city." We try to imagine a coexistence on the terms of vegetal life. Thinking along these lines brings us to learning from indigenous ways of understanding space and time.

Linda Tegg is an Australian artist who makes work out of inhabiting and reconfiguring the conditions of spectatorship. Within her immersive installations, plants, animals, images, and the built environment are brought into unlikely proximities to generate new points of orientation and relation. Interdisciplinary collaboration characterizes much of Tegg's work. She collaborated with Baracco+Wright Architects as the creative directors of *Repair* at the Venice Architecture Biennale in 2018 and grew *Grasslands*, a site-responsive public artwork at the State Library of Victoria with horticulturalist John Delpratt in 2014. Tegg holds degrees from SAIC, the University of Melbourne, and RMIT University.

Baracco+Wright Architects (founded in 2004) is a small, experimental architectural practice based in Melbourne, Australia. It seeks opportunities to position the architect in the role of strategic thinker across disciplinary boundaries exploring the whole built and natural environment. Its work sits between academia, practice, and multiple creative fields such as art and landscape architecture. In 2018, they were the creative directors in collaboration with Linda Tegg of the Australian Pavilion at the 16th Venice Biennale di Architettura with the theme *Repair*.

44

INTERVIEW WITH ANICKA YI

How do you identify the species of plants you decide to work with? What parameters guide your selection process and why?

ANICKA YI: I wouldn't say I decide to work with certain plants so much as I become captivated by them. The initial attraction I have for a certain species ranges from aesthetic appreciation to curiosity about a certain detail or feature. My 2016 video work *The Flavor Genome* was largely inspired by a fascination with orchids. The diversity of smells, forms, colors, and patterns that can be found in orchids is completely brain-wrinkling. I was particularly interested in the way that some orchids mimic the pheromones of insect species, seducing them into an interspecies cross-pollination ritual. On the other hand, some insects need to collect chemicals from the orchid in order to produce their own pheromones. Orchids use desire to cross species boundaries. They are the virtuosos of hybridization.

Do you ever consider plants as subjects in your work, and how does that change your approach to them?

AY: Yes, at times, especially a subject that is more a mythical presence or a force rather than a specific person or identity. This gives me the narrative freedom to combine aspects from many different species, according to my own imagination. In *The Flavor Genome*, one of the characters is an elusive animal–plant hybrid called the Saudaderrhiza. When the Saudade flower is pollinated by a wasp, it sets into motion a cascade of biochemical disturbances, from the release of a swarm of pathogenic bacteria, to the activation of fungal internet, to the ensnaring and digestion of human bodies in its vicinity. The molecular cocktail secreted by the Saudade's petals is so powerful that it can be used to create "chemical personas." These are aromas so overwhelming that they cause a hallucinogenic experience of being out of one's body, slipping instead into the body and the experience—the subjectivity—of an "other."

In your artistic practice, what have you learned from the plants themselves? In which ways does your art follow their movements, metamorphoses, and modes of being in the world? How does it interact with these vegetal processes?

AY: Plants guide me to imagine ways of being beyond my immediate human experience. Thinking of orchids again, the way some species have coevolved with their insect pollinators seems to make them more than simply plants. They are plants that have transgressed their biological "kingdom" and acquired animal characteristics. I am attracted to this fugitive quality in plants, their ability to shape-shift and resist categorization. Plants can use this interspecies ambiguity in a mutualist way, but it can also be violent or predatory. I have deep respect for this somewhat menacing aspect of plants.

For my exhibition at Fridericianum, *Jungle Stripe*, I debuted a series I like to call "chicken skins." These are silicone frames interlaced with pores and hairlike fibers. As the name suggests, they look very much like animal skin, yet strands of leaves and flowers dangle from the central orifice of the frame. One could say that these works express an animal longing toward the vegetal: to sprout, blossom, or take root.

What ethical or political considerations inform your work with plants? What are the ethical and political implications of this work?

AY: Yes, far too many to list here. I think about how plants are tied in with colonialism in the ways they are harvested, relocated, or driven to extinction. *The Flavor Genome* touched on how plants are extracted from their indigenous contexts; spliced, sometimes rather haphazardly, into new environments; and deployed for new industrial and scientific purposes. I think that working with living materials in general is extremely ethically fraught. But I do think that tension can be a fruitful space for exploration. It's very difficult for us as humans not to project our biases and desires onto other living things. Even when we are cultivating some kinds of life, we are making essentially curatorial decisions about other kinds of life.

What, if any, are the aspects of your work with plants related to the current global environmental and mass extinction crises?

AY: I would consider algae to be in the realm of the vegetal. My works with algae were tied to ideas of early earth ecosystems, but also to present-day environmental concerns such as industrial agriculture and massive "toxic" algae blooms. My first installation of kelp sculptures, *Biologizing the Machine (tentacular trouble)*, used panels of leather-like kelp that were covered in scratches and scars from being battered about in the ocean currents. The unique history displayed on each leaf reminded me of the primordial animal crawl from the sea, but also the threat of an untimely return to aquatic life, due to flooding and rising sea levels. Thinking of extinction, the kelp sculptures gave one the feeling of hovering on the edge of either a genesis or a disintegration.

Which pressing challenge, or challenges, has working with plants presented to you?

AY: Working with living plants is such a delicate process, especially when you are limited by a gallery or other institutional context. The context of fine art, with its emphasis on conservation and archivability, is quite opposed to the inclusion of mutable living creatures, let alone an entire ecosystem. Living things require care, and they can also become sick, or even die. The variables and potential pitfalls are infinite, which was a major challenge for my bioreactor sculptures. The bioreactor works harbored wild cultures of *Spirogyra* algae, which is incredibly beautiful and grows in massive glittering green clumps in the wild. However, once you remove it from those wild conditions, it suddenly transforms from a robust community into one that is much more vulnerable to the slightest disturbance. As soon as you remove something from "the wild" and you bring it into a highly controlled space like a gallery or lab, you learn very quickly to what extent the environment cannot be synthesized.

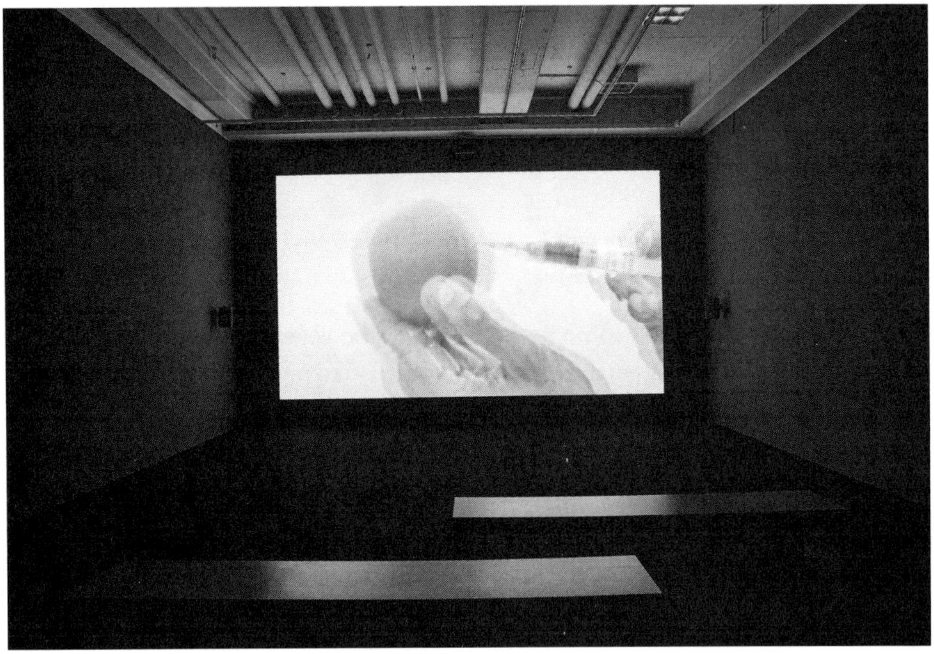

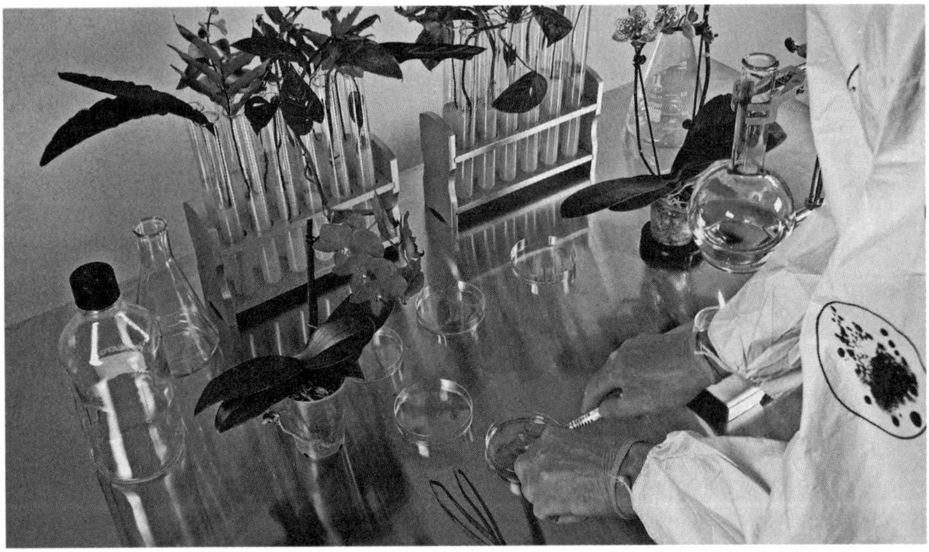

Anicka Yi is a conceptual artist whose work lies at the intersection of fragrance, cuisine, and science. She is known for installations that engage the senses, especially the sense of smell, and for her collaborations with biologists and chemists. Yi was the winner of the bi-annual 2016 Hugo Boss Prize presented by the Guggenheim. In 2017, Yi debuted at the Guggenheim with the exhibition *Life Is Cheap*, which explores her "sociopolitical interest in the olfactive." Yi lives and works in Los Angeles.

Stills from *The Flavor Genome*, 2016, Anicka Yi. Single-channel 3D video, 22 min. (Installation view, Fridericianum, Kassel, 2016. Image courtesy of the artist, 47 Canal, New York, and Fridericianum, Kassel. Photo: Fabian Frinzel.)

CONTRIBUTORS

Giovanni Aloi is an author, editor, and art curator specializing in the history and theory of photography, the representation of nature, and everyday objects in art. He has contributed to BBC radio programs and worked at Whitechapel Art Gallery and Tate Galleries in London, and he is the US correspondent for *Esse Magazine* and a regular public speaker at the Art Institute of Chicago. Aloi has curated exhibitions in the United States and Europe. He is the editor of *Antennae: The Journal of Nature in Visual Culture* and coeditor of the Art after Nature series for the University of Minnesota Press.

Marlene Atleo, *ʔeh ʔeh naa tuu kwiss*, a member of the Ahousaht First Nation, British Columbia, came to adult and postsecondary education after a career in the West Coast salmon fishing industry. Atleo's work in the design, development, delivery, and evaluation of Aboriginal education, training, and research gave her insight into the intractability of the "dirty, rotten problems" in Aboriginal education.

Monika Bakke is associate professor in the Philosophy Department at the Adam Mickiewicz University, Poznań, Poland. She writes on contemporary art and aesthetics, with a particular interest in posthumanist, transspecies, and gender perspectives. From 2001 to 2017, she was working as an editor of the Polish cultural journal *Czas Kultury* [*Time of Culture*].

Emily Blackmer, MSW, assistant professor in Azusa Pacific University's Department of Social Work, has worked in public child welfare for Los Angeles County in dependency investigation as well as intensive outpatient psychiatric treatment and residential treatment for youth involved with the juvenile justice system who experience co-occurring disorders. She also serves as a hospital social worker.

Jodi Brandt joined the Human-Environment Systems Research Center at Boise State University in 2015. The goal of her research is to better understand how human societies and healthy ecosystems can thrive on a rapidly changing planet. She focuses on quantifying human–environment interactions and whether they create sustainable environmental trajectories. She works with a wide range of people, including economists, ecologists, anthropologists, farmers, hunters, and tribal communities.

Teresa Castro is a lecturer in film and audiovisual studies at the Sorbonne Nouvelle University and a former postdoctoral researcher at the Musée du Quai Branly (Paris) and at the Max Planck Institute for the History of Science (Berlin). Part of her recent research focuses on the links between cinema and animism, ecocriticism, and forms of plant life in visual culture.

Dan Choffnes is associate professor of biology and Asian studies, and Director of Student Fellowships, Carthage College, in Kenosha, Wisconsin. He specializes in the relationships between people and plants (ethnobotany). He will teach the ASI4006 Asian Food and Cuisines Module for our students.

Braden Elliott is a PhD student in the Ecology, Evolution, Environment and Society Program at Dartmouth College.

Monica Gagliano is a research associate professor of evolutionary ecology at the Centre of Evolutionary Biology at the University of Western Australia, a research affiliate at the Sydney Environment Institute at the University of Sydney, and a former fellow of the Australian Research Council. She is the author of numerous scientific articles in the fields of animal and plant behavioral and evolutionary ecology.

Elaine Gan is an artist-scholar who teaches at XE: Experimental Humanities & Social Engagement at New York University, where she also directs the Multispecies Worldbuilding Lab with support from NYU's Office of Sustainability.

Prudence Gibson is a Sydney-based art and fiction writer and academic. She has published fiction in *Antipodes, Eureka Street*, and *Etchings.* She is author of the art book *The Rapture of Death* (2010) and *The Plant Contract* (2018) and has published art essays or articles in journals such as *Heat, The Australian, Vogue*, and *Art Monthly.*

Manuela Infante is a Chilean theater playwright, director, scriptwriter, and musician. She is well known for offering scenic articulations of complex theoretical issues. With her group Teatro de Chile (2002–2016), she wrote and directed work with the permanent support of the Chilean Funds for the Arts. She holds a Master of Arts in Cultural Analysis from University of Amsterdam.

Luce Irigaray is a highly influential French cultural theorist, philosopher, and psychoanalyst. Irigaray received a bachelor's degree from the University of Louvain in 1954 and a master's degree from the same university in 1956. Irigaray's work has influenced the feminist movement in France and Italy for several decades. Irigaray has published more than 40 books, which are translated into many languages.

Robin Wall Kimmerer is a mother, scientist, decorated professor, and enrolled member of the Citizen Potawatomi Nation. She is the author of *Braiding Sweetgrass: Indigenous Wisdom, Scientific Knowledge and the Teachings of Plants* and *Gathering Moss: A Natural and Cultural History of Mosses*. She lives in Syracuse, New York, where she is a SUNY Distinguished Teaching Professor of Environmental Biology and the founder and director of the Center for Native Peoples and the Environment.

Eduardo Kohn is associate professor of anthropology at McGill University and winner of the 2014 Gregory Bateson Prize. He is best known for the book *How Forests Think* (2013).

Wangari Muta Maathai obtained a degree in biological sciences from Mount St. Scholastica College in Atchison, Kansas (1964) and a master of science degree from the University of Pittsburgh (1966). He pursued doctoral studies in Germany and the University of Nairobi before obtaining a PhD (1971) from the University of Nairobi, where she also taught veterinary anatomy. The first woman in East and Central Africa to earn a doctorate degree, Professor Maathai became chair of the Department of Veterinary Anatomy and an associate professor in 1976 and 1977, respectively. In both cases, she was the first woman to attain those positions in the region.

Stefano Mancuso is the director of the International Laboratory of Plant Neurobiology (LINV) in Florence, Italy; a founder of the International Society for Plant Signaling and Behavior; and a professor at the University of Florence. His books and papers have been published in numerous international magazines and journals, and *La Repubblica* newspaper has listed him among the 20 people who will change our lives.

Michael Marder is Ikerbasque Research Professor of Philosophy at the University of the Basque Country, UPV/EHU, Vitoria-Gasteiz. His work spans the fields of environmental philosophy and ecological thought, political theory, and phenomenology.

Elaine P. Miller is professor of philosophy at Miami University in Oxford, Ohio. Her work lies at the confluence of the philosophy of nature, aesthetics, and feminist theory. She is currently executive director of *philo*SOPHIA, a society for continental feminism, and a member of the College of Fellows at the University of Western Sydney, Australia.

Mark Payne is interested in animal and plant studies; primitivism ancient and modern; and, most recently, speculative fiction. He is Chester D. Tripp Professor in Comparative Literature, Classics, and the Committee on Social Thought at the University of Chicago.

Allegra Pesenti is curator, Grunwald Center for the Graphic Arts, Hammer Museum. Pesenti was the curator of the Grunwald Center Curator from 2007 to 2013 and then gone chief curator and curator at large at the Menil Collection in Houston.

Michael Pollan grew up on Long Island and was educated at Bennington College, Oxford University, and Columbia University, from which he received a master's in English. Pollan has received an honorary doctorate from the University of Gastronomic Science and in 2015–2016 was a fellow at the Radcliffe Institute for Advanced Study at Harvard. He is the author of eight books, six of which have been *New York Times* bestsellers, and three of them (including his latest, *How to Change Your Mind*) were immediate number-one *New York Times* bestsellers.

Darren J. Ranco holds a joint appointment in the Department of Anthropology, the Senator George J. Mitchell Center for Sustainability Solutions, and Native American Programs, where he serves as chair of Native American Programs and coordinator of Native American Research. A member of the Penobscot Nation,

Ranco is particularly interested in how better research relationships can be established between universities, Native and non-Native researchers, and Indigenous communities.

Nicholas J. Reo is a citizen of the Sault Ste. Marie Tribe of Chippewa Indians. He is associate professor of Native American and Indigenous Studies and Environmental Studies at Dartmouth College. Reo studies Indigenous knowledge and ecological stewardship on Indigenous lands.

Angela Roothaan is a tenured assistant professor at the VU University Amsterdam. She has published on a wide range of subjects, such as philosophy of nature, spirit ontologies, value ethics, and (early) modern philosophy. As of recently, she publishes mostly on African and Intercultural philosophy—with a focus on environmentalism in an African context and (the epistemology) of Indigenous knowledge. Her most recent book is *Indigenous, Modern and Postcolonial Relations to Nature: Negotiating the Environment* (Routledge, 2019).

Marcela Salinas is an actress, known for *Todos Juntos* (2018), *The Pack* (2019), and *The Strong Ones* (2019).

Catriona A. H. Sandilands is a professor of environmental humanities in the Faculty of Environmental and Urban Change at York University, Toronto. Her writing on feminism, queer ecologies, ecocriticism, critical plant studies, and posthumanist thought includes the coedited anthology *Queer Ecologies: Sex, Nature, Politics, Desire* (2010) and the edited, creative collection *Rising Tides: Reflections for Climate Changing Times* (2019).

Elisabeth E. Schussler gained a PhD from Louisiana State University in 1997. She teaches at the University of Tennessee in Knoxville and is PI of the NSF-funded research coordination network (BioTAP) focused on improving GTA TPD.

Vandana Shiva is a scholar, environmental activist, food sovereignty advocate, ecofeminist, and antiglobalization author. Based in Delhi, Shiva has written more than 20 books. She is often referred to as the "Gandhi of grain" for her activism associated with the anti-GMO movement.

Krista Tippett is an American journalist, author, and entrepreneur. She created and hosts the public radio program and podcast *On Being*. In 2014, Tippett was awarded the National Humanities Medal by US President Barack Obama.

Anthony James Trewavas is Emeritus Professor in the School of Biological Sciences of the University of Edinburgh, best known for his research in the fields of plant physiology and molecular biology. His research investigates plant behavior.

Alessandra Viola is a scientific journalist, writer of documentaries, and television scriptwriter. In 2011, she directed the Genoa Science Festival. With Stefano Mancuso, she is the author of the bestselling book *Brilliant Green: The Surprising History and Science of Plant Intelligence* (2018).

Eduardo Batalha Viveiros de Castro is a Brazilian anthropologist and a professor at the National Museum of the Federal University of Rio de Janeiro. He has published many books and articles that are considered important in anthropology and in Americanist ethnology. Born in Rio de Janeiro, Viveiros de Castro taught at the École des Hautes Études en Sciences Sociales, the University of Chicago, and the University of Cambridge.

James Howard Wandersee earned a BS from Minnesota State University, Mankato in 1968. He continued his education at the University of Wisconsin–Milwaukee (MS, 1974) and Marquette University (PhD, 1978). After completing his doctorate, Jim and his young family moved to New Ulm, where he taught science for 11 years at Martin Luther College. In 1989, he had the opportunity to relocate to Baton Rouge to be a professor of biology education, focusing on plant science at Louisiana State University. He worked at Louisiana State University until 2012.

Lois Weinberger was an early and visionary critic of the upheavals of the Anthropocene and is considered a pioneer of a distinct, artistic ecology. From the 1990s onward, he played a significant role in shaping the discourse surrounding the relationship between nature and culture.

Kyle Whyte, citizen of Potawatomi Nation, is George Willis Pack Professor at the School for Environment and Sustainability, teaching in the SEAS environmental justice specialization. He is affiliate professor of Native American Studies and

Philosophy. His research addresses environmental justice, focusing on moral and political issues concerning climate policy and Indigenous peoples, the ethics of cooperative relationships between Indigenous peoples and science organizations, and problems of Indigenous justice in public and academic discussions of food sovereignty and the Anthropocene.

David Wood is W. Alton Jones Professor of Philosophy at Vanderbilt University, where he teaches continental and environmental philosophy. His many books include *Deep Time, Dark Times: On Being Geologically Human*; *Reoccupy Earth: Notes toward an Other Beginning*; and *Eco-Deconstruction: Derrida and Environmental Philosophy*, which he coedited. He is director of Yellow Bird Artscape in Tennessee.